DOS 4.5

Volume and File
Disk Management System

Second Edition

Walland Philip Vrbancic, Jr.

lulu

This Second Edition of the
DOS 4.5 Volume and File Disk Management System
is the
Confidential and Proprietary Intellectual Property
of
Walland Philip Vrbancic, Jr.

ISBN 979-8-218-39879-8

*I am very proud to dedicate this Second Edition of the
DOS 4.5 Volume and File Disk Management System
and all of my previous achievements
to my loving parents Walland and Melba Vrbancic
who continuously nourished my intellectual curiosities
with games, toys, books, education, and unconditional love.*

*I am truly fortunate for all of the love and the support
I have always received from my dear sister Marile.*

*I am also profoundly grateful to my partner
Carlton D. Wong
for his unconditional love
and who delightfully pretends to understand
what the Hell I am talking about!
Carlton is truly a most generous and kind human being.*

No problem can withstand the assault of sustained thinking.
~~~ Voltaire ~~~

Excellence is never an accident!
It is always the result of high intention, sincere effort, and intelligent execution;
it represents the wise choice of many alternatives;
choice, not chance, determines one's destiny.
~~~ Aristotle ~~~

If I have seen further than others it is because I have stood on the shoulders of giants.
~~~ Isaac Newton ~~~

Disclaimer of All Liability

Do not use the Second Edition of the DOS 4.5 Volume and File Disk Management System or the DOS 4.5 Build 06 software for any mission-critical applications or for any purpose in which a software error or a software failure could cause you financial or material loss. The Second Edition of the DOS 4.5 Volume and File Disk Management System and the DOS 4.5 Build 06 software are designed to enhance your Apple][computing experience, but they may contain design flaws that could inhibit the proper operation of your computer or they may result in the loss of recorded data on any storage device that is connected to your computer. You assume all of the risks that are associated with the operation of your computer and the potential loss of your recorded data when using the Second Edition of the DOS 4.5 Volume and File Disk Management System and the DOS 4.5 Build 06 software. If these terms are not acceptable to you, do not use the Second Edition of the DOS 4.5 Volume and File Disk Management System and the DOS 4.5 Build 06 software for any purpose, and remove this software from your computer.

Walland Philip Vrbancic, Jr., the administrator of www.applecored.net, makes no warranties either expressed or implied with respect to this Second Edition of the DOS 4.5 Volume and File Disk Management System and the DOS 4.5 Build 06 software, its quality, performance, or fitness for any particular purpose. Any risk of incidental or consequential damages that may result from the use of the information that is contained in this Second Edition of the DOS 4.5 Volume and File Disk Management System and the DOS 4.5 Build 06 software shall be assumed by you, the User. In no event shall Walland Philip Vrbancic, Jr., or www.applecored.net be liable for any direct, indirect, incidental, or consequential damages that may result from any defect, deficiency, or neglect that is found in the Second Edition of the DOS 4.5 Volume and File Disk Management System and the DOS 4.5 Build 06 software.

While all possible attempts have been made to ensure that the information that is contained within this publication and software is complete and accurate, the author shall have no liability or responsibility for any errors or omissions, or for any damages or the loss of recorded data that may result from the use of the information, figures, tables, circuit diagrams, and example software programs that are contained herein. The author reserves the right to implement any changes and/or any improvements to the contents of this Second Edition of the DOS 4.5 Volume and File Disk Management System and the DOS 4.5 Build 06 software at any time and without any prior notice to you, the User, or to the general Apple][community.

Preface

When Brian Wiser and Bill Martens discovered my original DOS 4.1 software and my DOS 4.1 documentation at www.applecored.net in 2017, they immediately contacted me and wanted Apple Pugetsound Program Library Exchange (*Call-A.P.P.L.E.*) to publish my DOS 4.1 Manual. Ha! If only this would have happened back in 1982. That's when my co-worker, Randy at Rockwell, and I were actively reading many publications featuring Apple software and hardware, and *Call-A.P.P.L.E.* was one of our favorite publications. Needless to say, to be published by any of those early computer journals would have been crazy exciting at that time, and it would have certainly been a cherished memory for a lifetime. I actually was very close to completing all of the capabilities that I wanted in DOS 4.1 when I agreed to have *Call-A.P.P.L.E.* publish the DOS 4.1 Manual for Build 45. I also provided *Call-A.P.P.L.E.* with demo diskette images for both DOS 4.1L and for DOS 4.1H. A month or two after the DOS 4.1 Build 45 manual was published and available to the public for purchase, I finalized DOS 4.1 with Build 46. Only the DOS 4.1 Build 46 documentation in PDF form and its companion software are available at www.applecored.net for download.

I remember explaining to Wiser and Martens that I wanted both versions of DOS 4.1 to provide the User with virtually the same computing experience, albeit the HELP command is found only in DOS 4.1H. This desire proved to be somewhat problematic in that I was limited in memory for DOS 4.1L, whereas I had ample memory for DOS 4.1H. Actually, it was the unused memory in DOS 4.1H that was the impetus to introduce the HELP command in the first place. At the onset of our negotiations, I warned Wiser and Martens that I could not stop creating more functionality in DOS 4.1, but they were rather insistent on publishing the DOS 4.1 Manual for the Apple][community in its current stage of development. In 2021 I had the opportunity to publish the Second Edition of the DOS 4.1 Manual in the format that I originally intended. The Second Edition features the publication of Build 46.

My next area of exploration for an Apple][DOS was the attempt to port DOS 4.1H to Auxiliary memory. I was absolutely successful, I might add, but I could not successfully design an interface between *Lisa*, my most favorite 65C02 assembler, and this new DOS that I had created to reside in Auxiliary memory. Over the course of several months of significant effort, I could not realize a viable solution that would be elegant, save memory, and provide the roadmap for interfacing other utilities and tools vis-s-vis this unique version of an Apple][DOS. But this effort was certainly not wasted! I documented what I had learned about Main and Auxiliary memory, its utilization and management, and I moved forward to other areas of exploration.

I had already decided to use DOS 4.1H as my initial model to begin development of DOS 4.3. Yes, DOS 4.3 does retain the "H" designation for "High" memory. However, I did not want to develop a companion "Low" memory DOS version in parallel, so I did **not** develop a DOS 4.3L. I simply refer to this new Apple][DOS as DOS 4.3. The question then became, can *Lisa* be ported to Auxiliary memory and function successfully in that memory space? The answer to that question turns out to be a resounding *"Yes!"* With DOS 4.3 residing in the memory of the Language Card partition in Main memory and *Lisa* residing in the memory of the Language Card partition in Auxiliary memory, the User has access to virtually all of Main memory below 0xBE00 for source code, object code, and the complete symbol table. I saw this exciting new configuration as the path forward to many potential and rewarding software possibilities.

If I can relocate *Lisa* to Auxiliary memory, what about performing a similar relocation for *Big Mac*? I have to say that that challenge was a bit uneventful because relocating *Big Mac* to the memory of the Language Card partition in Auxiliary memory was even easier to accomplish. My main focus in *Big Mac*, however, was to align *Big Mac* and *Sourceror* in terms of their respective *SWEET16* assembling and sourcing capabilities, though I do not believe *Big Mac* was ever able or was ever utilized to assemble all of its own unique *SWEET16* opcodes. This alignment task for *Big Mac* and *Sourceror* turned out to be an extraordinarily massive undertaking since I wanted *Big Mac* and *Sourceror* to assemble/disassemble my personal and well thought-out version for the unassigned *SWEET16* opcodes. I realized that *Big Mac* could not even assemble its own unique *SWEET16* EVAL opcode which was never created by Steven Wozniak in the first place. This tells me that Mr. Bredon probably could not even use *Big Mac* to assemble his own *Big Mac* source code unless he possibly hardcoded these unassigned opcodes as byt statements. I have to confess that there are still two *SWEET16* branches in my disassembled and verified *Big Mac* source code that are absolutely **wrong**, and I do not know their solution to this day. Furthermore, I have yet to discover how to force their execution in order to analyze the resulting behavior in *Big Mac*. I suspect that these particular code sequences may be part of MACRO handling, a set of pseudo opcodes that I have had no reason to use. After all is said and done, *Big Mac* and DOS 4.3 complemented each other beautifully.

While moving past DOS 4.3 in order to begin the development of the initial DOS 4.5 File and Volume Disk Management System, I discovered even more layers of File Manager functionality that I could code so much more effectively. DOS 4.3 certainly contains all of the necessary solutions to properly close files and flush volumes when the DOS CLOSE command is issued from within an Applesoft program. Yet, the coded solutions that are found in DOS 4.3 still do not exhaust my list of all of the additional capabilities that I wanted in my final release of an Apple][DOS. All of the capabilities that are contained in DOS 4.5 and specifically in DOS 4.5 Build 06 are detailed in Section I.2.

Finding any additional code space in DOS 4.5L Build 05 is simply not possible. Therefore, I chose to focus only on DOS 4.5H and I created a DOS 4.5 Build 06 project by redesigning yet again the DOS HELP Handler that resides in Bank 1 of the Language Card partition. Originally, I thought that it would be most advantageous to group the DOS commands into their six logical categories as I had done previously in the DOS 4.5 documentation, and to present the DOS commands in that format when the HELP command is issued. That feature, of course, required additional text table pointer space, column indexing, row indexing, and additional code routines in order to implement that particular design. In my opinion, that implementation and DOS command presentation within HELP was useful and effective; at that time there was no other practical use for the memory space. But when I conceived of several more DOS commands that required a practical use for that memory space, I had no other choice but to redesign HELP in order to recover the necessary code space in order to implement these new DOS commands. I did not want to sacrifice all of the important command utilization information that the HELP handler provides to the User. Could I obtain the necessary code space if I compromise the HELP command selection screen? Now that I had code solutions for fifty-two DOS commands, a new command selection screen was easy to visualize, design, and implement, and this new design implementation provides about 235 bytes of additional code space without sacrificing any DOS command information.

In most of my Apple][work during the past two years, I have been using DOS 4.5H Build 05 nearly 95% of the time. Even with *Lisa* and *Big Mac* residing in Auxiliary memory, I have yet to experience a program software failure. And in my most recent work I have been using DOS 4.5 Build 06 flawlessly 100% of the time, and still I have yet to experience a program software failure. There are many reasons not to use any part of lower Main memory for any version of an Apple][DOS, either DOS 3.3 or even DOS 4.5L: 1) the Applesoft interpreter does not process Applesoft code in the Language Card partition; 2) Applesoft programs may be far greater in size without having to rely on the DOS CHAIN command as often; 3) it is much easier to utilize assembly language routines when they reside in lower Main memory; and 4) several more DOS commands are available when DOS occupies the Language Card partition. These are the more obvious reasons why even ProDOS was moved to function natively in the Language Card partition. I find it somewhat amazing even today that it has taken me this long since I first envisioned DOS 4.1 to settle my concentration on a single version of an Apple][DOS. This version of an Apple][DOS, which is DOS 4.5 Build 06, installs its entire operating system natively into the Language Card partition, and it utilizes only two pages of memory in lower Main memory for its complete interface. DOS 4.5 Build 06 is truly a remarkable Disk Operating System for the Apple][computer, and it is a Disk Operating System that I am very proud to share with all of the Users in the entire Apple][community.

The Second Edition of the DOS 4.5 Volume and File Disk Management System and the DOS 4.5 Build 06 software represent the last and final release of my complete Disk Operating System for the Apple][computer.

I know the User will discover many, if not all of the fascinating developments and additions that I have designed, developed, and engineered into this final release of the Second Edition of the DOS 4.5 Volume and File Disk Management System. The User will be left wondering how he or she was able to previously accomplish nearly anything useful in a timely fashion without having had these magnificent achievements and developments that are now fully contained in this brilliant Apple][Disk Operating System. I know that this final release of my Disk Operating System for the Apple][computer and for the Apple //e computer is one of my greater accomplishments during my travels through time.

Enjoy the ride!

*I contend that a **good** hardware design is one in which software can most easily **utilize** and **flourish**.*

Table of Contents

*In order to design reliable and powerful software
for a particular machine or platform,
one must understand the complete
architecture of that machine.*

List of Figures

List of Tables

DOS 4.5 Volume and File Disk Management System Second Edition

I. Designing Another New DOS

This publication describes the process and the products I have created when I decided to design and program another enhanced Disk Operating System (DOS) for my Apple //e. Wherever I am able, I have included schematic diagrams, code samples, equations, figures, tables, and representative screen pictures to help explain what I have created and many of the reasons why I did so. As in my previous designs of an Apple][DOS, i.e. DOS 4.1 and DOS 4.3, this has been an incredible journey for me. With DOS 4.5 I have again re-imagined that time when I mostly lived, breathed, and worked on Apple][computers, hardware, and software development continuously for a good period of my life many, many years ago.

1. Introduction to DOS 4.5

I have been an avid Apple][computer enthusiast, hobbyist, and professional software programmer since 1983 when I became the proud owner of an Apple][+ computer. Besides the Apple][+ computer, my initial system included an Apple][Language Card, an Apple Disk][Drive with a Disk][Interface card, an Amdek color monitor, and an Epson MX100 printer with a Grappler+ Printer Interface card. During those early years I designed and built my own Apple][peripheral interface cards, I made electrical and hardware modifications to my Apple][+ motherboard and keyboard, and I wrote a substantial number of software programs initially using Applesoft BASIC (Applesoft hereafter). A few months later I started writng software in 6502 assembly language. I soon acquired a Videx UltraTerm video display card and a Microsoft Z80 Softcard. With the Z80 Softcard I was able to write complex Fortran programs that analyzed tomographic reconstructions of the human spinal column. A year or so later I added the Southern California Research Group quikLoader and PROmGRAMER cards to my system, a Johnathon Freeman Designs (JFD) Parallel Printer Buffer, and an Axlon RAM Disk 320 with its interface card.

I used C language in my professional programming career for the design and development of ultra-high-speed data collection engines for tactical radar and sensor development. Now that I am retired from the aerospace industry, I have always wanted to dig into, tear apart, and learn the software intricacies of the last available version of DOS 3.3 for the Apple][series of computers. I thought the last DOS 3.3 version was published on August 25, 1980. Then I recently came across another DOS 3.3 version that was published years later on January 1, 1983. That later DOS contains even more patches for the DOS APPEND command and for Apple //e initialization. What I learned from the 1980 publication totally flabbergasted me: the software is exciting in its originality and concept vis-à-vis it was released just after the publication of Integer BASIC. However, I found the software to be somewhat juvenile in its structure and in its implementation. Apparently, very little attention was given to software design and review. It appeared to me that Apple made a concerted drive to release *something or anything* to consumers and vendors in order to begin marketing software products on diskettes and hardware products in order to read and write those diskettes. And history does reveal that Apple Computer, Inc., did outsource DOS and contracted for it to be delivered within thirty-five days for $13,000 in April, 1978. Paul Laughton at Shepardson Microsystems wrote the initial Disk Operating System for Apple Computer using Hollerith cards, a card reader and a card writer, and a minicomputer.

Now that I have the time and the continuing curiosity to delve into Apple][DOS, I have the unique opportunity to create my own version of DOS that contains the power and the flexibility I always thought DOS ought to and could have. I call this final version of Apple][DOS, the DOS 4.5 Volume and File Disk Management System, and it requires an Apple][that contains memory in the Language Card partition for its complete operation. This publication describes my sixth build of DOS 4.5. What a ride I have been on! Why? To see what I could do for this brilliant machine and its equally magnificent architecture! I hope that you find my journey into DOS 4.5.06 as fascinating as I found in developing it.

2. Overview of the Improvements and Enhancements in DOS 4.5

I know there are a great many Apple ProDOS users in the global Apple][community, but I never became at all interested in ProDOS. The work I did at Hughes Aircraft in the mid 1980's consisted of using assembly language for programming an operating system executive and hardware interface driver routines on Gould SEL 2780, 6780, and 9780 mainframe computers. These computers hosted a proprietary operating system that allowed our team to simulate the flight of a Radar Digital Processor, an RDP, that is traveling above the surface of the earth in virtually real time. In order to accomplish that goal and simulate real time navigation, the file system of a Gould computer was essentially flat: every software developer had his or her own directory, and these user directories could not contain subdirectories. I was very comfortable with the idea of a flat file system as it was very much like the file system of Apple DOS 3.3. I was simply not comfortable with a slew of subdirectories exemplified by Apple ProDOS. My thought was always "How does one recall the path to follow in order to find anything again?" With the advent of the Macintosh computer and later when I became familiar with the UNIX file system, all of my subdirectory fears vanished and I cannot imagine a modern computer file system without having subdirectories. However, I still remain passionate about Apple][DOS and I leave Apple ProDOS to those who are comfortable with that Apple][operating system architecture. Though what I have seen of ProDOS recently, I believe it could definitely use a serious overhaul. I also believe that ProDOS is far better suited on a machine that has a 16-bit microprocessor much like what is found in the Apple //GS.

I am sure many are curious and want to know what is new and different in DOS 4.5.06, and what makes this version of the DOS Volume and File Disk Management System so special. Looking back over my previous publications of DOS 4.1 and DOS 4.3, I realized that I could have included this enhancement information with every version and with every software build, if only for historical reasons. Like, which version and build did I solve the Track 0x00 utilization quest? Which version and build did I start labeling volumes? Which version and build did I solve the Disk Full logic error? Taken all together, I have done an incredible amount of research, writing, and software development to reach the level of perfection that is contained in DOS 4.5 Build 06. And, to say the least, I have done an incredible amount of unit testing for each and every logical function under normal and abnormal and error conditions. However small the list of improvements and enhancements that are unique to DOS 4.5.06 may seem, I have spent countless hours developing and testing those improvements and enhancements alone and in concert with the overall DOS 4.5 command repertoire and its system functional managers and its interface routines.

Module	Description of Improvement or Enhancement
INCL	Added SUBCODEZ to page-zero 0xD7.
CMD1	Moved CMDINDX to CMDVALS and cleared keyboard variables before, not after parsing a new DOS command. No need to range check SV and USER parameters.
CMD2	Modified TS to read sector data into caller's specified buffer. Added ENTRMON routine that calls INITPTRS before entering the RAM Monitor. Removed COPYVALS after moving CD to File Manager with CDHNDLR. Moved DOADRINC to CMD2. Added DOS TIME command and it uses DATE and SV. Added DOS SSAVE and SLOAD commands where SSAVE uses WRITRNG and SLOAD uses RWRANGE2.
CMD3	Rewrote GREP so that it no longer requires a character string marker for a multiple-word character string search, and less code was required (Aha! Moment)
CMD4	FMDRVR now copies VALSPHAS to FMPHASE, CONFIG is set to default if R keyword is included, PHASE is set to default if R keyword is included, MAXFILES is set to default if R keyword is included, SAVALRD writes CONFIG, PHASE, and MAXFILES processed values into the Value Read buffer only if DOS is in the RUN mode, SV writes its processed values into the Value Read buffer only if DOS is in the RUN mode (Aha! Moment), CD uses File Manager to read VTOC for CONFIG value, PRTSDV now prints volume lock status.
MNGR1	External File Manager entry uses FILALC/NOFILALC values to set KEYWORD1 for file allocation control, now FMTBLJMP uses memory placement of File Manager routines to selectively copy FM Context Block SDV values to FMWORK since Byte Offset and Range Length are overloaded values in FMWORK.
MNGR2	DOS TOUCH handler only copies VALSCNFG to DOSCONFG if R keyword is included to save the DOS configuration, DOS DELETE handler rewritten and its logic reordered, DOS CATALOG handler shows NUMTRKS and FRSTSEC if FILETYPE set and does not show build information if DOSVRSN < 0x33 or DOSBUILD = 0, FREESECT now clears SECBTMAP before calling RORBITMP. Added CDHNDLR.
MNGR3	ALLOCSEC modified to perform up to 4 scans of the VTOC bitmap, ALLOCNTR moved to CMDVALS.
DATA1	Moved CMDUSER before CMDHELP, added CMDSSAVE, CMDSLOAD, and CMDTIME, set drive in KWRANGEH to 81 to support 8 GB CFFA.
BUFR1	Moved CMDINDX after MONVAL in keyword variables and put ALLOCNTR after CMDLNIDX where CMDINDX was, removed unused TRKNUMBR in FMWORK, set VALRDBUF to 8 bytes. File buffer is now 0x0245 bytes in size. Added 7-byte SCRCHTBL table (Aha! Moment) and adjusted SPAREBUF size.
BUFR2	Removed unused WATRKNUM in the Workarea buffer (parallel variable to TRKNUMBR).
RWTS1	If slot number index to SCRCHTBL is zero, RWTS Scratchpad RAM locations for track and phase are cleared for drives 1 and 2, and calls BLDNIBL when RWTS is called the first time for that slot number (Aha! Moment). BLDNIBL dynamically builds RDNIBL and WRNIBL tables in same page with NBUF2.
RWTS2	PHASE value better managed and DISKFMT now initially formats track 0x00, reduces SYNCNT, then formats entire volume starting with track 0x00.
INRF	Modified MNGEXVAL to return the Y-reg incremented twice when reading/writing 16-bit values and once when reading/writing 8-bit values found in the CMDVALS and FMWORK Data structures. Removed access to the INITVALS Data structure. Removed the call to CLRVALS in MNGEXVAL. The call to CLRVALS is now properly made by DOSINIT just prior to the COLDSTRT entry point.
HELP	Any key press other than ESCAPE, RETURN, or arrow keys selects the DOS 4.5.06 Management screen. The DOS 4.5.06 Commands screen lists all commands in alphabetical order by columns.
XFER	The DOS USER handler now resides in lower Main memory and its call to the USER address returns to re-enable RAM memory in the Language Card partition to complete its processing.

Table I.2.1. Major Improvements and Enhancements to DOS 4.5 and Build 06

DOS 4.5 Build 06 is designed to reside **ONLY** in the memory of the Language Card partition. DOS 4.5 Build 06 does **NOT** include a version that resides fully in lower Main memory. DOS 4.5 Build 06 occupies both Language Card partition banks from 0xD000 to 0xDFFF and the remaining memory from 0xE000 to 0xF7FF. The Apple][user has complete freedom to use all of Main memory below 0xBE00 where HIMEM is set. For the remainder of this Second Edition, the DOS 4.5 Volume and File Disk Management System will refer to DOS 4.5 Build 06, or DOS 4.5.06H, simply as DOS 4.5.

The foundation for DOS 4.5 is DOS 4.3 which includes the HELP command. In order to better appreciate all of the improvements and the enhancements that I have added to DOS 4.5, I have tabulated those changes according to each software module as shown in Table I.2.1. Please realize that nothing in DOS 4.3 was removed in order to provide the additional code space that is required by all of these improvements and enhancements. I simply spent a sizable amount of time and effort re-working certain modules to yield the same or better functionality using far less code space. I can truthfully say that I experienced several Aha! Moments that certainly assisted in making these improvements and enhancements to DOS 4.5 possible. Furthermore, I drastically simplified the HELP command interface without sacrificing any of the HELP data that is provided for each command. The new HELP command interface is functionally intuitive and it lists all fifty-two DOS commands in alphabetical order using four display columns.

3. Software Development Strategies Used in DOS 4.5

Let us begin with some software design and development strategies. In order to design reliable and powerful software for a particular machine or platform, one must understand the complete architecture of that machine. I believe this design approach is fully applicable even to the Apple][computer: either executable code or data occupies fixed addressable memory where some defined memory locations are reserved for the stack, text, graphics, control, and peripheral interface cards. Executable code is further restricted in the Apple][by the rather limited 6502-microprocessor Instruction Set. My obvious goal strategy is to design software in such a way as to create the most functionality using the least amount of code and data space. I believe this methodology yields the greatest level of code effectiveness.

I highly recommend obtaining and referring to a number of reference publications for the Apple][hardware and software. I have used the Apple][*Reference Manual*, the Apple //e *Reference Manual*, the Apple //e *Technical Reference Manual*, the Apple][*The DOS Manual* Disk Operating System, *Beneath Apple DOS* by Don Worth and Pieter Lechner, *Understanding the Apple][* by Jim Sather, and *What's Where in the APPLE A Complete Guide to the Apple Computer* by William F. Luebbert to obtain much of my understanding in how the Apple][hardware functions. I have also referred to Apple's *APPLESOFT][* manual to obtain my understanding of the Applesoft programming language. It is an absolutely required reference manual to have on hand in order to learn that BASIC programming language. These references provide the reader with a fairly complete understanding of the architecture of the Apple][computer as well as how to create software programs using the Applesoft language. No reference manual is perfect and people do make mistakes, but these manuals contain very few errors.

In order to study how other people have approached the hardware architecture of the Apple][in creating their software applications, it is necessary to obtain their source code or generate some source code from their object code, the code that actually executes from within the Apple][memory. Rarely have I ever found published source code. Glen Bredon designed *Sourceror* as a subsidiary tool to his assembler *Big Mac* that creates *Big Mac* source code files from assembly language object code files. *Big Mac* can also save source code as text files so that *Big Mac* source code can be migrated to other assemblers like *Lisa*.

To assist me in my assembly language programming, I use Gerard Putter's application Virtual][, Version 11.3.1, to create my software applications, and that is the platform that I use in order to perform my initial, though simulated software testing. Once I am satisfied with a software program or utility that is operating within the Virtual][environment, I transfer the volume image that contains that software program or utility to an Enhanced Apple //e. I have found some discrepancies between Virtual][and my Enhanced Apple //e particularly when I am enabling memory in the Language Card partition. For example, two successive *writes* to memory address 0xC083 does **not** write-enable Bank 2 in the Language Card partition in my Enhanced Apple //e as it does in Virtual][. Two successive *reads* of memory address 0xC083 function the same in both my Enhanced Apple //e and in Virtual][to enable Bank 2 memory. I have brought this to the attention of Mr. Putter. Also, Main memory is not initialized at power-up in quite the same way in my Enhanced Apple //e as it is in Virtual][. I believe DOS 3.3 always assumes that an Apple][will power up with all bytes in page-zero memory set to 0xFF. Virtual][also makes this same assumption. I know I have been caught unaware that all bytes in Auxiliary page-zero memory are not always set to 0xFF at power-up. Therefore, I have included a call to SETNORM during BOOT Stage 2 in order to ensure that page-zero memory location 0x32 is, indeed, set to 0xFF. I have used AUXMOVE to manually *stash* some Apple ProDOS code in Auxiliary memory from within Virtual][. The code disappears and becomes overwritten when I then BOOT into DOS. This does not happen in the Enhanced Apple //e: the ProDOS code or any stashed code can still be safely found in Auxiliary memory even after a DOS reBOOT. Always, always, always make unit and final software tests using **real** hardware. I am not so sure if it is truly possible to totally emulate real hardware using software.

Memory Page	Bank 2 Description	Bank 1 Description
0x00	Page-zero variables, pointers, routines, and special addressing modes	
0x01	Stack for the 6502-microprocessor	
0x02	INPUT buffer, Applesoft interpretation buffer	
0x03	User buffer, DOS interface routines and vectors	
0x04-0x07	Text or LORES graphics Page 1	
0x08-0x0B	Applesoft program start, Text or LORES graphics Page 2, or available for software	
0x0C-0x1F	Available for software	
0x20-0x3F	HIRES graphics Page 1, or available for software	
0x40-0x5F	HIRES graphics Page 2, or available for software	
0x60-0xBF	Available for software	
0xC0	System Soft Switches	
0xC1-0xC7	Peripheral-card ROM memory for slots 1-7, or CX ROM	
0xC8-0xCF	Peripheral-card expansion ROM memory for slots 1-7, or CX ROM	
0xD0-0xDF	ROM Applesoft Interpreter routines	not used
0xE0-0xEF	ROM Applesoft Interpreter routines	
0xF0-0xF7	ROM Applesoft Interpreter routines	
0xF8-0xFF	ROM Monitor routines	

Table I.3.1. Apple][Memory Utilization

Before beginning any discussion of a complicated subject like a volume and file disk management system for the Apple][computer, it is usually easier to understand such a system if each component of that system is shown as part of a Big Picture. That Big Picture is shown in the following two tables, Tables I.3.1 and I.3.2. Though certainly not to any particular scale, Table I.3.1 shows how memory is utilized in the Apple][and where the basic Apple][system hardware and software components can be found in lower Main memory and in the memory of the Language Card partition. The Language Card partition is shown in the bottom rows in both of these tables with a darker shade. The basic components that are shown in Table

I.3.1 are the 6502-microprocessor memory requirements, the DOS interface routines and vectors, text and LORES graphic pages, HIRES graphic pages, system Soft Switches, peripheral-card and CX ROM memory, where the ROM Applesoft interpreter is found, and where the ROM Monitor resides. If any of the components that are shown in Table I.3.1 are unfamiliar, it would be to your best advantage now to locate and study one or more of the above reference publications in order to refresh and increase your understanding of that component. Even the Apple][*Reference Manual* that was furnished with my Apple][+ computer contains invaluable information that is still applicable to the entire family of Apple][computers. I even own a few **SAMS** Publications that have provided me with more enhanced understanding of many of the components that are shown in Table I.3.1.

Memory Page	Bank 2 Description	Bank 1 Description
0x00-0x03	System, 6502-microprocessor memory utilization	
0x04-0x07	Text Page 1	
0x08-0xBD	Available for software	
0xBE-0xBF	DOS 4.5 HIMEM, DOS 4.5 Language Card partition software interface, DOS 4.5 bootstrap routines	
0xC0	System Soft Switches	
0xC1-0xCF	Peripheral-card ROM memory for slots, CX ROM	
0xD0-0xDF	RAM DOS 4.5 Command and File Managers	RAM DOS RWTS, HELP
0xE0-0xE6	RAM DOS 4.5 Command and File Managers	
0xE7-0xEC	RAM DOS 4.5 working variables and Workarea buffer	
0xED-0xF7	RAM DOS 4.5 file buffers	
0xF8-0xFF	RAM Monitor routines that are dynamically modified	

Table I.3.2. Apple][Memory Utilization with DOS 4.5 Installed

Table I.3.2 is similar to Table I.3.1 and it shows visually where DOS 4.5 and its components are placed in memory. In order to manage the DOS 4.5 routines that are located in the memory of both banks in the Language Card partition, a set of software interface routines that control the utilization of memory in the Language Card partition is located in Page 0xBE. Page 0xBF contains the DOS disk bootstrap routines.

The following sections discuss the utilization of Apple][memory in great detail. It may be helpful to occasionally refer to Tables I.3.1 and I.3.2 in order to fully understand how that memory utilization relates to the entire hardware and software management of the Apple][computer by the DOS 4.5 Volume and File Disk Management System. I prefer to view the hardware management of the Apple][computer by virtue of its microprocessor, its memory allocation, its Soft Switches, and its ROM architecture. And, I prefer to view the software management of the Apple][computer by virtue of its functional managers and interface routines. In my viewpoint, the functional managers that are provided by DOS 4.5 for the Apple][computer include the Boot Manager, the Volume and File Manager, the File Buffer Manager, the Memory Interface Manager, the RWTS Manager, the Variable Access Manager, the Data Buffer Manager, and the DOS Command Manager. The interface routines reside at 0x3D0:0x3FF and on Page 0xBF. The Apple][computer is truly a brilliantly designed machine and it has an equally magnificent hardware architecture. I sincerely believe that you will find my presentation of the Apple][computer vis-à-vis DOS 4.5 interesting, enlightening, and fundamentally useful in view of your own hardware and software experiences with this very delightful machine.

4. Page-Zero Utilization

The Instruction Set for the 6502-microprocessor as well as the 65C02-microprocessor includes certain microprocessor instructions that utilize variables that are located in the first 256 addressable memory bytes or page, or locations 0x0000 to 0x00FF. I designate this area of memory to be *page-zero*.

When Steven Wozniak designed the Apple ROM Monitor, a collection of low-level software routines, he allocated a number of page-zero locations for its variables and pointers. Similarly, Applesoft, DOS, and virtually all other assembly language routines use page-zero locations in order to utilize those specific microprocessor instructions. The 6502-microprocessor contains an accumulator called the A-register and two index registers called the X-register and the Y-register. Page-zero instructions using these registers include load and store instructions, indexed load and store instructions, indexed indirect addressing instructions using the X-register, and indirect indexed addressing instructions using the Y-register. Page-zero wraparound occurs with indexed and indexed indirect addressing instructions using the X-register and indexed addressing instructions of the X-register using the Y-register. Page-zero wraparound does **not** occur with indirect indexed addressing instructions using the Y-register. Yes, initially, addressing modes and their utilization can certainly be a little daunting, but these mode are also very logical.

0x	0	1	2	3	4	5	6	7	8	9	A	B	C	D	E	F
00	1234	134	34	34	34	4					4	4	4	4	4	4
10	4	4	4	4	4	4	4	4	4	4	4	4	4	24	2	3
20	134	134	134	134	1346	134	1456	1456	1346	1346	13456	13456	1456	1456	123456	123456
30	14	12	134	1246	123	1236	136	136	136	136	123	123	12345	12345	123456	123456
40	156	156	1236	1236	1236	1	1	1	1	1	56	56	6	6	13	13
50	346	346	4	4	4	4	24	24	24	24	46	6	6	6	4	4
60	4	4	4	4	4	4	4	46	46	46	46	46	46	346	346	346
70	346	4	4	346	346	4	46	4	4	4	4	4	4	4	4	4
80	4	4	4	4	4	4	4	4	4	4	4	4	4	4	4	4
90	4	4	4	4	34	34	4	4	4	4	4	34	34	4	4	4
A0	4	4	4	4	4	4	4	4	4	4	4	4	4	4	4	46
B0	46	4	4	4	4	4	4	4	4	4	4	4	4	4	4	4
C0	4	4	4	4	4	4	4	4	4	4	4	4	4	4		
D0	4	4	4	4	4	4	46	6	46	6	4	4	4	4	4	4
E0	4	4	4		4	4	4	4	34	34	4					
F0	4	4	4	14	14	4	4	4	4	4						34

Figure I.4.1. Page-Zero Memory Utilization

Key

1 – used by the ROM Monitor
2 – used by the Mini Assembler
3 – used by the Apple //e CX ROM

4 – used by ROM Applesoft
5 – used by RWTS
6 – used by DOS 4.5

When developing a new assembly language routine, it is critical to select page-zero locations that do not conflict with the Apple ROM Monitor, Applesoft, or DOS depending on whether those ROM routines and the routines that reside in the memory of the Language Card partition are important to the new program. Knowing which page-zero locations are used by or critical to ROM and resident routines can greatly simplify the selection of unused or available page-zero locations. Because DOS 3.3 supports Integer BASIC, a few page-zero locations are used to process that file Type. DOS 4.5 also uses those same page-zero locations for processing the Applesoft CHAIN command, for example, and to support many other DOS command enhancements. There are definitely obvious page-zero locations that cannot be used except for how they are intended, like the horizontal and vertical cursor locations CH and CV, respectively. Then, there are less obvious, rather dubious page-zero locations from 0x00 to 0x1F that are used by some Applesoft commands. These page-zero locations are fair game for any program that does not use the Applesoft interpreter or Steven Wozniak's *SWEET16* interpreter. Figure I.4.1 shows all of the used and unused page-zero locations, and the Key below Figure I.4.1 correlates those applications that use each particular page-zero location according to my references and the best of my ability to decipher which page-zero locations are utilized by ROM routines. The more shaded areas in Figure I.4.1 are unused page-zero locations that are most likely not used by the Apple //e ROM Monitor or by Applesoft, so those locations are more than likely the better page-zero locations to select for a new assembly language routine. Table I.4.1 summarizes all of the available page-zero locations that are not utilized by the ROM routines or by DOS 4.5 as shown in Figure I.4.1. Keep in mind that indirect indexed addressing mode instructions that use the Y-register **do** require a page-zero byte-pair, so it is even more critical that neither address byte is clobbered by software that is external to any new assembly language routine.

Start	End	Description
0x06	0x09	4 bytes free
0xCE	0xCF	2 bytes free
0xE3	0xE3	1 byte free
0xEB	0xEF	5 bytes free
0xFA	0xFE	5 bytes free

Table I.4.1. Available Page-Zero Locations Summary

Tables I.4.2 and I.4.3 list all of the page-zero locations that are utilized by DOS 4.5 and defined in the DOS 4.5 source code file INCL.L. There are certainly common page-zero locations that all software routines can use as temporary variables and pointers. The 6502-microprocessor is not time-shared and there is no context switching between routines. If a routine uses some common page-zero locations, that routine should complete all of its calculations and processing using those locations and the routine should not expect to find those same results sometime later. Examples of common page-zero locations would include A1L/A1H at 0x3C:0x3D, A2L/A2H at 0x3E:0x3F, A3L/A3H at 0x40:0x41, A4L/A4H at 0x42:0x43, OPRND at 0x44:0x45, and the first three bytes of DSCTMP at 0x9D:0x9F. As it is shown in Tables I.4.2 and I.4.3, all of these page-zero locations are defined in the DOS 4.5 file INCL.L and these page-zero locations are utilized in the DOS 4.5 source code. Using these page-zero locations to move or to copy data would be safe and using them for that purpose would not interfere with the ROM Monitor or Applesoft processing. Actually, several ROM Monitor routines require that some of these page-zero locations just mentioned contain user data before using those routines. The ROM Monitor MOVE routine at 0xFE2C is one such example that uses A1L/A1H and A2L/A2H in order to move data from one memory

8

location to another memory location. It is really up to the user to confirm and to verify that the selected page-zero memory locations do not interfere with other routines that may be external to and required by any new software that is developed by a user.

Address	Parameter	Description
0x24	CH	horizontal cursor location
0x25	CV	vertical cursor location
0x26	BUFRADRZ	ROM firmware BOOT DATA Field Data buffer address
0x26	TEMPZ	RWTS temporary 8-bit variable
0x27	TEMP2Z	RWTS temporary 8-bit variable
0x28	BASEZ	text screen line address
0x2A	ASPTRSAV	DOS CHAIN array descriptor addresses
0x2A	CURTRKZ	RWTS requested track
0x2B	SLOT16Z	BOOT slot * 16
0x2C	DRVFLAG	RWTS data -changing drive flag
0x2C	ADRDATMK	RWTS Address/Data mark
0x2C	ADRFIELD	RWTS sector Address Field header array
0x2D	SECFNDZ	RWTS sector Address Field header sector found
0x2E	TRKFNDZ	RWTS sector Address Field header track found
0x2F	VOLFNDZ	RWTS sector Address Field header volume found
0x32	INVFLG	text screen inverse/normal flag
0x33	PROMPT	text screen prompt character
0x34	PHASE	RWTS requested phase number
0x35	PAGECNT	BOOT/initialization DOS image page count
0x35	SAVXYREG	save X-reg or Y-reg 8-bit variable
0x35	SYNCNT	RWTS synchronization byte count
0x35	CMDINDXZ	Page-zero CMDINDX
0x36	CSWL	output device handler address
0x38	KSWL	input device handler address
0x3C	ROMTEMPZ	ROM firmware BOOT temporary 8-bit variable
0x3C	MOTORTIM	RWTS motor on-time, 16-bit count
0x3C	A1	general purpose temporary 16-bit variable
0x3D	ROMSECTR	ROM firmware BOOT requested sector
0x3E	BUFADR2Z	RWTS DATA Field Data buffer address
0x3E	ODDBITSZ	RWTS temporary 8-bit variable
0x3E	A2	general purpose temporary 16-bit variable
0x3F	SECTORZ	RWTS Address Field header sector
0x40	ROMDATA	ROM firmware BOOT Address Field header track found
0x40	FILEBUFZ	file Context Block parameter buffer address
0x40	TRACKZ	RWTS Address Field header track
0x41	ROMTRACK	ROM firmware BOOT requested track
0x41	VOLUMEZ	RWTS Address Field header volume

Table I.4.2. Page-Zero Utilization in DOS 4.5 – Part 1

Address	Parameter	Description
0x42	A4	general purpose temporary 16-bit variable
0x42	BUFADRZ	general purpose data buffer address
0x44	DIRINDX	VTOC and TSL data buffer index
0x4A	IOBADR	RWTS IOCB buffer address
0x4C	DOSPTR	DOS general purpose pointer address
0x50	LINNUM	Applesoft line number 16-bit variable
0x5A	DOSTEMP1	DOS general purpose 8-bit variable
0x5B	DOSTEMP2	DOS general purpose 8-bit variable
0x5C	DOSBUFR	DOS general purpose 16-bit variable/address
0x67	ASPGMST	Applesoft program start address
0x69	ASVARS	Applesoft simple variables pointer
0x6B	ASARYS	Applesoft array pointer
0x6D	ARYEND	Applesoft end of array pointer
0x6F	ASSTRS	Applesoft end of character string storage pointer
0x73	ASHIMEM	Applesoft HIMEM address
0x76	ASRUN	Applesoft RUN flag
0x9D	DSCTMP	Applesoft temporary character string descriptor data
0xAF	ASPEND	Applesoft end of program address
0xD6	PROTECT	Applesoft program write-protect 8-bit flag
0xD7	SUBCODEZ	Page-zero SUBCODE
0xD8	ASONERR	Applesoft ONERR 8-bit error flag
0xD9	RKEYWORD	DOS R keyword 8-bit variable

Table I.4.3. Page-Zero Utilization in DOS 4.5 – Part 2

0x	0	1	2	3	4	5	6	7	8	9	A	B	C	D	E	F
00	00	11	0F	33	03	00	FE	00	00	00	00	00	00	00	00	00
10	00	00	00	00	00	00	00	00	00	00	00	00	00	00	00	00
20	00	00	00	00	00	00	00	7A	00	00	00	00	00	00	00	00
30	12	01	00	00	23	10	00	01	00	00	00	00	00	00	00	00
40	00	00	00	00	FF	FF	00	00	FF	FF	00	00	FF	FF	00	00
50	FF	FF	00	00	FF	FF	00	00	FF	FF	00	00	FF	FF	00	00
60	FF	FF	00	00	FF	FF	00	00	FF	FF	00	00	FF	FF	00	00
70	FF	FF	00	00	FF	FF	00	00	FF	FF	00	00	00	00	00	00
80	3F	FF	00	00	FF	FF	00	00	FF	FF	00	00	FF	FF	00	00
90	FF	FF	00	00	FF	FF	00	00	FF	FF	00	00	FF	FF	00	00
A0	FF	FF	00	00	FF	FF	00	00	FF	FF	00	00	FF	FF	00	00
B0	FF	FF	00	00	FF	FF	00	00	FF	FF	00	00	FF	FF	00	00
C0	FF	FF	00	00	00	00	00	00	00	00	00	00	00	00	00	00
D0	00	00	00	00	00	00	00	00	00	00	00	00	00	00	00	00
E0	00	00	00	00	00	00	00	00	00	00	00	00	00	00	00	00
F0	00	00	00	00	00	00	00	00	00	00	00	00	00	00	00	00

Figure I.5.1. Disk Volume VTOC Structure in DOS 3.3

Byte	Name	Value	Description
0x00	VTOCSB	0x00	VTOC Structure Block
0x01	FRSTTRK	0x11	Track number of first catalog sector
0x02	FRSTSEC	0x0F	Sector number of first catalog sector (default = 0x0F)
0x03	DOSRLS1	0x33	DOS release #1 used to initialize this volume
0x04	DOSRLS2	0x03	DOS release #2 used to initialize this volume
0x05	DOSRLS3	0x00	DOS release #3 used to initialize this volume
0x06	DISKVOL	0xFE	Volume number assigned to this volume (default = 0xFE)
0x07-0x26	~	0x00	32 bytes are not used for anything
0x27	NUMTSENT	0x7A	Maximum number of T/S entry pairs in one TSL sector
0x28-0x2F	~	0x00	8 bytes are not used for anything
0x30	NXTTOALC	0x11	Last track used to allocate a sector for data or for a TSL
0x31	ALLCDIR	0x01	Track Allocation Direction (0x01 or 0xFF)
0x32-0x33	~	0x00	2 bytes are not used for anything
0x34	NUMTRKS	0x23	Number of tracks in this volume (always set to 0x23)
0x35	NUMSECS	0x10	Number of sectors per track in this volume (always set to 0x10)
0x36-0x37	BYTPRSEC	0x100	Number of bytes per sector (256) (Lo/Hi byte order)
0x38-0x3B	BITMAP	0x0000 0000	Bitmap of free sectors for track 0 (set to 0x0000 0000)
0x3C-0x43	:::	0x0000 0000	Bitmap of free sectors for tracks 1-2 (set to 0x0000 0000)
0x44-0x7B	:::	0xFFFF 0000	Bitmap of free sectors for tracks 3-16 (set to 0xFFFF 0000)
0x7C-0x7F	:::	0x0000 0000	Bitmap of VTOC and Catalog sectors for track 17 (0x0000 0000)
0x80-0xC3	:::	0xFFFF 0000	Bitmap of free sectors for tracks 18-34 (set to 0xFFFF 0000)
0xC4-0xFF		0x0000 0000	reserved for tracks 35-49 (set to 0x0000 0000)

Table I.5.1. VTOC Structure Block Definition in DOS 3.3

5. VTOC Structure in DOS 4.5

How I remember agonizing over how best to implement date and time stamping of disk volumes and their files! Preferably, I only wanted to update a date and time stamp when either the Volume Table Of Contents, or VTOC of a disk volume or a file in a disk volume has changed. I also wanted to date and time stamp a disk volume or disk image when that volume or image is first created and initialized. However, creating or updating a date and time stamp is only half of the task: the date and time stamp needs to be displayed in an appropriate format for an appropriate reason. So, when the contents of a Catalog directory of a volume are displayed, the date and time stamp of each file needs to be displayed along with its filename, its file Type, and its file size. Another reason to display a date and time stamp is for the date and time when a volume is first created and the date and time when the VTOC is last changed. Since the VTOC is basically the heart of the disk volume, I believe it is best to start the discussion with the VTOC and begin with how DOS 3.3 has implemented the VTOC and show its organization and its contents. Knowing the DOS 3.3 implementation will certainly help to explain the reasons behind the DOS 4.5 implementation and whether or not the unused VTOC resource space in the DOS 3.3 implementation was designed that way for a particular reason so that others, perhaps, may utilize that resource space in a future version.

The DOS 3.3 VTOC is defined to be located on track 0x11 and it includes all of sector 0x00 for its use, though it could be located in any sector on any track. The volume Catalog sectors may be any group of sectors on any track, but typically they are defined to be located on track 0x11 as well, and they are selected to be the remaining sectors of that same track just above the VTOC sector for optimal timing and access. Figure I.5.1 shows the VTOC for a typical DOS 3.3 volume and Table I.5.1 defines each entry that exists in that DOS 3.3 VTOC. All entries in this VTOC are essentially static in the sense that these entries are not variable and they are not subject to change: the number of volume Catalog sectors is always fifteen, the number of volume tracks is always thirty-five, and the number of sectors in a track is always sixteen. The remaining entries in the DOS 3.3 VTOC are used by DOS 3.3 routines in order to access volume resources to write or to update current files or to create new files on the volume.

It is quite obvious from Figure I.5.1 and Table I.5.1 that the DOS 3.3 VTOC contains a fair amount of unimagined resource space. Truly, did Apple leave the DOS 3.3 VTOC so barren hoping that others may find a usefulness in some of its unused resource space? I believe DOS 4.5 fully answers that question! The DOS 4.5 VTOC is defined to be located on track 0x11 and it includes all of sector 0x00 for its use, though it could be located in any sector on any track. The volume Catalog sectors may be any group of sectors on any track, but typically they are defined to be located on track 0x11 as well, and they are usually the lower sectors of that same track just above the VTOC sector for optimal timing and access. Figure I.5.2 shows the VTOC for a DATA volume that uses five sectors for its volume Catalog. A volume that does **not** contain a DOS 4.5 BOOT image on its BOOT tracks, or tracks 0x00 and 0x01 and ten sectors on track 0x02 for a total of 42 sectors, is defined as volume Type D for DATA volume. A volume that **does** contain a DOS 4.5 BOOT image on its BOOT tracks is defined as volume Type B for BOOT volume. Table I.5.2 defines each entry in the DOS 4.5 VTOC, Table I.5.3 defines the free sector bitmap for each initialized track that has sixteen sectors, Table I.5.4 defines the free sector bitmap for each initialized track that has thirty-two sectors, and Table I.5.5 defines the bytes of the six-byte date and time stamp in the order those bytes are stored in the VTOC and in the Catalog sectors. There is more information in Section I.6 about the free sector bitmap definition as it is utilized throughout DOS 4.5.

0x	0	1	2	3	4	5	6	7	8	9	A	B	C	D	E	F
00	00	11	05	45	06	C8	00	C4				Volume Name				
10							(24 characters)									
20	Date & Time Volume created						04	7A	LibNum		Date & Time VTOC last changed					
30	11	01	00	00	24	10	00	01	FF	FF	00	00	FF	FF	00	00
40	FF	FF	00	00	FF	FF	00	00	FF	FF	00	00	FF	FF	00	00
50	FF	FF	00	00	FF	FF	00	00	FF	FF	00	00	FF	FF	00	00
60	FF	FF	00	00	FF	FF	00	00	FF	FF	00	00	FF	FF	00	00
70	FF	FF	00	00	FF	FF	00	00	FF	FF	00	00	FF	C0	00	00
80	FF	FF	00	00	FF	FF	00	00	FF	FF	00	00	FF	FF	00	00
90	FF	FF	00	00	FF	FF	00	00	FF	FF	00	00	FF	FF	00	00
A0	FF	FF	00	00	FF	FF	00	00	FF	FF	00	00	FF	FF	00	00
B0	FF	FF	00	00	FF	FF	00	00	FF	FF	00	00	FF	FF	00	00
C0	FF	FF	00	00	FF	FF	00	00	00	00	00	00	00	00	00	00
D0	00	00	00	00	00	00	00	00	00	00	00	00	00	00	00	00
E0	00	00	00	00	00	00	00	00	00	00	00	00	00	00	00	00
F0	00	00	00	00	00	00	00	00	00	00	00	00	00	00	00	00

Figure I.5.2. Data Disk Volume VTOC Structure in DOS 4.5

Byte	Name	Value	Description
0x00	VTOCSB	0x00	VTOC Structure Block
0x01	FRSTTRK	0x11	Track number of first catalog sector
0x02	FRSTSEC	0x05	Sector number of first catalog sector (default = 0x05)
0x03	DOSVRSN	0x45	DOS version number used to initialize this volume
0x04	DOSBUILD	0x06	DOS build number used to initialize this volume
0x05	DOSRAM	0xC8	DOS RAM location used to initialize this volume (H)
0x06	DISKVOL	0x00	Volume number assigned to this volume (default = 0x00)
0x07	DISKTYPE	0xC4	Volume Type (B or D) for BOOT or DATA volume
0x08-0x1F	DISKNAME	~	Volume Name (24 ASCII characters), right filled with 0xA0
0x20-0x25	INITIME	~	Date and Time when volume was created/initialized
0x26	VTOCPHAS	0x04	Number of Half-Phases per track (1-16)
0x27	NUMTSENT	0x7A	Maximum number of T/S entry pairs in one TSL sector
0x28-0x29	DISKSUBJ	~	Volume Library (subject) (0x0000-0xFFFF) (Lo/Hi)
0x2A-0x2F	VTOCTIME	~	Date and Time VTOC was initialized or last changed
0x30	NXTTOALC	0x11	Last track used to allocate a sector for DATA or for a TSL
0x31	ALLOCDIR	0x01	Track Allocation Direction (0x01 or 0xFF)
0x32	DOSCONFG	0x00	DOS Configuration value (0x00-0xFF)
0x33	DISKLOCK	0x00	Disk Lock flag (0x00 for unlock and 0x80 for lock)
0x34	NUMTRKS	0x24	Number of tracks in this volume (maximum is 50)
0x35	NUMSECS	0x10	Number of sectors per track (16 or 32) in this volume
0x36-0x37	BYTPRSEC	0x100	Number of bytes per sector (256) (Lo/Hi byte order)
0x38-0x3B	BITMAP	~	Bitmap of free sectors for track 0
0x3C-0x7B	:::	~	Bitmap of free sectors for tracks 1-16
0x7C-0x7F	:::	~	Bitmap of free sectors for track 17 (VTOC and Catalog)
0x80-0xC7	:::	~	Bitmap of free sectors for tracks 18-35 (or NUMTRKS-1)
0xC8-0xFF		0x00	reserved for additional tracks (36-49 in this example)

Table I.5.2. VTOC Structure Block Definition in DOS 4.5

Byte	Sectors	Sector Order	Initial Value
0	0F-08	FEDCBA98	0xFF
1	07-00	76543210	0xFF
2	1F-18	FEDCBA98	0x00
3	17-10	76543210	0x00

Table I.5.3. Free Sector Bitmap for 16 Sectors per Track

Byte	Sectors	Sector Order	Initial Value
0	0F-08	FEDCBA98	0xFF
1	07-00	76543210	0xFF
2	1F-18	FEDCBA98	0xFF
3	17-10	76543210	0xFF

Table I.5.4. Free Sector Bitmap for 32 Sectors per Track

Byte	Value Range	Value
0	0x00 - 0x59	second
1	0x00 - 0x59	minute
2	0x00 - 0x23	hour
3	0x00 - 0x99	year
4	0x01 - 0x31	day
5	0x01 - 0x12	month

Table I.5.5. Date and Time Definition Shown in Variable Order

Nearly all of the entries in the DOS 4.5 VTOC are essentially dynamic such that these entries are variable and they can easily be changed for different VTOC configurations. As in DOS 3.3, many of the VTOC entries are used by DOS 4.5 routines in order to access volume resources to write or to update current files or to create new files on the volume. It is quite obvious from Figure I.5.2 and Table I.5.2 that the DOS 4.5 VTOC contains complete utilization for all of the unimagined resource space that exists in the DOS 3.3 VTOC. Truly, profound usefulness for each and every byte in the VTOC has been created for DOS 4.5 for each and every DOS 4.5 disk volume or disk image whether it is a BOOT or a DATA volume!

As shown in Table I.3.2, a simplified view of the contents of DOS include the Command Manager, the File Manager, RWTS, and an assortment of many other software routines that comprise DOS 4.5. In DOS 3.3, much code and valuable data space is dedicated to the manipulation of volume number beginning in the Command Manager, through the File Manager, and on to RWTS, and then back through the File Manager after RWTS processing. Since most positional parameters such as Volume, Address, and Length are initialized to zero by the Command Manager when a DOS 4.5 command is parsed, the default VOLVAL for the volume number keyword will always be zero. DOS 4.5 passes volume number through the File Manager and on to RWTS **unchanged**. Therefore, the **default** volume number that is displayed by DOS 4.5 is 000; the default volume number is never 254 or 0xFE as it is in DOS 3.3. The volume number at byte 0x06 in the VTOC sector is the **official** volume number that is assigned to that volume in DOS 4.5 and it is **not** the volume number that RWTS finds encoded in the Address Field header for any sector on any data or BOOTable diskette track. Disk images that are in file format do not contain an encoded Address Field header for its track sectors, so there is absolutely no available method to extract a volume number from any of this file data except from byte 0x06 in the VTOC sector. I will show throughout this book that VOLVAL plays a critical role in many other file systems that are external to DOS 4.5. Along with Drive number, Track number, and Sector number, Volume number is simply another required asset in all DVTS calculations for Logical Block Address conversions in file systems that utilize block number rather than sector number for data management.

Bytes 0x01 and 0x02 of the VTOC as shown in Figure I.5.2 are the track and sector numbers, respectively, that point to the first Catalog sector. As in DOS 3.3, DOS 4.5 uses byte 0x03 of the VTOC for the DOS Version Number, but unlike DOS 3.3, DOS 4.5 uses the unused byte at byte 0x04 for the DOS Build Number. Byte 0x05 is used to designate that H, or 0xC8, DOS RAM is the memory in which DOS 4.5 occupied when it creates or initializes another disk volume. Alternatively, byte 0x05 designates that L, or 0xCC, DOS RAM is the memory in which DOS 4.5L from Build 05 or earlier occupied when it creates or initializes another disk volume. DOS RAM does not have any further use in DOS 4.5 except to remind the user that DOS 4.5 Build 06 resides in the memory of the Language Card partition. From the above discussion, the volume number is found in byte 0x06. Byte 0x07 is used to specify the Disk Volume

Type, either B, or 0xC2, or D, or 0xC4, that designates whether the volume contains strictly DATA or a BOOT image. Bytes 0x08:0x1F are used for the 24-character Disk Volume Name or Disk Title and bytes 0x20:0x25 are used for the Disk Volume Date and Time stamp when the volume is first created or initialized. Bytes 0x2A:0x2F are used for the VTOC Date and Time stamp, and this time stamp is updated whenever DOS 4.5 changes anything in the VTOC for any reason. Byte 0x26 is the phase number and bytes 0x28:0x29 are used to assign a 16-bit Disk Library number in Lo/Hi byte order to the volume. Byte 0x32 is used to store the system CONFIG value and byte 0x33 is used to store the Disk Lock value for that volume. All other VTOC variables are still at their original, DOS 3.3 location. The number of Bytes per Sector that is found at bytes 0x36:0x37 is retained but it has no further internal or external use in DOS 4.5. All data manipulations are performed at the sector level where a sector is defined to contain 256 bytes of data.

6. The VTOC Bitmap Definition

The free sector bitmap of a volume is located in the VTOC of that volume starting at byte 0x38 as shown in Figure I.5.2. Four bytes are allocated for each of the tracks in a volume whose bits determine whether a sector on that track is utilized or not utilized for a BOOT sector, a Catalog sector, a Track/Sector List or TSL sector, or a sector that is comprised of data for a file. There are two routines where DOS 3.3 **uses** NUMSECS or byte 0x35 as shown in Table I.5.1, the VTOC variable that is equal to the number of sectors in a track: ALLOCSEC and RORBITMP. ALLOCSEC is a routine that finds, allocates, and reserves a disk track that contains at least one available sector. It uses the VTOC bitmap in order to find and reserve this identified track. RORBITMP is a routine that is used by FREESECT that sets or clears the assigned bit for a sector within the 4-byte bitmap of its track as shown in Table I.5.3. The ramifications of limiting these routines to the value found in NUMSECS causes the definition of the bit that is assigned to sector 0x00 to be different in 16-sector and 32-sector tracks. In DOS 3.3, sector 0x00 is assigned to the first bit or bit 0 in the **second** byte of the 4-byte bitmap for its track when NUMSECS is equal to sixteen, again as shown in Table I.5.3. However, when NUMSECS is equal to thirty-two, sector 0x00 is assigned to the first bit in the **fourth** byte of the 4-byte bitmap for its track as shown in Table I.6.1. Furthermore, *FID* has always assumed that NUMSECS is equal to sixteen and has always rotated the bitmap of every track accordingly. *FID*, as published by Apple, **cannot** copy files onto a DOS 3.3 volume that contains 32-sector tracks because it does not rotate the bitmap properly for volumes having 32-sector tracks!

Byte	Sector	Bitmap
0	1F-18	FEDCBA98
1	17-10	76543210
2	0F-08	FEDCBA98
3	07-00	76543210

Table I.6.1. Free Sector Bitmap for 32 Sectors per Track in DOS 3.3

Here is a confounded situation where the VTOC, presumably designed by Apple Computer, Inc., is not fully supported even by Apple designed utilities. I wonder if Apple thought as early as 1979 when it published *FID* that there would never be a device that would support 32-sector tracks? Were 32-sector tracks merely a placeholder in the VTOC? Did Apple give up on DOS 3.3 in preference to Apple ProDOS earlier than anyone suspected, or was *FID* designed and written by an incompetent person? As an aside, I have never been convinced that the family of Apple][computers was necessarily the optimal platform for the hierarchal directory structures that are created in ProDOS. I am even less convinced now. I maintain that ProDOS performs better on a platform that utilizes, at a minimum, a 16-bit microprocessor.

ALLOCSEC and RORBITMP manipulate the free sector bitmap for each track as shown in Table I.5.3 consistently in DOS 4.5 without regard to the value found in NUMSECS because 32-sector tracks is always implied even when a volume contains 16-sector tracks. DOS 4.5 only interacts with the VTOC bitmap by means of the variable NEXTSECR that is exclusively OR'd with the value of 0x10 in the routines ALLOCSEC and FREESECT. In other words, the bitmap is manipulated as if it looks like what is shown in Table I.6.1, but the bitmap appears in the VTOC as if it looks like what is shown in Table I.5.3. Whether a volume contains 16-sector or 32-sector tracks does not matter to the DOS 4.5 routines that utilize this programming strategy. When the bitmap is manipulated, or rotated consistently in this fashion, sector 0x00 is always assigned to the first bit in the **second** byte of the four-byte bitmap of its track as shown in Table I.5.3 but programmatically sector 0x00 is assigned to the first bit in the **fourth** byte of the four-byte bitmap of its track as shown in Table I.6.1.

For volumes that have 16-sector tracks, the 4-byte bitmap of each track in this volume that has all sixteen sectors available would be set to FF FF 00 00. For volumes having 32-sector tracks, the 4-byte bitmap of each track having all thirty-two sectors available would be set to FF FF FF FF. When the 4-byte bitmap of a track is not rotated consistently for 16-sector and 32-sector volumes, it puts an unnecessary burden on the DOS INIT handler to determine exactly which bit is assigned to sector 0x00 and which bit is assigned to sector 0x10. Utilizing and rotating the 4-byte bitmap of a track consistently puts no further throughput burden onto DOS 4.5. I have also incorporated the necessary bitmap utilization and the programming strategy changes into my modified version of *FID* that models how DOS 4.5 defines the 4-byte bitmap of a track and how that bitmap must be correctly manipulated. As to be expected, DOS 4.5 and my modified version of *FID* can fully read, copy, and write to a DOS 4.5 volume that has 16-sector tracks or to any other volume for that matter, without exception, even to a DOS 3.3 volume, whether that volume is formatted having tracks that contain 16 sectors or 32 sectors.

One of the most interesting aspects of the RORBITMP routine is that it plays a critical role in undeleting a file. Not only does RORBITMP reserve or unreserve a sector for file use, its intended purpose, but it can equally be used to preserve a sector in a file when that file is undeleted. I pay humble respects to my professor of Boolean Algebra for teaching me the power of the exclusive OR Boolean operation. I believe it is one of the most powerful instructions in the 6502-microprocessor command repertoire, for it certainly is most powerful when it is used in the RORBITMP routine. In normal processing, the Carry flag, or C-flag is used to allocate a sector when that flag is **clear** or to deallocate a sector when that flag is **set**. Identifying the intended sector to be allocated or deallocated and either clearing or setting its respective bit in the cache copy of the 4-byte bitmap of a track completes the first step of normal processing in RORBITMP. The next step is to update the 4-byte bitmap of the track that contains the target sector in the actual VTOC buffer. The RORBITMP routine simply OR's its cache copy with the actual 4-byte bitmap of the track. I cannot recall the source of my inspiration, but after the cache and actual bytes have been OR'd, and if the URMFLAG variable signals that the file is to be undeleted, that sum is exclusively OR'd with the cache bytes making it a simple, elegant, and powerful algorithm! With just eight additional bytes of code, not only are the data sectors of a file, but all of its TSL sectors are fully reserved again in the VTOC, and the complete file is restored in the Catalog. Truly, to be able to undelete a file so simply is an amazing feat to be sure!

Whenever one analyzes a mathematical function, the end-points of that function present the most difficulty, and perhaps the most interest. In a similar fashion, the routine ALLOCSEC presents some difficulty in processing sectors to allocate if NXTTOALC, or the next sector to allocate, happens to be the first track, or track 0x00, or the last track, or track NUMTRKS-1 of the operational range of tracks for that VTOC bitmap. Furthermore, track 0x00 needs to be processed and identified as track 0x40 as will be fully explained in Section I.7. DOS 4.5 initially assigns the value of 0x11, or the Catalog track to NXTTOALC and the value of 0x01, or *forward* to ALLOCDIR, the allocate direction variable. Once ALLOCSEC searches forward in increasing track number for free sectors in the VTOC bitmap and NXTTOALC reaches the last track of the VTOC bitmap, NXTTOALC is reassigned the value of 0x11 and ALLOCDIR is reassigned the value of 0xFF, or *backward*. So, whenever NXTTOALC becomes either the last track or the first track initially, an extra count must be decremented from ALLOCNTR, the allocate loop counter, which basically counts for nothing. DOS 3.3 utilized the flag variable ALLCFLG for its two-state counter which was sufficient because DOS 3.3 was not required to process track 0x00 as a *data* track. Therefore, to ensure that the entire VTOC bitmap is searched for free sectors in DOS 4.5, and to include the processing of the first track or the last track if they happen to be the initial search track, four half-passes through the VTOC bitmap must be counted. When ALLOCNTR is decremented to zero and a free sector has not yet been identified, the error message Volume Full can be correctly issued.

7. Catalog Structure in DOS 4.5

The first volume Catalog sector for DOS 4.5 is shown in Figure I.7.1. Bytes 0x01 and 0x02 of each Catalog sector point to the next Catalog sector as they do in the VTOC sector. The last Catalog sector, typically sector 0x01 on track 0x11, contains zero for these two bytes. A DOS 4.5 Catalog sector may define up to a maximum of seven file entries as they do in DOS 3.3. Table I.7.1 shows the content for each file entry. This table defines the first two bytes of a Catalog entry for a file to be the track and the sector values that point to the TSL for that file. The TSL lists all of the Track/Sector entry pairs for each of the sectors that comprise the *data* content for that file. The third byte of a Catalog entry for a file defines the Type parameter that is assigned to that file, and that byte is followed by the 24-character upper ASCII filename that is given to that file. The 3-byte time and 3-byte date stamp when the file was created or last modified follow the filename, and those bytes conform to the Date and Time definition that is shown in Table I.5.5. The last two bytes of a Catalog entry for a file defines the number of *data* sectors that are assigned to the file including its TSL sectors in low/high byte order. It is important to point out that 30-character DOS 3.3 filenames are not supported in DOS 4.5. Those DOS 3.3 filenames will be truncated to 24-characters and the last six characters will be misinterpreted as a date and time stamp.

Table I.7.2 lists the location of a file entry in the volume Catalog for each of the seven files that are contained in each Catalog sector. Table I.7.3 lists all of the possible file Type codes that DOS 4.5 can correctly process, the ASCII representation that is used in the DOS 4.5 volume Catalog, and a brief description for each file Type. DOS 4.5 can and does process an S Type file that is fully defined in sections III.4.6 and III.4.7. DOS 4.5 is purposefully not programmed to process Integer BASIC files and Relocatable, or R Type object files. There is absolutely no software support for these two file Type codes in DOS 4.5. Perhaps someone could quite easily utilize the memory space for the DOS 4.5 HELP command in order to correctly process the I and R file Type codes. First, a suitable definition for the R file Type code is necessary to even begin such a project. I have no idea whether the memory allocation of the HELP handler can even support a project such as this. I am positive a dedicated and passionate engineer can and will find the means to manage and complete such an interesting project if it is deemed useful.

0x	0	1	2	3	4	5	6	7	8	9	A	B	C	D	E	F
00		11	04									Trk 1	Sec 1	Type 1	Name 1->	-
10	-	-	-	-	-	-	-	-	-	-	-	-	-	-	-	-
20	-	-	-	-	-	Name <-1	Time 1->	-	Time <-1	Date 1->	-	Date <-1	LenL 1	LenH 1	Trk 2	Sec 2
30	Type 2	Name 2->	-	-	-	-	-	-	-	-	-	-	-	-	-	-
40	-	-	Sec 3	Type 3	Name 3->	-	-	-	Name <-2	Time 2->	-	Time <-2	Date 2->	-	Date <-2	LenL 2
50	LenH 2	Trk 3	-	-	-	-	-	-	-	-	-	-	-	-	-	-
60	-	-	LenL 3	LenH 3	Trk 4	Sec 4	Type 4	Name 4->	-	-	-	Name <-3	Time 3->	-	Time <-3	Date 3->
70	-	-	-	-	-	-	-	-	-	-	-	-	-	-	-	-
80	-	-	Date 4->	-	Date <-4	LenL 4	LenH 4	Trk 5	-	-	-	-	-	-	Name <-4	Time 4->
90	-	Time <-4	Time 5->	-	Time <-5	Date 5->	-	Date <-5	Sec 5	Type 5	Name 5->	-	-	-	-	-
A0	-	-	-	-	Name <-6	Time 6->	-	Time <-6	LenL 5	LenH 5	Trk 6	-	-	-	-	-
B0	-	Name <-5	-	-	-	-	-	-	Date 6->	-	-	Sec 6	Type 6	Name 6->	-	-
C0	-	-	-	-	-	-	-	Name <-7	-	-	Date <-6	-	-	-	-	-
D0	-	-	-	-	-	-	-	-	Time 7->	-	-	LenL 6	LenH 6	Trk 7	Sec 7	Type 7
E0	Name 7->	-	-	-	-	-	-	-	-	-	Time <-7	-	-	-	-	-
F0	-	-								-		Date 7->	-	Date <-7	LenL 7	LenH 7

Figure I.7.1. First Volume Catalog Sector Definition

Item	Offset	Length	Format	Description
Track	0x00	0x01	%DZTT TTTT	Delete bit, track Zero bit, TSL Track bits
Sector	0x01	0x01	%000S SSSS	TSL Sector bits
Type	0x02	0x01	%LTTT TTTT	Lock bit, Type bits
Name	0x03	0x18	upper ASCII	24-character ASCII filename with first Alpha character
Time	0x1B	0x03	0xSS MM HH	Seconds byte, Minute byte, Hour byte
Date	0x1E	0x03	0xYY DD MM	Year byte, Day byte, Month byte
Size	0x21	0x02	0xLL HH	2-byte file size in sectors, Low/High byte order

Table I.7.1. Catalog Entry Data Definitions

File	Track*	Sector	Type**	Name	Time	Date	Size
1	0x0B	0x0C	0x0D	0x0E-0x25	0x26-0x28	0x29-0x2B	0x2C-0x2D
2	0x2E	0x2F	0x30	0x31-0x48	0x49-0x4B	0x4C-0x4E	0x4F-0x50
3	0x51	0x52	0x53	0x54-0x6B	0x6C-0x6E	0x6F-0x71	0x72-0x73
4	0x74	0x75	0x76	0x77-0x8E	0x8F-0x91	0x92-0x94	0x95-0x96
5	0x97	0x98	0x99	0x9A-0xB1	0xB2-0xB4	0xB5-0xB7	0xB8-0xB9
6	0xBA	0xBB	0xBC	0xBD-0xD4	0xD5-0xD7	0xD8-0xDA	0xDB-0xDC
7	0xDD	0xDE	0xDF	0xE0-0xF7	0xF8-0xFA	0xFB-0xFD	0xFE-0xFF

* If the MSB is **set**, the file's Name shown is **Deleted**   ** If the MSB is **set**, the file's Name shown is **Locked**

Table I.7.2. Catalog Data Offsets for File Entries

File Type	Catalog	Description
00	T	T Type file and processed as a Text file
01	I	I Type file or Integer BASIC file (**not** supported in DOS 4.5)
02	A	A Type file and processed as an Applesoft file
04	B	B Type file and processed as a Binary or assembly language file
08	S	S Type file, now supported and processed as a Special file in DOS 4.5
10	R	R Type file or Relocatable object file (**not** supported in DOS 4.5)
20	A	A Type file and processed as an Applesoft file in DOS 4.5
40	L	L Type file, formally a B Type file, and processed as a *Lisa* file in DOS 4.5
80	*	File lock bit

Table I.7.3. File Type Definitions

File Type 0x08 is now used by DOS 4.5 to process Special Type files that are similar to Binary files except that these files lack the address and length bytes that are found in the first four bytes of the first data sector in Binary files. File Type 0x40 is used by DOS 4.5 to process *Lisa* files natively, and DOS 3.3 referred to these as B Type files. DOS 4.5 processes file Type 0x20 as an alternate A Type file for an Applesoft file. In DOS 4.5 a file is marked *deleted* when the most significant bit or bit 7 of its TSL track number is **set**. This is the track number of its **first** TSL sector, found in bytes 0x0B, 0x2E, 0x51, 0x74,

0x97, 0xBA, or 0xDD from Table I.7.2. DOS 4.5 stipulates that there will always be less than 64, or 0x3F or less tracks that comprise a volume, so that bit 6 of the TSL track number is available as a bit flag and this bit can be used to signify track 0x00 as in track 0x40 for ALLOCSEC processing. Using bit 6 to represent physical track 0x00 allows all of the File Manager logic testing for last *Track/Sector* entry pair in a TSL sector to remain virtually unchanged. This representation for track 0x00 also allows any sector on track 0x00 to be used for a TSL sector or for a file data sector just like any other sector on any other track. I have updated my version of *FID* to include this representation for track 0x00 and how a deleted file is determined and identified in the volume Catalog.

0x	0	1	2	3	4	5	6	7	8	9	A	B	C	D	E	F
00	00	Next TSL				Offset							T/S 00		T/S 01	
10	T/S 02		T/S 03													
20																
30																
40																
50																
60																
70																
80																
90																
A0																
B0																
C0																
D0																
E0																
F0															T/S 79	

Figure I.7.2. TSL Sector Definition

Byte	Name	Value	Description
0x00	TSLSB	0x00	start of TSL structure block
0x01	TSTRKOFF	0x00	Track to next TSL; 0x00 if no more TSL sectors
0x02	TSSECOFF	0x00	Sector to next TSL; 0x00 if no more TSL sectors
0x03-0x04		0x00	unused
0x05-0x06	TSRECOFF	0x00	TSL offset number (RELSLAST in FMWORK); 0x00/00 first TSL
0x07-0x0B		0x00	unused
0x0C-0x0D	TSLTSOFF	~	T/S entry pair for data sector 0x00; at least one entry is required
0x0E-0x0F		~	T/S entry pair for data sector 0x01; 0x00:0x00 if at end
0x10-0x11		~	T/S entry pair for data sector 0x02; 0x00:0x00 if at end
0x12-0xFD		~	T/S entry pairs for data sectors 0x03-0x78
0xFE-0xFF		~	T/S entry pair for data sector 0x79

Table I.7.4. TSL Structure Block Definition

20

If an attempt is made to LOAD or BLOAD a nonexistent file into memory when the volume Catalog is full, in other words, when all file entries within all Catalog sectors are fully utilized, DOS 3.3 erroneously prints the DISK FULL error message rather than the correct error message FILE NOT FOUND. If an attempt is made to SAVE or BSAVE a file when the volume Catalog is full, DOS 3.3 again erroneously prints the DISK FULL error message even when there are sufficient data sectors available in the volume for the data content of the file. Even though this situation is rarely encountered where all file entries within all Catalog sectors are fully utilized, having DOS issue the wrong or inappropriate error message could lead one to make erroneous conclusions. It would not have been difficult to devise a series of tests that would verify, at the unit level, the appropriate time under the correct conditions to generate any and all error messages.

DOS 4.5 initializes a volume with a default volume Catalog that consists of five data sectors which can contain thirty-file file entries and can, therefore, define up to thirty-five files. However, the volume Catalog may be made as small as one sector or as large as fifteen sectors by using the B keyword with the DOS INIT command. If the volume Catalog consists of one or two sectors, the volume Catalog will only support seven or fourteen files, respectively, and an erroneous DISK FULL error message can have significant consequences in this instance. I have identified and have rewritten the flawed DOS 3.3 routines when I designed DOS 4.3. Thus, DOS 4.5 also prints the correct error message File Not Found when a file truly does not exist in a volume Catalog regardless whether all of the file entries in the volume Catalog are utilized or not. DOS 4.5 also prints the correct error message Catalog Full when there is an attempt to save a file to a volume whose Catalog truly does not contain an available file entry regardless whether there are sufficient data sectors available in the volume for the data of that file.

At the heart of every file is its Track/Sector List buffer. This list of Track/Sector entry pairs is contained in the sector that every Catalog file entry points to which is its TSL. If a file exceeds 122 or 0x7A data sectors from NUMTSENT in Table I.5.2, the TSL sector has provisions to define a succeeding TSL sector in order to provide a location for additional Track/Sector entry pairs. And, for every increment of 122 data sectors, DOS 4.5 will create another chained TSL sector for that file and increase the sector resource count by one for that additional TSL sector.

Figure I.7.2 shows a typical TSL sector and Table I.7.4 defines each of the entries in that TSL sector. Bytes 0x01:0x02, or Next TSL point to the next chained TSL sector if it exists, otherwise these bytes are set to zero. Offset at bytes 0x05:0x06 is equal to 0x00:0x00 in the first TSL sector, and Offset increases by 0x007A for each succeeding chained TSL sector in Lo/Hi byte order. The Track/Sector List begins with its first entry pair at bytes 0x0C:0x0D, and all files must have at least one entry pair. Regardless whether the TSL contains additional Track/Sector entry pairs from previous file saves and/or file modifications, DOS only loads into memory the number of bytes that are specified by an Applesoft or by a Binary file. The DOS TLOAD command for a TEXT file, on the other hand, reads into memory **all** of its data sectors that are listed in its TSL sector without regard to the actual size of the TEXT file in bytes. The DOS TLOAD command only processes Sequential Text files which are always demarcated by a terminating NULL byte or character 0x00. For all file Types, if the next TSL track value in a Track/Sector entry pair is equal to a NULL byte or character 0x00, no further Track/Sector entry pairs are utilized and no further data is read into memory. Also, the TSL concludes when the DIRINDX index pointer that points to the next Track/Sector entry pair becomes zero and TSTRKOFF is also zero. I believe byte-pairs 0x08:0x09 or 0x09:0x0A could have been utilized for the value of the L keyword instead of requiring the L keyword to OPEN a Random-Access Data file as shown in Table III.6.0.1 and Figure III.6.1.1. At least that is how I might have designed the first TSL sector for a Random-Access Data file. I still do not fully understand what the benefit is in assigning 0x0C to TSLTSOFF and 0x7A to NUMTSENT when there is clearly room for perhaps 0x7B or even 0x7C Track/Sector entry pairs.

8. Booting DOS 4.5 into Memory

The BOOT image of DOS 4.5 occupies the first two tracks, tracks 0x00 and 0x01, and an additional ten sectors on track 0x02 of a volume, whether the volume has sixteen or thirty-two sectors per track. The remaining sectors on track 0x02 are made available in the VTOC by the initialization handler. When a DOS 4.5 volume BOOTs, the Disk][Interface Card firmware loads the bootstrap code from sector 0x00 on track 0x00 into memory at memory address 0x0800-0x08FF. This starts the BOOT Stage 0 processing and the X-register always contains the value of the slot number of the Interface Card times sixteen. The first byte of this bootstrap code must equal 0x01 for the BOOT process to continue and to read another sector into memory. Therefore, the BOOT Stage 0 processing instructions actually begin at memory address 0x0801 in order to initialize the BOOT Stage 1 software that is already now in memory. Bytes 0x08FE and 0x08FF are known as BOOTADR and BOOTPGS, respectively, as shown in Table I.8.1. These two bytes direct the BOOT Stage 1 software to read sectors 0x0F to 0x02 into Bank 1 memory at memory address 0xD000 to 0xDDFF and sectors 0x01 and 0x00 into memory at memory address 0xBE00 to 0xBFFF. There is nothing at all complex in using BOOTADR and BOOTPGS for reading all of track 0x00 into memory.

Address	Value	Variable	Instruction
0xBFF0	0x45	BLDVRSN	BYT VERSION
0xBFF1	0x06	BLDNMBR	BYT BUILD
0xBFF2	0xBE4A	MNGDISK	ADR EXMNGDSK
0xBFF4	0xBE50	MNGVALS	ADR EXMNGVAL
0xBFF6	0xBE56	MNGUSER	ADR EXMNGUSR
0xBFF8	0xBF58	INITDOS	ADR DOSINIT
0xBFFA	0xBEE2	INITVAL	ADR INITVALS
0xBFFC	0xE5	BCFGNDX	BYT BOOTCFG
0xBFFD	0xDE	NBUF1PG	HBY NBUF1
0xBFFE	0xD0	BOOTADR	HBY RWTSTART
0xBFFF	0x0F	BOOTPGS	HBY HELPEND-XFERSTRT

Table I.8.1. BOOT and DATA Management Data Structure Definition

Offset	Size	Value	Variable	Name	Description
0x00	0x01	0x01	CFGDNUM	DNUM	RWTS BOOT drive number
0x01	0x01	0x00	CFGVOLEX	VOLEXPT	RWTS BOOT volume expected
0x02	0x01	0x02	CFGTNUM	TNUM	RWTS initial BOOT track number
0x03	0x01	0x09	CFGSNUM	SNUM	RWTS initial BOOT sector number
0x04	0x02	0x0000		DCTADR	DCT address (unused)
0x06	0x02	0xF000	CFGUSRBF	USRBUF	RWTS initial BOOT start address
0x08	0x01	0x04	CFGPHASE	IOCBPHAS	RWTS half-phases per track
0x09	0x01	0x00	CFGBCNT	BYTCNT	RWTS bytes to read (256)
0x0A	0x01	0x01	CFGCCODE	CMDCODE	RWTS command code, read/write

Table I.8.2. BOOT Configuration Data Structure

```
    :              :           :
BF8D            195  ; Used by BOOT Stage 2 and the INIT command.
BF8D            196  ;
BF8D BD E5 BF   197  RWPAGES1 lda BOOTCFG,X
BF90 9D C4 BF   198           sta DNUM,X
BF93            199  ;
BF93 E8         200           inx
BF94            201  ;
BF94 88         202           dey
BF95 D0 F6      203           bne RWPAGES1
BF97            204  ;
BF97 A2 1A      205           ldx /DOSEND-DOSTART
BF99            206  ;
BF99 86 35      207  RWPAGES2 stx PAGECNT
BF9B            208  ;
BF9B 2C 8B C0   209  ^1       bit RAM1WE
BF9E            210  ;
BF9E 20 71 D2   211           jsr INTRWTS
BFA1 B0 E4      212           bcs RWERROR
BFA3            213  ;
BFA3 CE C7 BF   214           dec SNUM
BFA6 10 08      215  ;        bpl >2
BFA8            216  ;
BFA8 CE C6 BF   217           dec TNUM
BFAB            218  ;
BFAB A9 0F      219           lda #15
BFAD 8D C7 BF   220           sta SNUM
BFB0            221  ;
BFB0 EE CB BF   222  ^2       inc USRBUF+1
BFB3 D0 05      223           bne >3
BFB5            224  ;
BFB5 A9 E0      225           lda /PAGEE0
BFB7 8D CB BF   226           sta USRBUF+1
BFBA            227  ;
BFBA C6 35      228  ^3       dec PAGECNT
BFBC D0 DD      229           bne <1
BFBE            230  ;
BFBE 60         231           rts
    :              :           :
```

Figure I.8.1. RWPAGES Software Routine

A 16-byte sector interleave table is available to the BOOT Stage 1 software and to the RWTS routine whose Input/Output Context Block or IOCB structure is now in memory at Page 0xBF. Transfer of control passes to the BOOT Stage 2 software which is also in memory at Page 0xBF, and that software can now use RWTS which is located in Bank 1 of the Language Card partition in order to access any sector on any track in the volume. The initial RWTS IOCB values are copied from a BOOTCFG structure that is in memory at Page 0xBF. These values are used by the RWPAGES routine which is called by BOOT Stage 2 software to read the remaining twenty-six sectors into memory in ascending order of memory pages and descending order of volume sectors and tracks. Those twenty-six sectors begin with sector 0x09 on track 0x02 and end with sector 0x00 on track 0x01. The DOS 4.5 BOOTCFG table is shown in Table I.8.2 and the RWPAGES routine is shown in Figure I.8.1. When all of DOS 4.5 is in memory, ROM initialization is performed, the 80-column video is disabled and the normal character set is enabled, XMODE is initialized, the CSWL and KSWL interface pointers are initialized, a search is made for a clock card, and DOS is Cold-Started and is

23

now ready to execute the DOS `CMDVAL` command, a topic that is discussed further in Section I.9. As an aside, the DOS `INIT` command also uses the `RWPAGES` routine to write the pages of DOS onto an initialized volume in the same order its pages are read into memory when DOS is `BOOT`ed. The complete volume Track/Sector mapping to memory address for DOS 4.5 is shown in Table I.8.3.

Track	Sector	Address	Code	Track	Sector	Address	Code
0x00	0x00	0xBF00	BOOT	0x01	0x05	0xE400	MNGR
0x00	0x01	0xBE00	XFER	0x01	0x06	0xE300	MNGR
0x00	0x02	*0xDD00	HELP	0x01	0x07	0xE200	MNGR
0x00	0x03	*0xDC00	HELP	0x01	0x08	0xE100	MNGR
0x00	0x04	*0xDB00	HELP	0x01	0x09	0xE000	MNGR
0x00	0x05	*0xDA00	HELP	0x01	0x0A	0xDF00	MNGR
0x00	0x06	*0xD900	HELP	0x01	0x0B	0xDE00	MNGR
0x00	0x07	*0xD800	HELP	0x01	0x0C	0xDD00	MNGR
0x00	0x08	*0xD700	HELP	0x01	0x0D	0xDC00	CMD
0x00	0x09	*0xD600	INRF	0x01	0x0E	0xDB00	CMD
0x00	0x0A	*0xD500	INRF	0x01	0x0F	0xDA00	CMD
0x00	0x0B	*0xD400	RWTS	0x02	0x00	0xD900	CMD
0x00	0x0C	*0xD300	RWTS	0x02	0x01	0xD800	CMD
0x00	0x0D	*0xD200	RWTS	0x02	0x02	0xD700	CMD
0x00	0x0E	*0xD100	RWTS	0x02	0x03	0xD600	CMD
0x00	0x0F	*0xD000	RWTS	0x02	0x04	0xD500	CMD
0x01	0x00	0xE900	DATA	0x02	0x05	0xD400	CMD
0x01	0x01	0xE800	DATA	0x02	0x06	0xD300	CMD
0x01	0x02	0xE700	DATA	0x02	0x07	0xD200	CMD
0x01	0x03	0xE600	DATA	0x02	0x08	0xD100	CMD
0x01	0x04	0xE500	SPCL	0x02	0x09	0xD000	CMD

Table I.8.3. Disk Track/Sector Mapping to Memory Address

The internal entry point `INTRWTS` that is shown in line #211 in Figure I.8.1 for the call to RWTS simply loads the Y- and A-registers with the address of `TBLTYPE` before *falling into* the DORWTS routine. `TBLTYPE` is the internal structure for the RWTS IOCB that is shown later in Table I.10.1. According to Table I.8.2, the initial start address in USRBUF for DOS 4.5 is 0xF000. The first sixteen sectors that are read fill memory block 0xF0:FF, and when that occurs, RWPAGES2 changes the MSB address to 0xE0 as shown in line #225 in Figure I.8.1. The last ten sectors that are read fill memory block 0xE0:E9. Later, but before DOS COLDSTRT is initiated, the contents of memory block 0xF0:FF must be moved to memory block 0xD0:DF in Bank 2. It is simply not possible for RWTS, which is located in memory block 0xD0:D4 of Bank 1, to read disk sectors directly into memory block 0xD0:DF of Bank 2. Therefore, memory block 0xF0:FF serves as an intermediate assessable block of memory for BOOT Stage 2 and for the DOS INIT handler. That is, memory block 0xD0:DF is first copied to memory block 0xF0:FF before DOS 4.5 can be written to disk tracks 0x00 to 0x02 using RWPAGES. In DOS 4.5, DORWTS always exits into Bank 2 of the Language Card partition with Bank 2 in focus.

Offset	Address	Code	Offset	Address	Code
0x0000	0xD000	CMD	0x1500	0xE500	SPCL
0x0100	0xD100	CMD	0x1600	0xE600	DATA
0x0200	0xD200	CMD	0x1700	0xE700	DATA
0x0300	0xD300	CMD	0x1800	0xE800	DATA
0x0400	0xD400	CMD	0x1900	0xE900	DATA
0x0500	0xD500	CMD	0x1A00	*0xD000	RWTS
0x0600	0xD600	CMD	0x1B00	*0xD100	RWTS
0x0700	0xD700	CMD	0x1C00	*0xD200	RWTS
0x0800	0xD800	CMD	0x1D00	*0xD300	RWTS
0x0900	0xD900	CMD	0x1E00	*0xD400	RWTS
0x0A00	0xDA00	CMD	0x1F00	*0xD500	INRF
0x0B00	0xDB00	CMD	0x2000	*0xD600	INRF
0x0C00	0xDC00	CMD	0x2100	*0xD700	HELP
0x0D00	0xDD00	MNGR	0x2200	*0xD800	HELP
0x0E00	0xDE00	MNGR	0x2300	*0xD900	HELP
0x0F00	0xDF00	MNGR	0x2400	*0xDA00	HELP
0x1000	0xE000	MNGR	0x2500	*0xDB00	HELP
0x1100	0xE100	MNGR	0x2600	*0xDC00	HELP
0x1200	0xE200	MNGR	0x2700	*0xDD00	HELP
0x1300	0xE300	MNGR	0x2800	0xBE00	XFER
0x1400	0xE400	MNGR	0x2900	0xBF00	BOOT

Table I.8.4. File Image Mapping to Memory Address

```
  :            :         :
BFF2           7  MNGDISK  equ $BFF2
C020           8  RDENTRY  equ $C020          ; $C720
C900           9  RDPAGECX equ $C900          ; $C7
C901          10  RDSLOT   equ $C901          ; $07
  :            :         :
0940          24  ; Attach handler address.
0940 AE 01 C9 25           ldx RDSLOT
0943 A0 20    26           ldy #RDENTRY
0945 AD 00 C9 27           lda RDPAGECX
0948 38       28           sec
0949 20 90 09 29           jsr GETDISK
  :            :         :
0990 6C F2 BF 45  GETDISK  jmp (MNGDISK)
  :            :         :
```

Figure I.8.2. Attaching a Slot Card Handler Example

The file image of DOS 4.5 and how that image maps to memory is shown in Table I.8.4. This table correlates file offset to memory address, and it shows the basic function of the code that is found at that memory page, such as DOS Command handlers (CMD), DOS File Manager handlers (MNGR and SPCL), data buffers, tables, and variables (DATA), DOS Read/Write Track/Sector routines (RWTS), Interface Routine handlers (INRF), the DOS HELP handler (HELP), and the BOOT Stage 0, 1, and 2 routines (XFER and BOOT). The asterisk before those entries in Tables 1.8.3 and 1.8.4 indicates that those routines or structures reside in Bank 1 of the Language Card partition. The CMD and MNGR routines and the Data structures all reside in Bank 2 of the Language Card partition. Once DOS 4.5 is located in memory and has initialized, other data Input/Output or I/O disks or disk-emulating devices can easily attach their Slot Card handler address to DOS 4.5. Table I.8.1 shows where the RWTS disk management routine MNGDISK is located in DOS 4.5, which is at 0xBFF2 in order to set or to restore a DISKADRS table entry. To attach a Slot Card handler, simply make an indirect call to MNGDISK with the slot number in the X-register, the address of the Slot Card handler in the Y- and A-registers in Lo/Hi byte order, and **set** the C-flag. Alternatively, the X-register may contain the slot-times-sixteen value. The registers are returned unchanged. RWTS transfers control to the requested Slot Card handler for the desired data I/O based entirely on the slot-times-sixteen value that is found in the RWTS IOCB.

```
 :              :            :
0000            7  ZERO      equ $00
0800            8  ;
BFF2            9  MNGDISK   equ $BFF2
C020           10  RDENTRY   equ $C020          ; $C720
C900           11  RDPAGECX  equ $C900          ; $C7
C901           12  RDSLOT    equ $C901          ; $07
 :              :            :
0940           24  ; Request handler address.
0940 AE 01 C9  25            ldx RDSLOT
0943 A9 00     26            lda #ZERO
0945 38        27            sec
0946 20 90 09  28            jsr GETDISK
 :              :            :
0960           39  ; Detach a handler.
0960 AE 01 C9  40            ldx RDSLOT
0963 18        41            clc
0964 20 90 09  42            jsr GETDISK
 :              :            :
0990 6C F2 BF  65  GETDISK   jmp (MNGDISK)
 :              :            :
```

Figure I.8.3. Requesting and Detaching a Slot Card Handler Example

Figure I.8.2 shows an example assembly language routine that attaches the RAM Disk handler to DOS 4.5. The low byte address value of the handler is that of the routine RDENTRY, its high byte address is its CX page or 0xC7 for slot 7 and that value is found in RDPAGECX, and its slot number is found in RDSLOT. Figure I.8.3 shows an example assembly language routine that calls MNGDISK in order to request the address of the handler that is assigned to a particular slot into the Y- and A-registers because the routine initializes the A-register to zero and **sets** the C-flag. Then the routine calls MNGDISK again with the C-flag **clear** in order to disconnect that handler from DOS 4.5. Unlike the Manage Disk routine in DOS 4.1, it is not necessary to know where the DISKADRS table is located in memory, its structure, nor how to index it. MNGDISK takes care of all of that protocol which had to be done entirely by the DOS 4.1 user. MNGDISK always returns the C-flag clear as long as the X-register contains a valid slot number or a valid slot-times-sixteen number. If the X-register does not contain a valid slot number or a valid slot-time-sixteen number, the C-flag is returned **set**.

```
   :              :             :
03D0             9  DOSWARM  equ $3D0
BFF6            10  MNGUSER  equ $BFF6
BFF8            11  INITDOS  equ $BFF8
   :              :             :
0900 38         20           sec
0901 A0 80      21           ldy #SPCLCODE
0903 A9 09      22           lda /SPCLCODE
0905 20 B0 09   23           jsr SETUSER
0908 6C F8 BF   24           jmp (INITDOS)
   :              :             :
0980 18         43  SPCLCODE clc
0981 20 F6 BF   44           jsr SETUSER
0984 4C D0 03   45           jmp DOSWARM
   :              :             :
09B0 6C F6 BF   59  SETUSER  jmp (MNGUSER)
   :              :             :
```

Figure I.8.4. Using MNGUSER to Manage DOS 4.5 Example

Having an image of DOS 4.5 saved on disk as a Binary file can be very useful. For example, the DOS image could be read from a quikLoader and placed into memory according to Table I.8.4. Getting DOS 4.5 started is as easy as using an indirect JMP, such as JMP (INITDOS). Refer to Table I.8.1 for the address of the variable INITDOS. DOS 4.5 initializes, transfers control to Applesoft, and then Applesoft prints a carriage return or character 0x8D in order to initiate the execution of the first DOS command found in CMDVAL. Typically, that command will RUN the HELLO file. If, on the other hand, the user does not wish to lose control of DOS to Applesoft after DOS initialization, there is a very unique DOS 4.5 command that can be used to transfer control to a selected program after Applesoft initialization. The DOS USER command has been designed to provide a number of very powerful capabilities. One of the USER command capabilities is initiated when the RUN command in CMDVAL is replaced with the USER command so that the USER command is executed rather than the RUN command after Applesoft initialization. Whatever instructions that are at the address that is found in USERADR are executed rather than the HELLO file. Figure I.8.4 shows an example assembly language routine that calls MNGUSER to manage the initialization of DOS 4.5 which initializes CMDVAL with the USER command and USERADR with the address that is currently in the Y- and A-registers. In Figure I.8.4, the address that is put into USERADR is for the SPCLCODE routine that is found at line #43. Once DOS 4.5 has initialized and Applesoft is no longer in control, MNGUSER can be called again within SPCLCODE in order to restore the default values for CMDVAL and USERADR. This essentially restores DOS 4.5 to its default or initial state for CMDVAL/USERADR! Simply call MNGUSER with the C-flag **clear**.

Another powerful capability of the DOS USER command is initiated when the USER command is configured with the address of a specific routine or function. When the USER command is entered on the Apple Command Line followed by the RETURN or character 0x8D, that user specific routine or function is immediately entered and executed. Many historical software developers utilized the *Ampersand Handler*, or the USERAHAND routine in very much the same way. The utility Program Global Editor is an excellent example where the ampersand is used to bring that program into focus in order for the user to edit and modify a resident Applesoft program. Even DOS 4.5 is initially configured to utilize the USERAHAND routine in order to enter the REPEATCD routine that calls the DOS REPEAT function in order to repeat the last DOS command that was processed by the DOS DOCMD routine. Unlike the Ampersand handler, however, the DOS USER Command is a real DOS command and it carries with it all of the attributes and

27

the authorities of a real DOS command. The original DOS 3.3 version of the *Big Mac* assembler modified the DOS Command Table like the one shown in Table III.0.2 in order to utilize the code resources of the INIT command for a new ASSEM command. After exiting *Big Mac*, if the user entered the ASSEM command onto the Apple Command Line followed by the RETURN or character 0x8D, *Big Mac* was immediately brought into focus, and the user could continue using the assembler in order to modify and/or to develop additional assembly language code. This feature was designed to provide the user with an easy and very elegant method to develop assembly language code, test the code outside of the assembler, and then re-enter the assembler in order to continue assembly language code development. By design, DOS 4.5 does not provide a means to access the DOS Command Table in order to modify or to utilize the code resources of any of its commands. However, the USER command may be utilized to provide the identical capabilities of the DOS 3.3 ASSEM command. Figure I.8.5 shows precisely how the DOS 4.5 *Big Mac* loader utilizes MNGUSER in order to connect the DOS USER command to the re-entry address of *Big Mac*. The *Big Mac* loader is the task that manages Auxiliary memory and places the *Big Mac* executable code at its required address in the Language Card partition of Auxiliary memory. After the user has exited *Big Mac* and if the user enters the USER command on the Apple Command Line followed by RETURN or character 0x8D, *Big Mac* is then brought into focus.

```
:                    :              :
BC70                 9  REENTRY   equ $BC70
BFF6                10  MNGUSER   equ $BFF6
:                    :              :
097A A0 70         208            ldy #REENTRY
097C A9 BC         209            lda /REENTRY
097E 38            210            sec
097F 20 A7 09      211            jsr SETUSER
:                    :              :
09A7 6C F6 BF          SETUSER   jmp (MNGUSER)
:                    :              :
```

Figure I.8.5. Using MNGUSER in LOADMAC

The DOS 4.5 BOOT and DATA Management Data structure that is shown in Table I.8.1 contains a wealth of other vectors and values that have not yet been discussed. Ever since the publication of the DOS 4.1 Manual and during the development of the DOS 4.5 software, I thought there should be a far more convenient procedure in order to obtain the current DOS Version and Build information. One could parse the version and build values from the character string that is supplied by the RDCLKVSN function that is shown later in Table I.9.3, for example. But it is far more convenient to obtain these values directly, and BLDVRSN and BLDNMBR at 0xBFF0 and 0xBFF1, respectively, provide this information. MNGVALS, similar in function to MNGDISK, no longer provides an interface to access or change the INITVALS Data structure variables in DOS 4.5. This is fully discussed in Section I.12.

The INITVAL variable that is shown in Table I.8.1 contains the address of the variables that comprise the INITVALS Data structure that is shown in Table I.8.5. One should reference these variables indirectly and, therefore, more generally by using the address that is found at INITVAL and the offsets that are shown in Table I.8.5. Because the INITVALS Data structure resides in lower Main memory, these variables are somewhat easier to access in order to read and change their values directly rather than accessing those variables found in CMDVALS. The example assembly language routine that is shown in Figure I.8.6 copies

28

the address at INITVAL to a page-zero two-byte pointer. The Y-register is used to hold the desired offset that is found in Table I.8.5. The example routine first reads the value of RESETADR, saves it to RESETSAV, then changes it to another address. Table I.8.1 contains the offset BCFGNDX for the BOOTCFG Data structure that is shown in Table I.8.2. This Data structure may be accessed indirectly similar to the INITVALS Data structure knowing that this structure resides within Page 0xBF. A page-zero two-byte pointer to access this structure is shown in Figure I.8.7. The CFFA firmware I developed is one example that dynamically modifies the DNUM and VOLEXPT variables. Drive and volume numbers are critical parameters to the CFFA BOOT process, and being able to change those variables *on the fly* makes it possible for the CFFA to BOOT any of the volumes on any of its drives.

Offset	Size	Value	Variable	Description
0x00	0x02	0xD43C	WARMADR	ROM Soft Entry handler address
0x02	0x02	0xE000	COLDADR	ROM Hard Entry handler address
0x04	0x02	0xD865	ERRORADR	ROM Error handler address
0x06	0x02	0xD4F2	RESETADR	ROM Set/Reset handler address
0x08	0x02	0xD49A	USERADR	DOS USER handler address
0x0A	0x01	0x06	CMDVAL	DOS first-time Cold-Start command
0x0B	0x01	0x05	NMAXVAL	MAXFILES at initialization
0x0C	0x01	0x23	YEARVAL	Year value for Thunderclock card
0x0D	0x01	0x05	FIRSTCAT	First catalog sector (reference variable)
0x0E	0x01	0x23	LASTRACK	Number of tracks in volume (reference variable)
0x0F	0x01	0x05	SECVAL	First catalog sector (working variable)
0x10	0x01	0x23	ENDTRK	Number of tracks in volume (working variable)
0x11	0x02	0x0000	SUBJCT	Volume Library value (subject number)
0x13	0x01	0x11	TRKVAL	Catalog track number
0x14	0x01	0x45	VRSN	DOS Version number
0x15	0x01	0x06	BLD	DOS Build number
0x16	0x01	0xC8	RAMTYP	DOS RAM type
0x17	0x01	0x04	VALSPHAS	Half-phases per track
0x18	0x01	0x7A	TSPARS	Number of T/S entry pairs per sector
0x19	0x01	0x11	ALCTRK	Sector to allocate next
0x1A	0x01	0x01	ALCDIR	Sector allocation direction
0x1B	0x01	0x00	VALSCNFG	DOS Configuration byte
0x1C	0x01	0x10	ENDSEC	Number of sectors per track
0x1D	0x01	0x01	SECSIZ	(Bytes per sector) / 256

Table I.8.5. INITVALS Data Structure Definition

Table I.8.1 also contains the most significant byte of the memory address for NBUF1. NBUF1 is 256 bytes of memory on a page boundary that is used by the DOS 4.5 RWTS routines. This buffer resides in Bank 1 of the Language Card partition. This most significant address byte is included in order to provide easy access to a temporary page of memory as long as the RWTS routines are not invoked, which would obviously overwrite the data content of this particular buffer. The firmware I developed for the Rana disk drive makes excellent use of the NBUF1PG address byte. The CFFA firmware I developed also uses this buffer to temporarily save either the lower half or the upper half of a 512-byte data block.

```
 :            :        :
00EE          4  PTR      epz $EE
 :            :        :
0006         13  RESETOFF equ $06
008D         14  RETURN   equ $8D
 :            :        :
BFFA         20  INITVAL  equ $BFFA
 :            :        :
0940         26  ; Setup pointer.
0940 AD FA BF 27          lda INITVAL
0943 85 EE    28          sta PTR
0945 AD FB BF 29          lda INITVAL+1
0948 85 EF    30          sta PTR+1
094A         31  ;
094A         32  ; Get current entry and save.
094A A0 06    33          ldy #RESETOFF
094C B1 EE    34          lda (PTR),Y
094E 8D 90 09 35          sta RESETSAV
0951 C8       36          iny
0952 B1 EE    37          lda (PTR),Y
0954 8D 91 09 38          sta RESETSAV+1
0957         39  ;
0957         40  ; Change entry.
0957 A9 09    41          lda /MYRESET
0959 91 EE    42          sta (PTR),Y
095B 88       43          dey
095C A9 80    44          lda #MYRESET
095E 91 EE    45          sta (PTR),Y
 :            :        :
0980         50  ; My Reset Handler location.
0980 A9 8D    51  MYRESET  lda #RETURN
 :            :        :
0990 00 00    66  RESETSAV hex 0000
 :            :        :
```

Figure I.8.6. Accessing and Changing INITVALS Data Structure Example

I found that it was absolutely necessary to add two additional variables to the DOS 4.1 version of the INITVALS Data structure. These two variables are FIRSTCAT and LASTRACK at offsets 0x0D and 0x0E, respectively, that appear in Table I.8.5. At first glance, these two variables look exactly like SECVAL and ENDTRK which are part of the VTOCVALS substructure. The VTOCVALS substructure is shown in Table I.8.5 with a darker shade. In the DOS 4.5 source code, FIRSTCAT and SECVAL are set to the same value as are LASTRACK and ENDTRK. SECVAL and ENDTRK are working variables in that their values can be changed by the Command Manager or by an external File Manager user in order to modify the File Manager Context Block appropriately. FIRSTCAT and LASTRACK are reference variables in that their values are transferred to SECVAL and ENDTRK whenever the Command Manager determines that the values it finds in the A keyword or in the B keyword are out of range. Now, the user can set FIRSTCAT and LASTRACK to any default reference value without having the need to reassemble DOS 4.5.

```
    :                  :              :
  00EE               4  PTR        epz $EE
    :                  :              :
  0000              11  DNUMOFF    equ $00
    :                  :              :
  BFFC              16  BCFGNDX    equ $BFFC
    :                  :              :
  0940              24  ; Setup pointer.
  0940 AD FC BF     25             lda BCFGNDX
  0943 85 EE        26             sta PTR
  0945 A9 BF        27             lda /BCFGNDX
  0947 85 EF        28             sta PTR+1
  0949              29  ;
  0949              30  ; Change DNUM.
  0949 A0 00        31             ldy #DNUMOFF
  094B 85 12        32             lda #$12
  094D 91 EE        33             sta (PTR),Y
  094F              34  ;
  094F              35  ; Change VOLEXPT.
  094F C8           36             iny
  0950 85 A7        37             lda #$A7
  0952 91 EE        38             sta (PTR),Y
    :                  :              :
```

Figure I.8.7. Changing the BOOT Configuration Data Structure Example

9. Memory Initialization in DOS 4.5

DOS 4.5 memory initialization is a very complex procedure, and it begins even before the Disk][Interface Card firmware reads sector 0x00 on track 0x00 into memory. The Interface Card firmware must generate a RDNIBLBT table from 0x36C to 0x3D5 in order for the firmware to process the 342 *disk* bytes it reads that will generate a sector of 256 *data* bytes. This process is called *6 and 2* decoding or DATA Field Data Decoding, and this subject is thoroughly discussed in many publications on Apple DOS 3.3. Figure I.9.1 shows a snippet of firmware on the Disk][Interface Card that generates the RDNIBLBT table. The firmware reads the first 0x56 disk bytes to memory address 0x0300 which corresponds to an NBUF2-like buffer. Because the firmware saves the next 256 disk bytes to an address that is on a page boundary, a corresponding NBUF1-like buffer is not required. The post-nibblize routine uses the 0x56 bytes at memory address 0x300 and the 256 disk bytes to generate the data bytes at the same page-bounded address. Once the BOOT Stage 0 bootstrap code is in memory at address 0x0800, RWTS and all of its support routines must be read into memory by the Disk][firmware in order to have all of the necessary software routines placed into memory for BOOT Stage 2 so that RWTS can be used in order to move the read/write disk head and to access the rest of DOS on other disk tracks.

```
    :                  :              :
  C019 98           57             tya
  C01A 9D 56 03     58             sta RDNIBLBT-$16,X
    :                  :              :
```

Figure I.9.1. Generating the RDNIBLBT Table in Disk][Firmware

Slot	DRV0TRK	DRV1TRK	DRV0PHAS	DRV1PHAS
1	0x0479	0x04F9	0x0679	0x06F9
2	0x047A	0x04FA	0x067A	0x06FA
3	0x047B	0x04FB	0x067B	0x06FB
4	0x047C	0x04FC	0x067C	0x06FC
5	0x047D	0x04FD	0x067D	0x06FD
6	0x047E	0x04FE	0x067E	0x06FE
7	0x047F	0x04FF	0x067F	0x06FF

Table I.9.1. RWTS Scratchpad RAM Locations in DOS 4.5

BOOT Stage 2 begins by saving the X-register to SNUM16 and calling the CLRVALS routine primarily in order to initialize the seven byte Slot Scratchpad table called SCRCHTBL to zero. CLRVALS also initializes the CMDVALS Data structure and the File Manager FMWORK Data structure to zero. SCRCHTBL is used to determine if RWTS has been called previously on behalf of the slot number that is currently being used to BOOT DOS into memory. If this is the very first call to RWTS for that slot number, the Slot Scratchpad table entry for that slot number is decremented and the drive and the phase RWTS Scratchpad RAM locations for both Drive 1 and Drive 2 for that slot number are initialized to zero reflecting the current position of the read/write disk head onto track 0x00. Table I.9.1 shows the addresses for all of the RWTS Scratchpad RAM locations that are available for both disk drives for every slot number. It is at these RAM locations where the current track position of the read/write disk head is maintained in half-phase values for each drive and for each slot number that is utilized for a Disk][or a Disk][-like drive. Similarly, the spacing between tracks in half-phase values is maintained for each drive and for each slot number as well. The firmware I designed for a RanaSystems EliteThree disk drive simply expands Table I.9.1 to accommodate four disk drives. DOS 4.5 is unique among all previous Disk Operating Systems in that DOS 4.5 always initializes its RWTS Scratchpad RAM locations when RWTS accesses a disk drive for the very first time for each and every slot number.

BOOT Stage 2 utilizes the RWTS IOCB in order to stipulate what sector on which track to read for a page of data and where that data is placed into memory. Before any of that logic can take place, RWTS must establish where the read/write disk head is currently positioned. The ROM firmware has already utilized a low-level, though effective disk head recalibration routine that initially assumes the disk head is located on track forty or 0x28, and repositions the disk head onto track 0x00. From the IOCB, the DOS 4.5 RWTS extracts the slot-times-sixteen number and divides that number by sixteen in order to generate an index value which happens to also be the slot number. In this redesigned RWTS, the Slot Scratchpad table is used in combination with the calculated index value or slot number to determine if RWTS has been called previously on behalf of that slot number. Since this is currently the case, the appropriate RWTS Scratchpad RAM locations for the slot number that is used to BOOT a diskette as shown in Table I.9.1 is initialized to zero which happens to correspond to the current track position of the read/write disk head, which is at track 0x00. BOOT Stage 2 proceeds to read into memory the remaining twenty-six sectors of the DOS 4.5 executable code and data, and branches to the COLDSTRT entry point in order to bypass the DOSINIT entry point whose only function is to call the CLRVALS routine. Calling CLRVALS at this time would not be desirable because it would remove the critical information that is currently in SCRCHTBL and, therefore, the information in the RWTS Scratchpad RAM locations for the slot number that was just utilized in order to read into memory the remaining pages of DOS.

DOS 3.3, DOS 4.1, and even ProDOS read into memory a Read Translate table or RDNIBL and a Write Translate table or WRNIBL along with its DOS image when that DOS is booted. The RDNIBL table is 0x6A bytes in size and the WRNIBL table is 0x40 bytes in size. As alluded to above, the companion buffer to NBUF1, whose address is listed in Table I.8.1, is NBUF2, whose size is 0x56 bytes. When NBUF1 and NBUF2 are filled with data, 342 *disk* bytes have just been read. It is rather interesting and very fortunate that when taken together, NBUF2, RDNIBL, and WRNIBL all fit within one 256-byte page. One could utilize the Disk][Interface Card firmware to output its data to the RDNIBL address instead of to RDNIBLBT at 0x36C after the firmware BOOT of BOOT Stage 1 and before the software BOOT of BOOT Stage 2, but that still leaves having to read into memory the WRNIBL table. I was fascinated to discover (yes, certainly, a very joyous Aha! Moment indeed) that I could programmatically generate both tables at the same time. In other words, I could save having to read in 0xAA bytes of data at the expense of 0x25 bytes of code, thus saving over one-half page of disk space that could be used for other DOS functionality. The DOS 4.5 code snippet to generate both the RDNIBL and the WRNIBL tables is shown in Figure I.9.2. The BLDNIBL routine incorporates only six additional bytes to generate 0x40 bytes of essential data, and the routine directly follows the RWTS Scratchpad RAM initialization. Therefore, before RWTS is called for the very the first time, the RDNIBL and WRNIBL tables are manufactured *just in time*.

```
   :              :          :
D2CA 8A          823        txa
D2CB 09 80       824        ora #$80
D2CD 99 56 DF    825        sta WRNIBL,Y
D2D0             826     ;
D2D0 98          827        tya
D2D1 9D 80 DF    828        sta RDNIBL-$16,X
   :              :          :
```

Figure I.9.2. Generating the RDNIBL and WRNIBL Tables

Table I.9.2 shows the sequence of steps that are used by DOS 4.5 in order to BOOT and to read into memory its DOS image. Just prior to COLDSTRT initialization, DOS 4.5 copies the ROM Monitor into the RAM memory of the Language Card partition and changes the addresses at BASCONT and XBASIC to the corresponding addresses that are found at DOSWARM and DOSCOLD. Thus, when the ROM Monitor initialization routines are called at GOTOMON, the Applesoft verification test will fail, and the Apple][is forced into the Monitor at 0xFF65, albeit it is actually the **RAM** Monitor that is invoked. This is the purpose for GOTOMON in DOS 4.5 when the user wishes to inspect code in Bank 2 of the Language Card partition by calling 0xBE00, or when the user wishes to inspect code in Bank 1 of the Language Card partition by calling 0xBE08. It is phenomenal when the same routine can serve a dual purpose.

One of the major hardware design limitations in having two banks of memory in the Language Card partition, Bank 1 and Bank 2, at the same address, 0xD000, is that it is not possible to execute code in one bank and read or write data from or into the other bank concurrently and at the same time. Once DOS 4.5 RWTS is located in Bank 1 memory after BOOT Stage 1 has finished, BOOT Stage 2 reads the remaining twenty-six pages into memory in two sections: sixteen pages to 0xF0:FF and ten pages to 0xE0:E9. Those sixteen pages in 0xF0:FF need to be moved to 0xD0:DF in Bank 2. The ten pages at 0xE0:E9 are already where they need to be. This is how DOS 4.5 reads data using one bank and then copies that data into the other bank. Once DOS 4.5 is properly placed in memory, DOSINIT can begin the Cold-Start process.

Function	Description
BOOT Stage 0	Prepare STAG1MOD, BUFRADRZ+1
BOOT Stage 1	Select and write-enable Bank 1 in the Language Card partition; read in RWTS, INRF, HELP, XFER, and BOOT routines
BOOT Stage 2	Save X-register to SNUM16, call CLRVALS to initialize CMDVALS, FMWORK, and SCRCHTBL Data structures to zero, initialize RWTS IOCB, call RWTS to read into memory remaining DOS code, call HRAM2DOS to copy DOS to correct memory pages, branch to COLDSTRT
DOSINIT	Enable Bank 1 of the Language Card partition, call CLRVALS to initialize CMDVALS, FMWORK and SCRCHTBL Data structures to zero
COLDSTRT	Write-enable ROM Bank 2
Monitor Init/GOTOMON	Initialize stack pointer, XMODE, VID80OFF, ALTCHOFF, SETNORM, INIT, SETVID, SETKBD
Applesoft Verification	Verify ROM Applesoft; fall into Monitor if test fails (actually, the RAM Monitor)
Copy ROM Monitor and Addresses	Call COPYROM to copy ROM Monitor to RAM Monitor, call COPYDOS to copy DOSWARM and DOSCOLD addresses to RAM at BASCONT and XBASIC
Find Clock	Call FINDCLK to locate clock card and determine clock type
Cold-Start Init	Init SLOTVAL, DRVAL, VOLVAL
Begin Cold-Start	Set the C-flag, jump to COLDSTR2 to begin DOS 4.5 processing

Table I.9.2. BOOT Sequence Steps in DOS 4.5

ROM Monitor initialization has slightly changed as Apple introduced new platforms such as the Apple //e and the Apple //c. ROM Monitor initialization now includes initializing the variable XMODE to 0xFF for proper CX ROM space utilization and to access the variables VID80OFF and ALTCHOFF in order to deselect the 80-column display mode and to select the display of the main video character set. I have added a call to SETNORM to ensure that there is *normal* screen character display (**not** inverse or **not** flashing) along with the usual calls to INIT, SETVID, and SETKBD. I do not believe the order that these ROM Monitor routines are called actually matter. With the ROM Monitor now in focus, DOS 4.5 can verify the presence or the absence of ROM Applesoft. DOS 4.5 does not continue its initialization process if it does not find a JMP instruction opcode or 0x4C at the BASCLD address of 0xE000.

DOS 4.5 copies the entire Monitor that is in ROM from 0xF800 to 0xFFFF to the same address in the RAM of the Language Card partition. Obviously, having the Monitor in RAM saves DOS 4.5 having to manage memory using Soft Switches in order to gain access to common RAM Monitor routines. Unlike the Monitor routines in ROM, however, the Monitor routines in RAM can be modified and adjusted to provide better functionality that is totally unique to DOS 4.5. Therefore, DOS 4.5 copies the DOSWARM and DOSCOLD addresses shown in Table I.9.3 to the Monitor in RAM where 0xFEB0 is the Cold-Start location and 0xFEB3 is the Warm-Start location for Applesoft. DOS 4.5 can now begin its search for a clock card in one of the peripheral slots. Section I.13 is devoted entirely to clock card access in DOS 4.5. At this time, DOS 4.5 prepares for Cold-Start initialization by initializing the Command Manager with the slot, drive, and volume variables from the RWTS IOCB that was just utilized to BOOT DOS.

Software developers of my favorite utilities like *ADT*, *Big Mac*, *FID*, *Lisa*, *PGE*, *GPLE*, and *Sourceror* made use of the DOS 3.3 Initial Address table that is located at 0x9D00 to 0x9D0F, 0x9D56 to 0x9D83, and, unfortunately, direct entry points to many other internal DOS 3.3 variables and routines. One can directly modify the values in the DOS 4.5 INITVALS table that is shown in Table I.8.5 to tailor a DOS BOOT image specific to one's needs. That is, CMDVAL specifies the HELLO file command which is 0x06 for RUN, 0x14 for EXEC, and 0x34 for BRUN to name a few, NMAXVAL specifies what the initial MAXFILES

34

value is set to, and YEARVAL specifies the current year in order to support the Thunderclock card which lacks a year register. SECVAL defines how many sectors are used for the volume Catalog, ENDTRK specifies how many tracks are used to initialize the volume, and ENDSEC specifies whether a track has sixteen or thirty-two sectors. In order to support hardware that provides forty tracks per volume, simply change ENDTRK to forty or 0x28. If hardware supports thirty-two sectors per track, change ENDSEC to thirty-two or 0x20. Modify some or all of these parameters directly in memory or use the INIT keywords and initialize another disk volume with an appropriate HELLO file. Either a BOOT or a DATA volume can be created that has a volume Catalog that is structured according to the values that have been selected. DOS 4.5 offers so much capability so easily!

Address	Variable	DOS 4.5	Description
0x3D0:0x3D2	DOSWARM	jmp EXTWARM	DOS Warm-Start jmp
0x3D3:0x3D5	DOSCOLD	jmp COLDSTRT	DOS Cold-Start jmp
0x3D6:0x3D8	CALLFM	jmp EXTFM	File Manager jmp
0x3D9:0x3DB	CALLRWTS	jmp EXTRWTS	RWTS handler jmp
0x3DC:0x3E0	GETFMCB	ldy #FMVALS lda /FMVALS	Puts File Manager Input/Output Context Block address into #Y/A registers
0x3E1:0x3E2	RDCLKVSN	adr EXCLKVSN	address in #Y/A; Clock clc; Version sec
0x3E3:0x3E7	GETIOCB	ldy #TBLTYPE lda /TBLTYPE	Puts RWTS I/O Input/Output Context Block address into #Y/A registers
0x3E8:0x3E9	PRTERADR	adr EXTPRERR	Prints error message for error # in X-register
0x3EA:0x3EC	HOOKDOS	jmp EXTPTRS	DOS reconnect jmp
0x3ED:0x3EE	XFERADR	adr *-*	Used for the Apple //e DOXFER routine
0x3EF:0x3F1	AUTOBRK	jmp OLDBRK	ROM Break handler jmp
0x3F2:0x3F3	AUTORSET	adr EXTWARM	ROM auto-reset routine address
0x3F4	PWRSTATE	byt 0xA5^(0x3F3)	Power up byte
0x3F5:0x3F7	USRAHAND	jmp EXTRPEAT	Ampersand handler jmp
0x3F8:0x3FA	USRYHAND	jmp AUXMOVE	Ctrl-Y handler jmp to 0xC311
0x3FB:0x3FD	NMASKIRQ	jmp MON	Non-maskable IRQ jmp to 0xFF65
0x3FE:0x3FF	MASKIRQ	adr MON	Maskable IRQ routine address at 0xFF65

Table I.9.3. Page 0x03 Interface Routines and Vectors

When DOS 4.5 performs a Cold-Start, it sets MAXFILES equal to NMAXVAL, it initializes all five of the file buffers, it makes EXEC inactive, and it copies the contents of Table I.9.3 into memory beginning at memory address 0x3D0. It is in this structure where the important DOS interface routines and vectors are found for specific DOS functions, such as RWTS and the File Manager. This structure is essentially the same as that found in DOS 3.3 in order to maintain compatibility with virtually all previous software, but with some important additions. I have added "read DOS version" or "read clock routine" or RDCLKVSN at memory address 0x3E1, the "error printing routine" or PRTERROR at memory address 0x3E8, and the Apple //e "DOXFER address" or XFERADR at memory address 0x3ED. The RDCLKVSN and PRTERROR routines can be accessed using an indirect JMP instruction such as JMP (RDCLKVSN). The two routines GETFMCB and GETIOCB are changed somewhat in DOS 4.5 from their DOS 3.3 implementation, but they return the same information. That is, the address of the RWTS IOCB is put into the Y- and A-registers, and similarly, the address of the File Manager Context Block is put into the Y- and A-registers in Lo/Hi byte order. These two Context Blocks are shown in Tables I.10.1 and I.11.1, respectively. The routine RDCLKVSN copies the version of DOS that is currently in memory which is a 20-byte upper ASCII character string or DOS 4.5.06H 02/14/24, into a buffer whose address is in the Y- and A-registers when the C-flag is **set**. The routine RDCLKVSN reads the current date and time into a 6-byte buffer as shown in Table I.5.5 whose address is in the Y- and A-registers when the C-flag is **clear**. The routine PRTERROR prints the error messages as shown in Table I.11.7 whose index error number is in the X-register. Example code segments to read the current DOS version into a 20-byte buffer and the current date and time into a 6-byte buffer are shown in Figures I.9.3 and I.9.4, respectively. Figure I.9.5 shows how *Big Mac* prints all of its File Manager error codes.

```
   :              :         :
 03E1             5    RDCLKVSN equ $3E1
   :              :         :
 0900 A0 43       13            ldy #VSNBUFR
 0902 A9 09       14            lda /VSNBUFR
 0904 38          15            sec
 0905 20 40 09    16            jsr READVSN
   :              :         :
 0920 60          20            rts
   :              :         :
 0940 6C E1 03    40    READVSN  jmp (RDCLKVSN)
 0943 00 00 00    41    VSNBUFR  dfs 20,0
   :              :         :
```

Figure I.9.3. Reading the DOS Version Example

```
   :              :         :
 03E1             5    RDCLKVSN equ $3E1
   :              :         :
 0900 A0 43       13            ldy #CLKBUFR
 0902 A9 09       14            lda /CLKBUFR
 0904 18          15            clr
 0905 20 40 09    16            jsr READCLK
   :              :         :
 0920 60          20            rts
   :              :         :
 0940 6C E1 03    40    READCLK  jmp (RDCLKVSN)
 0943 00 00 00    41    CLKBUFR  dfs 6,0
   :              :         :
```

Figure I.9.4. Reading the Date and Time Example

It is worthwhile to note that the DOS 4.5 RWTS only supports Disk][-type hardware since there was no other device manufactured that was substantially any different. The Device Characteristics Table, or DCT was originally designed so that RWTS could support an array of disk devices each having different stepper motor phases per track that might have supported half-tracking or even different motor on-time requirements. I saw no need for DOS 4.5 to support something that simply does not, nor will ever exist.

36

I am aware that the RanaSystems EliteThree is a dual-headed disk drive with the ability to access eighty half-tracks on both sides of a double-sided, double-density diskette. Of course, the DCT for the Rana is different, but the Rana uses its own interface handler with its own PHASEON/PHASEOFF tables for its stepper motor operation, and its own number of stepper motor phases that accomplish its half-tracking capabilities. I even developed my own firmware for the Rana that formats a diskette with forty tracks on both sides of the diskette, with the lower sixteen sectors on side one and the upper sixteen sectors on side two, effectively creating a volume where each track contains thirty-two sectors. I was absolutely successful and, by design, the firmware attached to the DOS 4.5 RWTS DISKADRS table. I was able to obtain double-sided, double-density 5.25-inch floppy diskettes from www.floppydisk.com. As a word of caution, double-sided, double-density 5.25-inch floppy diskettes are manufactured with an inner reinforcement ring. Significantly better performance is achieved using those diskettes whether half-tracking is employed or not. In summary, DOS 4.5 does not utilize a DCT, and it ignores any DCT address that may be included in any RWTS IOCB for a Disk][or for any other Disk][-like drive.

```
   :               :            :
 0044            18  A5L       epz $44
 0045            19  A5H       epz $45
   :               :            :
 03D6            27  CALLFM    equ $3D6
 03DC            28  GETFMCB   equ $3DC
 03E8            29  PRTERADR  equ $3E8
   :               :            :
 D0B0 6C E8 03  101  PRTERROR  jmp (PRTERADR)
   :               :            :
 D12D 20 DC 03  131            jsr GETFMCB
 D130 84 44     132            sty A5L
 D132 85 45     133            sta A5H
   :               :            :
 E58A A2 01     316            ldx #1
 E58C 20 D6 03  317            jsr CALLFM
 E58F 90 40     318            bcc HE5D1
 E591 A0 0A     319            ldy #10
 E593 B1 44     320            lda (A5L),Y
 E595 AA        321            tax
   :               :            :
 E5BC 8A        361            txa
 E5BD 48        362            pha
   :               :            :
 E5C1 E8        366            inx
 E5C2 20 B0 D0  367            jsr PRTERROR
 E5C5 68        368            pla
 E5C6 AA        369            tax
 E5C7 20 B0 D0  370            jsr PRTERROR
 E5CA 20 8E FD  371            jsr CROUT
   :               :            :
 E5D1 A2 0E     394  HE5D1     ldx #$0E
   :               :            :
 FD8E A9 8D     586  CROUT     lda #$8D
   :               :            :
```

Figure I.9.5. Printing a File Manager Error in Big Mac Example

10. RWTS Interface in DOS 4.5

The DOS 4.5 RWTS interface is very straightforward and very simple to use. When a call is made to GETIOCB as shown in Table I.9.3, the Y- and A-registers point to the RWTS IOCB that is shown in Table I.10.1. Any other assessable memory address space may be utilized for an RWTS IOCB as well. Once the IOCB has been initialized with all required values, a call to CALLRWTS with the address of an external IOCB, or the address of the IOCB within DOS in the Y- and A-registers, begins RWTS processing. The RWTS handler pushes the current processor status onto the stack, disables interrupts, and saves the Y- and A-registers to the IOB page-zero address at 0x4A:0x4B, which is a different page-zero address than what is used in DOS 3.3.

Offset	Name	Size	Description
0x00	TBLTYPE	0x01	IOCB structure block
0x01	SNUM16	0x01	Slot number * 16
0x02	DNUM	0x01	Drive number
0x03	VOLEXPT	0x01	Volume number expected; 0x00 for any
0x04	TNUM	0x01	Track number
0x05	SNUM	0x01	Sector number
0x06	DCTADR	0x02	Address of Device Characteristics table (ignored)
0x08	USRBUF	0x02	Data buffer address
0x0A	IOCBPHAS	0x01	Half-phases per track; if 0x00, use default of 0x04
0x0B	BYTCNT	0x01	Bytes to read/write; 0x00 means 256 bytes
0x0C	CMDCODE	0x01	Command code
0x0D	ERRCODE	0x01	Return error code
0x0E	VOLFND	0x01	Return volume number found
0x0F	SLOTFND	0x01	Return slot number found
0x10	DRVFND	0x01	Return drive number found

Table I.10.1. RWTS Input/Output Context Block Definition

The official volume number for any DOS 4.5 volume is DISKVOL as shown in Table I.5.2, and not the value that is encoded in the Address Field header that prefaces each DATA Field header on a diskette, though these two values are typically the same for a physical diskette. In DOS 4.5, the encoded volume number is saved to the VOLFND variable in the IOCB as shown in Table I.10.1. Disk devices like the RAM Disk 320 or the CFFA do not require an Address Field header to preface each data sector or data block that contains data. Thus, the encoded volume number can only be ascertained from Disk][-like devices and there is **no** encoded volume number in other non-Disk][-type devices. In order for DOS 4.5 to determine volume number mismatch for **all** disk devices it must rely solely on the value that is found in DISKVOL. Because DISKVOL is external to RWTS, volume number mismatch can only be determined external to and **not** internal to RWTS. Therefore, the determination of volume number mismatch cannot be required of other disk devices and their established firmware algorithms. When RWTS returns to the File Manager with the C-flag **clear**, DOS 4.5 copies IOCBPHAS to VALSPHAS and then checks for volume number mismatch. If the requested volume number VOLEXPT is zero, no further processing is required and a return is made to the caller. If VOLEXPT is not zero, then its value is compared to DISKVOL, and if they are the same, no further processing is required and a return is made to the caller. If VOLEXPT and DISKVOL are not the same, the RWVOLERR error code is immediately submitted to the RWTS error code conversion routine, and the appropriate error number is reported to the File Manager. When the File Manager receives this error code, it displays the Volume Number Mismatch error message, it restores the stack pointer from STKSAVE, and the File Manager exits in order to allow DOS 4.5 to continue its normal processing. Because the VTOC is the very first structure that is read from a volume while DOS is processing I/O commands, DISKVOL becomes available *just in time* before it is compared to VOLEXPT in the IOCB. All further volume number checks will succeed while DOS continues processing the requested I/O command because the VTOC will not be read again until the next DOS I/O command is issued. The volume compare design strategy is unique to DOS 4.5.

After the Y- and A-registers have been saved to the 0x4A:0x4B IOB address, the RWTS handler extracts the supplied buffer address USRBUF from the IOCB and saves the address to BUFADR2Z and BUFADR2Z+1 at page-zero addresses 0x3E:0x3F. The handler also extracts the SNUM16 value, saves it to SLOTFND in the IOCB, divides it by sixteen, checks the Slot Scratchpad table SCRCHTBL for first-time slot number use, and calculates the low-order address byte for DISKJMP that is based on that original SNUM16 value. The RWTS handler then indirectly jumps to the routine whose address is located in the Disk Address table DISKADRS for the specified slot number. The assembler initializes all seven DISKADRS table entries to the address of RWTSENT so that it makes no difference into which physical slot or slots a Disk][or Disk][-like interface card may have been inserted.

Command	Value	Description
RWTSSEEK	0x00	Seek to track/sector command code
RWTSREAD	0x01	Read Track/Sector command code
RWTSWRIT	0x02	Write Track/Sector command code
RWTSFRMT	0x04	Format volume command code

Table I.10.2. RWTS Command Codes

Error	Value	Description
RWNOERR	0x00	RWTS No error
RWINITER	0x08	RWTS Initialization (format) error
RWPROTER	0x10	RWTS Write-protect error
RWVOLERR	0x20	RWTS Volume number mismatch error
RWSYNERR	0x30	RWTS Syntax error (out of range)
RWDRVERR	0x40	RWTS Drive error
RWREADER	0x80	RWTS Read error (obsolete)

Table I.10.3. RWTS Error Codes

The MOVEHD routine handles the placement of the read/write disk head and masks all track values it encounters with TRKMASK or 0x3F in order to remove the value of TRKZERO or 0x40 if it happens to be used in the IOCB. When RWTS completes its processing, it saves DRVFND and VOLFND and its processing results into the supplied IOCB at ERRCODE. The RWTS handler restores the original processor status and it either **clears** or **sets** the C-flag based on the return status results from RWTS. If interrupts were initially enabled before the call to the RWTS handler, interrupts are re-enabled when the RWTS handler exits. Table I.10.2 shows the four valid RWTS command codes and Table I.10.3 shows the six possible error codes that RWTS can generate. I have added the RWSYNERR error code for IOCBPHAS range checking errors and for errors found in the RAM Disk, Rana, and Sider firmware that perform their own range checking of their IOCB variables. If the volume number mismatch check fails at the conclusion of and external to RWTS, the error code RWVOLERR is issued. Once again, DOS 4.5 does not check for volume number mismatch with the volume number that is encoded in the Address Field header of a diskette. The astute reader will assuredly notice that I have utilized the spare byte in the RWTS IOCB for the IOCBPHAS variable. Furthermore, I have used the spare byte in the File Manager Input/Output Context Block for FMPHASE as shown later in Table I.11.1. Both variables, when encountered during their specific routine utilization, are range checked and copied to VALSPHAS as shown in Table I.8.5. The value entered with the DOS PHASE command is also copied to VALSPHAS. VALSPHAS is the key variable that is used to multiply the target track number in order to obtain the number of half-phases to which the read/write disk head is moved by MOVEHD before any input/output data can occur.

All physical tracks on a *physical* DOS diskette are separated by four half-phases, the equivalent of rotating the cam of the stepper motor 180 degrees as I prefer to imagine its operation. The stepper motor is used to move the read/write disk head along the radius of the diskette towards or away from the center of the diskette. A simplified representation of the Disk][read/write disk head mechanics is shown in Figure I.10.1. The read/write disk head is connected to the Carriage Rod and that rod travels along the radius of the diskette as the Cam Table is rotated by the Stepper Motor. The Cam Rider is also attached to the Carriage Rod and it essentially *rides* the Cam Channel. As the Cam Table rotates, the Cam Rider follows the Cam Channel, thereby pulling or pushing the Carriage Rod towards or away from the center of the diskette. The Stepper Motor can be made to rotate both clockwise and counter-clockwise in order to move the read/write disk head from track 0x00 to track 0x23, and then back to track 0x00.

About one year after the Disk][drive was first introduced in June, 1978, the Cam Table and supporting hardware were slightly modified in order to access a full thirty-six tracks rather than thirty-five tracks. For one reason or another this information never found its way into the general Apple user community.

The motor that is used to rotate the Cam Table in the Disk][is a general purpose 4-phase, 12-volt DC stepper motor. Each electromagnet or phase coil or sets of phase coils that are located inside the stepper motor can be energized individually or in pairs, as well as de-energized, in such a way as to cause the Cam Table to rotate. The illustration that is shown in Figure I.10.2 gives the location of the first twelve half-phases as well as the location where tracks 0x00, 0x01, 0x02, and 0x03 would occur along the Cam Channel as the Cam Table is rotated clockwise or counter-clockwise. These tracks conform to the normal spacing of four half-phases like the tracks that are found on a DOS Master diskette. On the other hand, the RanaSystems EliteThree has the ability to space tracks as close as two half-phases because the gap length of its read/write disk head is smaller than the gap length of the read/write disk head that is found in the Disk][. Actually, I empirically found that the gap length of the read/write disk head in the Disk][is somewhat equal to the size of three half-phases. Manufacturing read/write disk heads with this specification helps to minimize cross-talk between adjacent tracks that are spaced four or more half-phases apart.

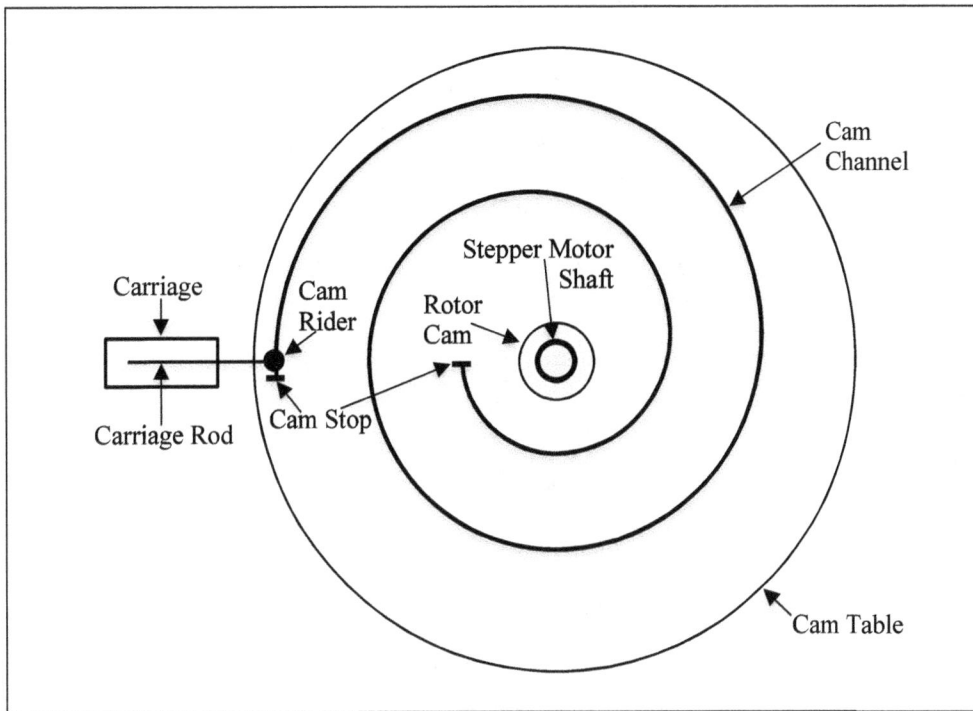

Figure I.10.1. Disk][Carriage and Cam Table

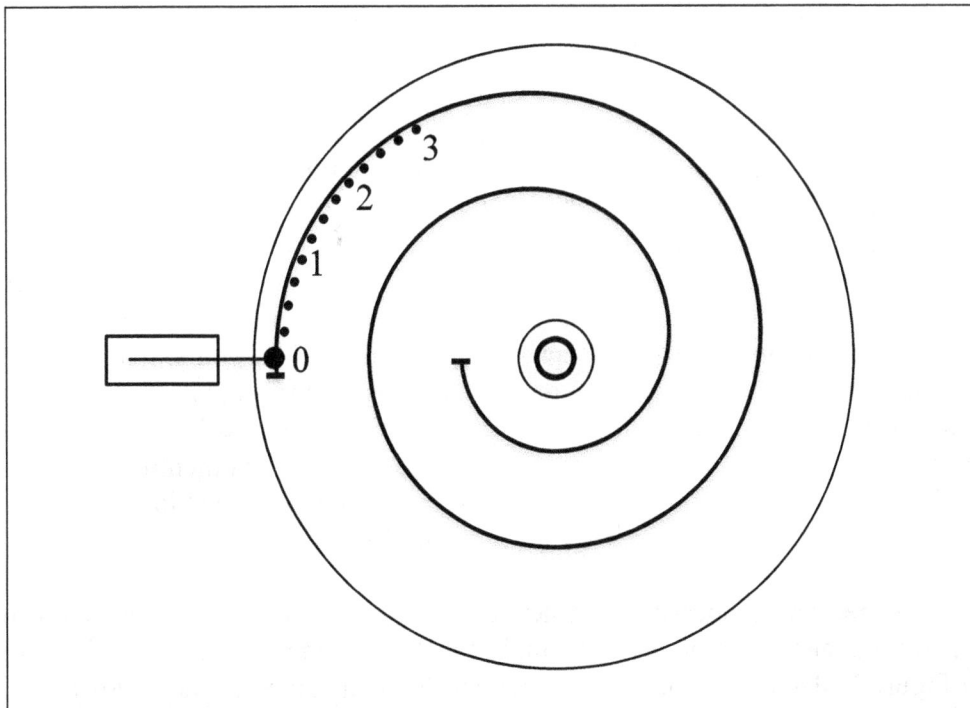

Figure I.10.2. Four Half-Phase Track Separation

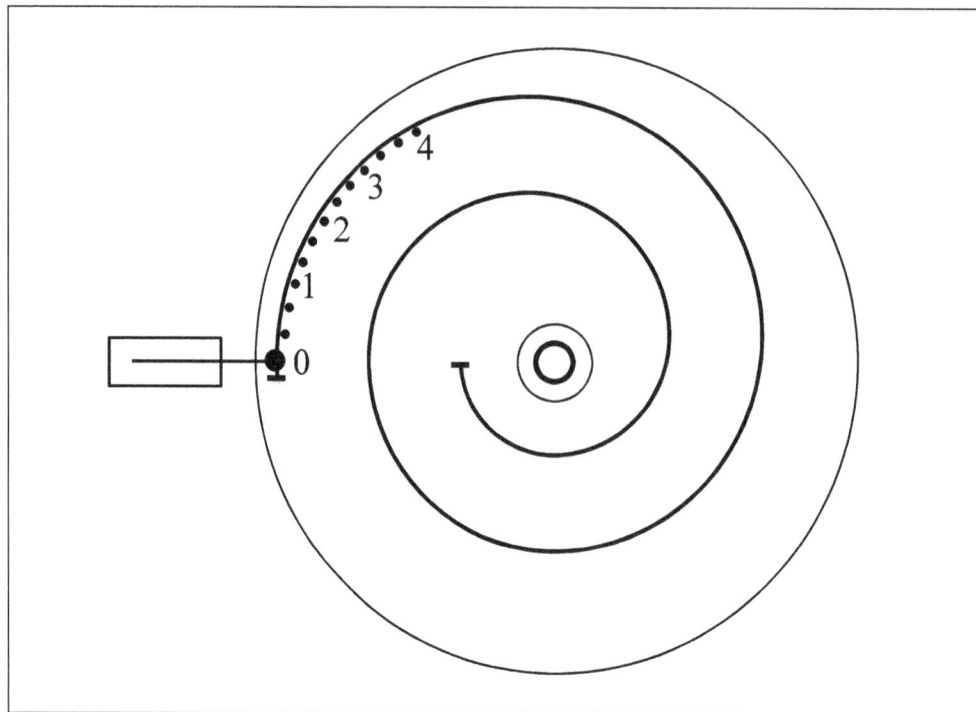

Figure I.10.3. Three Half-Phase Track Separation

In order to move the read/write disk head from track 0x00 to track 0x23, the stepper motor needs to rotate through a span of 140 half-phases, or 35 * 4 half-phases. *The span of tracks is always the number of available tracks minus one.* If tracks are separated by only three half-phases, it is conceivable that a diskette could possibly support up to forty-seven and perhaps even forty-eight physical tracks. Figure I.10.3 shows the same location of those first twelve half-phases as they were shown in Figure I.10.2, only now the tracks are spaced every three half-phases. Of course, this is merely an illustration until it can actually be demonstrated. There are a number of parameters to consider when designing software to actuate the stepper motor in the Disk][, or in any other similar disk drive implementation. These parameters may include current track location of the read/write disk head, direction of movement, distance of movement, desired acceleration if any, desired deceleration if any, desired maximum velocity, induced mechanical vibrations, and any controlled mechanical damping. The routine that moves the read/write disk head on behalf of RWTS may consider all or some of these parameters in order to consistently place the read/write disk head at the correct location or track as efficiently as possible without regard to direction of movement, distance, and the generation of any induced angular momentum. In other words, the read/write disk head must be totally stopped and it must be held at the correct location consistently before any data input or any data output can occur with any reliability.

I like to imagine the mechanical operation of a stepper motor as that represented by the illustrations shown in Figure I.10.4 for the sake of simplicity. The main functional components of this Disk][stepper motor are labeled in Figure I.10.4A. The permanent magnet that is attached to the Rotor Plate is attracted to each one of the four electromagnetic or phase coils as each coil is energized in succession. By design, the stepper motor is always at Phase 0 when the Cam Rider hits the outer Cam Stop which is the location of track 0x00. Figure I.10.4B shows the Rotor Cam positioned clockwise from Phase 0 at Phase Coil 2, effectively positioning the read/write disk head precisely over track 0x01 as shown in Figure I.10.2 where each track is separated by four half-phases. Essentially, the rotation of the Rotor Plate from one electromagnet to the next electromagnet amounts to one full phase or two half-phases. Every rotation of four half-phases moves the read/write disk head to the next or previous adjacent track. Figure I.10.4C shows the Rotor Cam positioned at three half-phases clockwise from Phase 0. This would position the read/write disk head precisely over track 0x01 as shown in Figure I.10.3 where each track is separated by three half-phases. Figure I.10.4D shows the Rotor Cam positioned clockwise from Phase 0 at Phase Coil 3 which would position the read/write disk head precisely over track 0x02, again for tracks separated by three half-phases.

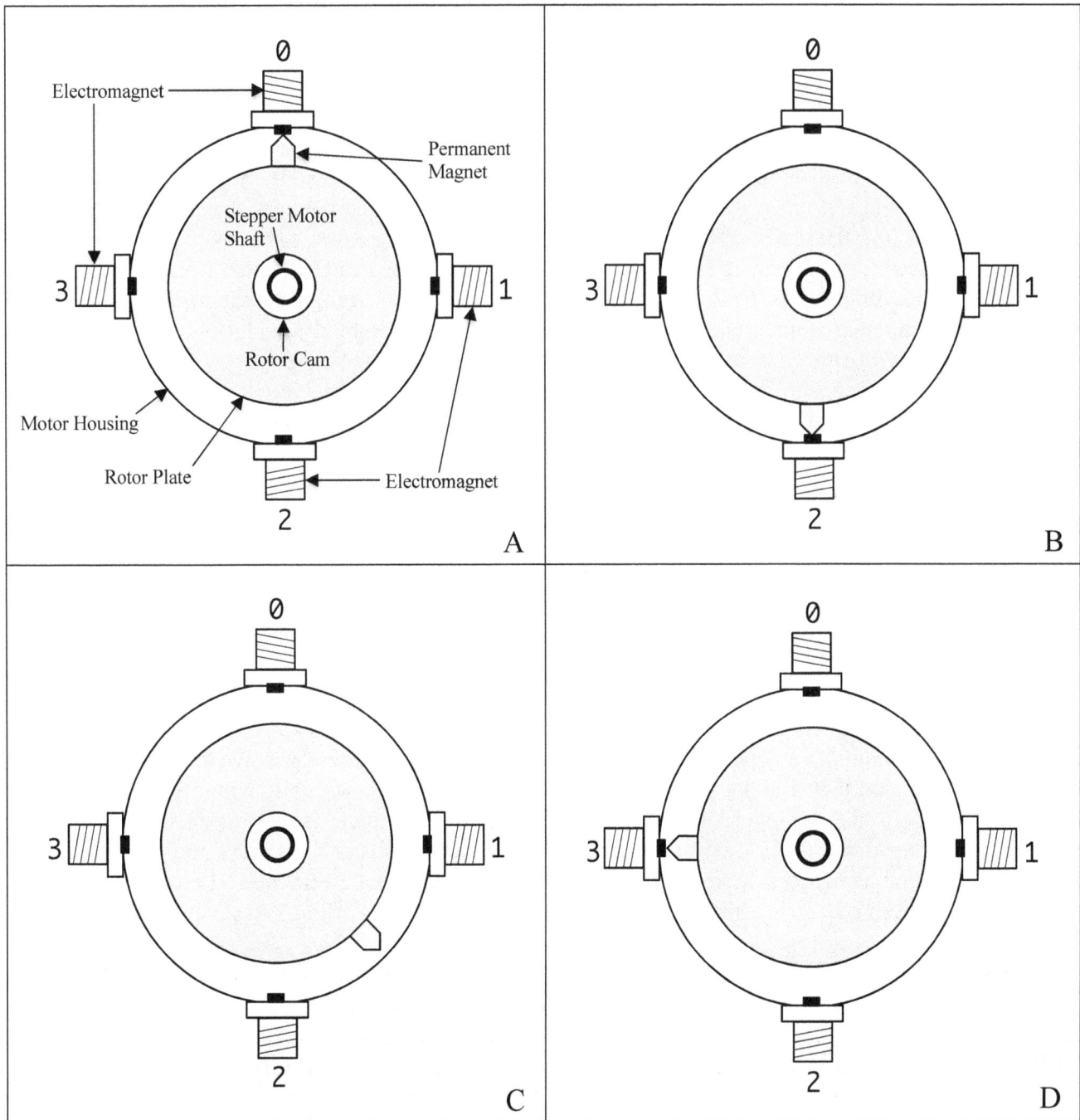

Figure I.10.4. Disk][Stepper Motor Illustration

The MOVEHD routine in DOS 4.1 is similar to the routine that is found in DOS 3.3 in that both routines move the read/write disk head to and from the even numbered phase coils 0 and 2. The odd numbered phase coils 1 and 3 simply assist in turning the Cam Table as accurately and as efficiency as possible. Both routines use an acceleration and deceleration algorithm that reaches maximum velocity after moving the read/write disk head through eight phases. That is, the current track and the target track are first doubled so that a computation is made every time the current track counter in incremented, and that would occur as every new phase is selected, thus, either a specific coil is energized or a specific coil is deenergized. The time to leave a specific coil energized or deenergized is determined by an entry from either an ONTBL or from an OFFTBL where there are eight values in each table. One can just as easily view the distance between two adjacent tracks as equal to four half-phases rather than equal to two full phases as in DOS 3.3 or in DOS 4.1. Since I claim that the individual half-phase is attainable, it is the more general expression, and Occam's Razor would favor the *half-phase* as the preferred designation.

The algorithm that is used in the DOS 4.5 MOVEHD routine is radically different from the algorithm that is used in DOS 4.1 in that a computation must be made every half-phase, and the time a coil is energized or deenergized is determined by an entry from a single ONOFFTBL table of twelve values. This table also provides the MOVEHD routine with an acceleration and deceleration component that reaches maximum velocity after moving the read/write disk head through twelve half-phases. The resulting movement of the Cam Table is also smooth and efficient. Once the read/write disk head is located at its destination, the Cam Table is held in place for nearly twenty-six milliseconds to ensure that all vibration transients and torque due to its angular momentum have been buffered and absorbed by the enclosure. The final coil or coils can then be deenergized to assure that the read/write disk head is held precisely over the requested track. The Carriage Rod and Carriage are designed to inhibit any further movement of the read/write disk head once the last coil or final coils have been deenergized. Some disk manufactures employ a tension band that can be adjusted to restrict movement of the Carriage Rod, but obviously not enough restriction that cannot be overcome by the strong startup torque of the stepper motor.

The direction of Cam Table movement in the DOS 4.5 MOVEHD routine determines the values for the NEXTON and NEXTOFF variables. One or the other variable is used every time the current track counter is incremented or decremented and a new computation is made, so either NEXTON is subtracted from or NEXTOFF is added to the track counter. When the read/write disk head has reached its final destination and held in place, and if the Permanent Magnet is at rest between two adjacent phase coils as shown in Figure I.10.4C, the coils are deenergized in a specific order. It does not matter whether the Cam Table is turned clockwise or counterclockwise because these two adjacent coils are always deenergized in the same order. Doing so minimizes any possible skewing of the read/write disk head relative to the absolute track location. Understand that it is not physically possible to deenergize two coils within the same stepper motor at precisely the same moment in time. Furthermore, there is no dependence on which microprocessor instructions are used to deenergize two adjacent coils at the same time. That is, a load accumulator absolute addressing instruction is no faster and induces no less skew than any load accumulator indexed addressing instruction regardless whether the X- or the Y-register is utilized.

Managing disk phase in RWTS is an exceedingly complex process particularly when copying files from diskette volumes that have been initialized with different phase values. Beginning with the initial BOOT for a volume, the start location of the read/write disk head for drive 1 is forced to be track 0x00 by the Disk][Interface Card firmware and the start location is set to be track 0x00 for both drive 1 and drive 2 in the Slot Scratchpad table when RWTS is called for the first time. The unique design of DOS 4.5 RWTS initializes the DRV0TRK and DRV1TRK variables as well as the DRV0PHAS and DRV1PHAS variables to zero at the beginning of BOOT Stage 2. DRV0TRK and DRV1TRK use the base addresses 0x0478 and 0x04F8, respectively, and DRV0PHAS and DRV1PHAS use the base addresses 0x0678 and 0x06F8, respectively. Of course, the slot number for the Disk][is used as an index from these base addresses. As an aside, the Rana uses 0x0578 and 0x05F8 as the base addresses for DRV2TRK and DRV3TRK, respectively, and 0x0778 and 0x07F8 for DRV2PHAS and DRV3PHAS, respectively.

In RWTS processing just prior to extracting the requested IOCB command, if the phase value that is saved at DRV0PHAS or DRV1PHAS, depending on drive number, is zero, it is set to DFLTPHAS, or four, and a page-zero PHASE variable is set to either the saved phase value or DFLTPHAS. Next, the IOCB phase value is extracted and if it is zero, it is replaced by PHASE, and then range checked not to exceed PHASMAX, or sixteen which is arbitrary. The IOCB phase value is again compared to PHASE, and if the values differ, the read/write disk head is moved to track 0x00 using the previously saved phase value or PHASE, and then moved to the requested track using the new IOCB phase value, which can then be saved to the scratchpad. If the PHASE and IOCB phase values do not differ, the read/write disk head is simply moved to the requested track using the PHASE value. If the phase value is changed, all further access to that drive now utilizes the new phase value. The additional logic to manage disk phase when the phase value does not change is still within the window that is established by the required number of 40-microsecond auto-synchronization bytes between an Address Field header and its DATA Field header. Establishing a new phase value for a Disk][or a Disk][-like drive occurs once, so the impact to a disk copying session is only slightly minimal. This re-phasing process happens so smoothly, so accurately, most users would probably never even notice its implementation.

The illustration that is shown in Figure I.10.3 suggests that a Disk][in pristine working order can conceivably access up to and possibly forty-eight tracks on a double-sided double-density diskette using a half-phase value of three. The DOS 4.5 INIT command can certainly initialize a diskette with that format flawlessly. And *FID*, after being modified to request phase number like it requests volume number, can be used to copy files from a phase-four diskette to a phase-three diskette. The new phase-three diskette BOOTs effortlessly because the DOS INIT handler copies the VALSPHAS value to CFGPHASE before it creates the new DOS image. Recall that CFGPHASE is copied to IOCBPHAS at the beginning of BOOT Stage 2. I have even created bootable diskettes that are initialized with VALSPHAS set to five and six. A phase-five diskette can only access at most twenty-nine tracks, or $1 + 140 / 5$, and a phase-six diskette can only access at most twenty-four tracks. Why would one desire this capability? First and foremost an odd-phased initialized diskette would be very difficult to copy and probably thwart a number of diskette copy applications. Because the DOS PHASE command is a DOS command in DOS 4.5, its value can be changed at any given moment, even while a *special* diskette is booting or while its first application is loading. Actually, the Application Loader could *adjust* phase to ensure its copy-protection routines are well protected and very difficult to access while it is loading the primary application. However, I have no doubt that John K. Morris can perfectly copy any DOS 4.5 phased diskette using his Applesauce floppy drive controller. And that is perfectly acceptable with me.

The software routines within RWTS that read and write the Address Field header, the DATA Field header, and the sector data of a Disk][diskette were all originally designed by Steven Wozniak. The critical timing these routines employ are entirely dependent on how Wozniak designed the companion Disk][Interface Card hardware, including its logic gate timing, its functional component requirements, and its data format restrictions. It has even been reported that Wozniak went so far as to modify the innovative design of his original interface card layout in order to reduce the number of feed-through holes from three to two! The most comprehensive discussions that I have found on RWTS and the Disk][Interface Card can be found in *Beneath Apple DOS* and *Beneath Apple ProDOS*, both books by Don Worth and Pieter Lechner, and *Understanding the Apple II* and *Understanding the Apple IIe*, both books by Jim Sather. I believe Sather's books are incredibly detailed because Sather uses tables, diagrams, and schematic drawings to explain the operation of the Apple][series of computers, and the Worth/Lechner books provide the reader with a number of excellent example routines that demonstrate how to use RWTS in software programs. In my opinion, even these references as well as others in my library do not adequately demonstrate how the Disk][Interface Card and its unique ROM manage to read data from and write data to a Disk][floppy diskette. That is, not until I took my own personal, deep dive into exploring how the logic circuits of the Disk][Interface Card interact with the data content of its 256-byte sequencer ROM did I fully appreciate, understand, and marvel at Wozniak's brilliant hardware design. I found the clearest schematic drawing of the Disk][Interface Card in the *Apple][The DOS Manual*. That reference book even provides the schematic drawing for the Disk][analog board.

The Disk][Interface Card contains the 256-byte P5 bootstrap BOOT Stage 0 firmware ROM, an 8-bit shift/storage data register, the 256-byte P6 8-bit logic state sequencer ROM, and an 8-bit addressable latch or command decoder. The schematic drawing of the Disk][Interface Card shows that the 8-bit *index byte* that is used to address the P6 sequencer ROM is composed of two bits from the command decoder, a negative pulse data bit from the Disk][analog board, a write-protect bit which is the QA output or the MSB from the shift/storage data register, and four bits from the 8-bit data byte that was previously read from the same P6 ROM. The connections to the bits of this index byte is shown pictorially in Figure I.10.5. The two bits from the command decoder that are named Q6 and Q7 provide the only means to control the logic state sequencer while using RWTS software. Table I.10.4 shows the definition of the sixteen peripheral-card I/O memory bytes that are dedicated to the Disk][Interface Card as switches, Q0 to Q7. The Disk][Interface Card circuitry and P6 ROM sequencing is specifically designed such that any reference to the Disk][peripheral-card I/O memory **must only** utilize indexed addressing instructions. Typically, the X-register is primarily used for this indexing, and this register contains the slot number of the Disk][Interface Card times sixteen. For a Disk][Interface Card that resides in slot 6, the address 0xC0E0 would be referenced when using the indexed addressing instruction $C080,X when the X-register is equal to 0x60. System RESET forces all eight switches into the OFF, or zero state.

A7	A6	A5	A4	A3	A2	A1	A0
Sequence Bit 3	Sequence Bit 2	Sequence Bit 0	Data Pulse	Q7	Q6	QA	Sequence Bit 1

Figure I.10.5. Index Byte Format for the P6 ROM

Switch	OFF Function	ON Function
Q0	$C080,X – PHASE 0 OFF	$C081,X – PHASE 0 ON
Q1	$C082,X – PHASE 1 OFF	$C083,X – PHASE 1 ON
Q2	$C084,X – PHASE 2 OFF	$C085,X – PHASE 2 ON
Q3	$C086,X – PHASE 3 OFF	$C087,X – PHASE 3 ON
Q4	$C088,X – selected drive OFF	$C089,X – selected drive ON
Q5	$C08A,X – select drive 1	$C08B,X – select drive 2
Q6	$C08C,X – read data or SHIFT while writing	$C08D,X – read write-protect state or LOAD data while writing
Q7	$C08E,X – enable READ sequencing	$C08F,X – enable WRITE sequencing

Table I.10.4. Disk][Interface I/O Switches Definition

One of the very first tasks the RWTS software performs when it begins its processing is to enable READ sequencing with the Disk][Interface Card regardless whether the call to RWTS will read or write data. Using Table I.10.4 as reference and the information that is shown in Table I.10.5, switches Q6 and Q7 must be both OFF in order to enable READ sequencing. This is shown in Figure I.10.6 which is taken from the DOS 4.5 RWTS software. Once the Disk][Interface Card has configured its sequencing to READ, it is now safe for RWTS to select the Drive using switch Q5 and to enable the drive motor using switch Q4 that rotates the diskette. The read/write disk head may now be safely positioned over the requested track using switches Q0 through Q3 in a controlled and precise sequence whose DOS 4.5 algorithm utilizes the requested phase number. If the call to RWTS is to read a sector of disk data, Figure I.10.7 shows a sample of code taken from the DOS 4.5 software that reads a disk byte. As will be shown later in this discussion, the MSB of a disk byte is not used as a data bit, but as a flag bit that indicates when valid disk data is available to be read from the shift and storage data register by software. Once a disk byte is read, the logic state sequencer immediately commands the shift register to clear, it commands the register to input a 1 bit and shift the register bits left, it commands the register to input a data pulse bit that is sent from the Disk][analog board that has been held for eight microseconds, and finally it shifts the register bits left again. Subsequent data pulse bits are input into the shift and storage data register and the register bits are shifted left every four microseconds which is equivalent to eight sequences of the logic state sequencer. The shift and storage data register and a 74LS174 latch that has six D-type flip-flops that contain the D4 through D7 data bits from the previous P6 ROM data byte are clocked by $Q3$ falling which has a frequency of 2 MHz that is synchronized to the 6502 or 65C02 PHASE 0 clock.

Q6		Q7		Sequencer Function
$C08C,X	SHIFT	$C08E,X	READ	Enable READ sequencing
$C08D,X	LOAD	$C08E,X	READ	Check state of write-protect switch and initialize the logic state sequencer before writing
$C08C,X	SHIFT	$C08F,X	WRITE	Shift data register after eight sequencer clocks while writing
$C08D,X	LOAD	$C08F,X	WRITE	Load data register after eight sequencer clocks while writing

Table I.10.5. Selectable Logic State Sequencer Functions

```
   :              :            :
D081            142  ; Return to read sequencing.
D081            143  ;        ;
D081 BD 8E C0   144  SETREAD  lda DATAIN,X    ; enable sequencer to READ
D084 BD 8C C0   145           lda STROBE,X    ; enable sequencer to SHIFT
   :              :            :
```

Figure I.10.6. Setting the Disk][Interface to READ Sequencing

If the call to RWTS is to write sector data, RWTS must manipulate the Disk][Interface Card switches in a prescribed manner in order to synchronize with what RWTS is about to write with what RWTS has previously read. In other words, RWTS has just read an Address Field header that contains the same values for the requested track, sector, and volume numbers, and it can now begin to write new sector data over the previous sector data. Once the new 40-microsecond auto-synchronization bytes, the new 32-microsecond prolog bytes, the sector data bytes, and the epilog bytes are written, the Disk][Interface Card must immediately set its sequencing to READ as shown in Figure I.10.6, otherwise the next series of auto-synchronization bytes and the next Address Field header will be destroyed. In order to sense the state of the current Disk][write-protection switch and to initialize the logic state sequencer before its sequencing can be set to WRITE, Q6 must be turned ON as in the code that is taken from the DOS 4.5 software as shown in Figure I.10.8.

```
  :              :             :
D123           320  ; Now read nibbles into NBUF1.
D123           321  ;
D123 BC 8C C0  322  ^8          ldy STROBE,X       ; read Data register latch
D126 10 FB     323              bpl <8             ; loop until MSB is set
  :              :             :
```

Figure I.10.7. Accessing the Disk][Interface to READ a Disk Byte

```
  :              :             :
D011           34   WRITSCTR sec                   ; set C-flag if write-protect
D012           35   ;
D012 BD 8D C0  36              lda LATCH,X          ; enable sequencer latch
D015 BD 8E C0  37              lda DATAIN,X         ; read sequencer latch
D018           38   ;
D018 30 67     39              bmi SETREAD          ; exit; C-flag and READ set
  :              :             :
```

Figure I.10.8. Accessing the Disk][Interface to SENSE Write Protect

According to the Worth/Lechner books, auto-synchronization can be achieved with no more than five auto-synchronization bytes written as 0b1111111100. Their books are excellent resources to fully understand diskette, track, and sector formatting. DOS 4.5 utilizes the same routine to write the auto-synchronization bytes and the three prolog bytes for the Address Field header data and the DATA Field header data where only the third prolog byte differs. In DOS 4.5, 128 auto-synchronization bytes are written before the Address Field header for sector 0x00 and a minimum of eight to a maximum of thirty-two auto-synchronization bytes are written before all other Address Field headers. Before every DATA Field header, six auto-synchronization bytes are written. This is certainly a very conservative design, but this design ensures that the data gaps that are created by the initial auto-synchronization bytes are wide enough to allow for the processing of Address Field header data values before a decision must be made to configure the sequencing of the Disk][Interface Card to WRITE. Re-written prolog header bytes and all sector data bytes can never be placed precisely over the original prolog and data bytes when the track was first initialized. This is particularly problematic when diskettes are read and written by a variety of different Disk][drives that may have different rotational speeds. However, the initial auto-synchronization byte gaps before and after sectors of data are sufficiently large enough when combined in order to allow for some decision making variations and/or variations in rotational speed that may occur in other versions of DOS and disk drives, respectively. The routine that actually sets the sequencing for the Disk][Interface Card to WRITE and then writes the prescribed number of auto-synchronization bytes that is held in the Y-register is shown in Figure I.10.9. This routine turns Q7 ON and selectively turns Q6

ON and OFF depending on how the routine must control the logic state sequencer. The software loop creates the prescribed number of 40-microsecond auto-synchronization disk bytes. Simply sum up the instruction cycles that are shown in parenthesis.

```
  :              :        :
  D0B6 85 34    204  WRITSYNC sta ADRDATMK    ; save third prolog byte
  D0B8          205  ;
  D0B8 A9 FF    206       lda #SYNCMARK       ; get SYNCMARK value
  D0BA          207  ;
  D0BA 9D 8F C0 208       sta DATAOUT,X       ; enable sequencer to WRITE
  D0BD 1D 8C C0 209       ora STROBE,X        ; enable sequencer to SHIFT
  D0C0          210  ;
  D0C0 48       211       pha                 ; waste 3 cycles
  D0C1 68       212       pla                 ; waste 4 cycles
  D0C2          213  ;
  D0C2 20 76 D2 214  ^1   jsr WAIT24          ; waste 24 cycles (24)
  D0C5          215  ;
  D0C5 9D 8D C0 216       sta LATCH,X         ; LOAD sequencer Data latch (5)
  D0C8 1D 8C C0 217       ora STROBE,X        ; enable sequencer to SHIFT (4)
  DOCB          218  ;
  DOCB EA       219       nop                 ; waste 2 cycles (2)
  D0CC          220  ;
  D0CC 88       221       dey                 ; decrement auto-sync count (2)
  D0CD D0 F3    222       bne <1              ; branch if not done (3|2)
  DOCF          223  ;
  DOCF          224  ;
  DOCF          225  ; Write Address/Data marks 0xD5, 0xAA, ADRDATMK to disk
  :              :        :
```

Figure I.10.9. Accessing the Disk][Interface to WRITE Auto-Sync Bytes

Once the 40-microsecond auto-synchronization disk bytes and the 32-microsecond DATA Field header prolog bytes have been written, the DATA Field Data disk bytes can now be written. Knowing that the RTS instruction from the WRITSYNC routine requires 6 cycles and it is issued before the LDX instruction on line #58 in Figure I.10.10, the time from when the third prolog byte 0xAD is written to the time the last nibble in NBUF2 is written on line #77 takes exactly thirty-two microseconds when all of these instructions execute. From that point on, the software loop to write each of the remaining nibbles in NBUF2 takes exactly thirty-two microseconds. The same routine in DOS 3.3 first begins with writing the last nibble in NBUF2 in thirty-six microseconds. In READ sequencing the logic state sequencer simply disregards the extra four microseconds that is attached to this first data disk byte. Extra attachments of anything other than four or eight microseconds is not tolerated by the logic state sequencer and synchronization to data disk bytes will be lost until the next series of auto-synchronization bytes are encountered. The DOS 3.3 routine is further penalized for accessing NBUF2 because the instruction at line #69 crosses a page-boundary: the Y-register is indexed 56:01 and not 55:00 as in DOS 4.5. In order to compensate for this five-cycle instruction, the instruction at line #74 must access a page-zero copy of SNUM16 that is put into TEMP2Z. In terms of the overall cost to the DOS 4.5 software routine to confine **all** of the prolog bytes and **all** of the data disk bytes to exactly thirty-two microseconds amounts to a single, additional program byte. Obviously, I considered the cost to be highly insignificant compared to the more significant **goal** to maintain overall timing precision when writing all header data and all disk nibble data in the DOS 4.5 WRITSCTR algorithm.

49

```
  :            :        :
D026            54  ; Checksum is cleared by writing the last byte of NBUF2.
D026            55  ; Apple originally published this routine using a 36 usec
D026            56  ; byte for this value.  I have changed this logic.
D026            57  ;
D026 AE 55 DF   58          ldx NBUF2+NBUF2SIZ-1 ; last nibble of NBUF2 (4)
D029            59  ;
D029 A0 55      60          ldy #NBUF2SIZ-1  ; point Y-reg to last byte (2)
D02B D0 07      61          bne >2           ; always taken (3)
D02D            62  ;
D02D            63  ;
D02D            64  ; Get next 6-bit nibble and XOR with current nibble to
D02D            65  ; form index into the write translate table.
D02D            66  ;
D02D B9 01 DF   67  ^1      lda NBUF2+1,Y    ; get next NBUF2 nibble (4)
D030            68  ;
D030 59 00 DF   69          eor NBUF2,Y      ; XOR with current nibble (4)
D033 AA         70          tax              ; make it an index (2)
D034            71  ;
D034 BD 56 DF   72  ^2      lda WRNIBL,X     ; get disk byte (4)
D037            73  ;
D037 AE C3 BF   74          ldx SNUM16       ; recall slot*16 (4)
D03A            75  ;
D03A 9D 8D C0   76          sta LATCH,X      ; LOAD sequencer latch (5)
D03D BD 8C C0   77          lda STROBE,X     ; enable sequencer to SHIFT (4)
D040            78  ;
D040 88         79          dey              ; point to next NBUF2 nibble (2)
D041 10 EA      80          bpl <1           ; branch if not done (3|2)
  :            :        :
```

Figure I.10.10. Accessing the Disk][Interface to WRITE Disk Bytes

Mr. Sather explains in his books how to extract the contents of the P6 sequencer ROM using a very cleaver procedure, by simply exchanging the P6 ROM with the P5 ROM since both ROMs are the same size. Using another Disk][Interface Card in another peripheral slot, the contents of the P6 ROM can be saved to a diskette as a Binary file. Close inspection of the schematic drawing for the Disk][Interface Card shows that address lines A5 and A7 are swapped as well as reverse ordering the D4 to D7 data lines that are connected to the P5 ROM socket. Wozniak certainly had his work cut out for him in order to write the BOOT Stage 0 firmware, swap the address lines A5 and A7, and reverse the order of the D4 to D7 data bits of the binary object code before the P5 ROM could be manufactured. So, whatever data that comprises the dump of the P6 ROM that uses Sather's method must take these schematic drawing observations into consideration if that data is to be displayed in any meaningful manner. The 8-bit logic state sequencer index byte that is shown pictorially in Figure I.10.5 must be redrawn with the bit connections to address lines A5 and A7 swapped as shown in Figure I.10.11 where the A5 and A7 address lines are presented with a darker shade.

A7	A6	A5	A4	A3	A2	A1	A0
Sequence Bit 0	Sequence Bit 2	Sequence Bit 3	Data Pulse	Q7	Q6	QA	Sequence Bit 1

Figure I.10.11. Adjusted Index Byte Format for the P6 ROM

50

A7	A6	A5	A4	A3	A2	A1	A0
Q7	Data Pulse	Q6	QA	Sequence Bit 3	Sequence Bit 2	Sequence Bit 1	Sequence Bit 0

Figure I.10.12. Functional Index Byte Format for the P6 ROM

Knowing that this sequencer index byte contains eight bits, it can reference a full 256 bytes of data. One can picture this ROM data as an array of sixteen different logic states where each state can have up to sixteen difference sequences. In order to utilize the Adjusted index byte that is shown in Figure I.10.11 as a more Functional index byte, a transformation of its bit order is needed to produce the bit order that is shown in Figure I.10.12. This transformation can easily be accomplished in software in order to display the data of the P6 ROM as it is used functionally by the Disk][Interface Card circuitry. The required transformation of the Adjusted index byte that is shown in Figure I.10.11 to produce the Functional index byte that is shown in Figure I.10.12 in 0:7 bit order would be 1, 4, 5, 7, 6, 3, 2, 0. Bit 0 content in Figure I.10.11 becomes Bit 1 content in Figure I.10.12, Bit 1 content becomes Bit 4 content, and Bit 7 content becomes Bit 0 content. And that is precisely how the Adjusted index byte becomes the Functional index byte. Once the Adjusted index byte bits have been transformed, the data from the P6 ROM can be presented separately as READ and WRITE data tables observing that address Bit 7 is Q7 which selects the READ or the WRITE sequencing for the Disk][Interface Card.

Data Bit 3 (CLR)	Data Bit 2 (SL)	Data Bit 1 (S0)	Data Bit 0 (S1)	CODE	Command Name and Data Register Operation	Data Register Before	Data Register After
0	0	0	0	0x0	CLR, clear data register	abcdefgh	00000000
1	0	0	0	0x8	NOP, no operation	abcdefgh	abcdefgh
1	0	0	1	0x9	SL0, shift left bringing in data Bit 2 which is a 0	abcdefgh	bcdefgh0
1	1	0	1	0xD	SL1, shift left bringing in data Bit 2 which is a 1	abcdefgh	bcdefgh1
1	0	1	0	0xA	SR, shift right, when Write-Protect bit is 0 shift right, when Write-Protect bit is 1	abcdefgh abcdefgh	0abcdefg 1abcdefg
1	0	1	1	0xB	LD, load data register from the data bus	abcdefgh	stuvwxyz

Table I.10.6. Shift/Storage Data Register Control Commands

Wozniak defined the lower four bits of the P6 ROM data as control bits that control the shift/storage data register and the upper four bits as the next sequence number for the logic state sequencer, though those upper four bits, D4 to D7, still need to be reverse ordered before the ROM data can be functionally displayed. Control Bits 0 and 1 control S1 and S0, respectively, Bit 2 controls SL, and Bit 3 controls CLR for the shift/storage data register. A simple truth table can be constructed using these bit controls and their functions, and labels can be assigned to specific groups of bits in their OFF/ON state as they appear in the ROM data. Table I.10.6 shows all of the labels for the distinct set of commands and/or functions that are used in the ROM data in order to control the shift/storage data register. Similar to the transformation of the address bits for the sequencer index byte, the upper four bits of the ROM data must be transformed in reverse order so that the ROM data can be displayed and shown to make functional sense. Sather wrote a comprehensive Applesoft program which he listed in his books that he used to display the P6 ROM data that he obtained when he swapped the P5 and P6 ROMs. As he did in generating the Address Bit Swap Table for address bit transformation to obtain Figure I.10.12 from Figure I.10.11, he generated a Data Bit Swap Table to transform the sixteen possible values he obtained from the four bits that are reverse ordered. This data order is 0, 8, 4, 12, 2, 10, 6, 14, 1, 9, 5, 13, 3, 11, 7, and 15 for the data bit transformation of ROM nibble data. For example, data nibble 0b0001 would be reverse ordered to 0b1000, 0b1011 to 0b1101, and 0b0101 to 0b1010. Ordering the swap table entries in 0:15 data order from left to right does indeed transform 1 to 8, 11 to 13, and 5 to 10.

```
                   ROM Read Index
Seq   0      1      2      3      4      5      6      7
      ----   ----   ----   ----   ----   ----   ----   ----
0    00:18  02:18  04:0A  06:0A  10:18  12:18  14:0A  16:0A
1    80:2D  82:38  84:0A  86:0A  90:2D  92:38  94:0A  96:0A
2    01:D8  03:08  05:0A  07:0A  11:38  13:28  15:0A  17:0A
3    81:D8  83:48  85:0A  87:0A  91:48  93:48  95:0A  97:0A
4    40:D8  42:D8  44:0A  46:0A  50:58  52:58  54:0A  56:0A
5    C0:D8  C2:D8  C4:0A  C6:0A  D0:68  D2:68  D4:0A  D6:0A
6    41:D8  43:D8  45:0A  47:0A  51:78  53:78  55:0A  57:0A
7    C1:D8  C3:D8  C5:0A  C7:0A  D1:88  D3:88  D5:0A  D7:0A
8    20:D8  22:D8  24:0A  26:0A  30:98  32:98  34:0A  36:0A
9    A0:D8  A2:D8  A4:0A  A6:0A  B0:29  B2:A8  B4:0A  B6:0A
A    21:CD  23:D8  25:0A  27:0A  31:BD  33:B8  35:0A  37:0A
B    A1:D9  A3:D8  A5:0A  A7:0A  B1:59  B3:C8  B5:0A  B7:0A
C    60:D9  62:D8  64:0A  66:0A  70:D9  72:A0  74:0A  76:0A
D    E0:D8  E2:E8  E4:0A  E6:0A  F0:08  F2:E8  F4:0A  F6:0A
E    61:FD  63:F8  65:0A  67:0A  71:FD  73:F8  75:0A  77:0A
F    E1:DD  E3:E0  E5:0A  E7:0A  F1:4D  F3:E0  F5:0A  F7:0A
```

Figure I.10.13. Functional ROM Read Index

```
                                ROM Read Data
     *--------------SHIFT---------------*---------------LOAD---------------*
     *------QA'-------*-------QA--------*------QA'-------*-------QA--------*
Seq  *--RP---*--NO RP--*--RP---*--NO RP--*--RP---*--NO RP--*--RP---*--NO RP-*
     ----    ----     ----    ----      ----    ----     ----    ----
0    18-NOP  18-NOP   18-NOP  18-NOP    0A-SR   0A-SR    0A-SR   0A-SR
1    2D-SL1  2D-SL1   38-NOP  38-NOP    0A-SR   0A-SR    0A-SR   0A-SR
2    D8-NOP  38-NOP   08-NOP  28-NOP    0A-SR   0A-SR    0A-SR   0A-SR
3    D8-NOP  48-NOP   48-NOP  48-NOP    0A-SR   0A-SR    0A-SR   0A-SR
4    D8-NOP  58-NOP   D8-NOP  58-NOP    0A-SR   0A-SR    0A-SR   0A-SR
5    D8-NOP  68-NOP   D8-NOP  68-NOP    0A-SR   0A-SR    0A-SR   0A-SR
6    D8-NOP  78-NOP   D8-NOP  78-NOP    0A-SR   0A-SR    0A-SR   0A-SR
7    D8-NOP  88-NOP   D8-NOP  88-NOP    0A-SR   0A-SR    0A-SR   0A-SR
8    D8-NOP  98-NOP   D8-NOP  98-NOP    0A-SR   0A-SR    0A-SR   0A-SR
9    D8-NOP  29-SL0   D8-NOP  A8-NOP    0A-SR   0A-SR    0A-SR   0A-SR
A    CD-SL1  BD-SL1   D8-NOP  B8-NOP    0A-SR   0A-SR    0A-SR   0A-SR
B    D9-SL0  59-SL0   D8-NOP  C8-NOP    0A-SR   0A-SR    0A-SR   0A-SR
C    D9-SL0  D9-SL0   D8-NOP  A0-CLR    0A-SR   0A-SR    0A-SR   0A-SR
D    D8-NOP  08-NOP   E8-NOP  E8-NOP    0A-SR   0A-SR    0A-SR   0A-SR
E    FD-SL1  FD-SL1   F8-NOP  F8-NOP    0A-SR   0A-SR    0A-SR   0A-SR
F    DD-SL1  4D-SL1   E0-CLR  E0-CLR    0A-SR   0A-SR    0A-SR   0A-SR
```

Figure I.10.14. Functional ROM Read Data

In order for me to fully understand what Sather was doing in his LOGIC STATE SEQUENCER ROM Applesoft program, I added some Applesoft statements to his program in order to create additional, intermediate listings of indices that were used to index through the ROM data. By convention, the ordering of bits in an index pointer value is typically performed from least significant bit or LSB to most significant bit or MSB from right to left, and that would also be the logical ordering of data from right to left. However, Sather chose to order his ROM data output display from left to right, which may have been driven by how more easily Applesoft indices are incremented and/or how more easily it is to write successive numerical data to the computer screen from left to right. Sather does describe the Data Pulse as an inverted, or *negative pulse* such that the Read Pulse, or RP for a column header means 0 and NO RP means 1. Also, QA means 1 and QA′ means 0. I found these format definitions to be rather odd, but nevertheless, I retained Sather's format definitions. When Q7, or Bit 7 in Figure I.10.12 is clear, READ sequencing is selected for the Disk][Interface Card. Sather thought it would be easier for the reader to understand the display of READ ROM data if the LOAD portion is separated from the SHIFT portion according to the value of Q6, and when QA′ is separated from QA. Figure I.10.13 shows the Index number along with its P6 ROM read data where the order of columns shown is 0:7, unaltered, and ordered by Data Pulse, Q6, and QA as shown in Figure I.10.12. Figure I.10.14 shows the same P6 ROM read data along with its shift/storage data register control command that is from Table I.10.6 which is found in the lower four bits of that data, and where the order of columns is now Q6, QA, and Data Pulse. The column indexes that are shown in Figure I.10.13 have been transformed to the column order-pairs of 0/4, 1/5, 2/6, and 3/7 that are shown in Figure I.10.14.

When Q7, or Bit 7 in Figure I.10.12 is set, WRITE sequencing is selected for the Disk][Interface Card. Figure I.10.15 shows the index number along with the P6 ROM write data where the order of columns shown is 8:F, unaltered, and ordered by Data Pulse, Q6, and QA. Figure I.10.16 shows the same P6 ROM write data along with its shift/storage data register control command that is from Table I.10.6 which is found in the lower four bits of that data, and where the order of columns remains unaltered. Whether a Data Pulse is present or not, according to Figure I.10.16 the write sequences and their order are precisely the same. In other words, the Data Pulse does not affect the logic state sequencer when it is configured in WRITE sequencing.

```
                ROM Write Index

Seq   8     9     A     B     C     D     E     F
    ----- ----- ----- ----- ----- ----- ----- -----
0   08:18 0A:18 0C:18 0E:18 18:18 1A:18 1C:18 1E:18
1   88:28 8A:28 8C:28 8E:28 98:28 9A:28 9C:28 9E:28
2   09:39 0B:39 0D:3B 0F:3B 19:39 1B:39 1D:3B 1F:3B
3   89:48 8B:48 8D:48 8F:48 99:48 9B:48 9D:48 9F:48
4   48:58 4A:58 4C:58 4E:58 58:58 5A:58 5C:58 5E:58
5   C8:68 CA:68 CC:68 CE:68 D8:68 DA:68 DC:68 DE:68
6   49:78 4B:78 4D:78 4F:78 59:78 5B:78 5D:78 5F:78
7   C9:08 CB:88 CD:08 CF:88 D9:08 DB:88 DD:08 DF:88
8   28:98 2A:98 2C:98 2E:98 38:98 3A:98 3C:98 3E:98
9   A8:A8 AA:A8 AC:A8 AE:A8 B8:A8 BA:A8 BC:A8 BE:A8
A   29:B9 2B:B9 2D:BB 2F:BB 39:B9 3B:B9 3D:BB 3F:BB
B   A9:C8 AB:C8 AD:C8 AF:C8 B9:C8 BB:C8 BD:C8 BF:C8
C   68:D8 6A:D8 6C:D8 6E:D8 78:D8 7A:D8 7C:D8 7E:D8
D   E8:E8 EA:E8 EC:E8 EE:E8 F8:E8 FA:E8 FC:E8 FE:E8
E   69:F8 6B:F8 6D:F8 6F:F8 79:F8 7B:F8 7D:F8 7F:F8
F   E9:88 EB:08 ED:88 EF:08 F9:88 FB:08 FD:88 FF:08
```

Figure I.10.15. Functional ROM Write Index

```
                              ROM Write Data
    *----------READ PULSE----------*----------NO READ PULSE----------*
    *------SHIFT------*------LOAD------*------SHIFT------*------LOAD------*
Seq *--QA'--*--QA---*--QA'---*--QA---*--QA'---*--QA---*--QA'--*--QA---*
---
0   18-NOP  18-NOP  18-NOP  18-NOP  18-NOP  18-NOP  18-NOP  18-NOP
1   28-NOP  28-NOP  28-NOP  28-NOP  28-NOP  28-NOP  28-NOP  28-NOP
2   39-SL0  39-SL0  3B-LD   3B-LD   39-SL0  39-SL0  3B-LD   3B-LD
3   48-NOP  48-NOP  48-NOP  48-NOP  48-NOP  48-NOP  48-NOP  48-NOP
4   58-NOP  58-NOP  58-NOP  58-NOP  58-NOP  58-NOP  58-NOP  58-NOP
5   68-NOP  68-NOP  68-NOP  68-NOP  68-NOP  68-NOP  68-NOP  68-NOP
6   78-NOP  78-NOP  78-NOP  78-NOP  78-NOP  78-NOP  78-NOP  78-NOP
7   08-NOP  88-NOP  08-NOP  88-NOP  08-NOP  88-NOP  08-NOP  88-NOP
8   98-NOP  98-NOP  98-NOP  98-NOP  98-NOP  98-NOP  98-NOP  98-NOP
9   A8-NOP  A8-NOP  A8-NOP  A8-NOP  A8-NOP  A8-NOP  A8-NOP  A8-NOP
A   B9-SL0  B9-SL0  BB-LD   BB-LD   B9-SL0  B9-SL0  BB-LD   BB-LD
B   C8-NOP  C8-NOP  C8-NOP  C8-NOP  C8-NOP  C8-NOP  C8-NOP  C8-NOP
C   D8-NOP  D8-NOP  D8-NOP  D8-NOP  D8-NOP  D8-NOP  D8-NOP  D8-NOP
D   E8-NOP  E8-NOP  E8-NOP  E8-NOP  E8-NOP  E8-NOP  E8-NOP  E8-NOP
E   F8-NOP  F8-NOP  F8-NOP  F8-NOP  F8-NOP  F8-NOP  F8-NOP  F8-NOP
F   88-NOP  08-NOP  88-NOP  08-NOP  88-NOP  08-NOP  88-NOP  08-NOP
```

Figure I.10.16. Functional ROM Write Data

The code snippet that is shown in Figure I.10.8 that senses the state of the write-protect switch is the only way software can initialize the sequence number of the logic state sequencer and set the sequencer to Sequence 0 while it is in READ sequencing. This is shown quite clearly in Figure I.10.14 in the right four columns where the upper four bits are set to zero and the command is set to SR. As soon as the data byte SYNCMARK, or 0xFF, is stored to DATAOUT,X, or sta 0xC08F,X in line #208 of Figure I.10.9, the logic state sequencer begins to execute the NOP command that is shown at the top of column three or column seven in 0:7 column order of Figure I.10.16. This is because the instruction at line #36 previously in Figure I.10.8 sets Q6 to one for LOAD and QA has already been determined to be zero, or not write-protected, and the state of the Data Pulse has already been determined not to matter. The logic state sequence progresses to Sequence 1, executes another NOP instruction, and progresses to Sequence 2. Because DATAOUT,X is an indexed absolute addressing instruction that requires five microprocessor cycles to execute, its data will now be available on the data bus by the time the logic state sequencer reaches Sequence 2. At Sequence 2, the shift/storage data register executes the LD control command which commands the data register to load whatever happens to be on the data bus at that moment in time, which, in this case is SYNCMARK. If an absolute addressing instruction such as 0xC0EF that requires four microprocessor cycles to execute had been used in line #208, its data would have been available only at Sequence 1 and never at Sequence 2, and, therefore, totally unavailable to the shift/storage data register. The 0xC08F,X instruction is the only valid addressing mode that is permitted by the logic state sequencer, and Sequence 9 ends when the 40-microsecond auto-synchronization disk byte has been written to disk.

The instruction at line #209 in Figure I.10.9 clears Q6 to zero for a SHIFT operation so that the next logic state sequencer command at Sequence 10 or 0x0A is an SL0 control command regardless whether QA, the current MSB of the data being written, is zero or one and regardless whether the Read Pulse is zero or one. The shift/storage data register is shifted left while a zero is loaded into its QH, or LSB bit. Whether the active sequencing is occurring in column 1 or 2 or in column 5 or 6 at this time, sequencing continues to Sequence 15 and the logic state sequencer either transitions to Sequence 0 or to Sequence 8. In either case an SL0 control command is issued to the shift/storage data register every four microseconds until new data is latched into its register as shown on line #76 in Figure I.10.10. When a new data disk byte is stored to LATCH,X or sta 0xC08D,X, three microseconds after the last SL0 control command is issued for the last bit of the previous data disk byte, Q6 is set to one, an LD control command is issued two microseconds later to the shift/storage data register, and after ten sequences, a load STROBE,X or lda 0xC08C,X program instruction must be issued that clears Q6 to zero. This begins another series of SL0 control commands that are issued every four microseconds in order to write that new data disk byte to the Disk][analog board one bit at a time.

If you have been conscientiously following this discussion and you now believe you have a better understanding of how Wozniak designed the Disk][Interface Card to operate in symbiosis with the RWTS read and write Address Field header, DATA Field header, and DATA Field Data sector software, you should be completely amazed and overwhelmed by his virtuosity. At least, that is my take-away after investing the time and the patience to undertake this deep dive into the deconstruction of the contents of the P6 ROM, the digital circuits of the Disk][Interface Card, and the specificity of the RWTS low level I/O routines and their chosen assembly language instructions. Only someone having very great skill at conceptualizing the flow of data and the simultaneous operation of many, many binary switches and gates could have conceived of the simplicity inherent in the design of the Disk][Interface Card and its software. To experience such cleverness could only be the result of massive intellectual curiosity in order to conceive of a computing device whose sole purpose is to accurately read and write data to and from a magnetic data storage medium. I simply cannot imagine the thrill and the glory Wozniak experienced when his intellectual conceptualization of this device became a reality. Like Tesla who designed his induction motor first as an intellectual conceptualization, Wozniak's similar innate intellectual ability is absolutely rare and uncommon. His genius has truly benefited all of mankind in one way or another to bring more information more easily to more people at any given time in history.

11. File Manager Interface in DOS 4.5

The DOS 4.5 File Manager interface is not as straightforward as the RWTS interface, and it is far more difficult to use. One look at the File Manager Command Parameter List as shown in Figure I.11.1 and another look at the File Manager Input/Output Context Block as shown in Table I.11.1 demonstrates how convoluted the File Manager interface is. Essentially, the Context Block is totally command driven and it is intended to be used with that in mind. So many of the Context Block entries are overloaded and the entry definitions and their usage strictly depends on the command in question. Figure I.11.1 also shows all of the buffers that are required by each of the File Manager commands. Table I.11.2 shows all eighteen command codes and their software handlers that are provided by the File Manager in DOS 4.5. The first thirteen command codes are the same as in DOS 3.3 in order to maintain compatibility with all previous software that utilizes the external File Manager interface. The last five command codes are new in DOS 4.5. These new File Manager commands can be used in the same fashion and in the same way as all of the other original File Manager commands by the external File Manager Command user.

0x Offset / Command	00 Op-code	01 Sub-code	02 03	04 Volume	05 Drive	06 Slot	07 File Type	08 09	0A Return Status	0B Phase	0C 0D Workarea Buffer Address	0E 0F T/S List Buffer Address	10 11 Date Sector Buffer Address
NO OPERATION	0x00												
OPEN	0x01		Record Length or 0x0000	V	D	S	File Type	Filename Address					
CLOSE	0x02												
READ	0x03	See Table I.11.4	Record Number	Byte Offset		Range Length		One Data Byte or Byte Range Address				T/S List Buffer Address	Data Sector Buffer Address
WRITE	0x04		Record Number	Byte Offset		Range Length		One Data Byte or Byte Range Address				T/S List Buffer Address	Data Sector Buffer Address
DELETE	0x05			V	D	S		Filename Address	Return Status				
CATALOG	0x06	RKEY-WORD		V	D	S	BKEY-WORD			Phase Value			
LOCK	0x07			V	D	S		Filename Address					
UNLOCK	0x08			V	D	S		Filename Address			Workarea Buffer Address		
RENAME	0x09		New Filename Address	V	D	S		Filename Address					
POSITION	0x0A		Record Number	Byte Offset									
INIT	0x0B	BOOT Type	Volume Title Address	V	D	S	SEC32 Flag	Filename Address					
VERIFY	0x0C			V	D	S		Filename Address					
URM	0x0D			V	D	S						T/S List Buffer Address	Data Sector Buffer Address
TOUCH	0x0E	RKEY-WORD		V	D	S							
TS	0x0F		Track Value	Sector Value	D	S	Data Byte						
WTS	0x10	Sector Index		V	D	S							
CD	0x11	RKEY-WORD		V	D	S						T/S List Buffer Address	Data Sector Buffer Address

Figure I.11.1. File Manager Command and Parameter List in DOS 4.5

55

Offset	Name	Size	Description
0x00	FMOPCOD	0x01	File Manager opcode
0x01	SUBCODE	0x01	File Manager subcode
0x02	RECNUM or FN2ADR	0x02 0x02	Record number or length value Secondary Filename buffer address
0x04	BYTOFFSET or VOLUME	0x02 0x01	Byte offset value (two bytes) Volume number (one byte)
0x05	DRIVE	0x01	Drive number
0x06	BYTRANGE or SLOT	0x02 0x01	Range length (two bytes) Slot number (one byte)
0x07	FILETYPE	0x01	File Type, SEC32 Flag, or data byte
0x08	DATADR or FNADR or DATBYTE	0x02 0x02 0x01	Data byte address (two bytes) Primary Filename buffer address (two bytes) Data byte (one byte)
0x0A	RTNCODE	0x01	Return code
0x0B	FMPHASE	0x01	Half-phases per track
0x0C	WBADR	0x02	Workarea buffer address
0x0E	TSLTSADR	0x02	Track/Sector List buffer address
0x10	DATASADR	0x02	Data buffer address

Table I.11.1. File Manager Input/Output Context Block Definition

Command	Value	Handler	Description
FMNOERR	0x00	NOERHNDL	File Manager No Operation code
FMOPENCD	0x01	OPNHNDLR	File Manager OPEN code
FMCLOSCD	0x02	CLSHNDLR	File Manager CLOSE code
FMREADCD	0x03	RDHNDLR	File Manager READ code
FMWRITCD	0x04	WRHNDLR	File Manager WRITE code
FMDELECD	0x05	DELHNDLR	File Manager DELETE code
FMCATACD	0x06	CATHNDLR	File Manager CATALOG code (modified)
FMLOCKCD	0x07	LCKHNDLR	File Manager LOCK code
FMUNLKCD	0x08	UNLKHNDL	File Manager UNLOCK code
FMRENMCD	0x09	RNMHNDLR	File Manager RENAME code
FMPOSICD	0x0A	POSHNDLR	File Manager POSITION code
FMINITCD	0x0B	INITHNDL	File Manager INIT code (modified)
FMVERICD	0x0C	VFYHNDLR	File Manager VERIFY code
FMURMCD	0x0D	URMHNDLR	File Manager URM code (new)
FMTCHCD	0x0E	TCHHNDLR	File Manager TOUCH code (new)
FMTSCD	0x0F	TSHNDLR	File Manager TS code (new)
FMWTSCD	0x10	WTSHNDLR	File Manager WTS code (new)
FMCDCD	0x11	CDHNDLR	File Manager CD code (new)

Table I.11.2. File Manager Command Codes

The command codes that are new in DOS 4.5 include FMURMCD, FMTCHCD, FMTSCD, FMWTSCD, and FMCDCD. The FMURMCD command code can be used to undelete a file that has been previously deleted from the volume Catalog by the FMDELECD command code. The File Manager Context Block entries for the FMURMCD command code are used in the same way as they are used for the FMDELECD command code where bytes 0x08:0x09 contain the address of the filename to be undeleted. Once the filename is undeleted, the sectors that are listed in the TSL sector(s) of the file as well as all of its TSL sectors are marked as used in the VTOC free sector bitmap. It is always prudent to undelete a deleted file before subsequent files can use those sectors that were made available when the file was deleted. A volume can be rendered unusable if a data sector should ever be interpreted as a TSL sector. **There is no harm in undeleting a file that already exists in the volume Catalog**. The FMTCHCD command code can be used to update the timestamp of a file. Processing a file with the FMTCHCD command code does **not** update the VTOC timestamp since nothing is changed in the VTOC, including the bitmap. If the SUBCODE is set to a non-zero value, the VALSCNFG value is copied to DOSCONFG and the VTOC is written back to the volume. The FMTSCD command code can be used to read any desired volume sector into a specified data buffer, DATASADR, where it can be processed for display. Similarly, the FMWTSCD command code can be used to read any desired volume sector into a specified data buffer, DATASADR, where one selected byte can be changed, and the result written back to the same volume sector. The FMCDCD command code can be used to set the Slot, Drive, and Volume variables without having to process a disk file. If the SUBCODE is set to a non-zero value, the VTOC is read in order to obtain the DOSCONFG value so that it can be copied to VALSCNFG. The File Manager has the unique capability to gracefully handle any volume access error or any I/O processing error if such an error should occur.

Some File Manager commands require a subcode to specify how the command is to be used. Table I.11.3 lists the five subcodes, one of which must be used with the READ and WRITE command codes FMREADCD and FMWRITCD, respectively. Table I.11.4 shows the other parameters that are required when using one of these five subcodes. For example, to read or write a range of bytes, the SUBCODE at offset 0x01 must be set to 0x02 and the Range Size and Range Address of the data must be entered into offsets 0x06:0x07 and 0x08:0x09 of the Context Block, respectively. Using the FMREADCD and FMWRITCD commands may appear daunting at first, but once the Context Block is configured, these two commands are quite powerful. I added a subcode to the FMCATACD command code in order to optionally display what the R keyword provides to the Command Manager. Simply save a non-zero value to the SUBCODE in the File Manager Context Block if that additional CATALOG information is desired. Similarly, save a non-zero value to the FILETYPE byte in the File Manager Context Block for the FMCATACD command code to optionally display what the B keyword provides to the Command Manager. The FMINITCD command code uses the SUBCODE for the BOOT Type information. The FMWTSCD command code uses the SUBCODE for its Sector Index parameter. The Sector Index is where the data byte, in the FILETYPE byte in the Context Block, is placed in the DATASADR buffer.

Command	Value	Description
FMNOOPSC	0x00	File Manager No Operation subcode
FMRW01SC	0x01	File Manager Read/Write 1-byte subcode
FMRWNBSC	0x02	File Manager Read/Write Range subcode
FMPOS1SC	0x03	File Manager Position and Read/Write 1-byte subcode
FMPOSRSC	0x04	File Manager Position and Read/Write Range subcode

Table I.11.3. File Manager Read and Write Command Subcodes

SUBCODE 0x01	File Manager Command Parameter List				Description
	0x02:0x03	0x04:0x05	0x06:0x07	0x08:0x09	
0x00					No operation
0x01				Byte Data	R/W 1-byte
0x02			Range Size	Range Address	R/W Range
0x03	Record Number	Byte Offset		Byte Data	Position, R/W 1 byte
0x04	Record Number	Byte Offset	Range Size	Range Address	Position, R/W Range

Table I.11.4. File Manager SUBCODE Utilization

Boot Type	DOS Installed	Description
0x00	No	DATA Disk D, all of track 0x00 can be used for data
0x06	Yes	BOOT Disk B, RUN; value 0x06 put into CMDVAL
0x10	Yes	BOOT Disk B, CLOSE; value 0x10 put into CMDVAL
0x14	Yes	BOOT Disk B, EXEC; value 0x14 put into CMDVAL
0x34	Yes	BOOT Disk B, BRUN; value 0x34 put into CMDVAL
0xN where 0x00≤N≤0x62	Yes	BOOT Disk B, any valid even-value within the DOS command table can be utilized for CMDVAL

Table I.11.5. File Manager FMINITCD BOOT Type for SUBCODE

The File Manager Context Block entries for the FMINITCD command code have been substantially modified from its DOS 3.3 version. Before the FMINITCD command code is even processed, the Command Manager initializes the Context Block to zero except for the FMOPCOD and SUBCODE fields. The Command Manager initializes the SUBCODE byte to one of the example values shown in Table I.11.5 for BOOT Type. In order to create a fully bootable DOS B Type volume, the SUBCODE byte must contain a non-zero value, the signal to the DOS INIT handler to write DOS to the volume. If the DOS INIT handler finds a zero value in the SUBCODE byte, a DOS D Type volume is created that does not contain a DOS. A DOS D Type volume does not BOOT, and all of track 0x00 is available for data. The Command Manager initializes bytes 0x02:0x03 with the address of the Volume Title SFNAME or FN2ADR, and it updates the SECVAL, ENDTRK, and SUBJCT values that are in the VTOCVALS substructure directly. The File Manager initializes bytes 0x08:0x09 of the Context Block with the address of FNAME or FNADR.

When the DOS INIT handler begins its processing, it knows whether it is processing on behalf of an external user or on behalf of the Command Manager by checking the MSB of the value that is found in KEYWORD1. If an external user is calling the File Manager, the DOS INIT handler uses the BUFADRZ buffer at 0x42:0x43 that has already been initialized by the FILEMNGR with the address of the Workarea buffer in order to copy the first four bytes of data to the VTOCVALS substructure as shown in Table I.11.6. The DOS INIT handler then begins its generic processing for both an external user and the Command Manager. If the value of the SEC32 Flag at offset 0x07 or FILETYPE byte is negative, a volume is initialized with thirty-two sectors per track, otherwise the volume is initialized with sixteen sectors per track. Once the volume is initialized, the VTOC bitmap is created and the volume is timestamped. The handler uses the address at offset 0x02:0x03 to copy a 24-character upper ASCII Volume Title to the VTOC and uses the address at offset 0x08:0x09 to copy a 24-character upper ASCII filename to FNAME.

Offset	Name	Size	Normal Range	Description
0x00	SECVAL	0x01	0x01–0x0F	number of sectors in volume Catalog
0x01	ENDTRK	0x01	0x12–0x30	number of tracks in volume
0x02	SUBJCT	0x02	0x0000–0xFFFF	volume library (subject) value

Table I.11.6. File Manager VTOCVALS Substructure Initialization Data

```
   :              :        :
  1300           395   FMVALS:
  1300 0B        396   FMOPCOD  byt FMINITCD
  1301 06        397   SUBCODE  byt BOOTYPE
  1302 2A 13     398   FN2ADR   adr VTITLE
  1304           399   ;
  1304 00        400   VOLUME   hex 00
  1305 01        401   DRIVE    hex 01
  1306 06        402   SLOT     hex 06
  1307 00        403   FILETYPE hex 00
  1308           404   ;
  1308 12 13     405   FNADR    adr FNAME
  130A 00        406   RTNCODE  hex 00
  130B 00        407   FMPHASE  hex 00
  130C           408   ;
  130C 42 13     409   WBADR    adr WORKAREA
  130E 00 00     410   TSLTSADR hex 0000
  1310 00 00     411   DATASADR hex 0000
  1312           412   ;
  1312 E8 E5 EC  413   FNAME    asc "hello"
  1315 EC EF
  1317           414            dfs FNLEN-5,SPACE
  132A           415   ;
  132A D4 E5 F3  416   VTITLE   asc "Test Disk"
       F4 A0 C4
       E9 F3 EB
  1342           417            dfs FNLEN-9,SPACE
  1342           418   ;
  1342           419   WORKAREA:
  1342 05        420   SECVAL   hex 05
  1343 23        421   ENDTRK   hex 23
  1344 34 12     422   SUBJCT   hex 3412
  1346           423            dfs FMWALEN-4,ZERO
   :              :        :
```

Figure I.11.2. File Manager Context Block for the INIT Command

In the present design of DOS 4.5, the File Manager knows nothing about the Command Manager and the values that the Command Manager parses from the DOS command keywords. All of the information the File Manager requires for processing its commands **must** come from its Context Block and from its Workarea buffer. And this is particularly true for DOS INIT handler processing. For **internal** File Manager INIT processing, the WBADR address at Context Block offsets 0x0C:0x0D and its Workarea buffer data are not utilized. However, for **external** users of the File Manager, WBADR must contain an address of a 37-byte Workarea buffer that begins with a 4-byte VTOCVALS substructure that contains the values for SECVAL, ENDTRK, and SUBJCT (in Lo/Hi byte order) as shown previously in Table I.11.6. Recall that SECVAL defines how many sectors are used for the volume Catalog, ENDTRK specifies the number of tracks in the volume, and SUBJCT is the two-byte Volume Library value. The 4-byte VTOCVALS substructure, the address for the BOOT filename or FNAME, the address for Volume Title, the BOOT Type, and the SEC32 Flag provide the same information the Command Manager obtains when it parses the A, B, L, and R keywords for the DOS INIT command. Figure I.11.2 shows an assembly language listing of a File Manager Context Block where bytes 0x0C:0x0D contain the address of a Workarea buffer, and the VTOCVALS substructure is placed at the beginning of that buffer. This protocol is different than in previous releases of DOS 4.1 and DOS 4.3, but it is a substantially superior protocol. As shown in Figures I.11.1 and I.11.2, the TSLTSADR and DATASADR addresses for these buffers are not required by the FMINITCD command code.

Error #	CMD	FM	RWTS	Error Message Text
0	√	√	√	Ring bell and print two carriage returns
1	√			Clock Not Found
2	√	√		Range Error
3			√ (0x08)	Volume Format Error
4	√		√ (0x10)	Volume Write Protected
5	√	√		End of Data
6		√		File Not Found
7		√ (0x20)		Volume Number Mismatch
8			√ (0x40)	I/O Error
9		√		Volume Full
10		√		File Locked
11	√		√ (0x30)	Syntax Error
12	√			No Buffers Available
13	√			File Type Mismatch
14	√			Program Too Large
15	√			Not Direct Command
16		√		Catalog Full
17		√		Volume Locked

Table I.11.7. Error Messages and Their Sources in DOS 4.5

Understand that the File Manager uses only its **own** Context Block that resides within DOS memory on Page 0xBF. GETFMCB can be called to obtain the address of that Context Block so that its individual fields can be modified. *FID* maintains its own **copy** of the 18-byte Context Block, modifies it as needed, and then copies it back in its entirety into DOS address space before calling CALLFM. Upon return from the File Manager, *FID* copies the entire Context Block again into its own address space before looking at the return code value RTNCODE. The File Manager Context Block resides in the BOOT page of DOS 4.5, an address space that is **not** within the memory of the Language Card partition, so the use of Soft Switches is unnecessary to read or to rewrite this Context Block.

Table I.11.7 shows all of the possible error codes that can be reported by DOS 4.5, and the source or the sources of those error codes, as from the Command Manager or CMD, from the File Manager or FM, or from RWTS. In DOS 4.5, the File Manager uses a table lookup algorithm to translate an RWTS error code into a File Manager error code that can be reported by DOS. The actual value of the RWTS error code is shown in parenthesis. I added an RWTS Initialization Error message Volume Format Error to the Error and Display Message Text table as well as the Catalog Full and the Volume Locked error messages.

It is *always* the responsibility of the user to utilize the RWTS Input Output Context Block and the File Manager Context Block rationally and with great care. When a Context Block value is used and that value is not within its normal range, unpredictable results should be expected. By design, the Command Manager always supplies rational values for these Context Blocks that are within their normal operational range. But the external user carries the full burden in selecting values for these Context Blocks that must provide the intended results. For example, if SECVAL is initialized to 0x00 or to any value greater than 0x0F, and the File Manager Context Block OPCODE byte is set to the FMINITCD command code, the VTOC in the target volume will never become initialized and DOS 4.5 will likely fail. Table I.11.6 shows that setting SECVAL to zero or to a value greater than 0x0F is not within its normal operational range and DOS 4.5 may very well produce unexpected results.

```
  :              :            :
1300           395  FMVALS:
1300 0D        396  FMOPCOD   byt FMURMCD
1301 00        397  SUBCODE   byt 00
1302 00 00     398  FN2ADR    hex 0000
1304           399  ;
1304 00        400  VOLUME    hex 00
1305 02        401  DRIVE     hex 02
1306 06        402  SLOT      hex 06
1307 00        403  FILETYPE  hex 00
1308           404  ;
1308 12 13     405  FNADR     adr FNAME
130A 00        406  RTNCODE   hex 00
130B 00        407  FMPHASE   hex 00
130C           408  ;
130C 2A 13     409  WBADR     adr WORKAREA
130E 4F 13     410  TSLTSADR  adr TSBUFFER
1310 00 00     411  DATASADR  hex 0000
1312           412  ;
1312 E8 E5 EC  413  FNAME     asc "urm file"
1315 EC EF
1317           414            dfs FNLEN-8,SPACE
132A           415  ;
132A           416  WORKAREA  dfs $25,ZERO
134F           417  TSBUFFER  dfs $100,ZERO
  :              :            :
```

Figure I.11.3. File Manager Context Block for the URM Command

A File Manager Context Block that is initialized by the external File Manager user to implement the DOS URM command is shown in Figure I.11.3. According to Figure I.11.1 and Table I.11.2 this Context Block uses the FMURMCD command code 0x0D, an address for a 24-character upper ASCII filename, and addresses for the Workarea buffer and the Track/Sector List buffer. As in most File Manager commands, this Context Block also requires values for Volume number, Drive number, and Slot number. The specified filename is the name of the file that is to be undeleted from the specified volume Catalog that is found at Slot s and Drive d having a Volume number v. If the filename is found in that volume Catalog, its Catalog entry is restored and the data sectors that are specified by the TSL entries of the file as well as all of the TSL sectors are marked as used in the VTOC free sector bitmap. For all intents and purposes, the file is restored in the volume Catalog as if it had never been previously deleted and its original timestamp is not altered, modified, or updated because the Catalog entry for the file and the content of the file has not been changed. The timestamp of the VTOC in the volume, however, is updated to the present date and time because the contents of the free sector bitmap of the VTOC have obviously changed.

```
    :            :         :
 1300          395  FMVALS:
 1300 0E       396  FMOPCOD  byt FMTCHCD
 1301 00       397  SUBCODE  byt RKEYWORD
 1302 00 00    398  FN2ADR   hex 0000
 1304          399  ;
 1304 00       400  VOLUME   hex 00
 1305 02       401  DRIVE    hex 02
 1306 06       402  SLOT     hex 06
 1307 00       403  FILETYPE hex 00
 1308          404  ;
 1308 12 13    405  FNADR    adr FNAME
 130A 00       406  RTNCODE  hex 00
 130B 00       407  FMPHASE  hex 00
 130C          408  ;
 130C 2A 13    409  WBADR    adr WORKAREA
 130E 4F 13    410  TSLTSADR adr TSBUFFER
 1310 00 00    411  DATASADR hex 0000
 1312          412  ;
 1312 E8 E5 EC 413  FNAME    asc "touch file"
 1315 EC EF
 1317          414           dfs FNLEN-10,SPACE
 132A          415  ;
 132A          416  WORKAREA dfs $25,ZERO
 134F          417  TSBUFFER dfs $100,ZERO
    :            :         :
```

Figure I.11.4. File Manager Context Block for the TOUCH Command

The DOS TOUCH command can be implemented by an external File Manager user by using a File Manager Context Block as shown in Figure I.11.4. According to Figure I.11.1 and Table I.11.2 the Context Block uses the FMTCHCD command code 0x0E, a SUBCODE value for the R keyword function, an address for a 24-character upper ASCII filename, and addresses for the Workarea buffer and the Track/Sector List buffer as well as values for Slot, Drive, and Volume. If a valid filename and file Type have been supplied for the specified volume Catalog that is found at Slot s and Drive d having a Volume number v, the File Manager updates the timestamp of this file to the present date and time. If the filename contains a SPACE or character 0xA0 for its first character at a minimum, the timestamp of the specified volume is updated to the present date and time. Only in this specific instance is the specified R keyword considered. That is, if a valid filename has been supplied, any R keyword that might also have been supplied is simply ignored. Otherwise, if no filename has been supplied and if the SUBCODE byte contains a non-zero value, VALSCNFG is copied to DOSCONFG before the timestamp of the volume is updated to the present date and time, and the modified VTOC is saved back to its specified volume.

An external File Manager user can implement the DOS TS command by using a File Manager Context Block that is initialized as shown in Figure I.11.5. According to Figure I.11.1 and Table I.11.2, the Context Block uses the FMTSCD command code 0x0F, and the Track and Sector parameters are saved to offsets 0x02 and 0x03, respectively, as well as values for the Slot, Drive, and Volume, and the Context Block can be copied back in its entirety into DOS address space before calling CALLFM. The File Manager reads the specified sector into the data buffer that is specified by the user at DATASADR. As in the DOS URM and the DOS TOUCH command processing, the Workarea buffer is a buffer that is required by the File Manager in order to utilize the Context Block variables throughout its processing.

```
   :                 :          :
   1300             395   FMVALS:
   1300 0F          396   FMOPCOD  byt FMTSCD
   1301 00          397   SUBCODE  hex 00
   1302             398   FN2ADR:
   1302 11          399   FMTSTRK  hex TRCKVAL
   1303 00          400   FMTSSEC  hex SECRVAL
   1304             401   ;
   1304 00          402   VOLUME   hex 00
   1305 02          403   DRIVE    hex 02
   1306 06          404   SLOT     hex 06
   1307 00          405   FILETYPE hex 00
   1308             406   ;
   1308 12 13       407   FNADR    hex 0000
   130A 00          408   RTNCODE  hex 00
   130B 00          409   FMPHASE  hex 00
   130C             410   ;
   130C 12 13       411   WBADR    adr WORKAREA
   130E 00 00       412   TSLTSADR hex 0000
   1310 37 13       413   DATASADR adr DATABUFR
   1312             414   ;
   1312             415   WORKAREA dfs $25,ZERO
   1337             416   DATABUFR dfs $100,ZERO
   :                 :          :
```

Figure I.11.5. File Manager Context Block for the TS Command

The DOS WTS command can be implemented by an external File Manager user by using a File Manager Context Block as shown in Figure I.11.6. According to Figure I.11.1 and Table I.11.2, the Context Block uses the FMWTSCD command code 0x10 and the Track and Sector parameters are saved to offsets 0x02 and 0x03, respectively, a Sector Index is saved to the SUBCODE byte at offset 0x01, and the Data Byte value is saved to the FILETYPE byte at offset 0x07, as well as values for the Slot, Drive, and Volume. Thus, whatever data that is supplied for the FILETYPE byte is copied to the specified sector at the offset that is found in the SUBCODE. The File Manager uses the specified data buffer address that is found in DATASADR to hold the content of the specified sector data, make the data byte change at the specified offset, and then write that modified sector data back to the same specified volume.

```
:                   :              :
1300              395   FMVALS:
1300 10           396   FMOPCOD   byt FMWTSCD
1301 00           397   SUBCODE   byt SECRNDX
1302              398   FN2ADR:
1302 11           399   FMTSTRK   hex TRCKVAL
1303 00           400   FMTSSEC   hex SECRVAL
1304              401   ;
1304 00           402   VOLUME    hex 00
1305 02           403   DRIVE     hex 02
1306 06           404   SLOT      hex 06
1307 00           405   FILETYPE  byt SECRBYT
1308              406   ;
1308 12 13        407   FNADR     hex 0000
130A 00           408   RTNCODE   hex 00
130B 00           409   FMPHASE   hex 00
130C              410   ;
130C 12 13        411   WBADR     adr WORKAREA
130E 00 00        412   TSLTSADR  hex 0000
1310 37 13        413   DATASADR  adr DATABUFR
1312              414   ;
1312              415   WORKAREA  dfs $25,ZERO
1337              416   DATABUFR  dfs $100,ZERO
:                   :              :
```

Figure I.11.6. File Manager Context Block for the WTS Command

```
:                   :              :
1300              395   FMVALS:
1300 11           396   FMOPCOD   byt FMCDCD
1301 00           397   SUBCODE   byt RKEYWORD
1302 00 00        398   FN2ADR    hex 0000
1304              399   ;
1304 00           400   VOLUME    hex 00
1305 02           401   DRIVE     hex 02
1306 06           402   SLOT      hex 06
1307 00           403   FILETYPE  hex 00
1308              404   ;
1308 00 00        405   FNADR     hex 0000
130A 00           406   RTNCODE   hex 00
130B 00           407   FMPHASE   hex 00
130C              408   ;
130C 12 13        409   WBADR     adr WORKAREA
130E 00 00        410   TSLTSADR  hex 0000
1310 00 00        411   DATASADR  hex 0000
1312              412   ;
1312              413   WORKAREA  dfs $25,ZERO
:                   :              :
```

Figure I.11.7. File Manager Context Block for the CD Command

For the last File Manager command, in order to implement the DOS CD command, an external File Manager user would initialize the File Manager Context Block like what is shown in Figure I.11.7. According to Figure I.11.1 and Table I.11.2 the Context Block uses the FMCDCD command code 0x11 and it requires a SUBCODE value for the R keyword function as well as values for the Slot, Drive, and Volume. The File Manager uses the supplied values for Slot, Drive, and Volume to change those parameters that are currently in memory in order to implement any subsequent volume access. The CD command does **not** return the Slot, Drive, and Volume parameter values that are currently in memory if they are initialized to zero in the Context Block and, therefore, not provided. If the SUBCODE byte contains a non-zero value, the VTOC of the specified volume is read and its DOSCONFG value is copied to VALSCNFG.

To what extent does an external user of RWTS or of the File Manager expect in *hand holding* vis-à-vis the values the user selects for any of the entries in either Context Block? That is the question I have grappled with in trying to decide whether I should try and *fix* incoherent values for a user, refuse to continue processing with those out of range values and issue a generic error message, or simply allow the processing to continue with those erroneous values knowing full well that something within DOS will undoubtedly fail. There is only so much code space, and *hand holding* can be very expensive code depending upon its depth and dimension. **DOS 4.5 is designed to provide its intended results when its Context Blocks contain rational values that are within their normal operational range.** That is all a user can and should expect! If a user is intent on breaking RWTS or the File Manager, nothing will stand in the way of that destructive user, and any *hand holding* would be a total waste of code space and the effort to implement any such features to any depth or to any dimension.

It is always a good policy to test and to experiment on diskette volumes that are clearly identified as Test Disk #NNN using real Apple][hardware when first testing a new program whether that program is written in Applesoft, assembly language, Fortran, or even Pascal. Even an EXEC file should be tested first on volumes that are exclusively used for experimentation. No one is immune to mistakes, but carelessly and irrationally using either one of these Context Blocks will surely cause very unwanted results, perhaps even the complete loss or destruction of critical data. Therefore, I say again, it is *always* the responsibility of the user to utilize both of these Context Blocks rationally and with very great care.

12. Data Structures in DOS 4.5

The Data structures in DOS 3.3, or areas of memory where data is found within the DOS 3.3 executable code, are spread out among the various functional managers. That is, those variables that are used by the Command Manager are generally found following the Command Manager. Those variables that are used by the File Manager are similarly found following the File Manager. The RWTS IOCB is found somewhere in the middle of all of the RWTS routines. I thought that DOS 4.5 should have far better organization of its various collections of variables and Data structures, and, therefore, reduce the number of addresses that are required to indirectly access any single variable or Data structure if that is what is desired or required by the user. The CMDVALS Data structure in DOS 4.5 is shown in Table I.12.1. Figure I.12.1 shows an example assembly language routine that can access and change the DRVAL variable that is shown with a darker shade in Table I.12.1. In Figure I.12.1, the MNGVALS routine reads or writes an 8-bit value using only the A-register. As long as the index value that is contained in the Y-register is less than CVALSLEN which is equal to 0x61, the MNGVALS routine will always return the C-flag **clear**. The Y-register is incremented each time a data byte is read from or written to the CMDVALS Data structure or read from or written to the FMWORK Data structure that is shown in Table I.12.2. Thus, the MNGVALS routine simplifies the user code when a range of data is read from or written to either one of these Data structures. The V-flag must be **cleared** in order to access only 8-bit values using the A-register.

Offset	Name	Size	Description
0x00	CURSTATE	0x01	0x00 = Warm-Start state 0x01 = READ state 0x02 = VALUE state 0x80 = Cold-Start state
0x01	CSWSTATE	0x01	CSWL intercept state number
0x02	CMDLNIDX	0x01	Apple Command Line offset
0x03	ALLOCNTR	0x01	VTOC scan allocation counter
0x04	KEYWORD1	0x01	First keyword table byte
0x05	KEYWORD2	0x01	Second keyword table byte
0x06	ASAVE	0x01	A-register save
0x07	XSAVE	0x01	X-register save
0x08	YSAVE	0x01	Y-register save
0x09	SSAVE	0x01	S-register save
0x0A	BUFRADR	0x02	Current file buffer address
0x0C	EXECBUFR	0x02	EXEC file buffer address
0x0E	CSWLSAV	0x02	True CSWL Interface handler address
0x10	KSWLSAV	0x02	True KSWL Interface handler address
0x12	MAXFILES	0x01	MAXFILES value
0x13	MONFLAGS	0x01	0x10 = Output 0x20 = Input 0x40 = Command
0x14	DIRTS	0x02	Catalog track and sector values
0x16	TSSAV	0x02	TS and WTS track and sector values
0x18	FRESPC	0x02	Last catalog free space value
0x1A	FILELAST	0x02	File end address
0x1C	FILESTRT	0x02	File start address
0x1E	FILELEN	0x02	File length in bytes
0x20	CLKSLOT	0x01	Clock slot
0x21	CLKINDEX	0x01	Clock data index
0x22	CLKTIME	0x06	See Table I.5.5 for variable order
0x28	SLOTVAL	0x02	S keyword, slot value
0x2A	DRVAL	0x02	D keyword, drive value
0x2C	VOLVAL	0x02	V keyword, volume value
0x2E	ADRVAL	0x02	A keyword, address value
0x30	LENVAL	0x02	L keyword, length value
0x32	RECVAL	0x02	R keyword, record value
0x34	BYTVAL	0x02	B keyword, byte value
0x36	LOADLEN	0x02	LOAD and BLOAD length
0x38	MONVAL	0x01	MON/NOMON value
0x39	CMDINDX	0x01	Index of last command * 2
0x3A	STKSAVE	0x01	Stack pointer save
0x3B	URMFLAG	0x01	Undelete flag

Table I.12.1. CMDVALS Data Structure Definition

```
    :            :         :
002A            19  DRVALOFF equ $2A
BFF4            20  MNGVALS  equ $BFF4
    :            :         :
094A            32  ; Get the DRVAL value.
094A 18         33          clc            ; read
094B A0 2A      33          ldy #DRVALOFF
094D 20 91 09   35          jsr MNGVAL8
0950 8E 90 09   36          sta DRIVE
0952            37  ;
0952            38  ; Change the DRVAL value.
0952 38         39          sec            ; write
0953 A0 2A      40          ldy #DRVALOFF
0955 AD 90 09   41          lda DRIVE
0958 20 91 09   42          jsr MNGVAL8
    :            :         :
0990            65  DRIVE    hex 00
0991 B8         66  MNGVAL8  clv            ; set 8-bit access
0992 6C F4 BF   67          jmp (MNGVALS)
    :            :         :
```

Figure I.12.1. Accessing and Changing 8-Bit CMDVALS Data Example

Offset	Name	Size	Description
0x3C	FRTSTRK	0x01	First T/S track number
0x3D	FRTSSEC	0x01	First T/S sector number
0x3E	CURTSTRK	0x01	Current T/S track number
0x3F	CURTSSEC	0x01	Current T/S sector number
0x40	CURDATRK	0x01	Current data track number
0x41	CURDASEC	0x01	Current data sector number
0x42	DSKFLAGS	0x01	0x00 = No pending activity 0x02 = VTOC/Catalog buffers have changed 0x40 = Data buffer has changed 0x80 = TSL buffer has changed
0x43	DIRSECIX	0x01	Directory sector index
0x44	DIRBYTIX	0x01	Directory byte index
0x45	SECPERTS	0x01	T/S entries in a sector
0x46	FILEBYTE	0x01	Current file byte offset
0x47	RELSFRST	0x02	Relative sector to first sector
0x49	RELSLAST	0x02	Relative sector to last sector
0x4B	RELSLRD	0x02	Relative sector to just read sector
0x4D	FILEPOSN	0x02	Current file position
0x4F	OPNRCLEN	0x02	File open record length
0x51	RECNUMBR	0x02	Current record number
0x53	BYTEOFFS	0x02	Current byte offset
0x55	SECCNT	0x02	Sector count
0x57	CURTRACK	0x01	Current track number
0x58	NEXTSECR	0x01	Next sector number
0x59	SECBTMAP	0x04	Sector bitmap of one track
0x5D	FYPTE	0x01	File Type (^0x80 = locked)
0x5E	SLOT16	0x01	Slot number times 16
0x5F	DRVNUMBR	0x01	Drive number
0x60	VOLNUMBR	0x01	Volume number

Table I.12.2. File Manager FMWORK Data Structure Definition

Offset	Name	Size	Description
Data buffer and Track/Sector List Buffer			
0x000	DATABUFR	0x100	I/O Data buffer
0x100	TSBUFFER	0x100	T/S List buffer
WORKAREA – File Manager Workarea Buffer Variables			
0x200	TSFRSTTS	0x02	T/S of first T/S List for file
0x202	TSCURRTS	0x02	T/S of current T/S List for file
0x204	TSCURDAT	0x02	T/S of current data sector
0x206	WAFLAGS	0x01	0x00 = No pending activity 0x02 = VTOC/Catalog buffers have changed 0x40 = DATA buffer has changed 0x80 = T/S List buffer has changed
0x207	SECATOFF	0x01	Sector offset into catalog
0x208	BYCATOFF	0x01	Byte offset into catalog
0x209	MAXTSECR	0x01	Maximum entries in one T/S list
0x20A	BYSECOFF	0x01	Current sector byte offset
0x20B	SECFRSTS	0x02	Offset of first sector in current T/S List
0x20D	SECLASTS	0x02	Offset of last sector in current T/S List
0x20F	SECLSTRD	0x02	Relative sector number last read
0x211	SECRPOST	0x02	Current relative position in sector
0x213	RECDLNGH	0x02	Fixed record length
0x215	RECURNUM	0x02	Current record number
0x217	BYRECOFF	0x02	Byte offset into current record
0x219	SECFILEN	0x02	Length of file in sectors
0x21B	CURALOTR	0x01	Current track that is allocated
0x21C	SECALOTR	0x01	Next sector to allocate in track
0x21D	SECFRETR	0x04	Bitmap of free sectors in CURALOTR track
0x221	WAFILTYP	0x01	File Type (^0x80 = locked)
0x222	WASLTNUM	0x01	Slot number times 16
0x223	WADRVNUM	0x01	Drive number
0x224	WAVOLNUM	0x01	Volume number
Filename Buffer			
0x225	FILNAMBF	0x18	Upper ASCII filename
Addresses of Buffer Locations			
0x23D	WABUFADR	0x02	Address of WORKAREA
0x23F	TSBUFADR	0x02	Address of TSBUFFER
0x241	DABUFADR	0x02	Address of DATABUFR
0x243	NXTFNADR	0x02	Address of next FILNAMBF

Table I.12.3. File Manager File Buffer Definition in DOS 4.5

The CMDVALS Data structure and the File Manager FMWORK Data structure both reside after the two pages of memory that are required for the working VTOC buffer and the Catalog buffer in DOS 4.5. The CMDVALS and FMWORK Data structures require nearly a half page of memory for their variables. The five File Manager file buffers follow the FMWORK Data structure. Quite a few software tools such as *Big Mac* and

Lisa require access to several internal variables from the `CMDVALS` Data structure. *Big Mac* requires the internal values of `DRVAL` and `LOADLEN`, and it needs the pointer addresses to what DOS considers to be the true `CSWL` and `KSWL` Interface handlers. *Lisa* also requires the internal values of `DRVAL` and `LOADLEN`. There is no telling how many other software utilities and programs that exist in many other software libraries which require specific values from these DOS internal Data structures in order to complete their processing functions. DOS 4.5 provides **easy access** protocols to any variable that is within the `CMDVALS` and the `FMWORK` Data structures that are shown in Tables I.12.1 and I.12.2, respectively. Even though these variables reside in Bank 2 of the Language Card partition, the `MNGVALS` routine that is shown in Table I.8.1 manages the Soft Switches in order to access or change the value of any of these variables.

DOS 4.5 must always have at least one File Manager file buffer allocated, which is all that *Lisa* actually requires and uses, surprisingly. Even to implement the DOS `CATALOG` command requires one free file buffer. However, reducing the number of file buffers in DOS 4.5 using the DOS `MAXFILES` command does **not** provide the user with any additional program memory as it does in DOS 3.3 or in DOS 4.5L. Table I.12.3 shows the contents of a file buffer which is 581 or 0x245 bytes in size where one memory page or 256 bytes is used for the data buffer `DATABUFR`, one memory page is used for the Track/Sector List buffer `TSBUFFER`, thirty-seven bytes are used for the working variables Workarea buffer `WORKAREA`, twenty-four bytes are used for the Filename buffer `FILNAMBF`, and eight bytes are used for the `WORKAREA`, `TSBUFFER`, `DATABUFR`, and `NXTFNADR` addresses. `NXTFNADR` contains the address of `FILNAMBF` for the next but not necessarily following file buffer, which functions like a single-direction linked-list. If the address in `NXTFNADR` is 0x0000, there are no more linked-list file buffers and the error message `No Buffers Available` is correctly displayed when DOS 4.5 is unable to locate an unused file buffer.

I have changed the order and the size of some of the variables in the Workarea buffers that are shown in Tables I.12.2 and I.12.3 from the order and the size in which they are found in DOS 3.3. I have removed `TRKNUMBR` from `FMWORK` and its complementary variable `WATRKNUM` from the Workarea buffer of a file since that variable is unused by the File Manager. As long as the Workarea buffer definition is consistent in both data buffers there will be **no** processing concerns. I made these changes to variable order and to variable size in order to reduce the number of routines that are necessary in order to copy certain variables to and from the Workarea buffer of a file and their complementary variables in the File Manager Workarea buffer. I provided *FID* with the same changes to the layout of its Workarea buffer as well.

The `MNGVALS` routine that is shown in Table I.8.1 was designed for DOS 4.3 in order to access the contents of the `CMDVALS` and the `FMWORK` Data structures as well as the contents of the `INITVALS` Data structure that is shown in Table I.8.5. To have the `MNGVALS` routine also access the contents of the `INITVALS` Data structure was actually an unnecessary redundancy. There is an excellent and perfectly valid procedure already in place to access and change the contents of the `INITVALS` Data structure as shown in Figure I.8.6. It has already been noted that one should reference the variables in the `INITVALS` Data structure indirectly and, therefore, more generally using the address that is found at `INITVAL` and the offsets that are shown in Table I.8.5. Because the `INITVALS` Data structure resides in lower Main memory, the variables in this Data structure are somewhat easier to access in order to directly read and to directly change than those variables that are found in `CMDVALS`. In DOS 4.5, the `CMDVALS` and the `FMWORK` Data structures reside in Bank 2 of the Language Card partition. Therefore, I have modified the `MNGVALS` routine in DOS 4.5 to **only** access the `CMDVALS` and the `FMWORK` Data structures. The routine uses the V-flag to read or to write 8-bit values when that flag is **clear** and to read or to write 16-bit values when that flag is **set**. Figure I.12.2 shows another assembly language example routine that is used in *Lisa* in order to obtain the 16-bit value of `LOADLEN` that is shown with a darker shade in Table I.12.1. The value of `LOADLEN` is added to the address of `BUFR` in order to obtain the final address where the data segment ends that was just read into memory from a volume. When the V-flag is **set**, the `MNGVALS` routine always returns

69

the requested 16-bit LSB value in the X-register and its MSB value in the A-register. As long as the index value that is contained in the Y-register is less than CVALSLEN which is equal to 0x61, the MNGVALS routine will always return the C-flag **clear**. The Y-register is incremented twice when a 16-bit data value is read from or written to the CMDVALS or the FMWORK Data structures, thus greatly simplifying the user code.

```
:            :            :
0002              3  BUFR      epz $02
:            :            :
000E              9  LDLENNDX  equ $36
BFF4             10  MNGVALS   equ $BFF4
:            :            :
0917 18          32            clc                ; read
0918 A0 36       33            ldy #LDLENNDX
091A 20 91 09    34            jsr MNGVAL16
091D 48          35            pha
091E 8A          36            txa
091F 65 02       37            adc BUFR
0921 85 02       38            sta BUFR
0923 68          39            pla
0924 65 03       40            adc BUFR+1
0926 85 03       41            sta BUFR+1
:            :            :
0991 2C 94 09    66  MNGVAL16  bit SETVFLAG        ; set 16-bit access
0994 6C F4 BF    67  SETVFLAG  jmp (MNGVALS)
:            :            :
```

Figure I.12.2. Reading a 16-Bit LOADLEN Value in Lisa

13. Clock Data Access in DOS 4.5

I applaud the individual (ah, rarely, if at all, do teams of individuals do anything significant as I have observed) who designed the concept of using signature and classification bytes in firmware in order to assist in the identification of a peripheral interface card. All clock cards made for the Apple][conform to the convention in using a PHP instruction for the first signature byte, an SEI instruction for the second signature byte, and either a 0x03 or a 0x07 for the classification byte which is the last byte in the peripheral-card ROM clock firmware. DOS 4.5 follows this convention to determine if a peripheral slot contains a clock card, and DOS 4.5 begins in slot 7 to search for a clock card and stops when and if a clock card has not been found after searching slot 1. When the FINDCLK search routine does find a clock card, FINDCLK calls the READCLK routine to issue a *Clock Colon Command*. This commands the clock card to generate its most generic date and time data which is mo/dd hh:mi:ss or mo/dd/yy hh:mi:ss. In this data, mo is month, dd is day, yy is year, hh is hour, mi is minute, and ss is second. Some peripheral clock card firmware generates the Day number of the week w before the Month data and some clock firmware might include a period after the Seconds' data followed by a three-digit millisecond suffix.

Clock cards from different manufactures may differ in the number of SPACE characters or 0xA0 that are used at the beginning of the data that their clock card generates. In order to increase the efficiency of the READCLK routine, the FINDCLK search routine parses the output of the generic clock data and determines an index value where the month data actually begins. The clock card I designed and built as well as the

70

TimeMaster clock card both model their generic data output after the Thunderclock card. These two clock cards produce a Year value whereas the Thunderclock card does not. Why the Thunderclock card became the de facto standard is beyond my comprehension. Maybe it was the first clock card that was marketed for the Apple][computer? So, what! Maybe it was well integrated into Apple ProDOS. Again, so what! Not including a Year value in its output data is just wrong and alarmingly shortsighted.

Clock Card	Index Value	Generic Character String
Thunderclock card	0	mo/dd hh;mi;ss
possible design clock card	1	mo/dd/yy hh:mi:ss
possible design clock card	2	x mo/dd/yy hh:mi:ss
Vrbancic Clock card	3	"w mo/dd/yy hh:mi:ss
TimeMaster Clock card	3	"w mo/dd/yy hh:mi:ss
possible design clock card	4	xxx mo/dd/yy hh:mi:ss
possible design clock card	5	xxxx mo/dd/yy hh:mi:ss

Table I.13.1. Supported Clock Cards in DOS 4.5

As I stated above, in order for DOS 4.5 to efficiently process clock data that is generated by a clock card, an index to where the Month data actually begins is determined by FINDCLK as there can be either no SPACE before the Month data or there can be a single SPACE before the Month data. It does not matter what precedes that SPACE and it does not matter what separators are used between the date and the time data values. The following separators can be used in clock data: " ", "/", ":", and even ";". Table I.13.1 lists all of the clock cards that I have tested with DOS 4.5. This table shows the generic character string the clock card generates when it issues a *Clock Colon Command* where **x** can be any data except for the SPACE character, and the table shows the Index Value that the FINDCLK routine generates for that character string. The READCLK routine uses that Index Value in order to begin extracting the date and time values from the clock data, and it substitutes in YEARVAL if it is parsing Thunderclock data. READCLK assumes that the date and the time data contains a Year value if it is **not** parsing Thunderclock data. See Table I.8.5 for YEARVAL which is a variable that is within the INITVALS Data structure.

```
10   D$ = CHR$( 4 )
20   S = 4
30   PRINT D$; "PR#"; S
     PRINT D$; "IN#"; S
40   INPUT ":"; A$
50   PRINT D$; "PR#0"
     PRINT D$; "IN#0"
60   PRINT
     PRINT A$
```

Figure I.13.1. Reading Generic Clock Data Using Applesoft

Years ago when I first started to investigate a process or a procedure to read a clock card within the assembly language software that I had started to develop for a new DOS, I found that it was not a very easy task. Developing an Applesoft program to read the generic date and time clock data was frightfully simple. Figure I.13.1 shows a programmatically generated listing of such an Applesoft program. The resulting output might be something like 02/14 08;28;48.000 when the Applesoft program is executed, for example, because this generic data is generated by a simulated Thunderclock card that is within the Virtual][program. Accomplishing this same task in assembly language takes far, far more work. Figure I.13.2 illustrates one solution in how this can be done using assembly language. Both programs yield the same information. However, the real task began sometime in early 2011 when I wanted to incorporate this general read clock logic into my first attempt to create a new version of Apple][DOS.

```
:            :          :
0906 A9 04   50            lda #4
0908 20 95 FE 51           jsr OUTPORT
090B A9 04   52            lda #4
090D 20 8B FE 53           jsr INPORT
0910         54 ;
0910 A9 BA   55            lda #COLON
0912         56 ;
0912 20 39 09 57 ^1        jsr RDCHAR
0915 C9 8D   58            cmp #RETURN
0917 D0 F9   59            bne <1
0919         60 ;
0919 A9 00   61            lda #ZERO
091B 20 95 FE 62           jsr OUTPORT
091E A9 00   63            lda #ZERO
0920 20 8B FE 64           jsr INPORT
0923         65 ;
0923 A0 00   66            ldy #ZERO
0925 B9 00 02 67 ^2        lda INPUT,Y
0928 20 ED FD 68           jsr COUT
092B C8      69            iny
092C C9 8D   70            cmp #RETURN
092E D0 F5   71            bne <2
:            :          :
0939 6C 38 00 85 RDCHAR    jmp (KSWL)
:            :          :
```

Figure I.13.2. Reading Generic Clock Data Using Assembly Language

When this read clock logic is inserted into DOS software, the primary issue centers around the modified content of the CSWL and KSWL interface pointers that are used to read the clock card and the restoration of these pointers. The READCLK routine must be able to support the BOOT process, all internal read clock processes, and the external read clock process. The initial content of these two interface pointers is not always the same before these particular processes are invoked. To what values are these two pointers restored was the primary question, and the two choices between the available routines LOADPTRS or INITPTRS could not be used reliably. Another concerning issue was the available code space that would be needed in order to connect to the clock card, to detach from the clock card, to restore the CSWL and KSWL interface pointers, and to determine the most economical method to extract and to store the clock data. As previously presented, Table I.5.5 shows that the order that the clock data is extracted and stored is in reverse order to how the data appears in the generic clock data output. The rationale for this observation is that when a data extraction loop register is decremented rather than incremented, and that register is also used to save the processed data within that logic loop, a single two-byte compare instruction is not required in order to terminate the data extraction loop and two bytes of code space is saved. It is an infinitesimal savings to be sure when the clock data is read and processed in this fashion, but there is another two-byte compare instruction savings every time that same clock data is displayed or copied. Note that the rules for indexed absolute addressing mode are different than for indexed page-zero wraparound addressing mode which prove to be quite useful as shown in Figure I.13.3.

```
   :              :           :
 E5E9           101   ; Save the CSWL and KSWL on the stack
 E5E9           102   ;
 E5E9 A2 03     103           ldx #3
 E5EB           104   ;
 E5EB B5 36     105   ^1        lda CSWL,X
 E5ED 48        106           pha
 E5EE           107   ;
 E5EE CA        108           dex
 E5EF 10 FA     109           bpl <1
   :              :           :
 E600           128   ; Restore the CSWL and KSWL from the stack
 E600           129   ;
 E600 A2 FC     130           ldx #!-4
 E602           131   ;
 E602 68        132   ^3        pla
 E603 95 3A     133           sta CSWL+4,X
 E605           134   ;
 E605 E8        135           inx
 E606 30 FA     136           bmi <3
   :              :           :
```

Figure I.13.3. Indexed Page-Zero Wraparound in Read Clock Algorithm

The READCLK routine combines both digits for each of the six pairs of date and time numbers using the Binary-Coded Decimal, or BCD format. There are many excellent reasons and advantages for doing so, and the first advantage is the ease at which the values can be displayed using the various hexadecimal printing routines that are available in the ROM Monitor. Secondly, the 6502-microprocessor and the 65C02-microprocessor can perform BCD arithmetic natively after the processor has been set to decimal mode by executing the SED instruction. Two BCD time buffers can be directly added or subtracted to obtain total time or elapsed time with very little effort. The microprocessor should be returned to hexadecimal mode by executing the CLD instruction after completing any BCD arithmetic. READCLK simply takes the first digit, multiplies it by sixteen using four ASL instructions, and saves that value to a temporary page-zero location. Then it takes the second digit and masks out the upper four bits using 0x0F, and OR's that value with the previously saved value. The newly formed BCD number can be saved to any six-byte buffer for date and time including VTOC initialization, VTOC update, file creation or update, current date and time display, and the request for current date and time from an external DOS 4.5 user.

The requirements in designing a READCLK routine must: save the pointers it receives for the intended target buffer, check a status flag to verify that there is an available clock card, save the current CSWL and

KSWL interface pointers, connect the CSWL and KSWL interface pointers to the clock card, issue the *Clock Colon Command*, read the generated generic clock data that is automatically saved to the INPUT buffer, restore the CSWL and KSWL interface pointers, extract the date and time data that is located in the INPUT buffer, and finally save this generated data in BCD format into the buffer whose pointers were initially provided. As I remarked earlier about developing a process or a procedure to read a clock card within DOS, I noted that it was not a very easy task. Every requirement must be satisfied and there can be no shortcuts. Either the CSWL and the KSWL interface pointers can be saved and restored from a memory location or from the stack. The stack is the more economical choice. And, it is better to save the pointers by decrementing a positive register and restoring those pointers by incrementing a negative register. This concept is illustrated nicely in Figure I.13.3. In order to extract the date and time from the generic clock data, the X-register is initialized to the Index Value that is determined by the FINDCLK search routine when it parses the clock data output in order to determine where the month data actually begins. The Y-register must always be initialized to five in order to point to the last value in the clock data buffer where the first BCD value is saved. While the X-register is incremented as the generic clock data is processed, the Y-register is decremented as the generated BCD values are saved.

The FINDCLK routine is 0x44 bytes in size in DOS 4.5, and it executes only when DOS 4.5 BOOTs or when DOS 4.5 is Cold-Started. The READCLK routine is 0x56 bytes in size, and it executes whenever the date and time is requested, which can be quite often actually, particularly in programs that create and/or modify a large number of data files. As previously mentioned, date and time values are required in DOS 4.5 for VTOC initialization, VTOC update, all file creation or update, the display of the current date and time, and the transfer of the current date and time values to a buffer for a user external to DOS 4.5. Knowing how important date and time is to DOS 4.5, particularly how important it is to the resources of the volume and to the resources of all of the files on that volume, one wonders why a more concerted effort was not undertaken early in the 1980's in order to integrate date and time into the next incremental version of DOS that would be issued after DOS 3.3, perhaps a DOS 3.4, but before Apple ProDOS was released. Certainly, there were clock cards available early enough for this integration to occur in a post-DOS 3.3 release. Whether the intuition of Apple Computer, Inc., was truly insightful may be a matter of opinion, but with the release of ProDOS came a rather steep learning curve. This ProDOS learning curve included having to understand how to organize one's files as system files, as executable program files, as data files, or as a myriad of other file Types that are maintained within a multiple-level hierarchical directory structure. At least the clock card gave ProDOS users a very clear understanding of all of the advantages for having date and time as an additional resource in the definition of ProDOS volumes, directories, and files. By now it should be very apparent that date and time is certainly a very welcomed and nearly indispensable resource in the definition of DOS 4.5 volumes and files. Would a clock card that was fully integrated into DOS 3.3+ have delayed the acceptance of Apple ProDOS? One wonders.

14. Error Processing in DOS 4.5

DOS 4.5 error processing is centered around Applesoft processing and whether or not an Applesoft program is running. DOS 4.5 determines if an Applesoft program is running by checking two page-zero locations called PROMPT at 0x33 and ASRUN at 0x76. PROMPT contains the upper ASCII character that is displayed on the Apple Command Line and ASRUN is equal to the most significant byte of the 16-bit page-zero variable called CURLIN, the Applesoft line number that is currently being interpreted. When an Applesoft program is not running, the ROM Applesoft interpreter puts the] character into PROMPT and sets CURLIN+1 or ASRUN to 0xFF, a very improbable line number MSB. The DOS routine ISBASRUN tests

PROMPT for 0xDD, the] character, and ASRUN for 0xFF. Therefore, when PROMPT is **not** equal to 0xDD **and** ASRUN is **not** equal to 0xFF, DOS 4.5 believes that Applesoft **is** running. Otherwise, DOS 4.5 believes that Applesoft **is not** running. In order to fool DOS 4.5 into thinking that Applesoft **is** running, PROMPT must **not** be equal to 0xDD **and** ASRUN must **not** be equal to 0xFF, but these two page-zero locations should be restored to their operational values once the programming charade has completed.

DOS 4.5 error processing begins by determining whether or not an Applesoft program is running. If an Applesoft program **is not** running or **not in** the RUN mode, DOS 4.5 processes ERRMSG00 that prints two carriage returns and issues a ctrl-G that beeps the speaker, prints the designated error message, and enters the DOS Warm-Start handler in order to enter the ROM Applesoft Warm-Start handler at WARMADR or 0xBEE2 that contains the address of ASROMWRM or 0xD43C . If an Applesoft program **is** running or is **in** the RUN mode, DOS 4.5 tests the value that is located in the page-zero ASONERR flag at 0xD8. If the value stored in ASONERR is positive so that the MSB of ASONERR is clear, the Applesoft program did **not** utilize the ONERR GOTO <*line number*> Applesoft statement in order to handle its own error processing to prevent program termination, and, instead, DOS 4.5 error processing is utilized as above to print ERRMSG00 and the designated error message. If, on the other hand, the value stored in ASONERR is negative, DOS 4.5 restores its control over the CSWL and the KSWL intercept pointers, sets CURSTATE to Warm-Start and sets CSWSTATE to zero, and DOS 4.5 exits to whatever address is stored at ERRORADR with the A-register containing the value of #$03. According to Table I.8.5 for the INITVALS Data structure, ERRORADR is initialized with the ROM Applesoft Error handler address of 0xD865, the routine that checks the MSB of ASONERR or ERRFLG in the ROM Applesoft code and the A-register for the value of #$03. Of course, ERRORADR at 0xBEE6 may contain a user provided address of any other Error handler in order to provide an error processing routine that is tailored to handle that Applesoft error.

Assembly language routines need to do a bit more work in order to handle their own DOS error processing: store 0xFF to ASONERR, zero to PROMPT and ASRUN, and replace the address stored at ERRORADR with the address of a specific error handler routine. DOS 4.5 loads the X-register with the appropriate DOS error number as shown in Table I.11.7 before it exits indirectly to ERRORADR or WARMADR for that matter if Applesoft is **not** in the RUN mode. As shown previously in Table I.9.3, calling PRTERADR at 0x3E8 using an indirect JMP instruction with the appropriate DOS error number stored in the X-register will print the corresponding DOS error message text without beeping the speaker and without printing a carriage return after the error message text. *Big Mac*, for example, utilizes PRTERADR for printing all DOS errors that it encounters as shown previously in Figure I.9.5. In that assembly language example routine, *Big Mac* loads the X-register with zero before the first call to PRTERROR in order to print two carriage returns and a ctrl-G. Then, *Big Mac* loads the X-register with the actual error number, calls PRTERROR, and ends the routine by printing a final carriage return at line #371. There is absolutely no need to duplicate the PRTERROR routine into the *Big Mac* source code because the Page 0x03 vector for PRTERADR is so conveniently located at memory address 0x3E8.

Section I.6 introduced the error message Volume Full in terms of the value in ALLOCNTR that is used in the ALLOCSEC routine and Section I.7 introduced the error message Catalog Full in terms of the value in the X-register for DIRINDX that is returned from the LCDIRENT routine. ALLOCSEC allocates a disk sector for a TSL sector or for a data sector for a file and LCDIRENT locates a filename in the volume Catalog. DIRINDX assumes one of the seven possible values for Track offset as shown in Table I.7.2. When DIRINDX becomes zero when calculating the offset for the next catalog entry and the last catalog sector is being processed, typically sector 0x01, and there are no deleted file entries to utilize, the volume Catalog is truly full. Both of these error conditions are reported as a DISK FULL error in DOS 3.3. Not that DOS 3.3 is seriously wrong in combining both error conditions into a single error message, I simply believe the user is far better off knowing what is actually triggering the error condition. DOS 4.5 accurately provides meaningful error messages whenever error conditions develop.

Both the Video Intercept routine and the Keyboard Intercept routine in the Command Manager save the contents of the registers and the current stack pointer into the CMDVALS Data structure before those intercept routines continue with their processing. The File Manager also saves the current stack pointer into its own variable in the CMDVALS Data structure before it continues with any of its processing. However, the supporting routines in both of these managers in DOS 3.3 strive to *maintain* the integrity of its stack pointer throughout its processing even though the stack pointer is eventually restored once the processing completes in either manager. Many, many unnecessary instructions such as PLA are utilized in order to maintain stack pointer integrity. For example, extra code and variables are utilized to save the value of a register in order to avoid using the stack in case an error condition develops. Even when error conditions do occur, great effort is made in order to maintain the integrity of that stack pointer. Why? Why bother saving the stack pointer in the first place if it isn't going to be seriously utilized when processing is complete? Error conditions in DOS 3.3 as well as error conditions in DOS 4.5 are always terminal conditions. There is simply no reason to continue any further processing when an error condition occurs because any processing results that are obtained thus far are probably wrong anyway. If Applesoft does not handle a DOS error, the DOS 4.5 Command Manager will print the error message text and perform a DOS Warm-Start which always initializes the stack pointer. Otherwise, the Command Manager restores its control over the CSWL and the KSWL intercept pointers, restores the stack pointer, and then restores all of the registers in order to exit normally. Whether or not the File Manager encounters any error conditions, it saves the contents of the A-register to RTNCODE, it saves the File Manager Workarea buffer to the Workarea buffer of the file that was just processed, and it restores the stack pointer with the error status in the C-flag. If the C-flag is **set**, the caller uses the value in RTNCODE in order to print the relevant error message. This is how both managers avoid stack overflow or underflow with or without encountering an error condition in DOS 4.5. There is absolutely **no need** to maintain stack pointer integrity throughout Command Manager or File Manager processing routines.

15. DOS CHAIN Command Utilization

DOS 4.5 includes a real CHAIN command in its command repertoire that is designed specifically for Applesoft programs that utilize real variables. Having a native CHAIN command is far more convenient than having to include an assembly language chain utility on each and every volume for those Applesoft programs that require this capability. However, several careful considerations should be addressed when designing Applesoft programs that chain to each other.

The purpose of the DOS CHAIN command is to move two areas of data variables where they reside in memory for the *Start* program to where they need to reside in memory for the *Chained* program. These two areas of data variables include the Simple Variables and the Array Variables, or Simple/Array Variables, or SAVs for short. Figure I.15.1 shows a typical Start Applesoft program that resides in memory beginning at memory address 0x0801. In that figure, Free Space exists because the Start Program, its SAVs, and its Character String Pool do not exceed the value that is stored in HIMEM at page-zero 0x73:0x74 minus 0x0801, the memory address where the Start and all other regular Applesoft programs begin. The Start program must **never chain** to a Chained program whose size along with the Start program SAVs and any additional SAVs and character strings from the Chained program exceed the available Free Space.

Page-Zero Pointer Addresses	Start Program	Small Program	Problematic Program	Large Program
	0x0000	0x0000	0x0000	0x0000
PRGTAB – 0x67:0x68	0x0801	0x0801	0x0801	0x0801
	Start Applesoft Program	Small Chained Applesoft Program	Problematic Chained Applesoft Program	Large Chained Applesoft Program
PRGEND – 0xAF:0xB0 VARTAB – 0x69:0x6A	Simple Variables			
ARYTAB – 0x6B:0x6C	Array Variables			
STREND – 0x6D:0x6E				
	Free Space			
FRETOP – 0x6F:0x70				
	Character String Pool			
HIMEM – 0x73:0x74				
	0xFFFF	0xFFFF	0xFFFF	0xFFFF

Figure I.15.1. Example Applesoft Program Layout in Memory

Applesoft uses a large number of byte-pair memory locations in page-zero for its use. Many of these memory locations are to store addresses in low/high byte order that can easily be used as pointers in memory management routines. DOS always loads an Applesoft program into memory at address 0x0801, which is the value that is found in PRGTAB at page-zero 0x67:0x68. The DOS LOAD command knows the file size of the Applesoft program in bytes before it actually loads the content of the file into memory because it reads the first data sector of the file and examines the first two bytes of that data sector where the size of the Applesoft program is located. Using the size of the Applesoft program, DOS can calculate the end address of the Applesoft program, and save that information in PRGEND at page-zero 0xAF:0xB0. Initially, DOS sets VARTAB to PRGEND and Applesoft sets ARYTAB and STREND to PRGEND and it sets FRETOP to HIMEM. The DOS MAXFILES command must **not** be used in an attempt to change HIMEM in DOS 4.5 because the address in HIMEM is fixed to 0xBE00. Thus, from Table III.1.1.1, all Applesoft programs that are written for DOS 4.5 should consider **setting** CONFIG Bit 3 in order to disable the DOS MAXFILES command, or simply not use the DOS MAXFILES command in any Applesoft program that executes within the DOS 4.5 environment.

When the Applesoft program begins to execute its instructions, the program begins to create simple variables that include real variables, integer variables, and character string variables. These variables reside in the Simple Variables area of memory as simple descriptors whose memory address is found in VARTAB at page-zero 0x69:0x6A. The definition of the descriptors for the variables that comprise the Simple Variables is shown in Table I.15.1. As more and more Simple Variable descriptors are added, the Array Variables area is pushed higher and higher **up** in memory that reduces the size of Free Space. Simple Variable descriptors are always seven bytes in size, and depending upon the variable type, some of the descriptor bytes may not be used. Table I.15.1 shows that real numbers require all seven bytes for the variable name, the exponent, and its 4-byte mantissa. Integer numbers require only four bytes for the variable name and its value in **high/low** byte order, leaving the remaining three bytes initialized to zero. Finally, simple character string variables require five bytes for the variable name, the 8-bit length of the character string in bytes, and the memory address in **low/high** byte order where the character string resides in memory, leaving the remaining two bytes initialized to zero. Obviously, a simple character string variable cannot contain more than 255 ASCII characters since the number of characters in the simple character string variable is limited to a single 8-bit quantity. Applesoft programs should never define a character string variable to contain more than 255 ASCII characters.

The definition of the descriptors for Applesoft Array Variables is shown In Table I.15.2. As shown in Figure I.15.1, the start address of the Array Variables area of memory is found in ARYTAB at page-zero 0x6B:0x6C and the end address of the Array Variables is found in STREND at page-zero 0x6D:0x6E. This area of memory contains single and multi-dimensioned Array Variable descriptors for arrays of real numbers, arrays of integer numbers, and arrays of character string variables. Table I.15.2 shows an example variable descriptor that has two dimensions. Successive Array Element dimension sizes **precede** each other with the first-dimension size in **high/low** byte order always coming **last**. The Array Variable descriptor grows in size as the number of dimensions increase in value. The nominal size of an Array Variable descriptor is seven bytes for a single dimension array. The descriptor increases in size by two additional bytes for each added dimension. Therefore, the dimension value that is found in Byte 5 of the Array Variable descriptor becomes a critical piece of information that is used to calculate where the Array Elements begin and end relative to the address of their Array Variable descriptor. The maximum number of dimensions for an Array Variable descriptor is 255 since this variable is limited to an 8-bit quantity.

Bytes 3 and 4 of the Array Variable descriptor give the offset in bytes to the beginning of the next, if any, Array Variable descriptor relative to the address in memory where the Array Variable descriptor is located. The Array Elements that belong to an Array Variable descriptor begin immediately after the descriptor whose descriptor size can easily be calculated knowing the value in Byte 5, or 5 + (value in Byte 5) * 2. The definition of each Array Element for each type of Array Variable descriptor is shown in Table I.15.3. These Array Element definitions are essentially the same as the definitions for the respective Simple Variable descriptors without including the name of the array variable. Obviously, the name for all of the Array Elements is the same, and this name is found only in its Array Variable descriptor. The Array Element for arrays of real numbers is five bytes in size and it contains the exponent and its 4-byte mantissa. The Array Element for arrays of integer numbers is two bytes in size and it contains its value in **high/low** byte order. The Array Element for arrays of character string variables is three bytes in size and it contains the 8-bit length of the character string in bytes and the memory address in **low/high** byte order where the character string resides in memory. It should be apparent that all of the character string elements of a character string array do not necessarily have to contain the same number of characters, but any single character string element cannot contain more than 255 characters since its dimension variable is limited to a single 8-bit quantity. Applesoft programs should never define a character string element to contain more than 255 ASCII characters.

Variable Type	Byte Definitions						
	Byte 1	**Byte 2**	**Byte 3**	**Byte 4**	**Byte 5**	**Byte 6**	**Byte 7**
Real Number	name1 +ASCII 65	name2 +ASCII 66	Exponent	Mantissa Byte 1	Mantissa Byte 2	Mantissa Byte 3	Mantissa Byte 4
Integer Number	name1 -ASCII 195	name2 -ASCII 196	High Value	Low Value	0	0	0
Simple Character String	name1 +ASCII 69	name2 -ASCII 198	String Length	Low Address	High Address	0	0

Table I.15.1. Simple Variable Descriptor Definitions in Applesoft

Variable Type	Byte Definitions								
	Byte 1	**Byte 2**	**Byte 3**	**Byte 4**	**Byte 5**	**Byte 6**	**Byte 7**	**Byte 8**	**Byte 9**
Real Array	name1 +ASCII 65	name2 +ASCII 66	Low Byte Offset	High Byte Offset	Number of Dimensions K	Size of Kth Dim High Byte	Size of Kth Dim Low Byte	Size of K-1 Dim High Byte	Size of K-1 Dim Low Byte
Integer Array	name1 -ASCII 195	name2 -ASCII 196	Low Byte Offset	High Byte Offset	Number of Dimensions K	Size of Kth Dim High Byte	Size of Kth Dim Low Byte	Size of K-1 Dim High Byte	Size of K-1 Dim Low Byte
Character String Array	name1 +ASCII 69	name2 -ASCII 198	Low Byte Offset	High Byte Offset	Number of Dimensions K	Size of Kth Dim High Byte	Size of Kth Dim Low Byte	Size of K-1 Dim High Byte	Size of K-1 Dim Low Byte

Table I.15.2. Array Variable Descriptor Definitions in Applesoft

Element Type	Byte Definitions				
	Byte 1	**Byte 2**	**Byte 3**	**Byte 4**	**Byte 5**
Real Number Element	Exponent	Mantissa Byte 1	Mantissa Byte 2	Mantissa Byte 3	Mantissa Byte 4
Integer Number Element	High Value	Low Value			
Character String Element	String Length	Low Address	High Address		

Table I.15.3. Single Array Element Descriptor Definitions in Applesoft

Quite often an Applesoft program contains the text of some character string variable. As long as there is **no** text operation on that character string variable such as A\$ = A\$ + B\$, for example, the text pointer address that is found in the Simple Variable or in the Array Element descriptor points to the actual character string text that is within the memory contents of the Applesoft program. In this particular case the character string variable can never be available to a Chained program. In order for this character string variable or array element variable to be available to a Chained program, the actual character string text must be relocated into the Character String Pool. A simple way to force this character string relocation is to perform some menial text operation on that character string variable or that array element variable, such as A$ = A$ + "" or A$(1) = A$(1) + "". This simple operation does nothing to the character string A$ or to A$(1) except to cause the actual text of A$ or A$(1) to be copied from within the contents of the Applesoft program into the contents of the Character String Pool.

The purpose of the DOS CHAIN command is to move the SAVs of the Start program to the end of the Chained program, and to update PRGEND, VARTAB, and ARYTAB with their new addresses so that the Chained program may access those real and integer variables and the character string variables of the Start program. Because of some required Applesoft calls, even FRETOP needs to be re-initialized. When the Chained program is smaller than the Start program or when the Chained program is larger than the Start program plus the size of the SAVs area, there is no problem in copying the SAVs directly to their new memory location. However, if the end of the Chained program occurs somewhere within the SAVs area of the Start program, there will be disaster if the SAVs are copied directly. Due to how the ROM Monitor memory move routine is implemented, if the SAVs area of memory is copied in this particular situation, the move routine will begin to overwrite the same area of memory it is attempting to copy. And this will certainly lead to disaster for the Chained program because some of the variable descriptors of the Start program will be overwritten and, therefore, destroyed. If the SAVs area is copied in reverse order from high memory to low memory to the end of this problematic Chained program, disaster will also occur when that algorithm is used to copy the SAVs area for a Chained program that is smaller than the Start program. The CHAIN routine can either refuse to perform the chain operation and signal an error message in those situations, or it can utilize another algorithm to copy the SAVs.

Another algorithm is to copy the SAVs to the address in STREND for the Start program and set PRGEND and VARTAB to that address as long as there is enough memory in Free Space. PRGEND does not necessarily have to be exactly the address where the Chained program ends in memory, technically at its triple-nulls. In fact, an Applesoft program may include attached assembly language routines that follow the Applesoft triple-null ending giving the program a larger physical length and a different physical end address. The DOS SAVE command uses PRGTAB and PRGEND to calculate the number of bytes to save that includes the Applesoft program and the attached assembly language routines, and it does not necessarily use the address where the triple-nulls occur in memory minus 0x0801 that would exclude the attached assembly language routines. However, this option does potentially waste a good deal of valuable memory if the SAVs area is quite large in size, even when there is adequate Free Space.

A better algorithm would be to always copy the SAVs up in memory to FRETOP and then copy them again down in memory to the PRGEND of the Chained program. Unfortunately, the first memory copy would require a unique negatively-indexed memory move algorithm that is **not** resident in the ROM Monitor where the pointers are decremented and not incremented, which is not for the faint-of-heart due to its difficulty and complexity. Also, a negatively-indexed memory move algorithm requires more CPU instructions than a simple positively-indexed memory move algorithm. The second memory copy would require a straight-forward positively-indexed memory move algorithm like the one that **is** resident in the ROM Monitor. Fortunately, there is enough code space in DOS 4.5 to implement this far superior and correct Applesoft chain algorithm. The user can utilize the DOS 4.5 CHAIN command to their heart's content and rest assured that DOS CHAIN always places the SAVs fully intact precisely where the Chained program ends with the single caveat already mentioned: the Start program must never chain to a Chained program whose size, including the Start program SAVs, will exceed available Free Space.

If the R keyword is **not** used with the DOS CHAIN command, DOS CHAIN calls the ROM Applesoft routine GARBAG at memory address 0xE484 before it moves the Simple Variable and Array Variable descriptors to their new memory location at the end of the Chained program. The GARBAG routine utilizes an algorithm similar in concept to a basic bubble sort algorithm in order to remove all unreferenced character string data from the Character String Pool, thus compacting the Character String Pool contents before DOS CHAIN relocates the SAVs in memory. The processing time for GARBAG to extract all of the little bits and pieces of unreferenced character strings and string characters is proportional to the square of the number of character strings that are currently in use. So, if there are one hundred active character strings it will take four times longer to process those character strings than if there are only fifty active character strings.

Many Garbage Collection algorithms have been previously published that accomplish the same results as GARBAG in far less time, but there can be a number of caveats when using some of these algorithms. For instance, normal Applesoft programs save all character string data in **lower** ASCII where the MSB is clear for each character byte in the string. Furthermore, normal Applesoft programs never allow more than one character string descriptor to point to the same character string data in memory. Multiple character string variable and array element descriptors may each point to identical character string data sets, but these identical sets of character string data must reside at different memory locations. Some Garbage Collection algorithms depend upon these constraints. If either constraint is not found to be true, a catastrophe will happen during the course of subsequent Applesoft processing! Of course, if the character string data of an Applesoft program is kept normal and these constraints are observed, there will be no subsequent processing problems. If assembly language routines, possible appendages to the Applesoft program, or other code segments perform exotic manipulations to the character string descriptors or to the contents of the Character String Pool, these constraints might very well be violated.

If an efficient Garbage Collection routine is available, the user should invoke that routine before using the DOS CHAIN command, and utilize the R keyword in order to bypass calling GARBAG from within the CHAIN processing. There is always the dilemma in finding that balance between either making the Applesoft Start program and its Chained programs smaller in order to accommodate an external and complex assembly language Garbage Collection routine, or enlarging the Applesoft Start program and its Chained programs and strategically placing many Applesoft FRE(aexpr) statements throughout the programs. The FRE(aexpr) statement forces a call to GARBAG which processes the Character String Pool contents more efficiently if there are fewer inactive character strings or few unreferenced character string data bytes. Again, there is always the dilemma in finding that balance for the best strategy in ensuring that memory is utilized as efficiently as possible. A more complete and detailed discussion of the Applesoft Garbage Collector can be found in Section II.4.

16. ProDOS Disk I/O Algorithm

I have no idea whether Apple or Axlon, the manufacture of the RAM Disk 320, developed the fast disk read algorithm. As described in section V.19, the Axlon RAM Disk initialization software can transfer the contents of an entire 35-track diskette to one of the RAM Disk drives in only seven seconds, the time to make thirty-five revolutions, one revolution for each track of a Disk][volume. The Axlon software locates track 0x00 on the Disk][volume, clears a sixteen byte *sector read* table, and reads the first sector address header it encounters. It does not matter which sector address header the routine finds first. The software notes the sector number from the address header information and proceeds to read the sector data that follows that header and it puts the first eighty-six bytes that it reads into a buffer called NBUF2 as shown in Table I.16.1. These eighty-six bytes contain the first two bits for each of the next three groups of data bytes that are about to be read. The first group of data bytes is comprised of another eighty-six bytes, where each byte is OR'd with its first two bits read from a BITNIBL table indexed by the respective byte from NBUF2, and stored directly into the designated RAM Disk sector. The second group of data bytes is comprised of the next eighty-six bytes of data that follow, similarly processed with the respective index byte from NBUF2, and stored in the designated RAM Disk sector. The last eighty-four bytes of data that follow are similarly processed and stored in the designated RAM Disk sector, now totaling 0x100 data bytes. The final byte read, or byte 343, is the checksum byte. If the checksum calculation is zero, no read error is flagged and the *sector read* table is updated with this sector number marked as read. Once the *sector read* table is complete, the Axlon software moves the Disk][read/write disk head to the next volume track, clears the *sector read* table, and begins to process that track in the same fashion. The Axlon software is finished when it has read and processed track 0x22.

Routine, Table, or Buffer	DOS 4.5		ProDOS	
	Bytes	Cycles	Bytes	Cycles
PRENIBL	36	10557	172	6331
POSTNIBL	23	9524	n/a	
READSCTR	84	11207	206	11248
WRITSCTR	128	11419	222	11420
RDNIBL	106		106	
WRTNIBL	64		n/a	
BITNIBL	n/a		256	
NBUF1	256		n/a	
NBUF2	86		86	
Total	783	42707	1048	28999

Table I.16.1. Comparison of DOS 4.5 and ProDOS RWTS

The Apple ProDOS version of the fast disk read algorithm is essentially the same as the Axlon version except that ProDOS incorporates the contents of the WRTNIBL table into the unused portion of its BITNIBL table. Since only three of every four bytes are needed for processing using the data in NBUF2, it made sense to utilize every fourth unused byte for the WRTNIBL table. Axlon did not provide a fast disk write algorithm so there was no reason or need to incorporate a WRTNIBL table within the Axlon BITNIBL table. Closer inspection of the two algorithms indicates to me that the Axlon version is a little cleaner programmatically. Perhaps Axlon obtained the ProDOS version and tweaked it some? If I had seen the ProDOS version initially, I probably would have made the same modifications Axlon did. I cannot imagine the reverse taking place where Apple obtained the Axlon version and purposefully sabotaged it. I could be wrong. Whatever the case, the basic algorithm is clever and it works well, and there is no need for a POSTNIBL routine when using either version of this algorithm. However, the READSCTR routine that implements the ProDOS fast disk read algorithm is nearly twice the size of the DOS 4.5 READSCTR and POSTNIBL routines combined, or 206 bytes versus a sum of 107 bytes, respectively. The ProDOS READSCTR routine also takes a few more startup processing cycles than the DOS 4.5 READSCTR routine. ProDOS requires the BITNIBL table for its data processing and DOS 4.5 requires the NBUF1 buffer for its data processing. The ProDOS BITNIBL table and the DOS 4.5 NBUF1 buffer are the same size, but the BITNIBL table also includes the WRTNIBL table, a table that is a standalone table in DOS 4.5. The ProDOS

BITNIBL and WRTNIBL tables cannot be programmatically generated as they are programmatically generated in DOS 4.5. To read and process a sector by DOS 4.5 requires 20,731 cycles or 20.73 milliseconds. ProDOS requires 11.25 milliseconds to read and process a sector. In order for ProDOS to read and process a block of data, ProDOS must read two sectors sequentially.

The processing time for the ProDOS version of its fast disk write algorithm is essentially the same as the DOS 4.5 write algorithm, and this is to be expected. Both algorithms must write at least five 40-microsecond auto-synchronization bytes, three 32-microsecond prologue bytes, 343 32-microsecond data and checksum bytes, three 32-microsecond epilogue bytes, and a final 32-microsecond synchronization byte. However, their algorithm sizes are substantially different and that is because NBUF1 lies on a page boundary for DOS 4.5 and the user data buffer may or may not lie on a page boundary for ProDOS. ProDOS must prenibblize its buffer data in the same way and for the same reason that DOS 4.5 prenibblizes its buffer data. However, ProDOS must modify its WRITSCTR code *on the fly* or dynamically because it does not utilize a page bounded intermediary NBUF1 buffer. ProDOS must determine whether the data buffer that is described by the RWTS IOCB lies on a page boundary, and if not, which pages contain what portion of the data buffer. There is one exception the ProDOS algorithm must also handle, and that is when the data buffer falls off of a page boundary by only one byte. The ProDOS fast disk write algorithm requires 394 bytes for its PRENIBL and WRITSCTR routines, and it gets its WRITNIBL table for free. On the other hand, DOS 4.5 requires a mere 164 bytes for its PRENIBL and WRITSCTR routines, but it requires a WRITNIBL table, for a total of 228 bytes which is still about 58% the size of the ProDOS memory requirements. To process and write a DOS 4.5 sector requires 21,976 cycles or 21.98 milliseconds. ProDOS requires 17,751 cycles to process and write a sector, or 17.75 milliseconds. In order for ProDOS to write a block of data it must write two sectors sequentially.

I have been referring to the data I collected for the information in Table I.16.1 in the above sizing and timing comparisons. Overall, the amount of software, table data, and buffer space that is required by DOS 4.5 to read from and write to a sector of diskette data totals 783 bytes. ProDOS requires 1048 bytes, a difference of 265 bytes, or an additional page of memory plus nine bytes. This difference in code and data amounts to a 25% increase in the memory requirements by ProDOS. The time to read and write a sector of data requires 42.71 milliseconds for DOS 4.5 and 29.00 milliseconds for ProDOS. The ProDOS algorithms are 32% faster than the DOS 4.5 algorithms overall. With these results, it is obvious that the extensive use of table data and self-modifying code alone cannot account for the visible and extraordinary differences the two operating systems demonstrate when reading and writing disk files.

ProDOS achieves its significant speed difference by employing a sector interleaving or skewing such that only two revolutions are required to read all eight data blocks on a track, similar to the technique Apple Fortran and Apple Pascal use for reading their data diskettes. The sectors are arranged such that there is one sector between each of the sector pairs that comprise a data block, and there is one sector between each successive data block. Data blocks are read and written in ascending block number or *Two Ascending skew* in ProDOS and sectors are read and written in descending sector number or *Two Descending skew* in DOS 4.5. DOS 4.5 employs a sector interleaving such that it is physically possible to read all sixteen sectors on a track in only two revolutions, but typically three revolutions are more realistic. For a more complete discussion on sector interleaving refer to *Beneath Apple DOS*, *Beneath Apple ProDOS*, and *Bag of Tricks* by Worth and Lechner. These references provide the reader with a thorough understanding of this rather complicated yet fascinating subject.

17. Using DOS 4.5 Commands

I have enhanced many of the original DOS 3.3 commands primarily using the R keyword as a command modifier or switch. This keyword has very limited usage in the original DOS command repertoire other than in the commands EXEC, POSITION, and the Random-Access Data file commands READ and WRITE. All DOS 4.5 commands and their arguments may be entered in a mixture of lowercase and uppercase ASCII on the Apple Command Line, in EXEC files, and in Applesoft programs and assembly language routines. Filenames may be entered in a mixture of lowercase and uppercase ASCII, and the filenames are treated as case sensitive. For example, the filenames HELLO and Hello are treated as two different files. In order to make full use of lowercase and uppercase in DOS 4.5, an Apple //e or similar computer is preferred. DOS 4.5 does function quite nicely on an Apple][or on an Apple][+ if it has a character generator ROM like, for example, the Dan Paymar *Lowercase Adaptor Interface PROM* that can display the complete lowercase and uppercase Latin character set. DOS 4.5 does print error messages in mixed case. The Enhanced Apple //e ROM also supports lowercase and/or uppercase entry for Applesoft statements. In my opinion, however, this ROM continues to retain at least two substantial deficiencies: there is no native DELETE key utilization and the HLIN drawing algorithm is hopelessly flawed.

There is no consistency in DOS 3.3 in whether to print one or two carriage returns after DOS completes its processing for a DOS command when that command is entered on the Apple Command Line. Certainly, it would be a mistake to print any additional carriage returns after DOS 4.5 completes its processing for a DOS command when that command is issued from within an Applesoft program or during the processing of an EXEC file. DOS 4.5 does print **one** carriage return after it completes its processing for a DOS command when that command is entered on the Apple Command Line. This policy is to ensure that there is at least one blank line between all DOS commands that are entered on the Apple Command Line. Having this blank line helps to keep each DOS command and its output information as legible as possible on the display screen. DOS commands that are issued from within assembly language routines using COUT will appear with the additional carriage return. One way to prevent DOS 4.5 from printing that additional carriage return is to clear the variables PROMPT at page-zero 0x33 and ASRUN at page-zero 0x76 to zero. When DOS 4.5 checks these variables after it completes its DOS command processing, it will appear to DOS that Applesoft is in the RUN mode, and therefore, DOS 4.5 will not print the additional carriage return. It is wise to restore these variables once routine processing is complete.

Both DOS 3.3 and DOS 4.5 save files to a volume Catalog using the TSL resources of the file if the file already exists in the volume Catalog. For example, if the file TEMP already exists and its TSL sector contains eight Track/Sector entry pairs, those same entries are used to save TEMP again whether TEMP is smaller or larger than its initial size. If TEMP is larger, the File Manager simply requests additional data sectors and adds those sectors to the file's TSL sector. If TEMP is edited and the file now uses only three data sectors, the first three Track/Sector entry pairs in the TSL sector are used to save the new content of the file and the remaining TSL entries are now unused. In other words, the last five TSL entries in this example remain allocated to the file and, therefore, these sectors are unavailable for use by any other file. This inherent resource wastefulness in DOS 3.3 and in DOS 4.5 is perpetuated by programs like *FID*. *FID* uses the File Manager to copy files in total, and it assumes that all Track/Sector entry pairs in a file's TSL sector belong to and are utilized by that file. But DOS 4.5 introduces a new strategy called *File Delete/File Save*. The DOS BSAVE, LSAVE, SAVE, SSAVE, and TSAVE commands can now utilize the B keyword to implement the *File Delete/File Save* strategy. This strategy first deletes the file from the volume and then saves the file to the same volume in order to ensure that the file's TSL sector contains only those Track/Sector entry pairs that are actually required and utilized by that file. *FID* can now expunge unused TSL entries by using the Verify Files and Expunge TSL option, or Option 8.

II. ROM Modifications in the Apple][

I presented all of my modifications to the Apple CX and D0:FF ROM space in the DOS 4.1 Manual and in my book *DOS 4.1 Disk Operating System Second Edition*. These ROM modifications include the changes I made to the HLIN Drawing Algorithm, the Delete Key Utilization, the Apple //e 80-Column Text Card, the Apple //e ROM Monitor, and the Apple Character Generator ROM. The DOS 4.1 Manual is available for download at www.applecored.net as a PDF. The DOS 4.1 *Second Edition* includes my last DOS 4.1 build, or Build 46, and it can be purchased from Lulu.com. If anyone is interested in exploring the benefits of the ROM modifications that I presented in both of these publications, those ROM images are available for download at www.applecored.net. The ROM images are located in the ROM2e folder which can be found in the appleXcode.tar TAR file.

The topics I have included in this section are important to DOS 4.5 and they are particularly important to me. I have edited all of these topics with DOS 4.5 specifically in mind.

In my version of the Apple //e firmware, or ROM source code, I use the variable HLINMOD for a conditional assembly directive that is used to optionally assemble the original, though hopelessly flawed ROM code or to assemble the modified or corrected ROM code. The generated object code can be programmed into either a single 27128 EPROM as found in the Enhanced and Platinum Apple //e or programmed into two 2764 EPROMs for the earlier version of the Apple //e. The modified contents of the Apple //e character generator ROM that defines each ASCII character in pixels can be programmed into a 2732 EPROM. An EPROM programmer is required in order to program new EPROMs in order to replace the Apple //e firmware ROM or ROMs and the character generator ROM. I have not sourced the Apple][+ Autostart ROM. I have no doubt that the contents of the Apple][+ Autostart ROM was the basis for the *Lisa* and the *Big Mac* Monitors, which I have sourced. I believe very little, if anything was changed in the Apple][+ version of the Applesoft interpreter to that found in the Apple //e firmware, except to support the CX ROM space and lowercase. There are no additions or deletions to the set of Applesoft commands that are contained in the Apple //e firmware. All Apple //e Applesoft commands in Applesoft statements function identically to how they function in Apple][and in Apple][+ Applesoft statements.

1. Corrected HLIN Drawing Algorithm

I have always disliked the unsymmetrical look of a HIRES diagonal line when it is drawn either in the horizontal or in the vertical direction ever since I acquired my Apple][+. And this same HLIN code persists in the Apple //e ROM Applesoft unchanged, which is shameful in my opinion. When I was assigned the task to provide all of the icons for HomeWord Speller at Sierra On-Line, I analyzed the HLIN algorithm and found that the algorithm does not correctly calculate the delta difference of the horizontal and the vertical start to end points before drawing the requested line. It is easy to demonstrate this error before and after installing my ROM modifications or by using an assembly language routine that contains the HLIN algorithm with and without my ROM modifications.

There are two memory locations that require a small code adjustment. The first code adjustment is made at 0xF57A and that adjustment is shown in Figure II.1.1. In that figure ZPGD4 is the page-zero memory location 0xD4 and HF465 is a label for an assembly language routine at memory address 0xF465.

```
0xF57A:
                .if HLINMOD
                bcs HF580                    ; branch to 0xF580 if carry is set
                asl                          ; times 2
                jsr HF465                    ; call 0xF465
HF580           clc                          ; prepare for delta, not diff
                lda ZPGD4                    ; load reg-A from 0xD4
                .el
                bcs HF581                    ; branch to 0xF581 if carry is set
                asl                          ; times 2
                jsr HF465                    ; call 0xF465
                sec                          ; prepare for diff, not delta
HF581           lda ZPGD4                    ; load reg-A from 0xD4
                .fi
```

Figure II.1.1. First HLIN Code Adjustment

```
0xF5A5:
                .if HLINMOD
                sec                          ; prepare for delta, not diff
                .el
                clc                          ; prepare for diff, not delta
                .fi
```

Figure II.1.2. Second HLIN Code Adjustment

```
10 HOME                                 300 HPLOT 100,110
20 HGR                                  310 HPLOT TO 101,151
30 HCOLOR= 3                            320 HPLOT TO 139,150
40 HPLOT 10,10                          330 HPLOT TO 140,111
50 HPLOT TO 50,10                       340 HPLOT TO 100,110
60 HPLOT TO 50,50                       350 GOSUB 1000
70 HPLOT TO 10,50                       400 HPLOT 200,15
80 HPLOT TO 10,10                       410 HPLOT TO 260,10
90 GOSUB 1000                           420 HPLOT TO 265,30
100 HPLOT 100,10                        430 HPLOT TO 250,35
110 HPLOT TO 140,11                     440 HPLOT TO 270,55
120 HPLOT TO 139,50                     450 HPLOT TO 255,75
130 HPLOT TO 101,51                     460 HPLOT TO 275,100
140 HPLOT TO 100,10                     470 HPLOT TO 245,115
150 GOSUB 1000                          480 HPLOT TO 215,117
200 HPLOT 10,110                        490 HPLOT TO 200,15
210 HPLOT TO 10,150                     500 GOSUB 1000
220 HPLOT TO 50,150                     900 TEXT : END
230 HPLOT TO 50,110                     1000 POKE 49168,0
240 HPLOT TO 10,110                     1010 WAIT 49152,128
250 GOSUB 1000                          1020 RETURN
```

Figure II.1.3. HLIN Demonstration Program in Applesoft

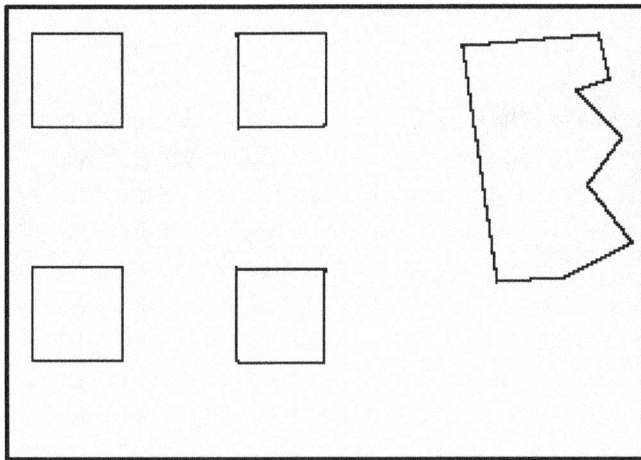

Figure II.1.4. Original ROM HLIN Routine   Figure II.1.5. Modified ROM HLIN Routine

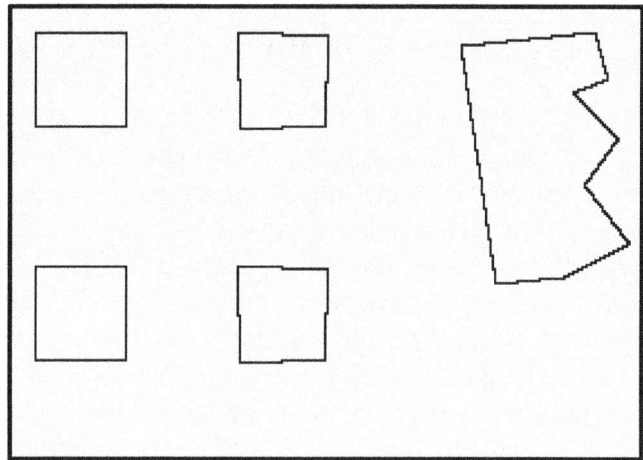

The second code adjustment is made at 0xF5A5 and that code adjustment is shown in Figure II.1.2. You will simply be amazed at how *lovely* and *symmetrical* diagonal lines are drawn either from left to right, from right to left, from top to bottom, or from bottom to top. And I am appalled that the old ROM code passed any sort of testing and/or code review vis-à-vis how trivial these two modification are and how elegant the results appear.

Figure II.1.3 shows a simple Applesoft program that can be used to demonstrate the visual differences between the original HLIN drawing algorithm and my corrected drawing algorithm. Figure II.1.4 shows what this Applesoft program visually produces when it is RUN on an Apple //e before the HLIN modifications are made to the Apple //e ROM code. In this figure, the two boxes on the left are square boxes and they draw perfectly no matter the direction in which the lines are drawn. The two middle boxes are nearly square boxes except that the horizontal and vertical line end points differ by one pixel. These boxes show different anomalies depending upon the direction in which the lines are drawn. That is, the upper middle box is drawn clockwise and the lower middle box is drawn counterclockwise from its upper left corner. The shape on the right is drawn clockwise from its upper left corner, and it shows many odd corner anomalies as the direction and the angle of the lines change.

Figure II.1.5 shows what this same Applesoft program produces visually when this program is RUN on the same Apple //e, but with the HLIN modifications made to the Apple //e ROM code. All corner anomalies disappear without regard to drawing direction, and when the lines are drawn diagonally, the lines are segmented equally. It is obvious from Figure II.1.5 that having the HLIN modifications allows one to draw any shape in any direction, and its lines may be drawn in any order without having to consider the possible introduction of any irregular corner anomalies and inconsistent line segmentation: they simply no longer exist when the HLIN modifications shown above are installed into the ROM code.

The two middle boxes in Figure II.1.5 visually show what precise line segmentation looks like. The shape on the right is far more representative of a very complex figure that shows precise corner detail as well as precise line segmentation. Even double-high-resolution graphics show some degree of line segmentation for diagonal lines that is inherent in the relatively low pixel density of the Apple //e display. In its day, Apple high-resolution graphics were totally awesome, and those graphic routines are still remarkable today as they were when they first appeared in the Apple][computer ROM code.

2. Soft Switches in the Apple //e

While I was working at Sierra On-Line, my parents purchased their Apple //e with the understanding that I would set up their system, teach them how to use its capabilities, fix and/or repair any software or hardware problems that might occur, and perform any regular maintenance as required. I didn't fully realize what I was getting myself into particularly when I attempted to teach my father how to use VisiCalc: his hands were quite large and his fingers were not keyboard-savvy, he had poor close-up vision, and he could not remember repetitive key-entry sequences very well. I designed his VisiCalc daily expenses spreadsheet for each month that required the wide paper in their Epson MX-100 printer and I wrote an Applesoft program to extract his monthly totals from his data files in order to create his annual summary file that displayed all of his summarized data. I provided him detailed instructions on how to begin his daily VisiCalc session and how to enter his data into each row and column. When he entered wrong data, or when he entered data in the wrong row and column, or when he skipped instructions, he would become rather agitated and blamed the computer for causing his errors. My mother would then enter the data for him to keep everyone calm. I should say that these were our typical family dynamics!

My parents purchased their Apple //e when it first became available, probably three or four years before the enhanced version was developed. I have no recall if we were even aware of an Enhanced Apple //e while I was at Sierra On-Line around 1983 and 1984. Because I was assisting another engineer in porting *ScreenWriter* to the Apple //e, I became very familiar with the 80-column text card, the routines AUXMOVE and XFER, and a whole gamut of new Soft Switches. Also, Ken Williams asked me to extract the data base from **the Dic-tio-nary**, the companion spell checker to *ScreenWriter*. He wanted this massive database for his new product called HomeWord Speller, the companion spell checker to HomeWord which he had already released. HomeWord and HomeWord Speller were both developed in-house. I made multiple calls to XFER within a printer driver I developed for **the Dic-tio-nary**, its only vulnerable access location at 0x300. My special driver extracted specific partitions of the database and copied the partition to Auxiliary memory instead of to a printer. Once I took control of the computer after the unorthodox data transfer, I was able to copy that database partition from Auxiliary memory back into Main memory, and then into a file onto a diskette. It is important to note that the XFER starting address is found at 0x3ED:0x3EE in the Page 0x03 Interface Routines and Vectors as shown in Table I.9.3.

I believe the Enhanced Apple //e provides MouseText characters in place of the alternate uppercase inverse characters and it also introduced double high-resolution graphics. Also, this Apple provides lowercase input for Applesoft and its new ROM Monitor allows lower ASCII input data to be stored in memory, it has a search command, and it contains the phenomenal Mini-Assembler from the original Apple][. The new ROM Monitor also supports a very sophisticated interrupt handler that captures the Apple //e memory configuration before the interrupt is processed as shown in Table IV.1.17.1. This is done by saving the current memory configuration state onto the stack at the time of the interrupt, placing the Apple in a standard memory configuration before calling the requested Interrupt handler, and then restoring the memory configuration state after the requested Interrupt handler has finished. However, I firmly believe Apple fell way short in not providing the ability to fully utilize the Mini-Assembler in order to enter and to display the complete 65C02 Instruction Set since the computer was designed to use and was shipped with a 65C02-microprocessor. What was Apple thinking about? Anyone knows that the Mini-Assembler is the gold standard when it is coupled with the ROM Monitor STEP and TRACE commands.

What was Apple thinking about when it continues to provide and to support the use of a cassette tape recorder in order to store and retrieve programs, multi-dimensioned integer and real arrays, and shape tables? I know of no software engineer in my professional career or among my personal friends who ever used a cassette tape recorder with any Apple computer for any reason. I designed a communication protocol for a programmable keyboard by means of a wire, which was similar to the output data to a cassette tape recorder. Other than programming a keyboard using an annunciator, I have never used a cassette tape recorder with any of my Apple computers. I have never used the Applesoft LOAD, RECALL, SAVE, STORE, or SHLOAD commands in any of my Applesoft programs, nor have I seen these commands used in any professional or commercial Applesoft programs. And, I have never used the ROM Monitor READ or WRITE commands at any time. Why would I use such a ridiculous and incredibly slow and error prone data archiving method when I have the Disk][, the Rana, the RAM Disk 320, the Sider, or the CFFA card to save programs and data in the form of files, visible within its media, and date and time stamped? Honestly, I derive no personal satisfaction in knowing that a user can read data into an Apple][computer from a cassette tape recorder port. I do have a few suggestions for what could replace the useless ROM Monitor READ and WRITE commands with something rather quite spectacular.

The Apple //e Main and Auxiliary memory together total 128 KB, and each 64 KB area can be controlled by means of an MMU and an IOU device using Soft Switches. By design, the memory of a 65C02 processor within the Apple //e hardware architecture can be naturally divided into four strategic areas: page-zero and the stack, 0x200 to 0xBFFF, 0xC000 to 0xCFFF, and 0xD000 to 0xFFFF which also includes the bank-switched 0xD000 to 0xDFFF memory space. These memory areas can be individually activated from Main or Auxiliary memory resources using the appropriate Soft Switches. What is also unique to the Apple //e is that the ROM Monitor firmware has been expanded to include additional ROM memory that is mapped to the 0xC100 to 0xCFFF address space called CX ROM. This address space is enabled or disabled using the appropriate Soft Switches. If there is a Display Slot Card that resides in Slot 3, the firmware of that card can be activated rather than using the internal 80-column text card firmware. Table II.2.1 summarizes the new memory management and video Soft Switches that are used to control Main and Auxiliary memory. Some data must be written to all of these Soft Switches in order to invoke their action. It does not matter what that data is because that data is not stored anywhere. Table II.2.2 summarizes the new Soft Switch status flags. It is by means of these status flags that one may determine the complete memory and video configuration of the Apple //e.

Address	Access	Name	Description	Notes
0xC000	W	STR80OFF	Disable 80-column store	1
0xC001	W	STR80ON	Enable 80-column store	1
0xC002	W	RAMRDOFF	Read-enable Main RAM, 0x0200-0xBFFF	2
0xC003	W	RAMRDON	Read-enable Auxiliary RAM, 0x0200-0xBFFF	2
0xC004	W	RAMWROFF	Write-enable Main RAM, 0x0200-0xBFFF	2
0xC005	W	RAMWRON	Write-enable Auxiliary RAM, 0x0200-0xBFFF	2
0xC006	W	CXROMOFF	Enable slot ROMs, slots 1-7, or 0xC100-0xC7FF	3
0xC007	W	CXROMON	Enable internal CX ROM, or 0xC100-0xCFFF	3
0xC008	W	AUXZPOFF	Enable Main ZP, stack, Language Card partition, Av1 BSR RAM	4
0xC009	W	AUXZPON	Enable Auxiliary ZP, stack, language card, Av1 BSR RAM	4
0xC00A	W	C3ROMOFF	Enable internal CX3 ROM, 0xC300-0xC3FF	
0xC00B	W	C3ROMON	Enable Slot Card ROM, 0xC300-0xC3FF	
0xC00C	W	VID80OFF	Disable 80-column video	
0xC00D	W	VID80ON	Enable 80-column video	
0xC00E	W	ALTCHOFF	Enable normal Apple character set	
0xC00F	W	ALTCHON	Enable alternate character set (no flash)	

Table II.2.1. New Memory and Video Management Soft Switches

Address	Access	Name	Description	MSB Clear	MSB Set	Notes
0xC000	R/R7	KEY	Read keyboard for keypress	None	Yes	
0xC010	R/R7	CLRKEY	Clear keyboard strobe, keypress	Yes	No	
0xC011	R7	RDBANK2	Which LC bank in use	Bank 1	Bank 2	
0xC012	R7	RDLCRAM	LC RAM or ROM read-enabled	ROM	RAM	
0xC013	R7	RDRAMRD	Main, AUX RAM read-enabled	AUX	Main	
0xC014	R7	RDRAMWR	Main, AUX RAM write-enabled	AUX	Main	
0xC015	R7	RDCXROM	Slot ROMs or internal ROM enabled	Slot	Internal	
0xC016	R7	RDAUXZP	Which ZP & LC enabled	Main	AUX	
0xC017	R7	RDC3ROM	Slot 3 or CX3 ROM enabled	Slot 3	CX3	
0xC018	R7	RDSTR80	State of STR80 switch	Off	On	
0xC019	R7	RDVRTBLK	State of vertical blanking	Off	On	
0xC01A	R7	RDTEXT	State of TEXT switch	Graphics	Text	
0xC01B	R7	RDMIXED	Read MIXED switch	Off	On	
0xC01C	R7	RDPAGE2	State of PAGE2 switch	Main	AUX	
0xC01D	R7	RDHIRES	State of Graphics resolution	LOWRES	HIRES	
0xC01E	R7	RDALTCH	State of Alternate Character Set	Off	On	
0xC01F	R7	RDVID80	State of VID80 video	Off	On	
0xC07E	R7	RDIOUDIS	Read IOUDIS switch	On	Off	5
0xC07F	R7	RDDHIRES	Read DHIRES switch	Off	On	5

Table II.2.2. New Soft Switch Status Flags

Address	Access	Name	Description	Notes
0xC020	R	TAPEOUT	Cassette output Toggle	
0xC030	R	SPKRTOGL	Speaker output Toggle	
0xC040	R	UTILTOGL	Utility Strobe; 1 ms. pulse, Game I/O pin 5	
0xC050	R/W	TEXTOFF	Display Graphics	
0xC051	R/W	TEXTON	Display Text	
0xC052	R/W	MIXEDOFF	Full Screen graphics	6
0xC053	R/W	MIXEDON	Text with graphics	6
0xC054	R/W	PAGE1ON	Display Page 1 or Main video memory	7
0xC055	R/W	PAGE2ON	Display Page 2 or Auxiliary video memory	7
0xC056	R/W	HIRESOFF	Select low resolution Graphics	6
0xC057	R/W	HIRESON	Select high resolution Graphics	6
0xC058	R/W	ANN1OFF	Annunciator 1 off (active if IOUDIS off)	
0xC059	R/W	ANN1ON	Annunciator 1 on (active if IOUDIS off)	
0xC05A	R/W	ANN2OFF	Annunciator 2 off (active if IOUDIS off)	
0xC05B	R/W	ANN2ON	Annunciator 2 on (active if IOUDIS off)	
0xC05C	R/W	ANN3OFF	Annunciator 3 off (active if IOUDIS off)	
0xC05D	R/W	ANN3ON	Annunciator 3 on (active if IOUDIS off)	
0xC05E	R/W	ANN4OFF	Annunciator 4 off (active if IOUDIS off)	
0xC05E	R/W	DHRESON	Double HIRES on (active if IOUDIS on)	
0xC05F	R/W	ANN4ON	Annunciator 4 on (active if IOUDIS off)	
0xC05F	R/W	DHRESOFF	Double HIRES off (active if IOUDIS on)	

Table II.2.3. Original Input/Output Control Soft Switches, Part 1

Address	Access	Name	Description	Notes
0xC060	R	TAPEIN	Cassette input	8
0xC061	R	PB1IN	Push Button 1 input	8
0xC062	R	PB2IN	Push Button 2 input	8
0xC063	R	PB3IN	Push Button 3 input	8
0xC064	R	GC1IN	Game Controller 1 input	9
0xC065	R	GC2IN	Game Controller 2 input	9
0xC066	R	GC3IN	Game Controller 3 input	9
0xC067	R	GC4IN	Game Controller 4 input	9
0xC070	R	GCTOGL	Game Controller Strobe; resets GC1IN-GC4IN	
0xC073	W	BANKSEL	RamWorks Bank Select; 64 KB Bank select	
0xC07E	W	IOUDISON	Disable annunciators, enable double HIRES	
0xC07F	W	IOUDISOFF	Enable annunciators, disable double HIRES	

Table II.2.4. Original Input/Output Control Soft Switches, Part 2

For completeness I have included Tables II.2.3, II.2.4, II.2.5, and II.2.6 showing the original Input/Output, memory management, and Disk][control Soft Switches. In all cases, the names of each Soft Switch are those that I use within the *Lisa* assembler because *Lisa* has an eight-character limitation for labels. Figure II.2.1 contains all notes that are referenced by Tables II.2.1 to II.2.6.

Address	Access	Name	Description	Notes
0xC080	R	RAM2WP	Select Bank 2; write-protect RAM	
0xC081	R|RR	ROM2WE	Deselect Bank 2; enable ROM | write-enable RAM	
0xC082	R	ROM2WP	Deselect Bank 2; enable ROM; write-protect RAM	
0xC083	R|RR	RAM2WE	Select Bank 2 | write-enable RAM	
0xC084			See 0xC080	
0xC085			See 0xC081	
0xC086			See 0xC082	
0xC087			See 0xC083	
0xC088	R	RAM1WP	Select Bank 1; write-protect RAM	
0xC089	R|RR	ROM1WE	Deselect Bank 1; enable ROM | write-enable RAM	
0xC08A	R	ROM1WP	Deselect Bank 1; enable ROM; write-protect RAM	
0xC08B	R|RR	RAM1WE	Select Bank 1 | write-enable RAM	
0xC08C			See 0xC088	
0xC08D			See 0xC089	
0xC08E			See 0xC08A	
0xC08F			See 0xC08B	

Table II.2.5. Original Memory Management Soft Switches

Address	Access	Name	Description	Notes
0xC080	R	PHAS0OFF	Turn stepper motor phase 1 off	
0xC081	R	PHAS0ON	Turn stepper motor phase 1 on	
0xC082	R	PHAS1OFF	Turn stepper motor phase 2 off	
0xC083	R	PHAS1ON	Turn stepper motor phase 2 on	
0xC084	R	PHAS2OFF	Turn stepper motor phase 3 off	
0xC085	R	PHAS2ON	Turn stepper motor phase 3 on	
0xC086	R	PHAS3OFF	Turn stepper motor phase 4 off	
0xC087	R	PHAS3ON	Turn stepper motor phase 4 on	
0xC088	R	MOTOROFF	Turn motor off	
0xC089	R	MOTORON	Turn motor on	
0xC08A	R	DRV0EN	Select Drive 1	
0xC08B	R	DRV1EN	Select Drive 2	
0xC08C	R	STROBE	Read data or shift while writing	
0xC08D	R/W	LATCH	Sense write-protect or load data while writing	
0xC08E	R	DATAIN	Prepare latch for input	10
0xC08F	W	DATAOUT	Prepare latch for output	11

Table II.2.6. Original Disk][Control Soft Switches

1) If STR80OFF, then access PAGE1/PAGE2 and use RAMRD and RAMWR; if STR80ON, then access Main or Auxiliary display page (0x400) using PAGE2.
2) If 80STORE is ON these switches do not affect video memory.
3) If INTCXROM is ON, then switch SLOTC3ROM is available; otherwise Main ROM is accessed.
4) Use bank enable and write-protect switches to control 0xD000-0xFFFF.
5) Triggers paddle timer and resets VBLINT.
6) This mode is only effective when TEXT switch is OFF.
7) This switch changes function when 80STORE is ON.
8) Data is on MSB only.
9) Read 0xC070 first, then count until MSB is zero.
10) DATAIN with STROBE for Read and DATAIN with LATCH for Sense Write-Protect.
11) DATAOUT with STROBE for Write and DATAOUT with LATCH for Load Write Latch.

Figure II.2.1. Notes for Tables II.2.1 to II.2.6

Table II.2.7 shows the Soft Switches that are used to control the *Zip Chip* if it is used in place of the 65C02-microprocessor. The *Zip Chip* includes a 65C02-microprocessor along with cache memory and a cache memory controller in order to execute processor instructions that are in cache and to manage some memory data that might also be in cache. Table II.2.8 shows the Soft Switches that are used to control the CFFA and Table II.2.9 shows the Soft Switches that are used to control the quikLoader. Table II.2.10 shows the Soft Switches that are used to control the Sider, RAM Disk 320, RAM Card, and Rana drives. Typically, the X-register contains the slot number in which the interface card or device resides times sixteen, and this register is used in combination with the addresses that are shown in Tables II.2.8, II.2.9, and II.2.10. Or, if speed is critical and the address space where the device driver is writable, the slot number of the device times sixteen can be added to the base addresses that are shown in these tables except in the case for the Disk][where indexed, absolute addressing instructions are **expected** and **must always** be used.

In addition to what is shown in Table II.2.10, the RanaSystems EliteThree Controller card also uses the original Disk][control Soft Switches as shown in Table II.2.6. The RanaSystems EliteThree Controller card uses a complicated algorithm where some of the PHASEON and PHASEOFF control Soft Switches are used in order to select its upper or lower playback/recording head and the 0xC800:0xC801 memory addresses are used to select a pair of drives, either drives 1 and 2 or drives 3 and 4.

Address	Access	Name	Description
0xC05A	W	ZIPCTRL	4 writes of 0x5A unlocks *Zip Chip*; 0xA5 locks *Zip Chip*
0xC05B	W	ZIPSTATS	Any byte written enables *Zip Chip*
0xC05B	R	ZIPSTATS	Bits 0 and 1 is RAM size: 0–8 KB, 1–16 KB, 2–32 KB, 3–64 KB; bit 3 for memory delay: 0 = fast mode (no delay), 1 = sync mode (delay); bit 4 is ZIP enable: 0 = enabled, 1 = disabled; bit 5 is paddle speed: 0 = fast, 1 = normal; bit 6 is cache update: 0 = no, 1 = yes; bit 7 is clock pulse every 1.0035 milliseconds
0xC05C	R/W	ZIPSLOTS	read/write speaker/slot speed: 0 = fast, 1 = normal. Bit 0 = speaker, bits 1 to 7 for slots 1 to 7
0xC05D	W	ZIPSPEED	Write speed: bit 2 = clk2/3, bit 3 = clk3/4, bit 4 = clk4/5, bit 5 = clk5/6, bit 6 = clk/2, bit 7 = clk/4
0xC05E	W	ZIPDELAY	Bit 7: 0 = enable delay, 1 = disable and reset delay
0xC05E	R	ZIPDELAY	Delay: 0 = OFF; 1 = ON. Bit 0 = ROMRD, bit 1 = RAMBNK, bit 2 = PAGE2, bit 3 = HIRES, bit 4 = 80STORE, bit 5 = MWR, bit 6 = MRD, bit 7 = ALTZP
0xC05F	W	ZIPCACHE	Bit 6 for paddle delay: 0 = disable, 1 = enable; bit 7 for Language Card partition cache: 0 = enable, 1 = disable

Table II.2.7. Zip Chip Control Soft Switches

Address	Access	Name	Description
0xC080	R/W	ATADATAH	Read or write high data byte register
0xC081	R	SETCSMSK	Disable pre-fetch register
0xC082	R	CLRCSMSK	Enable pre-fetch register
0xC086	R	ATASTAT2	Read alternate status register
0xC086	W	ATADEVCT	Write device control register
0xC088	R/W	ATADATAL	Read or write low data byte register
0xC089	R	ATAERROR	Read error register
0xC08A	W	ATASECCT	Write sector count register
0xC08B	W	ATASECTR	Write LBA3 (07:00) address register
0xC08C	W	ATACYLNL	Write LBA2 (15:08) address register
0xC08D	W	ATACYLNH	Write LBA1 (23:16) address register
0xC08E	W	ATAHEAD	Write LBA0 (27:24) address register and drive/head config
0xC08F	W	ATACMD	Write command register
0xC08F	R	ATASTAT	Read primary status register

Table II.2.8. CFFA Control Soft Switches

Address	Access	Name	Description
0xC080	W	QLSELC0	Select Banks 0 or 1, ON/OFF, USR, EPROM number
0xC081	W	QLSELC1	Select Banks 2 or 3, ON/OFF, USR, EPROM number
0xC082	W	QLSELC2	Select Banks 4 or 5, ON/OFF, USR, EPROM number
0xC083	W	QLSELC3	Select Banks 6 or 7, ON/OFF, USR, EPROM number

Table II.2.9. quikLoader Control Soft Switches

Address	Access	Name	Description
0xC080	R	SDINPUT	Sider read status
0xC080	W	SDINPUT	Write drive number, DCB data, input data
0xC081	R	SDOUTPUT	Sider read output data
0xC081	W	SDOUTPUT	Write start, flush, and stop commands
0xC080	W	RDSECTR	RAM Disk sector number
0xC081	W	RDTRACK	RAM Disk track number
0xC084	W	RAMCARD	RAM Card ON/OFF, track*2, sector/8
0xC800	W	ROMCODE1	Select Rana drive pairs 1 and 2
0xC801	W	ROMCODE2	Select Rana drive pairs 3 and 4

Table II.2.10. Sider, RAM Disk, RAM Card, and Rana Control Soft Switches

Even though the Apple //e has additional ROM memory in the CX ROM, that is, the 0xC100 to 0xCFFF address space, the original STEP and TRACE entry points are still disabled and they cannot be used in conjunction with the enabled Mini-Assembler command, the ! command. And, this ROM Monitor also contains a silly SEARCH command, the S command. In my opinion this SEARCH command is extremely limited for it can find at most two consecutive hexadecimal bytes or two consecutive lower ASCII data bytes in low/high byte order. And, I am most annoyed that the cassette tape recorder READ and WRITE commands are still retained in the Apple //e ROM Monitor. What disturbs me the most is that the ROM Monitor cannot even display the additional opcodes that are part of the 65C02 Instruction Set that pertains to the specific 65C02-microprocessor that is supplied in and utilized by the Apple //e. As an aside, the 65C02 Instruction Set was expanded even further in the Rockwell and WDC versions of that processor to include the BBR, BBS, RMB, and SMB mnemonics, thus adding thirty-two additional opcodes. However, these opcodes are not available in the Apple //e supplied 65C02-microprocessor.

In summary, it makes no sense to me to provide a computer to a user that utilizes a particular microprocessor and its firmware cannot even display the complete set of mnemonics for that microprocessor. What I would have done is to recommend to Apple Computer to retire the ROM Monitor READ and WRITE commands and to reintroduce the ROM Monitor STEP and TRACE commands, and to provide a more useful ROM Monitor command in addition to the SEARCH command if there is sufficient code space for such a command. And, of course, the ROM Monitor must be able to display all of its useable 65C02 mnemonics. Will retiring the ROM Monitor READ and WRITE commands provide enough code space for all of my suggestions? Can the new lower ASCII data input routine in the ROM Monitor be further enhanced? Let's find out. The ROM Monitor begins at 0xF800. The CX ROM routines along with the 80-column display routines are found in CX ROM memory from 0xC100 to 0xCFFF.

3. SWEET16 Metaprocessor

The *SWEET16* Metaprocessor is a "pseudo microprocessor" implemented in 6502 assembly language. Originally conceived and written by Steven Wozniak, *SWEET16* and Integer BASIC were included in the ROM firmware of the early Apple II computers. *SWEET16* is a really smart and useful extension to a 6502 or 65C02 based computer and it can be ported to other 6502 or 65C02 based systems in order to provide useful 16-bit functionality. It can be thought of as a virtual machine that gives the 65C02 programmer a 16-bit extension to the 8-bit microprocessor. *SWEET16* utilizes sixteen 16-bit registers or sixteen 16-bit pointers at the beginning of page-zero memory and *SWEET16* provides new instructions that use those registers or pointers. Although *SWEET16* instructions are not as fast as native 65C02 instructions, *SWEET16* can reduce the code size of programs and ease many programming difficulties.

Steven Wozniak wrote "While writing Apple BASIC for the 6502-microprocessor, I repeatedly encountered a variant of Murphy's Law. Briefly stated, any routine operating on 16-bit data will require at least twice the code that it should. Programs making extensive use of 16-bit pointers such as compilers, editors, and assemblers are included in this category. In my case, even the addition of a few double-byte instructions to the 6502's Instruction Set would have only slightly alleviated the problem. What I really needed was a hybrid of the MOS Technology 6502 and RCA 1800 architectures: a powerful 8-bit data handler complemented by an easy to use processor with an abundance of 16-bit registers and excellent pointer capability. My solution was to implement a non-existent 16-bit "metaprocessor" in software, interpreter style, which I call *SWEET16*. *SWEET16* is based around sixteen 16-bit registers called R0 to R15, which are actually implemented as thirty-two memory locations. R0 doubles as the *SWEET16* Accumulator (ACC), R15 as the Program Counter (PC), and R14 as the Status Register. R13 holds compare instruction results and R12 is the Subroutine Return stack pointer if *SWEET16* subroutines are used. All other *SWEET16* registers are at the user's unrestricted disposal.

"*SWEET16* instructions fall into register and non-register categories. The register instructions specify one of the sixteen registers to be used as either a data element or as a pointer to data in memory, depending on the specific instruction. For example, the instruction INR R5 uses R5 as a data register and ST @R7 uses R7 as a pointer register to data in memory. Except for the SET instruction, register instructions require one byte. The non-register instructions are primarily 6502 style branch operations with the second byte specifying a +/- 127-byte displacement relative to the address of the following instruction. If a Prior Register (PR) operation result meets a specified branch condition, the displacement is added to the *SWEET16* Program Counter, thus effecting a branch. *SWEET16* is intended as an enhancement package to the 6502 processor, not as a standalone processor. A 6502 program switches to *SWEET16* mode with a subroutine call, and subsequent code is interpreted as *SWEET16* instructions. The non-register instruction RTN returns the user program to the 6502's direct execution mode after restoring the A, X, Y, P, and S internal registers. Even though most opcodes are only one byte long, *SWEET16* runs approximately ten times slower than equivalent 6502 code, so it should be employed only when code is at a premium or execution is not. As an example of its usefulness, I have estimated that about 1K byte could be weeded out of my 5K byte Apple][BASIC interpreter with no observable performance degradation by selectively applying *SWEET16*."

SWEET16 was probably the least used and least understood function in the original Apple][. In exactly the same sense that the Integer and Applesoft BASICs are languages, *SWEET16* is also a language. Compared to the BASICs, however, *SWEET16* would be classified as a lower level language with a strong likeness to conventional 6502 or 65C02 assembly language. Obviously, to use *SWEET16*, one must learn the language. And according to Wozniak, "The opcode list is short and uncomplicated." *SWEET16* was

ROM based in every early Apple][and it resided in memory at 0xF689:0xF7FC. It uses the SAVE and the RESTORE routines in the ROM Monitor of the Apple in order to preserve the 6502 or 65C02 registers during its use, allowing *SWEET16* to be used as a subroutine. Table II.3.1 lists the *SWEET16* registers and the function of those registers. The complete *SWEET16* Instruction Set is shown in Tables II.3.2 and II.3.3. These tables list each opcode, its mnemonic, and a brief description of the instruction and what it does. Table II.3.2 lists the non-register instructions and Table II.3.3 lists the register instructions.

Glen Bredon utilized *SWEET16* extensively in his *Big Mac* software by incorporating the *SWEET16* interpreter within *Big Mac* since the interpreter did not exist in the Apple][+ or in the Apple //e ROMs. Mr. Bredon re-coded the NUL (not shown) and BNM1 opcodes to provide other functionality specific to his needs in *Big Mac*. He also did not use the R12 register as a Return from Subroutine stack pointer and he did not use the R14 register for the PR and Status functions. Rather than using a stack pointer at all, he simply saved the Return from Subroutine address at page-zero 0xDA:0xDB and the PR and Status at page-zero 0xFF.

Register	Description
R0	*SWEET16* Accumulator (ACC)
R1–R11	*SWEET16* user registers
R12	*SWEET16* subroutine return Stack Pointer (SP)
R13	*SWEET16* compare instruction results
R14	*SWEET16* Status (Prior) Register (PR & C-flag)
R15	*SWEET16* Program Counter (PC)

Table II.3.1. SWEET16 Register Descriptions

Opcode	Mnemonic	Instruction Description
0x00	RTN	Return to 6502 or 65C02 mode to process native 6502 or 65C02 instructions
0x01	BR rel	Branch always to PC+rel+2→PC
0x02	BNC rel	Branch if prior operation left carry clear to PC+rel+2→PC
0x03	BC rel	Branch if prior operation left carry set to PC+rel+2→PC
0x04	BP rel	Branch if Prior Register is positive to PC+rel+2→PC
0x05	BM rel	Branch if Prior Register is negative to PC+rel+2→PC
0x06	BZ rel	Branch if Prior Register is zero to PC+rel+2→PC
0x07	BNZ rel	Branch if Prior Register is not zero to PC+rel+2→PC
0x08	BM1 rel	Branch if Prior Register is minus one to PC+rel+2→PC
0x09	BNM1 rel	Branch if Prior Register is not minus one to PC+rel+2→PC
0x0A	SOUT chr	Send character chr to COUT (originally the BK opcode)
0x0B	RS	Return from Subroutine, and POPD @SP→PC, SP=SP-2
0x0C	BS rel	Branch to Subroutine, and PC→STD @SP, SP=SP+2, PC+rel+2→PC
0x0D	RSNS	Return from Subroutine without stack, and SP→PC (originally unassigned opcode)
0x0E	BSNS rel	Branch to Subroutine without stack, and PC→SP, PC+rel+2→PC (originally unassigned opcode)
0x0F	SJMP adr	Jump to 16-bit address, adr and adr-1→PC (originally unassigned opcode)

Table II.3.2. SWEET16 Non-Register Instructions

Opcode	Mnemonic	Instruction Description
0x1n	SET Rn,val	Load Rn with 16-bit value val
0x2n	LD Rn	Load ACC from Rn, PR=n
0x3n	ST Rn	Store ACC into Rn, PR=n
0x4n	LD @Rn	Load LO ACC indirectly using Rn, HO ACC=0, Rn=Rn+1, PR=0
0x5n	ST @Rn	Store LO ACC indirectly using Rn, Rn=Rn+1, PR=0
0x6n	LDD @Rn	Load ACC indirectly using Rn, Rn=Rn+2, PR=0
0x7n	STD @Rn	Store ACC indirectly using Rn, Rn=Rn+2, PR=0
0x8n	POP @Rn	Rn=Rn-1, load LO ACC indirectly using Rn, HO ACC=0, PR=0
0x9n	STP @Rn	Rn=Rn-1, store LO ACC indirectly using Rn, PR=0
0xAn	ADD Rn	ACC = ACC + Rn, status = carry, PR=0
0xBn	SUB Rn	ACC = ACC − Rn, status = carry, PR=0
0xCn	POPD @Rn	Rn=Rn-2, load ACC indirectly using Rn, PR=0
0xDn	CPR Rn	R13 = ACC − Rn, status = carry, PR=13
0xEn	INR Rn	Rn = Rn + 1, PR=n
0xFn	DCR Rn	Rn = Rn − 1, PR=n

Table II.3.3. SWEET16 Register Instructions

I am simply astounded at how easy it is to utilize the *SWEET16* instructions for any task that processes large sets of data, like an assembler. In fact, the early versions of the S-C or Sander-Cederlof Assembler II used *SWEET16* in several locations within its code. The TED/ASM assembler and all of its descendants, including the DOS Tool Kit, TED II+, Merlin, and many others, used *SWEET16* heavily. Several of the programs in the Apple Programmer's Aid ROM used *SWEET16* particularly for the Integer BASIC Renumber/Append programs.

As Tables II.3.2 and II.3.3 show, the *SWEET16* instruction set is short and uncomplicated. Except for relative branch displacements, hand assembly is trivial. All register instructions are formed by combining two hexadecimal digits, one for the opcode and one to specify a register. For example, register instructions 0x15 and 0x45 both specify register R5 while register instructions 0x23, 0x27, and 0x2B are all LD Rn instructions. Most register instructions are assigned in complementary pairs to facilitate remembering them. Thus, LD Rn and ST Rn are instructions 0x2n and 0x3n, while LD @Rn and ST @Rn are instructions 0x4n and 0x5n, respectively.

Opcodes 0x00 through 0x0F are assigned to the sixteen Non-Register Instructions and opcodes 0x1n through 0xFn are assigned to the fifteen Register Instructions. Except for the RTN or 0x00, SOUT or 0x0A, RS or 0x0B, RSNS or 0x0D, and SJMP or 0x0F opcodes, the non-register instructions are basic 6502 or 65C02 style branches. The second byte of a branch instruction contains a signed two's complement byte displacement value from -128 to +127 relative to the address of the instruction immediately following the branch. The RTN opcode calls the RESTORE routine in the ROM Monitor in order to restore the 6502 or 65C02 registers and return to 6502 or 65C02 processing mode using the *SWEET16* program counter. The *SWEET16* program counter contains the address for the 6502 or 65C02 instruction that immediately follows the initial call to *SWEET16*. The SOUT instruction sends its second byte to COUT at ROM Monitor address 0xFDED. Before the BS or RS instructions can be used, R12 must be initialized with the address to a stack buffer that is used for the return-from-subroutine 16-bit addresses. The stack buffer must be of sufficient size to hold n-levels of subroutine calls, or n-number of 16-bit addresses. Of course, the SJMP instruction, like the SET instruction, takes its second and third byte to form a 16-bit address, or a 16-bit value in the case of the SET instruction.

If a specified branch condition is met when using the Prior Register instruction result, the displacement is added to the Program Counter effecting a branch. Except for the BR or Branch always, the BS or Branch to a Subroutine, and the BSNS or Branch to a Subroutine using No Stack instructions, the branch instructions are assigned in complementary pairs like the register instructions, thus rendering them easily remembered for hand coding. For example, Branch if Plus and Branch if Minus are instructions 0x04 and 0x05 while Branch if Zero and Branch if Not Zero are instructions 0x06 and 0x07, respectively.

The original *SWEET16* software left the last three non-register instructions unassigned, where any of them could be used as a NUL instruction, and the BK instruction (BreaK or 0x0A) simply executed a 6502 or 65C02 BRK instruction. The PR and the C-flag were both combined in the high order or HO byte of R14. I chose to separate the PR and C-flag into separate bytes of the R14 register in order to reduce the code size and number of execution cycles for all of the non-register instructions. Doing this allowed the inclusion of more code to process four additional instructions within the limited, single memory page area that **must** contain all of the *SWEET16* routines. Those added routines send character to COUT, Branch to Subroutine using No Stack, Return from Subroutine using No Stack, and JuMP to address. Incidentally, one can jump to any memory address using other *SWEET16* instructions, but it requires using two of them, SET and ST, and the address must already be decremented by one, or decremented using a third instruction, DCR. The new instruction, SJMP ADR, loads the *SWEET16* Program Counter already decremented with ADR-1.

My implementation of *SWEET16* saves the Prior Register or PR number of the register that is receiving the value or change in value into the low order or LO byte of R14 when a register instruction is processed. If the register instruction is ADD, SUB, or CPR, I save the state of the C-flag in bit 0 of the HO byte of R14. I found that reasons for doing so were quite compelling. Originally, the LO byte of R14 is not utilized by the *SWEET16* interpreter, so it is available to the user. Personally, I found that that single unused byte is virtually useless. So, if there is a way to transform that byte into a more useful function, I am more inclined to adopt that strategy. Each time a non-register instruction is encountered, the original code uses nine cycles in five bytes for part of its setup code, and ten additional bytes are used for five of the branch instructions. My implementation requires only eight cycles in five bytes for the setup code, and **no** additional bytes for the same five branch instructions. This does not seem like very much of a savings; that is, one cycle for every invocation of a non-register instruction. However, in processing loops that execute many hundreds or thousands of times, a single cycle in savings does add up quickly. On the other hand, Mr. Bredon chose to use sixteen cycles in seven bytes for the same capability in *Big Mac*.

The SET command is another example where a few cycles can be saved just by using a different strategy. The original code uses thirteen cycles in ten bytes to increment the *SWEET16* Program Counter by two, not including the code for its RTS instruction. My implementation requires only eleven cycles in ten bytes every time the SET instruction is utilized. Mr. Bredon requires thirty-five cycles in seven bytes for the same functionality in *Big Mac*. To me, that seems like a lot of overhead just to save three bytes of code. This simply exemplifies the observable fact that when software is made extremely compact, the price paid is usually many more processing cycles, thus slower execution time overall.

As stated above, the original image of *SWEET16* was located in ROM Monitor at 0xF689:0xF7FC, so it required 372 bytes for its implementation, though the last three bytes in the 0xF7 page were set to 0xFF. My implementation of *SWEET16* requires exactly 400 bytes, though it includes four additional, and very useful instructions in my opinion. I believe that having the *SWEET16* Metaprocessor located in the Apple //e CX ROM memory rather than having the RESET diagnostic routines certainly makes far more sense to me. And, there is more than sufficient room for the *SWEET16* interpreter to reside at that location only if there is sufficient room for a calling and a return location in the ROM Monitor firmware. I believe a suitable ROM Monitor entry point for *SWEET16* is at 0xFA72. And, the *SWEET16* return address can follow at `0xFA78`. The DOS 4.1 Manual provides the details for why I chose these ROM Monitor address locations for *SWEET16*. My Apple //e ROM images include my implementation of *SWEET16*.

4. Garbage Collector in Applesoft

The Applesoft Garbage Collector routine `GARBAG` is located in ROM Applesoft at `0xE484:0xE596`, and that routine moves all currently active character string variables up in Character String Pool memory as far as possible. There are several Applesoft routines like the ROM Applesoft `FRE( aexpr )` command that relies on the garbage collector to consolidate the contents of the Character String Pool memory when there is not enough Free Space in memory as shown in Figure I.15.1 in order to perform the next requested character string variable manipulation. When certain conditions are met while these ROM Applesoft routines process character string data, `GARBAG` is called. Depending upon how many character string variables are active, the processing time for `GARBAG` is proportional to the square of the number of active character strings currently in use. This processing time may be a few seconds if there are less than fifty active character strings, or many minutes if there are hundreds of active character strings. It may even appear as if the Applesoft program has literally stopped, or hanged for no apparent reason. In Section I.15 I even suggested to strategically place multiple Applesoft `FRE( aexpr )` statements throughout an Applesoft program which may help to alleviate many processing delays.

Many years ago, Cornelis Bongers of Erasmus University in Rotterdam, Netherlands, published a brilliant Garbage Collector specification for Applesoft character strings in *Micro*, August, 1982. According to an article in *Apple Assembly Line*, March, 1984, the speed of his algorithm was incredible when compared to the `GARBAG` algorithm in ROM Applesoft. And, the processing time for his algorithm was directly proportional to the number of active character strings rather than to the number of active character strings squared. The only problem with his algorithm was that the magazine that published the algorithm owned the specification. Worse yet, the algorithm was tied to a program called Ampersoft, marketed by Microsparc, then publishers of *Nibble* magazine. It was reported that a license to use Bongers' algorithm was very expensive at that time.

Recall that Table I.15.1 shows the definition of a simple character string variable descriptor as it is found in the Simple Variables memory area and Table I.15.2 shows the definition of a character string array variable descriptor as it is found in the Array Variables memory area. After analyzing these two tables, Bongers specification introduced the idea of *marking* active character strings that are located in the Character String Pool. During the first pass through the Simple Variable and Array Variable descriptors storage area in memory and the Character String Pool, Bongers set the third byte in the character string data to its upper ASCII value and he swapped in the address of its character string descriptor in place of the first two bytes of the character string data. He saved those first two bytes of the character string data safely in the address field of its descriptor or character string element. The address that was previously in the address field of the descriptor would most likely be changed anyway after all of the character strings are moved up in memory to their final destination. During the second pass through the Simple Variable and Array Variable descriptors storage area in memory and the Character String Pool, he moved all active character strings up in memory as far as possible, he retrieved the first two characters from storage in its descriptor or character string element, and he updated the address field to the new memory location where that string now resides in the Character String Pool.

Bongers' algorithm is most efficient when the active character strings are a least three bytes in length, so one- and two-character strings require slightly different handling in his specification. During the first pass through the Simple Variable and Array Variable descriptors storage area in memory and the Character String Pool, he saved the first byte of character string data pointed to by these *short* descriptors into the character string length byte of its descriptor. If the character string length is two, he stored the second data byte into the low address byte of its descriptor. For single byte character strings, he flagged the low address byte with the value of 0xFF. He flagged the high address byte in all *short* descriptors with the value of 0xFF since no character string can have a memory address greater than 0xFF00. If he found *short* character strings during the first pass, he set a *short* descriptors flag and if that flag was found to be set after the second pass was completed, his specification initiated a third pass where he returned the *short* character strings to the Character String Pool with their descriptors updated to their new memory location. *Short* character strings do slow down Bongers' algorithm a little. However, the processing time is still directly proportional to the number of active character strings, and not to the number of active character strings squared. Tables II.4.1 and II.4.2 illustrate Bongers' specification during the first pass through the Simple Variable and Array Variable descriptors storage area in memory and the Character String Pool.

String Descriptor Before Pass 1							⇒	String Descriptor After Pass 1						
+AS	-AS	1	LSB	MSB	0	0		+AS	-AS	41	FF	FF	0	0

Character String Pool Before Pass 1							⇒	Character String Pool After Pass 1						
41								41						

String Descriptor Before Pass 1							⇒	String Descriptor After Pass 1						
+AS	-AS	2	LSB	MSB	0	0		+AS	-AS	41	42	FF	0	0

Character String Pool Before Pass 1							⇒	Character String Pool After Pass 1						
41	42							41	42					

String Descriptor at ADL/ADH Before Pass 1							⇒	String Descriptor at ADL/ADH After Pass 1						
+AS	-AS	LEN	LSB	MSB	0	0		+AS	-AS	LEN	41	42	0	0

Character String Pool Before Pass 1							⇒	Character String Pool After Pass 1						
41	42	43	44	45	46	47		ADL	ADH	C3	44	45	46	47

Table II.4.1. Bongers Simple Variable Descriptor Processing in Pass 1

Pass two in Bongers' specification uses only the information in the Character String Pool data in order to move all currently active character string variables up in Character String Pool memory as far as possible. This is accomplished by initializing a string pool pointer and a character string pointer beginning at HIMEM and searching down to FRETOP for any upper ASCII character bytes. Once an upper ASCII character byte is found, its character string descriptor is located at the memory location two bytes prior to the upper ASCII character byte. That character string descriptor contains the length of the character string and the first two ASCII characters of the character string. Those two characters may be safely moved back to its character string data and the upper ASCII character byte changed to its lower ASCII value. The character string length can now be subtracted from the current character string pointer address, the new character string address can be copied to the second and third bytes in its character string descriptor, and the character string data can be copied to its new Character String Pool location. However, the character string data must be copied from its last character to its first character rather than from its first character to its last character in order to prevent possibly overwriting part of the data of the character string. Once the string pool pointer reaches the original address in FRETOP, the current character string pointer address becomes the new address for FRETOP if the *short* descriptors flag is not set.

String Element Before Pass 1			⇒	String Element After Pass 1		
1	LSB	MSB		41	FF	FF

Character String Pool Before Pass 1			⇒	Character String Pool After Pass 1		
41				41		

String Element Before Pass 1			⇒	String Element After Pass 1		
2	LSB	MSB		41	42	FF

Character String Pool Before Pass 1			⇒	Character String Pool After Pass 1		
41	42			41	42	

String Element at ADL/ADH Before Pass 1			⇒	String Element at ADL/ADH After Pass 1		
LEN	LSB	MSB		LEN	41	42

Character String Pool Before Pass 1							⇒	Character String Pool After Pass 1						
41	42	43	44	45	46	47		ADL	ADH	C3	44	45	46	47

Table II.4.2. Bongers Array Variable Element Processing in Pass 1

If the *short* descriptors flag is set, then a third pass must be made through the Simple Variable and Array Variable descriptors storage area in memory and the Character String Pool according to Bongers' specification. A memory pointer is initialized to VARTAB and a search is made for the 0xFF byte in either the fifth byte of a Simple Variable descriptor or in the third byte of an Array Variable element. If the prior byte also contains an 0xFF byte, then the descriptor is for a single byte character string, otherwise the descriptor is for a two byte character string. The current character string pointer is adjusted for one or for two characters, the character string data is copied from its descriptor to the Character String Pool, and the character string pointer address is copied to its character string descriptor. Once the memory pointer reaches STREND, the current character string pointer address becomes the new address for FRETOP.

It must be emphasized that Bongers' specification depends upon two very important caveats: *normal Applesoft programs* save all character string data in **lower** ASCII, that is, with the MSB of each character byte cleared, and *normal Applesoft programs* never allow more than one character string descriptor to point to the same character string data in memory. Bongers' algorithm will **fail** if a user should program something like A$ = CHR$(193). Bongers' algorithm will **fail** if an assembly language routine should modify two character string descriptors to point to the same character string data in the Character String Pool. Therefore, reasonable care must be given when creating Applesoft programs and/or assembly language routines that take the above caveats seriously in order to exact the stupendous benefit in using a garbage collector routine that is based on Bongers' specification.

Armed with only these limited details of Bongers' specification that I just presented, my analysis of those details, and my complete understanding of Tables I.15.1, I.15.2, and I.15.3 as well as Tables II.4.1 and II.4.2, my attempt to recreate Bongers' algorithm resulted in an assembly language routine that was 0x200 bytes in size. This necessitated creating a suitable Applesoft test program that would verify the accuracy of my implementation of Bongers' specification and to confirm to my satisfaction that no character string was altered in length, modified in content, or destroyed during processing. My ultimate goal would be to replace GARBAG in ROM Applesoft with my version of Bongers' specification. GARBAG occupies 0x113 bytes of ROM Applesoft memory and there is 0x70 bytes of additional memory available in the CX ROM space at 0xC600:0xC66F just prior to where I placed the *SWEET16* program code at 0xC670. If the CX ROM space is used, then CX ROM memory management must also be incorporated into the new garbage routine. When all available memory is totaled, my garbage routine must fit within 0x183 bytes if it is to be located in ROM. On the other hand, my garbage routine, after some adjustment, could be attached to an Applesoft program and simply called prior to issuing the DOS CHAIN command providing that the R keyword is utilized with CHAIN. At least that would mitigate having to call GARBAG in this particular instance. Periodically, the Applesoft program could check the remaining Free Space and call its attached garbage routine based on reasonable criteria. There is still much indeterminacy whether a particular character string manipulation will trigger a call to GARBAG during Applesoft processing. If that should happen, Applesoft processing could come to a grinding halt until the Character String Pool data is processed without regard to the attached garbage routine to my Applesoft program. There is **no** flag available indicating when Applesoft intends to call GARBAG and there is **no** flag to suspend GARBAG.

In order to compact an assembly language routine, certain decisions must be made that, hopefully, do not cause the introduction of more processor cycles than absolutely necessary. Example strategies would be to limit subroutine calls in the inner-most loops and to limit the pushing and popping of variables onto the stack. Sometimes simply reorganizing the order of a number of processing loops can greatly simplify the routine and eliminate having to re-initialize registers. Keeping the MSB address of a variable in a register when addresses are often compared can help simplify and even accelerate the code as well. I have no doubt that Mr. Bongers could have condensed my initial attempt in programming his specification down from 0x200 bytes to 0x183 bytes where six of those bytes are required for CX ROM memory management. My initial attempt to condense my garbage routine could not meet the goal of 0x183 bytes unless I removed the *short* descriptors flag that signaled whether a third pass was necessary, so I always made a third pass. Many times it is helpful to just take a break from a difficult programming task like this one, walk away, and work on something else for a while. Thus, when I returned to my garbage routine, I took a fresh look and I found several additional strategies that could condense my code even further, and even allow the use of the *short* descriptors flag. Hurray! I was able to place one segment of the routine into the 0x70 bytes that are located in CX ROM and the other segment into the 0x113 bytes where GARBAG normally resides. All that was left for me to do was the testing, the timing, and the verification of the routine once the routine is installed in ROM Applesoft memory, or in an EPROM to be precise.

As mentioned earlier, a verification test must prove that no character string is altered in length, modified in content, or destroyed by the algorithm of the garbage collector routine. The test results of the new routine must be **identical** to the results that are obtained when using the original GARBAG algorithm. And since there is available a DOS 4.5 DATE command, each pass through the character string array variables can easily be time stamped. The Applesoft test that I wrote creates three two-dimension character string arrays where both dimensions are set to twenty-six. Each character string element is initialized with a single character that is *forced* into the Character String Pool. On each successive pass, another character is added to each character string element within the dimension that is being processed, from one to twenty-six. This causes the utilization of memory to grow larger on each successive pass. On each pass, I noted the size of Free Space. I issued the Applesoft FRE(aexpr) command if Free Space is less than 15,000 bytes thereby forcing the garbage collector to process the contents of the Character String Pool. I obtained identical results for each and every pass in my Applesoft test program whether I used the original GARBAG routine in ROM Applesoft or my new garbage routine in ROM Applesoft. The timing results are shown in Table II.4.3 for my test program. **Time** is shown in **minutes and seconds**. The three columns of timings to the right of **Pass Number** summarize the results that are obtained from the original GARBAG routine. The time each pass begins is shown in the first of the three columns starting at time 00:00. If Free Space falls below 15,000 bytes, I made another call to FRE(aexpr) before I recorded another timestamp. This timestamp is shown in the middle of the three columns. The delta time the routine required for its processing is shown in the third of the three columns. The right most three columns contain the same timing information as before but for my new garbage collector routine starting at time 00:00.

Pass Number	Original Garbage Collector			New Garbage Collector		
	Time	<15000	Delta	Time	<15000	Delta
0	00:00			00:00		
1	00:02			00:02		
2	00:05			00:05		
3	00:09			00:09		
4	00:14			00:14		
5	00:21			00:20		
6	00:28			00:28		
7	00:37			00:36		
8	00:47	01:26	00:39	00:46	00:47	00:01
9	02:37			00:58		
10	02:49	04:55	02:06	01:10	01:12	00:02
11	05:11			01:25		
12	05:25	07:57	02:32	01:39	01:41	00:02
13	08:13	11:08	02:55	01:56	01:58	00:02
14	11:29	14:31	03:02	02:15	02:16	00:01
15	14:59	18:12	03:13	02:34	02:36	00:02
16	18:36	21:59	03:23	02:55	02:56	00:01
17	22:27	26:00	03:33	03:17	03:19	00:02
18	30:27	34:14	03:47	03:42	03:43	00:01
	34:40			03:43		

Table II.4.3. Garbage Collector Comparison and Verification Timing Results

My implementation of Bongers' specification shows how truly amazing this algorithm actually is. Table II.4.3 shows only a small peek into the capacity of this algorithm. When I changed the Free Space parameter from 15,000 to 5,000 bytes, the Applesoft program calling the original GARBAG routine could not complete, even after an hour, and I simply terminated the program. The Applesoft program using my new garbage collector routine completed in 06:54 minutes, and twenty-four of the twenty-six possible passes finished before I finally terminated that program due to my impatience. This table shows that only the first eighteen of the twenty-six possible passes finished before insufficient memory remained when calling the original GARBAG routine. After every pass, I called a verification routine that simply confirms that the content of all arrays still contain the ASCII data that is expected to be there, and that no other data is present, and that there is no additional or missing data. Therefore, this verification test routine confirms and verifies that no character string is altered in length, modified in content, or destroyed by either the original GARBAG routine or by my new garbage collector routine. I acknowledge total and complete credit to Cornelis Bongers for creating the original concept for this brilliant Garbage Collector specification. I would be fascinated to know if my implementation is anything like Mr. Bongers' implementation of his specification and how much code space he required versus how much code space I required in order to create and realize a working algorithm. Someone may someday tell me the answers to these questions.

Start	End	Length	Applesoft Commands
0xD8B0	0xD8C8	0x19	SAVE
0xD8C9	0xD8EF	0x27	LOAD
0xD8F0	0xD911	0x22	SAVE and LOAD common routines
0xF39F	0xF3D7	0x39	STORE and RECALL
0xF775	0xF786	0x12	SHLOAD
0xF7D5	0xF7D8	0x04	free space
0xF7D9	0xF7E6	0x0E	GETARYPT
	Total	0xBF	Available bytes

Table II.5.1. Disabled ROM Applesoft Commands

5. Building a New Apple //e ROM

The DOS 4.1 Manual includes an in-depth analysis of the Apple //e ROM including the CX ROM space and the Apple //e 80-column text card. That Manual shows where some of the 0xF0 ROM routines are incorrectly coded using example code segments. My analysis begins with the BASCALC routine in order to ascertain sufficient memory space for my Delete Key handler and the new 65C02 16-byte FMT2 table and its data content. The GETFMT routine is also presented along with the TBLC and TBLL tables, as well as the MNEML and MNEMR tables which grew to be 0xA6 bytes larger in size. STEP and TRACE are introduced along with GETNSP and where these routines must now reside in memory. Also, an enhancement to the SEARCH routine is presented along with a new ROM Monitor routine called ZAPMEM that can initialize a range of memory to any single hexademimal value. These enhancements require changes to the LOOKASC routine that now offers both lower ASCII **and** upper ASCII data input support for SEARCH. I moved part of the ROM Monitor RESET handler into the CX ROM space in order to create additional memory space in the 0xF0 ROM for the entry and exit code that manages the CX ROM memory for the *SWEET16* Metaprocessor. Even the NXTCHR and OLDRST routines are discussed. Furthermore, I explain why the Applesoft LOAD, RECALL, SAVE, STORE, and SHLOAD commands are useless without the cassette tape READ and WRITE routines which I removed from the 0xC5 ROM in favor of having the STEP and TRACE routines. Instead of replacing the calls to the READ and WRITE routines with a call to IORTS at 0xFF58, for example, I replaced the addresses to these Applesoft commands with that of IORTS. This frees a total of 0xBF bytes from four locations for other processing and for other Applesoft commands. The entry addresses for

Applesoft commands are located at 0xD000:0xD0CF, and the ASCII text for Applesoft commands is located at 0xD0D0:0xD25F. Table II.5.1 shows the available ROM memory and its location when those Applesoft commands are disabled and effectively removed from Applesoft processing. As I said in that Manual, I have no doubt that I will innovate a terrific use for this ROM memory in the next development cycle. Section II.8 describes precisely what I have done to utilize this valuable ROM address space!

Table II.5.2 shows the migration, removal, and insertion of various routines and tables of data that transform the stock Apple //e ROM and CX ROM memory space into a new and more powerful Apple //e ROM in my most humble opinion. I call this new Apple //e ROM ROM2E.SW16GC.7 because Build 7 of the ROM source code contains the *SWEET16* Metaprocessor, the STEP and TRACE routines, the display and logic for all 65C02 mnemonics, the Delete Key handler, and the incredible Garbage Collector that is based on the specification that was developed by Cornelis Bongers. What this ROM does not contain are the Apple //e diagnostic routines DIAGS, the cassette tape recorder routines READ and WRITE, and all of the Applesoft commands that depend on the READ and WRITE routines. The ROM2E.SW16GC.7 ROM image has no provisions to read from or to write to an external cassette tape recorder. The TAPEOUT Soft Switch at 0xC020 as shown in Table II.2.3 and the TAPEIN Soft Switch at 0xC060 as shown in Table II.2.4 can certainly be used for other crafty external devices. Both of the cassette tape recorder external ports are unique in that they can be used to read and to write a stream of electrically buffered digital data. TAPEOUT is the electrically buffered output of a 74LS74 D-type flip flop. There is no way to know whether the output signal is high or low at any given moment when the 0xC020 Soft Switch is read. This behavior is more like the SPKRTOGL Soft Switch at 0xC030 than any of the four annunciators whose output follow address bit A0. TAPEIN is a capacitor filtered and electrically buffered input whose signal is amplified by a 741 operational amplifier. This operational amplifier requires a minimum input threshold voltage in order to create an ON state for data bit D7, otherwise data bit D7 is OFF. The value for data bit D7 is obtained by reading the 0xC060 Soft Switch. This behavior is totally unlike the four paddle inputs that are Resistor/Capacitor or R/C filtered and connected to a 558 Quad Timer device whose output is capable of sinking up to 100 mA of current.

I have been using the APPLE2E.SW16GC.7 ROM image for at least three years with Virtual][as well as having the equivalent ROM2E.SW16GC.7 ROM image programmed into an EPROM for an early Apple //e, for an Enhanced Apple //e, and for a Platinum Apple //e. In all instances, the ROM image has been totally stable. All Applesoft commands that rely on the READ and the WRITE routines simply return immediately and without error to the caller. I have no doubt that the individuals or the engineering teams of individuals who designed the Apple //e ROM firmware, and subsequently the Enhanced Apple //e ROM firmware, were given a momentous task. That task was to preserve sixteen *classic* ROM Monitor entry locations and to introduce a few new ROM Monitor routines in order to support 40-column *and* 80-column screen displays seamlessly. This ROM also must support most all previously written software for the Apple][and the Apple][+. Obviously, one can no longer expect reliable results when entering any of the previous ROM Monitor code that is *within* these *classic* ROM Monitor entry location addresses. For example, the ROM Monitor entry addresses for SETKBD, INPORT, SETVID, and OUTPORT are at their *classic* ROM Monitor entry locations, but the code that is *within* these ROM Monitor entry addresses has drastically changed that implement the use of CX ROM and to enable new routines that are found in that address space. **It is no longer safe to jump into any of the code that is *within* these *classic* ROM Monitor entry location addresses.** It must be understood and accepted that the location for some of the data tables in this new Apple //e ROM Monitor is not sacrosanct, and that these tables have been moved to other ROM memory location addresses. I believe it is fair to say that ROM memory is very, very precious. And, I believe that the Apple Computer, Inc., engineers did a remarkable job in building a quality Apple //e 80-column text card and firmware product that performs its task simply and elegantly.

ROM2E		ROM2E.SW16GC.7		Description
Start	End	Start	End	
0xC1B6	0xC1BD	0xC1B6	0xC1BC	add BASCALC support
0xC204	0xC209	0xC203	0xC207	modify VTAB support; saves Y-reg in BASL
0xC230	0xC230	0xC22E	0xC22E	add CLD before address calculation
0xC298	0xC29F	0xC297	0xC2A4	change DELETE (0xFF) to LARROW (0x88)
0xC2B0	0xC2ED	0xC2B5	0xC2EA	modify RESET support, remove DIAGS support
0xC2F2	0xC2FD	0xCE15	0xCE1E	move XRDKEYX routine near INVERT
0xC600	0xC66F	0xC600	0xC66F	remove DIAGS, add Bongers' algorithm Part 2
0xC670	0xC7FF	0xC670	0xC7FF	remove DIAGS, add SWEET16
0xC849	0xC84B	0xC849	0xC84B	add jump to CONTKEY
0xC9A4	0xC9A9	0xC2EF	0xC2F4	move KBDOUT
0xCA71	0xCA88	0xC5E7	0xC5FE	form mnemonic table index; put TBLC and TBLL
0xCC90	0xCC95	0xC9A4	0xC9A9	move XFF, put CONTKEY here
0xCE14	0xCE1E	0xCE15	0xCE1E	remove duplicate UPRCASE, put KRDKEYX here
0xCF16	0xCF16	0xCF16	0xCF18	fix logic for X-register
0xCF37	0xCF39	0xCF39	0xCF39	change 3 unused bytes to 1 unused bytes
0xD034	0xD035	0xD034	0xD035	use IORTS for SHLOAD address
0xD04E	0xD04F	0xD04E	0xD04F	use IORTS for RECALL address
0xD050	0xD051	0xD050	0xD051	use IORTS for STORE address
0xD06C	0xD06D	0xD06C	0xD06D	use IORTS for LOAD address
0xD06E	0xD06F	0xD06E	0xD06F	use IORTS for SAVE address
0xD8B0	0xD8C8	0xD8B0	0xD8C8	remove SAVE code; empty (0x19 bytes)
0xD8C9	0xD8EF	0xD8C9	0xD8EF	remove LOAD code; empty (0x27 bytes)
0xD8F0	0xD900	0xD8F0	0xD900	remove SAVE, LOAD code; empty (0x11 bytes)
0xE484	0xE596	0xE484	0xE596	replace GARBAG with Bongers' algorithm Part 1
0xF39F	0xF3BB	0xF39F	0xB3BB	remove STORE code; empty (0x1D bytes)
0xF3BC	0xF3D7	0xF3BC	0xF3D7	remove RECALL code; empty (0x1C bytes)
0xF57A	0xF582	0xF57A	0xF582	add HLINMOD
0xF5A5	0xF5A5	0xF5A5	0xF5A5	add HLINMOD
0xF775	0xF786	0xF775	0xF786	remove SHLOAD code; empty (0x12 bytes)
0xF7D5	0xF7E6	0xF7D5	0xF7E6	remove STORE, RECALL code; empty (0x12 bytes)
0xF9A6	0xF9B3	0xFBC7	0xFBD6	move FMT2 table, add (zpage), (absolute,X) modes
0xF9B4	0xF9BF	0xFA30	0xFA3B	move CHAR1 and CHAR2 tables
0xF9C0	0xFA3F	0xF9A6	0xFA2F	move MNEML and MNEMR tables (0xA6 added), CXOFF/RTN
0xFA62	0xFA81	0xFA62	0xFA81	modify RESET; add SWEET16, SW16RTN
0xFB08	0xFB18	0xFB08	0xFB18	remove Apple text; put RSETINIT, move XLTBL
0xFBC1	0xFBD8	0xFBC1	0xFBD8	use BASCALC in CX ROM (Y-reg = 2), add FMT2 table
0xFC5D	0xFC5F	0xFC5D	0xFC5F	unused bytes, add STEPRTN2
0xFCC9	0xFCD1	0xFCC9	0xFCD1	remove HEADR (rts); add STEPRTN
0xFEC2	0xFEC3	0xFEC2	0xFEC3	add TRACE
0xFEC4	0xFEC9	0xFA3C	0xFA3F	add STEP, move CXOFF, add CXRTN
0xFECD	0xFED6	0xFECD	0xFED6	remove WRITE, add ZAPMEM
0xFEF1	0xFEF5	0xFEFD	0xFF04	move MINIASM, modify SEARCH2
0xFEFD	0xFF12	0xFEFD	0xFF0E	remove READ, add MINIASM, modify TITLE
0xFF13	0xFF1A	0xC500	0xC507	move GETNSP to CX ROM
0xFF1B	0xFF2C	0xFF18	0xFF2C	enhance LOOKASC, add X search command
0xFFCC	0xFFE2	0xFFCC	0xFFE2	remove W & R, add T & Z, S for STEP

Table II.5.2. Transformations to Build a New Apple //e ROM

106

6. Apple][Character Generator ROM

Virtual][, Gerard Putter's MacOS application to emulate the Apple][computer, provides the capability to use a personally designed ASCII display input character set for the Apple][character display. The input character set is defined to be a character set bitmap that is either a PNG or a TIFF file that must be exactly 128 pixels wide and exactly 64 pixels high. The bitmap depth must be one or eight pixels. Each character in the bitmap is defined to be within a character cell that is eight pixels by eight pixels. Because characters displayed by the Apple][are only seven pixels wide, the right most column of the character cell is ignored by Virtual][. The black pixels within a character cell comprise the background of the character; all other pixels comprise the character itself. The directory that must contain this input character set bitmap file is at *Users/<username>/Library/Application Support/Virtual][/CharacterSets*. A filename that is suggested by the Virtual][documentation for this bitmap file is MyCharacters.tif. An XML file named International.plist must also be located in this same directory and it defines the actual name for the input character set bitmap file. This XML file may include the name of an icon bitmap file called MyCharSetIcon.tif whose size may be up to sixteen pixels wide by eleven pixels high. The icon bitmap is displayed in the upper left-hand corner of the Virtual][window. The XML file may also include a keyboard translation table if that is needed as well. The XML file I created is shown in Figure II.6.1, and it includes the resources for two different input character set bitmap files and one icon bitmap file.

Key	Type	Value
▼ Root	Dictionary	(2 items)
▼ My new character set	Dictionary	(3 items)
CharacterSet	String	MyNewCharacters.tif
Icon	String	MyCharSetIcon.tif
▶ KeyboardTranslation	Dictionary	(0 items)
▼ My old character set	Dictionary	(3 items)
CharacterSet	String	MyOldCharacters.tif
Icon	String	MyCharSetIcon.tif
▶ KeyboardTranslation	Dictionary	(0 items)

Figure II.6.1. International Character Set XML File

I used Xcode to easily create the XML file that is shown in Figure II.6.1. Any *Property List Editor* works as well. To create the TIFF bitmap files I used the MacOS *Paintbrush* application because it was available for download at no charge. I am certainly not an expert *Paintbrush* user and I had some difficulties with the application in order to produce what I wanted easily. Most of my difficulties occurred when I tried to save my work during incremental stages of testing. I found that if I used the Lasso tool to copy the entire bitmap area into the clipboard, I could save the content of the clipboard into a new bitmap file of the same size, and then discard the original file. I do not know why the *save* or *save as* option failed to save my incremental work to the original file, and I do not know why I had to save my work in such a round-about fashion. I used the Line tool configured for a *stroke* of one in order to toggle a pixel from black to white or from white to black. *Paintbrush* saves the bitmap file as a TIFF file having a Color Space of RGB, a Color Profile of Generic RGB Profile, and the Alpha Channel set to Yes. I have no idea what these specifications mean or imply, but Virtual][had no problem reading and utilizing all of the TIFF files that I created in this manner.

My greatest source of irritation came when I discovered that the *Library* directory specified in the above pathname for the *CharacterSets* directory is a hidden file by default. I lost more time putting the XML and TIFF files into the wrong folder because I could not see the hidden *Library* directory in my personal Users account. Once I realized that the *Library* directory is hidden, it was extremely easy to unhide the folder using Xquartz or the Terminal application that is found in the Utilities directory, which is located in the Applications directory. Simply launch the Terminal application and enter bash on the command line. This starts the GNU *Bourne-Again Shell*. Now, when you enter the UNIX command ls -AF at */Users/<username>*, all files including . files, hidden files, and directories are displayed. Now enter the command chflags nohidden Library and have a look at a Finder window for your personal Users account. You should now see a *Library* directory. Once you locate the XML and TIFF files properly and launch Virtual][, select *Quick settings>Character Set>My character set*. After selecting the desired character set bitmap file, be sure to save your Virtual][session when you are satisfied with its character display, and it will be selected and loaded every time Virtual][is launched again in the future.

Figure II.6.2. Character Set Bitmap TIFF File

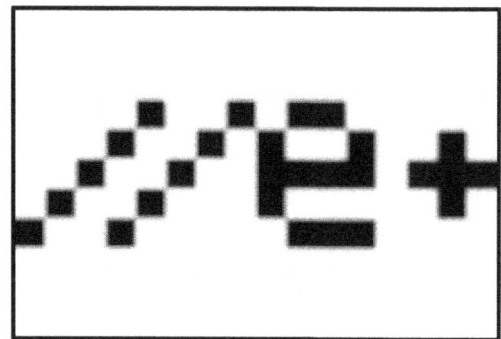

Figure II.6.3. Icon Bitmap TIFF File

Figure II.6.2 shows the inverse view of the MyNewCharacters.tif file and Figure II.6.3 shows the normal view of the MyCharSetIcon.tif file that I created for Virtual][. I used *Paintbrush* to modify a number of the ASCII characters to suit my preferences. Once I was satisfied with my input character set bitmap file, I created a simple Apple][tool using LORES graphics that allows me to create a 4 KB character ROM Binary data file. This LORES graphics tool is called *EDITROM*. The ROM file that *EDITROM* can edit must also contain the inverse characters as well as the alternate keyboard characters, though these characters are not included in Figure II.6.2. I found that it was easier to begin the editing process by reading the stock character ROM into a Binary file using the PROmGRAMER, for example. I can display the data for each character in the character ROM using *EDITROM* which also has the capability to modify any of the characters in that ROM data. Once I make all of the desired changes to the character data, I can save the character ROM data that is currently in memory to another Binary data file and program an equivalent sized 2732 EPROM with that new ROM data. My Apple][+ and all three of my Apple //e computers use the same character ROM data or a subset of that data as shown in Figure II.6.2.

To begin a ROM editing session with *EDITROM*, a suitable filename for ROM data may be entered as shown in Figure II.6.4. Simply press RETURN if there is no new ROM data file to read. The ROM data file is `0x1000` (or 4096) bytes in size and it is read into memory at memory address `0x1000`. Figure II.6.5 shows the LORES display of the first character entry in ROM data and four lines of Text at the bottom of the display. Line twenty-two in this display shows the location in memory where the first of eight bytes of character data begin, the value for each byte of data, and how the character is currently displayed by the Apple][hardware. There are only two modes of operation that can be used in *EDITROM*: Show Mode and Edit Mode. Show Mode simply duplicates the LORES character that is displayed on the left side of the LORES screen to the right side of the LORES screen. The data that is displayed on line twenty-two of the screen is copied to line twenty-four of the screen.

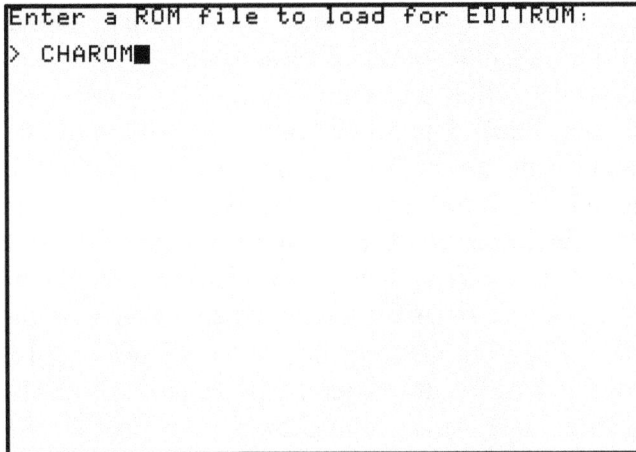

Figure II.6.4. Load ROM File for EDITROM

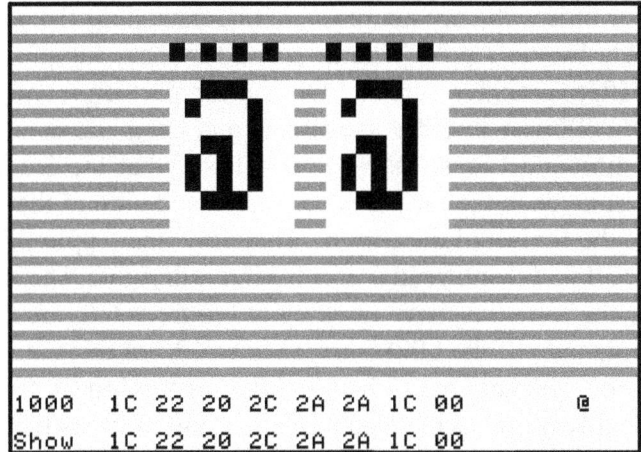

Figure II.6.5. ROM Data Show Mode

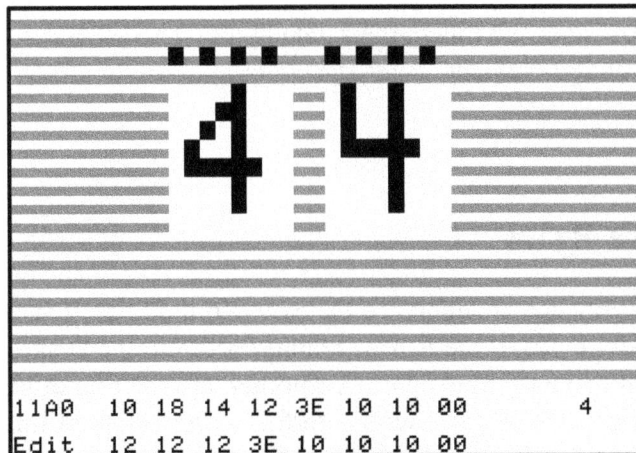

Figure II.6.6. ROM Data Edit Mode

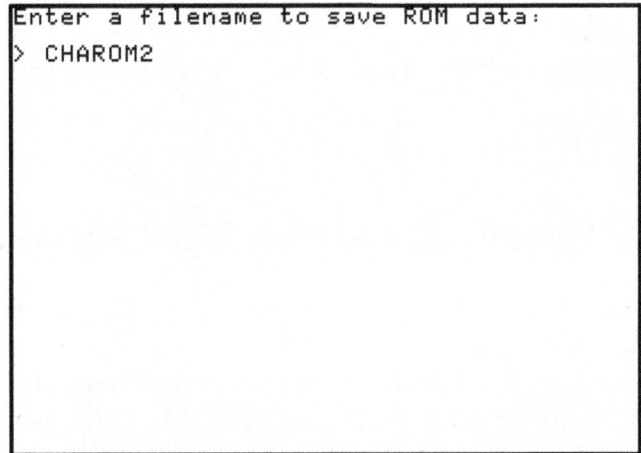

Figure II.6.7. Save ROM Data for EDITROM

There are only four commands that can be used in Show Mode: B goes back one character, E enters Edit Mode, RETURN displays the next character, and ESCAPE exits the program. There are only three commands along with the arrow keys that can be used in Edit Mode: SPACE toggles a character pixel, RETURN exits Edit Mode and saves all changes to memory, ESCAPE exits Edit Mode and discards all changes, and the arrow keys move the pixel cursor up and down or left and right. As shown in Figure II.6.6, Edit Mode displays the new character data on line twenty-four that corresponds to the LORES character that is displayed on the right side of the LORES screen as changes to that LORES character are made. Pressing RETURN will copy the new character data to memory and pressing ESCAPE will discard the new character data. Once all changes have been made to the ROM data, pressing ESCAPE will exit the editor and the *EDITROM* program will request the name of a filename in order to save the 4 KB of ROM data that is currently in memory as shown in Figure II.6.7. If a filename is not entered when *EDITROM* begins or when *EDITROM* exits, no file is read or saved, respectively. The DOS DIFF command can be used to compare both the input and the output ROM files in order to ensure that the output ROM file contains the desired changes that *EDITROM* made to the input ROM file.

For those who are interested in understanding the correspondence with ROM data and the display of that data by the Apple][hardware, a few data samples will easily illustrate their relationship by using the HIRES graphics screen. On the Apple Command Line, enter HGR and then CALL-151. Assure that MIXEDON or 0xC053 is enabled, and enter the data samples 2000:1 and 2400:40 on separate Monitor Command Lines. Now, you will see that the least significant bit, or bit 0 of the first data sample is displayed to the far left of the screen and bit 6 of the second data sample is displayed six pixels to the right of the far left of the screen. Therefore, the Apple][hardware processes data starting from the LSB to the MSB and displays that data from left to right. The same hardware logic displays the character ROM data in the same fashion. Looking at Figure II.6.6, the first three data bytes for the edited character 4 on the right side of the LORES screen is 0x12. In this data, the LSB or bit 0 is OFF and the far left pixel is also OFF. The next bit, or bit 1 is ON, thus turning ON the top pixel of the left column of the character 4. The next two bits in the data while moving towards the MSB are OFF, thus keeping the next two pixels OFF while moving from left to right on the display. Since bit 4 is ON in the data, the top pixel of the right column of the character 4 is also ON. The fourth data byte, or 0x3E turns the first pixel OFF, or the far left pixel, and moving to the right in the display, turns the next five pixels ON. All of the ASCII characters from 0x20 to 0x7F are designed to keep their far left pixel OFF, thus keeping the LSB in their data set to zero, and utilize only the next five bits in their data for the display of the character. But, some of the icon characters that are shown in Figure II.6.2 actually utilize all seven bits in their data bytes. The MSB for a character in ROM data is never utilized in the display of that character.

7. Peripheral Interface Card Signature Bytes

More than likely Apple Computer, Inc., designed the concept of Signature Bytes when the Disk][was first introduced to the Apple][consumer. The first eight bytes of the firmware that resides in the Disk][Interface Card ROM, the card that connects the Disk][drive to the Apple][computer, are the Signature Bytes for this peripheral interface card. Other manufactures of peripheral interface cards adopted this scheme such that each slot card could be potentially identified by inspecting those first eight bytes. Other manufactures who designed peripheral interface cards for their disk drives used the same scheme that was perhaps developed by Apple Computer. Manufactures of real time clock cards also used a signature byte scheme that was developed by ThunderClock. Similarly, signature byte schemes were developed for Printer Interface Slot Cards, Serial Data Interface Slot Cards, Mouse Interface Slot Cards, and Display Interface Slot Cards just to list a few examples. Each signature byte scheme utilizes a general pattern of bytes that contains identical portions bytes and unique portions of bytes. Table II.7.1 lists the signature bytes for a number of peripheral interface cards that I happen to own or I happen to know about.

Peripheral Slot Card	Signature Bytes							
	0	1	2	3	4	5	6	7
Disk][	LDX	#$20	LDY	#$00	LDX	#$03	STX	$3C
	0xA2	0x20	0xA0	0x00	0xA2	0x03	0x86	0x3C
SCSI][	LDX	#$20	LDX	#$00	LDX	#$03	LDX	#$00
	0xA2	0x20	0xA2	0x00	0xA2	0x03	0xA2	0x00
RANA	LDX	#$20	LDY	#$00	LDX	#$03	LDX	#$3C
	0xA2	0x20	0xA0	0x00	0xA2	0x03	0xA2	0x3C
SIDER	LDA	#$20	LDA	#$00	LDA	#$03	LDA	$3C
	0xA9	0x20	0xA9	0x00	0xA9	0x03	0xA9	0x3C
RAM Disk	LDX	#$20	LDY	#$00	LDX	#$03	STY	$3C
	0xA2	0x20	0xA0	0x00	0xA2	0x03	0x84	0x3C
CFFA	LDA	#$20	LDX	#$00	LDA	#$03	LDA	#$00
	0xA9	0x20	0xA2	0x00	0xA9	0x03	0xA9	0x00
ThunderClock	PHP	SEI	PLP	BIT	$FF58		BVS	⇒$Cs0D
	0x08	0x78	0x28	0x2C	0x58	0xFF	0x70	0x05
TimeMaster II	PHP	SEI	PLP	BIT	$FF58		BVS	⇒$Cs0D
	0x08	0x78	0x28	0x2C	0x58	0xFF	0x70	0x05
My Clock	PHP	SEI	BIT	$CFFF		CLR	BCC	⇒$Cs38
	0x08	0x78	0x2C	0xFF	0xCF	0x18	0x90	0x30
SuperSerial	BIT	$FF58		BVS	⇒$Cs11	SEC	BCC	⇒$Cs20
	0x2C	0x58	0xFF	0x70	0x0C	0x38	0x90	0x18
Grappler	CLC	BCS	⇒$Cs3B	BCC	⇒$Cs11	SEC	BCC	⇒$Cs20
	0x18	0xB0	0x38	0x90	0x0C	0x38	0x90	0x18
Mouse	BIT	$FF58		BVS	⇒$Cs20	SEC	BCC	⇒$Cs20
	0x2C	0x58	0xFF	0x70	0x1B	0x38	0x90	0x18
80-Column	BIT	$CE43		BCS	⇒$C317	SEC	BCC	⇒$C320
	0x2C	0x43	0xCE	0x70	0x12	0x38	0x90	0x18

Table II.7.1. Original Slot Card Signature Bytes

All of the odd signature bytes for peripheral slot cards that interface disk drives **must** be the same. This is done purposefully because the Autostart ROM that Apple Computer copyrighted in 1978 checks those four odd bytes during a system powerup or during a restart. However, the Autostart routine was modified for the Apple //e Video Firmware that was copyrighted in 1981 and in 1984. The specific firmware note for this modification is shown in Figure II.7.1. In other words, only the first three odd signature bytes are checked by the Apple //e Autostart ROM for a bootable disk drive. After analyzing the disk startup firmware that follows those first eight bytes in the Disk][Interface Card, the firmware shows, that upon entry, the Y-register **must contain** zero, the X-register **may contain** any value from 0x00 to 0x16, and the A-register **may contain** any value. The page-zero location 0x3C is a temporary storage location so any value may be stored there, which is done in the fourth instruction, STX $3C. The first instruction, LDX

#$20, does nothing useful since the third and critical instruction rewrites the value that is contained in the X-register which is used for and necessary in order to generate the RDNIBLBT table.

```
Check 3 ID bytes instead of 4.  Allows devices other
than Disk II's to be bootable.
```

Figure II.7.1. Video Firmware Note for the Apple //e

Peripheral Slot Card	Signature Bytes							
	0	1	2	3	4	5	6	7
Disk][	LDX	#$20	LDY	#$00	LDX	#$03	STX	$3C
(no change)	0xA2	0x20	0xA0	0x00	0xA2	0x03	0x86	0x3C
SCSI][	LDX	#$20	LDX	#$00	LDX	#$03	LDX	#$00
(no change)	0xA2	0x20	0xA2	0x00	0xA2	0x03	0xA2	0x00
RANA	ORA	#$20	LDY	#$00	LDX	#$03	STX	$3C
	0x09	0x20	0xA0	0x00	0xA2	0x03	0x86	0x3C
SIDER	AND	#$20	LDY	#$00	LDX	#$03	STX	$3C
	0x29	0x20	0xA0	0x00	0xA2	0x03	0x86	0x3C
RAM Disk	EOR	#$20	LDY	#$00	LDX	#$03	STX	$3C
	0x49	0x20	0xA0	0x00	0xA2	0x03	0x86	0x3C
CFFA	ADC	#$20	LDY	#$00	LDX	#$03	STX	$3C
	0x69	0x20	0xA0	0x00	0xA2	0x03	0x86	0x3C
available	LDY	#$20	LDY	#$00	LDX	#$03	STX	$3C
	0xA0	0x20	0xA0	0x00	0xA2	0x03	0x86	0x3C
available	LDA	#$20	LDY	#$00	LDX	#$03	STX	$3C
	0xA9	0x20	0xA0	0x00	0xA2	0x03	0x86	0x3C
available	CPY	#$20	LDY	#$00	LDX	#$03	STX	$3C
	0xC0	0x20	0xA0	0x00	0xA2	0x03	0x86	0x3C
available	CMP	#$20	LDY	#$00	LDX	#$03	STX	$3C
	0xC9	0x20	0xA0	0x00	0xA2	0x03	0x86	0x3C
available	CPX	#$20	LDY	#$00	LDX	#$03	STX	$3C
	0xE0	0x20	0xA0	0x00	0xA2	0x03	0x86	0x3C
available	SBC	#$20	LDY	#$00	LDX	#$03	STX	$3C
	0xE9	0x20	0xA0	0x00	0xA2	0x03	0x86	0x3C

Table II.7.2. Revised Disk Drive Peripheral Interface Card Signature Bytes

Applied Engineering used the same signature bytes for their TimeMaster II clock card as those signature bytes that are found in the ThunderClock card. Only the first two bytes are significant as well as the last byte, or classification byte in its first firmware page in order to detect the presence of a valid clock card. This last byte, or CLKID in the ThunderClock first firmware page is 0x07 and the last byte in the TimeMaster II first firmware page is 0x03. I also set the last byte in the first page of my clock card firmware to 0x03, thus my clock card appears identical to the TimeMaster II. It is these three bytes, the first two and the last byte in the first page of clock firmware that DOS 4.5 checks for a valid clock card. In many cases a peripheral interface card not only must be compatible with DOS, but possibly it must also be compatible with ProDOS, CP/M, Fortran, and Pascal as well. The peripheral-card ROM memory and the peripheral-card expansion ROM memory only provides nine pages of code space. Therefore, even the signature bytes may also perform a necessary computational function besides being unique to the particular peripheral interface card. In some cases, the signature bytes provide multiple return entry points for input and output data control. If the peripheral interface card supports Pascal, the offsets for the Pascal initialization, read, write, and status routines closely follow the initial signature bytes.

Since the operation of the first signature byte instruction is not utilized in the Disk][Interface Card for a data or for a logic operation, any of the other ten 6502 Immediate Addressing Mode instructions may be utilized as a product identifier within the Disk][signature byte scheme. Once I realized which were the critical and which were the non-critical bytes within the signature byte data, I could design a very simple strategy to quickly identify a Disk][product device. This strategy checks the first three odd bytes like the Autostart ROM does in the Apple //e, and then it extracts the very first instruction byte in order to select the actual product or device type. Table II.7.2 lists the revised signature bytes for my collection of Disk][, Disk][-like, and disk drive peripheral devices. I can use this strategy to easily identify a Disk][, a RANA, a SIDER, a RAM Disk, or a CFFA device and modify which routine or handler, if necessary, must be utilized in order to read data from or write data to that particular peripheral device. I seriously doubt that the six available choices that are shown in Table II.7.2 will ever be exhausted if a new Disk][-like device or devices should ever be developed any time in the near future.

8. The Apple //e ROM Monitor

I have no doubt that Steven Wozniak packaged his original Apple][with a ROM that is enabled for the top eight pages of memory, or 2048 bytes, which includes a collection of low-level software routines. The architecture of the 6502-microprocessor, and later the 65C02-microprocessor, addresses three vectors at the very top of its 16-bit address capability. These vectors include the non-maskable interrupt vector, or NMI vector at 0xFFFA:0xFFFB, the RESET vector at 0xFFFC:0xFFFD, and the maskable interrupt vector, or IRQ/BRK vector at 0xFFFE:0xFFFF. A non-maskable interrupt cannot be disabled or ignored using either processor instructions or software masks. On the other hand, a maskable interrupt can be disabled or ignored and then re-enabled, and the 6502 or the 65C02 instruction set contains the SEI instruction to disable a maskable interrupt and the CLI instruction to enable a maskable interrupt. The EPROM Reader, for example, depends on the address that is at the RESET vector location in order to execute the first instruction of *EOS+*. Actually, all three vector addresses point to that first instruction of *EOS+*. Throughout this book I have referred to these top eight pages of Wozniak's first ROM as the ROM Monitor. Indeed, this ROM Monitor contains some of the most universal routines that are utilized by every single software program ever written for the Apple][computer whether the author or authors of those programs realize it or not.

In Section II.5 I discuss the migration, removal, and insertion of various routines and tables of data that transform the stock Apple //e ROM and CX ROM memory space into a more powerful Apple //e ROM. Many parts of the ROM Monitor are included in this transformation. This ROM transformation includes the removal of all of the routines that depend on the READ and the WRITE routines that read data from and write data to a cassette tape recorder. I cannot overstate the importance of the ROM Monitor for DOS 4.5 and for assemblers such as *Big Mac* and *Lisa*. But I could not comprehend why Apple Computer retained the physical cassette data ports in the Apple //e; they are removed in the Apple][GS. I have benefitted far too much from having the STEP and TRACE commands as well as the Mini-Assembler command available for my immediate use in the ROM Monitor. And, I have had no equivalent use or need for the ROM Monitor READ and the WRITE commands. Essentially, I have justified the transformation of the Apple //e ROM, CX ROM, and ROM Monitor memory space for all of the functionality that I have most benefitted from in my Apple //e since doing so is my prerogative and it is within my expertise and my capabilities. Table II.5.1 contains a summary of all of the areas of ROM memory that became available once I completed this ROM transformation. I do recall previously writing in the DOS 4.1 Manual that "I have no doubt that I will innovate a terrific use for this ROM memory in the next development cycle." Unfortunately, I have yet to create a terrific new Applesoft command or commands that utilize this valuable ROM memory in order to implement a new functionality. However, I have recently stumbled across an extraordinary use for the cassette tape recorder Applesoft LOAD command.

There are two webpages, http://asciiexpress.net/diskserver/ and http://asciiexpress.net/gameserver/, that provide high frequency data waveforms for 1574 140 KB disk images and 249 games, respectively, for the Apple][. These disk images and games are transferred to an Apple][, an Apple][+, or to an Apple //e by means of the cassette data input port. The software tool that creates the high frequency data waveforms for these disk images and these games is called *c2t*. The source code for *c2t*, the research, history, and the technical specification for *c2t* can be downloaded from https://github.com/datajerk/c2t. In no uncertain terms, *c2t* is a remarkable game changer and this tool truly provides a unique and a reliable method for transferring a diskette image or a data file into an Apple][computer. The initial format of the input data waveform conforms to the specification that is used by Steven Wozniak's READ command for HEADER, SYNC, and DATA in order to load the Insta-Disk software that was developed by Egan Ford. The Insta-Disk software reads the remaining data waveform using another specification for HEADER, SYNC, and DATA. Instead of using Wozniak's specification that reads data at 1333 bps, Insta-Disk uses Ford's specification that reads data at 8000 bps in order to transfer complete disk images and games with remarkable speed. I cannot think of a better reason to re-install the Applesoft LOAD command and reactivate the ROM Monitor READ command in order to utilize the amazing data resources that are found in the above two webpages. The ROM Monitor WRITE command and all Applesoft commands that depend on the WRITE command are still useless in my opinion. The only rational method to transfer disk images and/or software products is to use *c2t* since its source code is freely available for download.

The ROM Monitor is a collection of low-level software routines as previously stated above. The ROM Monitor provides the ability to perform simple addition and subtraction of hexadecimal numbers; it can display the contents of the 6502 or 65C02 microprocessor registers; it can display the mnemonics, addressing modes, and the memory addresses and data for program instructions; it can process ctrl-B, ctrl-C, ctrl-E, ctrl-K, ctrl-P, and ctrl-Y inputs; it can easily set NORMAL or INVERSE display modes; it can display the contents of memory, move the contents of memory, verify the contents of memory, fill the contents of memory, and search the contents of memory for ASCII data and for numerical values; it can process an assembly language routine one instruction at a time or provide a complete trace of a routine; and the ROM Monitor can create executable code from any 6502/65C02 mnemonic with its data or address. Is it possible to include the READ command at its traditional ROM Monitor memory location of 0xFEFD without sacrificing **any** of the current capabilities of the presently transformed ROM Monitor?

Address	Value	Formula	Description
0xFFCC	0xBC	byt $89+$B0^$83	ctrl-C, jmp to 0xE003 or BASIC2
0xFFCD	0xB2	byt $89+$B0^$99	ctrl-Y, jmp to 0x3F8 or ctrl-Y handler (AUXMOVE)
0xFFCE	0xBE	byt $89+$B0^$85	ctrl-E, display registers
0xFFCF	0xED	byt $89+$B0^"T"	T, trace program execution
0xFFD0	0xEF	byt $89+$B0^"V"	V, verify memory
0xFFD1	0xC4	byt $89+$B0^$8B	ctrl-K, set input device slot
0xFFD2	0xEC	byt $89+$B0^"S"	S, step program execution
0xFFD3	0xA9	byt $89+$B0^$90	ctrl-P, set output device slot
0xFFD4	0xBB	byt $89+$B0^$82	ctrl-B, jmp to 0xE000 or BASIC
0xFFD5	0xA6	byt $89+$B0^"–"	-, math operator
0xFFD6	0xA4	byt $89+$B0^"+"	+, math operator
0xFFD7	0x06	byt $89+$B0^"M"	M, move contents of memory to another location
0xFFD8	0x95	byt $89+$B0^"<"	<, move direction
0xFFD9	0x07	byt $89+$B0^"N"	N, set normal display mode
0xFFDA	0x02	byt $89+$B0^"I"	I, set inverse display mode
0xFFDB	0x05	byt $89+$B0^"L"	L, list contents of memory
0xFFDC	0x9A	byt $89+$B0^"!"	!, enter Mini-Assembler
0xFFDD	0x00	byt $89+$B0^"G"	G, jmp to memory address
0xFFDE	0xF3	byt $89+$B0^"Z"	Z, fill contents of memory with value
0xFFDF	0x93	byt $89+$B0^":"	:, input instruction mode
0xFFE0	0xA7	byt $89+$B0^"."	., memory address delimiter
0xFFE1	0xC6	byt $89+$B0^$8D	CR, carriage return, the signal to process a command
0xFFE2	0x99	byt $89+$B0^" "	space, input instruction mode

Table II.8.1. ROM Monitor Command Table

Table II.8.1 summarizes the twenty-three commands that can be processed by the presently transformed ROM Monitor. The ROM Monitor command table is found at 0xFFCC:0xFFE2 and its companion LSB address table is found at 0xFFE3:0xFFF9 as shown in Table II.8.2. All entry addresses of the processing code for these ROM Monitor commands **must** reside on page 0xFE such that when 0xFE and the LSB-1 address for a command are pushed onto the stack and then popped from the stack using the RTS instruction by the routines TOSUB and ZMODE, the processing code for that command will be executed. The entry address for the routines IORTS, GETNUM, and ZMODE are fixed at 0xFF58, 0xFFA7, and 0xFFC7, respectively, and these address locations are all critical to the program *Sourceror*, for example. There is no wiggle room to add any additional commands to the ROM Monitor command table. Most people simply modify the values that exist in these two tables in order to have their desired commands as I have explicitly done. When the Apple //e ROM Monitor was developed, however, Apple Computer modified the NXTCHR routine in order to expand the ROM Monitor command table by using expensive Compare and Branch instructions for its new ASCII data and hexadecimal value SEARCH command. The SEARCH command, however, is not privy to having the Y-register set to zero by ZMODE as are the regular ROM Monitor commands. The command ZAPMEM depends on this particular feature of ZMODE so this command **must** reside in the ROM Monitor command table whereas the SEARCH command does not. Therefore, the Compare and Branch structure that Apple implemented for the SEARCH command would be the preferred way to reintroduce the READ command into the ROM Monitor. Table II.8.3 lists all of the commands that I have implemented by using the Compare and Branch structure extension that was introduced by Apple.

Address	Value	Routine	Usage Description
0xFFE3	0xB2	byt BASCONT-1	ctrl-C <cr>
0xFFE4	0xC9	byt USR-1	ctrl-Y <cr>
0xFFE5	0xBE	byt REGZ-1	ctrl-E <cr>
0xFFE6	0xC1	byt TRACE-1	T <cr>
0xFFE7	0x35	byt VFY-1	$dst<$strt.$end V <cr>
0xFFE8	0x8C	byt INPRT-1	#slot ctrl-K <cr>
0xFFE9	0xC3	byt STEPZ-1	S <cr>
0xFFEA	0x96	byt OUTPRT-1	#slot ctrl-P <cr>
0xFFEB	0xAF	byt XBASIC-1	ctrl-B <cr>
0xFFEC	0x17	byt SETMODE-1	$val-$val <cr>
0xFFED	0x17	byt SETMODE-1	$val+$val <cr>
0xFFEE	0x2B	byt MOVE-1	$dst<$strt.$end M <cr>
0xFFEF	0x1F	byt LT-1	$dst<$strt
0xFFF0	0x83	byt SETNORM-1	N <cr>
0xFFF1	0x7F	byt SETINV-1	I <cr>
0xFFF2	0x5D	byt LIST-1	$adr L <cr>
0xFFF3	0xF0	byt MINIASM-1	! <cr>
0xFFF4	0xB5	byt GO-1	$adr G <cr>
0xFFF5	0xAD	byt ZAPMEM-1	$val<$strt.$end Z <cr>
0xFFF6	0x17	byt SETMODE-1	$adr:$val <cr>
0xFFF7	0x17	byt SETMODE-1	$strt.$end
0xFFF8	0xF5	byt CRMON-1	<cr>
0xFFF9	0x03	byt BLANK	<space>

Table II.8.2. ROM Monitor LSB Address Table

Address	Value	Formula	Routine	Usage Description
0xFF5F	0x9B	byt $89+$B0^"""	LOOKASC1	" <cr>, QUOTE SEARCH
0xFF0F	0xEB	byt $89+$B0^"R"	READ	$strt.$end R <cr>, READ
0xFF13	0xA0	byt $89+$B0^' "	LOOKASC1	' <cr>, APOSTROPHE SEARCH
0xFECE	0xF1	byt $89+$B0^"X"	SEARCH	$val<$strt.$end X <cr>

Table II.8.3. ROM Monitor Additional Commands Table

Apple Computer tied the APOSTROPHE command to their SEARCH routine in order to search for and to find one or two ASCII characters whose most significant bit is turned OFF. As in the SEARCH for any $val, when memory is searched for two lower ASCII bytes that are specified by $val, the second lower ASCII byte is always found first. In other words, when memory is searched for a sixteen-bit value, the second byte in memory must precede the first byte as specified in $val. Why Apple limited its new SEARCH command to sixteen-bit values and to only lower ASCII bytes is worrisome and also very short-sighted. In response to this poorly thought-out design, I added the QUOTE command to the SEARCH routine in order to complete what Apple should have done initially. The APOSTROPHE command may be combined with the QUOTE command in order to search for any pair of ASCII bytes. Furthermore, I have utilized the ROM

Monitor S command for STEP and not for SEARCH, so instead, I use the ROM Monitor X command for SEARCH as shown in Table II.8.3. And, after relocating the character string TITLE or Apple //e+ from 0xFF05 to 0xF7D9 and ZAPMEM from 0xFECD to 0xFF05, seven bytes for the READ command fit comfortably at 0xFEFD, the original starting location for READ in the Apple][and in the Apple][+! This was all made possible by using the two unused bytes at 0xFEAE:0xFEAF in order to branch to the relocated ZAPMEM command which no longer resides in the 0xFE page. The character string TITLE now occupies ten bytes of the available fourteen bytes where I removed the GETARYPT routine.

Apple moved the original READ and WRITE routines that reside at 0xFEFD and 0xFECD, respectively, in the Apple][and in the Apple][+ ROM Monitors to the 0xC5 ROM in the Apple //e. That ROM space is now utilized by the fabulous Mini-Assembler. In order to process any of the high frequency data waveforms at the *diskserver* or the *gameserver* web pages, the Applesoft LOAD command along with the ROM Monitor READ command must both be made available to the user. It is elementary to re-install the Applesoft LOAD routine at its original address 0xD8C9 and the two routines the LOAD routine depends on at 0xD8F0 and 0xD903. Again, the GETARYPT code space is now used by TITLE. Both LOAD and READ depend on the READ routine which is 0x34 bytes in size and the READ routine depends on the RDBYTE routine which is 0x0E bytes in size and the RD2BIT routine which is 0x12 bytes in size. Using Table II.5.1 as a guide for memory location availability, the READ routine can be placed at 0xF39F where the Applesoft STORE and RECALL routines were removed, leaving 5 spare bytes. The RDBYTE routine can be placed at 0xF775 where the Applesoft SHLOAD routine was removed, leaving four spare bytes. Finally, the RD2BIT routine can be placed at 0xD8B7 where the Applesoft SAVE routine was removed, leaving seven spare bytes. All of these software additions as well as the new placement for TITLE are shown in Table II.8.4 which also shows the remaining free space at each memory location.

Start	End	Length	Applesoft Commands
0xD8B0	0xD8B6	0x07	free space
0xD8B7	0xD8C8	0x12	RD2BIT
0xD8C9	0xD8EF	0x27	Applesoft LOAD command
0xD8F0	0xD911	0x22	LOAD command pointer routines
0xF39F	0xF3D2	0x34	READ
0xF3D3	0xF3D7	0x05	free space
0xF775	0xF782	0x0E	RDBYTE
0xF783	0xF786	0x04	free space
0xF7D5	0xF7D8	0x04	free space
0xF7D9	0xF7E2	0x0A	TITLE
0xF7E3	0xF7E6	0x04	free space

Table II.8.4. Routines That Support Applesoft LOAD Command

The assembly of the Apple //e ROM source code includes the CX ROM, the ROM Applesoft, and the ROM Monitor software routines. This particular ROM project is titled ROM2E.SW16GCR.8 for this project includes the *SWEET16* interpreter, the Garbage Collector that is based on Cornelis Bongers' specification, the ROM Applesoft LOAD command, and the ROM Monitor READ command. This project is my eighth unique ROM build to date. The BLDROM tool that I developed creates a set of ROM files from the four output object files C0ROM, D0ROM, E0ROM, and F0ROM. These files are each 4096 bytes in size. The SW16GCR.CF.ROM image contains all four output object files so it is 16384 bytes in size. The SW16GCR.CD.ROM file contains the C0ROM and D0ROM output object files and the SW16GCR.EF.ROM file contains the E0ROM and F0ROM output object files. Both of these ROM images are 8192 bytes in size. The early Apple //e computers utilize two 8192-byte ROMs and the Enhanced and Platinum Apple //e computers utilize a single 16384-byte ROM. When I assemble my ROM source code, the very first page in the C0ROM output object file is set to zero. The SW16GCR.CF.ROM or the SW16GCR.CD.ROM is never enabled when any address in the 0xC000:0xC0FF range is placed on the address bus in any Apple //e by design. Having these ROM images on a physical diskette allows me to use the PROmGRAMER to easily write the SW16GCR.CF.ROM image to a 74128 EPROM. The PROmGRAMER can be used to write both the SW16GCR.CD.ROM and the SW16GCR.EF.ROM images to individual 7464 EPROMs. Building the APPLE2E.SW16GCR.8 ROM image from the four output object files C0ROM, D0ROM, E0ROM, and F0ROM for Virtual][is far more difficult, but easily handled in the XQuartz environment in a MacBook Pro. The challenge involved is to transfer the relevant files from the image of a Disk][diskette that is created by Virtual][into the UNIX file system of the MacBook Pro.

```
cat d0rom e0rom f0rom > romA
cat c0rom romA > SW16GCR.8.ROM
cat zeropage zeropage zeropage page3 > rom0
cat zeropage zeropage page6 zeropage > rom1
cat zeropage zeropage zeropage zeropage > rom2
cat zeropage zeropage zeropage zeropage > rom3
cat rom0 rom1 rom2 rom3 > romC0
cat romC0 romA SW16GCR.8.ROM > APPLE2E.SW16GCR.8.ROM
rm rom0 rom1 rom2 rom3 romA romC0
```

Figure II.8.1. Command File buildRom for Virtual][

It is certainly beyond the scope of this book to include and to describe all of the C language routines and programs that I have created in the XQuartz environment over the past few years that support and process Apple][DOS 4.5 volumes and files. Suffice it to say that a 35-track ~.dsk file is a simple binary file that is exactly 143360 bytes in size. This binary file begins with a 256-byte page of data for track 0x00, sector 0x00, and this binary file ends with a 256-byte page of data for track 0x22, sector 0x0F. Data headers, for example, are **not** utilized that might preface each of the 256-byte pages of data in order to label the data page with track and sector numbers. I found that it was most efficient to read a ~.dsk file into a three-dimensional array which I defined as UCHAR Disk[48][32][SECTOR_SIZE] and determine the Track and Sector index values based entirely on the size of the ~.dsk file using a call to stat() before the call to open(). When a ~.dsk file is exactly 143360 bytes in size after stat() is called, this file will consist of thirty-five tracks and each track will have exactly sixteen sectors. When a ~.dsk file is exactly 393216 bytes in size after stat() is called, this file will consist of forty-eight tracks and each track will have exactly thirty-two sectors. The global variable DiskSizes[6][3] contains the definition for six possible track and sector configurations that are simply based on a ~.dsk file size after stat() is called. Of course, there are other quite valid algorithms to choose from. My C language programs can extract Apple][program files from and insert Apple][program files onto any DOS 4.5 ~.dsk volume. This is possible by knowing the structural content of an Apple][program file that is based on filetype and the physical structure of the DOS 4.5 VTOC and its Catalog sectors. Once I extract all of the Apple][files from a volume such as ROM2E.SW16GCR.8.Image, I can easily create a ROM firmware file for Virtual][, like APPLE2E.SW16GCR.8.ROM. I prefer to utilize the UNIX tcsh C shell environment for processing my UNIX command files. The contents of the buildRom UNIX command file is shown in Figure II.8.1. The 256-byte files page3, page6, and zeropage also reside on the diskette that is named ROM2E.SW16GCR.8.Image. The file page3 is a direct copy of the Apple //e video firmware code at 0xC300:0xC3FF. The file page6 is a direct copy of the Disk][firmware code at 0xC600:0xC6FF. The file zeropage is simply a page of 256 bytes that are set to zero. Once buildRom has created the APPLE2E.SW16GCR.8.ROM file, this file can be copied to the Virtual][ROM directory that is found at

Users/<username>/Library/Application Support/Virtual][/ROM

All of my Apple //e related C language routines and programs may be downloaded from my website www.applecored.net as a TAR file which is called appleXcode.tar. After one establishes the UNIX tcsh C shell environment, copy the appleXcode.tar TAR file into a convenient directory, extract all of the contents in this file using the UNIX command tar xvf appleXcode.tar, and run the .config file in order to initialize specific global variables in your user environment and to utilize your C language compiler and linker. The C language compiler is utilized in the makefile that is found in the source directory and the C language linker is utilized in the makefile that is found in the binary directory. All of the Apple //e ROM images that I have developed over the years are found in the 2eRom directory. Several example ~.dsk files that are images of empty data disks are found in the dsk directory. These data disk files are created using Option #4 in the menu command file. I wrote menu in such a way so that I could establish an appleXcode directory on virtually every UNIX platform with which I am familiar. Very few if any modifications to the include files or to the makefiles are needed in order to recompile and relink all of the C language programs and utilities that are found in the appleXcode directory. I have generally observed that every software engineer has his or her preferred version for a C language makefile. I am sure that my preferred makefile version is unique, though rather straightforward and useable across many diverse computer platforms. There is certainly enough to contend with when establishing a UNIX directory in order to build C language products without having to fine-tune various include files and makefiles. There have been too many occasions when I have been left pondering whether the operation of a makefile is more art-craft or witch-craft. Hopefully, my makefiles are fairly easy to assimilate and they can certainly be easily modified in order to suit your particular preferences.

9. The Applesoft LOAD Command

The Apple][computer as designed by Steven Wozniak is centered around a common clock for microprocessor timing, RAM refresh timing, and video display timing. The two clock signals that Wozniak designed for the 6502 microprocessor in his computer are $\phi1$ and $\phi2$, and these two clock signals are complements of each other. Wozniak derived the basic timing for his computer with these two clock signals by dividing the crystal oscillator frequency that is running at 14.31818 MHz by fourteen. The COLOR REF signal that is used in a video display is simply this crystal oscillator frequency divided by four, or 3.579545 MHz. The horizontal video frequency that is also used in a video display is set to 15.734 KHz. When the crystal oscillator frequency is divided by this horizontal video frequency, or 14.31818

MHz ÷ 15.734 KHz = 910, the crystal oscillator makes 910 counts for each horizontal video line. Each of the eight horizontal video lines that comprise one ASCII character consists of seven pixels which are displayed within fourteen counts of the crystal oscillator. Thus, each horizontal video line has time to display a portion of the sixty-five ASCII characters, or 910 ÷ 14 = 65, though only forty ASCII characters are visible and the other twenty-five invisible characters are spent during horizontal blanking. The number of COLOR REF cycles that are used in order to display one horizontal line of video is 227.5 cycles, or 3.579545 MHz ÷ 15.734 KHz = 227.5, which is not a very convenient number for this very important ratio. If this horizontal video frequency is utilized in an Apple][computer, this frequency will cause COLOR REF to change phase for every horizontal line of video that is displayed. Wozniak compensated for this unusable frequency ratio by extending each horizontal line by one-half period of COLOR REF or two full periods of the crystal oscillator frequency. This ingenious solution is included among Wozniak's other critical solutions in US Patent #4136359. Extending each horizontal video line to 228 cycles produces a horizontal video frequency that is 3.579545 MHz ÷ 228 = 15.7 KHz which is close enough for most video displays to produce reasonably good looking color video. For the first sixty-four cycles of each horizontal video line, the period for each of these cycles is 14 ÷ 14.31818 MHz = 978 nanoseconds. The sixty-fifth cycle is extended by two clock cycles of the crystal oscillator, so its period is 16 ÷ 14.31818 MHz = 1117 nanoseconds. Therefore, the *average* microprocessor speed in the Apple][computer is

$$\frac{65 * 14.31818 \text{ MHz}}{(64 * 14) + 16} = 1.020484 \text{ MHz}$$

Data that is recorded onto a cassette tape or data that is delivered by means of a high frequency data waveform is formatted into individual records. Each record consists of about 10.4 seconds of a HEADER tone which is followed by a SYNC bit, a prescribed number of data bytes which may include a RUNFLAG byte and a CHKSUM byte. The ROM Monitor WRITE routine creates a single audio record for the number of data bytes that are specified with the WRITE command. The ROM Monitor READ routine reads a single audio record and saves the prescribed number of data bytes into memory that is specified with the READ command. The Applesoft SAVE routine creates two sequential audio records and the Applesoft LOAD routine reads two sequential audio records. The first audio record of three data bytes consists of the length of the Applesoft program in LSB/MSB byte order and saved to LINNUM at the page-zero locations 0x50:0x51 and the RUNFLAG byte is saved to the page-zero location 0xD6. These three data bytes are followed by a CHKSUM byte. The second audio record contains the data of the Applesoft program that is saved to PRGTAB or 0x0801 as shown in Figure I.15.1. These data bytes are also followed by a CHKSUM byte. The RUNFLAG byte from the first audio record is always set to 0x55 by the Applesoft SAVE routine. However, if the MSB of the RUNFLAG byte happens to be set ON, the Applesoft program that is transmitted in the second audio record is automatically set to RUN by Applesoft. This awesome feature that Wozniak included in the Applesoft LOAD command is exploited by Insta-Disk and it certainly makes the streaming of a high frequency data waveform appear to be seamless. Wozniak was quite precise in determining the various frequencies that his HEADER routine was capable of generating. He was obviously quite mindful of the *average* 6502 microprocessor speed that is utilized in the Apple][computer.

The ROM Monitor WRITE routine calls the HEADR routine with the A-register containing 0x40. That value in the A-register causes the HEADR routine to generate about 10.4 seconds of a square wave whose half cycles are approximately 650 microseconds. A tone that has a period of 1300 microseconds has a frequency of approximately 770 Hz, or 1 ÷ 1300 microseconds ≈ 770 Hz. When all of the HEADR byte counters become exhausted, HEADR generates a SYNC bit which consists of a half cycle that is 200 microseconds, or a frequency of 2500 Hz, and a half cycle that is 250 microseconds, or a frequency of 2000 Hz. The transmission of the prescribed data begins immediately and each byte is shifted such that the most significant bit is transmitted first and the least significant bit is transmitted last. Loop counters are adjusted in order to accommodate all housekeeping chores such that the frequencies that are used to transmit a zero bit or a one bit are always preserved. A zero bit is transmitted using a frequency of 2000 Hz and a one bit is transmitted using a frequency of 1000 Hz. All data is exclusively OR'd with each preceding byte that begins with an initial value of 0xFF in order to create a CHKSUM byte. After all data has been transmitted, the CHKSUM byte is transmitted last and there is no further data transmission. Therefore, the average cassette data frequency or rate of transmission for random cassette data that has an equal number of zero bits and one bits is given by

$$
\frac{2}{1/1000 + 1/2000} = 1333 \text{ Hz}
$$

The ROM Monitor READ routine calls the HEADR routine with the A-register containing 0x16. That value in the A-register causes the HEADR routine to generate about 3.54 seconds of a square wave whose half cycles are approximately 650 microseconds. There is **no** utility for this call to HEADR except to allow 3.54 seconds of HEADER to pass before the READ routine begins in earnest to detect the SYNC bit. Once the SYNC bit is detected, READ begins to read zero bits and one bits that comprise a byte value. Each byte value is exclusively OR'd with the preceding byte value beginning with an initial value of 0xFF in order to create a CHKSUM byte. When the data length counter becomes exhausted, READ reads the transmitted CHKSUM byte and compares that value with its own internal value. In order to install all of the routines that support the Applesoft LOAD command as shown in Table II.8.4, there is simply not enough ROM space for the 35-byte HEADR routine. In place of the seven bytes that are used in the READ routine to initialize the A-register with 0x16, or the call to HEADR and the initialization of CHKSUM, READ now uses five additional bytes in order to initialize CHKSUM with 0xFF and to setup a simple loop counter in order to call the ROM Monitor WAIT routine at 0xFCA8 eighteen times. The original size of READ is 0x2F bytes. Now, with five additional bytes, READ is 0x34 bytes in size as shown in Figure II.8.4. This simple loop counter completes in 3,011,562 microprocessor cycles or 3011562 ÷ 1020484 = 2.95 seconds. The ROM Monitor WAIT routine always returns with the A-register set to zero, so WAIT can be called successively knowing that the routine will provide the longest delay possible for that call. The Delay in microprocessor cycles by the ROM Monitor WAIT routine is given by

$$
\text{Delay} = 2.5 * A * A + 13.5 * A + 13 \text{ cycles}
$$

$$
A = (\text{Delay} \div 2.5 + 2.09)^{0.5} - 2.7
$$

The second equation above is only valid when Delay is less than or equal to 167309, when WAIT is called having a value of zero in the A-register which is equivalent to 256. For example, to create a delay of exactly eight seconds, a loop counter having forty-nine counts that begins with the A-register initialized to 0xE4 will accomplish that desired delay.

Wozniak chose to detect a change in the cassette data waveform whether that change is from positive to negative or from negative to positive by using the EOR microprocessor instruction in the RD2BIT routine. The cassette data input port signal is AC coupled using a 0.1 μF capacitor and the signal is attenuated to half its amplitude using two 12 KΩ resistors before the filtered signal enters the inverting input of a general purpose 741 operational amplifier. This operational amplifier is wired to behave as a voltage comparator that has an average comparator threshold of 0 volts and about 100 mV of hysteresis for the non-inverting input to the comparator. The non-inverting input hysteresis accounts for the time it takes this comparator to react to a change in input voltage. This circuit is typically called a zero crossing detector where the minimum input voltage is about 1 volt peak-to-peak in order to produce acceptable results and to clearly detect a change in voltage. The current that is generated by this comparator is limited by a 12 KΩ resistor before the output signal enters the S0 input of a 74LS251 8-input multiplexer integrated circuit. This IC is enabled when 0xC06n is put onto the address bus by the 6502 or 65C02 microprocessor. Reading the value of TAPEIN at 0xC060 and examining its most significant bit provides all of the necessary information about the input data waveform and whether the waveform is changing from positive to negative or from negative to positive at that moment in time. All Wozniak cared about was whether the data waveform changed polarities and **not** whether the waveform was indeed positive or negative at that given moment. This is not the case for the Insta-Disk routines which are loaded into Apple][memory from a high frequency data waveform that is created by the *c2t* software routines. Insta-Disk routines look for specific polarities of the input data waveform.

Some of the Insta-Disk routines also count register loops as in Wozniak's READ routine in order to detect zero bits and one bits while the routines look for specific voltage transitions in the input data waveform. And some of the Insta-Disk routines utilize self-modifying code for the memory address of the data byte whose bits are shifted in response to the specific value that is found in the Y-register because the current bit value is determined by a register compare instruction. After loading an Insta-Disk routine using Wozniak's ROM Monitor READ routine, Insta-Disk loops forever as long as it reads a *positive* value from TAPEIN. As soon as Insta-Disk detects a *negative* value from TAPEIN, Insta-Disk has detected the first half-cycle of a SYNC bit or of a preamble bit. As soon as Insta-Disk detects a *positive* value from TAPEIN, it has detected the second half-cycle of the SYNC bit, a preamble bit, or every single data bit that will forever be read until the routine terminates. After the SYNC bit is found, the read routine has detected the beginning of the data in the input data waveform, and the read routine will loop forever as long as it reads a *negative* value from TAPEIN. For all intents and purposes, it does not matter how long TAPEIN remains negative, though there are practical considerations that are employed by Insta-Disk. While TAPEIN remains *positive*, the Y-register is incremented creating a register loop that is nine cycles in size. Upon receipt of a *negative* value from TAPEIN, the value that resides in the Y-register corresponds to the frequency of a half-cycle of the input data waveform at that moment in time.

The Insta-Disk routine terminates if the Y-register is equal to or greater than 0x40 and Insta-Disk computes a checksum for the data that has already been read and the routine verifies that it has received all of the data that was requested. Having this termination value in the Y-register, the frequency for this half-cycle would be 886 Hz or less, or 1020484 ÷ (9 * 64 * 2) = 885.8 Hz. According to the *c2t* documentation, a programmed loop value of 0x49 would be consistent with an approximate frequency of 770 Hz in order to designate the End of Data. If the Y-register is less than 0x40 but equal to or greater than 0x15, the Insta-Disk preamble is still being transmitted and the routine branches to the beginning of the read routine where it waits for the input waveform to become *positive* again. The Insta-Disk preamble is transmitted at 2000 Hz according to the *c2t* documentation. At this point in the Insta-Disk logic, the input waveform contains either a one bit or a zero bit. If the Y-register is less than 0x15 but equal to or greater than 0x07, this register compare will **set** the C-flag. Otherwise, this compare instruction will **clear** the C-flag when the contents of the Y-register is less than 0x07. The ROL instruction that is indexed by the X-register is used to incorporate the value of the C-flag into the data value that is at the currently indexed memory address. The A-register is initialized with 0x01, thus the bit counter for a data byte utilizes the A-register when it is shifted left eight times until the C-flag becomes **set** from that initial value.

The X-register serves as the page index and it is incremented once a data byte is saved to memory. When a page of data has been saved, the page memory address is incremented. All of these tasks comprise the housekeeping chores that are performed while the input waveform is still *negative*. A one bit is transmitted at 6000 Hz and a zero bit is transmitted at 12000 Hz according to *c2t* documentation.

I studied the code for the DISKLOAD8000 routine which I just described above and the code for the DISKLOAD9600 routine. DISKLOAD8000 has an average data throughput of 8000 bps assuming there is a random mixture of data. DISKLOAD9600 uses 8000 Hz to transmit a one bit and 12000 Hz to transmit a zero bit. Its average data throughput is 9600 bps for random data. I found good ideas in both routines but I still prefer to use an indirect indexed addressing store instruction that uses the Y-register rather than a modified absolute addressing store instruction that uses the X-register. Storing values with an indirect indexed addressing instruction that uses the Y-register requires six cycles rather than five cycles when using an absolute addressing instruction that uses the X-register. However, incrementing a page-zero address for an indirect indexed instruction requires only three cycles rather than four cycles when incrementing a memory address using an absolute instruction. It all boils down to personal preference and whether a critical timing analysis will support that preference. If the negative half-cycle is transmitted at 12000 Hz regardless whether a one bit or a zero bit is transmitted, the effective rate of transmission becomes 8000 Hz for a one bit in the DISKLOAD8000 routine. Therefore, the average rate of transmission for random data could very well be 9600 bps. According to the *c2t* documentation, the indexing register should contain a value of 0x04 or 0x05 for a zero bit and a value of 0x09 or 0x0A for a one bit. Due to many complexities such as amplitude, sample rate, frequency, operational amplifier hysteresis, and the sine trigonometric function that is used in the *appendtone* routine all contribute in crushing the waveform from its theoretical presentation to its actual presentation. I found that DISKLOAD8000 broke when the indexing register compare value was set to three or to eight. A better value for this register compare is 0x06 for this particular routine.

The routine DISKLOAD9600 uses a totally different strategy in order to detect a one bit versus a zero bit in a transmitted data waveform. The register indexing loop that is used in DISKLOAD8000 is nine cycles in size. DISKLOAD9600 makes multiple inquiries of TAPEIN and uses branch instructions that together are only six cycles in size except when the branch is taken. This methodology can dial in more accurately the size of the waveform that is currently being measured. Furthermore, this technique requires that *c2t* transmit a HEADER bit at 6000 Hz rather than at 2000 Hz as it does for DISKLOAD8000. If a non-symmetrical wave for a one bit is utilized in DISKLOAD9600, the average rate of transmission for random data could very well be 10667 bps.

While in the XQuartz environment, I did successfully integrate the *c2t* software program and its supporting routines into my C language Apple][directory. Only a few changes were necessary to the *c2t* supporting routines in order to fully compile and link a new *c2t* executable without error. I did incorporate the ability for *c2t* to create a non-symmetrical wave for a one bit for the *dsk* function on demand. At this early stage in my analysis of *ct2*, only the DISKLOAD8000 routine that is configured to use a symmetrical wave for a one bit is able to transmit successfully the image of a diskette from my MacBook Pro to my Apple //e. The DISKLOAD9600 routine continuously failed. Troubleshooting why a 12000 Hz zero bit is successfully detected and not a non-symmetrical one bit whose second half of its waveform is identical to a zero bit is a difficult task. There is never too much data or too many experiments that provide even more data when analyzing such a confounded situation. Why? Why? As I mentioned earlier, there are many complexities that are involved in creating a high frequency data waveform that can be successfully transmitted to and decoded by an Apple][computer. Can the timing of the iTunes or the Music software waver while processing data at a sample rate frequency of 48 KHz when playing an AIFF file? Can the audio amplification circuitry of the MacBook Pro insert transients? Can the audio cable that is used between the MacBook Pro and the Apple computer have capacitive and/or inductive effects on the higher audio frequencies that are utilized by *c2t*? Can any mismatch in impedance between the MacBook Pro and the cassette data input port cause any significant changes to parts of the transmitted high frequency data waveform? These are all possible problems with the transmission of high frequency data.

Quality audio preamplifiers in general can provide up to 1.0 to 1.5 volts peak-to-peak of audio signal into 10 KΩ of output impedance in order to provide sufficient gain across the audio bandwidth. Similarly, quality cassette recorders provide at least 10 KΩ of matching input impedance so that audio information is efficiently transferred for most audible frequencies. These voltages and impedances are referred to as line level specifications and RCA-type cables and connectors are utilized in order to properly connect a preamplifier to a cassette recorder. The Apple][cassette recorder input and output connections strive to meet these general line level specifications. Certainly, any cassette recorder is **not** designed to receive an audio input signal from a headphone jack. Headphone jacks are typically designed to drive headphones or micro-speakers that are inserted into one's ears, and these usually have an input impedance from 10 Ω to 100 Ω. Attempting to drive a cassette recorder's input port with an audio signal that has an impedance, at best, of 100 Ω would require substantial gain. Employing such levels of gain may also introduce many audio complexities such as noise, distortion, and lower amplitude of the higher audible frequencies. There are many solutions to better match the Apple][cassette recorder input port impedance with an audio signal that is derived from the typical headphone jack of a laptop computer.

I happen to own several high quality audio transformers that are similar to the audio transformers that are utilized in a vintage Dynaco ST-70 power amplifier. Such transformers are rather large in size and they can weigh several pounds, but they have the ability to pass the audible frequency spectrum with little degradation. Their purpose is to isolate the very high DC bias voltages that are utilized in a tube audio amplifier from reaching a speaker or a set of speakers. The Dynaco ST-70 audio transformers, for example, have one set of windings for its input audio signal and multiple sets of windings for its speaker outputs. Modern speaker systems are designed to have an input impedance of 4, 8, or even 16 Ω, and the ST-70 could drive any of those speakers and correctly match their rated input impedance. There is nothing to prevent a high quality audio transformer from being used opposite to how such a transformer is normally intended. My audio transformers have multiple high impedance windings of 500, 1000, 1500, and 2000 Ω, and they have multiple low impedance windings of 8 Ω and 16 Ω. The high and low impedance windings each have a common ground connection and these connections are separate from each other. I connected the two separate ground taps, the laptop headphone jack to the 16 Ω tap by means of a 4.7 μF, 35 volt capacitor, and the cassette recorder input to the 2000 Ω tap. I also connected a 5000 Ω load resistor across the 2000 Ω tap and the common ground. Instead of having to drive the headphone jack to a maximum volume level in order to obtain **any** *c2t* information in the Apple computer, I can relax the volume down to as low as 45% of maximum and obtain perfect *c2t* data transmission into my Apple //e. At this volume level, I measured approximately 0.3 volts AC across the 5000 Ω load resistor when the data waveform first begins. I prefer a volume level that provides approximately 0.5 volts AC initially.

Obviously, this audio transformer is not actively amplifying the *c2t* audio signals since the transformer is a passive device only. What this audio transformer is providing is a better impedance match to both the laptop's headphone jack signal and to the cassette recorder's input port circuitry in the Apple computer. It is certainly not the best impedance match to the cassette recorder input port, but it is many, many times better than connecting the cassette recorder input port directly to the laptop's headphone jack. Jameco Electronics, for example, offers a number of replacement audio transformers specifically for tube amplifiers. The Hammond 1750PA audio transformer has an 8400 Ω center-tap primary and 4, 8, and 16 Ω secondaries. This particular transformer would be a far better choice, in my opinion, in order to better drive the cassette recorder input port in an Apple][computer. Utilizing the 4.7 μF capacitor protects the audio transformer from any unwanted DC voltages.

I have found throughout my engineering career that Voltaire was absolutely correct when he said "No problem can withstand the assault of sustained thinking." I did require a substantial amount of sustained testing, measuring, and the development of more and more software logic within *c2t*. Whenever I have had to augment someone else's software in order for me to understand the particular funtionality of their routines, I have found that it is a unique opportunity to become totally familiar with that software. I can utilize clever ways in order to generate even more information in addition to the actual data that is being generated by that software. I proved to myself that the data that *c2t* generates for a zero bit is identical to the data that it generates for the second half of a one bit when a non-symmetrical one bit is selected. I realized that a number of other forces must be acting on this non-symmetrical waveform such that it may appear different to either the DISKLOAD8000 routine or to the DISKLOAD9600 routine. An oscilloscope might assist and make the appearance of this data waveform far more easy to analyze. I did wonder why *c2t* sets the amplitude of the data waveform to 0.75 for the *dsk* function and to 1.00 for the fast 44.1 KHz/16 bit fuction that is used to burn a compact disk. After I changed the value of amplitude from 0.75 to 1.00 for all *c2t* functions, I started to obtain amazing results. Now, after building a new *c2t* executable, both the DISKLOAD8000 and the DISKLOAD9600 routines are able to detect all data waveforms flawlessly. Even when both routines were configured with non-symmetrical one bits, both routines were still able to detect all data waveforms. I even began work on a new DISKLOAD routine that uses 16000 Hz for a zero bit and 8000 Hz for a one bit, and I set the sampling rate frequency to 64 KHz in *c2t*. When non-symmetrical one bits are selected, this routine occasionally fails, but not always. So more work is needed in order to determine if it is even possible for the Apple][computer or the Apple //e computer to detect data waveforms at these extraordinarily high frequencies. It is totally amazing that the Apple computer can even detect data waveforms consistently at 10667 bps.

I captured *c2t* verson 2.13.3 from the Build from Source section at https://github.com/datajerk/c2t. I did successfully integrate the *c2t* software program and its supporting routines into my C language Apple][directory. As expected, Insta-Disk installs a version of DOS 3.3 into Apple][memory before it transfers the disk image which is sectioned into five segments where each segment contains the data for seven tracks. Table II.9.1 lists all of the components that are utilized by Insta-Disk, their operational memory location, their size in bytes, and a brief description of each component. These software components transfer a complete disk image whether the data is compressed or not using DOS 3.3 as its Disk Operating System. A simple Applesoft program is attached to DISKLOAD which precedes either the DISKLOAD8000 routine or the DISKLOAD9600 routine, and they are all loaded together into memory starting at 0x0801 using Wozniak's Applesoft LOAD command and his READ protocol. DISKLOAD now resides in page 0x08 and it is 0x4D bytes in size. This routine copies the attached DATALOAD routine that is specific to its processing algorithm to 0x9000. Now, DISKLOAD can utilize DATALOAD at 0x9000 in order to read into memory beginning at 0x96D0 the remaining *c2t* routines as well as DOS 3.3 which is, all together, 0x292F bytes in size. As denoted by the asterisk after DOSBOOT2 in Table II.9.1, the last byte of DOS 3.3 is deleted in the c2t.h include file in order to provide a memory location for the CHKSUM byte. That last byte of DOS 3.3, or 0xB3, must be restored by the DISKLOADCODE2 routine which also copies DOSBOOT1 to 0x3D0. DISKLOADCODE2 is now able to utilize the resources of the File Manager in order to initialize a disk volume if that option is selected in *c2t* and the resources of RWTS in order to write specific memory pages of data to specific sectors and tracks on the target disk volume.

I used a slightly different approach and created a version of *c2t* that loads and installs DOS 4.5 rather than DOS 3.3. My approach had to accommodate the additional size of DOS 4.5 and the fact that it is assembled as a noncontiguous image. Table II.9.2 lists all of the components that are utilized by Insta-Disk, their load memory location, their operational memory location, their size in bytes, and a brief description of each component. These software components transfer a complete disk image whether the data is compressed or not using DOS 4.5 as its Disk Operating System. I chose to enlarge the simple Applesoft program to 0x0F bytes in order to include an END statement, so now the DATALOAD80 program or the DATALOAD96 program begins at 0x0810. Both programs function similar to their DOS 3.3 versions except that they copy their specific DATALOAD routine to 0xB000. Both programs call DATALOAD at 0xB000 in order to load DISKCOPY to 0x2000 and to conditionally load INFLATE to 0x2600 and to conditionally load DOS45H to 0x2600 or to 0x2800. I chose to have *c2t* add the load time in seconds to the end of DATALOAD80 or to DATALOAD96 instead of writing these two bytes somewhere in the middle of the program as it does in the DOS 3.3 version.

Name	Start	Size	Description
BASIC	0x0801	0x000B	Applesoft program to CALL 2060 (0x80C)
DISKLOAD8000	0x080C	0x010D	Copies attached 0xC0 code to DATALOAD; jmp to DISKLOADCODE2
DISKLOAD9600	0x080C	0x013F	Copies attached 0xF2 code to DATALOAD; jmp to DISKLOADCODE2
DATALOAD	0x9000	variable	Specific DISKLOAD routine to read data waveform
BUFFER1	0x9200	0x0100	Used by DISKLOADCODE3 (INFLATE)
BUFFER2	0x9300	0x0100	Used by DISKLOADCODE3 (INFLATE)
BUFFER3	0x9400	0x0100	Used by DISKLOADCODE3 (INFLATE)
DOSBOOT1	0x96D0	0x0030	Page 0x03 DOS 3.3 vectors that are copied to 0x3D0
DISKLOADCODE2	0x9700	0x0400	Routine that calls DATALOAD, INFLATE, FM, and RWTS
DISKLOADCODE3	0x9B00	0x0200	INFLATE routine; uses BUFFER1, BUFFER2, and BUFFER3
DOSBOOT2*	0x9D00	0x22FF	DOS 3.3 contiguous image
CHKSUM	0xBFFF	0x0001	CHKSUM byte for initial program/DOS load

Table II.9.1. Insta-Disk Structure for DOS 3.3

Name	Load	Move	Size	Description
BASIC	0x0801	0x0801	0x000F	Applesoft program to CALL 2064 (0x810)
DATALOAD80	0x0810	0x0810	0x01F8	Copies attached 0x13C bytes to DATALOAD; jmp to DISKCOPY
DATALOAD96	0x0810	0x0810	0x0219	Copies attached 0x181 bytes to DATALOAD; jmp to DISKCOPY
DATALOAD	0x091F	0xB000	variable	Specific DATALOAD routine to read data waveform
DISKCOPY	0x2000	0xB200	0x0600	Routine that calls DATALOAD, INFLATE, and RWTS
INFLATE	0x2600	0xB800	0x0200	INFLATE routine; uses BUFFER1, BUFFER2, and BUFFER3
DOS45H	0x2800	LC	0x2A00	DOS 4.5 noncontiguous image
CHKSUM	0x5200	0x5200	0x0001	CHKSUM byte for initial program/DOS load
BUFFER1		0xBA00	0x0100	Used by INFLATE
BUFFER2		0xBB00	0x0100	Used by INFLATE
BUFFER3		0xBC00	0x0100	Used by INFLATE

Table II.9.2. Insta-Disk Structure for DOS 4.5

Up to `0x5201` bytes are read from the data waveform by `DATALOAD` which includes the `CHKSUM` byte. There is no need to replace any missing byte in `DOS45H` as a placeholder for the `CHKSUM` byte as in the DOS 3.3 version. Once `DISKCOPY`, `INFLATE`, and `DOS45H` are in memory, `DISKCOPY` can be moved to `0xB200`, `INFLATE` can be moved to `0xB800` if it was loaded into memory, and `DOS45H` can be installed into both banks of the Language Card partition and to `0xBE00:0xBFFF` if it was loaded into memory, their normal operational memory locations as shown in Table I.8.4. Of course, initializing DOS 4.5.06H in order to create its Page `0x03` vectors, initialize Applesoft, and create the keyboard and the video vectors are all **easily** accomplished by utilizing the DOS `USER` command by means of the `MNGUSER` vector at `0xBFF6:0xBFF7` and the `INITDOS` vector at `0xBFF8:0xBFF9`, all fully documented in Sections IV.3.5 and IV.3.6, respectively. The time that is required to move these programs into their operational memory location and to initialize DOS 4.5 and Applesoft is surprisingly fast, in less than one second. I also augmented *c2t* to include the actual end address for each track segment and the time to decompress each track segment to the end of `DISKCOPY`. There is certainly enough memory space for all of these variable additions since *c2t* pads the end of `DISKCOPY` with `zeros` in order to make it precisely `0x600` bytes in size. My version of `DISKCOPY` does **not** utilize the File Manager in order to initialize a disk volume. Rather, `DISKCOPY` utilizes `RWTS` to initialize a disk volume because it is **not** necessary to write a copy of DOS onto this volume: the content of the target disk volume is being replaced anyway with whatever DOS, if any, is utilized on the selected processed ~.`dsk` volume. Lastly, my version of *c2t* prints a summary that indicates whether the target disk track segments are compressed, whether the target disk volume is formatted, and the sampling rate frequency that *c2t* utilizes. My version of *c2t* also summaries and presents the total time to transfer the selected processed ~.`dsk` volume and the total time to transfer all of the track segments that are contained in the AIFF or WAVE file as shown in Table II.9.3.

Routine	f0	f1	favg	Sample Rate	Data Time	Overhead	Total Time
28	12 KHz	6 KHz	8.0 KHz	48 KHz	136.8	76.9	213.7
28n	12 KHz	6 KHz	8.0 KHz	48 KHz	136.8	55.9	192.7
28no	12 KHz	6 KHz	9.6 KHz	48 KHz	118.1	54.1	172.1
28cn	12 KHz	6 KHz	8.0 KHz	48 KHz	130.1	49.2	179.3
28cno	12 KHz	6 KHz	9.6 KHz	48 KHz	115.0	47.3	162.3
29	12 KHz	8 KHz	9.6 KHz	48 KHz	118.1	75.2	193.3
29n	12 KHz	8 KHz	9.6 KHz	48 KHz	118.1	54.2	172.3
29no	12 KHz	8 KHz	10.7 KHz	48 KHz	108.7	53.3	162.0
29cn	12 KHz	8 KHz	9.6 KHz	48 KHz	115.0	47.4	162.4
29cno	12 KHz	8 KHz	12.8 KHz	48 KHz	107.4	46.5	153.9
2	16 KHz	8 KHz	10.6 KHz	64 KHz	103.6	74.1	177.6
2n	16 KHz	8 KHz	10.6 KHz	64 KHz	103.6	53.1	156.6
2no	16 KHz	8 KHz	12.8 KHz	64 KHz	89.5	51.7	141.2
2cn	16 KHz	8 KHz	10.6 KHz	64 KHz	107.4	46.3	153.7
2cno	16 KHz	8 KHz	12.8 KHz	64 KHz	96.1	44.9	140.9

Table II.9.3. Insta-Disk Routine Timing for DOS 4.5

The results that are shown in Table II.9.3 illustrate some very interesting behaviors of the various data load routines. I chose to process the DOS 4.5 `Tools Disk` that contains 35 tracks whose sectors are completely filled with data. These tracks are divided into five seven-track segments. The 28 routines use the DATALOAD80 algorithm, the 29 routines use the DATALOAD96 algorithm, and the 2 routines use the DATALOAD10 algorithm which is based on the DATALOAD96 algorithm with a sampling rate of 64 KHz. The routine names that include the character n do not initialize a diskette. The routine names that include the character o use a non-symmetrical one bit. The routine names that include the character c compress the track segments. In all cases, the time to load INFLATE, compress the track segments, and decompress the track segments all help to reduce the total data transmission time, but not significantly for the routines that use DATALOAD10. INFLATE helps the DATALOAD80 routines between 6% and 7% and INFLATE helps the DATALOAD96 routines between 5% and 6%. All of the routines show that exactly 21.0 seconds is required for RWTS to initialize a diskette which confirms the delay value that is used in the *c2t* software. That is, from the **Overhead** timings, the difference from **Routines** 28 and 28n, 29 and 29n, and 2 and 2n is 21.0 seconds. The **Total Time** shows this same difference for these same routines as well. The 29 routines are between 9% and 10% faster than the 28 routines except when a non-symmetrical one bit is used, and for these routines, the 29 routines are only 5% to 6% faster. The DATALOAD10 routines are highly volatile and they only prove that data **can** be transmitted at these frequencies using the AIFF file format from an Apple MacBook Pro to an Apple //e under the most **perfect** conditions. It is not always possible to recreate these data transmissions on a regular basis. The DATALOAD96 routines that do not use a non-symmetrical one bit are the most stable and the most reliable for that algorithm. Surprisingly, **all** of the DATALOAD80 routines are the most stable and the most reliable for any of the algorithms.

```
#
# c2t.cfg c2t Configuration File
#

# Valid value for diskType is 0:3.
# 0 - Disk ][, 1 - CFFA, 2 - unk, 3 - unk
# diskType: 1

# Valid values for dosLoad is 0 or 1.
# 0 - DOS is not loaded into memory.
# dosLoad: 0

# Valid range of segTracks is 2:9.
# segTracks: 4

# Valid values for segSectors is 16 or 32.
# segSectors: 32

# Valid range of slotNumber is 1:7.
# slotNumber: 5

# Valid range of driveNumber is 1:81.
# driveNumber: 3

# Valid range of volumeNumber is 0:255.
# volumeNumber: 47

# Valid values for slotConnect is 0 or 1.
# Use this when diskType is not a Disk ][ drive.
# slotConnect: 1
#
```

Figure II.9.1. c2t.cfg Configuration File

I have added a host of other modifications to *c2t* other than adding a non-symmetrical one bit and printing summaries for data transmission time, data overhead time, and total data transmission time. These additional modifications include the search for a possible c2t.cfg file on the command line, the saving of all compressed segments to individual files for post analysis, and the printing of offsets where an internal output value may be located in the output AIFF file. A typical input c2t.cfg configuration file is shown in Figure II.9.1. This configuration file provides all of the input variables that are necessary when transmitting a ~.dsk volume image that is intended for a CFFA volume. This data transmission assumes, of course, that the CFFA drive is utilizing the firmware that I created and designed which is compatible with the DOS 4.5 Disk Operating System. Whether DOS 4.5 is installed or not reinstalled into the Language Card memory during data transmission, the CFFA must be enabled and its RWTS interface address must be entered into the DOS 4.5 Disk Address table. Either the MNGDISK Vector address as described in Section IV.3.3 or the ROMHOOK routine as shown in Table V.13.3 may be utilized in order to perform this simple installation. Enabling the slotConnect variable as shown in Figure II.9.1 will execute the ROMHOOK routine on behalf of DISKCOPY. When *c2t* transmits data to the Apple][for the CFFA volume and thirty-two sector tracks are specified for the segSectors variable, only four tracks or less can be specified for segTracks. There is only enough memory for 144 sectors per segment, or nine tracks of data when each track contains sixteen sectors. Four tracks that have thirty-two sectors amount to 128 total sectors whereas five tracks that have thirty-two sectors amount to 160 total sectors. Therefore, four tracks that have thirty-two sectors is the largest number of tracks that can be specified for each track segment for a CFFA volume. Slot number, drive number, and volume number are all necessary variables so that the image of a diskette volume may be transmitted to any CFFA volume on any CFFA drive.

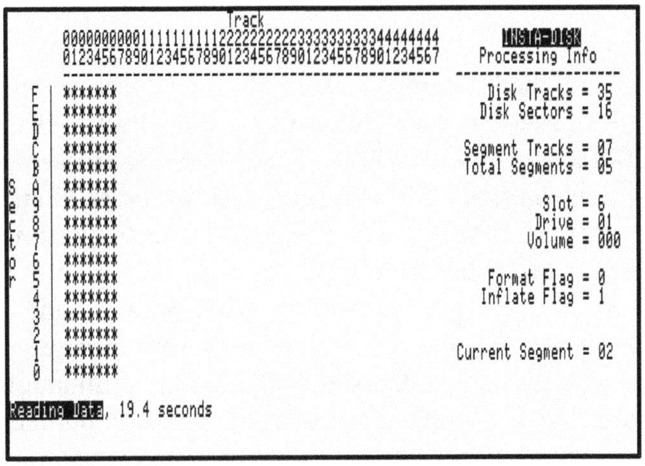

Figure II.9.2. Insta-Disk Reading Data

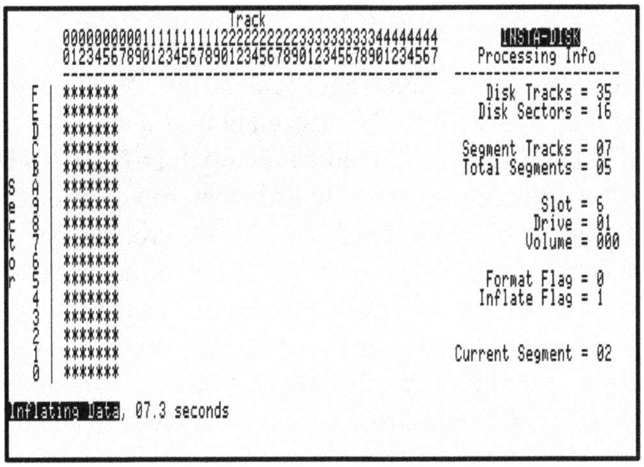

Figure II.9.3. Insta-Disk Inflating Data

The memory layout of the Insta-Disk routines that are shown in Table II.9.2 provides up to six memory pages for DISKCOPY which must also include the c2t.cfg configuration values, flags, start and end addresses, and the LOAD and the INFLATE times that are displayed. DISKLOADCODE2, the equivalent DISKCOPY routine for DOS 3.3, requires only four memory pages for its design. My design for Insta-Disk as well as the modifications that I have created for the *c2t* software has put DOS 4.5 and the CFFA up front as the major design drivers. I seriously desire to be able to transmit a data waveform that contains the data for a CFFA volume that can be configured with up to forty-eight tracks where each track contains thirty-two sectors. This is a staggering amount of data and a staggering requirement to be able to transfer

129

this amount of data without a single bit error. It is my belief that the 28cno routine is capable of transmitting this amount of data without incurring a single bit error. Figures II.9.2 through II.9.5 display the various stages of Insta-Disk processing for the data of a 35 track volume having sixteen sectors per track and whose data is written onto a diskette in a Disk][drive whose slot interface card resides in an Apple //e computer. The 80-column display is perfect for showing the stages of this high frequency data transfer. This volume is sectioned with seven tracks per segment and the INFLATE routine is utilized.

```
                  Track                                              Track
0000000000111111111122222222223333333333344444444     INSTA-DISK     0000000000111111111122222222223333333333344444444     INSTA-DISK
0123456789012345678901234567890123456789012345678   Processing Info   0123456789012345678901234567890123456789012345678   Processing Info
-------------------------------------------------   ----------------   -------------------------------------------------   ----------------
F |**********                          Disk Tracks = 35     F |***********************************      Disk Tracks = 35
E |**********                          Disk Sectors = 16    E |***********************************      Disk Sectors = 16
D |**********                                                D |***********************************
C |**********                          Segment Tracks = 07   C |***********************************      Segment Tracks = 07
B |**********                          Total Segments = 05   B |***********************************      Total Segments = 05
A |**********                                                A |***********************************
9 |**********                                Slot = 6        9 |***********************************           Slot = 6
8 |**********                                Drive = 01      8 |***********************************           Drive = 01
7 |**********                               Volume = 000     7 |***********************************          Volume = 000
6 |**********                                                6 |***********************************
5 |**********                          Format Flag = 0       5 |***********************************      Format Flag = 0
4 |**********                          Inflate Flag = 1       4 |***********************************      Inflate Flag = 1
3 |**********                                                3 |***********************************
2 |*********                                                 2 |***********************************
1 |*********                        Current Segment = 02     1 |***********************************    Current Segment = 05
0 |**********                                                0 |***********************************

Writing Data                                          Press <RTN> to Boot this Disk or

                                                      Press <ESC> to Enter DOS 4.5.06H. ■
```

Figure II.9.4. Insta-Disk Writing Data   Figure II.9.5. Insta-Disk Data Transfer Complete

It can be ascertained from Figures II.9.2 through II.9.5 that the 80-column display is the perfect vehicle for displaying all of the information of a data wave transmission in order to easily monitor its progress. DISKCOPY requires far more memory than DISKLOADCODE2 because DISKCOPY contains far more amazing software features. Because RWTS can more efficiently write a track of data starting with sector 0x0F and ending with sector 0x00, DISKCOPY utilizes that strategy. DISKCOPY also displays its sector writing progress using a top/down approach so that is why sectors are listed from top to bottom in high to low sector number. As evidenced from these figures, there is sufficient room in the display to include a maximum of forty-eight tracks and the Processing Information shows how these tracks are segmented along with the destination slot, drive, and volume numbers. The flags that show whether the destination volume is formatted and whether INFLATE is utilized are also displayed. The Current Segment number identifies which segment is currently being read, decompressed, and written to the destination volume. DISKCOPY provides two options to the user after all data has been transmitted to DISKCOPY and written to the destination volume by RWTS. The user may press RETURN in order to BOOT this volume or the user may press ESCAPE in order to enter DOS 4.5 with an Apple Command Line PROMPT and DOS available for use. Only these two options are accepted. In both cases, the display is returned to 40-column mode. Additional data waveforms may be transmitted to an Apple][computer or to an Apple //e computer simply by entering DOS 4.5, replacing the diskette with another diskette, entering the RAM Monitor by issuing the DOS MON command, and entering 3D3G on the Monitor Command Line in order to Cold-Start DOS. The Cold-Start function in DOS 4.5 is unique and it will initialize the computer such that another LOAD command may be successfully issued on the Apple Command Line. Any number of data waveforms may be transmitted to the Apple][or to the Apple //e computer successively in this fashion.

```
                 Track                        INSTA-DISK
     00000000001111111111222222222233333333334444444
     01234567890123456789012345678901234567890123456   Processing Info
     ----------------------------------------         ------------------
   1F    ********+                                     Disk Tracks  = 48
   1E    ********+                                     Disk Sectors = 32
   1D    ********+
   1C    ********+                                     Segment Tracks = 04
   1B    ********+                                     Total Segments = 12
S  1A    ********+
e  19    ********+                                             Slot = 5
c  18    ********+                                            Drive = 03
t  17    *******                                             Volume = 123
o  16    *******
r  15    *******                                        Format Flag = 0
   14    *******                                        Inflate Flag = 1
   13    *******
   12    *******
   11    *******                                      Current Segment = 02
   10    *******
 Writing Data
```

Figure II.9.6. Insta-Disk Writing Upper Tracks

```
                 Track                        INSTA-DISK
     00000000001111111111222222222233333333334444444
     01234567890123456789012345678901234567890123456   Processing Info
     ----------------------------------------         ------------------
   0F    ********                                      Disk Tracks  = 48
   0E    ********                                      Disk Sectors = 32
   0D    ********
   0C    ********                                      Segment Tracks = 04
   0B    ********                                      Total Segments = 12
S  0A    ********+
e  09    ********+                                             Slot = 5
c  08    ********+                                            Drive = 03
t  07    ********+                                            Volume = 123
o  06    ********+
r  05    ********+                                       Format Flag = 0
   04    ********+                                       Inflate Flag = 1
   03    ********+
   02    ********+
   01    ********+                                     Current Segment = 02
   00    ********+
 Writing Data
```

Figure II.9.7. Insta-Disk Writing Lower Tracks

```
                 Track                        INSTA-DISK
     00000000001111111111222222222233333333334444444
     01234567890123456789012345678901234567890123456   Processing Info
     ----------------------------------------         ------------------
   1F    ****************************************+      Disk Tracks  = 48
   1E    ****************************************+      Disk Sectors = 32
   1D    ****************************************+
   1C    ****************************************+      Segment Tracks = 04
   1B    ****************************************+      Total Segments = 12
S  1A    ****************************************+
e  19    ****************************************+              Slot = 5
c  18    ****************************************+             Drive = 03
t  17    ****************************************+             Volume = 123
o  16    ****************************************+
r  15    ****************************************       Format Flag = 0
   14    ****************************************       Inflate Flag = 1
   13    ****************************************
   12    ****************************************
   11    ****************************************     Current Segment = 12
   10    ****************************************
 Writing Data
```

Figure II.9.8. Insta-Disk Writing Last Track

```
                 Track                        INSTA-DISK
     00000000001111111111222222222233333333334444444
     01234567890123456789012345678901234567890123456   Processing Info
     ----------------------------------------         ------------------
   0F    ****************************************       Disk Tracks  = 48
   0E    ****************************************       Disk Sectors = 32
   0D    ****************************************
   0C    ****************************************       Segment Tracks = 04
   0B    ****************************************       Total Segments = 12
S  0A    ****************************************
e  09    ****************************************               Slot = 5
c  08    ****************************************              Drive = 03
t  07    ****************************************              Volume = 123
o  06    ****************************************
r  05    ****************************************        Format Flag = 0
   04    ****************************************        Inflate Flag = 1
   03    ****************************************
   02    ****************************************
   01    ****************************************      Current Segment = 12
   00    ****************************************

 Press <RTN> to Boot this Disk or

 Press <ESC> to Enter DOS 4.5.06H. ■
```

Figure II.9.9. Insta-Disk 48 Track Complete

DISKCOPY utilizes the 80-column display natively for all volumes that contain tracks that have sixteen sectors. What about volumes that contain tracks that have thirty-two sectors? DISKCOPY slightly modifies the 80-column display when a destination volume contains tracks that have thirty-two sectors into two groups: tracks 0x1F to 0x10 and tracks 0x0F to 0x00. DISKCOPY always writes tracks 0x1F to 0x10 **first** using the character + and then writes tracks 0x0F to 0x00 **second** using the character *. Figures II.9.6 through II.9.9 display the various stages of Insta-Disk processing for a 48 track destination volume that contains tracks that have thirty-two sectors. The data that is extracted from a data wave transmission is transferred to a CFFA drive that resides in an Apple //e. In Figure II.9.6, all of the single digit sector numbers are preceded with the number 1 and the + character is used to show when a sector is being written by RWTS. In Figure II.9.7, all of the single digit sector numbers are now preceded with the number 0 and the * character is used to overwrite the previous + character in order to show when a sector is written by RWTS. Figure II.9.8 displays a data wave transmission that is nearly complete. Figure II.9.9 displays a data wave transmission that has successfully completed. As in Figure II.9.5, DISKCOPY provides two options to the user after all data has been transmitted to DISKCOPY and written to the destination volume by RWTS as shown in Figure II.9.9.

In addition to all of the changes that I have added to *c2t*, the modifications that I made to DATALOAD80, to DATALOAD96, and to DISKCOPY, utilizing DOS 4.5 for the Disk Operating System in transmitting a disk volume, adding the additional logic to *c2t* in order to optionally include a non-symmetrical wave for a one bit, and processing a c2t.cfg input configuration file, I have performed an analysis on all of the internal variables that are used internal to *c2t* and whether those variables actually need to be typed as sixty-four bit integers and floating point numbers. In response to that data type analysis and after reviewing the data sizes for all of my AIFF output files, I decided to modify *c2t* and utilize only thirty-two bit variables in place of the sixty-four bit variables. I compared AIFF output files and found only a handful of differences of ± 1 in the active sine data. All AIFF output files when *c2t* utilizes thirty-two bit variables perform the same as the AIFF output files when *c2t* utilizes sixty-four bit variables. I could **not** determine any rationale to continue to utilize any sixty-four bit variable within *c2t* except in the ConvertToIeeeExtended32 routine that is called by the Write_AIFF32 routine for the common chunk data before the sound data chunk or SSND is written to the AIFF output file. The common chunk data has absolutely no impact on the SSND data and the transmission of that SSND data to an Apple][computer.

Another major conversion that I made to *c2t* was to its include file, fake6502.h. I found this file to be most interesting and very amenable for source code conversion and transforming it into a C language program which I called fake65C02.c. In performing this conversion, I was able to remove all of the undocumented 6502 instructions, I removed all of the support for the 6502 Nintendo Entertainment System, and I enabled the support for Binary-Coded Decimal. Furthermore, I added to fake65C02.c the support for all of the missing 65C02 instructions that are found in the 65C02 microprocessor that resides in the Apple //e. This conversion required substantial modifications to the addrtable, optable, and ticktable tables, each with 256 entries, in order to remove the undocumented instructions, add in the missing 65C02 instructions, and to adjust some of the timing entries for the redesigned 6502 instructions that are found in the Apple //e 65C02 microprocessor. It was simply a conversion exercise that I had never before performed. The output data throughput documentation for all of my generated AIFF output files did not change whatsoever as a result of converting fake6502.h to fake65C02.c. I also included the variables instructions and clockTicks65C02 as external unsigned thirty-two bit integers in *c2t*. I was **not able** to measure any detectable change in the *c2t* data processing time for any data segment once *c2t* has received and begun to process all of its data input values.

I am certainly very impressed with what Egan Ford has accomplished with his *c2t* program and his ancillary routines. I find it most exhilarating to be able to utilize many of the Apple XQuartz environment resources on a MacBook Pro in order to modify such a versatile program that can interface the Apple][computer or the Apple //e computer in such a fundamental manner. The Applesoft LOAD command is indeed absolutely necessary in order to provide this delightful connection to the outside world. The far-reaching wisdom of Wozniak to include the RUNFLAG byte with the READ command processing and his technique to discern a zero bit from a one bit as a high frequency data waveform is being processed in the Apple][or in the Apple //e computer is totally genius. I can hardly summarize the pleasure that I have received in learning about and working with this data waveform technology and to be able to contribute my understanding of DOS 4.5 in transforming *c2t* to quite another level of execution. I know that others will find their adventure into *c2t* processing an overwhelmingly delightful experience as I have. All of the time that I have spent developing, creating, testing, and documenting my contributions in order to expand *c2t* using DOS 4.5 as the favored Disk Operating System has literally passed with barely taking a breath. I cannot thank Egan Ford enough for giving me and others like me an incredible journey and an opportunity to further develop a technology for what I initially considered to be a useless cassette data input port. How wrong I was!

III. Commands Used in DOS 4.5.06

DOS 4.5 provides a set of commands that are in addition to the ROM Applesoft commands. As in ROM Applesoft commands, DOS commands and their keywords may be utilized in uppercase and/or in lowercase. DOS 4.5 uses a number of data tables in order to parse a valid DOS command when that command is found in the DOS Command Name Text table. This table consists of the DCI ASCII name for each DOS command in the order of command index value that is generally the same as in DOS 3.3. The Command Valid Keyword table is used to determine which keywords if any are required or may be used in conjunction with each command that is based on its index value. In this table, each command has a two-byte entry, thus providing sixteen possible bit flags including a new two-bit flag that indicates which keywords are legal, or, for example, if a filename is expected. The bit settings for the DOS Command Valid Keyword table are defined in Table III.0.1. The legal keywords have been ordered in a more logical, hierarchical, and useful way than in the order that is used by DOS 3.3. Before processing a valid DOS 4.5 command, the value of the R keyword is copied to the File Manager SUBCODE variable. This allows the user of the external File Manager interface to utilize the SUBCODE in order to simulate the R keyword for the File Manager command codes FMCATACD for CATALOG, FMTCHCD for TOUCH, FMWTSCD for WTS, and FMCDCD for CD. The DOS INIT command, however, overwrites the SUBCODE variable with a BOOTYPE value for its specific use as shown in Figures I.11.1 and I.11.2.

Valid Keyword bits 10 and 11 form a new two-bit flag, and these two bits are mutually exclusive in that no DOS 3.3 or DOS 4.5 command uses both of these bits together in any single command. I chose to identify a special non-keyword *integer value* category by setting both of these bits in the DOS 4.5 CONFIG, PHASE, SV, and USER commands. This special category of *integer value* commands is easily identified and range-checked as appropriate in the DOS 4.5 Command Manager routine GETPRMS.

Bit	Bit Position	Value	Flag Bit Description
15	%1000 0000 0000 0000	0x8000	Filename legal but optional
14	%0100 0000 0000 0000	0x4000	Command has no positional operands
13	%0010 0000 0000 0000	0x2000	Filename #1 is expected
12	%0001 0000 0000 0000	0x1000	Filename #2 is expected
11	%0000 1000 0000 0000	0x0800	Slot number positional operand is expected
11 & 10	%0000 1100 0000 0000	0x0C00	Non-keyword *integer value* number is expected
10	%0000 0100 0000 0000	0x0400	MAXFILES value positional operand is expected
9	%0000 0010 0000 0000	0x0200	Command is only issued from within a program
8	%0000 0001 0000 0000	0x0100	Command creates a new file if file is not found in the Catalog
7	%0000 0000 1000 0000	0x0080	C, I, 0 keywords are legal
6	%0000 0000 0100 0000	0x0040	S keyword is legal but not necessarily expected
5	%0000 0000 0010 0000	0x0020	D keyword is legal but not necessarily expected
4	%0000 0000 0001 0000	0x0010	V keyword is legal but not necessarily expected
3	%0000 0000 0000 1000	0x0008	A keyword is legal but not necessarily expected
2	%0000 0000 0000 0100	0x0004	L keyword is legal but not necessarily expected
1	%0000 0000 0000 0010	0x0002	R keyword is legal but not necessarily expected
0	%0000 0000 0000 0001	0x0001	B keyword is legal but not necessarily expected

Table III.0.1. Valid Command Keyword Table in DOS 4.5

Command Name	Index	ASCII Text	Handler Name	Keyword
CMDINIT	0x00	INIT	DOINIT	0x317F
CMDLOAD	0x02	LOAD	DOLOAD	0xA072
CMDSAVE	0x04	SAVE	DOSAVE	0xA173
CMDRUN	0x06	RUN	DORUN	0xA074
CMDCHAIN	0x08	CHAIN	DOCHAIN	0x2276
CMDDELET	0x0A	DELETE	DODELETE	0x2072
CMDLOCK	0x0C	LOCK	DOLOCK	0x6070
CMDUNLCK	0x0E	UNLOCK	DOUNLOCK	0x6070
CMDCLOSE	0x10	CLOSE	DOCLOSE	0x6000
CMDREAD	0x12	READ	DOREAD	0x2203
CMDEXEC	0x14	EXEC	DOEXEC	0x2073
CMDWRITE	0x16	WRITE	DOWRITE	0x2203
CMDPOSTN	0x18	POSITION	DOPSTION	0x2202
CMDOPEN	0x1A	OPEN	DOOPENTX	0x2374
CMDAPND	0x1C	APPEND	DOAPND	0x2270
CMDRENAM	0x1E	RENAME	DORENAME	0x3072
CMDCAT	0x20	CATALOG	DOCAT	0x4073
CMDMON	0x22	MON	DOMON	0x4080
CMDNOMON	0x24	NOMON	DONOMON	0x4080
CMDPRNUM	0x26	PR#	DOPRNUM	0x4800
CMDINNUM	0x28	IN#	DOINNUM	0x4800
CMDMXFLS	0x2A	MAXFILES	DOMXFLS	0x4402
CMDDATE	0x2C	DATE	DODATE	0x4000
CMDLIST	0x2E	LIST	DOLIST	0x2077
CMDBSAVE	0x30	BSAVE	DOBSAVE	0x217F
CMDBLOAD	0x32	BLOAD	DOBLOAD	0x207A
CMDBRUN	0x34	BRUN	DOBRUN	0x2078
CMDVERFY	0x36	VERIFY	DOVERIFY	0x2072
CMDLSAVE	0x38	LSAVE	DOLSAVE	0x217F
CMDLLOAD	0x3A	LLOAD	DOLLOAD	0x207A
CMDTSAVE	0x3C	TSAVE	DOTSAVE	0x2173
CMDTLOAD	0x3E	TLOAD	DOTLOAD	0x207F
CMDDIFF	0x40	DIFF	DODIFF	0x3070
CMDGREP	0x42	GREP	DOGREP	0x3070
CMDMORE	0x44	MORE	DOLIST	0x2077
CMDCAT2	0x46	CAT	DOCAT	0x4073
CMDURM	0x48	URM	DOURM	0x2070
CMDCD	0x4A	CD	DOCD	0x4072
CMDLS	0x4C	LS	DOCAT	0x4073
CMDMV	0x4E	MV	DORENAME	0x3072
CMDRM	0x50	RM	DODELETE	0x2072
CMDSV	0x52	SV	DOSV	0x4C00
CMDTS	0x54	TS	DOTS	0x407F
CMDWTS	0x56	WTS	DOWTS	0x407F
CMDTW	0x58	TW	DOTW	0x2170
CMDPHASE	0x5A	PHASE	DOPHASE	0x4C02
CMDTOUCH	0x5C	TOUCH	DOTOUCH	0x6072
CMDCONFG	0x5E	CONFIG	DOCONFIG	0x4C02
CMDUSER	0x60	USER	DOUSER	0x4C00
CMDSSAVE	0x62	SSAVE	D0SSAVE	0x217D
CMDSLOAD	0x64	SLOAD	DOSLOAD	0x207C
CMDTIME	0x66	TIME	DOTIME	0x4000
CMDHELP	0x68	HELP	DOHELP	0x4000

Table III.0.2. Command and Handler Table in DOS 4.5

Table III.0.2 is a comprehensive listing of the complete set of DOS 4.5 commands in command index order showing the command name, its command index value, its ASCII text, its command handler name, and the value of its two-byte keyword. CMDHELP is available in DOS 4.5 because there is additional memory in Bank 1 of the Language Card partition where RWTS is located. This additional memory seemed like an ideal location for placing a DOS HELP handler in order to provide instant syntactical usage information for all DOS 4.5 commands. DOS 4.5 requires one page of lower Main memory for the interface that controls the utilization of the Language Card partition. Therefore, the DOS image requires at least one sector on track 0x02. Why not use a few more sectors on track 0x02 for something quite useful like the DOS HELP handler? Another DOS developer may choose to eliminate the DOS HELP handler and utilize that memory and/or those volume data sectors for other DOS functionality.

DOS 4.5 uses four tables in order to parse valid keywords, ascertain the bit positions within the keyword variable KYWRDFND, and determine if the value of a keyword is within a minimum and a maximum range. The four tables include PPARMS, PARMBITS, KWRANGEL, and KWRANGEH. The content of these four tables is summarized in Table III.0.3. Unlike DOS 3.3, DOS 4.5 allows up to 81 drives on any given slot in order to support the CFFA firmware and the Volume Manager software for a Compact Flash card that has up to 8 GB of memory. DOS 4.5 also allows default volume numbers to be zero and BSAVE, LSAVE, and SSAVE can write files that are up to 0xFFFF bytes in size. The Bit Positions for the keywords C, I, and O are used directly in order to generate the variable MONVAL once the MSB of the bit position value is cleared. The other Bit Positions are added to the variable KYWRDFND as each keyword is parsed. Therefore, keywords and their parameter values may be used within a DOS command in any order. It is **no** accident that the lower byte Bit Position of each Command Keyword in Table III.0.1 is identical to the Bit Position of that same keyword in the lower byte of each Keyword Value as shown in Table III.0.3.

Keyword Name	Bit Position – Value	Minimum Value	Maximum Value
C	%1100 0000 – 0xC0	-	-
I	%1010 0000 – 0xA0	-	-
O	%1001 0000 – 0x90	-	-
MON/NOMON	%1000 0000 – 0x80	-	-
S	%0100 0000 – 0x40	1 (0x01)	7 (0x0007)
D	%0010 0000 – 0x20	1 (0x01)	81 (0x0051)
V	%0001 0000 – 0x10	0 (0x00)	255 (0x00FF)
A	%0000 1000 – 0x08	0 (0x00)	65535 (0xFFFF)
L	%0000 0100 – 0x04	0 (0x00)	65535 (0xFFFF)
R	%0000 0010 – 0x02	0 (0x00)	32767 (0x7FFF)
B	%0000 0001 – 0x01	0 (0x00)	32767 (0x7FFF)

Table III.0.3. Keyword Name and Range Table in DOS 4.5

The syntax of a DOS 4.5 command begins with the command, and the command is immediately followed by one or two filenames if they are required. All keywords and their parameter values, whether they are required or optional, must follow the filename(s), or they must follow the command if there are no required filename(s), and usually a comma must delineate each keyword that is coupled with its parameter value. Table III.0.4 lists all keywords, the keyword name, and a brief description of that keyword. In all of the

DOS 4.5 command definitions that are given throughout this section, optional keywords and their parameter values are contained in square brackets, as in [,Vv]. Commands and keywords are shown in "UPPERCASE" letters and keyword parameter values are shown in "lowercase" letters for ease of explanation. The lowercase letters that represent keyword parameter values are, of course, replaced by valid numerical values when they are actually used in a DOS command. Keyword parameter numerical values may be entered as a decimal or as a hexadecimal number. Input hexadecimal numbers are always prefaced by the dollar sign $ as in $1234. However, DOS 4.5 usually prints hexadecimal numbers prefaced with 0x as in 0x1234 unless an uppercase keyword precedes the hexadecimal number as in A$1234. There are times when the value of zero is shown as 0x00 for ease of explanation.

Keyword	Name	Description
S	Slot	Keyword followed by slot number
D	Drive	Keyword followed by drive number
V	Volume	Keyword followed by volume number
A	Address	Keyword followed by address value
L	Length	Keyword followed by length value
R	Record	Keyword followed by record number or value
B	Byte	Keyword followed by byte value
C	Command	Keyword to display or not to display DOS commands
I	Input	Keyword to display or not to display input data
O	Output	Keyword to display or not to display output data
f	filename	Must begin with ASCII A or greater and be 1-24 characters in length
f2	2nd filename	Must begin with ASCII A or greater and be 1-24 characters in length
s	slot number	Slot number of a peripheral interface card, value range 1-7
d	drive number	Initialized to 1, value range 1-81 (for CFFA and Volume Manager use)
v	volume number	Initialized to 0, value range 0-255
a	address value	Initialized to 0, value range 0-65535
l	length value	Initialized to 0, value range 0-65535
r	record value	Initialized to 0, value range 0-32767
b	byte value	Initialized to 0, value range 0-32767
n	number	Some numerical value that is required by some commands

Table III.0.4. Keywords and Their Definition in DOS 4.5

In keeping with the original DOS 3.3 documentation,
DOS 4.5 commands may be grouped into six categories
and those categories are shown on the following page.

DOS System Commands

CONFIG	DATE	HELP	IN#
MAXFILES	MON	NOMON	PHASE
PR#	SV	TIME	USER

File System Commands

CAT	CATALOG	CD	DELETE
DIFF	GREP	INIT	LIST
LOCK	LS	MORE	MV
RENAME	RM	TOUCH	TS
UNLOCK	URM	VERIFY	WTS

Applesoft File Commands

CHAIN	LOAD	RUN	SAVE

Binary File Commands

BLOAD	BRUN	BSAVE	LLOAD
LSAVE	SLOAD	SSAVE	

Sequential Text File Commands

APPEND	CLOSE	EXEC	OPEN
POSITION	READ	TLOAD	TSAVE
TW	WRITE		

Random-Access Data File Commands

CLOSE	OPEN	READ	WRITE

Command	Default Value	Command Syntax
CONFIG	0x00	[n][,R]
DATE		
HELP		
IN#		s
MAXFILES	0x05	[n][,R]
MON		[,C][,I][,O]
NOMON		[,C][,I][,O]
PHASE	0x04	[n][,R]
PR#		s
SV		[n]
TIME		
USER		[n]

Table III.1.0.1. DOS System Commands in DOS 4.5

1. DOS System Commands

The DOS System commands in the DOS 4.5 command repertoire consist of those commands that manage the general operation of DOS 4.5 in an Apple][computer. The DOS CONFIG command provides the user with the ability to configure the operation of eight key processing elements within DOS. The DOS DATE and TIME commands access the real time clock if a clock card is found in one of the Apple][peripheral slots. The DOS HELP command provides syntactical usage for all DOS commands. The DOS IN# and PR# commands direct the Input keyboard data and the Output display data streams, respectively. The DOS MAXFILES command selects and initializes the number of available data file buffers. The DOS MON and NOMON commands enable or disable, respectively, the display of commands, input data, and output data to the display screen. The DOS PHASE command sets the physical track size in half-phases to read data from and write data to a Disk][or a Disk][-like disk drive. The DOS SV command converts either decimal or hexadecimal values to hexadecimal and decimal. The DOS USER command is designed to provide a number of modes of operation that include initializing DOS, re-entering a program, calling an assembly language routine with various input data, and many other possible uses.

The syntax of the DOS System commands is shown in Table III.1.0.1. The DOS CONFIG, PHASE, SV, and USER commands belong to a special non-keyword *integer value* category of commands. Either decimal or hexadecimal values that are prefaced by a dollar sign $ can be used with this category of commands because they have **no** required keywords for their associated parameter values. If the R keyword, even with a parameter value, is entered after the DOS CONFIG, MAXFILES, or PHASE commands followed by a comma, the operational value that is associated with that DOS command is *reset* to its **default** value. DOS 4.5 will issue a Syntax Error if a comma is not used between these particular DOS commands and the R keyword. All of the DOS System commands including the DOS HELP command are permitted to be used from within an Applesoft program, an assembly language routine, or in an EXEC file as well as on the Apple Command Line. Be aware that the DOS HELP handler does call the ROM Monitor HOME routine when the user exits DOS HELP.

138

1. CONFIG Command

```
CONFIG      [n][,R]

Example:    CONFIG
            CONFIG,R
            CONFIG 123
            CONFIG $C7
```

This command is not available in DOS 3.3 for DOS System commands and was initially developed for DOS 4.3, and this command has been enhanced in DOS 4.5 to accept the R keyword. The DOS CONFIG command provides the user with the ability to configure the operation of eight key processing elements within DOS with an operational value for n. The value for n may be entered as a decimal number or as a hexadecimal number that is preceded by the dollar sign $. Input CONFIG values for n may be entered directly on the Apple Command Line or within an Applesoft program or an assembly language routine. If no value or zero is entered for n with the DOS CONFIG command, its current or operational value is displayed in decimal if its value is less than ten, otherwise its value is displayed in hexadecimal and prefaced by 0x on the Apple Command Line when DOS 4.5 **is not** in the RUN mode. When DOS **is** in the RUN mode and the DOS CONFIG command is issued from within a program, the current operational value of the CONFIG command may be obtained and displayed according to the design of that program because the DOS CONFIG command belongs to a special non-keyword *integer value* category of commands.

```
]config = 000

]config 9
]config = 009
]

]config 239
]CONFIG = 0XEF
]SV 239 = 0X00EF = 00239
]

]LS

S=6 D=02 V=123 F=0504 02/14/24 08:28:48

  A 002 CONFIG TEST1    02/14/24 08:28:48
  A 002 CONFIG TEST2    02/14/24 08:28:48
  A 002 CONFIG TEST3    02/14/24 08:28:48
  A 002 CONFIG TEST4    02/14/24 08:28:48
]CONFIG,R

]config = 000

]*
```

Figure III.1.1.1. CONFIG Command Display

```
10 D$ =   CHR$ (4)
20   PRINT D$;"CONFIG,R": GOSUB 1
     00
30 A = 1: PRINT D$;"CONFIG ",A: GOSUB
     100
40 A$ = "$99": PRINT D$;"CONFIG
     ",A$: GOSUB 100
50   PRINT D$;"CONFIG,R": GOSUB 1
     00: END
100   PRINT D$;"CONFIG": INPUT IN
     : PRINT "CONFIG value:  ";IN
     : RETURN
]RUN

CONFIG value:   0

CONFIG value:   1

CONFIG value:   153

CONFIG value:   0

]*
```

Figure III.1.1.2. Capturing CONFIG Values

Several examples in using the DOS CONFIG command on the Apple Command Line such that DOS 4.5 **is not** in the RUN mode are shown in Figure III.1.1.1. When DOS **is** in the RUN mode and the DOS CONFIG command is issued from within an Applesoft program or an assembly language routine, the operational value of CONFIG may be obtained and displayed as shown in Figure III.1.1.2. The Value Read buffer is utilized by the DOS CONFIG handler in order to store the operational value of CONFIG when DOS **is** in the RUN mode. The Applesoft statement INPUT can be used to read its value.

Bit	Off	On	Description
0	Enable	Disable	Manage the extra carriage return between DOS commands
1	Enable	Disable	Manage DOS VERIFY after a DOS SAVE, BSAVE, LSAVE, SSAVE, or TSAVE
2	Enable	Disable	Manage the PROMPT character] during EXEC processing
3	Enable	Disable	Manage the DOS MAXFILES command
4	Enable	Disable	Manage all volume and file locks
5	Enable	Disable	Manage pushing the DOSWARM-1 address onto the stack before a DOS BRUN
6	Disable	Enable	Manage the case of output characters
7	Disable	Enable	Manage the case of input characters

Table III.1.1.1. CONFIG Command Bit Definitions

Each of the eight available bits that comprise the CONFIG operational value controls one of the DOS 4.5 processing elements. As shown in Table III.1.1.1, the LSB, or Bit 0 controls the first processing element that is listed in the table. The MSB, or Bit 7 controls the last processing element that is listed in Table III.1.1.1. If the R keyword, even with a parameter value, is entered after the DOS CONFIG command followed by a comma, all of the bits in the operational value of the CONFIG command are *reset* to zero which is its **default** value. DOS 4.5 will issue a Syntax Error if a comma is not used between the DOS CONFIG command and the R keyword.

CONFIG Bit 0, when set or ON, eliminates the extra carriage return that is normally issued between command entries on the Apple Command Line.

CONFIG Bit 1, when set or ON, bypasses the DOS VERIFY command for a file after that file has been saved to a volume when using the DOS SAVE, BSAVE, LSAVE, SSAVE, or TSAVE commands. Enabling this bit visibly reduces the amount of time that is required in order to save a file to a volume, but it eliminates the verification that that file can be read into memory without error.

CONFIG Bit 2, when set or ON, eliminates printing the PROMPT which is usually character] while EXEC is processing its file. Setting this bit will not change how EXEC processes DOS commands.

CONFIG Bit 3, when set or ON, bypasses the DOS MAXFILES command when that command is issued in an Applesoft program or in an assembly language routine. However, if the DOS MAXFILES command is issued without a value, the command functions as normal without regard to CONFIG Bit 3. There is no benefit in changing the value of MAXFILES in DOS 4.5. DOS 4.5 builds five file buffers within the memory of the Language Card partition that should not be used for any other purpose. Reducing the number of file buffers in DOS 4.5 does not provide any additional memory for Applesoft programs.

CONFIG Bit 4, when set or ON, bypasses all disk and file lock enforcement routines.

CONFIG Bit 5, when set or ON, does not push the DOSWARM-1 address onto the stack before entering the start address for a DOS BRUN. Pushing the DOSWARM-1 address onto the stack simply ensures that DOS is reconnected to its keyboard and video intercepts after a DOS BRUN has finished its processing.

CONFIG Bit 6, when set or ON, converts all DOS 4.5 output characters to uppercase. For example, all DOS 4.5 error messages will appear in uppercase when Bit 6 is set. Even text that is printed using an Applesoft

PRINT command will appear in uppercase. Essentially, everything that is printed to the display will appear in uppercase when CONFIG Bit 6 is set.

CONFIG Bit 7, when set or ON, converts all DOS 4.5 input filename characters to uppercase. In other words, whether the caps lock key is enabled or not, all input filenames are converted to uppercase. This makes it possible to load or to save uppercase filenames while the keyboard is configured for lowercase utilization when CONFIG Bit 7 is set.

2. DATE Command

DATE

Example: DATE

This command is not available in DOS 3.3 for DOS System commands and this command was initially developed for DOS 4.1. The DOS DATE command displays on the screen the current date and time as shown in Figure III.1.2.1 when the command is issued on the Apple Command Line. DOS 4.5 supports at least three clock cards and possibly others: Thunderclock, TimeMaster, and the clock card I designed and built. The major difference in these clock cards is the index to where the date and time data begin in their respective raw data character output string that each card generates. Figure III.1.2.1 also shows an example Applesoft program that displays the raw data character output string for a Thunderclock card that resides in slot 4. The index that points to where the date and time data begin for this clock card is 0x00 from Table I.13.1. The TimeMaster clock card and my clock card both have an index of 0x03 that points to where their date and time data begin. DOS 4.5 supports any clock card whose firmware contains the standard signature bytes and a classification byte or CLKID of 0x03 or 0x07. When the generic raw data character output string of a clock card is examined, it will yield an index value from 0x00 to 0x05. That index value points to where the date and the time data begin in the clock data that that clock card generates.

```
]date = 02/14/24 08:28:48
]load read clock
]list

10 D$ =   CHR$ (4)
20 SLOT = 4
30   PRINT D$;"pr#";SLOT
40   PRINT D$;"in#";SLOT
50   INPUT ":";A$
60   PRINT D$;"pr#0"
70   PRINT D$;"in#0"
80   PRINT
90   PRINT A$
]run

02/14 08;28;48.000
]*
```

Figure III.1.2.1. DATE Command for Thunderclock

```
]DATE = 02/14/24 08:28:48
]LOAD GET CLOCK5
]LIST

10 D$ =   CHR$ (4): GOSUB 1000
20   VTAB 21: PRINT "Date and Tim
     e is ";DT$
999  END
1000  VTAB 1: HTAB 1: PRINT D$;"
      DATE":DT$ = "":DT = 1024
1010 CH =   PEEK (DT): POKE DT,16
     0:DT$ = DT$ +   CHR$ (CH - 12
     8):DT = DT + 1: IF (DT < >
     1041) THEN  GOTO 1010
1020  HTAB 1: RETURN
]RUN
Date and Time is 02/14/24 08:28:48
]*
```

Figure III.1.2.2. Capturing DATE Data

141

When the DOS DATE command is issued from within an Applesoft program, DOS 4.5 only prints the date and time information; the equal sign is not printed as it is printed on the Apple Command Line. The program that is shown in Figure III.1.2.2 captures the date and time information from the resident clock card. It saves that information starting at memory address 0x0400 to memory address 0x0411 when the DOS DATE command is issued in the subroutine that begins on line #1000. The subroutine places the cursor at memory address 0x0400 using the Applesoft VTAB and HTAB statements, issues the DOS DATE command, it initializes the date and time character string DT$, it extracts each character of the date and time information from memory, and it stores a SPACE or character 0xA0 over each data byte that it reads. When all of the date and time information is extracted from memory, the subroutine moves the cursor back to memory address 0x0400 and returns to the caller. This technique cleverly extracts the date and time information from memory while it hides or covers up that same information. The program prints the contents of the DT$ character string on display line #21.

Notice that in line #1010 the character string DT$ is constructed by adding one character at a time to DT$ after it first clears the MSB for each added character by subtracting 128. Section I.15 thoroughly explains why a normal Applesoft program must save all character string data in **lower** ASCII such that the MSB of each character byte is **cleared**. This program simply adheres to that fundamental policy in case Applesoft calls the garbage collection GARBAG routine that is based on Bongers' specification.

3. HELP Command

HELP

Example: HELP

This command is not available in DOS 3.3 for DOS System commands and this command was initially developed for DOS 4.1H and has been modified once again for the benefit of DOS 4.5 Build 06. This new DOS HELP handler provides the same instant syntactical usage information for all DOS 4.5 commands. The handler displays all of the DOS 4.5 Build 06 commands alphabetically rather than by category as in DOS 4.3 or DOS 4.5 Build 05. When the DOS HELP command is entered onto the Apple Command Line, Figure III.1.3.1 is displayed and it shows the entire DOS 4.5 Build 06 command repertoire. Arrow keys must be used in order to navigate to the specific DOS command for which HELP is desired. The left/right arrow keys step through rows of commands either backwards or forwards, respectively. The up/down arrow keys step through a column of commands either upwards or downwards, respectively. Stepping backwards from the first command APPEND navigates to the last command WTS, and vice versa. Pressing the carriage return selects the command that is shown in inverse and displays its help content. Pressing the ESCAPE key while viewing the list of commands, DOS Management, or the help content of a DOS command will exit the DOS HELP handler. Pressing any other key displays the DOS 4.5 Build 06 Management contents as shown in Figure III.1.3.2.

Two example displays of help content are shown in Figures III.1.3.3 and III.1.3.4 for the DOS INIT and LSAVE commands, respectively. It is certainly not possible with the limited memory resources of the Apple][to provide any further help content than what this command can already provide. The DOS HELP command is intended to display sufficient information in how each command is correctly used and all of the legal keywords that are associated with that command. Keywords that have been added to a DOS command are defined. At least one example is given showing how that command can be used in an

Applesoft program. If more information is required for a DOS command, the Second Edition of the DOS 4.5 Volume and File Disk Management System book is always available and that book is always the ultimate resource for DOS 4.5 Build 06 detailed command utilization.

```
        DOS 4.5.06 Commands

APPEND      EXEC       MV          SV
BLOAD       GREP       NOMON       TIME
BRUN        INIT       OPEN        TLOAD
BSAVE       IN#        PHASE       TOUCH
CAT         LIST       POSITION    TS
CATALOG     LLOAD      PR#         TSAVE
CD          LOAD       READ        TW
CHAIN       LOCK       RENAME      UNLOCK
CLOSE       LS         RM          URM
CONFIG      LSAVE      RUN         USER
DATE        MAXFILES   SAVE        VERIFY
DELETE      MON        SLOAD       WRITE
DIFF        MORE       SSAVE       WTS
```

Figure III.1.3.1. HELP Display DOS Commands

```
        DOS 4.5.06 Management

*BE00G - RAM Bank 2
*BE08G - RAM Bank 1

0xBFF0 - DOS Version Number
0xBFF1 - DOS Build Number

0xBFF2 - Manage Disk Address Table
0xBFF4 - Manage all DOS Values
0xBFF6 - Manage DOS USER Command

0xBFF8 - DOS Initialization Address
0xBFFA - DOS Init Values Address

0xBFFC - Boot Config Table Offset
0xBFFD - NBUF1 Page MSB Address

0xBFFE - Boot MSB Address
0xBFFF - Boot Sector Number
```

Figure III.1.3.2. HELP Display DOS Management

```
INIT f, f2 [,Ss][,Dd][,Vv][,An][,Bn]
           [,Ln][,R[n]]

INIT HELLO,<Title>,L$1234        (Boot)

INIT HELLO,<Title>,A40,B4,R      (Data)

INIT HELLO,<Title>,R$14          (EXEC)

A = Volume Tracks
B = Sectors/Track Flag|Catalog Sectors
L = Volume Subject
R = Volume Type
```

Figure III.1.3.3. HELP Display INIT Command

```
LSAVE f [,Ss][,Dd][,Vv][,Aa][,B][,L1]
        [,R[1]]

LSAVE TEST

LSAVE TEST,A$1234,L$1234,R

LSAVE TEST,B,R1

B  = file delete/save strategy
R  = show Address, Length
R1 = show Address, Length, Sectors Read
```

Figure III.1.3.4. HELP Display LSAVE Command

Because the DOS HELP command currently displays the list of DOS commands alphabetically rather than by category, three DOS commands must be displayed that show both of their unique software utilizations. These three commands are the Sequential Text File and Random-Access Data File commands OPEN, READ, and WRITE. The Sequential Text File utilization for each of these commands is always displayed first, followed by a separator, and then the Random-Access Data File utilization is displayed next. The help content for the DOS OPEN command is shown in Figure III.1.3.5 and the help content for the DOS READ command is shown in Figure III.1.3.6. The DOS CLOSE command does not depend on whether the file is a Sequential Text File nor a Random-Access Data File. The help content for the DOS WRITE command is virtually the same as for the DOS READ command.

```
OPEN f [,Ss][,Dd][,Vv]

OPEN TEST

-----

OPEN f, Ll [,Ss][,Dd][,Vv]

OPEN TEST,L10
```

```
READ f [,Bb]

READ TEST
READ TEST,B4

-----

READ f, Rr [,Bb]

READ TEST,R4
READ TEST,R1,B4
```

Figure III.1.3.5. HELP Display OPEN Command   Figure III.1.3.6. HELP Display READ Command

4. IN# Command

IN#   s

Example: IN# 4

This command is available in DOS 3.3 for DOS System commands and no enhancements have been made to this command so it functions in the same manner in DOS 4.5. The DOS IN# handler configures the KSWL interface pointer to receive all subsequent data from the peripheral device that resides in the specified peripheral slot s instead of receiving data from the Apple keyboard.

The DOS IN# handler makes a call to the ROM Monitor INPORT routine at 0xFE8B with the value of the slot number s in the A-register. The ROM Monitor INPORT routine directly follows the ROM Monitor SETKBD routine at 0xFE89 that simply loads the A-register with zero in order to reconnect the Apple keyboard to the KSWL interface pointer. The ROM Monitor SETKBD routine is one of several ROM Monitor routines that is called during the BOOT sequence for DOS 4.5 as shown in Table I.9.2.

Figure III.1.2.1 shows an example Applesoft program that uses the DOS IN# command in order to configure the KSWL interface pointer to slot 4 in order to communicate with the Thunderclock card that resides in slot 4.

144

5. MAXFILES Command

```
MAXFILES   [n][,R]

Example:   MAXFILES
           MAXFILES,R
           MAXFILES 3
           MAXFILES $4
```

This command is available in DOS 3.3 for DOS System commands and it functions in the same manner as it did in DOS 4.1 to accept an input value of zero for n. This DOS command has been further enhanced to accept the R keyword in DOS 4.5. The DOS MAXFILES command specifies the number of file buffers n that can be active at any given time up to a maximum value of five file buffers in DOS 4.5. The value for n may be entered as a decimal number or as a hexadecimal number that is preceded by the dollar sign $. MAXFILES values for n may be entered directly on the Apple Command Line or within an Applesoft program or an assembly language routine. If no value or zero is entered with the DOS MAXFILES command, the current number of active file buffers is displayed in decimal on the Apple Command Line when DOS 4.5 **is not** in the RUN mode. When DOS **is** in the RUN mode and the DOS MAXFILES command is issued from within an Applesoft program without a parameter n, the current number of active file buffers may be obtained and displayed according to the design of that program.

Several examples in using the DOS MAXFILES command on the Apple Command Line when DOS 4.5 **is not** in the RUN mode are shown in Figure III.1.5.1. Figure III.1.5.1 shows that changing the number of file buffers in DOS 4.5 **does not** change the address that is in HIMEM at 0x73:0x74, and it remains set at 0xBE00. When DOS **is** in the RUN mode and the DOS MAXFILES command is issued from within an Applesoft program or an assembly language routine, the number of file buffers may be obtained and displayed as shown in Figure III.1.5.2. The Value Read buffer is utilized by the DOS MAXFILES handler in order to store the operational value of MAXFILES when DOS **is** in the RUN mode. The Applesoft statement INPUT can be used to read its value. The number of file buffers can never be zero. Even the CATALOG command requires a file buffer for the File Manager CLOSOPEN routine.

```
]MAXFILES = 5

]PRINT PEEK(116);",";PEEK(115)
190,0

]PRINT 190*256+0
48640

]SV 48640 = 0xBE00 = 48640

]MAXFILES 4

]MAXFILES = 4

]PRINT PEEK(116);",";PEEK(115)
190,0

]PRINT 190*256+0
48640

]SV 48640 = 0xBE00 = 48640

]
```

```
10  D$ = CHR$ (4)
20  PRINT D$;"MAXFILES,R": GOSUB
    100
30  PRINT D$;"MAXFILES 1": GOSUB
    100
40  PRINT D$;"MAXFILES $3": GOSUB
    100
50  PRINT D$;"MAXFILES,R": GOSUB
    100: END
100  PRINT D$;"MAXFILES": INPUT
     A: PRINT "MAXFILES value:  "
     ;A: RETURN

]RUN

MAXFILES value:  5

MAXFILES value:  1

MAXFILES value:  3

MAXFILES value:  5

]※
```

Figure III.1.5.1. MAXFILES Command Display   Figure III.1.5.2. Capturing the MAXFILES Value

Buffer	Data Buffer	TS Buffer	Workarea	Filename	Addresses
1	0xECA0-0xED9F	0xEDA0-0xEE9F	0xEEA0-0xEEC4	0xEEC5-0xEEDC	0xEEDD-0xEEE4
2	0xEEE5-0xEFE4	0xEFE5-0xF0E4	0xF0E5-0xF109	0xF10A-0xF121	0xF122-0xF129
3	0xF12A-0xF229	0xF22A-0xF329	0xF32A-0xF34E	0xF34F-0xF366	0xF367-0xF36E
4	0xF36F-0xF46E	0xF46F-0xF56E	0xF56F-0xF593	0xF594-0xF5AB	0xF5AC-0xF5B3
5	0xF5B4-0xF6B3	0xF6B4-0xF7B3	0xF7B4-0xF7D8	0xF7D9-0xF7F0	0xF7F1-0xF7F8

Table III.1.5.1. DOS 4.5 File Buffer Contents and Their Locations

When DOS 4.5 BOOTs into memory, the default number of active file buffers is configured by using the NMAXVAL variable as shown in Table I.8.5. This default value is set to five in the DOS 4.5 source code. Each file buffer requires 581 or 0x245 bytes of memory. DOS 4.5 builds its file buffers **up** in the Language Card partition beginning at address 0xECA0. DOS 4.5 was designed this way such that setting MAXFILES to three allows the installation of the MiniAssembler and its monitor in the Language Card partition at memory address 0xF500 and not perturb any of the three active file buffers that reside in memory below 0xF500. Apple][memory is very precious, and specifying fewer than five file buffers in DOS 4.5 does **not** provide any additional memory for programs in lower Main memory. HIMEM is always set to memory address 0xBE00 regardless how many file buffers are configured. Table III.1.5.1 shows the file buffer contents and their memory locations for all five file buffers in DOS 4.5. There is just enough memory space for the 32-byte SECMAP buffer at 0xEC80 to precede the DOS file buffers that begin at 0xECA0 and the file buffers end at 0xF7F8, which is seven bytes before the beginning of the ROM Monitor routines. As a reminder, reducing the number of file buffers in DOS 4.5 does not provide any additional memory for software programs because all five active file buffers reside in the memory of the Language Card partition. Before the MAXFILES handler rebuilds all of the file buffers so that they can be utilized by DOS, DOS 4.5 terminates any active EXEC file and closes all open files. If the DOS MAXFILES command is ever issued within an active EXEC file, the EXEC file is immediately terminated and closed, and any remaining commands in the EXEC file are not processed before the DOS MAXFILES handler rebuilds the designated number of file buffers.

If CONFIG Bit 3 is **set** in order to disable the DOS MAXFILES command as shown in Table III.1.1.1, the DOS 4.5 Command Manager bypasses the processing of the DOS MAXFILES handler when the DOS MAXFILES command is encountered **with** a parameter n. Processing of the DOS MAXFILES handler is **not** bypassed when the DOS MAXFILES command is encountered **without** a parameter n. In this instance DOS 4.5 will still display the current number of active file buffers on the Apple Command Line when DOS 4.5 **is not** in the RUN mode. When DOS **is** in the RUN mode and the DOS MAXFILES command is issued from within a program **without** a parameter n, the number of file buffers may be obtained by reading the Value Read buffer as shown in Figure III.1.5.2. Setting CONFIG Bit 3 is far easier to implement rather than having to modify or to edit a software program in order to eliminate all DOS MAXFILES commands thereby transforming the program to be far more suitable when operating within the DOS 4.5 processing environment. If the R keyword, even with a parameter value, is entered after the DOS MAXFILES command followed by a comma, the operational value of the MAXFILES command is *reset* to its **default** value of IMAXFLS, which is the value of 0x05, **except** when CONFIG Bit 3 is set, and in this case the R keyword is ignored and the operational value of the MAXFILES command is **not** reset. DOS 4.5 will issue a Syntax Error if a comma is not used between the DOS MAXFILES command and the R keyword.

6. MON Command

MON   [,C][,I][,O]

Example: MON
          MON C,I,O

This command is available in DOS 3.3 for DOS System commands and it functions in the same manner as it did in DOS 4.1 which is designed to also accept **no** input parameters. The DOS MON command enables the display of Commands, Input data, and Output data to the screen. All programmatically executed DOS commands are displayed if the C keyword is included with the DOS MON command. All Input data from a volume is displayed if the I keyword is included with the DOS MON command. All Output data to a volume is displayed if the O keyword is included with the DOS MON command. Figure III.1.6.1 shows an example in using the DOS MON command before processing an EXEC file. In this example the DOS MON command enables the C, I, and O keywords, the EXEC file EXECFILE is listed to show its contents, and finally the EXEC file is processed. Each statement in EXECFILE is echoed to the screen as if that statement had been entered directly onto the Apple Command Line. Each statement in this EXEC file is terminated by a carriage return that initiates DOS to process that statement.

If no keywords are included with the MON command, DOS enters the GOTOMON routine by means of ENTRMON. ENTRMON prints a carriage return and then calls INITPTRS to restore the DOS control over the CSWL and KSWL interface pointers before entering the GOTOMON routine. The GOTOMON routine initializes the stack pointer and XMODE to 0xFF, selects the main video and deselects the alternate character set, sets the video output to normal, initializes the text and graphics modes, sets the window operating parameters, and initializes the DOS CSWL and KSWL interface pointers. Because the Language Card partition is **enabled**, the verification check for ROM Applesoft **fails** in GOTOMON as it is designed to do. Otherwise, if the ROM is enabled as during the BOOT of DOS 4.5, the verification check for ROM Applesoft will **pass**. Thus, GOTOMON enters the RAM Monitor at memory address 0xFF65. If a ctrl-C is entered from within the RAM Monitor, DOS's control over the CSWL and KSWL interface pointers is re-enabled and DOS 4.5 is available and ready to process the next DOS command.

```
]MON C,I,O

]LIST EXECFILE
MON C,I,O
LIST TEXTFILE.TXT


]EXEC EXECFILE

]MON C,I,O

]LIST TEXTFILE.TXT

This is line 1.
This is line 2.
This is line 3.

]

]*
```

```
]NOMON C,I,O

]LIST EXECFILE2
NOMON C,I,O
LIST TEXTFILE.TXT


]EXEC EXECFILE2
]
]

This is line 1.
This is line 2.
This is line 3.
]

]*
```

Figure III.1.6.1. MON Command Display   Figure III.1.7.1. NOMON Command Display

147

7. NOMON Command

NOMON   [,C][,I][,O]

Example: NOMON
             NOMON C,I,O

This command is available in DOS 3.3 for DOS System commands and it functions in the same manner as it did in DOS 4.1 which is designed to also accept **no** input parameters. The DOS NOMON command disables the display of Commands, Input data, and Output data to the screen. All programmatically executed DOS commands are no longer displayed if the C keyword is included with the DOS NOMON command. All Input data from a volume is no longer displayed if the I keyword is included with the DOS NOMON command. All Output data to a volume is no longer displayed if the O keyword is included with the DOS NOMON command. Figure III.1.7.1 shows an example in using the DOS NOMON command before processing an EXEC file. In this example the DOS NOMON command disables the C, I, and O keywords, the EXEC file EXECFILE2 is listed to show its contents, and finally the EXEC file is processed. Each statement in EXECFILE2 is no longer echoed to the screen. Each statement in this EXEC file is terminated by a carriage return that initiates DOS to process that statement.

If no keywords are included with the NOMON command, DOS enters the GOTOMON routine by means of ENTRMON. ENTRMON prints a carriage return and then calls INITPTRS to restore the DOS control over the CSWL and KSWL interface pointers before entering the GOTOMON routine. The GOTOMON routine initializes the stack pointer and XMODE to 0xFF, selects the main video and deselects the alternate character set, sets the video output to normal, initializes the text and graphics modes, sets the window operating parameters, and initializes the DOS CSWL and KSWL interface pointers. Because the Language Card partition is **enabled**, the verification check for ROM Applesoft **fails** in GOTOMON as it is designed to do. Otherwise, if the ROM is enabled as during the BOOT of DOS 4.5, the verification check for ROM Applesoft will **pass**. Thus, GOTOMON enters the RAM Monitor at memory address 0xFF65. If a ctrl-C is entered from within the RAM Monitor, DOS's control over the CSWL and KSWL interface pointers is re-enabled and DOS 4.5 is available and ready to process the next DOS command.

8. PHASE Command

PHASE   [n][,R]

Example: PHASE
             PHASE,R
             PHASE 4
             PHASE $A

This command is not available in DOS 3.3 for DOS System commands and was initially developed for DOS 4.3, and this command has been enhanced in DOS 4.5 to accept the R keyword. The DOS PHASE command provides the means to establish the number of half-phases n that define the width of disk tracks in a DOS volume when that volume is first initialized. The value for n may be entered as a decimal number or as a hexadecimal number that is preceded by the dollar sign $. PHASE values for n may be entered directly on the Apple Command Line or within an Applesoft program or an assembly language routine. If no value or zero is entered with the DOS PHASE command for n, its current or operational value is displayed in decimal if its value is less than ten, otherwise its value is displayed in hexadecimal and prefaced by 0x on the Apple Command Line when DOS 4.5 **is not** in the RUN mode. When DOS **is** in the RUN mode and the DOS PHASE command is issued from within a program without a parameter n, the current operational value of the PHASE command may be obtained and displayed according to the design of that program because the DOS PHASE command belongs to a special non-keyword *integer value* category of commands.

Once a volume is initialized with a particular phase value other than the default value of 0x04, that phase value must be re-established in DOS 4.5 prior to accessing that volume for any data I/O to occur. The phase value for an Apple Master DOS diskette is equal to the default value of DFLTPHAS which is defined to be 0x04. It is quite possible to initialize a volume with multiple phase values where the software that resides on this unique volume knows when to change the phase value before it accesses those particular tracks. Figure III.1.8.1 shows a volume that is initialized with a phase value of 0x03, and this volume will contain forty-eight tracks within the same disk magnetic area that volumes having a phase value of 0x04 contain in thirty-six tracks. Figure III.1.8.2 shows the VTOC of this same volume after the volume has been initialized with forty-eight tracks. If the R keyword, even with a parameter value, is entered after the DOS PHASE command followed by a comma, the operational value of the PHASE command is *reset* to its **default** value of DFLTPHAS, which is the value of 0x04. DOS 4.5 will issue a Syntax Error if a comma is not used between the DOS PHASE command and the R keyword.

```
]PHASE 3
]INIT HELLO,PHASE Figure,A48,L$F00B,D2
]LSB Available = 0x30,0x05
S=6 D=02 V=000 F=0718 02/14/24 08:28:48
 A 002 HELLO              02/14/24 08:28:48
]LSR
B=4506H boot T=PHASE Figure
M=4506H P=03 L=0xF00B 02/14/24 08:28:48
S=6 D=02 V=000 F=0718 02/14/24 08:28:48
 001 0x12,0x0F HELLO
]※
```

Figure III.1.8.1. PHASE Command Display

```
]PHASE 3
]TS A17
0011 0545 06C8 00C2 D0C8 C1D3 C5A0 C6E9
E7F5 F2E5 A0A0 A0A0 A0A0 A0A0 A0A0 A0A0
4828 0824 1402 037A 0BF0 4828 0824 1402
1201 0000 3010 0001 0000 0000 0000 0000
FC00 0000 FFFF 0000 FFFF 0000 FFFF 0000
FFFF 0000 FFFF 0000 FFFF 0000 FFFF 0000
FFFF 0000 FFFF 0000 FFFF 0000 FFC0 0000
3FFF 0000 FFFF 0000 FFFF 0000 FFFF 0000
FFFF 0000 FFFF 0000 FFFF 0000 FFFF 0000
FFFF 0000 FFFF 0000 FFFF 0000 FFFF 0000
FFFF 0000 FFFF 0000 FFFF 0000 FFFF 0000
FFFF 0000 FFFF 0000 FFFF 0000 FFFF 0000
FFFF 0000 FFFF 0000 0000 0000 0000 0000
TS = 0x11,0x00
]
```

Figure III.1.8.2. PHASE 3 VTOC Display

I spent a significant amount of time once again analyzing the algorithm that DOS 3.3 and DOS 4.1 use in order to move the Disk][read/write disk head from one track to an adjacent track and from one track to many distant tracks in either direction. This algorithm includes an acceleration and deceleration component to ensure that radial movements to and from distant tracks occur accurately and in the least amount of time. When moving the read/write disk head to distant tracks, it is necessary to account for all induced momentum and all mechanical reluctance in the Cam Rider and in the Carriage Rod as shown in Figure I.10.1. I literally opened a Disk][drive enclosure and marked where tracks 0, 1, 2, 3, and 4 are located along the Cam Channel on the Cam Table. After much trial and error and experimentation, I developed an algorithm to move the Cam Rider in half-phase steps perfectly and repeatably in either direction. Lastly, I added in the acceleration and deceleration components to the algorithm that have sufficient electromagnetic holding time in order to buffer any induced momentum and mechanical reluctance, and to provide accurate and efficient target track movements.

In order to obtain the highest signal-to-noise ratio for the recording and playback of data onto a diskette, Apple designed the Disk][read/write disk head to be somewhat smaller than the width of a nominal, four half-phase track. Actually, Apple manufactured their read/write disk heads approximately the size of three half-phases. As an aside, Rana manufactured their read/write disk heads for their Rana drives slightly smaller than the size of two half-phases. A Disk][is **not** capable of reading and writing tracks that are spaced less than three half-phases due to the extreme crosstalk between adjacent tracks. However, the Disk][is capable of reading and writing tracks that are spaced three half-phases or more. The RWTS MOVHD algorithm I designed is capable of de-energizing two adjacent electromagnetic poles within four microseconds, and the position of the read/write disk head is maintained between those electromagnetic poles by mechanical reluctance of the Carriage Rod. The operational value of the DOS PHASE command, normally set to 0x04 as its **default**, can be *reset* from 0x01 to 0x10 half-phases.

Virtual][is capable of storing data in the WOZ 1.0 and in the WOZ 2.0 disk image formats. These formats are basically an offshoot of the Applesauce project started by John K. Morris, and they duplicate the way data is stored on a physical diskette. Using Virtual][, a WOZ 2.0 volume may be initialized by DOS 4.5 using an operational PHASE value other than 0x04 in order to create unique volume images.

9. PR# Command

PR   s

Example: PR#7

This command is available in DOS 3.3 for DOS System commands and no enhancements have been made to this command so it functions in the same manner in DOS 4.5. The DOS PR# handler configures the CSWL interface pointer to send all subsequent data to the peripheral device that resides in the specified peripheral slot s instead of to the Apple display.

The DOS PR# handler makes a call to the ROM Monitor OUTPORT routine at 0xFE95 with the value of the slot number s in the A-register. The ROM Monitor OUTPORT routine directly follows the ROM Monitor SETVID routine at 0xFE93 that simply loads the A-register with zero in order to reconnect the Apple display to the CSWL interface pointer. The ROM Monitor SETVID routine is one of several ROM Monitor routines that is called during the BOOT sequence for DOS 4.5 as shown in Table I.9.2.

Figure III.1.2.1 shows an example Applesoft program that uses the DOS PR# command in order to configure the CSWL interface pointer to slot 4 in order to communicate with the Thunderclock card that resides in slot 4.

10. SV Command

SV   [n]

Example: SV
              SV 1234
              SV $1234

This command is not available in DOS 3.3 for DOS System commands and was initially developed as a File System command for DOS 4.1, and this command has been enhanced as a DOS System command in DOS 4.3. The DOS SV or Show Value command displays on the Apple Command Line the decimal and hexadecimal values for the number n. The value for n may be entered as a decimal number or as a hexadecimal number that is preceded by the dollar sign $. SV values for n may be entered directly on the Apple Command Line or within an Applesoft program or an assembly language routine. If no value or a value up to and including 65535 or 0xFFFF is entered for n for the DOS SV command, the value of n is redisplayed as a 16-bit hexadecimal number that is prefaced by 0x as well as a zero-prefaced five digit decimal number on the Apple Command Line when DOS 4.5 **is not** in the RUN mode. When DOS **is** in the RUN mode and the DOS SV command is issued from within an Applesoft program or an assembly language routine, the current value of the SV command may be obtained and displayed according to the design of that program because the DOS SV command belongs to a special non-keyword *integer value* category of commands.

Figure III.1.10.1 shows how the DOS SV command can be used on the Apple Command Line. The DOS SV command is a convenient way to convert numbers from decimal to hexadecimal or from hexadecimal to decimal without having to reach for the hexadecimal calculator. The DOS SV command can also be utilized from within an Applesoft program or an assembly language routine. A simple Applesoft program that displays several examples in how the DOS SV command can be utilized is shown in Figure III.1.10.2. Real, Integer, and Simple Strings can certainly be used for the input SV command value. The Value Read buffer is utilized by the DOS SV handler in order to store its operational value only when DOS is in the RUN mode.

```
]LS

S=6 D=02 V=000 F=0548 02/14/24 08:28:48

 A 002 SV TEST1        02/14/24 08:28:48
 A 002 SV TEST2        02/14/24 08:28:48
 A 002 SV TEST3        02/14/24 08:28:48
]SV 1234 = 0x04D2 = 01234

]SV $1234 = 0x1234 = 04660

]SV = 0x0000 = 00000

]sv $ffff = 0xFFFF = 65535

]▓
```

```
10 D$ = CHR$ (4)
20 PRINT D$;"SV 123": GOSUB 100

30 B = 1234: PRINT D$;"SV ";B: GOSUB
   100
40 C$ = "$1234": PRINT D$;"SV ";
   C$: GOSUB 100
50 D% = 4321: PRINT D$;"SV ";D%:
   GOSUB 100
90 END
100 INPUT SV: PRINT "SV = ";SV:
    RETURN
]run
SV = 123

SV = 1234

SV = 4660

SV = 4321

]
```

Figure III.1.10.1. SV Command Display   Figure III.1.10.2. SV Command Program

The Print Decimal PRTDEC routine is severely flawed in DOS 3.3, and it can only convert 8-bit hexadecimal values to decimal. DOS 4.5 requires the conversion of 16-bit hexadecimal values to decimal in order to selectively print numbers that have up to five zero-prefaced decimal digits. The DOS SV handler is an example of one of several routines that is required to print up to five zero-prefaced decimal digits to the display. The algorithm I designed for the DOS 4.5 PRTDEC routine requires one additional program byte and one additional data byte for the low-order Decimal Table bytes DECTBLL and five additional data bytes for the added high-order Decimal Table bytes DECTBLH.

11. TIME Command

TIME

Example: TIME

This command is not available in DOS 3.3 for DOS System commands and this command was initially developed for DOS 4.5 Build 06. The DOS TIME command calculates the number of seconds that have elapsed from the preceding 12 AM hour or midnight or from the preceding 12 PM hour or noon. A 16-bit parameter in the Apple][is not large enough to contain the number of seconds in twenty-four hours, but it may contain the number of seconds in twelve hours which is 0xA8C0 or 43200. When the DOS TIME command is issued on the Apple Command Line when DOS 4.5 **is not** in the RUN mode, the number of seconds that have elapsed from the preceding 12 AM hour or 12 PM hour is displayed in hexadecimal and in decimal. When DOS **is** in the RUN mode and the DOS TIME command is issued from within an Applesoft program or an assembly language routine, the current value of the TIME parameter may be obtained and displayed according to the design of that program. The Value Read buffer is used by the DOS TIME handler in order to store its operational value only when DOS is in the RUN mode.

Many times it is useful or necessary to know how much time in seconds certain software routines or programs require for their processing. It is quite possible, though somewhat cumbersome, to obtain this information by capturing and parsing the output of the DOS DATE command before and after the event under analysis, and calculating for each time the number of seconds from the preceding 12 AM hour or 12 PM hour by extracting the current hour, minute, and second values. This is precisely how the DOS TIME handler calculates the number of seconds that have elapsed from the preceding 12 AM hour or 12 PM hour. Using the DOS TIME command to obtain both the before and the after time values in seconds for the event and then subtracting those values will provide the elapsed number in seconds for that event. This is now trivial it is to use the DOS TIME command to measure the elapsed time for any event.

When the DOS TIME command is utilized on the Apple Command Line and DOS **is not** in the RUN mode, several examples that show the current date using the DOS DATE command and the current processed time using the DOS TIME command are shown in Figure III.1.11.1. The elapsed time from 12 PM is calculated from the current time and that is equal to the processing time. When the DOS TIME command is utilized from within an Applesoft program or an assembly language routine and DOS **is** in the RUN mode, the number of elapsed seconds that is calculated by the DOS TIME handler can be obtained from the Value Read buffer. A simple Applesoft program that shows how to obtain the processing time that is stored in the Value Read buffer is shown in Figure III.1.11.2. The Value Read buffer is used by the DOS TIME handler in order to store its processing time value only when DOS **is** in the RUN mode.

```
]LS

S=6 D=02 V=000 F=0546 02/14/24 08:28:48

 A 002 TIME TEST1        02/14/24 08:28:48
 A 002 TIME TEST2        02/14/24 08:28:48
 A 002 TIME TEST3        02/14/24 08:28:48
 A 002 TIME TEST2B       02/14/24 08:28:48

]DATE = 02/14/24 12:50:34

]TIME = 0x0BDA = 03034

]PRINT 0*3600 + 50*60 + 34
3034

]DATE = 02/14/24 12:51:47

]TIME = 0x0C23 = 03107

]PRINT 0*3600 + 51*60 + 47
3107

]※
```

```
10 D$ =  CHR$ (4): PRINT
20  PRINT D$;"DATE": GOSUB 100:A
    = TI: PRINT "A = ";A
30  FOR I = 1 TO 1000:J = (I + 1
    ) * 2: NEXT : PRINT
40  PRINT D$;"DATE": GOSUB 100:B
    = TI: PRINT "B = ";B
50 C = B - A: PRINT : PRINT "B-A
    = ";C
90  END
100  PRINT D$;"TIME": INPUT TI: RETURN

]RUN

02/14/24 13:00:40
A = 3640

02/14/24 13:00:46
B = 3646

B-A = 6

]
```

Figure III.1.11.1. TIME Command Display   Figure III.1.11.2. TIME Command Program

12. USER Command

USER   [n]

Example: USER
            USER 1234
            USER $1234

This command is not available in DOS 3.3 for DOS System commands and this command was initially developed for DOS 4.5 Build 05. The DOS USER command provides the user with the ability to configure the page-zero DOSBUFR parameter with a 16-bit operational value n. The value for n may be entered as a decimal number or as a hexadecimal number that is preceded by the dollar sign $. USER operational values for n may be entered directly on the Apple Command Line or within an Applesoft program or an assembly language routine. If no value is entered with the DOS USER command, the operational value for USER is set to zero. The DOS USER command works in concert with the INITVALS parameters USERADR and CMDVAL as shown in Table I.8.5 and the MNGUSER routine as shown in Table I.8.1.

The DOS USER command belongs to a special non-keyword *integer value* category of commands and the DOS USER handler may be configured by the user or by a program to function in several different ways. The default configuration of the DOS USER handler is established by those values that are initially set for USERADR and CMDVAL when DOS 4.5 first BOOTs. The routine MNGUSER also establishes those same default configuration values when the routine is called with the C-flag **clear** regardless what values are currently in the registers. USERADR is set to the address of ENTRMON, or 0xD49A, and CMDVAL is set to CMDRUN-CMDTBL, or 0x06 when DOS 4.5 first BOOTs. ENTRMON is the same routine that the DOS MON and NOMON handlers use when no keywords are included with those DOS commands in order to enter the ROM Monitor at memory address 0xFF65. The DOS USER handler loads the X-register with the LSB of the USER value n from DOSBUFR and the A-register with the MSB of the USER value n from DOSBUFR+1 before making a call to the CALLUSER routine. The CALLUSER routine is simply an indirect jump to the address found in USERADR.

153

The DOS USER command has already been presented to perform two modes of operation that are shown in Figures I.8.4 and I.8.5. Figure I.8.4 shows an example assembly language routine that calls MNGUSER to manage the initialization of DOS 4.5 to BOOT in a very special way. MNGUSER is called to initialize USERADR with the address for the SPCLCODE routine in the Y- and A-registers, and CMDVAL is initialized with the CMDUSER-CMDTBL value, or 0x60. When DOS 4.5 BOOTs, instead of calling the DOS RUN handler, the DOS USER handler is called instead. Once DOS 4.5 has initialized and Applesoft is no longer in control, the SPCLCODE routine is processed. The SPCLCODE routine can call MNGUSER again, this time with the C-flag **clear** in order to restore the default values for USERADR and CMDVAL. The EPROM Operating System I designed for the SCRG quikLoader utilizes this mode of operation in order to load DOS into memory from the quikLoader, initialize DOS, and allow EOS to remain in control. Figure I.8.5 shows a second mode of operation for the DOS USER command. The DOS 4.5 *Big Mac* loader is an assembly language routine that utilizes MNGUSER in order to connect the DOS USER command to the re-entry address of *Big Mac*. The *Big Mac* loader is the task that manages Auxiliary memory and places the *Big Mac* executable code at its required address in the Language Card partition of Auxiliary memory. After the user has exited *Big Mac* and if the user enters USER on the Apple Command Line followed by a carriage return, *Big Mac* is immediately brought back into focus. Figure III.1.12.1 shows the exit message for *Big Mac* that informs the *Big Mac* user how to restart *Big Mac* using the DOS USER command.

The DOS USER command may also be associated with an assembly language routine in order to process selected functions within that assembly language routine as a third mode of operation. USER values for n may include direct, integer, real, or simple string variables. Figure III.1.12.2 shows an example Applesoft program where the DOS USER command passes various numerical values using direct, real, and simple string variables to the assembly language routine USERMNG that is designed to print those values that it receives by means of the DOS USER command. Every time the Applesoft program references the DOS USER command, the DOS USER handler calls the routine that is located at 0x404C by means of an indirect jump instruction at CALLUSER that is within the DOS 4.5 Language Card partition interface. Creative program design possibilities are virtually infinite in how the DOS USER command may be utilized as a conduit between an Applesoft program and a multi-functioned assembly language routine. The assembly language routine may process different algorithms that are based on the value that is passed from the Applesoft program by means of the DOS USER command.

```
Type 'USER' to restart Big Mac


]LS,D2

S=6 D=02 V=000 F=0535 02/14/24 08:28:48

 L  008  USERMNG.L      02/14/24  08:28:48
 B  003  USERMNG        02/14/24  08:28:48
 A  002  PGMUSER        02/14/24  08:28:48
 A  002  PGMUSER2       02/14/24  08:28:48
 A  002  PGMUSER3       02/14/24  08:28:48
 A  002  PGMUSER4       02/14/24  08:28:48
]*
```

Figure III.1.12.1. USER Command Display

```
10 D$ =   CHR$ (4):A$ = "$1234":A
      = 65535: PRINT D$;"BLOAD US
   ERMNG,A$4000": CALL 16384
30   PRINT D$;"USER"
40   PRINT D$;"USER 1234"
50   PRINT D$;"USER ";A$
60   PRINT D$;"USER ";A
]RUN
Activating the USERMNG program.
Content of USERADR variable:  0xD49A

Call MNGUSER with USERPGM address.
Content of USERADR variable:  0x404C

Entered USER function, value = 0x0000
Entered USER function, value = 0x04D2
Entered USER function, value = 0x1234
Entered USER function, value = 0xFFFF

Call MNGUSER to reset USERADR, exiting.
Content of USERADR variable:  0xD49A
]*
```

Figure III.1.12.2. USER Command Program

Command	Command Syntax
CATALOG CAT LS	[,Ss][,Dd][Vv][,B][,R] [,Ss][,Dd][Vv][,B][,R] [,Ss][,Dd][Vv][,B][,R]
CD	[,Ss][,Dd][Vv][,R]
DELETE RM	f [,Ss][,Dd][,Vv][,R] f [,Ss][,Dd][,Vv][,R]
DIFF	f, f2 [,Ss][,Dd][,Vv]
GREP	f, f2 [,Ss][,Dd][,Vv]
INIT	f, f2 [,Ss][,Dd][,Vv][,An][,Bn][,Ln][,R[n]]
LIST MORE	f [,Ss][,Dd][,Vv][,Aa][,Bb][,Ll][,R] [f] [,Ss][,Dd][,Vv][,Aa][,Bb][,Ll][,R]
LOCK	[f] [,Ss][,Dd][,Vv]
RENAME MV	f, f2 [,Ss][,Dd][,Vv][,R] f, f2 [,Ss][,Dd][,Vv][,R]
TOUCH	[f] [,Ss][,Dd][,Vv][,R]
TS	[,Ss][,Dd][,Vv][,An][,Bn][,L][,R]
UNLOCK	[f] [,Ss][,Dd][,Vv]
URM	f [,Ss][,Dd][,Vv]
VERIFY	f [,Ss][,Dd][,Vv][,R1]
WTS	Ln, Rn [,Ss][,Dd][,Vv][,An][,Bn]

Table III.2.0.1. File System Commands in DOS 4.5

2. File System Commands

The File System commands in the DOS 4.5 command repertoire consist of those commands that manage the general operation of the file system for a disk volume in an Apple][computer. The DOS CATALOG command can display the basic contents of a disk volume. The DOS CD Command can manage the directory parameters Slot, Drive, and Volume. The DOS DELETE and URM commands can remove or restore a file, respectively, on a disk volume. The DOS DIFF command can compare two files on a disk volume and show where they are different. The DOS GREP command can show the location of specific string data that is found in a disk file. The DOS INIT command can initialize a disk volume to BOOT or to exclusively store DATA. The DOS LIST command can display the contents of any disk file. The DOS LOCK and UNLOCK commands can either lock or unlock, respectively, a disk file or a disk volume.   The DOS RENAME command can change the name of a disk file. The DOS TOUCH command can update the date and time stamp of a disk file or of a disk volume. The DOS TS and WTS commands can display and modify, respectively, a single disk volume sector. The DOS VERIFY command can read the TSL and data sectors of a disk file in order to confirm that there are no RWTS errors when reading that disk file.

The syntax of the File System commands is shown in Table III.2.0.1. All of the File System commands are permitted to be used from within an Applesoft program or an assembly language routine as well as on the Apple Command Line. The majority of the File System Commands depend on a specific File Manager handler. Either the Command Manager or the external File Manager user can implement all of the functionality of a specific File System Command by means of a File Manager handler. For example, the File Manager FMCATACD command directs the File Manager CATHNDLR handler to implement all of the functionality for the DOS CATALOG command. The DOS DIFF, GREP, and LIST commands do not depend on a specific File Manager handler. These File System commands depend primarily on the File Manager CMDHNDLR, DOSECLEN, RDTEXT, and RD2BYT routines. The DOSECLEN routine calls the CMDHNDLR routine among its many functions, the RDTEXT routine reads a single byte of data from an open Text file, and the RD2BYT routine reads two bytes of data from any open file. The CMDHNDLR routine closes the requested file if it is already open, locates an unused file buffer, builds the File Manager Context Block, and calls the File Manager driver with the requested File Manager command such as FMOPENCD, FMCLOSCD, FMREADCD, or FMWRITCD as shown in Table I.11.2.

1. CATALOG Command

CATALOG	[,Ss][,Dd][,Vv][,B][,R]	
CAT	[,Ss][,Dd][,Vv][,B][,R]	; short version
LS	[,Ss][,Dd][,Vv][,B][,R]	; UNIX version

Example: CATALOG S6,D2
           CAT D1
           LS B
           LS,R

This command is available in DOS 3.3 for File System commands and was initially enhanced for DOS 4.1 to accept the R keyword, and this command has been further enhanced to accept the B keyword in DOS 4.5. The DOS CATALOG command depends on the File Manager CATHNDLR handler. This handler displays a wealth of information for the specified volume, and it shows the current slot as S=, the current drive as D=, and the current volume number as V=, the remaining free space as F=, the date and time the VTOC was last modified, and a list of all files that are resident in the volume. Each file is displayed with its lock/unlock status, its file Type, its size in sectors including all TSL sectors, the first fourteen ASCII characters of its filename, and the date and time when the file was either created or last modified. Table I.7.3 lists all file Types that are native to DOS 4.5. Since the DOS CATALOG command does not expect a filename, this command does not require a comma or a space before the first keyword. However, a comma or a space may be used after the DOS CATALOG command and before a keyword.

Figure III.2.1.1 shows an example display of the DOS CATALOG command. Notice that the asterisk before the file Type designates that the files DOS4.5 and INSTALL are both locked. This figure also shows an example of the DOS CAT command when the B keyword is included with this command. As a reminder, DOS 4.5 commands may be entered in lowercase. The B keyword shows that this volume has been initialized with 0x23 or 35 tracks and five sectors are available for its catalog. Therefore, the catalog on this volume has the capacity to contain up to thirty-five file entries whether or not there is sufficient data sectors on this volume for the data that is specified in the TSL sectors of thirty-five files.

If the R keyword is included with the DOS CATALOG command, the display shows the version and build of the DOS that created this volume as B=, the volume Type as boot or as data, the twenty-four ASCII character volume title as T=, the version of DOS that is currently in memory as M=, the phase value that was used to initialize this volume as P=, the volume library value that is assigned to this volume as L=, and the date and time this volume was created, followed by a list of all of the files and another set of information for each file that is resident in this volume. With the R keyword, each file is displayed with its lock/unlock status as before, its volume sequence number, the track and sector values of its first TSL sector, and **all** twenty-four ASCII characters of its filename. Figure III.2.1.2 shows an example display of the DOS LS R command. Having the track and sector values of the first TSL sector for a file is absolutely necessary in order to begin any investigation of that file, its TSL sector resources, and the location of all of the data sectors that are currently assigned to that file.

```
]CATALOG S6,D2

S=6 D=02 V=000 F=0488 02/14/24 08:28:48

*B 044 DOS4.5            02/14/24 08:28:48
 L 013 INSTALL.L         02/14/24 08:28:48
*B 003 INSTALL           02/14/24 08:28:48
 L 006 MOVEDOS.L         02/14/24 08:28:48

]cat,b Available = 0x23,0x05

S=6 D=02 V=000 F=0488 02/14/24 08:28:48

*B 044 DOS4.5            02/14/24 08:28:48
 L 013 INSTALL.L         02/14/24 08:28:48
*B 003 INSTALL           02/14/24 08:28:48
 L 006 MOVEDOS.L         02/14/24 08:28:48

]*
```

Figure III.2.1.1. CATALOG and CAT Commands

```
]LS R

B=4506H data T=CATALOG Figure

M=4506H P=04 L=0xF001 02/14/24 08:28:48

S=6 D=02 V=000 F=0488 02/14/24 08:28:48

*001 0x12,0x0F DOS4.5
 002 0x15,0x0F INSTALL.L
*003 0x16,0x0F INSTALL
 004 0x17,0x0F MOVEDOS.L
x005 0x18,0x0F DOS2TO1

]*
```

Figure III.2.1.2. LS R Command Display

When DOS 4.5 initializes a disk volume, RWTS is designed to create sixteen sectors on each disk track starting with sector 0x00 and incrementing sector number sequentially up to and including sector 0x0F. However, RWTS utilizes a sector interleave table that translates this physical sector number to an operational sector number that is used by the Volume Manager and the Command Manager for TSL and data sectors that are assigned to a file. The sector interleave table provides a Two Descending skew for each sector number. This skew optimizes the reading of data from and the writing of data to a disk sector when the operational sector number begins with sector 0x0F and is sequentially decremented down to include sector 0x00. The DOS 4.5 File Manager is purposefully designed to create a new file on a disk volume and utilize sector 0x0F on any available track for the first TSL sector that is assigned to that file. The data for the file is stored on the remaining sectors of that same track, and those sectors are sequentially decremented down and listed in that order in the TSL sector. This process continues to utilize the next available track and use those sectors beginning with sector 0x0F. If another TSL sector is required after 0x7A or 122 data sectors have been written, the next following sector on that same track is utilized for another TSL sector. The first or previous TSL sector is updated with the track/sector information of that second or following TSL sector. The Two Descending skew that is utilized for this design procedure that optimizes the reading and writing of files in a DOS 4.5 file system will significantly accelerate disk I/O. Having the DOS CATALOG command provide the track and sector values for the first TSL sector of a given file is necessary in order to begin any analysis of the sector resources that DOS 4.5 has allocated to that file. Knowing and understanding the design and logic that DOS 4.5 utilizes in order to allocate resources to any file makes this analytical procedure easy to follow.

2. CD Command

```
CD          [,Ss][,Dd][,Vv][,R]

Example:    CD
            CD,R
            CD S6,D2,V3
```

This command is not available in DOS 3.3 for File System commands and this command was initially developed for DOS 4.1 and was enhanced for DOS 4.3 to accept the R keyword, and this command was further enhanced for DOS 4.5 to utilize the newly created File Manager FMCDCD command or 0x11 for the new File Manager CDHNDLR handler. This handler can change the current slot, drive, and volume parameters that are used by the Command Manager and by the File Manager to a different value for slot, drive, or volume. If no keywords are used with the DOS CD command, the current slot, drive, and volume parameters are displayed on the Apple Command Line after the DOS CD command. Two values are displayed for volume. The first value comes from DISKVOL as shown in Table I.5.2 and the second value comes from VOLNUMBR as shown in Table I.12.2. DISKVOL is the actual volume number value that is used in the VTOC and VOLNUMBR is the volume number value that is used in an RWTS IOCB by the File Manager. When these values differ and VOLNUMBR is not zero, the Volume Number Mismatch error message is issued as shown in Figure III.2.2.1. This figure shows two examples in using the DOS CD command. When the DOS CD command is used **with** keywords, the keyword values are stored in the CMDVALS Data structure to be utilized by subsequent DOS commands and nothing further is displayed on the Apple Command Line.

When the R keyword is included with the DOS CD command followed by a space or comma or neither, the VTOC of the volume that is currently in focus is read and its variable DOSCONFG as shown in Table I.5.2 is copied to the variable VALSCNFG as shown in Table I.8.5. Using the DOS CD command with the R keyword can restore the DOS configuration that was employed when this volume was initialized. The value of VALSCNFG can be displayed by using the DOS CONFIG command without arguments.

```
]CD S6,D2,V123
]LS
S=6 D=02 V=123 F=0518 02/14/24 08:28:48
 A 004 HELLO              02/14/24 08:28:48
]
]CD = S=6 D=02 V=123 123
]
]LS V23
Volume Number Mismatch
]cd = S=6 D=02 V=123 023
]
```

Figure III.2.2.1. CD Command Display

```
]DELETE DOS1TO2
]CAT
S=6 D=02 V=000 F=0510 02/14/24 08:28:50
 B 044 DOS4.5             02/14/24 08:28:48
]
]CAT,R
B=4506H data T=DELETE Figure
M=4506H P=04 L=0xF005 02/14/24 08:28:48
S=6 D=02 V=000 F=0510 02/14/24 08:28:50
 001 0x12,0x0F DOS4.5
x002 0x15,0x0F DOS1TO2
]
```

Figure III.2.3.1. DELETE Command Display

158

3. DELETE Command

```
DELETE     f [,Ss][,Dd][,Vv][,R]
RM         f [,Ss][,Dd][,Vv][,R]                              ; UNIX version

Example:   DELETE COPYDOS
           RM COPYDOS,R
```

This command is available in DOS 3.3 for File System commands and this command was enhanced for DOS 4.3 to accept the R keyword. The DOS DELETE command depends on the File Manager DELHNDLR handler. This handler removes the filename f entry from the specified volume Catalog if the filename exists by **setting** the most significant bit of its TSL track byte, and marking the data sectors that are listed in the TSL sector(s) of file f as well as all of its TSL sectors as available in the VTOC. Refer to Figure I.7.1 that shows the components of a volume Catalog entry.

Figure III.2.3.1 shows an example of a file that is deleted. In that figure the file DOS1TO2 is marked with the character x where the asterisk is used to mark a locked file. **A deleted file is never a locked file.** It is prudent to undelete a deleted file as soon as possible because the data sectors that are listed in the TSL sector(s) of file f as well as all of its TSL sectors are now available in the VTOC, and those sectors may be utilized by another file. A locked file cannot be deleted unless the file is first unlocked or the R keyword is used to override the lock status.

When the R keyword is included with the DOS DELETE command, the specified filename f is marked as deleted in the volume Catalog regardless whether the file is locked or not. That is, the R keyword can be used to override the lock status for any file when that file is deleted. This capability is quite useful when a series of files must be deleted without regard to their lock status or without having to determine what that lock status is. Locking a file still provides a level of protection from an accidental file deletion. Providing the capability of deleting a file without regard to its lock status by using the R keyword must not be used indiscriminately, but only when the power and the versatility of the R keyword is fully understood and properly appreciated.

4. DIFF Command

```
DIFF       f, f2 [,Ss][,Dd][,Vv]

Example:   DIFF TEST1,TEST2
```

This command is not available in DOS 3.3 for File System commands and was initially developed for DOS 4.1, and this command was enhanced for DOS 4.5. The DOS DIFF command compares any two files f and f2 in the specified volume up to the end of SECCNT-1 sectors for the second file, f2. The variable SECCNT is the sector count in the File Manager FMWORK Data structure as shown in Table I.12.2. The command displays the number of bytes that are compared on the Apple Command Line after the DOS DIFF command, the offsets(s) where the two files differ and the bytes that differ, and the total number of mismatched bytes. **The two specified files f and f2 must reside on the same volume.** The offset(s)

159

where the files differ are the number of bytes from the beginning of each file. The first differing byte comes from the first file, or f, and the second differing byte comes from the second file, or f2. Displayed values are all shown in hexadecimal. The DOS DIFF handler will not compare the same file. In this case, if file f and file f2 are the same filename, a Syntax Error is displayed.

Figure III.2.4.1 shows an example of three sets of files that are compared using the DOS DIFF command and one pair of files having the same filename. The first pair of files are identical and the display shows that 0x0100 bytes were compared even though the files themselves are only 0x0080 bytes in size. The DOS DIFF handler compares whole data sectors and the total number of mismatched bytes is zero. The second pair of files are exactly 0x1000 bytes in size but the DOS DIFF handler compared 0x1100 bytes. Because these are Binary files their address and length bytes occupy the first four bytes in the first data sector for each file, thus making the files actually 0x1004 bytes in length. Whole data sectors are compared, and the last four bytes of data for each file reside in that additional data sector. The total number of mismatched bytes shown for these two files is one. The third pair of files are actually 0x300 bytes in size, the offsets where each file differs is shown, and the number of mismatched bytes for these two files is three. Lastly, the DOS DIFF command compares the same file F1. The DOS DIFF handler displays the Syntax Error message because the same file is specified.

The DOS DIFF handler does not have the capability to re-establish synchronization for two files if one of the files contains an extra byte or a deleted byte somewhere within its data. In this case, a substantial number of bytes after the first difference that is encountered by the handler would be listed to the display and shown in the number of mismatches. The inserted or deleted byte would become very apparent and the DOS DIFF command will have actually served its purpose. In this instance, it is appropriate to enable the printer so that the address can be calculated from the displayed offset where the loss of file synchronization occurs, thus pointing to the location in the source code where the extra or missing byte can be located. Once the error is corrected, the DOS DIFF command will certainly show that the two files under inspection are once again identical. The DOS DIFF command can also be used to verify minor changes that are made to source code by comparing its generated object code file to its previous object code version. The object code does not even need to execute in order to be convinced that the intended changes that are made to the source code can indeed be found in the generated object code where they are expected to occur.

```
]DIFF F1,F2 = 0x0100
Number Mismatch = 00000
]DIFF N1,N2 = 0x1100
0x0F84 = 0x00,0xFF
Number Mismatch = 00001
]DIFF Z1,Z2 = 0x0400
0x0104 = 0x00,0xFF
0x0184 = 0x00,0xFF
0x0204 = 0x00,0xFF
Number Mismatch = 00003
]DIFF F1,F1
Syntax Error
]※
```

Figure III.2.4.1. DIFF Command Display

```
]GREP HELLO,WINDOW = 0x0500
0x0449
Found = 00001
]GREP VOLMGR,Images,D2 = 0x3700
0x22C9
0x256D
0x3372
0x33E8
Found = 00004
]GREP VOLMGR,Drive Information = 0x3700
0x32A7
0x32C0
Found = 00002
]
```

Figure III.2.5.1. GREP Command Display

160

5. GREP Command

GREP   f, f2 [,Ss][,Dd][,Vv]

Example: GREP HELLO,TEST
            GREP TEST1,Manage Test

This command is not available in DOS 3.3 for File System commands and was initially developed for DOS 4.1, and this command was enhanced for DOS 4.5. The DOS GREP command is designed to search file f for the single or multiple word ASCII character string f2 in the specified volume up to the end of SECCNT-1 sectors for file f. The DOS GREP handler displays on the Apple Command Line after the GREP command the number of bytes that will be searched in file f, and after this information the GREP handler displays each offset where the character string f2 is found in the file and the total number of times the character string f2 is found. Each offset where f2 is found is the number of bytes from the beginning of the file to the first character of f2. Displayed offset values are all shown in hexadecimal. The character string f2 must conform to the format and maximum length of a filename.

Figure III.2.5.1 shows an example of three DOS GREP command searches on two files. The first search is on an Applesoft file. The second and third searches are on a Binary file. The third search uses a multiple word character string for f2. The DOS GREP handler searches whole data sectors. Regardless how many actual bytes that are associated with the file in its last data sector, the entire last data sector is included in the data search. The DOS GREP handler is case sensitive as shown in Figure III.2.5.1. However, this handler masks out the MSB of all data that is read from file f such that the lower ASCII character 0x41 matches the upper ASCII character 0xC1. DOS 4.5 expects the character string that is contained in f2 to conform to the format and maximum length of a filename. Therefore, the first character must be an alpha character from A to Z or from a to z, and all characters after the first alpha character must be equal to or greater than the SPACE character 0xA0. If f2 does not conform to the format of a filename, processing of the Apple Command Line will pass from DOS to Applesoft. The maximum length of f2 is twenty-four characters. In the first example in Figure III.2.5.1, the DOS GREP command found one occurrence of WINDOW in the file HELLO, four occurrences of Images in the file VOLMGR, and two occurrences of Drive Information in the same file VOLMGR.

6. INIT Command

INIT   f, f2 [,Ss][,Dd][,Vv][,An][,Bn][,Ln][,R[n]]

Example: INIT HELLO,<title>,V123,L$101   ; creates Volume Type B
            INIT EXECFILE,<title>,R$14   ; creates Volume Type B
            INIT Hello,<title>,V123,r   ; creates Volume Type D

This command is available in DOS 3.3 for File System commands and was initially developed for DOS 4.1, and this command was enhanced for DOS 4.5. The DOS INIT command depends on the File Manager INITHNDL handler. This handler initializes the specified volume with the required filename f and a volume title f2, and the handler is able to write a DOS 4.5 image onto tracks 0x00 and 0x01, and ten

161

additional sectors onto track 0x02. A BOOT volume, or Volume Type B, is created having a DOS 4.5 image when the R keyword is **not** included or the value of the R keyword is **not** equal to zero. When the R keyword **is** included or the value of the R keyword **is** equal to zero, a DATA volume, or Volume Type D, is created **without** having a DOS 4.5 image. If the A or B keyword is not used or they are included with a value of zero, the default initialization values for ENDTRK and SECVAL come from LASTRACK and FIRSTCAT, respectively. The L keyword is used to specify a Library Value or subject value for the initialized volume. The L keyword value n is set to zero if that keyword is not included with the DOS INIT command.

Figure III.2.6.1 shows the initialization of a BOOT volume that has a DOS 4.5 image because the R keyword is **not** included with the DOS INIT command. The Applesoft program that is currently in memory is saved to the volume and its filename f is entered into the new volume Catalog. All initialized volumes are titled with the required upper ASCII character string that is contained in f2. The parameter v is assigned to the volume number if the V keyword is included; otherwise, the volume is initialized with a volume number of zero. In Figure III.2.6.1 the DOS CATALOG command with the R keyword shows that a BOOT volume has been created. The B keyword shows that this volume contains 0x23 tracks and five sectors are allocated for the volume Catalog. Figure III.2.6.2 shows the initialization of a DATA volume that does not have a DOS 4.5 image because the R keyword **is** included without a parameter with the DOS INIT command. An initialized DATA volume contains an empty volume Catalog because no file is saved to the volume even if there is an Applesoft file currently in memory. The filename f is simply a placeholder and its character string is discarded. All DATA volume sectors are available for data storage including all sectors on track 0x00. In Figure III.2.6.2 the DOS CATALOG command with the R keyword shows that a DATA volume has been created. The B keyword shows that this volume contains 0x23 tracks and five sectors are allocated for the volume Catalog.

```
]INIT HELLO,Boot Disk,D2,V123,L$F007
]
]CAT R
B=4506H boot T=Boot Disk
M=4506H P=04 L=0xF007 02/14/24 08:28:48
S=6 D=02 V=123 F=0510 02/14/24 08:28:48
 001 0x12,0x0F HELLO
]
]CAT B Available = 0x23,0x05
S=6 D=02 V=123 F=0510 02/14/24 08:28:48
 A 002 HELLO          02/14/24 08:28:48
]※
```

Figure III.2.6.1. INIT BOOT Volume Command

```
]init hello,Data Disk,v101,1$e009,r
]
]cat r
B=4506H data T=Data Disk
M=4506H P=04 L=0xE009 02/14/24 08:28:48
S=6 D=02 V=101 F=0554 02/14/24 08:28:48
]
]cat b Available = 0x23,0x05
S=6 D=02 V=101 F=0554 02/14/24 08:28:48
]※
```

Figure III.2.6.2. INIT DATA Volume Command

If the R keyword is included with a non-zero value, that value is copied to the variable CMDVAL that is found in the CMDVALS Data structure, and a BOOT volume is initialized that has a DOS 4.5 image. No HELLO or BOOT file is saved to that volume if BOOT Type or SUBCODE does not equal 0x06, the DOS RUN command, even if there is an Applesoft file currently in memory. This logic is new in DOS 4.5. The user is required to copy an EXEC file to the volume if R$14 is used or copy a Binary file to the volume if R$34 is used as its HELLO or BOOT file. Other possible values for the R keyword could include R$10 for CLOSE, R$2C for DATE, and R$2E for LIST, all obtained from Table III.0.2.

The complete set of DOS INIT handler initialization values, or INITVALS, is available at the address found in INITVAL at 0xBFFA. These initialization values are found in lower Main memory and they can be modified directly or indirectly before invoking the DOS INIT command in order to tailor a DOS 4.5 volume specific to ones needs and that of the target disk hardware. The INITVALS Data structure is found at memory address 0xBEE2 for DOS 4.5. See Table I.8.5 for a list of all of the available initialization variables. If the A or the B keyword is not used, its variable n value is set to zero, respectively. The A keyword value is used to specify a new ENDTRK, the *accepted* number of tracks in a DOS volume, and if the keyword value is zero, the default initialization value comes from LASTRACK. The lower four bits of the B keyword value is used to specify a new SECVAL, the number of Catalog sectors from 1 to 15, and if the keyword value is zero, the default initialization value comes from FIRSTCAT. The MSB of the B keyword value is used to select either 16-sector or 32-sector tracks. When the MSB is **clear**, then 16-sector tracks are selected, otherwise when the MSB is **set**, then 32-sector tracks are selected. The default setting is for 16-sector tracks. The L keyword is used to specify a Library Value from 0x0000 to 0xFFFF if it is included, otherwise the Library Value is set to zero. Once an initialization parameter has been changed, it remains equal to that value except for CMDVAL, SECVAL, ENDTRK, SUBJCT, and ENDSEC. There is no process or procedure in DOS 4.5 except for a total reBOOT of DOS 4.5 that can reset the following variables in the INITVALS Data structure to their *default* setting: NMAXVAL, YEARVAL, TRKVAL, VRSN, BLD, RAMTYP, VALSPHAS, TSPARS, ALCTRK, ALCDIR, VALSCNFG, and SECSIZ as shown in Table I.8.5. Please, use common sense when modifying these variables and only use those values that are within the normal operational values for these variables. Unexpected results may occur that could very well prevent DOS 4.5 the ability to read or to write a volume if irrational values are ever utilized.

SECVAL	Catalog Sectors	16 Sectors/Track		32 Sectors/Track	
		BOOT	DATA	BOOT	DATA
0x01	1	532	574	1108	1150
0x02	2	531	573	1107	1149
0x03	3	530	572	1106	1148
0x04	4	529	571	1105	1147
0x05	5	528	570	1104	1146
0x06	6	527	569	1103	1145
0x07	7	526	568	1102	1144
0x08	8	525	567	1101	1143
0x09	9	524	566	1100	1142
0x0A	10	523	565	1099	1141
0x0B	11	522	564	1098	1140
0x0C	12	521	563	1097	1139
0x0D	13	520	562	1096	1138
0x0E	14	519	561	1095	1137
0x0F	15	518	560	1094	1136

Table III.2.6.1. Available Sectors in BOOT and DATA Volumes

Tracks/Volume	16 Sectors/Track	32 Sectors/Track
35	560	1120
36	576	1152
40	640	1280
48	768	1536

Table III.2.6.2. Total Sectors in an Initialized Volume

The value in SECVAL determines the number of sectors that are used for the volume Catalog not including the VTOC sector. The useable values for SECVAL are 1≤SECVAL≤15. If its value is greater than fifteen, then SECVAL mod 0x0F Catalog sectors are allocated. Table III.2.6.1 shows the number of available data sectors and TSL sectors in a volume based on Volume Type for volumes having **thirty-six** tracks and with sixteen or thirty-two sectors per track. A few disk drives, either physical or solid state, were manufactured to access forty tracks for a volume. Set ENDTRK to 0x28, and either use A40 or A$28 to provide access to all forty tracks, or set ENDTRK to 0x30, and either use A48 or A$30 to access forty-eight tracks if they are available on the target device, such as an initialized volume in the CFFA using the *VOLMGR*. The VTOC is designed to manage up to fifty tracks per volume as shown previously in Figure I.5.2. Table III.2.6.2 shows the total number of sectors in a volume that have thirty-five, thirty-six, forty, or forty-eight tracks and with sixteen or thirty-two sectors per track. It is truly amazing the capabilities that are incorporated into the VTOC of an Apple][disk volume. It is quite a shame that these VTOC capabilities were never fully exploited in the early years of DOS 3.3 development and also for Apple][peripheral hardware development in order to utilize this amazing format even further.

7. LIST Command

```
LIST      f  [,Ss][,Dd][,Vv][,Aa][,Bb][,Ll][,R]
MORE      [f] [,Ss][,Dd][,Vv][,Aa][,Bb][,Ll][,R]          ; UNIX version

Example:  LIST EXECFILE
          LIST TESTFILE,B8,L10,R
```

This command is not available in DOS 3.3 for File System commands and was initially developed for DOS 4.1, and this command was enhanced for DOS 4.5. The DOS LIST command displays on the screen the data in ASCII that is contained in file f in the specified volume if the file Type is a Text file or the command displays the data that is contained in file f in hexadecimal for all other file Types. Table I.7.3 lists all of the file Types that are native in DOS 4.5. If the R keyword is included with the DOS LIST command, the data of a Text file is displayed in hexadecimal rather than in ASCII. If the B keyword is included, that number of data bytes b from the beginning of the file is skipped. If the L keyword is included, that number of data bytes l are displayed, or until the end of the file, whichever occurs first. The DOS LIST handler displays a complete data sector at a time, and the handler can be terminated at any time by pressing the ESCAPE key. The DOS LIST command displays the contents of file f whereas the Applesoft LIST command displays the contents of an Applesoft program if such a program currently resides in memory.

```
]LIST EXECFILE.T
MON CIO
BLOAD FOO
NOMON CIO

]

]LIST EXECFILE.T,L6
MON CI

]

]LIST EXECFILE.T,B9,L7
LOAD FO

]LIST EXECFILE.T,B9,L7,R
CCCF C1C4 A0C6 CFCF

]※
```

Figure III.2.7.1. LIST Text File Command

```
]LOAD STEST,R
A$0801,L$008A
]LIST STEST
8A00 2008 0A00 4424 D0E7 2834 293A 4624
D022 5354 4553 542E 5422 3AA5 AB31 3030
0033 0814 00BA 4424 3B22 4F50 454E 2022
3B46 2400 4708 1E00 BA44 243B 2257 5249
5445 2022 3B46 2400 6E08 2800 BA22 5468
6973 2069 7320 6120 7365 7175 656E 7469
616C 2054 4558 5420 6669 6C65 2E22 0082
0832 00BA 4424 3B22 434C 4F53 4520 223B
4624 0088 0864 0080 0000 000A 0000 0000
0000 0000 0000 0000 0000 0000 0000 0000
0000 0000 0000 0000 0000 0000 0000 0000
0000 0000 0000 0000 0000 0000 0000 0000
0000 0000 0000 0000 0000 0000 0000 0000
0000 0000 0000 0000 0000 0000 0000 0000
※
```

Figure III.2.7.2. LIST Applesoft File Command

The DOS LIST command is also capable of displaying data that resides at any memory location in either ASCII or in hexadecimal. DOS 4.5 now permits the direct display of data that resides in memory when the A keyword is used to specify a memory address with the DOS LIST command. Because the DOS LIST command is overloaded by DOS and by Applesoft, in order to display the contents of memory, the DOS MORE command is far more suitable because a filename is not required. If the A keyword is used with the DOS LIST command, however, any filename of any length or any set of characters must be included simply as a filename placeholder. This filename placeholder is discarded by the DOS LIST handler when the A keyword is processed. The B keyword as well as the L keyword may be utilized with the A keyword in order to skip b memory bytes and to display l memory bytes, respectively.

Figure III.2.7.1 shows examples of using the DOS LIST command on a Text file while utilizing the various keywords. First, the entire file is displayed. Next, the first six bytes of the file are displayed. Then, the first nine bytes are skipped and the next seven bytes are displayed. Finally, those same seven bytes are displayed as hexadecimal data. Hexadecimal data is always displayed as byte-pairs. Thus, the L in the data word BLOAD is the first hexadecimal byte that is displayed. Because byte-pairs are displayed together, eight hexadecimal bytes are displayed rather than the requested seven data bytes. The second O in the data word FOO is added to the displayed byte-pairs. Remember to count the carriage return or character 0x8D because it is also an ASCII character and this character is part of the data. The DOS LIST handler does **not** skip over a NULL byte or character 0x00, and the handler does **not** process a NULL byte or character 0x00 that is found in Random Access Data files when that file Type is displayed in ASCII. Random Access Data files should only be displayed in hexadecimal in order to display the complete contents of the records that are contained in the data of that file Type. Figure III.2.7.2 shows the length in bytes for the Applesoft file STEST which are the first two bytes that are found in the first data sector. The Applesoft file STEST is first read into memory using the R keyword in order to display its length in bytes, and then the DOS LIST command is used to display its first data sector, or the first 256 bytes of data in the file STEST. Figure III.2.7.3 uses the DOS TLOAD command to read the Text file EXECFILE.T into memory and then utilize the DOS MORE command to display the contents of memory. The results are identical to Figure III.2.7.1. The same procedure uses the DOS LOAD command in Figure III.2.7.4 in order to load the Applesoft file STEST into memory and then display the contents of memory using the DOS MORE command. Again, the results are identical to Figure III.2.7.2. The address 0x07FF was chosen in order to account for the file size that was shown in Figure III.2.7.2.

165

```
]TLOAD EXECFILE.T,R            ]LOAD STEST,R
A$0900,L$001B                  A$0801,L$008A
]MORE ,A$900,L$1B              ]MORE ,A$7FF,L$100,R

MON CIO                        0000 2008 0A00 4424 D0E7 2834 293A 4624
BLOAD FOO                      D022 5354 4553 542E 5422 3AA5 AB31 3030
NOMON CIO                      0033 0814 00BA 4424 3B22 4F50 454E 2022
                               3B46 2400 4708 1E00 BA44 243B 2257 5249
]MORE ,A$900,L6                5445 2022 3B46 2400 6E08 2800 BA22 5468
                               6973 2069 7320 6120 7365 7175 656E 7469
MON CI                         616C 2054 4558 5420 6669 6C65 2E22 0082
                               0832 00BA 4424 3B22 434C 4F53 4520 223B
]MORE ,A$900,B9,L7             4624 0088 0864 0080 0000 000A 0000 0000
                               0000 0000 0000 0000 0000 0000 0000 0000
LOAD FO                        0000 0000 0000 0000 0000 0000 0000 0000
                               0000 0000 0000 0000 0000 0000 0000 0000
]MORE ,A$900,B9,L7,R           0000 0000 0000 0000 0000 0000 0000 0000
                               0000 0000 0000 0000 0000 0000 0000 0000
CCCF C1C4 A0C6 CFCF            0000 0000 0000 0000 0000 0000 0000 0000

]                              ※
```

Figure III.2.7.3. MORE Text Memory Command   Figure III.2.7.4. MORE Memory Command

8. LOCK Command

LOCK   [f] [,Ss][,Dd][,Vv]

Example: LOCK
            LOCK TEST

This command is available in DOS 3.3 for File System commands and this command was enhanced for DOS 4.3 so that a filename f is not required. The DOS LOCK command depends on the File Manager LCKHNDLR handler. This handler **sets** the most significant bit of the Type byte of the file f in the specified volume Catalog as shown in Tables I.7.1 and I.7.2. A locked file cannot be deleted, renamed, or touched until the file is unlocked. The lock status of a file is indicated in the volume Catalog by using an asterisk before the Type character in the display entry for the file. The date and time stamp of a file **is** updated when a file f is locked. The date and time stamp for the VTOC **is not** updated when a file is locked because nothing is changed in the VTOC.

Figure III.2.8.1 shows how to use the DOS LOCK command in order to lock the file DOS4.5. The first volume Catalog shows that the Binary file DOS4.5 is not a locked file. After this file is locked using the DOS LOCK command, a second volume Catalog shows the asterisk before the Type character B for the display entry of this file. The presence of that asterisk indicates that the file DOS4.5 is now locked. There is **no** harm in locking a file that is already locked, and conversely, there is **no** harm in unlocking a file that is already unlocked.

When the DOS LOCK command is used in DOS 4.5 without specifying a filename, the **volume** that is currently in focus is locked. The keywords for Slot, Drive, and Volume may be used in order to specify a particular volume to be locked. The DOS LOCK command may be preceded by the DOS CD command in order to utilize its command capabilities in selecting the intended volume to be locked. When a volume is locked, the DATA and TSL buffers are flushed, the VTOC sector of the volume that is in focus is read into memory, the MSB is **set** for the VTOC DISKLOCK flag as shown in Table I.5.2, the VTOC is updated with a current date and time stamp, and the modified VTOC is written back to the same volume that is in focus. A locked volume may still be read at any time but DOS 4.5 is no longer able to write to the volume until the volume is unlocked. Understand that this procedure of locking a volume is simply a software lock implementation and not a hardware lock implementation. Other versions of DOS may ignore or be totally unaware of the status or the existence of the DISKLOCK flag in the VTOC.

```
]CAT

S=6 D=02 V=000 F=0486 02/14/24 08:28:48

 B 044 DOS4.5          02/14/24 08:28:48
 L 013 INSTALL.L       02/14/24 08:28:48
 B 003 INSTALL         02/14/24 08:28:48
 L 006 MOVEDOS.L       02/14/24 08:28:48
 B 002 DOS1TO2         02/14/24 08:28:48

]LOCK DOS4.5

]CAT

S=6 D=02 V=000 F=0486 02/14/24 08:28:48

*B 044 DOS4.5          02/14/24 08:28:50
 L 013 INSTALL.L       02/14/24 08:28:48
 B 003 INSTALL         02/14/24 08:28:48
 L 006 MOVEDOS.L       02/14/24 08:28:48
 B 002 DOS1TO2         02/14/24 08:28:48

]※
```

```
]CD = S=6 D=02 V=000 000

]LOCK

]LS R

B=4506H data T=LOCK Figure

M=4506H P=04 L=0xF00A 02/14/24 08:28:48

*S6 D=02 V=000 F=0486 02/14/24 08:28:50

*001 0x1B,0x0F DOS4.5
 002 0x1E,0x0F INSTALL.L
 003 0x1F,0x0F INSTALL
 004 0x20,0x0F MOVEDOS.L
 005 0x21,0x0F DOS1TO2

]DELETE DOS1TO2

Volume Locked

]※
```

Figure III.2.8.1. LOCK File Command Display   Figure III.2.8.2. LOCK Volume Command Display

Figure III.2.8.2 shows the same volume from Figure III.2.8.1 and the procedure that is used to lock this volume. Once a volume is locked, files may not be deleted, renamed, touched, or even saved to a locked volume in DOS 4.5. Even though a volume is locked, files may still be read into memory or displayed using the DOS LIST command. In Figure III.2.8.2 the DISKLOCK flag status is shown in the S=6 catalog information line where it uses an asterisk, and the lock status is displayed as *S6. The lock status asterisk for a volume is conveniently placed in the first column of the Catalog information line that contains the date and time stamp for the VTOC, and that first column happens to be the same column that is used to display the lock status asterisk for a file when a file is locked. The date and time stamp for the VTOC is updated since the VTOC is changed because the VTOC DISKLOCK flag is changed to the lock value or 0x80. There is **no** harm in locking a volume that is already locked, and conversely, there is **no** harm in unlocking a volume that is already unlocked.

9. RENAME Command

RENAME   f, f2 [,Ss][,Dd][,Vv][,R]
MV   f, f2 [,Ss][,Dd][,Vv][,R]   ; UNIX version

Example: RENAME COPYDOS,COPYDOS.EXEC
           mv test1,test2,r

This command is available in DOS 3.3 for File System commands and this command was enhanced for DOS 4.3 to accept the R keyword. The DOS RENAME command depends on the File Manager RNMHNDLR handler. This handler changes the name of the file f to f2 in the specified volume if the file f exists. The date and time stamp of the file f is also updated as shown in Figure III.2.9.1 where the file INSTALL is renamed to the file Put DOS 4.5. A locked file cannot be renamed unless the R keyword is used to override the lock status of the file. A file cannot be renamed when it resides in a volume that is locked unless the volume is first unlocked or when CONFIG Bit 4 is **set** which disables all volume and file locks. The VTOC date and time stamp remains **unchanged** when a file is renamed because nothing in the VTOC is changed. There is **no** harm in renaming a file to its own name. There is **no** harm in renaming a file to a filename that **already** exists in the volume Catalog. All this does is cause confusion for the user when files are processed since the first of two identically named files will always be selected whether that is intended or not. DOS 4.5 does not check or verify a volume Catalog in order to prevent the creation of duplicate file names when using the DOS RENAME command.

```
]LS

S=6 D=02 V=000 F=0488 02/14/24 08:28:48

 B 044 DOS4.5          02/14/24 08:28:48
 L 013 INSTALL.L       02/14/24 08:28:48
 B 003 INSTALL         02/14/24 08:28:48
 L 006 MOVEDOS.L       02/14/24 08:28:48
]

]RENAME INSTALL,Put DOS 4.5

]LS

S=6 D=02 V=000 F=0488 02/14/24 08:28:48

 B 044 DOS4.5          02/14/24 08:28:48
 L 013 INSTALL.L       02/14/24 08:28:48
 B 003 Put DOS 4.5     02/14/24 08:28:50
 L 006 MOVEDOS.L       02/14/24 08:28:48
]※
```

Figure III.2.9.1. RENAME Command Display

```
]LS

S=6 D=02 V=000 F=0494 02/14/24 08:28:48

*B 044 DOS4.5          02/14/24 08:28:48
 L 013 INSTALL.L       02/14/24 08:28:48
*B 003 INSTALL         02/14/24 08:28:48
]TOUCH DOS4.5

File Locked

]TOUCH DOS4.5,R

]LS

S=6 D=02 V=000 F=0494 02/14/24 08:28:48

*B 044 DOS4.5          02/14/24 08:28:50
 L 013 INSTALL.L       02/14/24 08:28:48
*B 003 INSTALL         02/14/24 08:28:48
]※
```

Figure III.2.10.1. TOUCH Command Display

10. TOUCH Command

TOUCH   [f] [,Ss][,Dd][,Vv][,R]

Example: TOUCH
            TOUCH,R
            TOUCH TESTFILE

This command is not available in DOS 3.3 for File System commands and this command was initially developed for DOS 4.3 in order to utilize the newly created File Manager FMTCHCD command or 0x0E for the new File Manager TCHHNDLR handler. This handler updates the date and time stamp of the file f in the specified volume if the file f exists. Figure III.2.10.1 shows an example in using the DOS TOUCH command. The DOS TOUCH handler cannot update the date and time stamp of a locked file unless the R keyword is used to override the lock status of the file. The date and time stamp for the VTOC remains **unchanged** when the DOS TOUCH command is used because this command does not change anything in the VTOC. When the DOS TOUCH command is used without specifying a filename, the date and time stamp of the VTOC for the specified volume is updated. If only keywords including the R keyword are included with the DOS TOUCH command followed by a comma, the DOS 4.5 internal variable VALSCNFG as shown

168

in Table I.8.5 is copied to the VTOC Configuration variable DOSCONFG as shown in Table I.5.2, the date and time stamp of the VTOC is updated, and the modified VTOC is written to the specified volume. Using the DOS TOUCH command in this way saves the current DOS Configuration variable VALSCNFG to the specified volume. The VTOC Configuration variable DOSCONFG of a volume cannot be updated when the specified volume is locked. The specified volume must be unlocked before any attempt is made to update the VTOC Configuration variable DOSCONFG.

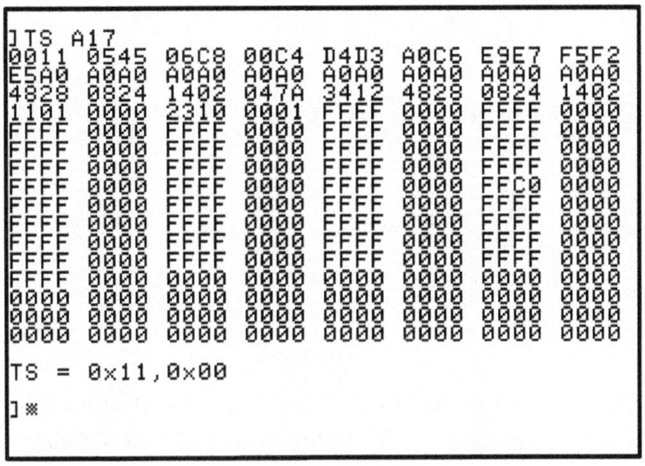

Figure III.2.11.1. TS Command Display

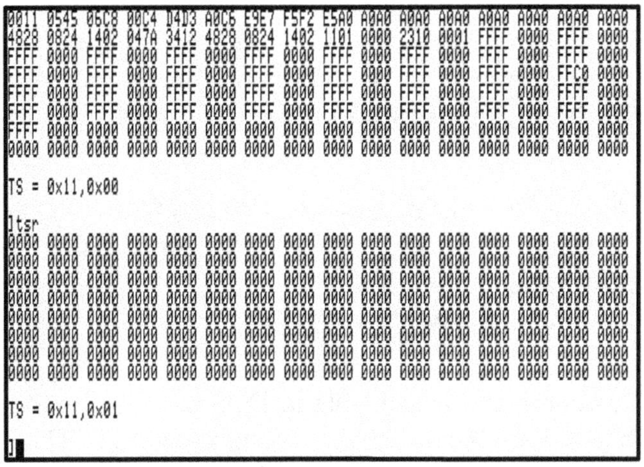

Figure III.2.11.2. TS Command in 80-Column

11. TS Command

TS   [,Ss][,Dd][,Vv][,An][,Bn][,L][,R]

Example: TS
           TS A$11,B7
           TS L

This command is not available in DOS 3.3 for File System commands and this command was initially developed for DOS 4.1 and no enhancements have been made for DOS 4.5. The DOS TS command depends on the File Manager TSHNDLR handler. This handler displays on the screen the contents of the specified sector and track in hexadecimal for the specified volume. The A keyword is used to specify a track value n and the B keyword is used to specify a sector value n, and if these keywords are not included with the DOS TS command, their keyword values are zero. The value n for these keywords may be entered in decimal or in hexadecimal, and range checking is done against the VTOC parameters NUMTRKS, or the number of tracks in the volume, and NUMSECS, or the number of sectors in a track, of the specified volume. It is critical that a suitable DOS command, like DOS CATALOG for example, has been previously issued in order to ensure that the VTOC of the specified volume has already been read and is currently in memory so that NUMTRKS and NUMSECS have relevant values when the DOS TS command is processed. If the L or the R keyword is included with the DOS TS command, then any A or B keyword is ignored if they also happen to be included with this command. The R keyword takes precedence over the L keyword if both keywords are included. The L keyword displays the previous sector, or to the Left or down, and the R keyword displays the next sector, or to the Right or up.

Figure III.2.11.1 shows a typical DOS TS view of an initialized DATA disk VTOC whose volume contains no files at this time. The sector data is displayed in hexadecimal byte-pairs followed by the TS command and the track and sector values that were specified with the DOS TS command, both shown in hexadecimal for the requested sector data. The DOS TS command is designed to view two complete sectors of data when the 80-column display is in view as shown in Figure III.2.11.2.

12. UNLOCK Command

UNLOCK   [f] [,Ss][,Dd][,Vv]

Example: UNLOCK
           UNLOCK TEST

This command is available in DOS 3.3 for File System commands and this command was enhanced for DOS 4.3 so that a filename f is not required. The DOS UNLOCK command depends on the File Manager UNLKHNDL handler. This handler **clears** the most significant bit of the Type byte of the file f in the specified volume Catalog as shown in Tables I.7.1 and I.7.2. A locked file cannot be deleted, renamed, or touched until the file is unlocked. The lock status of a file is indicated in the volume Catalog by using an asterisk before the Type character in the display entry for the file. The date and time stamp of the file **is** updated when a file f is unlocked. The date and time stamp for the VTOC is **not** updated when a file is unlocked because nothing is changed in the VTOC.

Figure III.2.12.1 shows how to use the DOS UNLOCK command in order to unlock the file DOS4.5. The first volume Catalog shows that the Binary file DOS4.5 is a locked file because of the presence of an asterisk before the Type character B for the display entry of this file. After this file is unlocked using the DOS UNLOCK command, a second volume Catalog shows that there is no longer an asterisk before the Type character B for the display entry of the Binary file DOS4.5. The absence of that asterisk indicates that the file DOS4.5 is now unlocked. There is **no** harm in unlocking a file that is already unlocked, and conversely, there is **no** harm in locking a file that is already locked.

When the DOS UNLOCK command is used in DOS 4.5 without specifying a filename, the **volume** that is currently in focus is unlocked. The keywords for Slot, Drive, and Volume may be used in order to specify a particular volume to be unlocked. The DOS UNLOCK command may be preceded by the DOS CD command in order to utilize its command capabilities in selecting the intended volume to be unlocked. When a volume is unlocked, the DATA and TSL buffers are flushed, the VTOC sector of the volume that is in focus is read into memory, the MSB is **cleared** for the VTOC DISKLOCK flag as shown in Table I.5.2, the VTOC is updated with a current date and time stamp, and the modified VTOC is written back to the same volume that is in focus. Files may be written to an unlocked volume at any time in DOS 4.5. Understand that this procedure of unlocking a volume is simply a software unlock implementation and not a hardware unlock implementation. Other versions of DOS may ignore or be totally unaware of the status or the existence of the DISKLOCK flag in the VTOC.

```
]LS                                        ]LSR

S=6  D=02  V=000  F=0486  02/14/24  08:28:48    B=4506H  data  T=UNLOCK  Figure 2

*B  044  DOS4.5         02/14/24  08:28:48    M=4506H  P=04  L=0xF00A  02/14/24  08:28:48
 L  013  INSTALL.L      02/14/24  08:28:48
 B  003  INSTALL        02/14/24  08:28:48    *S6  D=02  V=000  F=0510  02/14/24  08:28:48
 L  006  MOVEDOS.L      02/14/24  08:28:48
 B  002  DOS1TO2        02/14/24  08:28:48    *001  0x12,0x0F  DOS4.5

]UNLOCK DOS4.5                             ]UNLOCK

]LS                                        ]LSR

S=6  D=02  V=000  F=0486  02/14/24  08:28:48    B=4506H  data  T=UNLOCK  Figure 2

 B  044  DOS4.5         02/14/24  08:28:50    M=4506H  P=04  L=0xF00A  02/14/24  08:28:48
 L  013  INSTALL.L      02/14/24  08:28:48
 B  003  INSTALL        02/14/24  08:28:48    S=6  D=02  V=000  F=0510  02/14/24  08:28:50
 L  006  MOVEDOS.L      02/14/24  08:28:48
 B  002  DOS1TO2        02/14/24  08:28:48    *001  0x12,0x0F  DOS4.5

]※                                         ]
```

Figure III.2.12.1. UNLOCK File Command   Figure III.2.12.2. UNLOCK Volume Command

Figure III.2.12.2 shows the procedure that is used to unlock a volume. Once a volume is locked, files may not be deleted, renamed, touched, or even saved to a locked volume in DOS 4.5. Even though a volume is locked, files may still be read into memory or displayed using the DOS LIST command. In Figure III.2.12.2 the DISKLOCK flag status is shown in the S=6 catalog information line where it uses an asterisk, and the lock status is displayed as *S6. The lock status asterisk for a volume is conveniently placed in the first column of the Catalog information line that contains the date and time stamp for the VTOC, and that first column happens to be the same column that is used to display the lock status asterisk for a file when a file is locked. The date and time stamp for the VTOC is updated since the VTOC is changed because the VTOC DISKLOCK flag is changed to the unlock value or 0x00. There is **no** harm in unlocking a volume that is already unlocked, and conversely, there is **no** harm in locking a volume that is already locked.

13. URM Command

URM   f [,Ss][,Dd][,Vv]

Example: URM MOVEDOS

This command is not available in DOS 3.3 for File System commands and this command was initially developed for DOS 4.1 and no enhancements have been made for DOS 4.5. The DOS URM command depends on the File Manager URMHNDLR handler. This handler restores the filename f to the specified volume Catalog by **clearing** the most significant bit of its TSL track byte, and marking the data sectors that are listed in the TSL sector(s) of file f as well as all of its TSL sectors as used in the VTOC. Refer to Figure I.7.1 that shows the components of a volume Catalog entry.

Figure III.2.13.1 shows an example of a file that is deleted. In that figure the file INSTALL is marked with the character x where the asterisk is used to mark a locked file. **A deleted file is never a locked file**. It is prudent to undelete a deleted file as soon as possible because the data sectors that are listed in the TSL sector(s) of file f as well as all of its TSL sectors are now available in the VTOC, and those sectors may be utilized by another file. **There is no harm in undeleting a file that already exists in the volume Catalog**.

Once a file is undeleted and restored using the DOS URM command, the character x that is displayed in the first column of the entry for file f is removed and the free sectors that are currently in the specified volume are reduced by the number of DATA and TSL sectors of the restored file. The DOS 4.5 File Manager URMHNDLR handler manages the restoration of a file much like the File Manager DELHNDLR handler manages the deletion of a file. The date and time stamp for the VTOC is updated because the VTOC is changed when a file is restored. The date and time stamp for the restored file is **not** updated even when the URM command is used to restore a file that is already displayed in the volume Catalog.

```
]cat r
B=4506H data T=URM Figure
M=4506H P=04 L=0xF00D 02/14/24 08:28:48
S=6 D=02 V=000 F=0510 02/14/24 08:28:48
 001 0x12,0x0F DOS4.5
x002 0x15,0x0F INSTALL
]urm INSTALL
]LS
S=6 D=02 V=000 F=0507 02/14/24 08:28:50
 B 044 DOS4.5            02/14/24 08:28:48
 B 003 INSTALL           02/14/24 08:28:48
]
```

Figure III.2.13.1. URM Command Display

```
]CAT
S=6 D=02 V=000 F=0507 02/14/24 08:28:48
 B 044 DOS4.5            02/14/24 08:28:48
 B 003 INSTALL           02/14/24 08:28:48
]
]VERIFY DOS4.5
]VERIFY DOS4.5,R1 = 043
]LS
S=6 D=02 V=000 F=0507 02/14/24 08:28:48
 B 044 DOS4.5            02/14/24 08:28:48
 B 003 INSTALL           02/14/24 08:28:48
]
```

Figure III.2.14.1. VERIFY Command Display

14. VERIFY Command

VERIFY   f [,Ss][,Dd][,Vv][,R1]

Example: VERIFY DOS4.1,R1

This command is available in DOS 3.3 for File System commands and this command was enhanced for DOS 4.1 and no enhancements have been made for DOS 4.5. The DOS VERIFY command depends on the File Manager VFYHNDLR handler. This handler reads into memory each data sector that is listed in the TSL sector(s) of file f in the specified volume. The RWTS READ handler simply reads each selected sector in order to verify the sector checksum. No data is copied to another memory location, the data is **not** modified, and the date and time stamp of the file is **not** changed. The TSL sector(s) of file f are indirectly verified since the TSL sector is read into a DOS TS buffer and it is used to obtain the list of Track/Sector entry pairs where each entry pair points to a data sector that comprises the file, but the TSL sector(s) are **not** included in the verified sector count. The number of verified sectors are displayed on the Apple Command Line following the DOS VERIFY command only when a **non-zero** R keyword is included with the DOS VERIFY command.

Figure III.2.14.1 shows how to use the DOS VERIFY command. Nothing else is displayed following that command. However, when the DOS VERIFY command includes a non-zero R keyword with the command, the number of verified sectors are displayed on the Apple Command Line following the DOS command. If a non-zero R keyword is included with the DOS SAVE, BSAVE, LSAVE, SSAVE, or TSAVE commands, not only is the address and length information displayed, but also the number of verified sectors are displayed as well. The VTOC and the date and time stamp of a verified file remain **unchanged** because nothing in the VTOC or in the file is changed. This is shown in Figure III.2.14.1

If CONFIG Bit 1 is set in order to disable file verification as shown in Table III.1.1.1, DOS 4.5 bypasses the automatic verification of a file after the file is saved to a volume when using the DOS SAVE, BSAVE, LSAVE, SSAVE, or TSAVE commands. Disabling the automatic verification of a file visibly reduces the total amount of time that it requires to save a file to a volume, but it eliminates the verification that the file can be read into memory without error.

15. WTS Command

WTS	Ln, Rn [,Ss][,Dd][,Vv][,An][,Bn]
Example:	WTS A17,L4,R3
	WTS L0,R1

This command is not available in DOS 3.3 for File System commands and this command was initially developed for DOS 4.3 and no enhancements have been made for DOS 4.5. The DOS WTS command depends on the File Manager WTSHNDLR handler. This handler provides the user the ability to modify a single byte on any sector of the specified volume and it displays on the screen the contents of the specified sector and track in hexadecimal. Both the L and the R keywords are required by the DOS WTS command, and they provide the sector index n and the data byte value n, respectively, that is used by the DOS WTS handler in order to modify the specified sector. As in the DOS TS command, the A keyword is used to specify a track value n and the B keyword is used to specify a sector value n, and if these keywords are not included with the DOS WTS command, their keyword values are zero. The value n for all four keywords may be entered in decimal or in hexadecimal. Range checking is done against the A and the B keywords for the VTOC parameters NUMTRKS, or the number of tracks in the volume, and NUMSECS, or the number of sectors in a track, respectively, of the specified volume. It is critical that a suitable DOS command, like DOS CATALOG for example, has been previously issued in order to ensure that the VTOC of the specified volume has already been read and is currently in memory so that NUMTRKS and NUMSECS have relevant values when the DOS WTS command is processed.

Figure III.2.15.1 shows a BOOT sector, or sector 0x00 on track 0x00, that has been modified using the DOS WTS command. This BOOT image is no longer valid and the volume will no longer BOOT because the first byte is changed from 0x01 to 0x02. Once the DOS WTS handler modifies the specified byte, the handler saves the sector to the specified volume and then displays the contents of the sector in hexadecimal byte-pairs followed by the WTS command and the track and sector values that were specified with the DOS command, both shown in hexadecimal for the requested sector data. The DOS WTS command is designed to view two complete sectors of data when the 80-column display is in view as shown in Figure III.2.15.2. In this figure, the VTOC sector on track 0x11 is modified at byte 0xF0 with the value of 0x96. Then, the

DOS WTS command is used a second time in order to change byte 0xF0 again, and it restores that same byte to its original value of 0x00. The DOS WTS command makes the task of simple sector data modification easy to implement.

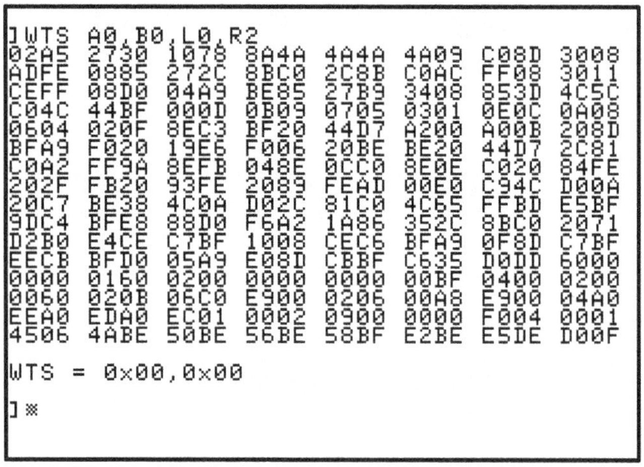

Figure III.2.15.1. WTS Command Display

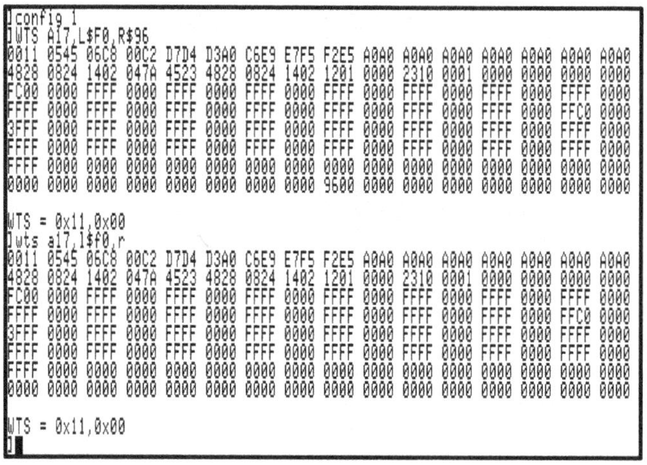

Figure III.2.15.2. WTS Command in 80-Column

Command	Command Syntax
CHAIN	f [,Ss][,Dd][,Vv][,Ll][,R]
LOAD	f [,Ss][,Dd][,Vv][,R]
RUN	f [,Ss][,Dd][,Vv][,Ll]
SAVE	f [,Ss][,Dd][,Vv][,B][,R[1]]

Table III.3.0.1. Applesoft File Commands in DOS 4.5

3. Applesoft File Commands

The Applesoft File commands in the DOS 4.5 command repertoire consist of those commands that manage the general operation of Applesoft files. The DOS CHAIN command loads an Applesoft file into memory and preserves the variables of the previous Applesoft program. The DOS LOAD command loads an Applesoft file into memory. The DOS RUN command loads an Applesoft file into memory before it begins the execution of the Applesoft statements that now reside in memory. The DOS SAVE command saves the Applesoft program that currently resides in memory to a file in a disk volume.

The syntax of the Applesoft File commands is shown in Table III.3.0.1. The Applesoft File commands are permitted to be used from within an Applesoft program or an assembly language routine as well as on the Apple Command Line. However, the DOS CHAIN command is not permitted to be used on the Apple Command Line.

1. CHAIN Command

CHAIN   f [,Ss][,Dd][,Vv][,Ll][,R]

Example: CHAIN TESTPART2,D2

This command is not available in DOS 3.3 for Applesoft File commands and this command was initially developed for DOS 4.1 and no enhancements have been made for DOS 4.5. The DOS CHAIN command can only be used from within an Applesoft program or an assembly language routine. This Applesoft File command will read into memory the Applesoft file f in the specified volume and then begin execution of the Applesoft program in a unique way such that the DOS CHAIN handler does not clear the value(s) of any previous Applesoft program variable(s). Therefore, the Applesoft file f can utilize the numerical and the string data results from the previous Applesoft program(s) and the Applesoft file f can provide its numerical and its string data results to any following Applesoft program(s) that may be sequentially processed by the DOS CHAIN handler. If the L keyword is included with the DOS CHAIN command, Applesoft processing will begin at that line number within the Applesoft file f only if that line number exists, otherwise the Applesoft interpreter will report an error and terminate further Applesoft processing. Obviously, this capability opens up a multitude of selective programming capabilities. If the R keyword is **not** used with the DOS CHAIN command, the DOS CHAIN handler will call the ROM Applesoft GARBAG routine at memory address 0xE484 before the DOS CHAIN handler moves the Simple Variable and the Array Variable descriptors to their new location at the end of file f. Using the R keyword will bypass the call to ROM Applesoft GARBAG and it allows the user to utilize another method or process in order to collect and remove character string data garbage before or after using the DOS CHAIN command. It is critical that the Applesoft program that invokes the DOS CHAIN command to locate or to *cause* to move all of its simple character string variables and character string array variables to the Character String Pool that are to be utilized in the next Applesoft program. All character string data that safely resides in the Character String Pool will be available to the next Applesoft program when the DOS CHAIN command is invoked. See Section I.15 for a more thorough discussion of the DOS CHAIN command.

```
]load START
]list

 10 D$ =   CHR$ (4):AB = 123:CD% =
    456:EF$ = "Test Chain" + ""
 20 PRINT : PRINT "This is the S
    TART program to test CHAIN":
    PRINT
 30 PRINT "AB = ";AB;", CD% = ";
    CD%;", EF$ = ";EF$: PRINT
 40 PRINT D$;"CHAIN PROGRAM2"

]load PROGRAM2
]list

 10 PRINT : PRINT "Now running p
    rogram PROGRAM2": PRINT
 20 PRINT "AB = ";AB;", CD% = ";
    CD%;", EF$ = ";EF$
 30 PRINT D$;"CATALOG": PRINT

]
```

```
]run START
This is the START program to test CHAIN

AB = 123, CD% = 456, EF$ = Test Chain

Now running program PROGRAM2

AB = 123, CD% = 456, EF$ = Test Chain

S=6 D=02 V=000 F=0550 02/14/24 08:28:48

 A 002 START            02/14/24 08:28:48
 A 002 PROGRAM2         02/14/24 08:28:48
]*
```

Figure III.3.1.1. START & PROGRAM2 Listing   Figure III.3.1.2. START & PROGRAM2 Output

Figure III.3.1.1 shows the program list of two Applesoft programs named START and PROGRAM2. The Applesoft program START defines four simple variables D$, AB, CD%, and EF$. The character string variable EF$ is defined in such a way as to *cause* the Applesoft interpreter to relocate that string variable into the Character String Pool where that variable can be safely stored. The interpreter also moves the variable D$ to the Character String Pool before that variable is utilized with the DOS CHAIN command. All four variables will be available to Applesoft program PROGRAM2 when the DOS CHAIN command is issued as shown in line 40 in Figure III.3.1.1. Figure III.3.1.2 shows the text output of the Applesoft program START after the program is RUN. Applesoft program PROGRAM2 clearly shows the values of the four simple variables from Applesoft program START, and that these variables and their values have been totally preserved. Even the value for the variable D$ has been preserved, otherwise the DOS CATALOG command in Applesoft program PROGRAM2 would fail.

Table I.15.1 shows the definition of the descriptor for simple variables that are used in Applesoft programs. The character string descriptor consists of only the first two characters of the character string name, so care must be given in naming all Applesoft variables, the character string length, the address in low/high byte order where that character string currently resides in memory, and two filler bytes that contain zero. Character string descriptors for array variables are shown in Table I.15.2 and each character string element contains the character string length and the address in low/high byte order where that character string currently resides in memory. The address in the character string descriptor or in the character string element is initially the location where the character string data resides within the contents of the Applesoft program. Once the DOS CHAIN command has replaced the current Applesoft program in memory with the next Applesoft program that is specified by file f, the resident character string data would be overwritten and lost, and its address or its location in memory, would become invalid. Therefore, caution must be exercised when using character string variables whose address is still within an Applesoft program and the DOS CHAIN command. When those character string variables are **not** *caused* to be moved, that is, when they are **not** copied from within the contents of an Applesoft program to the Character String Pool and safely stored in that memory location, those character string variables will **never** be available for general access by other chained Applesoft programs.

2. LOAD Command

LOAD   f [,Ss][,Dd][,Vv][,R]

Example   LOAD HELLO
                    LOAD HELLO,R

This command is available in DOS 3.3 for Applesoft File commands and this command was enhanced for DOS 4.1 to accept the R keyword. This Applesoft file command reads the Applesoft file f in the specified volume into memory always at address 0x0801 unless certain page-zero locations are modified in order to utilize another load address. Applesoft files are file Type 0x02 as shown in Table I.7.3. The DOS LOAD command will also process A Type files, or file Type 0x20, as an Applesoft program in the same way these files are processed in DOS 3.3. If the R keyword is included with the DOS LOAD command, the memory load address and the number of bytes that are read into memory are displayed after the DOS command. Figure III.3.2.1 shows the DOS LOAD command with the file HELLO and the R keyword. In this example, the file HELLO is loaded into memory at address 0x0801 and the number of bytes that are read from this file is shown to be 0x0494.

```
]CATALOG
S=6 D=02 V=000 F=0500 02/14/24 08:28:48

 A 006 HELLO           02/14/24 08:28:48
 A 006 HELLO2          02/14/24 08:28:48
]LOAD HELLO
]LOAD HELLO,R
A$0801,L$0494
]SAVE HELLO2
]SAVE HELLO2,R
A$0801,L$0494
]SAVE HELLO2,R1
A$0801,L$0494 = 005
]
```

Figure III.3.2.1. LOAD and SAVE Commands

```
]load HELLO
]save HELLO3
]save HELLO3,r1
A$0801,L$0494 = 005
]config 2
]config = 002
]save HELLO3,r1
A$0801,L$0494
]config,r
]config = 000
]※
```

Figure III.3.4.1. SAVE Command Display

3. RUN Command

RUN   f [,Ss][,Dd][,Vv][,Ll]

Example: RUN
           RUN START

This command is available in DOS 3.3 for Applesoft File commands and this command was not enhanced for DOS 4.1 and no enhancements have been made to this command for DOS 4.5. The DOS RUN command loads the Applesoft file f in the specified volume into memory always at address 0x0801 and begins program execution. The DOS RUN handler calls the ROM ASROMCLR routine at memory address 0xD665 in order to initialize all Applesoft pointers which include PRGEND, VARTAB, ARYTAB, and STREND. The handler then calls the ROM ASROMSET routine at memory address 0xD955 in order to initialize LINNUM, it clears the PROMPT and ASONERR flags, and finally the handler jumps to the ROM ASROMNEW routine at memory address 0xD7D2 in order to begin Applesoft program execution. If the L keyword is included with the DOS RUN command, Applesoft processing will begin at that line number within the Applesoft file f only if that line number exists, otherwise the Applesoft interpreter will report an error and terminate further Applesoft processing. An example in using the RUN command is shown in Figure III.3.1.2.

4. SAVE Command

SAVE   f [,Ss][,Dd][,Vv][,B][,R[1]]

Example: SAVE HELLO2
            SAVE HELLO2,R
            SAVE HELLO2,R1

This command is available in DOS 3.3 for Applesoft File commands and was enhanced for DOS 4.1 to accept the B and the R keywords, and this command was further enhanced for DOS 4.3. The DOS SAVE command saves the Applesoft program that currently resides in memory to file f to the specified volume. If the R keyword is included with the DOS SAVE command, the save address, which is always 0x0801, and the number of bytes that are written to the file are displayed as shown previously in Figure III.3.2.1 which is 0x0494 bytes as shown in the example. If a non-zero R keyword is included with the DOS SAVE command, the number of verified sectors is also displayed after the number of bytes saved, again as shown previously in Figure III.3.2.1. The B keyword can be used with the DOS SAVE command in order to implement the *File Delete/File Save* strategy. That is, the Applesoft file f is deleted from the volume and then saved to the same volume in order to ensure that the TSL sector(s) of file f contain only those Track/Sector entry pairs that are required and utilized by the file. If CONFIG Bit 1 is **set**, the Applesoft file is **not** verified after it is saved. Figure III.3.4.1 shows that even when a non-zero R keyword is used with the DOS SAVE command, no sectors are verified when CONFIG Bit 1 is set. The VALSCNFG variable as shown in Table I.8.5 can be cleared by using the R keyword with the DOS CONFIG command followed by a comma as shown in Figure III.3.4.1.

Command	Command Syntax
BLOAD	f [,Ss][,Dd][,Vv][,Aa][,R]
BRUN	f [,Ss][,Dd][,Vv][,Aa]
BSAVE	f [,Ss][,Dd][,Vv][,Aa][,B][,Ll][,R[1]]
LLOAD	f [,Ss][,Dd][,Vv][,Aa][,R]
LSAVE	f [,Ss][,Dd][,Vv][,Aa][,B][,Ll][,R[1]]
SLOAD	f, Aa, Ll [,Ss][,Dd][,Vv]
SSAVE	f, Aa, Ll [,Ss][,Dd][,Vv][,B]

Table III.4.0.1. Binary File Commands in DOS 4.5

4. Binary File Commands

The Binary File commands in the DOS 4.5 command repertoire consist of those commands that manage the general operation of Binary or assembly language files. The DOS BLOAD command loads a Binary file into memory. The DOS BRUN command loads a Binary file into memory before it begins the execution of the instructions that now reside in memory. The DOS BSAVE command saves the Binary program that currently resides in memory into a file in a disk volume. The DOS LLOAD command loads a *Lisa* Binary file into memory. The DOS LSAVE command saves the *Lisa* Binary program that currently resides in memory into a file in a disk volume. The DOS SLOAD command loads a Special Binary file into memory. The DOS SSAVE command saves the Special Binary program that currently resides in memory into a file in a disk volume.

The syntax of the Binary File commands is shown in Table III.4.0.1. All of the Binary File commands are permitted to be used from within an Applesoft program or an assembly language routine as well as on the Apple Command Line.

1. BLOAD Command

```
BLOAD      f [,Ss][,Dd][,Vv][,Aa][,R]

Example:   BLOAD RD
           BLOAD RD,R
           BLOAD RD,A$1000,R
```

This command is available in DOS 3.3 for Binary File commands and this command was enhanced for DOS 4.1 to accept the R keyword. The DOS BLOAD command reads into memory the Binary file f in the specified volume at address a if the A keyword is included. If the A keyword is not included with the DOS BLOAD command, the Binary file f is read into memory at the address the file was originally saved or last saved. Binary files are file Type 0x04 as shown in Table I.7.3.

Figure III.4.1.1 shows an example of using the DOS BLOAD command, and if the R keyword is included with this command, the memory load address and the number of bytes that are read into memory are displayed. A Binary file utilizes the first four bytes in its first data sector for its memory load address and for its length in bytes where both pairs of bytes are saved in Lo/Hi byte order. Therefore, when the A keyword is not included with the DOS BLOAD command, the memory load address information is obtained from the first pair of bytes in its first data sector. The DOS BLOAD handler always obtains the number of bytes to read into memory from the second pair of bytes in its first data sector.

```
]BLOAD RD,R
A$4000,L$1B00
]BLOAD RD,A$1000,R
A$1000,L$1B00
]BSAVE RD2
]BSAVE RD3,R
A$1000,L$1B00
]BSAVE RD4,A$4000,L$1B00,R1
A$4000,L$1B00 = 028
]DIFF RD,RD4 = 0x1C00
Number Mismatch = 00000
]※
```

```
]BRUN INSTALL
Reading DOS 4.5H image into memory.

DOS 4.5H image now in memory.

Insert diskette into Slot 6, Drive 2.
Press any key to continue.

Installing DOS 4.5H.
. . . . . . . . . . . . . . . . . . . . . . . . . . . .
. .
Installation of DOS 4.5H is complete.
]
```

Figure III.4.1.1. BLOAD and BSAVE Commands   Figure III.4.2.1. BRUN Command Display

179

2. BRUN Command

```
BRUN        f [,Ss][,Dd][,Vv][,Aa]

Example:    BRUN INSTALL
            BRUN INSTALL,A$1000
```

This command is available in DOS 3.3 for Binary File commands and this command was not enhanced for DOS 4.1 and no enhancements have been made to this command for DOS 4.5. The DOS BRUN command reads the Binary file f in the specified volume into memory at address a if the A keyword is included, and begins program execution at address a. If the A keyword is not included, the Binary file f is loaded into memory at the address the file was originally saved or last saved, and execution begins at that address. In the DOS BRUN handler the DOSWARM address is pushed onto the stack before the handler processes an indirect jump to ADRVAL, the Binary file memory load address, to guarantee that DOS 4.5 is in control when the Binary program exits. In order to disable this unique feature that is part of the DOS BRUN handler, simply **set** CONFIG Bit 5 as shown in Table III.1.1.1 before using the DOS BRUN command.

Figure III.4.2.1 shows an example of using the DOS BRUN command to BLOAD the Binary file INSTALL and begin processing its instructions immediately after the file has been read into memory. As explained in the DOS BLOAD command, when the A keyword is not included with the DOS BRUN command, the memory load address information is obtained from the first pair of bytes in its first data sector. The DOS BRUN handler always obtains the number of bytes to read into memory from the second pair of bytes in its first data sector.

3. BSAVE Command

```
BSAVE       f [,Ss][,Dd][,Vv][,Aa][,B][,Ll][,R[1]]

Example:    BSAVE RD2
            BSAVE RD2,R
            BSAVE RD3,A$4000,L$1C00,R1
```

This command is available in DOS 3.3 for Binary File commands and was enhanced for DOS 4.1 to accept the B and the R keywords, and this command was further enhanced for DOS 4.3. The DOS BSAVE command saves the Binary file f to the specified volume using the memory address a and the length l in bytes if the A and the L keywords are included, respectively. In DOS 4.5 these keywords are **optional**, but if they are included **both** keyword values are required. If the A and the L keywords are not included, the address a and the length l values of the previous BLOAD or BSAVE command are utilized. If the R keyword is included with the DOS BSAVE command, the memory save address and the number of bytes that are written to the specified file f are displayed as shown previously in Figure III.4.1.1. If a non-zero R keyword is included, the number of verified sectors is also displayed as shown in Figure III.4.1.1. If CONFIG Bit 1 is **set** the Binary file is **not** verified after it is saved as shown previously for the DOS SAVE command in Figure III.3.4.1.

180

Figure III.4.1.1 shows a byte comparison of the two files RD and RD4 using the DOS DIFF command. The DOS DIFF command proves that both of these saved files are identical because no differences are shown. The B keyword can be used with the DOS BSAVE command in order to implement the *File Delete/File Save* strategy. That is, the Binary file f is deleted from the volume and then saved to the same volume in order to ensure that the TSL sector(s) of file f contain only those Track/Sector entry pairs that are required and utilized by the file.

4. LLOAD Command

LLOAD   f [,Ss][,Dd][,Vv][,Aa][,R]

Example: LLOAD README.L
            LLOAD README.L,R
            LLOAD README.L,A$1000,R

This command is not available in DOS 3.3 for Binary File commands and this command was initially developed for DOS 4.1 and no further enhancements have been made to this command for DOS 4.5. The DOS LLOAD command reads into memory the *Lisa* Binary file f in the specified volume at memory address a if the A keyword is included. If the A keyword is not included with the DOS LLOAD command, the *Lisa* Binary file f is read into memory at the address the file was originally saved or last saved. *Lisa* Binary files are file Type 0x40 as shown in Table I.7.3.

Figure III.4.4.1 shows an example of using the DOS LLOAD command, and if the R keyword is included with this command, the memory load address and the number of bytes that are read into memory are displayed. A *Lisa* Binary file utilizes the first four bytes in its first data sector for its memory load address and for its length in bytes where both pair of bytes are in Lo/Hi byte order. Therefore, when the A keyword is not included with the DOS LLOAD command, the memory load address information is obtained from the first pair of bytes in its first data sector. The DOS LLOAD handler always obtains the number of bytes to read into memory from the second pair of bytes in its first data sector.

5. LSAVE Command

LSAVE   f [,Ss][,Dd][,Vv][,Aa][,B][,Ll][,R[1]]

Example: LSAVE README2.L
            LSAVE README2.L,R
            LSAVE README3.L,A$2100,L$CED,R1

This command is not available in DOS 3.3 for Binary File commands and was enhanced for DOS 4.1 to accept the B and the R keywords, and this command was further enhanced for DOS 4.3. The DOS LSAVE command saves the *Lisa* Binary file f to the specified volume using the memory address a and the length l in bytes if the A and the L keywords are included, respectively. In DOS 4.5 these keywords are **optional**,

181

but if they are included, **both** values are required. If the A and the L keywords are not included, the address a and the length l values of the previous LLOAD or LSAVE command are utilized. If the R keyword is included with the DOS LSAVE command, the memory save address and the number of bytes that are written to the specified volume are displayed as shown in Figure III.4.4.1. If a non-zero R keyword is included, the number of verified sectors is also displayed as shown in Figure III.4.4.1. If CONFIG Bit 1 is **set**, the *Lisa* Binary file f is **not** verified after it is saved as shown previously for the DOS SAVE command in Figure III.3.4.1.

Figure III.4.4.1 shows a byte comparison of the two files README.L and README4.L using the DOS DIFF command. The DOS DIFF command proves that both of these saved files are identical because no differences are shown. The B keyword can be used with the DOS LSAVE command in order to implement the *File Delete/File Save* strategy. That is, the *Lisa* Binary file f is deleted from the volume and then saved to the same volume in order to ensure that the TSL sector(s) of file f contain only those Track/Sector entry pairs that are required and utilized by the file.

```
]LLOAD README.L,R
A$3800,L$1627
]LLOAD README.L,A$1000,R
A$1000,L$1627
]LSAVE README2.L
]LSAVE README3.L,R
A$1000,L$1627
]LSAVE README4.L,A$3800,L$1627,R1
A$3800,L$1627 = 023
]DIFF README.L,README4.L = 0x1700
Number Mismatch = 00000
]※
```

```
]LSB Available = 0x23,0x05
S=6 D=02 V=000 F=0530 02/14/24 08:28:48
 S 024 README.S      02/14/24 08:28:48
]SLOAD README.S,R
Syntax Error
]SLOAD README.S,A$2000,L$1700
]SSAVE README2.S,A$2000,L$1700
]SLOAD README.S,A$4000,L$1700
]SSAVE README3.S,A$4000,L$1700
]DIFF README2.S,README3.S = 0x1700
Number Mismatch = 00000
]※
```

Figure III.4.4.1. LLOAD and LSAVE Commands   Figure III.4.6.1. SLOAD and SSAVE Commands

6. SLOAD Command

SLOAD   f, Aa, Ll [,Ss][,Dd][,Vv]

Example: SLOAD GAMECODE,A$900,L$3800

This command is not available in DOS 3.3 for Binary File commands and this command was initially developed for DOS 4.5. The DOS SLOAD command reads into memory the *Special* Binary file f in the specified volume using the required keywords A and L for memory address a and the length l in bytes, respectively. If either the A keyword or the L keyword is not included with the DOS SLOAD command, a Syntax Error is displayed. The user is required to already know and to provide the values for both the A and the L keywords. *Special* Binary files are file Type 0x08 as shown in Table I.7.3.

Figure III.4.6.1 shows an example in using the DOS SLOAD command, and if the R keyword is included with this command, a Syntax Error is displayed. A *Special* Binary file does **not** utilize the first four bytes in its first data sector for its memory load address and for its length in bytes. The memory load address and the length in bytes for a *Special* Binary file must be already known in order to load this file into memory. Figure III.4.6.1 shows that files README2.S and README3.S are identical even though these two files have been saved from different areas of memory. The DOS SLOAD handler is not required to read the first four bytes from the first data sector in order to begin processing a *Special* Binary file in order to load this file into memory. The handler can immediately take advantage of the fact that each sector that comprises a *Special* Binary file may be read directly into memory and that individual bytes of data are never required to be processed. A *Special* Binary file will be read directly into memory in the least amount of time that is possible for a Two Descending skew of the sector interleave table.

A great deal of effort went into a project at Sierra On-Line in order to modify DOS 3.3 that would load a Binary file directly into memory. This effort produced a modified DOS BLOAD command that utilized additional keywords that would provide the necessary parameters to achieve these desired results, much like the desired results of the DOS 4.5 SLOAD command. Unfortunately, I have no further information on the additional keywords that were utilized and the extent of the modifications that went into DOS 3.3, the DOS BLOAD command, and the Valid Keyword table. Binary files could be loaded into memory in a surprisingly accelerated rate by this modified DOS 3.3. The DOS 4.5 SLOAD command is very competitive and can also read into memory a *Special* Binary file in a surprisingly accelerated rate.

7. SSAVE Command

SSAVE   f, Aa, Ll [,Ss][,Dd][,Vv][,B]

Example: SSAVE GAMECODE,A$900,L$3800
                   SSAVE GAMECODE,A$900,L$3800,B

This command is not available in DOS 3.3 for Binary File commands and this command was initially developed for DOS 4.5. The DOS SSAVE command saves the *Special* Binary file f in the specified volume using the required keywords A and L for memory address a and the number of bytes l, respectively. If either the A keyword or the L keyword is not included with the DOS SSAVE command, a Syntax Error is displayed. The user is required to already know and to provide the values for both the A and the L keywords. *Special* Binary files are file Type 0x08 as shown in Table I.7.3. If CONFIG Bit 1 is **set**, the *Special* Binary file is **not** verified after it is saved as shown previously for the DOS SAVE command in Figure III.3.4.1.

A *Special* Binary file does **not** utilize the first four bytes in its first data sector for its memory save address and for its length in bytes. The memory save address and the length in bytes for a *Special* Binary file must be already known in order to save this file onto a disk volume. Figure III.4.6.1 shows that files README2.S and README3.S are identical even though these two files have been saved from different areas of memory. The DOS SSAVE handler is not required to obtain the FILESTRT and the FILELAST values from the CMDVALS Data structure in order to provide the memory save address and the length in bytes in order to begin processing a *Special* Binary file so that this file can be saved automatically to a disk volume. Rather, the memory save address and the length in bytes must be already known and must be supplied to the DOS

SSAVE handler. The handler can immediately take advantage of the fact that each page of memory that comprises a *Special* Binary file may be saved directly to a disk sector on a specified disk volume, and that individual bytes of data are never required to be processed. A *Special* Binary file will be saved directly to a disk volume in the least amount of time that is possible for a Two Descending skew of the sector interleave table. The B keyword can be used with the DOS SSAVE command in order to implement the *File Delete/File Save* strategy. That is, the *Special* Binary file f is deleted from the volume and then saved to the same volume.

Command	Command Syntax
APPEND*	f [,Ss][,Dd][,Vv]
CLOSE	[f]
EXEC	f [,Ss][,Dd][,Vv][,Rr]
OPEN*	f [,Ss][,Dd][,Vv]
POSITION*	f [,Rr]
READ*	f [,Bb]
TLOAD	f [,Ss][,Dd][,Vv][,A][,Bb][,Ll][,R]
TSAVE	f [,Ss][,Dd][,Vv][,B][,R[1]]
TW	f [,Ss][,Dd][,Vv]
WRITE*	f [,Bb]

Table III.5.0.1. Sequential Text File Commands in DOS 4.5

5. Sequential Text File Commands

The Sequential Text File commands in the DOS 4.5 command repertoire consist of those commands that manage the general operation of Sequential Text files. The DOS APPEND command can add more ASCII data to the end of a Sequential Text file. The DOS CLOSE command can flush and de-allocate the file buffer that is associated with a Sequential Text file. The DOS EXEC command can execute Applesoft or DOS commands as if the commands are issued on the Apple Command Line. The DOS OPEN command can allocate a file buffer and associate that buffer with a Sequential Text file. The DOS POSITION command can place the data pointer after any carriage return within a Sequential Text file. The DOS READ command can read ASCII data from a Sequential Text file into a character string variable. The DOS TLOAD command can read ASCII data from a Sequential Text file into memory. The DOS TSAVE command can save ASCII data from memory into a Sequential Text file. The DOS TW command can save ASCII data that is entered on the Apple Command Line directly into a Sequential Text file. The DOS WRITE command can save the ASCII data that is in a character string variable into a Sequential Text file.

The syntax of the Sequential Text File commands is shown in Table III.5.0.1. All Sequential Text File commands shown in Table III.5.0.1 are permitted to be used from within an Applesoft program or an assembly language routine. Those commands shown **without** an asterisk in Table III.5.0.1 **are** permitted to be used on the Apple Command Line. Those Sequential Text File commands that are shown **with** an asterisk are **not** permitted to be used on the Apple Command Line. Sequential Text files are comprised of sequential records of ASCII characters where a carriage return or character 0x8D terminates each record, and a NULL or character 0x00 terminates the Sequential Text file.

DOS 4.5 differentiates between Sequential Text files and Random-Access Data files in how the file is opened. If the L keyword is **not** included with the DOS OPEN command, the file is treated as a Sequential Text file and the DOS READ and the DOS WRITE commands **must not include** the R keyword as shown in Table III.5.0.1. See Table III.6.0.1 that shows the syntax of the Random-Access Data file READ and WRITE commands in order to understand how those commands are syntactically different from the Sequential Text file READ and WRITE commands.

Data may be read from or written to a Sequential Text file immediately after the file is opened, after the file pointer has been positioned to a particular byte location, or after the file pointer has been positioned to a particular record location. If the B keyword is included with the DOS READ or DOS WRITE command, that keyword takes precedence over any previous DOS POSITION command. That is, even though the file pointer may be positioned at the beginning of the rth record as specified by a previous DOS POSITION command, the B keyword, if it is included with a subsequent DOS READ or DOS WRITE command, will force the recalculation of the file pointer location such that the file pointer will now point to the bth byte relative to the beginning of the file.

Many DOS commands utilize the File Manager in order to open a Text file, which is typically handled by the File Manager CMNOPEN Common Open routine. This routine initializes the File Manager Workarea buffer, checks if the RECNUM value as shown in Table I.11.1 is zero, and allocates a new file if the requested filename is not found in the volume Catalog. If RECNUM does equal zero, DOS 3.3 sets the value of OPNRCLEN as shown in Table I.12.2 to 0x0001. On the other hand, when RECNUM equals zero, DOS 4.5 sets the value of OPNRCLEN equal to 0x0100. This is a far better and more logical design value because Text file records are rarely, if ever one byte in size, and using 0x0100 for an initial record size, the size of a memory page, is far closer to reality. The actual record sizes will eventually be determined by the ASCII data content that resides in the records of a Sequential Text file.

1. APPEND Command

APPEND   f [,Ss][,Dd][,Vv]

Example: APPEND STEST.T

This command is available in DOS 3.3 for Sequential Text File commands and no enhancements have been made for DOS 4.5. The DOS APPEND command opens the Sequential Text file f in the specified volume if it is not already open. The DOS APPEND command must be followed by a DOS WRITE command for the same filename f. The DOS APPEND command reads the entire file f, discards that data, and then positions the file pointer before the first NULL or character 0x00 that it finds in that file. Typically, a carriage return character 0x8D will precede the NULL character 0x00 when records are written normally to a Sequential Text file. The DOS APPEND handler writes all subsequent input data to file f at the location given by the file pointer.

Figure III.5.1.1 shows an example Applesoft program that uses the DOS OPEN, WRITE, and CLOSE commands in order to create the Sequential Text file STEST.T. Figure III.5.1.2 shows another example Applesoft program that is similar to the program that is shown in Figure III.5.1.1 except that this program uses the DOS APPEND command in order to add more information to the end of the Sequential Text file STEST.T.

The APPEND command is flawed in several locations within the DOS 3.3 source code which requires multiple software patches in order to correct the flawed manipulation of the File Manager Context Block variables BYTOFFST and RECNUM. The DOS 4.5 source code manipulates these variables correctly both within the File Manager FMDRVR driver routine and within the File Manager CMNOPEN Common Open routine. The original DOS 3.3 File Manager CALPOSN Calculate Position routine fails to ensure that the C-flag must be **clear** before the routine manipulates its variables in order to calculate the requested file position within a Sequential Text file. DOS 4.5 guarantees that the File Manager CALPOSN routine correctly manages the C-flag in order to correctly manipulate the routine variables that are required to calculate the requested file position within a Sequential Text file with absolute mathematical precision.

```
]LOAD STEST
]LIST

 10 D$ =   CHR$ (4):F$ = "STEST.T"
    : ONERR  GOTO 100
 20   PRINT D$;"OPEN ";F$
 30   PRINT D$;"WRITE ";F$
 40   PRINT "This is a sequential
    TEXT file."
 50  PRINT D$;"CLOSE ";F$
 100  END
]RUN

]LIST STEST.T

This is a sequential TEXT file.

]※
```

Figure III.5.1.1. OPEN, WRITE, and CLOSE

```
]LOAD STEST2
]LIST

 10 D$ =   CHR$ (4):F$ = "STEST.T"
    : ONERR  GOTO 100
 20   PRINT D$;"OPEN ";F$
 30   PRINT D$;"APPEND ";F$
 40   PRINT D$;"WRITE ";F$
 50   PRINT "This is an appended l
    ine."
 60  PRINT D$;"CLOSE ";F$
 100  END
]RUN

]LIST STEST.T

This is a sequential TEXT file.
This is an appended line.

]
```

Figure III.5.1.2. APPEND Command Display

2. CLOSE Command

CLOSE   [f]

Example: CLOSE
             CLOSE STEST.T

This command is available in DOS 3.3 for Sequential Text File commands and no enhancements have been made for DOS 4.5. The DOS CLOSE command flushes and de-allocates the file buffer that is associated with the Sequential Text file f, thereby closing the file from any further data input or data output. If a filename f is not supplied with the DOS CLOSE command, **all** open files regardless of their file Type are closed except for an open EXEC file. The File Manager FMCLOSCD command for the File Manager CLSHNDLR handler utilizes two routines, CHKBUF and CHKTSL. These routines test whether two specific bits are **set** or **clear** in the DSKFLAGS variable, DATAFLAG and TSLFLAG, respectively. See Table I.12.2 that defines the FMWORK variable DSKFLAGS where DATAFLAG has a value of 0x40 and TSLFLAG has a value of 0x80. If either one of these two bits are **set**, either the current data buffer or the TSL buffer needs to be written to the volume that is currently in focus. DSKFLAGS also contains a bit reserved for CATFLAG that has a value of 0x02, and if that bit is **set**, both the VTOC and the Catalog buffers also need

186

to be written to the volume that is currently in focus. This entire process is referred to as *flushing a file buffer*.

In DOS 4.5 the process of closing a file after the DATA and TSL buffers have been written to the volume that is in focus also includes updating the size of the file from SECCNT and updating the date and time stamp of the file. Once these updates have been made to the Catalog buffer on behalf of the file, the Catalog buffer can be written to the volume. All buffer resources that are allocated to the Sequential Text file f are relinquished immediately when a zero is written to the first character of FNAME that corresponds to the filename f that was used in the initial DOS OPEN command. If a file f is open for data input, a CLOSE command forces all of the remaining data that currently resides in the data buffer of file f to be written to file f and then file f is closed. Figures III.5.1.1 and III.5.1.2 show examples of using the DOS CLOSE command in an Applesoft program.

```
]LIST ETEST.T
print "This is ETEST running."
mon c
brun BTEST
date

]EXEC ETEST.T
]This is ETEST running.

]

]
]This is an example Binary program.
Clock data:  02/14/24 08:28:48
End of Binary program.

] = 02/14/24 08:28:48
]

]*
```

Figure III.5.3.1. EXEC Command Display

```
]CONFIG 4
]EXEC ETEST.T
]This is ETEST running.


]This is an example Binary program.
Clock data:  02/14/24 08:28:48
End of Binary program.

 = 02/14/24 08:28:48

]EXEC ETEST.T,R3
 = 02/14/24 08:28:48

]CONFIG,R
]*
```

Figure III.5.3.2. No PROMPT, EXEC,Rr Display

3. EXEC Command

EXEC   f [,Ss][,Dd][,Vv][,Rr]

Example: EXEC ETEST.T
            EXEC ETEST.T,R3

This command is available in DOS 3.3 for Sequential Text File commands and no enhancements have been made for DOS 4.5. The DOS EXEC command opens the file f in the specified volume with the expectation of reading either Applesoft statements or DOS 4.5 commands as if the statements or commands have been issued from the Apple Command Line. There can be only **one** active EXEC file, but an EXEC file may transfer its control to another EXEC file. If the R keyword is included with the DOS EXEC command, the file pointer is positioned that number of ASCII records r from the beginning of the file. EXEC files are Sequential Text files that are composed of sequential records where each record is terminated with a carriage return or character 0x8D. Figure III.5.3.1 shows an example of an EXEC file and its output.

187

There is one obvious and undesirable feature that is shown in Figure III.5.3.1, and that is the presence of the PROMPT or character] on nearly every line of the EXEC file output. I vividly remember my co-worker in 1982 asking me "Why? Why is that PROMPT character] there in the first place?" Now, I can honestly answer that formidable question! In EXEC file processing, DOS immediately prepares the Apple Command Line for the next command to be issued after DOS has output the carriage return character 0x8D when EXEC processing has completed the previous command. Thus, DOS immediately outputs a new PROMPT character]. The output of the EXEC file then proceeds to *type in* the data for the next command to be processed after that new PROMPT character]. When CONFIG Bit 2 is **set** in order to disable the printing of the PROMPT character] during EXEC processing as shown in Table III.1.1.1, DOS 4.5 simply bypasses the routine that prints the PROMPT character] whenever there is an active EXEC file. The same EXEC file is processed again in Figure III.5.3.2 except that CONFIG Bit 2 is **set**. Figure III.5.3.2 shows that the PROMPT character] is not printed during EXEC processing and that there is a remarkable difference in the look of the screen output. Figure III.5.3.2 also shows the utilization of the R keyword for DOS EXEC processing. In this example, the file pointer is positioned at the first character after counting three carriage return characters of 0x8D, thus ignoring those records. All subsequent commands are issued from that point on from the EXEC file f. That is, the first three commands in ETEST.T are skipped and only the DOS DATE command is processed and only its data is printed.

If the DOS MAXFILES command is used in an EXEC file, EXEC file command processing terminates immediately and the EXEC file is closed. The DOS MAXFILES command initializes the entire file buffer chain. Since the DOS EXEC command utilizes a file buffer, EXEC cannot continue processing after its file buffer has been initialized. In Figures III.5.3.1 and III.5.3.2 command line spacing is set to single spacing while an EXEC file is open. DOS 4.5 returns to double spacing between successive DOS commands after an EXEC file is closed unless CONFIG Bit 0 is **set**.

4. OPEN Command

OPEN   f [,Ss][,Dd][,Vv]

Example: OPEN STEST.T

This command is available in DOS 3.3 for Sequential Text File commands and no enhancements have been made for DOS 4.5. The DOS OPEN command allocates one of the available file buffers, which is 0x245 or 581 bytes in size, for the Sequential Text file f in the specified volume. This file buffer is initialized to read data from or write data to the beginning of file f. If there is **no** available file buffer, the Applesoft program can handle this situation by using the Applesoft statement ONERR GOTO or have the Applesoft interpreter print the No Buffers Available error message. If this file f does not exist in the specified volume, file f is created and an entry is made into the volume Catalog. If this file is already open, the file f is flushed so that any remaining data in its data buffer is written to the file before the file is closed, and the specified file f is again opened. Previous Figures III.5.1.1 and III.5.1.2 show examples in using the DOS OPEN command in order to open a Sequential Text File in an Applesoft program. The L keyword must **not** be included with the DOS OPEN command when reading data from or writing data to a Sequential Text file.

5. POSITION Command

POSITION f [,Rr]

Example: POSITION STEST.T,R1

This command is available in DOS 3.3 for Sequential Text File commands and no enhancements have been made for DOS 4.5. The DOS POSITION command must follow a DOS OPEN command for the Sequential Text file f. The DOS POSITION command reads the ASCII data in file f and places the file pointer position after reading r records from the current file pointer position. A record is a sequence of ASCII characters that are terminated with a carriage return or character 0x8D. Figure III.5.5.1 shows an example Applesoft program where the file pointer is positioned at the first character in the record after counting one carriage return character relative to the current file pointer position which is the beginning of the file STEST.T. Otherwise, the file pointer is positioned at the first character in the record after counting r records ahead relative to the current file pointer position within file f.

```
]LIST STEST.T
This is a sequential TEXT file.
This is an appended line.

]LOAD STEST3
]LIST

 10 D$ =   CHR$ (4):F$ = "STEST.T"
    : ONERR  GOTO 100
 20   PRINT D$;"OPEN ";F$
 30   PRINT D$;"POSITION ";F$;",R1"
 40   PRINT D$;"READ ";F$
 50   INPUT A$: PRINT A$
 60   GOTO 50
 100   PRINT D$;"CLOSE ";F$: END
]RUN
This is an appended line.

]
```

```
]LIST STEST.T
This is a sequential TEXT file.
This is an appended line.

]LOAD STEST4
]LIST

 10 D$ =   CHR$ (4):F$ = "STEST.T"
    : ONERR  GOTO 100
 20   PRINT D$;"OPEN ";F$
 30   PRINT D$;"READ ";F$;",B3"
 40   INPUT A$: PRINT A$
 50   GOTO 40
 100   PRINT D$;"CLOSE ";F$: END
]RUN
s is a sequential TEXT file.
This is an appended line.

]*
```

Figure III.5.5.1. POSITION and READ Commands   Figure III.5.6.1. READ, Bb Command Display

6. READ Command

READ   f [,Bb]

Example: READ STEST.T

This command is available in DOS 3.3 for Sequential Text File commands and no enhancements have been made for DOS 4.5. The DOS READ command configures the Sequential Text file data buffer for file f such that all input data is read from that file. If the B keyword is included with the DOS READ command, the file pointer position is located that many actual bytes b from the beginning of the file before any data is read from file f. Figure III.5.6.1 shows an example Applesoft program that uses the DOS READ command to read a Sequential Text file using a byte b offset. Any previous DOS POSITION command

and calculated file pointer position value is ignored when the B keyword is included with the DOS READ command, and a new file pointer position is calculated using the value of the B keyword.

7. TLOAD Command

TLOAD   f [,Ss][,Dd][,Vv][,A][,Bb][,Ll][,R]

Example: TLOAD ETEST.T,L31
                 TLOAD STEST,A,R
                 TLOAD ETEST.T,A,B31

This command is not available in DOS 3.3 for Sequential Text File commands and this command was initially developed for DOS 4.1 and no enhancements have been made for DOS 4.5. The DOS TLOAD command reads into memory the data of the Sequential Text file f in the specified volume starting at memory address 0x0900. Memory address 0x0900 is internal to DOS 4.5 and its value is not a parameter and, therefore, its value cannot be changed. If the A keyword is included in a subsequent DOS TLOAD command, the data in that Sequential Text file f is **appended** to the Sequential Text file data that is already in memory from any number of previously read Sequential Text files as long as the internal variable FILELAST+1 is not zero. If FILELAST+1 is zero, the flag that there is no Sequential Text file data yet in memory, and the A keyword is included, the data of the Text file f is simply read into memory starting at memory address 0x0900. If the B keyword is included with the DOS TLOAD command, that number of data bytes b is skipped before reading the remaining data contents of the file into memory. If the L keyword is included with the DOS TLOAD command, that number of data bytes l is read into memory, or until the end of the file if that should occur first. If the R keyword is included with the DOS TLOAD command, the start address and the total number of ASCII data bytes that currently reside in memory are displayed once the DOS TLOAD handler completes its processing.

```
]TLOAD ETEST.T,L31
]TLOAD STEST.T,A,R
A$0900,L$0059
]TLOAD ETEST.T,A,B31
]TSAVE TOTAL.T,R1
A$0900,L$006F = 001
]LIST TOTAL.T
print "This is ETEST running."
This is a sequential TEXT file.
This is an appended line.
mon c
brun BTEST
date

]
```

Figure III.5.7.1. TLOAD and TSAVE Commands

In Figure III.5.7.1 the first thirty-one ASCII bytes of the file ETEST.T are read into memory starting at memory address 0x0900. The entire data contents of the file STEST.T is read into memory next and appended to the previous ASCII data that is already in memory because the A keyword is included. The total ASCII data that now resides in memory is 0x59 or 89 bytes. Finally, the first thirty-one data bytes of the file ETEST.T are skipped and the remaining data contents of the file ETEST.T is appended to all of the previous ASCII data that is already in memory. All of the Sequential Text data is written to the file TOTAL.T, and all 0x6F or 111 bytes are displayed using the DOS LIST command. It is quite apparent that a complete Sequential Text file may be easily constructed by extracting pieces of other Sequential Text files using the DOS TLOAD command and its very powerful set of keywords.

8. TSAVE Command

TSAVE   f [,Ss][,Dd][,Vv][,B][,R[1]]

Example: TSAVE TOTAL.T,R
            TSAVE TOTAL2.T,R1

This command is not available in DOS 3.3 for Sequential Text File commands and this command was initially developed for DOS 4.1 and no enhancements have been made for DOS 4.5. The DOS TSAVE command saves the Sequential Text data that is currently in memory to the file f in the specified volume. The start address and the total number of ASCII data bytes that is currently in memory is internal to DOS 4.5, and DOS 4.5 uses the variables FILESTRT and FILELEN in the CMDVALS Data structure as shown in Table I.12.1. If the R keyword is included with the DOS TSAVE command, the start address and the total number of Sequential Text data bytes that are currently in memory is displayed as shown in Figure III.5.7.1 once the DOS TSAVE command completes its processing. If a non-zero R keyword is included with the DOS TSAVE command, the number of verified sectors is also displayed. If CONFIG Bit 1 is **set**, the Sequential Text file f is **not** verified after it is saved. The B keyword can be used with the DOS TSAVE command in order to implement the *File Delete/File Save* strategy. That is, the Sequential Text file f is deleted from the volume and then saved to the same volume in order to ensure that the TSL sector(s) of file f contain only those Track/Sector entry pairs that are required and utilized by the file.

9. TW Command

TW   f [,Ss][,Dd][,Vv]

Example: TW ETEST

This command is not available in DOS 3.3 for Sequential Text File commands and this command was initially developed for DOS 4.1 and no enhancements have been made to this command for DOS 4.5. The DOS TW or Text Write command records all keystrokes that are typed on the Apple Command Line after the PROMPT or character >. Those ASCII characters are sequentially added into the data buffer of the Sequential Text file f in the specified volume. If file f does not exist in the specified volume, file f is created, otherwise the file is always opened in APPEND mode and all keystrokes that are typed are saved directly into the data buffer for that file. The file is flushed and closed when the ESCAPE key or 0x9B is typed. That is, when the ESCAPE key is typed, all buffered data is flushed and written to the Sequential Text file f, and then the file is closed. No line editing capability is provided with the DOS TW command, and **all** keystrokes, including arrow keystrokes like the left arrow keystroke that is used for quasi editing, are captured and recorded into the data buffer of the file. The DOS TW command provides a very convenient and very expeditious method to create or to append an EXEC file or any other Sequential Text file with additional ASCII data as shown in Figure III.5.9.1.

```
]LIST TEST.T
PRINT "This is TEST.T running."
PRINT "Ready to run BTEST."
BRUN BTEST

]TW TEST.T
>DATE
>

]LIST TEST.T
PRINT "This is TEST.T running."
PRINT "Ready to run BTEST."
BRUN BTEST
DATE

]*
```

Figure III.5.9.1. TW Command Display

10.WRITE Command

WRITE   f [,Bb]

Example: WRITE STEST.TXT

This command is available in DOS 3.3 for Sequential Text File commands and no enhancements have been made for DOS 4.5. The DOS WRITE command configures the Sequential Text file data buffer for file f such that all output data is written to that file. If the B keyword is included with the DOS WRITE command, the file pointer position is located that many actual bytes b from the beginning of the file before any data is written to file f. Any previous data that existed in the Sequential Text file f is overwritten starting at the bth byte from the beginning of the file. Any previous DOS POSITION command and calculated file pointer position value is ignored when the B keyword is included with the DOS WRITE command, and a new file pointer position is calculated using the value of the B keyword. Previous Figures III.5.1.1 and III.5.1.2 show examples in using the DOS WRITE command in an Applesoft program.

Command	Command Syntax
CLOSE	[f]
OPEN*	f, Ll [,Ss][,Dd][,Vv]
READ*	f, Rr [,Bb]
WRITE*	f, Rr [,Bb]

Table III.6.0.1. Random-Access Data File Commands in DOS 4.5

6. Random-Access Data File Commands

The Random-Access Data File commands in the DOS 4.5 command repertoire consist of those commands that manage the general operation of Random-Access Data files. The DOS CLOSE command can flush and de-allocate the file buffer that is associated with a Random-Access Data file. The DOS OPEN command can allocate a file buffer and associate that buffer with a Random-Access Data file. The DOS READ command can read Text fields, numerical data fields, unallocated data bytes, or a combination of all three from a Random-Access Data file into appropriate data variables. The DOS WRITE command can save the Text fields and numerical data fields that are found in various data variables to a Random-Access Data file.

The syntax of the Random-Access Data File commands is shown in Table III.6.0.1. All Random-Access Data File commands that are shown in Table III.6.0.1 are permitted to be used from within an Applesoft program or an assembly language routine. Those commands that are shown **without** an asterisk in Table III.6.0.1 **are** permitted to be used on the Apple Command Line. Those commands that are shown **with** an asterisk are **not** permitted to be used on the Apple Command Line. Random-Access Data files are composed of data records where an individual record has a specified size in bytes. A data record may be comprised of Text fields, numerical data fields, unallocated data bytes, or a combination of all three. A data record can be as small as one byte or as large as 32767 or 0x7FFF bytes in size. The data record size is established by the OPEN command using the required L keyword where the data record size in bytes is determined by the l value. Two bytes are provided for the l value which is stored in the variable RECDLNGH. RECDLNGH is located at offset 0x213 in the File Manager Workarea buffer of a file as shown in Table I.12.3. A Text field is any number of sequential ASCII characters that are terminated with a carriage return or character 0x8D. A numerical data field may be any number of digits, either integer values or floating point values in decimal, hexadecimal, or expressed in scientific notation as real and/or as imaginary floating point numbers. All data fields including any unallocated data bytes must reside within the specified size of the data record. All data records that comprise a file f are not required to contain the same number of data fields, the same type of data fields, or the same order of data fields. **All data records within a file f must be the same size. Only those records that contain any data whatsoever will actually exist within file f**. That is, a data record is created only whenever any data is generated and supplied for that data record. DOS 4.5 allows the R keyword value r for the DOS READ and the DOS WRITE commands to be any value up to and including 65535, thus permitting up to 65536 data records in a single file f. The only mathematical limitation for the maximum number of data records is the size of a 16-bit integer that is contained in two bytes. However, the maximum number of data records in DOS 3.3 is set to 32767, and there is no mathematical or logical reason for this limitation. The R keyword value r is stored in the variable RECURNUM which is located at offset 0x215 as shown in Table I.12.3. Two bytes are provided for this variable.

DOS 4.5 differentiates Sequential Text files and Random-Access Data files in how the file is opened. If the L keyword is **included** with the DOS OPEN command, the file is treated as a Random-Access Data file and the DOS READ and the DOS WRITE commands **must include** the R keyword as shown in Table III.6.0.1. See Table III.5.0.1 that shows the syntax for the Sequential Text file READ and WRITE commands in order to understand how those commands are syntactically different from the Random-Access Data file READ and WRITE commands. Applesoft programs or assembly language routines that access a Random-Access Data file must always open this file with the same record size l using the L keyword. Otherwise, the necessary computations that locate a specific record will result in obtaining unpredictable record data and the program quite likely will have disastrous results as the file is processed further. DOS 3.3 could have provided the value for l in the first TSL sector for a Random-Access Data file. There certainly is enough room for that value in that file structure, particularly at offset 0x08:0x09.

Data records are created as necessary on data sectors and the Track/Sector entry pairs for those sectors are added to a respective TSL sector when any data whatsoever is supplied to a Random-Access Data File record. The file pointer value is calculated based on record size l and the supplied record number r. Using the file pointer value, the necessary TSL index is also determined, and if there is no Track/Sector entry for the respective data sector, a data sector is obtained from the volume Catalog and an entry is made into the appropriate TSL sector for that new data sector. Any numerical remainder from the TSL index calculation plus any b index value from a B keyword that may have been included with the READ or the WRITE command determines the byte offset within the data sector where the supplied data is written for the specified data record. If the complete data record requires additional data sectors to contain the supplied data, those data sectors are also obtained from the volume Catalog and their Track/Sector entry pairs are added to the respective TSL sector.

1. CLOSE Command

CLOSE   [f]

Example: CLOSE RTEST.T

This command is available in DOS 3.3 for Random-Access Data File commands and no enhancements have been made for DOS 4.5. The DOS CLOSE command flushes and de-allocates the file buffer that is associated with the Random-Access Data file f, thereby closing the file from any further data input or any data output. If a filename f is not supplied with the DOS CLOSE command, **all** open files regardless of their file Type are closed except for an open EXEC file. The File Manager FMCLOSCD command for the File Manager CLSHNDLR handler utilizes two routines, CHKBUF and CHKTSL. These routines test whether two specific bits are **set** or **clear** in the DSKFLAGS variable, DATAFLAG and TSLFLAG, respectively. See Table I.12.2 that defines the FMWORK variable DSKFLAGS where DATAFLAG has a value of 0x40 and TSLFLAG has a value of 0x80. If either one of these two bits are **set**, either the current data buffer or the TSL buffer needs to be written to the volume that is currently in focus. DSKFLAGS also contains a bit that is reserved for CATFLAG which has a value of 0x02, and if that bit is **set**, both the VTOC and the Catalog buffers also need to be written to the volume that is currently in focus. This process is referred to as *flushing a file buffer*.

In DOS 4.5 the process of closing a file after the DATA and TSL buffers have been written to the volume that is in focus also includes updating the size of the file from SECCNT and updating the date and time stamp of the file. Once these updates have been made to the Catalog buffer on behalf of the file, the Catalog buffer can be written to the volume. All buffer resources that are allocated to the Random-Access Data file f are relinquished immediately when a zero is written to the first character of FNAME that corresponds to filename f that was used in the initial DOS OPEN command. If a file f is open for data input, a CLOSE command forces all of the remaining data that currently resides in the data buffer for file f to be written to file f and then file f is closed. Figure III.6.1.1 shows an example of using the DOS CLOSE command in an Applesoft program.

```
]LOAD RTEST
]LIST

 10 D$ =   CHR$ (4):F$ = "RTEST.T"
    :L = 32: ONERR  GOTO 60
 20  PRINT D$;"OPEN ";F$;", L";L
 30  PRINT D$;"WRITE ";F$;", R3"
 35  PRINT "This is Record 3."
 40  PRINT D$;"WRITE ";F$;", R2,
     B6"
 45  PRINT "This is Record 2."
 50  PRINT D$;"WRITE ";F$;", R1,
     B12"
 55  PRINT "This is Record 1."
 60  PRINT D$;"CLOSE ";F$: END

]RUN

]
```

Figure III.6.1.1. OPEN, WRITE, and CLOSE

2. OPEN Command

OPEN   f, Ll [,Ss][,Dd][,Vv]

Example: OPEN RTEST.T, L32

This command is available in DOS 3.3 for Random-Access Data File commands and no enhancements have been made for DOS 4.5. The DOS OPEN command allocates one of the available file buffers, which is 0x245 or 581 bytes in size, for the Random-Access Data file f in the specified volume, and sets the record length to the number of bytes l that are specified by the required L keyword. This file buffer is initialized to read data from or write data to the beginning of file f. If there is **no** available file buffer, the Applesoft program can handle this situation by using the Applesoft statement ONERR GOTO or have the Applesoft interpreter print the No Buffers Available error message from DOS. If this file f does not exist in the specified volume, file f is created and an entry is made into the volume Catalog. If this file is already open, file f is flushed so that any remaining data that resides in its data buffer is written to the file before the file is closed, and the specified file f is again opened. Figures III.6.1.1 and III.6.3.2 show examples in using the DOS OPEN command in order to open a Random-Access Data File in an Applesoft program. The L keyword **must** be included with the DOS OPEN command when reading data from or writing data to a Random-Access Data file.

```
]LIST RTEST.T,R

0000 0000 0000 0000 0000 0000 0000 0000
0000 0000 0000 0000 0000 0000 0000 0000
0000 0000 0000 0000 0000 0000 D4E8 E9F3
A0E9 F3A0 D2E5 E3EF F2E4 A0B1 AE8D 0000
0000 0000 0000 D4E8 E9F3 A0E9 F3A0 D2E5
E3EF F2E4 A0B2 AE8D 0000 0000 0000 0000
D4E8 E9F3 A0E9 F3A0 D2E5 E3EF F2E4 A0B3
AE8D 0000 0000 0000 0000 0000 0000 0000
0000 0000 0000 0000 0000 0000 0000 0000
0000 0000 0000 0000 0000 0000 0000 0000
0000 0000 0000 0000 0000 0000 0000 0000
0000 0000 0000 0000 0000 0000 0000 0000
0000 0000 0000 0000 0000 0000 0000 0000
0000 0000 0000 0000 0000 0000 0000 0000
0000 0000 0000 0000 0000 0000 0000 0000

]
```

Figure III.6.3.1. Display of RTEST.T

```
]LOAD RTEST2
]LIST

10  D$ =   CHR$ (4):F$ = "RTEST.T"
    :L = 32: ONERR  GOTO 60
20  PRINT  D$;"OPEN ";F$;", L";L
30  PRINT  D$;"READ ";F$;", R2, B
    6": INPUT D2$
40  PRINT  D$;"READ ";F$;", R3": INPUT
    D3$
50  PRINT  D$;"READ ";F$;", R1, B
    12": INPUT D1$
60  PRINT  D$;"CLOSE ";F$
70  PRINT : PRINT D1$: PRINT D2$
    : PRINT D3$: END

]RUN

This is Record 1.
This is Record 2.
This is Record 3.
]
```

Figure III.6.3.2. READ Command Display

3. READ Command

| READ | f, Rr [,Bb] |

Example: READ RTEST.T,R1,B12

This command is available in DOS 3.3 for Random-Access Data File commands and no enhancements have been made for DOS 4.5. The DOS READ command configures the Random-Access Data file buffer for file f such that all input data is read from that file. Data is read from the specified Record r, one field at a time. If the R keyword is **not** included with the DOS READ command, no error is generated within DOS and the file pointer is simply positioned at the beginning of file f. DOS 4.5 does not check for the presence or the absence of the R keyword; it simply utilizes its value if it is provided. However, even though the R keyword is initialized to zero before any DOS command is parsed, the practice of not including the R keyword with the DOS READ command for a Random-Access Data file is strongly **not** advised. If the B keyword is included along with the DOS READ command, the file pointer position is located that many actual bytes b from the beginning of the specified R keyword Record r before any data is read from that record. Note that this usage of the B keyword is **very different** in Random-Access Data files than how the B keyword is utilized in Sequential Text files.

Figure III.6.3.1 shows a hexadecimal listing of the contents of RTEST.T using the DOS LIST command that includes the R keyword. The R keyword for the DOS LIST command selects hexadecimal data output rather than ASCII data output for a Text Type file. It is easy to observe that each record is thirty-two bytes in size and that Record 0 ranges from byte 0x00 to byte 0x1F in Figure III.6.3.1. There is no data in Record 0, the first record in the file. There is data in Record 1 that begins at offset byte 0x0C (see line 50 in Figure III.6.3.2); there is data in Record 2 that begins at offset byte 0x06 (see line 30 in Figure III.6.3.2); there is data in Record 3 that begins at offset byte 0x00 (see line 40 in Figure III.6.3.2). Figure III.6.3.2 shows an example Applesoft program that uses the DOS READ command for a Random-Access Data file. The data records may be read from the Random-Access Data file in any order, hence the descriptive term *random-access* data file. Figure III.6.3.2 also shows the results of running the RTEST2 Applesoft program.

4. WRITE Command

WRITE   f, Rr [,Bb]

Example: WRITE RTEST.T,R1,B12

This command is available in DOS 3.3 for Random-Access Data File commands and no enhancements have been made for DOS 4.5. The DOS WRITE command configures the Random-Access Data file data buffer for file f such that all output data is written to that file. Data is written to the specified Record r, one field at a time. If the R keyword is **not** included with the DOS WRITE command, no error is generated within DOS and the file pointer is simply positioned at the beginning of file f. DOS 4.5 does not check for the presence or the absence of the R keyword; it simply utilizes its value if it is provided. However, even though the R keyword is initialized to zero before any DOS command is parsed, the practice of not including the R keyword with the DOS WRITE command for a Random-Access Data file is strongly **not** advised. If the B keyword is included with the DOS WRITE command, the file pointer position is located that many actual bytes b from the beginning of the specified R keyword Record r before any data is written to the record. Note that this usage of the B keyword is **very different** in Random-Access Data files than how the B keyword is utilized in Sequential Text files. Figure III.6.1.1 shows an example in using the DOS WRITE command for a Random-Access Data file in an Applesoft program where data records are defined to be 32 bytes in size. The data records may be written to the Random-Access Data file in any order, hence the descriptive term *random-access* data file.

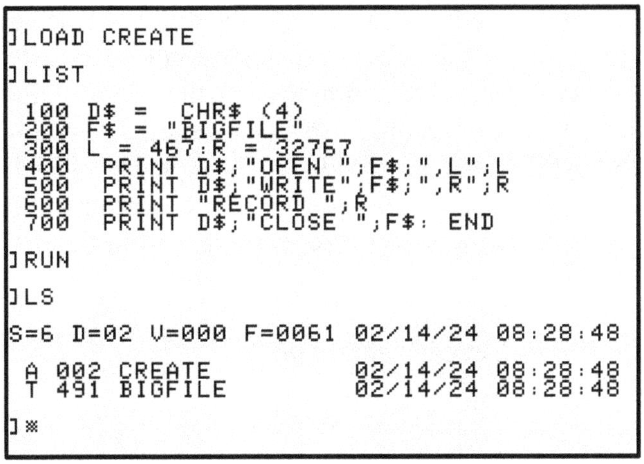

Figure III.7.1. Program CREATE Display

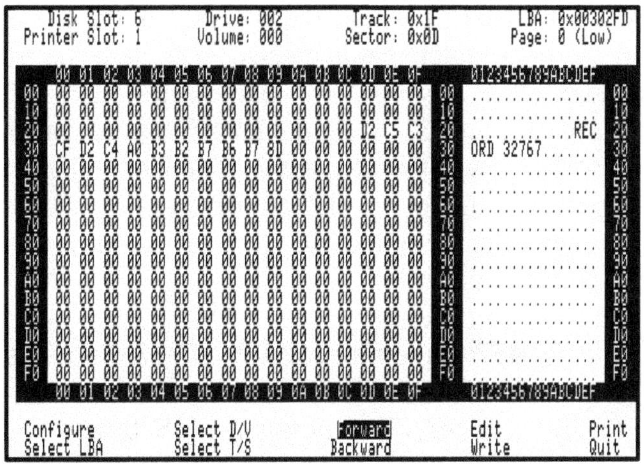

Figure III.7.2. Record 32767 Display

7. Random-Access Data File Design Considerations

Denis Molony, a citizen of Australia and the author of the extraordinarily useful tool *DiskBrowser*, provided me with an excellent example of an Applesoft program that creates a Random-Access Data file that quickly becomes useless after a few records are written to that file. Figure III.7.1 shows Molony's Applesoft program that he saved onto a volume that he initialized with DOS 3.3. I copied his Applesoft program CREATE onto a volume that I initialized with DOS 4.5. His program certainly looks simple enough until you realize that this program writes to the last possible record that is permitted by DOS 3.3 which is record 32767 or 0x7FFF, or the 32768th record. Just to be clear, DOS 4.5 changes the record specification size from 32767 to 65535 which is 0x7FFF to 0xFFFF, but this does not in any way alter the results of this program nor does it alter the concepts this program teaches. When DOS first creates a Random-Access Data file, only the first TSL sector is created as shown in line 400 in Figure III.7.1. The value of the L keyword, 467 in this example, is saved in the File Manager Workarea buffer for BIGFILE in the RECDLNGH variable as shown in Table I.12.3 at offset 0x213. When BIGFILE is reopened sometime in the future, BIGFILE must be opened with the **same** L keyword value in order to accurately locate the desired data records and the desired data fields that are contained in those data records. When Molony's program writes to record 32767 in line 500, a file pointer is calculated and sufficient TSL sectors are created for the BIGFILE file in order to save that particular data record to its designated data sector at its designated data sector offset, and save its Track/Sector entry pairs for that particular data sector in its designated TSL sector.

How many TSL sectors are created in order to write a single data field to record 32767 may seem puzzling at first, though it is easy to determine that value. Each TSL sector contains 122 or 0x7A Track/Sector entry pairs. These TSL sector entries are for **sectors of data**, not for **records of data**. Each sector of data contains 256 or 0x100 bytes of information. Including record 0, therefore,

```
{ ( 467 bytes/record * 32768 records ) / 256 bytes/sector } /

    122 sectors/TSL sector = 490 TSL sectors
```

When the Text field is actually written to the file in line 600, an entry is made into the 490th TSL sector for the data sector that is created to contain the provided Text field. The Text field is not necessarily written to the very first byte of the sector, but in this instance it is written to byte 45, which comes after the end of record 32766, or the 32767th record, and is the first byte of record 32767. The entire data record of 467 bytes is **not** written to the file but only the single Text field that is provided in the Applesoft PRINT statement in line 600 which amounts to only twelve data bytes and a carriage return or character 0x8D. The byte offset into the data sector where these thirteen bytes are written is the remainder from the data file pointer calculation

```
( 467 bytes/record * 32767 records ) / 256 bytes/sector =

    59,774 sectors + 45 bytes
```

Figure III.7.1 shows that BIGFILE is 491 sectors in size, currently composed of 490 TSL sectors and one data sector. Figure III.7.2 shows the actual data sector that contains the Text field that is written by line 600. There are only sixty-one sectors free on this DOS 4.5 data volume which originally contained 554 sectors when it was first initialized. Why does DOS create all these TSL sectors? It seems rather ludicrous, because 59,774 sectors are required to contain all of the data for the previous 32767 records if the program CREATE writes at least one data field to all of these data records in BIGFILE. This would require a volume having at least 3,736 additional disk tracks. At the very least, DOS has created the minimum number of required linked-list TSL sectors in order to write a single Text field to record number 32767 and enter that data sector as a single Track/Sector entry pair into a TSL sector. It is rather obvious that BIGFILE is not at all suitable to contain all of the data fields that the Applesoft program CREATE intended. Therefore, it is critical to properly size a Random-Access Data file to the volume in which that data file is to be stored.

Family Roots by Stephen C. Vorenberg and marketed by Quinsept, Inc., utilizes Sequential Text files and Random-Access Data files for its *Family Roots* database. Each data volume contains a minimum of three files: CONTROL, NAMELIST, and FAMILY. The Random-Access Data file NAMELIST uses twenty-six sectors. The Sequential Text file CONTROL uses two sectors, and it contains the Start and the End record numbers that exist within the Random-Access Data file FAMILY whose records have been pre-initialized using a 256-byte empty buffer. The CONTROL file also contains the size of the FAMILY file records, and a few other operating parameters, so that the file FAMILY is always opened with the correct value l for the L keyword. Essentially, each FAMILY file contains 224 records and each record is configured to be two sectors in size so that a maximum of 512 bytes can be utilized for each record. The equations that are required to verify whether there is sufficient disk space for this Random-Access Data file when all of its records are filled with at least one data field can be expressed as follows

```
( 224 records * 512 bytes/record ) / 256 bytes/sector = 448 sectors

448 sectors / 122 sectors/TSL sector = 4 TSL sectors
```

Since *Family Roots* utilizes the DOS 3.3 Disk Operating System, tracks 0x00, 0x01, and 0x02 are not available for data since they are reserved for DOS 3.3, and the VTOC and Catalog sectors combined require another sixteen sectors. This leaves 496 sectors for data in a volume that has thirty-five tracks. Using the above results, each data volume for *Family Roots* requires 26 + 2 + 448 + 4 = 480 sectors. Therefore, at least sixteen sectors should be available in each data volume that could be used for any additional files. A few data volumes did contain one or two additional files: LASTID and DATE. These files were only two sectors each in size and they appeared transitory. Vorenberg sized his data files such that 96.8% of each data volume is utilized, thus giving the program *Family Roots* a little margin of safety for the size of these Random-Access Data files.

The Molony and Vorenberg data volume examples demonstrate how important it is to consider whether a single data volume can provide sufficient room in order to store the data records of a particular Random-Access Data file, or whether several volumes would be required to store all of the generated data records when using multiple Random-Access Data files. Performing the file sizing analysis upfront certainly saves much grief later on when and if a Random-Access Data file should exceed its storage media capacity. Certainly, a Random-Access Data file cannot grow endlessly and it must have boundaries built into its design and its capacity.

Given R for the number of records, L for the size or length of each record in bytes, and S for the number of available sectors where each sector contains 256 bytes of data, the Random-Access Data file sizing equations that also incorporate TSL sector overhead can be expressed as follows

```
S = ( R * L * 123 ) / ( 256 * 122 ) sectors        (always round up)

R = ( S * 256 * 122 ) / ( L * 123 ) records        (always round down)

L = ( S * 256 * 122 ) / ( R * 123 ) bytes          (always round down)
```

Inserting Vorenberg's parameters into these equations where R = 224 and L = 512:

$$S = (224 * 512 * 123) / (256 * 122) = 451.67 => 452 \text{ sectors}$$

This is precisely the same value obtained above: 448 data sectors + 4 TSL sectors = 452 sectors.

For Molony's example program, the required number of sectors for his Random-Access Data file is

$$S = (32768 * 467 * 123) / (256 * 122) => 60,266 \text{ sectors}$$

A single 35-track volume is hardly the appropriate media for this Random-Access Data file.

Now, assuming Molony's data file can be spread over several 36-track volumes each providing 570 sectors when using DOS 4.5, the number of records on each volume would be

$$R = (570 * 256 * 122) / (467 * 123) => 309 \text{ records} \quad (\text{round } \textbf{down})$$

And, the number of volumes required for all of these records would be

$$32768 \text{ records } / 309 \text{ records/volume} => 106 \text{ volumes} \quad (\text{round } \textbf{up})$$

A database of this magnitude would require quite a substantial programing effort, but easily managed on the CFFA when a CF card is initialized using the *VOLMGR* and each volume is initialized for DOS 4.5 utilization. Vorenberg strongly recommended using the Sider with *Family Roots* and that is precisely the hard drive my mother utilized with her copy of *Family Roots* in order to digitize our family tree which happens to be rather extensive in size. My mother was able to obtain family history and documentation on individuals where some in our family tree arrived to America on the *Mayflower*. My parents traveled through several parts of Scotland and Ireland searching for any records my mother could find for her great-great-great-grandparents. She was able to create an amazing database for our family tree using *Family Roots* on her Apple //e computer that hosted her Sider hard disk drive.

8. Using Real and Imaginary Floating Point Numbers

Applesoft stores and processes floating point numbers using four bytes or thirty-two bits for the mantissa and one byte or eight bits for the exponent for a total of five bytes as shown in Table I.15.1. As in all floating point number notations, the most significant mantissa bit and the most significant exponent bit are sign bits, and if that bit is OFF in either case, the respective value is positive. Also, the mantissa utilizes an implicit high-order one bit to yield a full 32-bit significand. Applesoft floating point numbers have a numerical range from 10^{-38} to 10^{38} and they have over nine digits of accuracy. When using floating point numbers in Applesoft, those numbers must be within this numerical range or Applesoft will flag an error or simply convert the number to zero. Applesoft understands scientific notation when a floating point number is either too large or too small to express the number in decimal form. The format of a floating pointer number is SD.FFFFFFFFESTT in Applesoft scientific notation. Both the single digit decimal number D and the double digit exponent TT utilize the sign bit S. If the floating point number is positive, no plus sign is used before the number. However, the sign of the exponent TT is always given in Applesoft scientific notation whether the exponent is positive or negative. The letter E separates the decimal number D and its fractional part FFFFFFFF from the exponent TT. Applesoft does not identify imaginary floating point numbers as any different from real floating point numbers. And, Applesoft does not provide for either double precision integer numbers or double precision floating point numbers.

Applesoft mathematical routines and functions that operate on very small floating point numbers can become problematic. These routines and functions exhibit non-commutative addition, non-commutative multiplication, non-reflexive equality evaluation, irregularities of the exponent when the exponent is very large or very small, bugs in the multiplication algorithm, errors in the binary to decimal conversion, and significant errors in the trigonometric functions involving very small arguments. Some intermediate arguments depend on a full 40-bit significand since these arguments utilize guard bytes. On the other hand, other intermediate arguments are rounded and pushed onto the stack using only their 32-bit significand. Sticky bits are not utilized in Applesoft mathematical routines and functions in order to make numerical rounding decisions. Since the trigonometric functions depend solely on the sine function, the cosine and tangent functions are equally flawed, if not more so. The Applesoft mathematical routines and functions can provide acceptable results if very small or very large arguments are avoided and if the number of significant digits are limited to only what is acceptable given the total **range** of the numerical values of all arguments.

S. Keller and L. D'Addario published the *Complex Math Package for Apple II Plus Computers* in January, 1982. This publication was Internal Report No. 226 from the Electronics Division of the National Radio Astronomy Observatory in Charlottesville, Virginia. The *Complex Math Package for Apple II Plus Computers* publication provides an Introduction, a Calling Sequence, Descriptions of Individual Subroutines, Memory Requirements and Addresses, Timing, and Examples and Suggestions. Tables are also provided for Entry Point Addresses in Binary Library Version 2.0 and for Subroutine Execution Times. When I inquired about the availability of any further information on Report No. 226 and perhaps the source code for the complex math subroutines, I have yet to receive a response from the observatory.

The complex math package is an extension to Applesoft and the package includes functions for adding, multiplying, dividing, and converting coordinate systems that utilize complex floating point numbers, as well as adding, subtracting, multiplying, and inverting complex floating point number 2-by-2 matrices. The assembly language routines are accessed by means of a CALL statement that uses a special format in order to allow the passing of parameters to the various algorithms. The report states that the execution time for these assembly language routines are two to eight times faster than the equivalent Applesoft routine. Understand that these routines operate on two Applesoft floating point numbers that comprise a complex floating point number at the same time. If the same routines were utilized in Applesoft, twice as many or more operations would be necessary in order to evaluate the same complex floating point number routines. Operations on 2-by-2 matrices must be handled uniquely because they involve specific operations on the matrix complex floating point values. The inversion of a 2-by-2 matrix is very difficult. The conversion of polar coordinates, in phase/quadrature measurements, current lag in inductive loads, and voltage lag in capacitive loads all require complex mathematical solutions.

It is indeed a shame that the *Complex Math Package for Apple II Plus Computers* appears to be **no longer** available to the Apple][enthusiast. I suspect that this might be a very interesting project to try and recreate. It might be easy! And it certainly would be educational and a whole lot of fun, indeed!

*In no other Apple][Disk Operating System will the user find
a more powerful set of initialization and data management routines
that puts DOS 4.5 literally at the forefront of any other
Disk Operating System that is fully compatible with the
disk and sector structure that was originally created for DOS 3.3.*

IV. Assembly Language Routines in DOS 4.5

DOS 4.5 provides unapparelled support for assembly language routines when they need to acquire or to change the value of a particular operational variable whether it is used locally in a single software routine or it is used throughout the DOS 4.5 software and functional handlers. DOS 4.5 also provides direct access to interface routines and vectors that handle error reporting, obtaining the date and time, and for displaying the DOS version and build information easily. Even though the Page 0x03 Interface Routines, Vectors, and DATA Management functions have been previously discussed and even utilized in example programs, I have found it to be exceedingly informative to present all of these routines, vectors, entry points, and variables together, in one section, showing their address, the registers and values they require and/or utilize, and the processor flags that are necessary upon entry that support their various processing capabilities, and the registers, their values, and processor flags that are returned to the user.

There are two basic approaches that a user may call or to invoke an assembly language routine or vector: the Direct Approach or the Indirect Approach. The Direct Approach is simply to use the JSR instruction in order to **jump directly** to a routine. The Indirect Approach is to use the JSR instruction coupled with an indirect JMP instruction such as JMP(ADR) in order to **jump indirectly** to a routine. Figure IV.0.1 shows both approaches that a user may utilize in order to call or to invoke a DOS 4.5 assembly language routine or vector. Depending upon how the assembly language routine or vector is entered either by a JSR or by a JMP instruction or how the routine or vector is specified by an address or by a vector usually determines which approach is more favorable to use within the software that the user is developing.

```
   :           :        :
  03E1         10  RDCLKVSN equ $3E1
  03EA         11  HOOKDOS  equ $3EA
   :           :        :
   :           :        :
  1000        100  ; Direct subroutine approach.
  1000 20 EA 03 101        jsr HOOKDOS
   :           :        :
   :           :        :
  2000        200  ; Indirect vector approach.
  2000 A0 83  201        ldy #VSNBUFR
  2002 A9 20  202        lda /VSNBUFR
  2004 38     203        sec
  2005 20 80 20 204        jsr READVSN
   :           :        :
   :           :        :
  2080 6C E1 03 300  READVSN  jmp (RDCLKVSN)
  2083 00 00 00 301  VSNBUFR  dfs 20,0
   :           :        :
```

Figure IV.0.1. Direct and Indirect Approach to Call a Subroutine

I have always viewed software development as a set of very complex strategies that involve highly developed problem solving techniques. To develop such programming skills requires passion, perseverance, and practice. One cannot be expected to perform a Fiorillo Caprice overnight without expending a little passion, a little perseverance, and a little practice. Learning how to utilize and manage the memory of the Language Card partition in the Apple][machine is, in itself, very complicated, problematic, and certainly not intuitive. When that memory is managed correctly, the utilization of the Language Card partition provides great opportunities to expand one's programming skills. But those skills are still considerably simple compared to the skills that are required to utilize and manage Auxiliary memory. Only with passion, perseverance, and practice will the Apple][hardware reveal itself and yield its total computational power to that competent software and hardware engineer.

The DOS 4.5 Assembly Language Routines are found collectively in three distinct memory locations that are either external to or they are internal to DOS 4.5. The routines, vectors, entry points, and variables that are available to the DOS 4.5 user and found external to DOS 4.5 are the Page 0x03 Interface Routines and Vectors as shown in Table I.9.3. Those routines, vectors, entry points, and variables that are found internal to DOS 4.5 are the Page 0xBE Main Memory and Language Card Memory Interface Routines as shown in Table IV.2.0.1 and the Page 0xBF BOOT and DATA Management Vectors and Bytes as shown in Table I.8.1.

1. Page 0x03 Interface Routines and Vectors

The Page 0x03 Interface Routines and Vectors are part of the DOS 4.5 Data structures that are found at the end of the executable object code that resides in Bank 2 of Language Card memory. These routines are copied in bulk from DOS 4.5 into lower Main memory to 0x03D0:0x03FF. All of the Page 0x03 Interface Routines and Vectors reside within this memory location. When DOS 4.5 BOOTs or when DOS 4.5 is Cold-Started, the CURSTATE variable is made negative and this variable initiates the entry into the FRSTIME routine after Applesoft has initialized. FRSTIME completes the DOS 4.5 Cold-Start initialization after the Cold-Start routine initializes the DOS file buffers, establishes the CURSTATE, CSWSTATE, and RKEYWORD variables, and copies the Page 0x03 Interface Routines and Vectors to 0x03D0:0x03FF. It is in this Interface structure where the important routines and vectors are found for a variety of important DOS functions. This Interface structure is essentially the same as that found in DOS 3.3 and it exists for DOS 4.5 in order to maintain compatibility with virtually all previously written software for the Apple][. Just to be clear, all of the Page 0x03 Interface Routines and Vectors are available to DOS 4.5 and to the DOS 4.5 user **only after** DOS 4.5 has BOOTed and has fully initialized.

1. DOSWARM Routine

Function	Address	X-reg	Y-reg	A-reg	C-flag	Description
Entry	0x03D0	–	–	–	–	Enters (WARMADR) handler
ASROMWRM	0xD43C	–	–	–	–	Applesoft Warm-Start

The DOSWARM routine at memory address 0x3D0 as shown in Table I.9.3 enters the DOS WARMSTRT routine by means of the DOS EXTWARM routine. In DOS 4.5 the DOSWARM routine directly enters the DOS EXTWARM routine that is found in the Page 0xBE Interface Routines that write-enables Bank 2 of the Language Card partition in order to directly enter the DOS WARMSTRT routine. The DOS WARMSTRT routine sets the stack pointer to 0xFF, resets the state machine, initializes the MON flags and the keyboard and video intercepts, turns ROM memory ON, and exits indirectly by means of the DOS WARMADR vector in the Page 0xBE INITVALS Data structure as shown in Table I.8.5.

The assembler sets the WARMADR vector to memory address 0xD43C, the address of the Applesoft ASROMWRM routine. The ROM ASROMWRM routine performs a partial re-initialization of Applesoft. This ROM Applesoft routine does not return to the caller. The user is encouraged to modify the address at WARMADR or 0xBEE2 in order to tailor the DOSWARM routine not to exit into ROM Applesoft, but to enter a user specific routine initially, and then exit into the ROM ASROMWRM routine.

Use the Direct Approach in order to utilize the DOS DOSWARM routine at 0x3D0.

2. DOSCOLD Routine

Function	Address	X-reg	Y-reg	A-reg	C-flag	Description
Entry	0x03D3	-	-	-	-	Enters (COLDADR) handler
BASCLD	0xE000	-	-	-	-	Applesoft Cold-Start

The DOSCOLD routine at memory address 0x3D3 as shown in Table I.9.3 enters the DOS COLDSTR2 routine by means of the DOS COLDSTRT routine. In DOS 4.5 the DOSCOLD routine directly enters the DOS COLDSTRT routine that is found on Page 0xBF that initializes the stack pointer and XMODE to 0xFF, selects the main video and deselects the alternate character set, sets the video output to normal, initializes the text and graphic modes and sets the window operating parameters, initializes the CSWL and KSWL interface pointers, verifies that Applesoft is in ROM, copies the ROM Monitor to the RAM Monitor, searches for a clock card, and initializes SLOTVAL, DRVAL, and VOLVAL in order to directly enter the DOS COLDSTR2 routine. The DOS COLDSTR2 routine sets the stack pointer to 0xFF, resets the state machine, initializes the MON flags and the keyboard and video intercepts, turns ROM memory ON, and exits indirectly by means of the DOS COLDADR vector in the Page 0xBE INITVALS Data structure as shown in Table I.8.5.

The assembler sets the COLDADR vector to memory address 0xE000, the address of the ROM BASCLD routine. The ROM BASCLD routine performs a complete re-initialization of Applesoft. This ROM Applesoft routine does not return to the caller. The user is encouraged to modify the address at COLDADR or 0xBEE4 in order to tailor the DOS COLDSTRT routine not to exit into ROM Applesoft, but to enter a user specific routine initially, and then exit into the ROM BASCLD routine.

Use the Direct Approach in order to utilize the DOSCOLD routine at 0x3D3.

3. CALLFM Routine

Function	Address	X-reg	Y-reg	A-reg	C-flag	Description
Entry	0x03D6	File Flag	-	-	-	Set RAM Bank 2 ON, call FMHNDLR routine
Return	-	Error #	-	-	Status	Set ROM Bank 2 WP and return to caller

The CALLFM routine at memory address 0x3D6 as shown in Table I.9.3 enters the DOS FMHNDLR handler by means of the DOS EXTFM routine. In DOS 4.5 the CALLFM routine directly enters the DOS EXTFM routine that is found in the Page 0xBE Interface Routines that write-enables Bank 2 of the Language Card partition in order to directly enter the DOS FMHNDLR handler. The DOS FMHNDLR handler loads the FILALC flag value, or 0x81, when the File Flag in the X-register is set to zero, otherwise it loads the

NOFILALC flag value, or 0x80, and saves that value to KEYWORD1. Both file flags have their MSB **set** which tells the INIT INITHNDL handler that the call to the DOS FMHNDLR handler was by means of CALLFM and not from within DOS. All registers are saved and the CSWL and the KSWL interface pointers to DOS are disconnected. Processing continues in the DOS FILEMNGR routine that directly follows the DOS FMHNDLR handler.

When all File Manager processing is complete, the DOS FILEMNGR routine preserves its final status in the C-flag and its final error code value in the X-register, and the routine returns to the caller. For the external caller in DOS 4.5, the DOS FMHNDLR handler returns to the Page 0xBE Interface Routines, enters directly the DOS INITPTRS routine in order to restore control over the DOS CSWL and KSWL interface pointers, and enables ROM memory in order to return to the external caller. If the final status that is returned in the C-flag from the DOS FILEMNGR routine is **set**, the X-register contains an error code value, otherwise the C-flag is **clear** and the X-register is set to zero. The File Manager uses its **own** Context Block in order to process a File Manager command from DOS 4.5 or from an external caller.

Use the Direct Approach in order to utilize the CALLFM routine at 0x3D6.

4. CALLRWTS Routine

Function	Address	X-reg	Y-reg	A-reg	C-flag	Description
Entry	0x03D9	–	#IOCB	/IOCB	–	Set RAM Bank 1 ON, call DORWTS routine
Return	–	–	–	Error #	Status	Set ROM Bank 2 WP and return to caller

The CALLRWTS routine at memory address 0x3D9 as shown in Table I.9.3 enters the DOS DORWTS routine by means of the DOS EXTRWTS routine. In DOS 4.5 the CALLRWTS routine directly enters the DOS EXTRWTS routine that is found in the Page 0xBE Interface Routines that write-enables Bank 1 of the Language Card partition in order to directly enter the DOS DORWTS routine. The DOS DORWTS routine disables interrupts, saves the Y- and A-registers that contain the address of the user's IOCB to the IOBADR pointer, extracts the USRBUF address from the IOCB and saves that address to the BUFADR2Z pointer, extracts the SNUM16 slot-times-sixteen value from the IOCB and saves it to SLOT16Z and back to the IOCB at SLOTFND, divides the SNUM16 value by sixteen and copies it to the X-register, and the routine formulates the DISKJMP indirect JMP address. The SCRCHTBL Scratch Pad table, indexed using the same X-register slot value, is checked to determine whether the scratch pad RAM locations have been initialized for this slot, and the BLDNIBFG flag is checked to determine whether the DOS BLDNIBL routine has been called in order to generate the RDNIBL and WRNIBL nibble tables. The BLDNIBFG flag ensures that the DOS BLDNIBL routine is entered only once. The X-register is restored from SLOT16Z, the Y- and A-registers are restored from the IOBADR pointer, and the requested RWTS Slot handler is indirectly entered by means of DISKJMP.

When the requested RWTS Slot handler processing is complete, the DOS DORWTS routine restores the processor status and **clears** the C-flag if the returned error code contains a zero value, otherwise the routine **sets** the C-flag. For the external caller in DOS 4.5, the DOS DORWTS routine returns to the Page 0xBE Interface Routines, enables ROM memory, and returns to the caller. DOS RWTS can use any Context Block that is located anywhere within lower Main memory, even the RWTS I/O Context Block within Page 0xBF as long as the Y- and A-registers contain the address of that Context Block.

Use the Direct Approach in order to utilize the CALLRWTS routine at 0x3D9.

5. GETFMCB Routine

Function	Address	X-reg	Y-reg	A-reg	C-flag	Description
Entry	0x03DC	-	-	-	-	Gets the FMVALS address
Return	0x03E0	-	#FMVALS	/FMVALS	-	Return to caller

The GETFMCB routine at memory address 0x3DC as shown in Table I.9.3 loads the Y- and A-registers with the address of the File Manager FMVALS Context Block. The FMVALS Context Block resides within Page 0xBF and this Context Block immediately follows the internal RWTS Input/Output Context Block. The File Manager uses **only** this FMVALS Context Block in order to process a File Manager command from DOS 4.5 or from an external caller. *FID*, for example, maintains its own copy of the 18-byte FMVALS Context Block, modifies selected variables of the Context Block as needed, and then copies the Context Block in its entirety back into DOS address space that is within Page 0xBF before entering the File Manager CALLFM routine. Upon return from File Manager processing, *FID* copies the entire FMVALS Context Block again into its own address space before processing the RTNCODE return code value in order for *FID* to select its next processing step.

Use the Direct Approach in order to utilize the GETFMCB routine at 0x3DC.

6. RDCLKVSN Vector Address

Function	Address	X-reg	Y-reg	A-reg	C-flag	Description
Entry	0x03E1	-	#CLKBUF	/CLKBUF	clear	Set RAM Bank 2 ON, call READCLK routine
Return	-	-	-	-	-	Set ROM Bank 2 WP and return to caller
Entry	0x03E1	-	#VSNBUF	/VSNBUF	set	Set RAM Bank 2 ON, call READVSN routine
Return	-					Set ROM Bank 2 WP and return to caller

The RDCLKVSN vector address at memory address 0x3E1 as shown in Table I.9.3 enters the DOS DOCLKVSN routine by means of the DOS EXCLKVSN routine. In DOS 4.5 the caller, using the RDCLKVSN vector address, indirectly enters the DOS EXCLKVSN routine that is found in the Page 0xBE Interface Routines that write-enables Bank 2 of the Language Card partition in order to directly enter the DOS DOCLKVSN routine. The DOS DOCLKVSN routine saves the address that is in the Y- and A-registers to the DOSPTR pointer. If the C-flag is **clear**, the DOSPTR pointer contains the address of a 6-byte clock buffer in order to capture the current date and time values, and processing continues in the DOS READCLK routine. If the C-flag is **set**, the DOSPTR pointer contains the address of a 20-byte version buffer in order to capture the 20-byte DOS Version ASCII character string, and processing continues in the DOS READVSN routine. The supplied 20-byte DOS Version ASCII character string will contain only upper ASCII characters for the string data, and the character string will not contain a carriage return character 0x8D or a termination NULL byte 0x00, nor is the character string data in DCI format. Once processing is complete in either DOS routine, the DOCLKVSN routine returns to the Page 0xBE Interface Routines, enables ROM memory, and returns to the caller.

Use the Indirect Approach in order to utilize the RDCLKVSN vector address at 0x3E1.

7. GETIOCB Routine

Function	Address	X-reg	Y-reg	A-reg	C-flag	Description
Entry	0x03E3	-	-	-	-	Gets RWTS IOCB address
Return	0x03E7	-	#IOCB	/IOCB	-	Return to caller

The GETIOCB routine at memory address 0x3E3 as shown in Table I.9.3 loads the Y- and A-registers with the address of the RWTS Input/Output Context Block. The RWTS IOCB resides within page 0xBF immediately before the internal File Manager FMVALS Context Block. DOS RWTS uses the 17-byte Context Block in order to process a DOS RWTS command either from DOS 4.5 or from an external caller. DOS RWTS can use virtually any lower Main memory address space for its IOCB as long as the Y- and A-registers contain the address for that Context Block.

Use the Direct Approach in order to utilize the GETIOCB routine at 0x3E3.

8. PRERRADR Vector Address

Function	Address	X-reg	Y-reg	A-reg	C-flag	Description
Entry	0x03E8	Error #	-	-	-	Set RAM Bank 2 ON, call DOPRTERR routine
Return	-	-	-	-	-	Set ROM Bank 2 WP and return to caller

The PRERRADR vector address at memory address 0x3E8 as shown in Table I.9.3 enters the DOS DOPRTERR routine by means of the DOS EXTPRERR routine. In DOS 4.5 the caller, using the PRERRADR vector address, indirectly enters the DOS EXTPRERR routine that is found in the Page 0xBE Interface Routines that write-enables Bank 2 of the Language Card partition and disconnects the CSWL and the KSWL interface pointers from DOS and directly enters the DOS DOPRTERR routine. The DOS DOPRTERR routine saves the registers, range checks the error number value in the X-register verifying that it is less than 0x12, and prints the ASCII character string that is based on the respective error number value as shown in Table I.11.7. No carriage return or character 0x8D is printed after printing the ASCII character string. Once processing is complete, the DOPRTERR routine returns to the Page 0xBE Interface Routines, restores the registers and restores the control over the DOS CSWL and the KSWL interface pointers, enables ROM memory, and returns to the caller.

Use the Indirect Approach in order to utilize the PRTERADR vector address at 0x3E8.

9. HOOKDOS Routine

Function	Address	X-reg	Y-reg	A-reg	C-flag	Description
Entry	0x03EA	-	-	-	-	Set RAM Bank 2 ON, call INITPTRS routine
Return	-	-	-	-	-	Set ROM Bank 2 WP and return to caller

The HOOKDOS routine at memory address 0x3EA as shown in Table I.9.3 enters the DOS INITPTRS routine by means of the DOS EXTPTRS routine. In DOS 4.5 the HOOKDOS routine directly enters the DOS EXTPTRS routine that is found in the Page 0xBE Interface Routines that write-enables Bank 2 of the Language Card partition in order to directly enter the DOS INITPTRS routine. The INITPTRS routine restores the control over the DOS CSWL and KSWL interface pointers. Once processing is complete, the DOS INITPTRS routine returns to the Page 0xBE Interface Routines, enables ROM memory, and returns to the caller.

Use the Direct Approach in order to utilize the HOOKDOS routine at 0x3EA.

10. XFERADR Transfer Address Pointer

Function	Address	X-reg	Y-reg	A-reg	C-flag	V-flag	Description
Address	0x03ED	-	-	-	Xfer Dir	page-zero	Set target address
Return	-	-	-	-	-	-	-

The XFERADR transfer address pointer at memory address 0x3ED as shown in Table I.9.3 is utilized by the ROM XFER routine that is found at memory address 0xC314. The ROM XFER routine directly enters the ROM DOXFER routine at 0xC3C3. The ROM DOXFER routine uses the XFERADR address pointer in order to indirectly enter its destination address and transfer control to a target routine that exists in either Main or in Auxiliary memory. Three parameters must be initialized before the user can utilize ROM XFER: the destination address that is stored in the XFERADR pointer, the memory where the target routine exists (Main or Auxiliary memory), and which page-zero/stack the target routine must use (Main or Auxiliary memory). The C-flag controls the memory where the target routine exists and the Overflow flag or V-flag controls which page-zero/stack the target routine must use. The A-, X-, and Y-registers are maintained without change by the ROM XFER routine when control is transferred to the target routine.

The destination address of the target routine must be stored in the XFERADR pointer in Lo/Hi byte order. The C-flag must be **set** in order to transfer control from Main memory to the target routine that is in Auxiliary memory, or the C-flag must be **clear** in order to transfer control from Auxiliary memory to the target routine that is in Main memory. The Overflow flag must be **set** in order for the target routine to use the page-zero/stack in Auxiliary memory or the Overflow flag must be **clear** in order for the target routine to use the page-zero/stack in Main memory.

The 6502 and 65C02 Instruction Set **does** contain a native **clear** Overflow flag instruction or CLV. Unfortunately, the Instruction Set **does not** contain a native **set** Overflow flag instruction. I am not sure why this microprocessor operation is missing. Truthfully, I believe there is **no** rationale for this shortcoming. Generally, many have used the BIT IORTS command to easily achieve setting the Overflow flag. The ROM IORTS address is the address for the RTS instruction in the ROM Monitor at memory address 0xFF58. One can utilize *any* RTS instruction within *any* routine in order to achieve the same result.

The ROM XFER routine saves the address in the XFERADR pointer into the requested stack, enables the requested memory space where the target routine exists, restores the address that was in the XFERADR pointer from the stack and saves that address back to the XFERADR pointer for the target routine that resides in that memory space, enables the requested page-zero/stack memory, and indirectly enters the target routine using the JMP (XFERADR) instruction. Processor control is henceforth taken over by the target routine in the requested memory space using the requested page-zero/stack memory.

11. AUTOBRK Routine

Function	Address	X-reg	Y-reg	A-reg	C-flag	Description
Entry	0x03EF	-	-	-	-	Enter OLDBRK (0xFA59) routine
OLDBRK	0xFA59	-	-	-	-	No return to caller

The AUTOBRK routine at memory address 0x3EF as shown in Table I.9.3 enters the ROM OLDBRK routine at memory address 0xFA59. In DOS 4.5 the AUTOBRK routine directly enters the ROM OLDBRK routine. The ROM OLDBRK routine prints the current program counter and the contents of all processor registers, and then directly enters the ROM Monitor MON routine at memory address 0xFF65. The ROM Monitor MON routine does not return to the caller.

Use the Direct Approach in order to utilize the AUTOBRK routine at 0x3EF.

12. AUTORSET Vector Address

Function	Address	X-reg	Y-reg	A-reg	C-flag	Description
Entry	0x03F2	-	-	-	-	Enter (WARMADR) handler
ASROMWRM	0xD43C	-	-	-	-	Applesoft Warm-Start

The AUTORSET vector address at memory address 0x3F2 as shown in Table I.9.3 enters the DOS WARMSTRT routine by means of the DOS EXTWARM routine. The AUTORSET vector address is used by the Autostart ROM whenever a ROM reset is issued. The Autostart ROM indirectly enters the routine whose address is contained in the AUTORSET vector. In DOS 4.5 the caller, using the AUTORSET vector address, indirectly enters the DOS EXTWARM routine that is found in the Page 0xBE Interface Routines that write-enables Bank 2 of the Language Card partition in order to directly enter the DOS WARMSTRT routine. The DOS WARMSTRT routine sets the stack pointer to 0xFF, resets the state machine, initializes the MON flags and the keyboard and video intercepts, turns ROM memory ON, and exits indirectly by means of the WARMADR vector in the Page 0xBE INITVALS Data structure as shown in Table I.8.5.

The assembler sets the WARMADR vector to memory address 0xD43C, the address of the Applesoft ASROMWRM routine. The Applesoft ASROMWRM routine performs a partial re-initialization of Applesoft. This ROM Applesoft routine does not return to the caller. The user is encouraged to modify the address at WARMADR or 0xBEE2 in order to tailor the DOSWARM routine not to exit into ROM Applesoft, but enter into a user specific routine initially, and then exit into the Applesoft ASROMWRM routine.

Use the Indirect Approach in order to utilize the AUTORSET vector address at 0x3F2.

13. PWRSTATE Variable Byte

Function	Address	X-reg	Y-reg	A-reg	C-flag	Description
Verification	0x03F4	-	-	-	-	View or change power up byte

The PWRSTATE variable byte at memory address 0x3F4 as shown in Table I.9.3 is used to verify whether the Apple][hardware is currently in the process of powering up or if the hardware is already powered up. When pin 40 of the 6502-microprocessor or 65C02-microprocessor is brought low, the microprocessor is designed to indirectly enter a Reset handler by using the address that is found in the RESET Vector at memory address 0xFFFC:0xFFFD. The address at 0xFFFC:0xFFFD in the Autostart ROM is for the ROM RESET handler that is found at memory address 0xFA62. After the ROM RESET handler has initialized the annunciators, the window specifications, the DOS CSWL and KSWL interface pointers, and XMODE, the handler directly enters the ROM NEWMON routine at memory address 0xFA81. After ringing the bell at 0xFF3A, the ROM NEWMON routine calculates its own PWRSTATE value and compares that calculation to the value it finds at 0x3F4. If the comparison fails, the hardware is powering up and the ROM NEWMON routine branches to the ROM PWRUP routine at memory address 0xFAA6. The ROM PWRUP routine copies the ROM OLDBRK vector, the BASIC vector, and a calculated PWRSTATE value to 0x3EF through 0x3F4. Finally, the ROM PWRUP routine locates a disk bootable device and directly enters the Slot handler firmware if such a bootable device is found.

There is a 1-in-256 probability that this logic will fail to sense a real power-up condition. The PWRSTATE variable at 0x3F4 may randomly equal the PWRSTATE value that the ROM NEWMON routine calculates when the Apple][hardware is first turned ON or when the computer is physically reset. The probability of this logic failing to detect a real reset condition is virtually inconsequential. The ROM SETPWRC routine at memory address 0xFB6F calculates the power-up state variable and saves that value to the PWRSTATE variable at 0x3F4.

The assembler calculates the PWRSTATE variable using the following statement

    PWRSTATE byt PWRUPBYT^EXTWARM/PAGESIZE

where PWRUPBYT is defined to be 0xA5, the address for the EXTWARM routine is 0xBE3E, the value of PAGESIZE is 0x100, and the ^ operator is for exclusive OR (XOR).

The PWRSTATE variable is calculated from 0xA5 XOR 0xBE, which is computed to be 0x1B.

14. USRAHAND Routine

Function	Address	X-reg	Y-reg	A-reg	C-flag	Description
Entry	0x03F5	-	-	-	-	Set RAM Bank 2 ON, call REPEATCD routine
REPEATCD	-	-	-	-	-	No return to caller

The USRAHAND routine at memory address 0x3F5 as shown in Table I.9.3 enters the DOS REPEATCD routine by means of the DOS EXTRPEAT routine. In DOS 4.5 the USRAHAND routine directly enters the DOS EXTRPEAT routine that is found in the Page 0xBE Interface Routines that write-enables Bank 2 of the Language Card partition in order to directly enter the DOS REPEATCD routine. The DOS REPEATCD routine saves the registers, disconnects the CSWL and the KSWL interface pointers from DOS, and loads the Y-register from the CMDINDX variable which is the index of the last DOS command that DOS processed, and directly enters the DOS DOCMD routine. After the DOS DOCMD routine finishes its processing, processor control returns to the DOS REPEATCD routine and processor control directly falls into the DOS WARMSTRT routine.

The USRAHAND routine is known as the *Ampersand Handler* and it is a favorite vehicle for many software programs and utilities in order to utilize the AMPERSAND character &. Software programs can initialize the address in the USRAHAND routine in order to easily and quickly enter any processing routine in that software. The Program Global Editor is one example of a software program that is designed to utilize the USRAHAND routine in order to enter its main processing routine when the AMPERSAND character & is entered on the Apple Command Line. When DOS 4.5 is first initialized, the USERAHAND routine is initialized with the address of the DOS REPEATCD routine in order to repeat the last DOS command when the AMPERSAND character & is entered on the Apple Command Line. The USRAHAND routine does not return to the caller.

Use the Direct Approach in order to utilize the USRAHAND routine at 0x3F5.

15. USRYHAND Routine

Function	Address	X-reg	Y-reg	A-reg	C-flag	Description
Entry	0x03F8	-	-	-	Direction	Enter AUXMOVE (0xC311) routine
Return	-	same	same	same	-	Return to caller

The USRYHAND routine at memory address 0x3F8 as shown in Table I.9.3 directly enters the ROM AUXMOVE routine at memory address 0xC311. The AUXMOVE routine is a ROM routine that can copy blocks of data from Main memory to Auxiliary memory or from Auxiliary memory to Main memory. Before AUXMOVE can be utilized, three byte-pair locations in page-zero must be initialized with the starting and ending addresses of the data source and the starting address of the data destination. The C-flag is used to select the direction of transfer. The USRYHAND routine returns with the A-, X-, and Y-registers unchanged to the caller.

If the C-flag is **set**, data is moved from Main memory to Auxiliary memory and if the C-flag is **clear** data is moved from Auxiliary memory to Main memory. Page-zero A1 at 0x3C:0x3D must contain the data source starting address, page-zero A2 at 0x3E:0x3F must contain the data source ending address, and page-zero A4 at 0x42:0x43 must contain the data destination starting address. All three page-zero byte-pair locations expect the address to be saved in Lo/Hi byte order.

Use the Direct Approach in order to utilize the USRYHAND routine at 0x3F8.

16. NMASKIRQ Routine

Function	Address	X-reg	Y-reg	A-reg	C-flag	Description
Entry	0x03FB	-	-	-	-	Enter MON (0xFF65) or IRQ handler
Return	0xFF65	-	-	-	-	Return to interrupted code by IRQ handler

The NMASKIRQ routine at memory address 0x3FB as shown in Table I.9.3 directly enters a non-maskable IRQ handler and then enters the ROM Monitor MON routine at memory address 0xFF65. The address for the NMIRTN non-maskable IRQ routine, or 0x3FB, is hardcoded in ROM at the 0xFFFA:0xFFFB non-maskable IRQ vector location. Whenever the microprocessor receives a non-maskable IRQ interrupt, the microprocessor indirectly enters the NMASKIRQ routine in order to handle the IRQ interrupt.

When a non-maskable IRQ interrupt handler routine first executes, it must initialize 0x3FC:0x3FD with the entry address in Lo/Hi byte order for the non-maskable IRQ routine that will handle a non-maskable IRQ interrupt. An intelligently written non-maskable IRQ interrupt handler **will** return to the instruction that immediately follows the instruction that was interrupted by means of the RTI instruction when the microprocessor receives a non-maskable IRQ interrupt.

Use the Direct Approach in order to utilize the NMASKIRQ routine at 0x3FB.

17. MASKIRQ Vector Address

Function	Address	X-reg	Y-reg	A-reg	C-flag	Description
Entry	0x03FE	-	-	-	-	Enter (MON) (0xFF65) or IRQ handler
Return	0xFF65	-	-	-	-	Return to interrupted code by IRQ handler

The MASKIRQ vector at memory address 0x3FE as shown in Table I.9.3 contains the address for the maskable IRQ handler and it is used to indirectly enter the ROM Monitor MON routine at memory address 0xFF65. The address for the IRQRTN maskable IRQ handler routine, or 0xC3FA, is hardcoded in ROM at the 0xFFFE:0xFFFF maskable IRQ vector location. Whenever the microprocessor receives a maskable IRQ interrupt, the microprocessor indirectly enters the IRQRTN routine in order to handle the IRQ interrupt. The IRQRTN routine must **read-enable** the internal CX ROM space so that ROM Page 0xC4 is in focus for interrupt processing.

The Apple //e interrupt handler is highly complex and it begins its processing at memory address 0xC400. This interrupt handler creates a System Status byte that is saved to page-zero 0x44. If a system function is found to be turned ON, that function is turned OFF during interrupt handler processing, and the state of that system function is captured in the System Status byte. RAM memory of the Language Card partition is always turned OFF. Table IV.1.17.1 summarizes the system function that each bit represents in the System Status byte. There are two caveats to Table IV.1.17.1.

1) If bit 3 is OFF, then bits 1 and 2 are both OFF.

2) If bit 3 is ON, then bit 1 **or** bit 2 is ON and the other bit is OFF.

The Main and Auxiliary memory stack pointers are both saved along with the System Status byte at page-zero 0x44. The processor status is restored and the interrupt handler directly enters the GOTOIRQ routine at memory address 0xFC74. The GOTOIRQ routine disables the CX ROM space and it indirectly enters the address that is found at the MASKIRQ vector at 0x3FE:0x3FF.

When a maskable IRQ interrupt handler routine first executes, it must initialize the MASKIRQ vector with the entry address in Lo/Hi byte order for the maskable IRQ interrupt handler routine that will handle a maskable IRQ interrupt. An intelligently written maskable IRQ interrupt handler **will** return to the instruction that immediately follows the instruction that was interrupted by means of the RTI instruction when the microprocessor receives a maskable IRQ interrupt.

Use the Indirect Approach in order to utilize the DOS MASKIRQ vector address at 0x3FE.

Bit	Name	If Bit is OFF	If Bit is ON	Function Address
0	RDCXROM	Slot ROM enabled	Internal ROM enabled	read 0xC015
1	RDBANK2	LC Bank 1 is OFF	either bit 1 or bit 2 is ON, the other bit is OFF	read 0xC011, LC Bank 1
2		LC Bank 2 is OFF		read 0xC011, LC Bank 2
3	RDLCRAM	LC ROM read-enabled	LC RAM read-enabled	read 0xC012
4	RDRAMWR	AUX RAM write-enabled	Main RAM write-enabled	read 0xC014
5	RDRAMRD	AUX RAM read-enabled	Main RAM read-enabled	read 0xC013
6	RDPAGE2	Main PAGE2 enabled	AUX PAGE2 enabled	read 0xC01C
7	RDAUXZP	Main ZP/stack enabled	AUX ZP/stack enabled	read 0xC016

Table IV.1.17.1. Interrupt Handler System Status Byte Definition

2. Language Card and ROM Interface Routines

DOS 4.5 is fully resident in the memory of the Language Card partition for Main memory except for two memory pages that are located in lower Main memory at Page 0xBE and at Page 0xBF. Page 0xBE contains the page of Interface Routines for DOS 4.5 that performs all of the necessary Bank switching protocol that is required in order to put into focus the memory of the particular Language Card Bank or ROM in order to access the routine or routines for the requested processing. All of the Language Card and ROM Interface Routines are shown in Table IV.2.0.1. The five file buffers that are available for DOS 4.5 utilize the memory in the Language Card partition at 0xECA0:0xF7F8. The remaining RAM memory provides sufficient room for the eight pages of memory that are required in order to maintain a copy of the ROM Monitor in order for it to reside in RAM memory at precisely the same memory location which is at 0xF800:0xFFFF.

When the COLDSTRT routine is called, the ROM Monitor is fully copied into RAM memory in the Language Card partition before the routine searches for a clock card. Having a copy of the ROM Monitor in the RAM memory of the Language Card partition provides many, many benefits to the DOS user. It allows the user to inspect, modify, copy, and move the contents of memory in either RAM Bank of the Language Card partition using the same tools and in the same fashion as one inspects, modifies, copies, and moves the contents of lower Main memory. There is no need having to remember which Soft Switches are required in order to read-enable and/or to write-enable the memory of a particular RAM Bank in the Language Card partition.

Address	Function	Description
0xBE00	GOTOMON2	Set RAM Bank 2 ON, enter GOTOMON routine
0xBE08	GOTOMON1	Set RAM Bank 1 ON, enter GOTOMON routine
0xBE0E	EXTRWTS	Set RAM Bank 1 ON, enter DORWTS
0xBE17	EXTFM	Set RAM Bank 2 ON, enter FMHNDLR routine
0xBE1D	EXTPTRS	Set RAM Bank 2 ON, enter INITPTRS routine
0xBE20	EXTPTRS2	Set RAM Bank 2 ON, enter INITPTRS routine
0xBE26	EXTVIDIN	Set RAM Bank 2 ON, enter VIDINTRC routine
0xBE2F	EXTKBDIN	Set RAM Bank 2 ON, enter KBDINTRC routine
0xBE38	EXTRPEAT	Set RAM Bank 2 ON, enter REPEATCD routine
0xBE3E	EXTWARM	Set RAM Bank 2 ON, enter WARMSTRT routine
0xBE44	EXTPRERR	Set RAM Bank 2 ON, enter DOPRTERR routine
0xBE4A	EXMNGDSK	Set RAM Bank 1 ON, enter MNGEXDSK routine
0xBE50	EXMNGVAL	Set RAM Bank 1 ON, enter MNGEXVAL routine
0xBE56	EXMNGUSR	Set RAM Bank 1 ON, enter MNGEXUSR routine
0xBE5C	EXCLKVSN	Set RAM Bank 2 ON, enter DOCLKVSN routine
0xBE62	GOTOROM	Set ROM Bank 2 WP and return to caller
0xBE66	DOROMSRT	Set ROM Bank 2 WP, enter WARMADR or COLDADR routine
0xBE71	DOROMERR	Set ROM Bank 2 WP, enter ERRORADR routine
0xBE77	DOGARBGE	Set ROM Bank 2 WP, enter DOGARBGE routine
0xBE80	DOROMCLR	Set ROM Bank 2 WP, enter DOROMCLR routine
0xBE8C	DOROMRST	Set ROM Bank 2 WP, enter DOROMRST routine
0xBE96	DOCLRNEW	Set ROM Bank 2 WP, enter ASROMCLR routine
0xBE9B	DOROMNEW	Process LENVAL for LINNUM, enter ASROMNEW routine
0xBEB5	RAM2ON	Set RAM Bank 2 ON and return to caller
0xBEBE	RAM1ON	Set RAM Bank 1 ON and return to caller

Table IV.2.0.1. Language Card and ROM Interface Routines

DOS 4.5 is so elegantly designed that the contents of memory in the Language Card partition, whether it is part of Main memory or part of Auxiliary memory, can be inspected, modified, copied, and moved easily, and with virtually no extra knowledge of which Soft Switches to employ. Another advantage of having the ROM Monitor in RAM memory of the Language Card partition is that the DOSWARM and the DOSCOLD addresses can be copied from the Page 0x03 Interface Routines to 0xFEB4 and 0xFEB1, respectively, instead of having the Applesoft routines at 0xE003 and 0xE000, respectively, handle a RAM Warm-Start or a RAM Cold-Start. Certainly, a seasoned assembly language programmer will celebrate the ease at which software can be developed and inspected anywhere within the memory of the Language Card partition, specifically code that is designed to be resident in Auxiliary memory. Auxiliary memory, to be sure, is unique, perhaps the most difficult memory to manage, yet it is available for many brilliant, unimagined uses that could create highly versatile and extraordinary tools, utilities, and games. Just to be clear, all of the Language Card and ROM Interface Routines are available to DOS 4.5 and to the DOS 4.5 user **only after** DOS 4.5 has BOOTed and has fully initialized.

1. GOTOMON2 Routine

Function	Address	X-reg	Y-reg	A-reg	C-flag	Description
Entry	0xBE00	-	-	-	-	Set RAM Bank 2 ON, enter GOTOMON routine
RAM MON	-	-	-	-	-	No return to caller

The DOS GOTOMON2 routine at memory address 0xBE00 write-enables **Bank 2** of the Language Card partition and then directly enters the DOS GOTOMON routine that is found in Page 0xBF. The DOS GOTOMON routine is an integral part of the DOS COLDSTRT Cold-Start initialization routine that is used when DOS 4.5 BOOTs or when a user utilizes the INITDOS vector at 0xBFF8 in order to initialize DOS. The DOS GOTOMON routine initializes the stack pointer and XMODE to 0xFF, selects the main video and deselects the alternate character set, sets the video output to normal, initializes the text and graphics modes, sets the window operating parameters, and initializes the DOS CSWL and KSWL interface pointers. Because the Language Card partition is enabled, the verification check for ROM Applesoft **fails** in the DOS GOTOMON routine as it is designed to do. Otherwise, if the ROM is enabled as it is during the BOOT process of DOS 4.5, the verification check for ROM Applesoft will **pass**.

The verification byte at RAM memory address 0xE000 in DOS 4.5 happens to be set to 0x20 from jsr ALLOCSEC, and that byte value is certainly **not** equal to the 0x4C value that is found at ROM memory address 0xE000. Because RAM memory in the Language Card partition is enabled when the DOS GOTOMON2 routine is entered, the DOS GOTOMON routine deliberately fails the ROM Applesoft verification check and it enters RAM MON at 0xFF65. RAM MON is the normal entry address for the RAM Monitor and it does not return to the caller. Bank 2 in the Language Card partition remains in focus. If a ctrl-C is entered from within the RAM Monitor, DOS's control over the CSWL and the KSWL interface pointers is re-enabled and DOS 4.5 is available and ready to process the next DOS command.

Use the Direct Approach in order to utilize the DOS GOTOMON2 routine at 0xBE00. This is typically done by entering BE00G on the Monitor Command Line.

2. GOTOMON1 Routine

Function	Address	X-reg	Y-reg	A-reg	C-flag	Description
Entry	0xBE08	-	-	-	-	Set RAM Bank 1 ON, enter GOTOMON routine
RAM MON	-	-	-	-	-	No return to caller

The DOS GOTOMON1 routine at memory address 0xBE08 write-enables **Bank 1** of the Language Card partition and then directly enters the DOS GOTOMON routine that is found in Page 0xBF. The DOS GOTOMON routine is an integral part of the DOS COLDSTRT Cold-Start initialization routine that is used when DOS 4.5 BOOTs or when a user utilizes the INITDOS vector at 0xBFF8 in order to initialize DOS. The DOS GOTOMON routine initializes the stack pointer and XMODE to 0xFF, selects the main video and deselects the alternate character set, sets the video output to normal, initializes the text and graphics modes, sets the window operating parameters, and initializes the DOS CSWL and KSWL interface pointers. Because the Language Card partition is enabled, the verification check for ROM Applesoft **fails** in the DOS GOTOMON routine as it is designed to do. Otherwise, if the ROM is enabled as it is during the BOOT process of DOS 4.5, the verification check for ROM Applesoft will **pass**.

The verification byte at RAM memory address 0xE000 in DOS 4.5 happens to be set to 0x20 from jsr ALLOCSEC, and that byte value is certainly **not** equal to the 0x4C value that is found at ROM memory address 0xE000. Because RAM memory in the Language Card partition is enabled when the DOS GOTOMON1 routine is entered, the DOS GOTOMON routine deliberately fails the ROM Applesoft verification check and it enters RAM MON at 0xFF65. RAM MON is the normal entry address for the RAM Monitor and it does not return to the caller. Bank 1 in the Language Card partition remains in focus. If a ctrl-C is entered from within the RAM Monitor, DOS's control over the CSWL and the KSWL interface pointers is re-enabled and DOS 4.5 is available and ready to process the next DOS command.

Use the Direct Approach in order to utilize the DOS GOTOMON1 routine at 0xBE08. This is typically done by entering BE08G on the Monitor Command Line.

3. EXTRWTS Routine

Function	Address	X-reg	Y-reg	A-reg	C-flag	Description
Entry	0xBE0E	-	#IOCB	/IOCB	-	Set RAM Bank 1 ON, enter DORWTS routine
Return	-	-	-	Error #	Status	Set ROM Bank 2 WP and return to caller

The CALLRWTS routine at memory address 0x3D9 as shown in Table I.9.3 enters the DOS DORWTS routine by means of the DOS EXTRWTS routine. In DOS 4.5 the CALLRWTS routine directly enters the DOS EXTRWTS routine that is found in the Page 0xBE Interface Routines that write-enables Bank 1 of the Language Card partition in order to directly enter the DOS DORWTS routine.

When the requested RWTS Slot handler processing is complete, the DOS DORWTS routine restores the processor status and **clears** the C-flag if the returned error code contains a zero value, otherwise the routine **sets** the C-flag. For the external caller in DOS 4.5, the DOS DORWTS routine returns to the Page 0xBE Interface Routines and directly enters the DOS GOTOROM routine in order to enable ROM memory and return to the external caller.

Use the Direct Approach in order to utilize the DOS EXTRWTS routine at 0xBE0E.

4. EXTFM Routine

Function	Address	X-reg	Y-reg	A-reg	C-flag	Description
Entry	0xBE17	File Flag	-	-	-	Set RAM Bank 2 ON, enter FMHNDLR routine
Return	-	Error #	-	-	Status	Set ROM Bank 2 WP and return to caller

The CALLFM routine at memory address 0x3D6 as shown in Table I.9.3 enters the DOS FMHNDLR handler by means of the DOS EXTFM routine. In DOS 4.5 the CALLFM routine directly enters the DOS EXTFM routine that is found in the Page 0xBE Interface Routines that write-enables Bank 2 of the Language Card partition in order to directly enter the DOS FMHNDLR handler.

When all File Manager processing is complete, the DOS FILEMNGR routine preserves its final status in the C-flag and its final error code value in the X-register. If the final status that is returned in the C-flag is **set**, the X-register contains an error code value, otherwise the C-flag is **clear** and the X-register is set to zero. For the external caller in DOS 4.5, the DOS FMHNDLR handler returns to the Page 0xBE Interface Routines and directly enters the DOS EXTPTRS routine. The DOS EXTPTRS routine write-enables Bank 2 of the Language Card partition in order to process the DOS INITPTRS routine in order to restore control over the DOS CSWL and the KSWL interface pointers. Once that processing is complete, the DOS EXTPTRS routine directly enters the DOS GOTOROM routine in order to enable ROM memory and return to the external caller. The final status in the C-flag and the error code value in the X-register, both from File Manager processing, are returned to the external caller for analysis.

Use the Direct Approach in order to utilize the DOS EXTFM routine at 0xBE17.

5. EXTPTRS Routine

Function	Address	X-reg	Y-reg	A-reg	C-flag	Description
Entry	0xBE1D	-	-	-	-	Set RAM Bank 2 ON, enter INITPTRS routine
Return	-	-	-	-	-	Set ROM Bank 2 WP and return to caller

The HOOKDOS routine at memory address 0x3EA as shown in Table I.9.3 enters the DOS INITPTRS routine by means of the DOS EXTPTRS routine. In DOS 4.5 the HOOKDOS routine directly enters the DOS EXTPTRS routine that is found in the Page 0xBE Interface Routines that write-enables Bank 2 of the Language Card partition in order to directly enter the DOS INITPTRS routine that restores the control over the DOS CSWL and KSWL interface pointers.

Once processing is complete, the DOS INITPTRS routine returns to the Page 0xBE Interface Routines and directly enters the DOS GOTOROM routine in order to enable ROM memory and return to the external caller.

Use the Direct Approach in order to utilize the DOS EXTPTRS routine at 0xBE1D.

6. EXTPTRS2 Routine

Function	Address	X-reg	Y-reg	A-reg	C-flag	Description
Entry	0xBE20	-	-	-	-	Set RAM Bank 2 ON, enter INITPTRS routine
Return	-	-	-	-	-	Set ROM Bank 2 WP and return to caller

The PRERRADR vector address at memory address 0x3E8 as shown in Table I.9.3 enters the DOS DOPRTERR routine by means of the DOS EXTPRERR routine. In DOS 4.5 the caller, using the PRERRADR vector address, indirectly enters the DOS EXTPRERR routine that is found in the Page 0xBE Interface Routines that write-enables Bank 2 of the Language Card partition and disconnects the CSWL and KSWL interface pointers from DOS in order to directly enter the DOS DOPRTERR routine.

Once processing is complete, the DOS DOPRTERR routine returns to the Page 0xBE Interface Routines by means of the DOS EXTPTRS2 routine. The DOS EXTPTRS2 routine directly enters the DOS INITPTRS routine that restores the control over the DOS CSWL and KSWL interface pointers. Once that processing is complete, the DOS INITPTRS routine directly enters the DOS GOTOROM routine in order to enable ROM memory and return to the external caller.

Use the Direct Approach in order to utilize the DOS EXTPTRS2 routine at 0xBE20.

7. EXTVIDIN Routine

Function	Address	X-reg	Y-reg	A-reg	C-flag	Description
Entry	0xBE26	-	-	-	-	Set RAM Bank 2 ON, enter VIDINTRC routine
Return	-	-	-	-	-	Set ROM Bank 2 WP and return to caller

The address of the DOS EXTVIDIN routine is used by the DOS INITPTRS routine in order to initialize the CSWL pointer that handles the data that is written to the display device. The DOS INITPTRS routine safely stores the current address that is in the CSWL pointer to the CSWLSAV variable that is in the CMDVALS Data structure at offset 0x0E as shown in Table I.12.1 before changing the address in the CSWL pointer. The DOS EXTVIDIN routine write-enables Bank 2 of the Language Card partition and directly enters the DOS VIDINTRC routine.

Once processing is complete, the DOS VIDINTRC routine returns to the Page 0xBE Interface Routines and directly enters the DOS GOTOROM routine in order to enable ROM memory and return to the external caller.

Use the Direct Approach in order to utilize the DOS EXTVIDIN routine at 0xBE26.

8. EXTKBDIN Routine

Function	Address	X-reg	Y-reg	A-reg	C-flag	Description
Entry	0xBE2F	-	-	-	-	Set RAM Bank 2 ON, enter KBDINTRC routine
Return	-	-	-	-	-	Set ROM Bank 2 WP and return to caller

The address of the DOS EXTKBDIN routine is used by the DOS INITPTRS routine in order to initialize the KSWL pointer that handles the data that is read from the keyboard device. The DOS INITPTRS routine safely stores the current address that is in the KSWL pointer to the KSWLSAV variable that is in the CMDVALS Data structure at offset 0x10 as shown in Table I.12.1 before changing the address in the KSWL pointer. The DOS EXTKBDIN routine write-enables Bank 2 of the Language Card partition and directly enters the DOS KBDINTRC routine.

Once processing is complete, the DOS KBDINTRC routine returns to the Page 0xBE Interface Routines and directly enters the DOS GOTOROM routine in order to enable ROM memory and return to the external caller.

Use the Direct Approach in order to utilize the DOS EXTKBDIN routine at 0xBE2F.

9. EXTRPEAT Routine

Function	Address	X-reg	Y-reg	A-reg	C-flag	Description
Entry	0xBE38	-	-	-	-	Set RAM Bank 2 ON, enter REPEATCD routine
Return	-	-	-	-	-	No return to caller

The USRAHAND routine at memory address 0x3F5 as shown in Table I.9.3 enters the DOS REPEATCD routine by means of the DOS EXTRPEAT routine. In DOS 4.5 the USRAHAND routine directly enters the DOS EXTRPEAT routine that is found in the Page 0xBE Interface Routines that write-enables Bank 2 of the Language Card partition in order to directly enter the DOS REPEATCD routine.

The DOS REPEATCD routine does **not** return to the Page 0xBE Interface Routines and the routine does **not** return to the external caller.

Use the Direct Approach in order to utilize the DOS EXTRPEAT routine at 0xBE38.

10. EXTWARM Routine

Function	Address	X-reg	Y-reg	A-reg	C-flag	Description
Entry	0xBE3E	-	-	-	-	Set RAM Bank 2 ON, enter WARMSTRT routine
Return	-	-	-	-	-	No return to caller

The DOSWARM routine at memory address 0x3D0 as shown in Table I.9.3 enters the DOS WARMSTRT routine by means of the DOS EXTWARM routine. In DOS 4.5 the DOSWARM routine directly enters the DOS EXTWARM routine that is found in the Page 0xBE Interface Routines that write-enables Bank 2 of the Language Card partition in order to directly enter the DOS WARMSTRT routine.

The DOS WARMSTRT routine does **not** return to the Page 0xBE Interface Routines and the routine does **not** return to the external caller.

Use the Direct Approach in order to utilize the DOS EXTWARM routine at 0xBE3E.

11. EXTPRERR Routine

Function	Address	X-reg	Y-reg	A-reg	C-flag	Description
Entry	0xBE44	-	-	-	-	Set RAM Bank 2 ON, enter DOPRTERR routine
Return	-	-	-	-	-	Set ROM Bank 2 WP and return to caller

The PRERRADR vector address at memory address 0x3E8 as shown in Table I.9.3 enters the DOS DOPRTERR routine by means of the DOS EXTPRERR routine. In DOS 4.5 the caller, using the PRERRADR vector address, indirectly enters the DOS EXTPRERR routine that is found in the Page 0xBE Interface Routines that write-enables Bank 2 of the Language Card partition and disconnects the CSWL and KSWL interface pointers from DOS in order to directly enter the DOS DOPRTERR routine.

Once processing is complete, the DOS DOPRTERR routine returns to the Page 0xBE Interface Routines by means of the DOS EXTPTRS2 routine. The DOS EXTPTRS2 routine directly enters the DOS INITPTRS routine that restores the control over the DOS CSWL and the KSWL interface pointers. Once that processing is complete, the DOS INITPTRS routine directly enters the DOS GOTOROM routine in order to enable ROM memory and return to the external caller.

Use the Direct Approach in order to utilize the DOS EXTPRERR routine at 0xBE44.

12. EXMNGDSK Routine

Function	Address	X-reg	Y-reg	A-reg	C-flag	Description
Entry	0xBE4A	-	-	-	-	Set RAM Bank 1 ON, enter MNGEXDSK routine
Return	-	-	-	-	-	Set ROM Bank 2 WP and return to caller

The DOS MNGDISK vector at memory address 0xBFF2 as shown in Table I.8.1 is used to indirectly enter the DOS MNGEXDSK routine by means of the DOS EXMNGDSK routine. In DOS 4.5 the DOS MNGDISK vector is used to indirectly enter the DOS EXMNGDSK routine that is found in the Page 0xBE Interface Routines that write-enables Bank 1 of the Language Card partition in order to directly enter the DOS MNGEXDSK routine.

Once processing is complete, the DOS MNGEXDSK routine returns to the Page 0xBE Interface Routines by means of the DOS GOTOROM routine in order to enable ROM memory and return to the external caller.

Use the Direct Approach in order to utilize the DOS EXMNGDSK routine at 0xBE4A.

13. EXMNGVAL Routine

Function	Address	X-reg	Y-reg	A-reg	C-flag	Description
Entry	0xBE50	-	-	-	-	Set RAM Bank 1 ON, enter MNGEXVAL routine
Return	-	-	-	-	-	Set ROM Bank 2 WP and return to caller

The DOS MNGVALS vector at memory address 0xBFF4 as shown in Table I.8.1 is used to indirectly enter the DOS MNGEXVAL routine by means of the DOS EXMNGVAL routine. In DOS 4.5 the DOS MNGVALS vector is used to indirectly enter the DOS EXMNGVAL routine that is found in the Page 0xBE Interface Routines that write-enables Bank 1 of the Language Card partition in order to directly enter the DOS MNGEXVAL routine.

Once processing is complete, the DOS MNGEXVAL routine returns to the Page 0xBE Interface Routines by means of the DOS GOTOROM routine in order to enable ROM memory and return to the external caller.

Use the Direct Approach in order to utilize the DOS EXMNGVAL routine at 0xBE50.

14.EXMNGUSR Routine

Function	Address	X-reg	Y-reg	A-reg	C-flag	Description
Entry	0xBE56	-	-	-	-	Set RAM Bank 1 ON, enter MNGEXUSR routine
Return	-	-	-	-	-	Set ROM Bank 2 WP and return to caller

The DOS MNGUSER vector at memory address 0xBFF6 as shown in Table I.8.1 is used to indirectly enter the DOS MNGEXUSR routine by means of the DOS EXMNGUSR routine. In DOS 4.5 the DOS MNGUSER vector is used to indirectly enter the DOS EXMNGUSR routine that is found in the Page 0xBE Interface Routines that write-enables Bank 1 of the Language Card partition in order to directly enter the DOS MNGEXUSR routine.

Once processing is complete, the DOS MNGEXUSR routine returns to the Page 0xBE Interface Routines by means of the DOS GOTOROM routine in order to enable ROM memory and return to the external caller.

Use the Direct Approach in order to utilize the DOS EXMNGUSR routine at 0xBE56.

15.EXCLKVSN Routine

Function	Address	X-reg	Y-reg	A-reg	C-flag	Description
Entry	0xBE5C	-	-	-	-	Set RAM Bank 2 ON, enter DOCLKVSN routine
Return	-	-	-	-	-	Set ROM Bank 2 WP and return to caller

The RDCLKVSN vector address at memory address 0x3E1 as shown in Table I.9.3 enters the DOS DOCLKVSN routine by means of the DOS EXCLKVSN routine. In DOS 4.5 the caller, using the RDCLKVSN vector address, indirectly enters the DOS EXCLKVSN routine that is found in the Page 0xBE Interface Routines that write-enables Bank 2 of the Language Card partition in order to directly enter the DOS DOCLKVSN routine.

Once DOS processing is complete, the DOCLKVSN routine returns to the Page 0xBE Interface Routines by means of the DOS GOTOROM routine in order to enable ROM memory and return to the external caller.

Use the Direct Approach in order to utilize the DOS EXCLKVSN routine at 0xBE5C.

16.GOTOROM Routine

Function	Address	X-reg	Y-reg	A-reg	C-flag	Description
Entry	0xBE62	-	-	-	-	Set ROM Bank 2 write-protect
Return	-	-	-	-	-	Return to caller

The DOS GOTOROM routine is at memory address 0xBE62 and this routine is used by a number of routines that are within DOS and by a number of routines that are among the Page 0xBE Interface Routines. The DOS GOTOROM routine is very simple in that it enables ROM memory with a BIT ROM2WP instruction and it uses an RTS instruction to return to the caller.

Use the Direct Approach in order to utilize the DOS GOTOROM routine at 0xBE62.

17.DOROMSRT Routine

Function	Address	X-reg	Y-reg	A-reg	C-flag	Description
Entry	0xBE66	-	-	-	-	Set ROM Bank 2 write-protect
Exit	-	-	-	-	inspect	Enter WARMADR or COLDADR routine

The DOS DOROMSRT routine is at memory address 0xBE66 and it is one of three routines among the Page 0xBE Interface Routines that utilizes the first two vector entries in the INITVALS Data structure, namely WARMADR and COLDADR. The DOS CSWL and KSWL interface pointers have already been setup in order to point to their respective Page 0xBE Interface Routines EXTVIDIN and EXTKBDIN, respectively. Therefore, outside of DOS 4.5 the Apple][machine is always configured with ROM memory enabled. The DOS DOROMSRT routine is the exit routine that the DOS WARMSTRT and the DOS COLDSTR2 routines enter in order to disable RAM Bank 2 memory and to enable ROM memory, and the routine directly enters the ROM Applesoft Warm-Start or Cold-Start routine by means of the WARMADR or the COLDADR vector, respectively. The decision to enter the ROM Applesoft Warm-Start or Cold-Start routine is easily determined by inspecting the state of the C-flag.

Use the Direct Approach in order to utilize the DOS DOROMSRT routine at 0xBE66.

18.DOROMERR Routine

Function	Address	X-reg	Y-reg	A-reg	C-flag	Description
Entry	0xBE71	-	-	-	-	Set ROM Bank 2 write-protect
Exit	-	-	-	-	-	Enter ERRORADR routine

The DOS DOROMERR routine is at memory address 0xBE71 and it is one of three routines among the Page 0xBE Interface Routines that utilizes the third vector entry in the INITVALS Data structure, or ERRORADR. When Applesoft is currently running and the ASONERR flag is enabled, the general print error DOS DOERROR routine restores the keyboard and video intercepts, initializes the A-register with the value of 0x03, and exits directly into the DOS DOROMERR routine. Only when the ASONERR flag is **not** enabled does the value in the A-register matter in the ROM routine at 0xD86C. Therefore, initializing the A-register with the value of 0x03 causes Applesoft at 0xD86C to copy TXTPTR at 0xB8:0xB9 to TEXTPTR at 0x79:0x7A, copy CURLIN at 0x75:0x76 to OLDLIN at 0x77:0x78, and re-enter Applesoft processing at 0xD43C. The DOROMERR routine enables ROM memory and the routine indirectly enters the Applesoft error handler by means of the ERRORADR vector at 0xBEE6.

Use the Direct Approach in order to utilize the DOS DOROMERR routine at 0xBE71.

19. DOGARBGE Routine

Function	Address	X-reg	Y-reg	A-reg	C-flag	Description
Entry	0xBE77	-	-	-	-	Set ROM Bank 2 WP, enter DOGARBGE routine
Return	-	-	-	-	-	Set RAM Bank 2 ON and return to CHAIN

The DOS DOGARBGE routine is at memory address 0xBE77 and it is the first of three routines among the Page 0xBE Interface Routines that utilizes the first of two ROM Applesoft routines that is designed specifically for the chaining of Applesoft programs. The DOS DOGARBGE routine is used by the DOS CHAIN handler that programmatically chains one Applesoft program to another Applesoft program. A parameter flag is set to 0xC0 for the DOS CHAIN command, 0x80 for the DOS RUN command, or 0x00 for the DOS LOAD command that allows the BIT instruction to easily identify which DOS command is being processed throughout the entire DOS CHAIN/RUN/LOAD handler. If the R-keyword is not utilized with the DOS CHAIN command, the DOS DOGARBGE routine will be directly entered. The DOS DOGARBGE routine enables ROM memory and it directly enters the ROM Applesoft GARBAGE routine at 0xE484. Once ROM processing is complete, the DOS DOGARBGE routine uses the DOS RAM2ON routine in order to enable RAM Bank 2 memory so that the routine can return to the DOS CHAIN handler that is about to move the simple variable and the array variable descriptors to another location in memory.

Use the Direct Approach in order to utilize the DOS DOGARBGE routine at 0xBE77.

20. DOROMCLR Routine

Function	Address	X-reg	Y-reg	A-reg	C-flag	Description
Entry	0xBE80	-	-	-	-	Set ROM Bank 2 WP, enter DOROMCLR routine
Return	-	-	-	-	-	Set RAM Bank 2 ON and return to CHAIN

The DOS DOROMCLR routine is at memory address 0xBE80 and it is the second of three routines among the Page 0xBE Interface Routines that utilizes the second of two ROM Applesoft routines that is designed specifically for the chaining of Applesoft programs. The DOS DOROMCLR routine is used by the DOS CHAIN handler that programmatically chains one Applesoft program to another Applesoft program. A parameter flag is set to 0xC0 for the DOS CHAIN command, 0x80 for the DOS RUN command, or 0x00 for the DOS LOAD command that allows the BIT instruction to easily identify which DOS command is being processed throughout the entire DOS CHAIN/RUN/LOAD handler. After the DOS CHAIN/RUN/LOAD handler has read the first two data bytes in the first data sector for the program size value of the requested Applesoft program, the handler can calculate the end address for the ASPEND pointer and the handler can test if the DOS CHAIN command is being processed. If so, DOS 4.5 utilizes unique and special code that has been designed and developed in order to move the simple variable and the array variable descriptors to where they need to be located in memory for the Applesoft program that is about to be read into memory. Once the simple variable and the array variable descriptors are where they need to be in memory, the DOS CHAIN routine must initialize all of the simple variable and the array variable pointers as well as a few system pointers. This initialization is accomplished by the DOS DOROMCLR routine.

The DOS DOROMCLR routine enables ROM memory and it directly enters the ROM ASROMCLR routine at 0xD665. The ROM ASROMCLR routine clears all of the simple variable and the array variable descriptors by initializing the simple variable and the array variable pointers. This means that the routine initializes the TXTPTR at 0xB8:0xB9 from PRGTAB at 0x67:0x68, FRETOP at 0x6F:0x70 from MEMSIZE at 0x73:0x74, and ARYTAB at 0x6B:0x6D and STREND at 0x6D:0x6E from VARTAB at 0x69:0x6A. Also, the routine calls the ROM RESTORE routine in order to copy PRGTAB at 0x67:0x68 to DATPTR at 0x7d:0x7E. What makes the ROM ASROMCLR routine so incredibly difficult to utilize is the annoying fact that it initializes the stack pointer to 0xF8 at the end of its processing. This alone makes it impossible to directly enter the DOS DOROMCLR routine using a JSR/RTS construction. Rather, a JMP/JMP construction is necessary and the stack pointer is avoided altogether. The DOS CHAIN handler uses a JMP instruction to directly enter the DOS DOROMCLR routine and the DOS DOROMCLR routine also uses a JMP instruction to return directly to the DOS CHAIN handler by means of a BACK2CHN label at the strategic location just after the first JMP instruction in the DOS CHAIN handler.

Once ROM processing is complete, the DOS DOROMCLR routine uses the DOS RAM2ON routine in order to enable RAM Bank 2 memory so that the routine can return to the DOS CHAIN handler. That handler is about to restore all of the old descriptor addresses at their new location in memory since the ROM ASROMCLR routine initialized those simple variable and array variable pointers. Because the stack pointer has now been modified and is therefore corrupted, the only safe way to directly return to the DOS CHAIN handler is by means of a label that is placed just after the JMP instruction to the DOS DOROMCLR routine.

Use the Direct Approach in order to utilize the DOS DOROMCLR routine at 0xBE80.

21. DOROMRST Routine

Function	Address	X-reg	Y-reg	A-reg	C-flag	Description
Entry	0xBE8C	-	-	-	-	Set ROM Bank 2 WP, enter DOROMRST routine
Return	-	-	-	-	-	Set ROM Bank 2 WP and return to caller

The DOS DOROMRST routine is at memory address 0xBE8C and it is the third of three routines among the Page 0xBE Interface Routines that utilizes the fourth vector entry in the INITVALS Data structure, or RESETADR. The DOS CHAIN/RUN/LOAD handler utilizes the DOS INITPTRS routine in order to restore the video and keyboard intercepts so that the handler may exit by means of a direct entry into the DOS DOROMRST routine. The DOS DOROMRST routine enables ROM memory and the routine indirectly enters the ROM Applesoft reset handler by means of the RESETADR vector at 0xBEE8 only when the DOS LOAD command is processed.

Use the Direct Approach in order to utilize the DOS DOROMRST routine at 0xBE8C.

22. DOCLRNEW Routine

Function	Address	X-reg	Y-reg	A-reg	V-flag	Description
Entry	0xBE96	-	-	-	clear	Set ROM Bank 2 WP, enter ASROMCLR routine
Exit	-	-	-	-	-	Enter DOROMNEW routine

The DOS DOCLRNEW routine is at memory address 0xBE96 and it is utilized by the DOS DOROMRST routine which is among the Page 0xBE Interface Routines. A parameter flag is set to 0xC0 for the DOS CHAIN command, 0x80 for the DOS RUN command, and 0x00 for the DOS LOAD command that allows the BIT instruction to easily identify which DOS command is being processed throughout the entire DOS CHAIN/RUN/LOAD handler. When the DOS DOROMRST routine finds that the N-flag is **clear** after the BIT instruction tests this parameter flag, the routine indirectly enters the ROM Applesoft reset handler by means of the RESETADR vector at 0xBEE8 since only the DOS LOAD command is being processed. Otherwise, when the N-flag is **set**, DOS DOROMRST processing continues in the DOS DOCLRNEW routine and that routine tests the V-flag. If the V-flag is clear, then the DOS DOCLRNEW routine directly enters the ROM ASROMCLR routine at 0xD665. If the V-flag is **set**, then processing continues in the DOS DOROMNEW routine which follows the DOS DOCLRNEW routine.

This simple test of the V-flag in the DOS DOCLRNEW routine filters out DOS CHAIN commands in order to utilize the ROM ASROMCLR routine for all DOS RUN commands. The ROM ASROMCLR routine is fully described in the DOS DOROMCLR routine. It makes no difference whether the ROM ASROMCLR routine modifies or corrupts the stack pointer since ROM memory has already been enabled previously by the DOS DOROMRST routine and the stack will not be utilized for a return to DOS.

Use the Direct Approach in order to utilize the DOS DOCLRNEW routine at 0xBE96.

23. DOROMNEW Routine

Function	Address	X-reg	Y-reg	A-reg	C-flag	Description
Entry	0xBE9B	-	-	-	-	Process LENVAL for LINNUM
Exit	-	-	-	-	-	Enter ASROMNEW routine

The DOS DOROMNEW routine is at memory address 0xBE9B and it follows the DOS DOCLRNEW routine which is among the Page 0xBE Interface Routines, and this routine is the final processing destination for both the DOS CHAIN and the DOS RUN common handler. One of the very last functions that the DOS CHAIN/RUN handler performs before the handler leaves RAM Bank 2 by means of the DOS DOROMRST routine, is to copy the 16-bit parameter that resides in LENVAL to the 2-byte pointer LINNUM at 0x50:0x51. The parameter LENVAL is the L keyword value that corresponds to the program line number where Applesoft processing is required to begin. The page-zero pointer LINNUM must be initialized with this L keyword value in order for Applesoft to perform this function. The handler also mathematically ORs the MSB byte of LINNUM with its LSB byte and saves that to a DOS temporary variable DOSBUFR+1. In the DOS DOROMNEW routine, if the value in DOSBUFR+1 is not zero, then the ROM ASROMSET routine at 0xD955 is directly entered in order to search the Applesoft program for the program line number that corresponds to the value found in LINNUM. The address where that program line number occurs is then transferred to the page-zero variable TXTPTR at 0xB8:0xB9. If the program line number is not found in the Applesoft program, the ROM ASROMSET routine prints the UNDEF'D STATEMENT ERROR message and Applesoft processing terminates. If the program line number is found, the DOS DOROMNEW routine concludes its processing and the handler directly enters the ROM ASROMNEW routine in order to initiate Applesoft processing for the new Applesoft program that currently resides in memory.

Use the Direct Approach in order to utilize the DOS DOROMNEW routine at 0xBE9B.

24. RAM2ON Routine

Function	Address	X-reg	Y-reg	A-reg	C-flag	Description
Entry	0xBEB5	-	-	-	-	Set RAM Bank 2
Return	-	-	-	-	-	Return to caller

The RAM2ON routine is a short utility routine that write-enables and turns RAM Bank 2 memory ON. The routine pushes the processor status onto the stack, executes two BIT instructions for the variable RAM2WE or 0xC083, and pulls the processor status back from the stack. No registers are changed and no processor flags are changed. The RAM2ON routine returns directly to the caller.

Use the Direct Approach in order to utilize the DOS RAM2ON routine at 0xBEB5.

25. RAM1ON Routine

Function	Address	X-reg	Y-reg	A-reg	C-flag	Description
Entry	0xBEBE	-	-	-	-	Set RAM Bank 1
Return	-	-	-	-	-	Return to caller

The RAM1ON routine is a short utility routine that write-enables and turns RAM Bank 1 memory ON. The routine pushes the processor status onto the stack, executes two BIT instructions for the variable RAM1WE or 0xC08B, and pulls the processor status back from the stack. No registers are changed and no processor flags are changed. The RAM1ON routine returns directly to the caller.

Use the Direct Approach in order to utilize the DOS RAM1ON routine at 0xBEBE.

3. BOOT and DATA Management Vectors and Bytes

DOS 4.5 is fully resident in the memory of the Language Card partition for Main memory except for two memory pages that are located in lower Main memory at Page 0xBE and at Page 0xBF. Page 0xBF contains the bootstrap Stage 0 routine that is followed by the Stage 1 and the Stage 2 routines in order to read DOS 4.5 from the BOOT tracks of a DOS bootable volume and place DOS directly into the Language Card partition of Main memory. Page 0xBF also contains the read/write sector interleave table, the fundamental DOS initialization routines, the routine to read from and write to the BOOT sectors of a volume, the RWTS IOCB, the File Manger Context Block, the BOOT CFG table, and the BOOT and DATA Management Vectors and Bytes. The BOOT and DATA Management Vectors and Bytes occupy the last sixteen bytes in Page 0xBF and the BOOT and DATA Management Data structure is shown in Table I.8.1. Each vector and data byte in this Data structure has been carefully selected in order to provide the user with access to the most advanced DATA management routines and parameters than those found in any previously published Disk Operating System for the Apple][computer. In no other Apple][Disk Operating System will the user find a more powerful set of initialization and DATA management routines that puts DOS 4.5 literally at the forefront of any other Disk Operating System that is fully compatible with the disk and sector structure that was originally created for DOS 3.3. Just to be clear, all of the BOOT and DATA Management Vectors and Bytes are available to DOS 4.5 and to the DOS 4.5 user **only after** DOS 4.5 has BOOTed or has been copied into memory.

1. BLDVRSN Variable Byte

Function	Address	X-reg	Y-reg	A-reg	C-flag	Description
Identification	0xBFF0	-	-	-	-	Read DOS Version number

The DOS BLDVRSN variable byte at memory address 0xBFF0 as shown in Table I.8.1 identifies the DOS version number for the DOS that currently resides in memory. Using this variable byte to identify the DOS version that currently resides in memory is far more convenient than having to parse the DOS version number from the DOS Version character string that is provided by indirectly entering the RDCLKVSN routine at memory address 0x3E1 and supplying the address of a 20-byte buffer.

Use the Direct Approach in order to utilize the DOS BLDVRSN variable byte at 0xBFF0.

2. BLDNMBR Variable Byte

Function	Address	X-reg	Y-reg	A-reg	C-flag	Description
Identification	0xBFF1	-	-	-	-	Read DOS Build number

The DOS BLDNMBR variable byte at memory address 0xBFF1 as shown in Table I.8.1 identifies the DOS build number for the DOS that currently resides in memory. Using this variable byte to identify the DOS build that currently resides in memory is far more convenient than having to parse the DOS build number from the DOS Version character string that is provided by indirectly entering the RDCLKVSN routine at memory address 0x3E1 and supplying the address of a 20-byte buffer.

Use the Direct Approach in order to utilize the DOS BLDNUMBR variable byte at 0xBFF1.

3. MNGDISK Vector Address

Function	Address	X-reg	Y-reg	A-reg	C-flag	Description
Entry	0xBFF2	slot #	#handler	/handler	set	Set RAM Bank 1 ON, attach handler
Return	-	same	same	same	clear	Set ROM Bank 2 WP and return to caller
Entry	0xBFF2	slot #	-	0x00	set	Set RAM Bank 1 ON, get DISKADRS entry
Return	-	same	#handler	/handler	clear	Set ROM Bank 2 WP and return to caller
Entry	0xBFF2	slot #	-	-	clear	Set RAM Bank 1 ON, detach handler
Return	-	same	#RWTSENT	/RWTSENT	clear	Set ROM Bank 2 WP and return to caller

The DOS MNGDISK vector address at memory address 0xBFF2 as shown in Table I.8.1 enters the DOS MNGEXDSK routine by means of the DOS EXMNGDSK routine. In DOS 4.5 the caller, using the DOS

MNGDISK vector address, indirectly enters the DOS EXMNGDSK routine that is found in the Page 0xBE Interface Routines that write-enables Bank 1 of the Language Card partition in order to directly enter the DOS MNGEXDSK routine. The DOS MNGEXDSK routine reads, writes, or restores the specified DISKADRS table entry.

In order to attach the address of a Peripheral Interface Disk Drive handler, that address must be entered into the DISKADRS table in order for RWTS to utilize that Disk Drive handler. In order to utilize the DOS MNGDISK vector address, the user must initialize the X-register with the Peripheral Interface slot number or the slot-times-sixteen number, place the address of the Interface Disk Drive handler in the Y- and A-registers in Lo/Hi byte order, and **set** the C-flag. The registers are returned unchanged and the C-flag is returned **clear**. RWTS transfers control to the Interface Disk Drive handler for the requested I/O based entirely on the slot-times-sixteen value that is found in the RWTS IOCB. Figure I.8.2 shows an example assembly language routine that attaches the RAM Disk Drive handler to RWTS. Figure I.8.3 shows an example assembly language routine that uses the DOS MNGDISK vector address in order to request the address of the handler that is currently assigned to a particular slot number, and that address is returned in the Y- and A-registers. Thus, to obtain the address for any entry in the DISKADRS table, utilize the DOS MNGDISK vector address with the interface slot number or the slot-times-sixteen number in the X-register, the A-register set to zero, and the C-flag **set**. The X-register will be returned unchanged and the Y- and A-registers will contain the address of the current Disk handler for that slot number, and the C-flag will be returned **clear**. The same example in Figure I.8.3 shows how to detach an entry address in the DISKADRS table. Simply utilize the DOS MNGDISK vector address with the interface slot number or the slot-times-sixteen number in the X-register and the C-flag **cleared**. The X-register will be returned unchanged and the Y- and A-registers will contain the address of RWTSENT. The selected DISKADRS table entry will be replaced with the default Disk Drive handler address which is the address of the internal RWTS Disk Drive handler routine RWTSENT that resides at 0xD2F3 in DOS 4.5.

For all DOS MNGDISK functions, the X-register must contain a valid slot number or a valid slot-times-sixteen number. A valid slot number is any number in the range from one to seven. If DOS MNGDISK processing determines that the X-register contains an invalid value, DOS MNGDISK immediately returns to the caller with the C-flag **set** before any further processing occurs. Otherwise, DOS MNGDISK returns to the caller with the C-flag **clear**.

Unlike DOS 4.1, it is not necessary to know where the DISKADRS table resides within DOS 4.5 memory nor how that table is accessed, utilized, and protected. The DOS MNGEXDSK routine takes care of all of the necessary protocol that had to be handled entirely by the DOS 4.1 user. The DOS MNGEXDSK routine always returns the C-flag **clear** unless the X-register contains an invalid value, and that is the only time when the C-flag is returned **set**. Once processing is complete, the MNGEXDSK routine returns to the Page 0xBE Interface Routines, enables ROM memory, and then returns directly to the caller. The X-register is returned to the user unchanged and the Y- and A-registers are returned containing the appropriate or requested values to the user.

Use the Indirect Approach in order to utilize the DOS MNGDISK vector address at 0xBFF2.

4. MNGVALS Vector Address

Function	Address	X-reg	Y-reg	A-reg	C-flag	V-flag	Description
Entry	0xBFF4	-	<0x61	variable	set	clear	Set RAM Bank 1 ON, write one
Return	-	same	++1	same	clear	clear	Set ROM Bank 2 WP, return
Entry	0xBFF4	-	<0x61	-	clear	clear	Set RAM Bank 1 ON, read one
Return	-	same	++1	variable	clear	clear	Set ROM Bank 2 WP, return
Entry	0xBFF4	variable	<0x61	variable+1	set	set	Set RAM Bank 1 ON, write two
Return	-	same	++2	same	clear	set	Set ROM Bank 2 WP, return
Entry	0xBFF4	-	<0x61	-	clear	set	Set RAM Bank 1 ON, read two
Return	-	variable	++2	variable+1	clear	set	Set ROM Bank 2 WP, return

The DOS MNGVALS vector address at memory address 0xBFF4 as shown in Table I.8.1 enters the DOS MNGEXVAL routine by means of the DOS EXMNGVAL routine. In DOS 4.5 the caller, using the DOS MNGVALS vector address, indirectly enters the DOS EXMNGVAL routine that is found in the Page 0xBE Interface Routines that write-enables Bank 1 of the Language Card partition in order to directly enter the DOS MNGEXVAL routine. The DOS MNGEXVAL routine reads or writes selected variables in the CMDVALS Data structure and variables in the File Manager Workarea buffer as shown in Tables I.12.1 and I.12.2, respectively. In all cases, the Y-register is range checked, and if its value is equal to or greater than CVALSLEN or 0x61, the DOS MNGVALS routine returns to the user with the C-flag **set**, otherwise the DOS MNGVALS routine always returns to the user with the C-flag **clear**.

In order to **change** or **write** new data to a single variable in the CMDVALS Data structure or to a single variable in the Workarea buffer, the A-register must contain the new data, the Y-register must contain the index to the desired variable that is to be changed, the C-flag must be **set**, and the Overflow flag or V-flag must be **clear**. The Y-register is returned and incremented by one. Variable indices for variables in the CMDVALS Data structure and variables in the File Manager Workarea buffer are shown in Tables I.12.1 and I.12.2, respectively. In order to **access** and to **read** the value of a single variable in the CMDVALS Data structure or a single variable in the Workarea buffer, the Y-register must contain the index to the desired variable that is to be read, the C-flag must be **clear**, and the Overflow flag must be **clear**. The data for the desired variable is returned in the A-register and the Y-register is returned and incremented by one. The DOS MNGEXVAL routine always returns to the caller with the C-flag **clear** unless the Y-register contains an invalid value, and then the C-flag is returned **set**.

When the V-flag is **set**, the Y-register is range checked, the Y-register must be less than CVALSLEN, and the Y-register must contain the index to the first variable that is to be read or written. The DOS MNGEXVAL routine reads or writes two consecutive variables from either the CMDVALS Data structure or from the File Manager Workarea buffer. When the C-flag is **set**, the two data variables that currently reside in the X- and A-registers are **written** consecutively to the CMDVALS Data structure or to the File Manager Workarea buffer. The variable that is in the X-register is written first and it is followed by the variable in the A-register. The Y-register is returned after being incremented twice. When the C-flag is **clear**, two consecutive variables are **read** from the CMDVALS Data structure or from the File Manager Workarea buffer and returned in the X- and A-registers. The first variable that is read is copied into the X-register and it is followed by the second variable that is read and copied into the A-register. The Y-register is returned after being incremented twice. The DOS MNGEXVAL routine returns to the caller with the C-flag **clear** unless the Y-register contains an invalid value, and then the C-flag is returned **set**. It is possible to read or to write a single byte variable that is beyond the File Manager Workarea buffer when the Y-register is equal to 0x60 and the V-flag is **set**. A SPAREVAL byte is located immediately following VOLNUMBR that ensures that no unintentional critical data is ever read or modified. Figures I.12.1 and I.12.2 show example assembly language routines in how to access and how to change the value of any variable in the CMDVALS Data structure or in the File Manager Workarea buffer using the DOS MNGVALS vector. In all cases the Overflow flag is returned unchanged.

The 6502 and 65C02 Instruction Set **does** contain a native **clear** Overflow flag instruction or CLV. Unfortunately, the Instruction Set **does not** contain a native **set** Overflow flag instruction. I am not sure why this microprocessor operation is missing. Truthfully, I believe there is **no** rationale for this shortcoming. Generally, many have used the BIT IORTS instruction to easily achieve setting the Overflow flag. The ROM IORTS address is the address for the RTS instruction in the ROM Monitor at memory address 0xFF58. One can utilize *any* RTS instruction within *any* routine in order to achieve the same result.

Use the Indirect Approach in order to utilize the DOS MNGVALS vector address at 0xBFF4.

5. MNGUSER Vector Address

Function	Address	X-reg	Y-reg	A-reg	C-flag	Description
Entry	0xBFF6	–	#USERADR	/USERADR	set	Set RAM Bank 1 ON, change
Return	–	#USERADR	same	same	clear	Set ROM Bank 2 WP, return
Entry	0xBFF6	–	–	–	clear	Set RAM Bank 1 ON, restore
Return	–	#CMDRUN-CMDTBL	#GOTOMON	/GOTOMON	clear	Set ROM Bank 2 WP, return

The MNGUSER vector address at memory address 0xBFF6 as shown in Table I.8.1 enters the DOS MNGEXUSR routine by means of the DOS EXMNGUSR routine. In DOS 4.5 the caller, using the DOS MNGUSER vector address, indirectly enters the DOS EXMNGUSR routine that is found in the Page 0xBE Interface Routines that write-enables Bank 1 of the Language Card partition in order to directly enter the DOS MNGEXUSR routine. The DOS MNGEXUSR routine changes or restores the USERADR and the CMDVAL variables which are found in the INITVALS Data structure as shown in Table I.8.5. In either function the DOS MNGEXUSR routine returns to the caller with the C-flag **clear**.

In order to utilize the DOS CMDUSER command during the DOS 4.5 BOOT process, the Y- and A-registers must contain the address of a user post-initialization routine in Lo/Hi byte order and the C-flag must be **set**. The MNGEXUSR routine initializes the CMDVAL command variable with the value of the DOS CMDUSER command or 0x60 and copies the address of the user post-initialization routine that is found in the Y- and A-registers to the USERADR variable. If the C-flag is **clear**, the MNGEXUSR routine restores the values of the variables USERADR and CMDVAL to their default values: USERADR contains the address of the internal DOS ENTRMON routine at 0xD49A in Bank 2 and CMDVAL contains the value of CMDRUN-CMDTBL which is 0x06. The DOS ENTRMON routine prints a carriage return, initializes the DOS CSWL and KSWL interface pointers, and enters the DOS GOTOMON routine.

A user post-initialization routine is extremely useful and valuable to a user who wishes to load DOS 4.5 or copy a DOS 4.5 image into memory and then initialize DOS such that the initialization process returns control to the user instead of normally losing control to Applesoft. In the normal BOOT scenario, DOS 4.5

loads the value that is found in CMDVAL in order to initiate the first DOS command, typically a RUN command of an Applesoft program whose filename is found in FNAME, the HELLO filename. On the other hand, after copying the DOS 4.5 image into memory, the DOS MNGUSER vector address can be utilized in order to initialize USERADR with the address of a user post-initialization routine, and then DOS can be immediately initialized by utilizing the DOS INITDOS vector address. DOS will find the CMDUSER value in CMDVAL and initiate the processing of that DOS command. For CMDUSER processing, DOS simply utilizes the vector address that is found in USERADR in order to indirectly enter the post-initialization routine that is provided by the user. What could be easier? One of the first tasks in the user post-initialization routine could be to utilize the DOS MNGUSER routine with the C-flag **clear**. This action would restore the values that are normally found in the USERADR and the CMDVAL variables and effectively restore DOS to its unmodified state. Finally, that same post-initialization routine could utilize the DOS INITDOS vector address in order to clear the CMDVALS Data structure and Cold-Start DOS to begin normal HELLO file processing or any number of other initial processing options. The list of initial processing options is virtually limitless using one's imagination. Figure I.8.4 shows an example assembly language routine in how to utilize the MNGUSER vector address for a user post-initialization routine.

The default address that is found in USERADR is for the DOS ENTRMON routine. Whenever DOS parses the Apple Command Line and finds the USER command as shown in Table III.0.2, DOS begins CMDUSER processing which simply loads the X- and A-registers with the decimal or the hexadecimal number that is used in conjunction with the USER command, if any, as in USER $1234. The address that is found in USERADR is utilized in order to transfer processing to that memory location, normally the DOS ENTRMON routine that transfers the user into the ROM or the RAM Monitor. The address that is found in USERADR can point to any routine that must execute whenever DOS parses the USER command on the Apple Command Line or from within an Applesoft program, an assembly language routine, or an EXEC file as shown in Figure III.1.12.2. *Big Mac*, for example, uses the USER command in order to restart the *Big Mac* program once the user has exited *Big Mac* to DOS. The DOS USER command may be utilized for **any** programmed command function or requirement that is invoked by DOS whenever DOS utilizes the address that it finds in USERADR.

Use the Indirect Approach in order to utilize the DOS MNGUSER vector address at 0xBFF6.

6. INITDOS Vector Address

Function	Address	X-reg	Y-reg	A-reg	C-flag	Description
Entry	0xBFF8	-	-	-	-	Initialize (Cold-Start) DOS
Return	0xE000	-	-	-	-	Enter BASCLD (no return to caller)

The INITDOS vector address at memory address 0xBFF8 as shown in Table I.8.1 indirectly enters the DOS DOSINIT routine that resides in memory Page 0xBF. The DOSINIT routine uses the RAM1ON routine in order to write-enable and turn RAM Bank 1 memory ON, directly enter the DOS CLRVALS routine that clears the CMDVALS Data structure, and DOSINIT enters the DOS COLDSTRT routine. The DOS COLDSTRT routine is also found on Page 0xBF and this routine initializes the stack pointer and XMODE to 0xFF, selects the main video and deselects the alternate character set, sets the video output to normal, initializes the text and graphic modes and sets the window operating parameters, initializes the CSWL and KSWL interface pointers, verifies that Applesoft is in ROM, copies the ROM Monitor to the RAM Monitor, searches for a clock card, and initializes SLOTVAL, DRVAL, and VOLVAL in order to directly enter the DOS COLDSTR2 routine.

When DOS COLDSTRT and DOS COLDSTR2 processing is complete, DOS exits indirectly into Applesoft by means of the DOS COLDADR vector in the Page 0xBE INITVALS Data structure as shown in Table I.8.5. The assembler initially sets the COLDADR vector to memory address 0xE000, the address of ROM Applesoft BASCLD. The BASCLD routine is entered at the Applesoft Cold-Start entry address in ROM that performs a complete re-initialization of Applesoft, and this routine does not return to the caller. The user is encouraged to change the address that is in the variable COLDADR at 0xBEE4 in order to tailor the DOS COLDSTRT routine not to exit into ROM Applesoft, but rather, to enter a user specific routine, and then exit into the ROM BASCLD routine. Figure I.8.4 shows an example assembly language routine in how to utilize the DOS INITDOS vector address.

Use the Indirect Approach in order to utilize the DOS INITDOS vector address at 0xBFF8.

7. INITVAL Vector Address

Function	Address	X-reg	Y-reg	A-reg	C-flag	Description
Address	0xBFFA	-	-	-	-	Address of INITVALS Data structure

The INITVAL vector address at memory address 0xBFFA as shown in Table I.8.1 is the address of the DOS INITVALS Data structure as shown in Table I.8.5. The DOS INITVALS Data structure resides within Page 0xBE in DOS 4.5 such that the variables in this Data structure may be modified directly without having to manage any Soft Switches in order to access their value. However, accessing and changing the values of the variables in this Data structure is far easier and far more general using a page-zero pointer as shown in the example assembly language routine in Figure I.8.6. The DOS INITVAL vector address is simply copied to a page-zero pointer in Lo/Hi byte order and any or all of the variables within the DOS INITVALS Data structure may be accessed using the offsets or indices for those variables as shown in Table I.8.5. The address for the INITVAL vector address or 0xBFFA will not change in any version of DOS 4.5, but the vector address that is at that memory location may, indeed, change.

Use the Indirect Approach in order to utilize the DOS INITVAL vector address at 0xBFFA.

8. BCFGNDX Least Significant Address Byte

Function	Address	X-reg	Y-reg	A-reg	C-flag	Description
#Address	0xBFFC	-	-	-	-	BOOTCFG table offset

The BCFGNDX least significant address byte at memory address 0xBFFC as shown in Table I.8.1 is the page offset for the DOS 4.5 BOOT Configuration BOOTCFG Data structure that always resides within memory Page 0xBF as shown in Table I.8.2. This Data structure may be accessed indirectly by using a page-zero pointer as shown in Figure I.8.7.

The BOOT Stage 1 process can be easily monitored, and at the appropriate moment when the BOOT Stage 1 process has just completed, the DOS BOOTCFG Data structure can be tailored or modified specifically for the BOOT Stage 2 process that is about to begin. As Figure I.8.7 shows by example, the variables DNUM and VOLEXPT can be dynamically modified before the BOOT Stage 2 process begins by using the CFFA drive and volume values, respectively, such that **any** volume number on **any** drive number may be selected and BOOTed into memory no matter what the DOS version may be.

BOOT Stage 1 sectors are directly read into memory by the CFFA firmware. However, BOOT Stage 2 is unique for each BOOT volume, and that BOOT volume process must be tailored for its own unique DOS that is currently BOOTing. When the BOOT Stage 2 process begins, the RWPAGES routine is now correctly configured dynamically by means of the RWTS IOCB content that is found in the DOS BOOTCFG Data structure. Once DOS is read into memory, DOS can then initialize and properly execute its initial HELLO program.

Use the Direct Approach in order to utilize the DOS BCFGNDX least significant address byte at 0xBFFC.

9. NBUF1PG Most Significant Address Byte

Function	Address	X-reg	Y-reg	A-reg	C-flag	Description
/Address	0xBFFD	-	-	-	-	NBUF1 MSB Address

The NBUF1PG most significant address byte at memory address 0xBFFD as shown in Table I.8.1 is the most significant address byte of the memory location for the 256-byte NBUF1 nibble buffer. DOS NBUF1 is a unique buffer because it is defined to begin on a page boundary and this buffer is exclusively used for RWTS processing. In DOS 4.5 this buffer is one of the very last memory pages in Bank 1 that resides in the Language Card partition. The most significant address byte of the DOS NBUF1 nibble buffer is included in the BOOT and DATA Management Vectors and Bytes in order to provide very easy access to the most significant address byte of the memory location address for a temporary page of memory. If RWTS processing is invoked while using the DOS NBUF1 buffer, the contents of this buffer would obviously be overwritten and be of little or no value.

The NBUF1PG address byte can be copied to the MSB of a page-zero pointer in order to utilize this page of memory, and Bank 1 in the Language Card partition must be write-enabled. The LSB of this page-zero pointer should be set to zero. Oftentimes, having access to a temporary buffer that is a full page which begins on a page boundary can alleviate a very difficult programming situation. This full page buffer can also be used to temporally hold a page of data that must be swapped for another page of data. This type of buffer utilization is necessary in the CFFA where either the first half or the second half of a 512-byte sector must be temporally saved while the other half of the 512-byte sector is modified.

In order to write-enable NBUF1 in DOS 4.5, the Soft Switch 0xC08B must be read twice consecutively. In an assembly language routine, this would be written as follows

```
BIT $C08B
BIT $C08B
```

The processor flag settings that would result from these two assembly language instructions are of **no** value because there is no physical memory that is connected to this particular address, or to the address of any Soft Switch in the Apple][computer hardware.

Use the Direct Approach in order to utilize the DOS NBUF1PG most significant address byte at 0xBFFD.

10. BOOTADR Most Significant Address Byte

Function	Address	X-reg	Y-reg	A-reg	C-flag	Description
/Address	0xBFFE	-	-	-	-	BOOT Stage 0 MSB Address

The DOS BOOTADR most significant address byte at memory address 0xBFFE as shown in Table I.8.1 is configured and set by the assembler and it is equal to the most significant memory address byte of the page of data that is contained in the initial data sector that is read from track 0x00 during BOOT Stage 1. That initial data sector is read from a BOOT volume and copied to Page 0xD0 in DOS 4.5. Therefore, the DOS BOOTADR address byte is 0xD0 in DOS 4.5. In BOOT Stage 0 the DOS BOOTADR address byte is copied into the MSB byte of the page-zero BUFRADRZ+1 pointer at address 0x27. The Disk][firmware has already set the LSB address 0x26 to zero. The BUFRADRZ+1 pointer is incremented in the Disk][firmware at 0xCnEB, where **n** is the slot number of the Disk][peripheral interface card.

DOS 4.5 is unique in that as the BUFRADRZ+1 pointer is incremented, the next sector number to be read is decremented during the BOOT Stage 1 BOOT process as shown in Table I.8.3. The DOS 3.3 BOOT Stage 1 algorithm BOOTs in a totally opposite fashion in that the BUFRADRZ+1 pointer is decremented while the sector number is incremented. DOS 4.5 takes advantage of all of the native firmware logic that is found in the Disk][peripheral interface card which increments both the BUFRADRZ+1 pointer and the sector number. However, sector number is not utilized directly in a linear fashion like the BUFRADRZ+1 pointer is utilized. In DOS 3.3 as well as in DOS 4.5 the sector number is decremented sequentially and utilized as in index into a sector interleave table in order to accelerate the loading of volume sectors that are resident in a given track. The remaining DOS 4.5 BOOT image is read into memory during the BOOT Stage 2 process starting with sector 0x09 on track 0x02 and ending with sector 0x00 on track 0x01. Every file that is saved to a DOS 4.5 volume attempts to save the first TSL sector of a file to sector 0x0F on any given track and all of the data sectors of a file are saved in a sequentially decremented order entirely for the purpose to accelerate read sector and write sector processing. ProDOS, Fortran, and Pascal utilize specific and unique sector interleave tables that are different from the sector interleave table that is used in DOS 3.3 and in DOS 4.5. DOS 4.5 uses the same sector interleave table that is used in DOS 3.3 only to remain compatible with all previously initialized DOS 3.3 volumes.

Use the Direct Approach in order to utilize the DOS BOOTADR most significant address byte at 0xBFFE.

11. BOOTPGS Variable Sector Number Byte

Function	Address	X-reg	Y-reg	A-reg	C-flag	Description
Sectors	0xBFFF	-	-	-	-	BOOT Stage 1 sectors read

The DOS BOOTPGS variable sector number byte at memory address 0xBFFF as shown in Table I.8.1 is configured and set by the assembler and is equal to the number of sectors that must be consecutively read from track 0x00 during the BOOT Stage 1 process. The first sector that is read from a BOOT volume on track 0x00 is sector 0x0F in DOS 4.5. Therefore, the DOS BOOTPGS variable sector number byte is 0x0F in DOS 4.5. In BOOT Stage 1 the DOS BOOTPGS variable sector number byte serves both as a counter and as the next sector index into the sector interleave table in order to obtain the value for the next physical sector number that the BOOTPGS routine is about to read. The value of the DOS BOOTPGS variable sector number byte is also used to determine when to change the address value in the BUFRADRZ+1 pointer from 0xDE to 0xBE. Table I.8.3 shows the relationship of track 0x00 sector value and its corresponding memory page MSB for a DOS 4.5 BOOT image. In other words, DOS 4.5 always loads sector 0x01 on track 0x00 to Page 0xBE and sector 0x00 on track 0x00 to Page 0xBF.

Use the Direct Approach in order to utilize the DOS BOOTPGS variable sector number byte at 0xBFFF.

V. Operational Environment Using DOS 4.5

DOS 4.5 Build 06 provides a far more advanced operational environment than what DOS 4.1, DOS 4.3, and even DOS 4.5 Build 05 were capable of providing for the design of the entire genre of Apple][software. For example, whether it is used for the design of software tools, utilities, games, and firmware, the operational environment inherent in DOS 4.5 is unchallenged particularly when any software development project utilizes the architectural and design elements that I have presented for DOS 4.5. I have developed my own software projects and programs such as *Applesoft Formatter*, Binary File Installation (*BFI*), *Real Time Clock* using my own clock hardware, *Disk Window*, EPROM Operating System (*EOS*), Volume Manager for the CFFA card including *BOOTVOL* and *BOOTDOS*, VTOC Manager (*VMGR*), *TrackScan*, and *ICON Maker*. Furthermore, I have created my own source code programs from the object code of commercial programs that include Asynchronous Data Transfer (*ADT*), *Big Mac*, PROmGRAMER, firmware for the CFFA card, File Developer (*FID*), Lazer's Interactive Symbolic Assembler (*Lisa*), Program Global Editor (*PGE*), Global Program Line Editor (*GPLE*), firmware for the RAM Disk 320, firmware for the RanaSystems EliteThree disk drive, firmware for the Sider hard disk drive, and *Sourceror*. All of these commercially available software tools, utilities, and firmware now utilize the operational environment features that are built and engineered into DOS 4.5 Build 06.

Many of the above-mentioned commercially published software projects and programs are based on software that was available from the early 1980's when it became affordable to own an Apple][computer. Because so much time has now passed since these programs were first available, I did not even consider seeking permission from the respective publishers of this object code in order to *source* this software. I am sure, sadly, that many of the original software authors may have already passed on. My primary intent was to understand and to document all of the internal dependencies that these commercially published software programs had on DOS 3.3. Collectively, all of these dependencies on DOS 3.3 assisted in driving my initial design of DOS 4.1, and now these dependencies continue to assist me in my design of DOS 4.5. It was also my intent to provide enough visibility into the DOS 4.5 processing routines, its Data structures, and its command architecture that these authors required in order to address the requirements of their software programs. As it is said, *The proof is in the pudding!* I have successfully modified all the above-mentioned commercially available software tools, utilities, and firmware to be fully DOS 4.5 compliant as if DOS 4.5 is some black box with sufficient special access means to its data. There should be absolutely no need to know anything about DOS 4.5 nor any need to directly access any of the internal routines in DOS 4.5. I created many of these source code files from the commercially available object code files for my own intellectual edification and, initially, for my own private utilization. I am simply acknowledging the effort and the time that I have invested in order to understand and to appreciate what I consider to be valuable software programs written by other brilliant Apple][software programmers. Furthermore, I am showing by example how I have modified these particular software programs in order to function successfully within the operational environment of DOS 4.5, its processing routines, its Data structures, and its command architecture.

I did spend a considerable amount of time attempting to relocate DOS 4.3 into Auxiliary memory. I was absolutely successful in this exercise! However, I could not successfully create a viable interface for this DOS such that either *Big Mac* or *Lisa* could reside in Main memory. The interface routines became unwieldy and they started to consume precious code space in lower Main memory that became too significant. My next option was to leave DOS 4.3 in the Language Card partition in Main memory and relocate *Lisa* to the Language Card partition in Auxiliary memory. This proved to be far easier than I anticipated given the number of previous interface challenges. Now that I have fully developed the Auxiliary memory interface routines for *Lisa* and have amassed considerable experience working with

Auxiliary memory, I attempted to relocate *Big Mac* to the Language Card partition in Auxiliary memory as well. This proved to be far easier to accomplish, and the Auxiliary memory interface routines that support *Big Mac* are very similar to the routines I developed for *Lisa*. Furthermore, I was able to design, develop, and implement all of the routines that are needed in order to fully support the *SWEET16* Metaprocessor Instruction Set in both *Sourceror* and in *Big Mac*. I considered this to be an original major shortcoming to both software programs before I added the complete *SWEET16* support to *Sourceror* and to *Big Mac*. The complete *SWEET16* Metaprocessor Instruction Set is found in Section II.3.

The achievements that I have accomplished during the development of DOS 4.3 came easier because I had far more memory available to work with. I found it burdensome during DOS 4.1 development having substantially less memory for DOS 4.1L than I had for DOS 4.1H. Keeping DOS 4.1L and DOS 4.1H synchronized consumed a great deal of energy. Having more memory for DOS 4.1H gave me all of the right reasons for developing the first version of the DOS HELP command. When it came to developing DOS 4.3, not having to develop a DOS 4.3L version in parallel allowed me to utilize all of my time far more efficiently. For this, I am grateful because developing DOS 4.3 gave me the opportunity to begin my investigation into Auxiliary memory and what I might be able to do with that memory.

I did find that I could, with some clever rearrangement of the Build 05 source code, produce a useful DOS 4.5L that only added one additional data sector to its disk BOOT image. I was so enamored with the fact that DOS 4.1L and early DOS 4.5L only require two tracks for their complete BOOT image. Considering the fact that DOS 3.3 commandeered three complete tracks for its thirty-seven sector BOOT image, adding an additional sector to the BOOT image for DOS 4.5L did not seem that severe of a penalty. In addition to the extra BOOT sector, DOS 4.5L uses more critical program memory such that it became necessary to sacrifice one default file buffer in order to reduce the critical program memory utilization. Unfortunately, the *final and last* new contents and capabilities that I wanted to engineer into DOS 4.5H Build 06 could never be realized in a version for DOS 4.5L Build 06 because the sacrifices to critical program memory and to DOS functionality were simply not acceptable. I adopted the same rationale that I utilized for the development of DOS 4.3 and I concentrated on the *final and last* release of DOS 4.5 with Build 06 that requires forty-two BOOT sectors that BOOT natively into the Language Card partition in Main memory.

When I first wrote Section V for *The DOS 4.1 Manual*, I wrote each chapter as if their subject followed a time-line that matched the programs that I wrote and the various hardware that I added to my Apple][+ as I developed and utilized my general computer skills. I have no idea why I changed the presentation order for these chapters in my following publication, *DOS 4.3 File Management System*. And, I even retained this modified chapter order in my next publication, *DOS 4.5 File and Volume Disk Management System*. This new chapter ordering was not using very good sense at all. I believe the original order that I utilized for presenting the chapters in Section V was done for a very good reason, and I have returned to that original presentation order for these chapters in the publication of this *Second Edition*. I have made a few modifications to that original presentation order that helps to clarify some of these particular subjects. The chapter on *Apple][+ Keyboard Modification* now follows the chapter on *Apple][+ Memory Upgrade*. The original chapter on *EPROM Operating System for quikLoader* is now divided into two separate chapters. I discuss the *SCRG quikLoader Card* hardware separately from the *EPROM Operating System* software. The three chapters on *ClientServer*, *CHAR Editor*, and *ICON Maker* were some of the last major programs that I have designed and developed or redesigned and redeveloped after I published the *DOS 4.3 File Management System*. The EPROM Reader card and *EOS+* are some of my final projects in this publication. My very last software project was to reintroduce the Applesoft LOAD command into ROM firmware that is found in Section II.9. Taken all together, Section V contains a vast amount of knowledge, effort, and proficiency in my understanding of the magnificent Apple][computer that I rely on in order to develop, produce, and create this diverse array of software tools, utilities, and firmware.

238

1. Applesoft Formatter Program

After about six months of writing test and demonstration Applesoft programs on my new Apple][+, I began thinking about writing a serious Applesoft program. Binary File Installation was that program, but it became a hybrid program because it included many attached assembly language routines as described next in Section V.2. I also thought I was now capable of writing a standalone assembly language routine. How an Applesoft program appears when it is listed on a display or how an Applesoft program appears when it is printed by my printer literally appalled me, and I was determined to use assembly language in order to design and write an *Applesoft Formatter* program. I wanted *Applesoft Formatter* to align program line numbers and to consistently space all parentheses the way I liked them spaced. My spacing of parentheses actually carried over to how I formatted and wrote all of my future C language software during my professional engineering career. One feature of this program is to optionally split multiple Applesoft statements that have the same line number and are separated by a colon character : such that each Applesoft statement would appear on separate lines. Another feature is to optionally indent Applesoft statements within a FOR/NEXT loop no matter how nested the loops become. Since I owned an Epson MX100 printer, I could easily print up to 120 characters on each line when I use wide paper. Basically, this program became an exercise in parsing Applesoft tokens, keeping track of FOR/NEXT loops, and counting quote characters like '. As an interesting aside, I wrote this software so that it could execute at virtually any memory location. It was certainly an intriguing exercise in order to develop and practice my skills at writing relocatable object code for the Apple][computer.

```
]LOAD TEST

]LIST

 10  MN = 1:MX = 10: PRINT
 20  I = 0: FOR I = MN TO MX: IF I
     = 5 THEN  GOSUB 100
 30  S$ = "Entry #" +  STR$ (I):J =
     I + 7
 40  T$ = S$ +  STR$ (J): NEXT
 50  END
 100  PRINT "I = ";I;", J = ";J;"
     , S$ = ";S$: RETURN

]

]RUN

I = 5, J = 11, S$ = Entry #4

]
```

Figure V.1.1. Applesoft Test Program Listing

```
Maximum Characters/Line (<161):   31
Split Line (Y,N):  Y
Indent (Y,N):  Y
Echo to Screen (Y,N):  Y
    10     MN = 1
           MX = 10
           PRINT
    20     I = 0
           FOR I = MN TO MX
              IF I = 5 THEN GOSUB 100
    30        S$ = "Entry #" + STR$( I )
              J = I + 7
    40        T$ = S$ + STR$( J )
           NEXT
    50     END
    100    PRINT "I = "; I; ", J = "; J;
           ", S$ = "; S$
           RETURN
] ※
```

Figure V.1.2. Applesoft Formatted Program

A very simple, unimaginative Applesoft test program is shown in Figure V.1.1 along with some results when that program is RUN. I have purposefully combined several Applesoft statements having the same line number and I have embedded a FOR/NEXT loop within other Applesoft statements where the loop spans multiple line numbers. Even when this program is listed to a printer, it appears just as awkward and difficult to read. Needless to say, a program many times this size would be exceedingly difficult to read, to debug, and to analyze. I am sure there must have been at least one utility if not more that was available in the early 1980's similar to the Apple-Doc program by Roger Wagner, that could format and document Applesoft programs using multiple formatting options. And, I am sure those programs did their task work magnificently, too. But that was not my intention, to purchase the labor and product of someone else. I

239

wanted to perform the labor of writing my own program and I wanted to own the results, or the product of that labor. Someone else may indeed choose differently.

I wanted to understand the organization of an Applesoft program as it is found in memory. Therefore, I needed to know about all of the rules in how an Applesoft program is constructed from the very first Applesoft statement that has a line number to the very last Applesoft statement that also has a line number. I learned about the triple-NULL bytes and how they terminate an Applesoft program. The very first line of Applesoft statements in an Applesoft program begins at memory address 0x0801. At memory address 0x0801 there is a two-byte value in low/high byte order that is the address for the beginning of the next line of Applesoft statements such as 0x13, 0x08. These two bytes, when reversed, form the memory address 0x0813. This two-byte address is followed by a two-byte line number, again expressed in low/high byte order. So, if the first line of Applesoft statements is 10, then the two-byte line number would be found in memory as 0x0A, 0x00. To reiterate, memory addresses as well as line numbers are expressed in low/high byte order in Applesoft programs. All text data that is contained in an Applesoft program is always found in lower ASCII where the MSB turned OFF for each character byte. On the other hand, all Applesoft statements, that is, their Applesoft tokens, are always found in upper ASCII with the MSB turned ON. For example, the first token in the list of BASIC statements in the ROM Applesoft interpreter is for the END statement, and its token value is 0x80. The last token in the token list is for the MID$ statement, and its token value is 0xEA. The token values for all of the other Applesoft statements are within these two values. At the end of each Applesoft statement that has a line number, there is a single byte NULL character 0x00. That NULL character 0x00 terminates that Applesoft statement. In other words, if the memory address to the next Applesoft statement that has a line number is found to be 0x0813, there will be a NULL character 0x00 at memory address 0x0812.

The format for an Applesoft statement that has a line number does not include the memory address for the beginning of the previous Applesoft statement that has a line number. Applesoft statements that have a line number are organized in a single direction format, or linked list. To find line number 1000 when parsing for the statement GOTO 1000, the Applesoft interpreter must start at the beginning of the Applesoft program at memory address 0x0801, and follow the linked list of memory addresses until it finds line number 0x03E8 in memory. This organization of Applesoft statements that have a line number suggests that highly utilized subroutines or functions should be placed early in an Applesoft program. I still find this surprisingly counter-intuitive even though I routinely place all of my subroutines and functions at the beginning of my C language programs with Main always coming last.

Now that I have a basic understanding of the organization of an Applesoft program as it is found in memory, I understand how to parse an Applesoft program using assembly language, and I understand how to separate Applesoft tokens from variable names and embedded ASCII text. This exercise required me to do a little research, a little data and memory analysis, and a little hard work in order to develop the *Applesoft Formatter* program. Figure V.1.2 displays the output of *Applesoft Formatter* when the *Split Line* and the *Indent* options are both enabled. Seriously, the generated listing is totally easier to read, easier to debug, and far easier to analyze now that the Applesoft test program is formatted into an appealing and precise composition. I also gained an exceptional understanding of assembly language programming for the 6502-microprocessor, how best to use an assembler, and how to create relocatable object code so that *Applesoft Formatter* is able to execute at virtually any memory location. Obviously, the lessons learned in designing and writing *Applesoft Formatter* early in my ownership of an Apple][+ computer are forever invaluable to me. Furthermore, the effort that I put into developing this program has paid off handsomely throughout my entire professional software career. I am still thankful today in having had the experience in designing and in writing *Applesoft Formatter*.

2. Binary File Installation Program

Binary File Installation or *BFI* was my first often used Applesoft program that I wrote for my Apple][+ computer. I began writing Applesoft programs initially, but I soon started to explore assembly language for various data sort algorithms and disk I/O routines that fascinated me. If I wrote the data sort algorithms and the disk I/O routines such that they could execute at any memory location, then I could attach their assembly language code to the end of an Applesoft program, modify some page-zero pointers, and save the composite, albeit hybrid program to disk. Later, whenever I ran the Applesoft program, its initial program logic was designed to obtain its program size from certain page-zero locations and then calculate the locations in memory for the attached binary code routines simply by knowing their length in bytes and the address for the end of the Applesoft program. A CALL statement could then be made directly to the start address of a data sort algorithm or of a disk I/O routine from any location within the Applesoft program. This capability of being able to CALL any of my relocatable assembly language routines anywhere within an Applesoft program was exhilarating. I talked about this Applesoft programming capability to all of my co-workers who would listen, or to those who were patient with my *Apple computer* programming excitement and enthusiasm.

I learned I could even pass parameters to an assembly language routine and also have calculated values returned to the Applesoft program. Any number of relocatable routines could be attached to the end of an Applesoft program and CALLed as long as their start location in memory could be precisely determined. I thought that a utility could more easily and precisely handle this attachment process, so I created *BFI* to programmatically perform any assembly language file attachments to any Applesoft program. The user tells *BFI* which Applesoft program to target which is the program that is to receive all of the assembly language file attachments, and then the user is offered a selection of all of the relocatable assembly language files that can be attached. *BFI* modifies the size of the Applesoft program on disk, its first two bytes in its sector data, and calls the File Manager to append the assembly language files directly to the end of the Applesoft program on disk just after its last three NULL bytes: simple, clean, and efficient. Once the attachment process is done, *BFI* prints the order and the size of all of the assembly language files it attached. The Applesoft program can still be edited or changed at any time using the Apple Command Line and cursor move routines. Unfortunately, if a tool such as *GPLE* or *PGE* is used to edit the Applesoft program, any attached assembly language files are stripped from the Applesoft program when the edited file is saved back to disk. I have yet to explore how to disable this feature in both *GPLE* and *PGE*. Figures V.2.1, V.2.2, and V.2.3 show the *BFI* initial Splash Screen, the Main Menu, and how the user selects the external devices for *BFI*. *BFI* only utilizes the disk drive or disk drives that are located in slot 6. When the Install icon is selected as shown in Figure V.2.2, the Applesoft program instructional screen as shown in Figure V.2.4 is displayed in order to allow the user time to locate and insert the desired diskette containing the target Applesoft program.

Applesoft Program selection is fairly straightforward using the left and right arrow keys. The Applesoft program that is highlighted when the RETURN key is pressed becomes the target Applesoft program as shown in Figure V.2.5. The Binary file instructional screen as shown in Figure V.2.6 is displayed next in order to allow the user time to locate and insert the desired diskette containing the first Binary file to install. Once again, Binary file selection is fairly straightforward using the left and the right arrow keys. The Binary file that is highlighted when the RETURN key is pressed becomes the selected file to attach to the target Applesoft program as shown in Figure V.2.7. A graphic screen is displayed next which is called the Intermediate Installation screen as shown in Figure V.2.8. This screen graphically displays the remaining free memory space and the remaining free disk space on which the target Applesoft program resides.

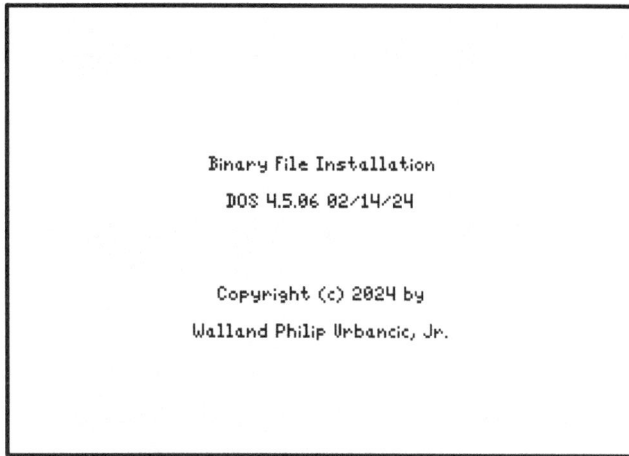

Figure V.2.1. BFI Splash Screen

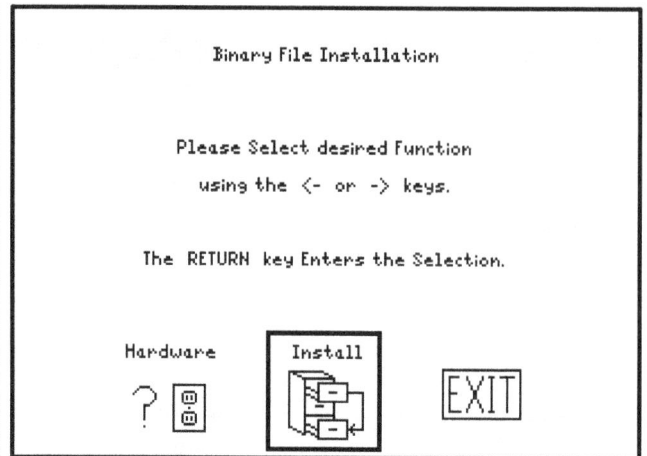

Figure V.2.2. BFI Main Menu

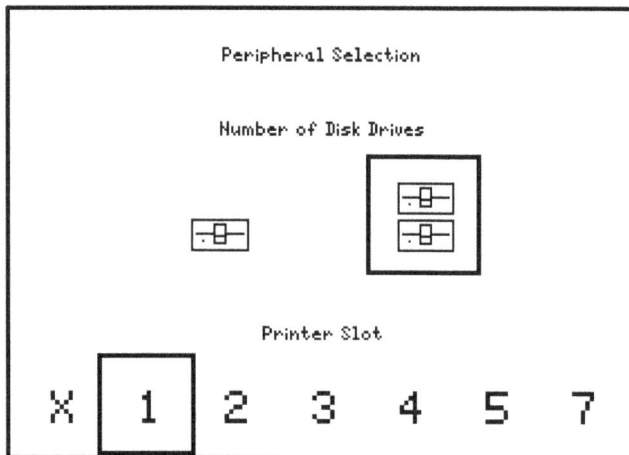

Figure V.2.3. BFI Peripheral Selection

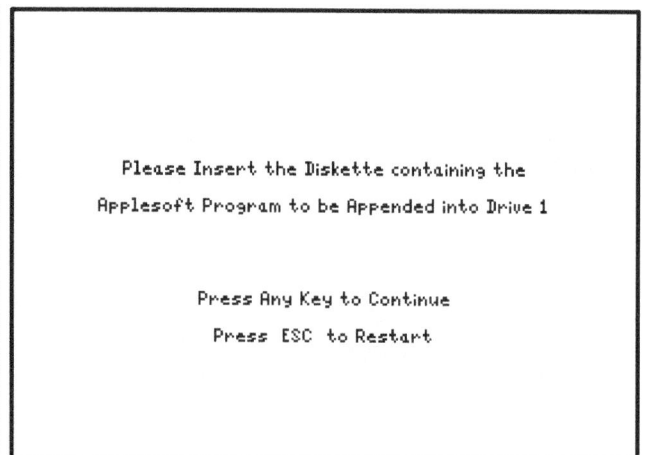

Figure V.2.4. Applesoft Program Directions

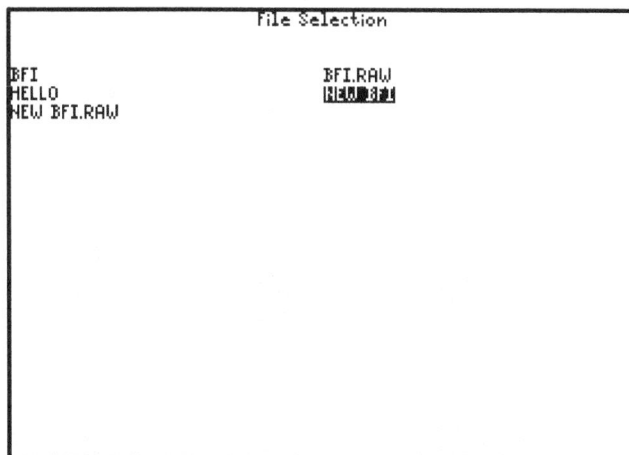

Figure V.2.5. Applesoft Program Selection

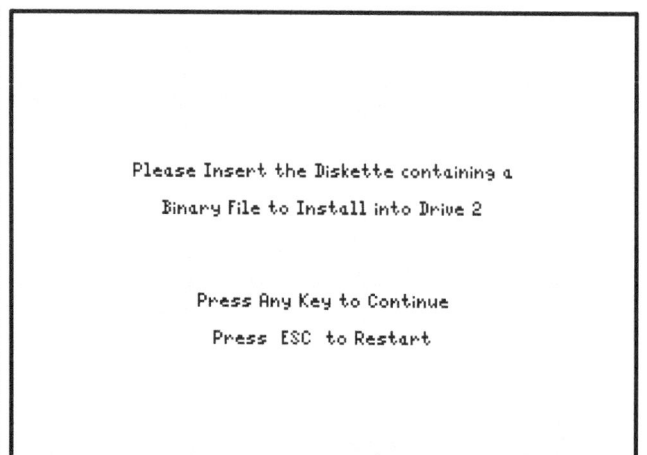

Figure V.2.6. Binary File Directions

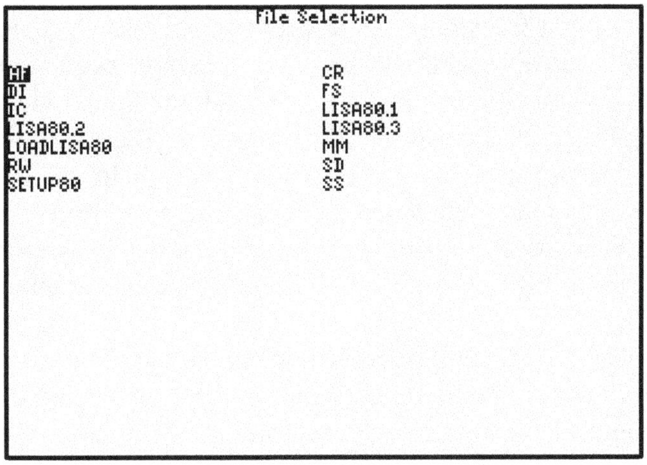

Figure V.2.7. Binary File Selection

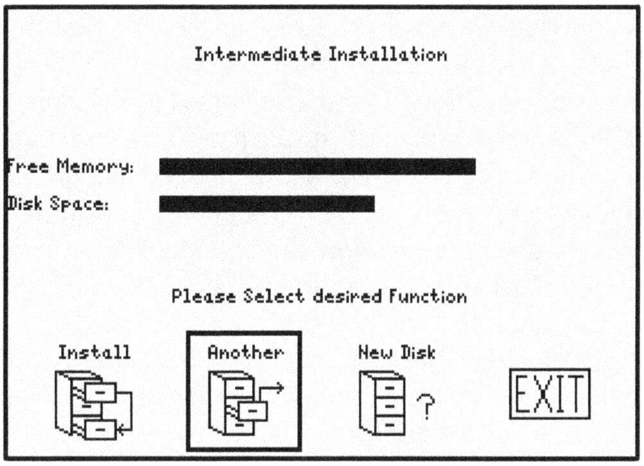

Figure V.2.8. Intermediate Installation Screen

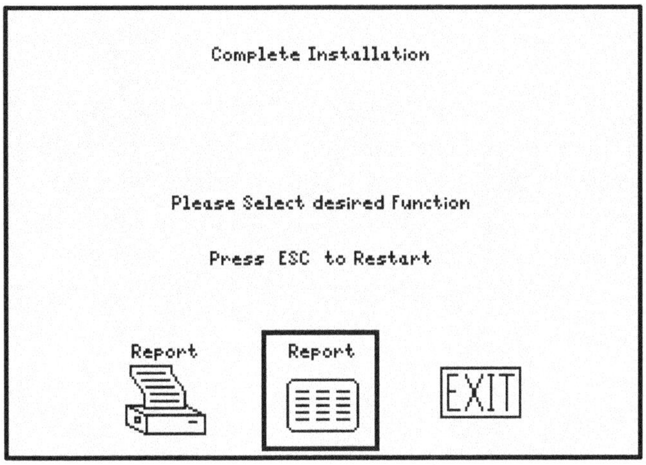

Figure V.2.9. BFI Complete

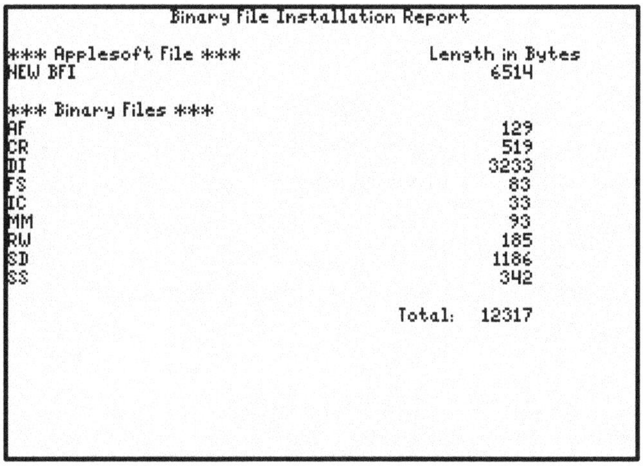

Figure V.2.10. BFI Final Report

The target Applesoft program is not read into memory, however, but all of the selected Binary files must be read into memory. Using DOS 4.5 will provide a far greater memory reservoir for selecting Binary files. Those selected Binary files must be appended to the target Applesoft program. Therefore, the diskette that contains the target Applesoft program must have sufficient disk space for the additional program code that is attached to that Applesoft program. The Intermediate Installation screen also provides the option to perform the Binary File Installation using all presently selected files, select another Binary file from the same diskette, change to another diskette that contains additional Binary files, or cancel the installation and exit. If a New Disk is selected, Figure V.2.6 is displayed again before reading the catalog of the new diskette and displaying an alphabetized list of all of the Binary files that reside on that diskette. Figure V.2.9 is displayed **after** *BFI* has completed the installation of all selected Binary files to the target Applesoft file, and Figure V.2.10 is displayed when the Report icon is selected showing the Binary File Installation Report. The Binary File Installation Report includes the name and the size of the target Applesoft program as well as the names of all of the selected Binary files, their installation order, and their file size.

As previously explained, *BFI* modifies the first two bytes of the target Applesoft program's sector data directly on disk. Furthermore, *BFI* calls the File Manager to append the Binary files that have been read into memory directly to the end of the target Applesoft program on disk just after its last three NULL bytes. *BFI* does not perform that much work. Essentially, *BFI* uses the power of Applesoft to keep lists of filenames, file sizes, and the memory locations of various assembly language tools that help *BFI* to conduct its processing. The task that *BFI* performs is to read selected Binary files into memory from one or more diskettes and write the content of those selected Binary files to another diskette at a precise sector location that amounts to simply appending a target Applesoft program. Thus, *BFI* orchestrates a number of activities that can be performed manually, but those activities are highly prone to error and to miscalculation. Still, the user can ruin all of the good work *BFI* accomplishes in not calculating the correct locations where the attached assembly language file routines reside in memory during Applesoft program execution. Furthermore, if the attached assembly language files are not relocatable assembly language routines, the resulting Applesoft program will not function properly no matter what it calculates for any of the start memory locations. Clearly, one of the first statements in the Applesoft program would be something like

```
10    PE = PEEK( 175 ) + PEEK( 176 ) * 256
```

When DOS reads an Applesoft program into memory, DOS copies the size in bytes of the Applesoft program that is found in its first two bytes plus 0x0801 to the page-zero locations 0xAF:0xB0 in low/high byte order as shown in Figure I.15.1. And, this is precisely the page-zero location where the program statement above uses in order to calculate the value for PE, or Program End. According to the Binary File Installation Report that *BFI* produces as shown in Figure V.2.10, the precise start memory location for each of the attached assembly language file routines may be determined as follows, starting with the last attached routine and going forward

```
15    SS = PE - 342
20    SD = SS - 1186
25    RW = SD - 185
30    MM = RW - 93
35    IC = MM - 33
40    FS = IC - 83
45    DI = FS - 3233
50    CR = DI - 519
55    AF = CR - 129
```

As I have increased my knowledge of the VTOC and of RWTS as well as the HIRES screen and the HIRES drawing routines, I have modified *BFI* a number of times. The experience that I gained from assisting in moving the Sierra On-Line *ScreenWriter* product from the Apple][+ to the Apple //e allowed me the opportunity to study the HIRES screen font that was used in the Apple][+ *ScreenWriter* product. I adapted that HIRES screen font for *BFI* as well as develop the *CHAR Editor* and *LENGTH* tools. *BFI* also uses an adaptation of the HIRES icon drawing routines that I developed for Sierra On-Line's *HomeWord Speller* product. I even wrote the icon development and editing tool *ICON Maker* that I use to generate the *shape table* data for all of the screen icons that I use in *BFI*. I probably learned more about the design of my Apple][hardware and firmware from this single Applesoft hybrid program. Essentially, *BFI* became the development tool where I combined all of the talents that I had perfected from working on a number of very interesting and very successful products that were included in the Sierra On-Line catalog.

The String Draw or SD and the Draw ICON or DI programs are large in size and it would be impractical to write these two programs as relocatable assembly language routines. SD resides at 0x6000 and DI resides at 0x6500 in memory. BFI uses the second HIRES graphics page that resides in memory at 0x4000 to 0x5FFF. Either BFI can BLOAD SD and/or DI to their operational memory address or BFI can move both of these routines from their attachment memory address to their operational memory address. I did not favor having to carry around additional routines with BFI, so attaching SD and DI to BFI and moving both of these routines to their operational memory address appealed to me. That necessitated having to develop a Memory Move or MM routine just for that purpose.

The raw version of BFI, or the version without any assembly language file attachments, is not the typical file Type that can be easily manipulated like a Text file. Access to the File Manager is absolutely necessary in order to utilize any Applesoft file as if it were a Text file and I use its three byte NULL ending as simply a file location that has a byte offset. Therefore, I created the small relocatable assembly language routine Append File or AF that performs the Binary file attachment to any Applesoft program. Another useful relocatable assembly language routine is Catalog Read or CR that reads the diskette catalog. Catalog Read reads a list of catalog filenames into a character string array and reads a list of file Types, a list of the TSL track and sectors, and a list of file sizes into their respective integer number arrays. The descriptors for character string arrays and integer number arrays are well defined in Table I.15.2. Assembly language provides easy access to Applesoft variables and arrays simply by passing the Applesoft variable name or the array name in the CALL statement.

It is important for BFI to know if there will be sufficient disk space for BFI to attach all of the selected assembly language files to the selected target Applesoft program. The relocatable assembly language routine Free Space or FS calculates the free sector space of a diskette by processing the VTOC data in the default INPUT page at 0x0200. This routine and many other functions within BFI depend heavily on the relocatable assembly language routine Read/Write RWTS or RW. This routine will read or write any sector on any track of any drive in any slot using any memory page. It returns the error number that is generated by RWTS. I found that Applesoft does not have an unformatted input character command in its command repertoire. Therefore, I created a relocatable assembly language routine called Input Character or IC for that very purpose in BFI. In my discussion of the Applesoft Garbage Collector I made it quite clear that all Applesoft character string variables and character string arrays are composed of ASCII characters that have their MSB turned OFF. Therefore, the IC routine is designed specifically for Applesoft programs in that IC returns the ASCII of any keypress with its MSB turned OFF.

How I cherish my memories of that time early in owning an Apple][+ when I started looking at various algorithms that sorted character strings. I am not entirely sure why sort algorithms caught my attention, but these algorithms certainly provided a wonderful vehicle for me to learn what an algorithm was and how one can convert an algorithm into lines of code that will capitalize on the intellectual concepts employed by that algorithm. Alphabetical sorting of the filenames in a diskette catalog is certainly not a fundamental requirement of BFI, but I found it to be a rather nice feature in order to display the filenames of a diskette in alphabetical order. My relocatable assembly language routine String Sort or SS can sort the entries of an Applesoft character string array in either direction from A to Z or Z to A. The entries of the character string array are not actually moved in memory. Instead, I return an integer array whose entries are the sorted index to the character string array. Doing so prevents unnecessarily filling the Character String Pool if, indeed, the entries to the character string array are heavily swapped during the sorting process. Admittedly, the algorithm I chose to implement for sorting character strings is the classic Bubble Sort. As a general rule of thumb, when there are less than fifty character string items to sort, the Bubble Sort algorithm is a practical design choice. A thirty-five or thirty-six track diskette catalog will probably never exceed fifty filenames. Furthermore, BFI dimensions its filename, track, sector, and index arrays to fifty. In SS processing, only when two character strings do not differ in length does the algorithm start comparing the bytes of the two strings.

Hopefully, this general overview of *BFI* and its assembly language file attachments will give you some idea on how powerful a hybrid program such as *BFI* can become. *BFI* takes advantage of the numerical and character string arrays and program organization that is inherent in a high level language such as Applesoft and the processing speed of assembly language for sorting and drawing icons that include a character font on the HIRES graphics screen in the Apple][. Each routine has been specifically designed to exact the most productivity in the least amount of memory space. Certainly, the memory space of an Apple][is a significant aspect in all program designs and its proper management must be considered at all times. The speed of Applesoft can be daunting in certain applications, thus using assembly language where appropriate can definitely relieve Applesoft of many of its potential bottlenecks. I believe *BFI* demonstrates how effective the Applesoft language is when it is paired with assembly language routines in order to create a useful and powerful hybrid tool that can be used to create even more useful and more powerful hybrid tools for the Apple][computer.

3. Apple][+ Memory Upgrade

As an Electrical Engineering graduate student in the early 1980's, I wanted to utilize my Apple][+ as an opportunity to make some practical hardware modifications to its motherboard and to the circuit board of its keyboard. First and foremost I wanted to incorporate a shift key modification, add in keyboard repeat logic, and provide an *alt* key circuit to the keyboard that would set or clear specific bits in the keyboard data byte. Thus, the *alt* key would generate all of the other ASCII characters that the Apple][+ keyboard could not generate. This project naturally gave me the idea to program my own character generator EPROM that would include lowercase characters, rather similar to what Dan Paymar was selling as his *Lowercase Adaptor Interface PROM*. Then, I fixed the glitch that I noticed when I switched modes from TEXT, LOWRES, and HIRES by adding a couple of additional logic gates that added an additional timing delay to match the timing delay that was created when the display mode is switched by the Apple hardware. Sometimes a minimalistic hardware design is not always the better choice particularly when video glitches are easily seen. I reached a level of competence when I decided to remove all twenty-four 16 Kb DRAM ICs from my Apple][+ motherboard and replace them with eight 64 Kb DRAM ICs. This required cutting some foil traces, rerouting power, and building a satellite circuit board that would generate an additional DRAM row/column refresh/data address line. The satellite circuit even includes the logic that is necessary in order to model the Soft Switches that control the memory of the Language Card partition. These Soft Switches emulate the action of certain addresses that control whether ROM is active or RAM is active, and which RAM bank is active in the Language Card partition. In theory, it all worked perfectly in my head, of course. The satellite circuit I developed is shown in Figure V.3.1. I paused a very, very long moment before applying power to my modified motherboard the very first time. I was pleased, if not absolutely delighted to find that my 48 KB Apple][+ was now fully 64 KB functional as if a Language Card resides in Slot 0. There was no blue smoke that went *Puff*. Wow! Even today I marvel at how gutsy I was to implement this drastic modification to the motherboard of my beloved Apple][+.

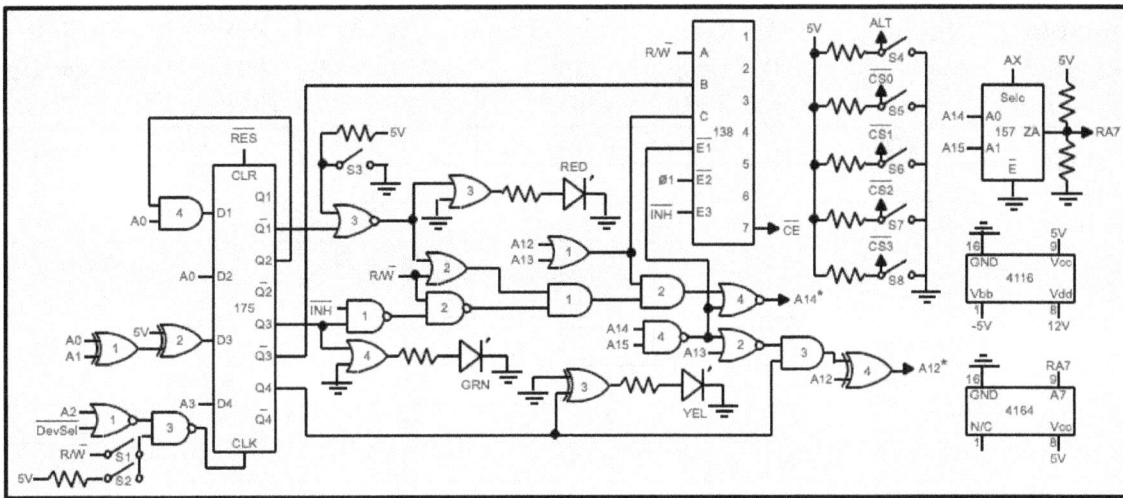

Figure V.3.1. Apple][+ Satellite Circuit Diagram

Signal	Location	Signal	Location
ø1	B1,6 (74LS175)	A12	H4,3 (8T97)
AX	C2,14 (74LS195)	A13	H5,3 (8T97)
DevSel	H2,15 (74LS138, Slot 0)	A14	J1,9 (74LS257)
INH	F3,18 (ROM-E8)	A15	J1,12 (74LS257)
RES	A7,3 (keyboard socket)	A12*	to C1,3 (74LS157)
R/W	H5,5 (8T97)	A14*	to F2,14 (74LS139)
A0	H5,11 (8T97)	RA7	to all 4164,9
A1	H4,5 (8T97)	CE	to all EPROM's CE
A2	H5,7 (8T97)	ALT	to all EPROM's A14
A3	H5,9 (8T97)	CS0-CS3	to each EPROM CS

Table V.3.1. Apple][+ Satellite Circuit Board Connections

As shown in Figure V.3.1, the satellite circuit board contains eight logic ICs, three LEDs, eight DIP switches, and a 26-pin connector for all of the signals that are shown in Table V.3.1, along with power and ground. Either DIP switch 1 or 2 must be closed, but not both. If DIP switch 1 is closed then the 74LS175 configuration register is clocked only with a read to 0xC08n, where **n** can be 0x0 to 0xF. If DIP switch 2 is closed then the configuration register is clocked with either a read or a write to 0xC08n. RAM memory in the Language Card partition is enabled if 0xC080, 0xC083, 0xC088, or 0xC08B is read, and, as a result, the green LED glows. If RAM Bank 1 is enabled by reading 0xC088 to 0xC08F, the yellow LED glows as a result. RAM is write-enabled when 0xC081, 0xC083, 0xC089, or 0xC08B is read twice, and when DIP switch 3 is closed, the red LED glows as a result. Opening DIP switch 3 will absolutely electrically write-protect RAM memory in the Language Card partition. This RAM write-protect feature is quite useful when stashing some particular code into the Language Card partition, resetting the computer to BOOT a useful DOS, and then properly managing that bit of special code all the while RAM memory is fully protected from any further changes.

Input to 74LS175 Latch	Input Address Bus	Red LED State	Grn LED State	Yel LED State	Final A12* State	RAM Enabled		ROM Read Enable	Output Address Bus RAM/ROM
						R	W		
0xC080 RAM2 WP 0b0100	<0xC000	0	1	0	A12	1	1	0	<0xC000
	0xCnnn	0	1	0	0	0	0	0	0xCnnn
	0xDnnn	0	1	0	1	1	0	0	0xDnnn
	0xEnnn	0	1	0	0	1	0	0	0xEnnn
	0xFnnn	0	1	0	1	1	0	0	0xFnnn
0xC081 ROM2 WP 0b0010	<0xC000	0	0	0	A12	1	1	0	<0xC000
	0xCnnn	0	0	0	0	0	0	0	0xCnnn
	0xDnnn	0	0	0	1	0	0	1	0xDnnn
	0xEnnn	0	0	0	0	0	0	1	0xEnnn
	0xFnnn	0	0	0	1	0	0	1	0xFnnn
0xC081 0xC081 ROM2 WE 0b0011	<0xC000	1	0	0	A12	1	1	0	<0xC000
	0xCnnn	1	0	0	0	0	0	0	0xCnnn
	0xDnnn	1	0	0	1	0	1	1	0xDnnn
	0xEnnn	1	0	0	0	0	1	1	0xEnnn
	0xFnnn	1	0	0	1	0	1	1	0xFnnn
0xC082 ROM2 WP 0b0000	<0xC000	0	0	0	A12	1	1	0	<0xC000
	0xCnnn	0	0	0	0	0	0	0	0xCnnn
	0xDnnn	0	0	0	1	0	0	1	0xDnnn
	0xEnnn	0	0	0	0	0	0	1	0xEnnn
	0xFnnn	0	0	0	1	0	0	1	0xFnnn
0xC083 RAM2 WP 0b0110	<0xC000	0	1	0	A12	1	1	0	<0xC000
	0xCnnn	0	1	0	0	0	0	0	0xCnnn
	0xDnnn	0	1	0	1	1	0	0	0xDnnn
	0xEnnn	0	1	0	0	1	0	0	0xEnnn
	0xFnnn	0	1	0	1	1	0	0	0xFnnn
0xC083 0xC083 RAM2 WE 0b0111	<0xC000	1	1	0	A12	1	1	0	<0xC000
	0xCnnn	1	1	0	0	0	0	0	0xCnnn
	0xDnnn	1	1	0	1	1	1	0	0xDnnn
	0xEnnn	1	1	0	0	1	1	0	0xEnnn
	0xFnnn	1	1	0	1	1	1	0	0xFnnn
0b0001	This configuration is not possible to select, so it is not valid.								
0b0101	This configuration is not possible to select, so it is not valid.								

Table V.3.2. Apple][+ Satellite Circuit Board Operation, Part 1

Table V.3.1 lists all of the signals that I required and the location on the Apple][+ motherboard where I obtained that signal. In order to provide two banks of RAM memory in the Language Card partition for the 0xD000 to 0xDFFF address range, address lines A12* and A14* must be derived from the outputs of the 74LS175 configuration register on the satellite circuit board, and from the real A12, A13, A14, and A15 address lines. The A14 and A15 address line are from a 74LS257 at motherboard location J1, and they also support memory data access and memory data refresh. The two derived address lines A12* and A14* are connected directly to the pins of C1,3 and F2,14, respectively. Memory refresh for the 4164 64 Kb DRAM ICs is accomplished using the current RA0 through RA6 refresh signals on the motherboard without regard to the derived RA7 signal. The RA7 signal simply provides the eighth row and eighth column address in order to access the full 64 Kb of each DRAM IC.

Input to 74LS175 Latch	Input Address Bus	Red LED State	Grn LED State	Yel LED State	Final A12* State	RAM Enabled R	RAM Enabled W	ROM Read Enable	Output Address Bus RAM/ROM
0xC088 RAM1 WP 0b1100	<0xC000	0	1	1	A12	1	1	0	<0xC000
	0xCnnn	0	1	1	1	0	0	0	0xDnnn
	0xDnnn	0	1	1	0	1	0	0	0xCnnn
	0xEnnn	0	1	1	0	1	0	0	0xEnnn
	0xFnnn	0	1	1	1	1	0	0	0xFnnn
0xC089 ROM1 WP 0b1010	<0xC000	0	0	1	A12	1	1	0	<0xC000
	0xCnnn	0	0	1	1	0	0	0	0xDnnn
	0xDnnn	0	0	1	0	0	0	1	0xCnnn
	0xEnnn	0	0	1	0	0	0	1	0xEnnn
	0xFnnn	0	0	1	1	0	0	1	0xFnnn
0xC089 0xC089 ROM1 WE 0b1011	<0xC000	1	0	1	A12	1	1	0	<0xC000
	0xCnnn	1	0	1	1	0	0	0	0xDnnn
	0xDnnn	1	0	1	0	0	1	1	0xCnnn
	0xEnnn	1	0	1	0	0	1	1	0xEnnn
	0xFnnn	1	0	1	1	0	1	1	0xFnnn
0xC08A ROM1 WP 0b1000	<0xC000	0	0	1	A12	1	1	0	<0xC000
	0xCnnn	0	0	1	1	0	0	0	0xDnnn
	0xDnnn	0	0	1	0	0	0	1	0xCnnn
	0xEnnn	0	0	1	0	0	0	1	0xEnnn
	0xFnnn	0	0	1	1	0	0	1	0xFnnn
0xC08B RAM1 WP 0b1110	<0xC000	0	1	1	A12	1	1	0	<0xC000
	0xCnnn	0	1	1	1	0	0	0	0xDnnn
	0xDnnn	0	1	1	0	1	0	0	0xCnnn
	0xEnnn	0	1	1	0	1	0	0	0xEnnn
	0xFnnn	0	1	1	1	1	0	0	0xFnnn
0xC08B 0xC08B RAM1 WE 0b1111	<0xC000	1	1	1	A12	1	1	0	<0xC000
	0xCnnn	1	1	1	1	0	0	0	0xDnnn
	0xDnnn	1	1	1	0	1	1	0	0xCnnn
	0xEnnn	1	1	1	0	1	1	0	0xEnnn
	0xFnnn	1	1	1	1	1	1	0	0xFnnn
0b1001	This configuration is not possible to select, so it is not valid.								
0b1101	This configuration is not possible to select, so it is not valid.								

Table V.3.3. Apple][+ Satellite Circuit Board Operation, Part 2

Tables V.3.2 and V.3.3 provide the details of the operation of the Apple][+ Satellite Circuit Board vis-á-vis the input address bus, the state of each LED, whether RAM is read-enabled or write-enabled, whether ROM is read-enabled, and the effective memory address that is generated for all other motherboard logic. A 27128 EPROM is the minimum size that can hold the ROM firmware from 0xD000 to 0xFFFF, although the first 4 KB of this EPROM is never addressed. When a 27256 EPROM is used to contain two ROM firmware images, DIP switch 4 connects A14 to pin 27 and it can be used to select the desired image. If DIP switch 4 is closed, the lower image is selected. DIP switches 5, 6, 7, and 8 select one of four possible EPROMs that reside on the Apple][+ motherboard. I removed all six 24-pin ROM sockets and installed four 28-pin EPROM sockets ensuring that pins 1, 2, 27, and 28 were electrically isolated from the motherboard. Only one of these four DIP switches should be closed, otherwise multiple EPROMs would be enabled simultaneously. Honestly, I ended up preparing and programming only a single 27256 EPROM that contains two ROM images. Providing access to three more similar EPROMs never became necessary and the design was slightly over-kill. I should have placed a single 28-pin EPROM socket on the Satellite Circuit Board and left the six 24-pin ROM sockets on the Apple][+ motherboard alone. I initially thought it was better to have too much than too little EPROM expansion capabilities!

4. Apple][+ Keyboard Modification

After I started programming on my new Apple][+ computer, my coworker Randy at Rockwell let me borrow a few of his computer magazines. I wanted to read all about the latest enhancements that were available for my computer. The Dan Paymar *Lowercase Adaptor Interface PROM* fascinated me and that adaptor was instrumental in encouraging me to invest in an EPROM programmer so that I could design my own lowercase character set. I was also very interested in adding some additional hardware logic to the piggy-back circuit board of my Apple][+ keyboard. One possible addition to this circuit board is to provide a CapLock function, and I thought that adding a tiny LED to the inside of the cap that sits over the SHIFT key would be totally awesome in order to visually show the state of the SHIFT key. I also wanted to add a pushbutton to the left of the left SHIFT key. That small pushbutton would set or clear a specific bit in the keyboard data byte in order to generate all of the other ASCII characters that the Apple][+ keyboard could not generate.

When I started to design the keyboard modification circuit, I had just accepted employment in the Digital Simulation Laboratory at Hughes Aircraft, and I had access to virtually any data book available. Also, I was not hesitant at all in opening up my Apple][+ and doing some initial testing on the piggy-back circuit board of the keyboard and connecting that circuit board to a few logic integrated circuits from my growing toolbox. I had a Heathkit oscilloscope so I could actually view some of the signals on this circuit board. *The Apple][Circuit Description* by Winston D. Gayler helped me to understand the function of S2 and a 6-pad connector on the piggy-back circuit board that contains two electrical bowties that must be cut in order to modify bits 4 and 5 of the keyboard data byte. If I recall correctly, my keyboard logic testing was more trial and error rather than from experience when I began designing the keyboard modification circuit that is shown in Figure V.4.1.

The 74LS153 dual 1-of-4 data selector device is the perfect integrated circuit that can be used in order to generate all of the ASCII characters that are unavailable on the Apple][+ keyboard. The truth table for the 74LS153 data selector device is shown in Table V.4.1. Select Input A is controlled by the Pushbutton switch I placed to the left of the left SHIFT key and Select Input B is controlled by the state of the CapLock flip-flop that is shown in Figure V.4.1. Both of these signals are enabled by a Double-Pole Double-Throw, or DPDT switch that I added to my keyboard modification circuit. The 74LS153 along with S2 and the 6-pad connector pass bit 5 of the generated keyboard data byte back into the keyboard logic in order to derive the lowercase characters. On the other hand, bit 4 must be inverted in order to derive the ASCII characters that *are not* available on the Apple][+ keyboard from those characters that *are* available on the Apple][+ keyboard.

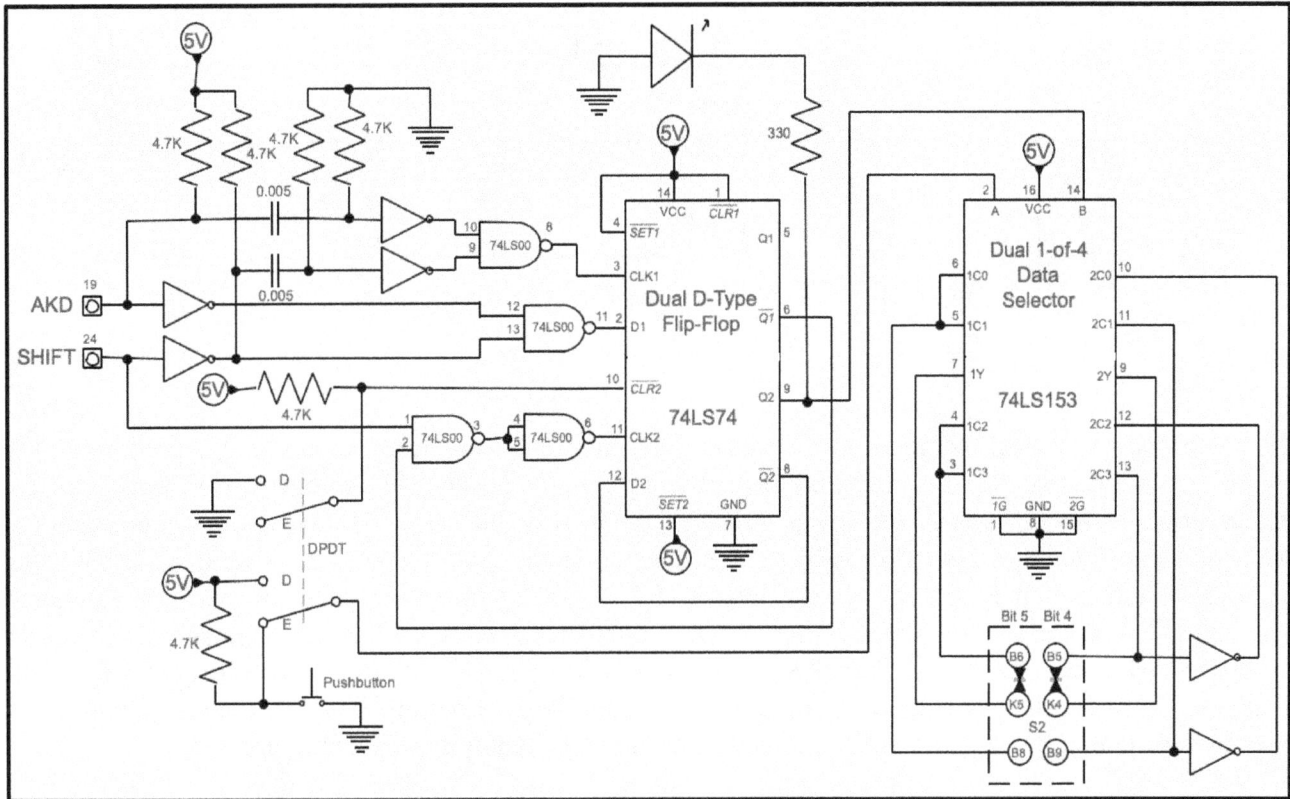

Figure V.4.1. Apple][+ Keyboard Modification Circuit

Select Input		Data Inputs				Strobe	Output
B	A	C0	C1	C2	C3	G	Y
X	X	X	X	X	X	H	L
L	L	L	X	X	X	L	L
L	L	H	X	X	X	L	H
L	H	X	L	X	X	L	L
L	H	X	H	X	X	L	H
H	L	X	X	L	X	L	L
H	L	X	X	H	X	L	H
H	H	X	X	X	L	L	L
H	H	X	X	X	H	L	H

Table V.4.1. 74LS153 Truth Table

251

Push Button	SHIFT Key	CTRL Key	Input Character	Input ASCII	Output ASCII	Output Character
ON	ON	ON	L	0x0C	0x1C	fs
ON	ON	ON	O	0x0F	0x1F	us
ON	ON	OFF	K	0x4B	0x5B	[
ON	ON	OFF	L	0x4C	0x5C	\
ON	ON	OFF	M	0x4D	0x5D	]
ON	ON	OFF	O	0x4F	0x5F	_
ON	OFF	OFF	k	0x6B	0x7B	{
ON	OFF	OFF	l	0x6C	0x7C	|
ON	OFF	OFF	m	0x6D	0x7D	}
ON	OFF	OFF	n	0x6E	0x7E	~
ON	OFF	OFF	o	0x6F	0x7F	rub
ON	OFF	OFF	p	0x70	0x60	`

Table V.4.2. Generation of Unavailable Characters

Bit 5 is properly handled by means of S2 connectivity in order to create lowercase and uppercase ASCII characters. Of course, this assumes that the character generator EPROM contains the bit images or the pixels for the characters that are normally found in the 0x60 to 0x7F ASCII range and not for a repeat of the characters found in the 0x40 to 0x5F ASCII range. The inversion of bit 4 is accomplished by using the Pushbutton switch to the left of the left SHIFT key in combination with an available keyboard character. This is very much like deriving a control character using the CTRL key with another available keyboard character. Table V.4.2 shows how to derive the unavailable keyboard characters from the available keyboard characters by using the SHIFT key and the Pushbutton. The Pushbutton is a normally open switch so that it does not modify normal keyboard logic when it is not being pressed.

The piggy-back circuit board contains a 555 timer circuit for the REPEAT key that is connected to a signal called Any Key Down or AKD. The REPEAT key in combination with any keyboard key generates multiple instances of that pressed key. My keyboard modification circuit uses the AKD signal along with an inverted SHIFT key signal in order to provide automatic toggling of CapLock when the SHIFT key is held a bit longer than during normal typing. This is accomplished by generating a digital pulse using a half-monostable circuit made up of a capacitor, a resister, and an inverter for both of these signals. When CapLock is ON, an LED that is mounted in left SHIFT key cap glows. The DPDT switch disables CapLock simply by pulling the CLR input of the CapLock flip-flop to ground in order to force its output low. The DPDT switch disables the Pushbutton by connecting Select Input A to Vcc.

There is sufficient room to mount the keyboard modification circuit board to the left side of the piggy-back circuit board which in turn is connected to the keyboard using a 40-pin dual incline connector. I use a short length of 10-connector ribbon cable between the keyboard modification circuit board and the piggy-back circuit board. The ten signals include Vcc, ground, SHIFT, AKD, and the 6-pad connector. Also, the LED and the Pushbutton each require two leads to the keyboard modification circuit board and the DPDT slide switch is mounted directly onto the keyboard modification circuit board. I have no idea why anyone would choose to disable the CapLock function or disable the ability to generate those additional ASCII characters that are unavailable on the Apple][+ keyboard. Regardless, the keyboard modification circuitry can be selectively disabled D or enabled E if and when it is desired.

5. Real Time Clock Card

The experience I gained in building the memory upgrade for my Apple][+ that is described previously in Section V.3 encouraged me to design and build my own *Real Time Clock* peripheral interface card. I had to learn some new skills in order to build a peripheral interface card that would fit within the dimensions that are allowed for such a card in the Apple][+ computer. I had never etched a double-sided copper clad board that large nor had I thought about how to place TTL components in terms of organization, data and control signal flow, wire length, and clean power. I also had to include and manage additional circuitry to charge the onboard rechargeable batteries. All of these ideas mattered one way or another I am sure, but honestly, I didn't have much of a clue. In hindsight I should have taken a class in TTL circuit board design and layout before I was graduated with my degree in Electrical Engineering. My garage was my ultimate laboratory and workshop! But most importantly I wanted the hardware design of my *Real Time Clock* card to provide a simple, elegant, and thoroughly *elementary* hardware interface to the onboard firmware that communicates with external software routines.

I wanted to design my *Real Time Clock* card around the SaRonix RTC58321 Real Time Clock module, which I probably obtained from Jameco Electronics in the mid 1980's. The pinout of the RTC58321 is shown in Table V.5.1 and this clock module incorporates an internal quartz crystal in a single 16-pin DIP package thereby eliminating the need for an external crystal and timing circuit. This clock module provided me with everything I needed in order to read and to write the date and the time values, and the module provided an external *BUSY* signal. I wanted the firmware interface to be as simple as possible so I designed the hardware logic of my clock card so that the hardware would negotiate the setup time for the data and the address requirements of the RTC58321. Unfortunately, the 6502-clock read/write period happens to be far too short for the data and the address setup time that the RTC58321 requires.

Pin	Name	Function
1	CS2	IC select #2, active high, low to disable
2	WRITE	write port, active high to write data, 2.0 μsec minimum
3	READ	read port, active high to read data, 1.0 μsec minimum
4	D3	read and write data bit 3
5	D2	read and write data bit 2
6	D1	read and write data bit 1
7	D0	read and write data bit 0
8	Vss	ground connection
9	ADRWRT	address write port, active high to latch address, hold time 0.1 μsec, pulse time 0.5 μsec
10	*BUSY*	active low, wait until high to continue
11	STOP	stop enable port, active high, low to run
12	TEST	test enable port, active high, low to test
13	CS1	IC select #1, active high, low to disable
14	NC	no connection
15	NC	no connection
16	Vdd	+5 volt connection

Table V.5.1. SaRonix RTC58321 Real Time Clock Pinout

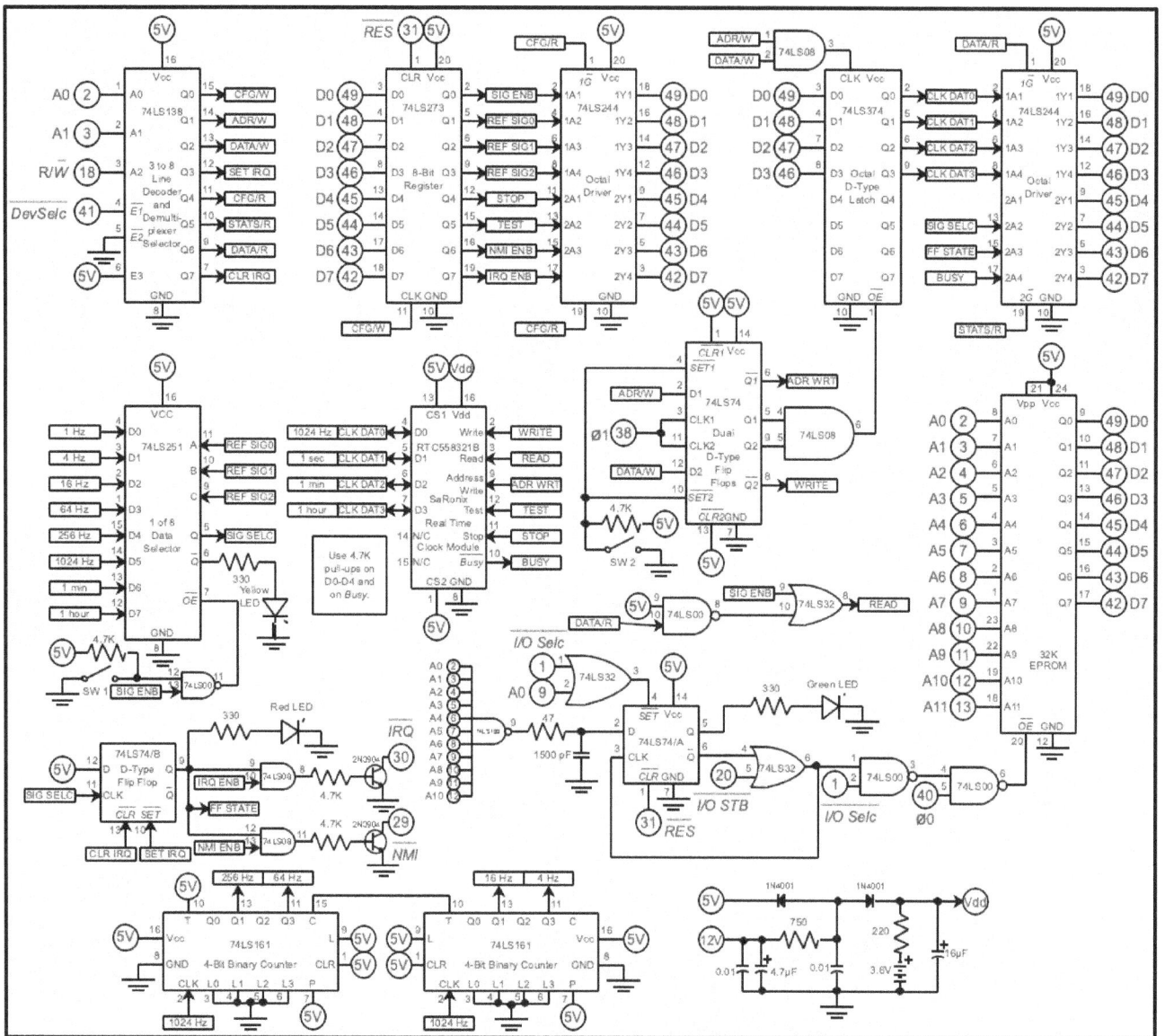

Figure V.5.1. Real Time Clock Circuit Diagram

I used a breadboard to connect the initial TTL logic components in order to figure out how to best negotiate with the RTC58321 using a full 6502-clock period and increasing the time of that clock period by utilizing a flip-flop. Then I wrote the slot interface firmware for the onboard 2732 EPROM. I modeled my general user Applesoft interface after the Applied Engineering TimeMaster II Applesoft interface. Whatever commands the TimeMaster could manage, I made sure my clock card could manage as well, including all of the other commands and capabilities that I could devise and process in the available EPROM memory. And I figured out how to make use of the standard signals that are generated by the RTC58321 that can be used to pull the IRQ line and/or the NMI line low in order to initiate a hardware interrupt. Once I had the schematic diagram drawn and the components nicely organized, I drilled all of the necessary holes for the IC sockets and the components, and I etched the copper clad for the power, ground, and a few of the basic logic lines. I hand-wired and soldered the remaining connections to the slot finger of the interface board, IC sockets, transistors, batteries, LEDs, configuration block, resistors, and capacitors. *Whew*! My *Real Time Clock* card is fully operational today even as it was over thirty-six years ago. I've only had to replace the rechargeable batteries a couple of times! Figure V.5.1 shows the complete schematic diagram for my *Real Time Clock* card that I had originally drawn and dated 1988 March 20.

Only four of the sixteen peripheral-card I/O memory locations are used for clock configuration, clock address, clock status, clock register, clock data, interrupt clear, and interrupt set. Table V.5.2 shows the description of those memory locations where **s** is equal to the slot number where the *Real Time Clock* card resides plus eight. Only memory address bits A0 and A1 are captured so it does not matter what is used for memory address bits A2 and A3. Addresses 0xC0s4, 0xC0s8, and 0xC0sC are all valid for address 0xC0s0 in order to read and write the *Real Time Clock* configuration register. Table V.5.3 shows the description of the configuration register bits. This register retains its configuration until it is changed by another write to 0xC0s0 or when RESET is pressed. When RESET is pressed this register is cleared to zero. Before loading the clock data registers it is important to stop the clock by setting the STOP Enable bit to one. Once the clock is loaded with its data, the configuration register can be restored with its previous configuration data. Table V.5.4 shows the description of the eight interrupt rates that are available for the generation of IRQ interrupts and/or NMI interrupts. The selected interrupt rate is made active by setting the Interrupt Enable bit to one as shown in Table V.5.3. For interrupts to be generated either the NMI Enable bit and/or the IRQ Enable bit must be set to one. The configuration register also provides control of the TEST enable port of the RTC58321. Unfortunately, I am no longer able to locate any documentation that describes how to test the RTC58321 using the TEST enable port.

Address	Operation	Description
0xC0s0	read	Read configuration register
0xC0s0	write	Write configuration register
0xC0s1	read	Read clock status register
0xC0s1	write	Write clock register address
0xC0s2	read	Read clock data register
0xC0s2	write	Write clock data register
0xC0s3	read	Clear interrupt flip-flop
0xC0s3	write	Arm interrupt flip-flop

Table V.5.2. Real Time Clock Peripheral Interface Card I/O Addresses

Bit	Description
0	Interrupt enable, 0 = OFF
1	Interrupt rate select A
2	Interrupt rate select B
3	Interrupt rate select C
4	STOP enable, 0 = RUN
5	TEST enable, 0 = normal operation
6	NMI enable, 0 = OFF
7	IRQ enable, 0 = OFF

Table V.5.3. Real Time Clock Configuration Register

C	B	A	Description
0	0	0	1 Hz interrupt rate
0	0	1	4 Hz interrupt rate
0	1	0	16 Hz interrupt rate
0	1	1	64 Hz interrupt rate
1	0	0	256 Hz interrupt rate
1	0	1	1024 Hz interrupt rate
1	1	0	1 minute interrupt rate
1	1	1	1 hour interrupt rate

Table V.5.4. Interrupt Rate Selection

Reg	A3	A2	A1	A0	Name	D3	D2	D1	D0	Count	Notes
00	0	0	0	0	S1	s8	s4	s2	s1	0 to 9	1-second digit
01	0	0	0	1	S10	-	s40	s20	s10	0 to 5	10-second digit
02	0	0	1	0	MI1	mi8	mi4	mi2	mi1	0 to 9	1-minute digit
03	0	0	1	1	MI10	-	mi40	mi20	mi10	0 to 5	10-minute digit
04	0	1	0	0	H1	h8	h4	h2	h1	0 to 9	1-hour digit
05	0	1	0	1	H10	24/12	PM/AM	h20	h10	0 to 2 0 to 1	10-hour digit
06	0	1	1	0	W	-	w4	w2	w1	0 to 6	week digit
07	0	1	1	1	D1	d8	d4	d2	d1	0 to 9	1-day digit
08	1	0	0	0	D10	leap year		d20	d10	0 to 3	10-day digit
09	1	0	0	1	MO01	mo8	mo4	mo2	mo1	0 to 9	1-month digit
0A	1	0	1	0	MO010	-	-	-	mo10	0 to 1	10-month digit
0B	1	0	1	1	Y1	y8	y4	y2	y1	0 to 9	1-year digit
0C	1	1	0	0	Y10	y80	y40	y20	y10	0 to 9	10-year digit
0D	1	1	0	1	Reset	-	-	-	-		reset register
0E	1	1	1	0	Idle	1	1	1	1024		standard signal register
0F	1	1	1	1	Idle	hour	min.	sec.	Hz		

Table V.5.5. Real Time Clock Registers

Table V.5.5 lists the sixteen registers that are available in the RTC58321. Any time when an 0x0E or an 0x0F register number is latched, the clock module is put into its Idle state and the standard clock signals that are shown in Table V.5.5 are available at its data port when the READ port of the RTC58321 is set to one. Setting the READ port of the RTC58321 to one is accomplished by setting the Interrupt Enable bit or Bit 0 in the configuration register to one as shown in Table V.5.3. The 1024 Hz signal at data bit D0 of the RTC58321 is divided by two 74LS161 binary counters in order to obtain the rest of the interrupt rates that are shown in Table V.5.4 which can be selected by the configuration register. Even though the *Real Time Clock* card can also generate an NMI interrupt, the firmware in the EPROM only has provisions to manage an IRQ interrupt. Nevertheless, the user can easily provide the necessary software in order to utilize an NMI interrupt if there is an occasion for such an interrupt to be generated.

Setting data bit D3 in register 0x05 of the RTC58321 to one selects 24-hour mode. Setting data bit D3 clears data bit D2 to zero in the same register. If 12-hour mode is selected by clearing data bit D3 to zero, then data bit D2 selects PM if data bit D2 is set to one or AM if data bit D2 is cleared to zero. The RTC58321 divides the 10-year digit Y10 in register 0x0C by 4 in order to determine leap year. The remainder of this division is saved to data bits D2 and D3 of register 0x08. If the remainder is zero then leap year is selected. The RTC58321 may be reset by latching register 0x0D and writing any data to that register. This sets the WRITE port of the RTC58321 to one as shown in Table V.5.1. The firmware in the EPROM has no reason to ever RESET the RTC58321.

The *Real Time Clock* card utilizes two switches to control its function. Closing Switch 1 disables the frequency data selector module and blocks the output of the selected interrupt rate. Therefore, the clock card cannot generate an interrupt even if the NMI enable bit or the IRQ enable bit is set to one in the configuration register. Closing Switch 2 disables the Address Write and Data Write flip-flops. Therefore, the data in the clock module cannot be changed, thus rendering the RTC58321 write-protected. The clock card utilizes three LEDs to indicate what function the clock card is performing at that moment. The Green LED glows whenever the 2732 EPROM is accessed. The Yellow LED glows at the same frequency as the selected interrupt rate if the frequency data selector module is enabled by the Interrupt Enable bit in the configuration register only if Switch 1 is open. The Red LED glows whenever the output of the Interrupt Flip-Flop is set to one, or armed, regardless whether the NMI enable bit or the IRQ enable bit is set to one in the configuration register. If either bit is set to one, the base of a 2N3904 general purpose transistor is pulled high thereby allowing its collector-emitter junction to conduct and pull the respective interrupt line safely to ground. I placed an R/C network between the output of the 74LS133 and the data input to the EPROM enable flip-flop in order to slightly extend the derived CLRROM signal because of the slight delay that is inherent in the clock pulse to that flip-flop.

The first half of the 2732 EPROM is used for eight copies of the same interface firmware for the peripheral-card ROM memory, one copy for each possible slot in which the Clock card could reside. The second half of the EPROM maps into the peripheral-card expansion ROM memory. Whenever the 6502-microprocessor fetches an instruction only in the first half of the peripheral-card ROM memory, 0xCs00 to 0xCs7F, where **s** is the slot number where the Clock card resides, the peripheral-card expansion ROM memory, 0xC800 to 0xCFFF, is enabled. The peripheral-card expansion ROM memory is **not** re-enabled when CLRROM is used in the second half of the peripheral-card ROM memory, a hardware design trick I learned from the hardware design of the RAM Disk 320 peripheral interface card. Table V.5.6 shows all of the entry points in the firmware in the EPROM for the *Real Time Clock* card. This firmware conforms to the clock card protocol where the first two instructions are PHP and SEI, and the last byte, the clock ID byte, is set to 0x03. The Clock ID byte can also be set to 0x07. DOS 4.5 accepts either the 0x03 or the 0x07 value as a valid Clock ID byte.

The program *Set Clock* utilizes some of the special features that I designed into the *Real Time Clock* card firmware. Its primary purpose is to set the clock card with the current date and time, of course. The program also displays the current date and time that is stored in the clock registers, and those values may be automatically selected or new values may be entered for each of the data registers. The surprising feature of this program is that it utilizes an interrupt handler. The clock card is configured to generate an IRQ interrupt every second. Every time an interrupt occurs, its handler reads the clock registers and displays the date and time data. Once the desired date and time data is selected, that data can be written to the clock registers. The handler continues to display the current date and time data that is contained in the clock registers while the *Real Time Clock* continues to update its internal registers. Before *Set Clock* exits, it restores the data that it originally found at MASKIRQ, or 0x3FE as shown in Table I.9.3 and sets the clock card configuration register as shown in Table V.5.3 to zero.

Offset	Name	Description
0x00	MAINSELC	PHP instruction, DOS PR# and DOS IN# handlers
0x01		SEI instruction
0x02	INITSELC	Issues CLRROM, branches to INITCLK
0x08	WRITSELC	Issues CLRROM, branches to LOADCLK
0x10	READSELC	Issues CLRROM, branches to READCLK
0x18	MODESELC	Issues CLRROM, branches to SETMODE
0x20	IRQSELC	Issues CLRROM, branches to SETIRQ
0x28	STRTSELC	Issues CLRROM, branches to STRTCLK
0x30	STOPSELC	Issues CLRROM, branches to STOPCLK
0x38	INITCLK	Saves registers, branches to HNDLINIT
0x3F	LOADCLK	Saves registers, branches to HNDLLOAD
0x46	READCLK	Saves registers, branches to HNDLREAD
0x4D	SETMODE	Saves registers, branches to HNDLMODE
0x54	SETIRQ	Saves registers, branches to HNDLIRQ
0x5B	STRTCLK	Saves registers, branches to HNDLSTRT
0x62	STOPCLK	Saves registers, branches to HNDLSTOP
0x69	WRITCLK	Issues CLRROM, branches to HNDLWRIT
0x71	SETRTN	Issues CLRROM, branches to HNDLRTN
0x79	IRQHNDLR	Issues CLRROM, branches to EXECIRQ
0x80	EXIT	Restores registers, issues CLRROM, returns to caller
0x8A	HNDLINIT	Gets slot, processes input command
0x93	HNDLLOAD	Gets slot, writes clock buffer at 0x2F0-0x2FC to clock
0x9C	HNDLREAD	Gets slot, reads clock to clock buffer at 0x2F0-0x2FC
0xA5	HNDLMODE	Gets slot, stores mode value 0x21-0x3E to MODE, 0x478
0xAE	HNDLIRQ	Gets slot, sets IRQ 0-7, clears IRQBUF, 0x2FD-0x2FF
0xB7	HNDLSTRT	Gets slot, updates clock config, puts SETRTN address in KSWL
0xC0	HNDLSTOP	Gets slot, stops clock, puts SETRTN address in KSWL
0xC9	HNDLWRIT	Saves registers, gets slot, stop CLK, write CLK register, start CLK
0xD7	HNDLRTN	Saves registers, gets slot, puts "RTN" at 0x200-0x201
0xE5	EXECIRQ	Saves registers, gets slot, updates IRQBUF at 0x2FD-0x2FF, restores registers, issues CLRROM, returns with RTI instruction
0xFA	VERSION	upper ASCII "45"
0xFC	CLKNAME	upper ASCII "RTC"
0xFF	CLKID	0x03

Table V.5.6. Clock Firmware Entry Points

The *Set Clock* program first issues the SEI instruction to the 6502-microprocessor in order to inhibit all further interrupts. *Set Clock* copies the address that is found at MASKIRQ to a safe location and then sets MASKIRQ as shown in Table I.9.3 to the address of the interrupt handler that is part of *Set Clock*. *Set Clock* then sets the clock card configuration register to 0b10000001 in order to enable interrupts and to specifically enable the IRQ interrupt. See Section IV.1.17 for a thorough discussion on using MASKIRQ. Once the initialization routine issues the CLI instruction to the 6502-microprocessor, the interrupt handler in *Set Clock* is now able to field all incoming IRQ interrupts while the user is setting the data registers in the RTC58321 with various values for the current date and time. When the interrupt handler is invoked, it first issues the CLD instruction to the 6502-microprocessor, it pushes the X- and Y-registers onto the stack, it clears the IRQ interrupt by reading the appropriate peripheral-card I/O memory location, it reads the *Real Time Clock* card date and time registers, it displays the date and time data that the handler just obtained, it restores the X- and Y-registers from the stack, it restores the A-register from the page-zero location 0x45, and it issues the RTI instruction to the 6502-microprocessor. It is amazing to me how simple it is to utilize interrupts in this assembly language routine. Of course, the well-thought-out hardware design and the well-thought-out firmware design of the *Real Time Clock* card helps to make the utilization of interrupts on the Apple][computer so easy and so much fun!

6. Disk Window Program

I have no doubt that Don Worth and Pieter Lechner inspired thousands of computer hobbyists like me with their Example Programs that are found in their book *Beneath Apple DOS*, for these authors certainly inspired me. The learning curve was a bit steep as I recall, diskettes were expensive at that time, and I had some preconceived underlying fears that I could possibly destroy something precious, be it hardware or software, if I casually started to tinker around with RWTS back in 1981. Patience was certainly a virtue, and when one is examining the sectors and tracks of a diskette, it was like peering through some sort of digital microscope. The idea of reading a specific sector on a diskette and being able to display that sector content was awe-inspiring. Furthermore, having a utility that could edit those sector bytes and write those edits back to that same sector, or to any other sector for that matter, was totally mind blowing. *What can of worms would that capability open?* Worth's and Lechner's utility Zap did inspire me to design *Disk Window*, what I call my fancy Zap program. It is like having a digital window focused on any device, track, sector, or Logical Block Address or LBA of my choosing.

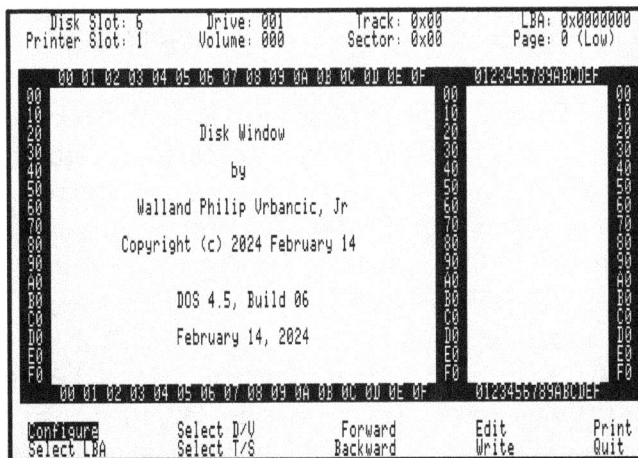

Figure V.6.1. Disk Window Startup Display

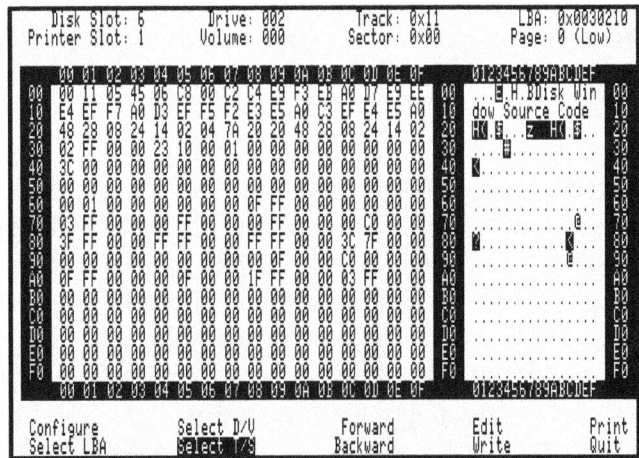

Figure V.6.2. Select T/S Mode Display

The current version of *Disk Window* now supports the reading and writing of any valid LBA sector on a CFFA card. If a CFFA card is detected and resident in the selected slot, LBA mode is utilized for reading and writing **block** data. If a Disk][interface or similar peripheral-card is detected and resident in the selected slot, track-sector mode is utilized for reading and writing **sector** data. Regardless which mode is utilized to read and write device data, the appropriate LBA for the selected volume-track-sector is displayed according to the conversion algorithm that I developed for the CFFA card. The startup screen for *Disk Window* is displayed as shown in Figure V.6.1. The four commands at the bottom of the screen are Configure, Select LBA, Select D/V, and Select T/S and they utilize the respective variables at the top of the screen. The commands Forward and Backward simply increment or decrement the Track/Sector values if in track-sector mode or LBA values if in LBA mode. The commands Edit, Write, and Print display a respective command screen for each of their functions.

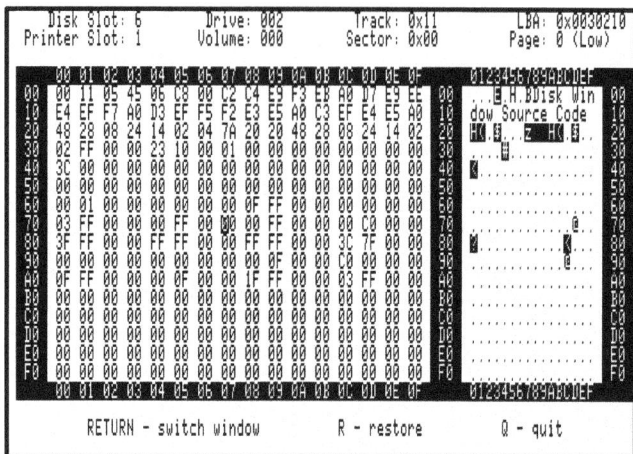

Figure V.6.3. Edit Data Display

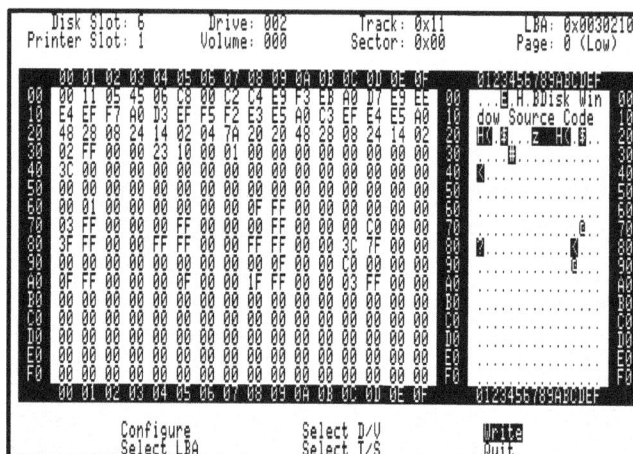

Figure V.6.4. Write Sector Data Display

Figure V.6.2 shows the display of the VTOC DATA for the diskette that is located in Drive 2 of a Disk][whose peripheral interface card resides in Slot 6. The data is displayed both in hexadecimal and in ASCII, unless the ASCII data byte is a control character. The hexadecimal values from 0x00 to 0x1F and from 0x80 to 0x9F are displayed as an ASCII PERIOD character . . Lower ASCII values from 0x20 to 0x7F are displayed in inverse text and upper ASCII values from 0xA0 to 0xFF are displayed in normal text. If Edit is selected as shown in Figure V.6.3, the same VTOC data is displayed and the cursor is initially placed on row 0x70 and in column 0x07. After all edits have been applied, the Write command can write the sector data to the selected sector or to any other sector or LBA as shown in Figure V.6.4. Note that LBA blocks are 512 bytes in size. *Page 0* refers to the first 256 bytes of an LBA block and *Page 1* refers to the second 256 bytes of an LBA block. Thus, CFFA sectors 0x00-0x0F reside on Page 0 and CFFA sectors 0x10-0x1F reside on Page 1. The 256-byte sector data may be saved to any available LBA, either on Page 0 or on Page 1 when LBA mode is enabled. Page 0 is selected by pressing the 0 or L key and Page 1 is selected by pressing the 1 or H key. The data that is shown on the display can also be printed using the Print command as shown in Figure V.6.5. The command Configure at the bottom and to the left of Figure V.6.5 allows the user to change the configuration values like Printer Slot if desired without having to return to the main menu display as shown in Figure V.6.1. If an RWTS error should occur during *Disk Window* processing, the error is prominently displayed in the center of the hexadecimal data display window as shown in Figure V.6.6. I purposefully opened the diskette door of the Disk][drive in order to cause a disk drive error before any data could be written to the diskette. According to Table I.9.4, an RWTS error having a value of 0x40 is an RWTS Drive error. The error message remains displayed until any key is pressed on the keyboard.

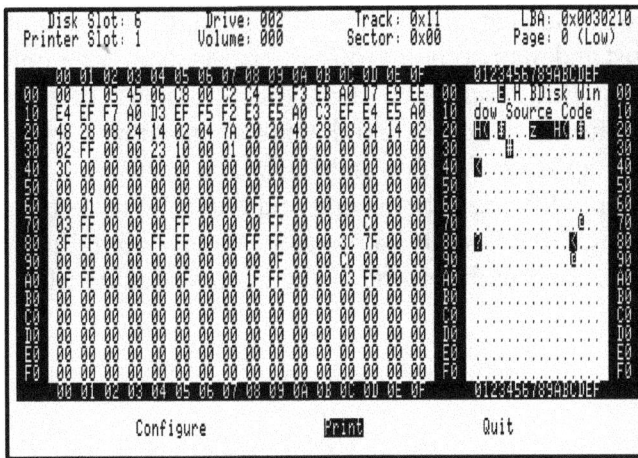

Figure V.6.5. Print Sector Data Display

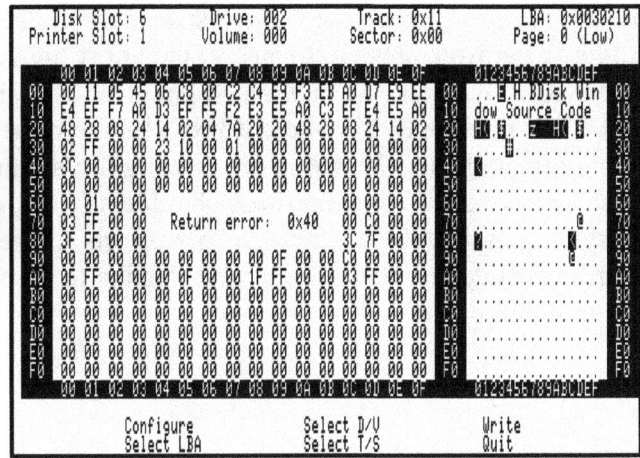

Figure V.6.6. Disk Window Error Message

I originally wrote *Disk Window* after I purchased the Videx UltraTerm video display card for my Apple][+. This video card has a number of beautiful character sets with inverse display for both upper and lower case ASCII characters. The cursor can be placed anywhere on the screen using a simple GOTO routine that I developed since the normal CH and CV page-zero locations cannot be used because their values are outside of the normal Apple][+ 40-column screen locations. I believe this video display card is well worth every penny and the firmware is very well thought out. When I began working at Sierra On-Line, I was provided with an Apple //e and, unfortunately, all of my 80-column screen handling code that I had developed for *Disk Window* did not function correctly by the Apple //e 80-column display card. The task of modifying *Disk Window* to support the Apple //e 80-column display gave me a first-hand view of how dumbed-down the Apple //e display is when it is compared to the magnificent design of the Videx UltraTerm display. As a result, I have mixed opinions as to Apple's solution in doubling the number of column characters by doubling the computer memory and using what Apple calls Auxiliary memory which is a mirror image of Main memory. I also question Apple's logic in retaining its **wide** selection of upper case display options such as *flashing* and *inverse* and a very **limited** selection of lower case display options such as only *inverse*. Would Wozniak have designed the Apple //e display differently? I wonder if his opinion was even solicited. Probably Apple Computer, Inc., knew better than to ask!

Apple did have a tremendous responsibility on the other hand when it developed its 80-column display solution so that it was simplistic and cost effective, and its new ROM routines had to provide great compatibility with all previous software that was written for the basic Apple][platform. Auxiliary memory does offer a unique solution that is easily managed by the Memory Management Unit or MMU that generates the address signals for the added CXROM and the 65C02-microprocessor, and by the Input/Output Unit or IOU that generates the complex address signals for the video display. These units, the MMU and the IOU, are not strictly independent of each other, but they work together cohesively in order to generate all of the required addressing signals that are used throughout the entire hardware design. The third integrated circuit in the Apple //e is the Programmed Array Logic device or PAL that generates all of the critical timing and control signals for the Apple //e hardware and for any peripheral interface card that is connected to the Apple //e hardware. These three integrated circuits not only serve in the formulation of the 80-column display solution, but they also serve in the management of the vast array of new Soft Switches like those shown in Figures II.2.1 and II.2.2 as well as all of the original Soft Switches. I believe Apple integrated all of the functionality that is found in the Apple //e smartly and with an eye on simplicity and cohesiveness. The Videx UltraTerm as well as the Videx VideoTerm are 80-column high fidelity peripheral interface video display cards. These display cards cannot be integrated into the overall Apple //e hardware design because of their very high cost and their complete disassociation from the Apple //e MMU, IOU, and PAL integrated circuits. My Videx UltraTerm video display card remains seated in Slot #3 of my Apple][+ where it provides the most beautiful, flexible, and dynamic high fidelity video display imaginable. *Disk Window* is certainly a giant leap from Worth's and Lechner's utility Zap, but these authors are the giants whose shoulders I stand on in utilizing their insight and their enthusiasm for everything Apple][. I know that my efforts in creating *Disk Window* serve to genuinely compliment Worth and Lechner and to return my thanks to them for their early efforts in the history making of the Apple][computer.

7. SCRG quikLoader Card

Southern California Research Group or SCRG developed and marketed the quikLoader as well as the PROmGRAMER, and they were must-have peripheral interface cards when they first appeared in the early 1980's. Without question, data can be loaded many, many times faster from the Disk][than data can be loaded from cassette tape. But data can be loaded many, many times faster from a quikLoader EPROM than data can be loaded from the Disk][. Literally, in a fraction of a second, any version of a Disk Operating System can be loaded into memory from any quikLoader EPROM, the DOS can be initialized, and the DOS can begin its Apple Command Line processing almost immediately. I attended a Los Angeles computer convention where I bought the quikLoader after I witnessed several demonstrations in how fast data can be loaded into the memory of an Apple Computer from various EPROMs. Essentially, the quikLoader is a very simple, though elegantly designed peripheral interface card that can hold up to eight 2716 to 27512 EPROMs. The card contains some hardware logic that maps the selected EPROM into the 0xC100 to 0xFFFF memory address space according to the quikLoader Reference Manual that is written by Jim Sather and dated on 12/12/83. Regardless what this manual states, Table V.7.1 shows what I observed when I enabled the quikLoader in slot 4, configured it for EPROM 0 and Bank 0 access. I did not observe EPROM data in the 0xC100 to 0xC7FF address range except for the data from slot 4, and I observed a duplication of EPROM data in the 0xD000 to 0xDFFF from the 0xF000 to 0xFFFF address range when I captured data from the quikLoader.

Address	quikLoader Data	EOS Data
0xC100-0xC1FF	No EPROM data, Super Serial Card data	No EPROM data, Super Serial Card data
0xC200-0xC2FF	No EPROM data, Clock Card data	No EPROM data, Clock Card data
0xC300-0xC3FF	No EPROM data, CXROM slot 3	No EPROM data, CXROM slot 3
0xC400-0xC4FF	Yes, EPROM offset 0x0400-0x04FF	Yes, slot 4 EPROM ASEOS interface
0xC500-0xC5FF	No EPROM data, CFFA Card data	No EPROM data, CFFA Card data
0xC600-0xC6FF	No EPROM data, Disk][Card data	No EPROM data, Disk][Card data
0xC700-0xC7FF	No EPROM data, RAM Disk Card data	No, RAM Disk Card data
0xC800-0xCFFF	Yes, EPROM offset 0x0800-0x0FFF	Yes, EOS code 0xE800-0xEFFF
0xD000-0xDFFF	Yes, EPROM offset 0x1000-0x1FFF	Yes, EOS code 0xF000-0xFFFF
0xE000-0xEFFF	Yes, EPROM offset 0x0000-0x0FFF	Yes, EOS code 0xE000-0xEFFF
0xF000-0xFFFF	Yes, EPROM offset 0x1000-0x1FFF	Yes, EOS code 0xF000-0xFFFF

Table V.7.1. quikLoader EPROM 0 and Bank 0 Access

Using the USR bit and address bits A0 and A1, the bank switching of the quikLoader is performed as follows:

Bank	A1	A0	USR	EPROM Offset	Memory Address
0	0	0	0	0x0000-0x1FFF	0xE000-0xFFFF
1	0	0	1	0x2000-0x3FFF	0xE000-0xFFFF
2	0	1	0	0x4000-0x5FFF	0xE000-0xFFFF
3	0	1	1	0x6000-0x7FFF	0xE000-0xFFFF
4	1	0	0	0x8000-0x9FFF	0xE000-0xFFFF
5	1	0	1	0xA000-0xBFFF	0xE000-0xFFFF
6	1	1	0	0xC000-0xDFFF	0xE000-0xFFFF
7	1	1	1	0xE000-0xFFFF	0xE000-0xFFFF

Figure V.7.1 quikLoader Schematic with Circuit Modifications

I had fortunately acquired the *improved* quikLoader, model #10030 that is capable of addressing a 27512 EPROM. A 74LS74 dual D flip-flop was added to the original circuit in order to capture the state of the 6502 A1 address line when writing to the 74LS174 control register of the quikLoader, and to ever so slightly delay the 6502 ϕ3 clock edge for latching EPROM data. The control register data byte can be written to any of the sixteen I/O memory locations that are dedicated to any slot from 0xC0n0 through 0xC0nF where n is equal to the slot number where the quikLoader resides plus eight. However, only the first four address locations or their relatives do anything different since the control register only latches the state of address line A0 while the added 74LS74 latches the state of address line A1. The state of address lines A2 and A3 are not latched, so therefore their values cannot be utilized. Data lines D0, D1, and D2 are latched by the control register and they enable one of eight EPROM sockets that reside on the quikLoader. Data line D3 is latched for the USR bit and data line D4 is latched to turn the quikLoader hardware ON or OFF. If data line D4 is zero, the quikLoader is turned ON and its EPROM capabilities are enabled. The state of data lines D5, D6, and D7 are not latched and are not utilized.

The control and management software that SCRG provided with the quikLoader resides in the first EPROM or EPROM 0, and this EPROM has sufficient room for a few additional programs as well. The SCRG documentation explains how to organize the contents of all of the programs and the utilities that may reside in any other EPROM and how to build a Catalog for those EPROM contents. Once an EPROM is programmed with its software contents and its Catalog, and seated in one of the quikLoader EPROM sockets, a selected *Primary* program is loaded into computer memory when the user presses and holds its EPROM number followed by pressing the RESET key. Alternatively, the EPROM Catalog is displayed when the letter Q is pressed followed by pressing the RESET key. I prepared several quikLoader EPROMs using the SCRG software interface, but I found this process to be tedious and cumbersome, and I thought I might be able to design a far better software interface. Once I sourced the SCRG EPROM control code, I realized, perhaps, that their software interface could have been better thought out. But I discovered that there was absolutely no way to programmatically access any of the quikLoader EPROM contents using the *current SCRG hardware* unless I included a substantial portion of their EPROM control code routines within my software. Unfortunately, the EPROM control code routines are not actually published, so that made accessing the quikLoader contents even more tenuous.

Peripheral interface cards for the Apple][computer typically incorporate and utilize firmware code in its peripheral-card ROM memory from 0xCs00 to 0xCsFF where s is the slot number where the peripheral interface card resides. Also, when the appropriate hardware logic is included, a peripheral interface card can use its peripheral-card expansion ROM memory from 0xC800 to 0xCFFF for additional firmware code when the interface card is enabled. As an aside, if 0xCFFF or CLRROM is put onto the address bus, a peripheral interface card is **required** to disable its peripheral-card expansion ROM memory. This allows another peripheral interface card, enabled by accessing its peripheral-card ROM memory, to utilize its peripheral-card expansion ROM memory. This protocol prevents data contention when addressing multiple peripheral interface cards. Unless the quikLoader is turned ON, the quikLoader hardware did not have the ability to display any of its EPROM contents while addressing its peripheral-card ROM memory. This inability is simply a hardware design *choice*, but I viewed it as a hardware design and a hardware logic *deficiency*.

I did find one unused 74LS08 AND gate on the quikLoader. That single AND gate allowed me to modify the quikLoader hardware logic such that it is now possible to access its peripheral-card ROM memory that is mapped to a single page of quikLoader EPROM data in each of its eight data banks. Now I had an additional hardware capability I could work with, and this simple hardware logic modification allowed me to develop the EPROM Operating System or *EOS* that is presented next in Section V.8. In addition to this simple hardware logic modification, I added an LED to glow whenever the quikLoader is enabled and an SPDT switch to physically disable the quikLoader hardware without having to actually remove the quikLoader from the computer. The complete circuit diagram of my modified quikLoader that includes the settings for data bank selection is shown in Figure V.7.1.

Referring to the settings for data bank selection that are shown in Figure V.7.1, I would replace address line A1 with address line A2, address line A0 with address line A1, and the USR bit that is latched from data line D3 with address line A0. With this configuration, an EPROM would still be selected using data lines D0, D1, and D2 that are captured from the control register data byte and the quikLoader would still be enabled or disabled using data line D4 that is also captured from the control register data byte. All other bits in the control register data byte, or D3, D5, D6, and D7, serve no purpose in the quikLoader. Perhaps I might even consider replacing data line D4 with data line D7 in order to turn the quikLoader ON or OFF. These circuit board changes would dramatically simplify the protocol that *EOS* must utilize in order to configure the A-register and the X-register that control EPROM selection and data bank selection for the selected EPROM. With the circuit changes I propose, EPROM selection could simply be handled by loading the EPROM number into the A-register, data bank selection could be handled by loading the data bank number into the X-register, and the A-register could be saved, using absolute indexed addressing, to the base I/O memory location that is dedicated to the slot in which the quikLoader resides. I contend that a *good* hardware design is one in which software can most easily *utilize* and *flourish*.

8. EPROM Operating System

The SCRG documentation describes how an area of quikLoader EPROM memory at a given offset is mapped to the 0xC100 to 0xFFFF memory address space in the Apple][computer. I found that using the first half of this memory address space was strange and confusing to me, and this address space was not very amenable to programmatic utilization. Rather, I found that I could access an entire 27512 EPROM simply by identifying eight 8 KB data banks, where each data bank uses the upper 0xE000 to 0xFFFF memory address space. The SCRG described function of the USR bit was also strange and confusing to me as well as the role it is designed to perform according to the provided documentation. The USR bit is intended to be used as a master/slave bit-flag when multiple quikLoaders are seated in the same computer. For the moment I have quite a few programs that I routinely rely on, and all of those programs along with *EOS* fit comfortably into three 27512 EPROMs. I cannot imagine requiring more than one quikLoader in my computer, so my vision of *EOS* became even more tailored when I limited *EOS* to manage a single quikLoader and utilize the USR bit only for data bank selection. Table V.8.1 expands on the data bank selection settings that are shown in Figure V.7.1. This table lists the six EPROM memory sizes that the quikLoader hardware can address, their associated data banks, and the latched data from the data control register 74LS174 and the high bank select register 74LS74 that are necessary to obtain USR or D3, A0, and A1 in order to access up to eight data banks in one EPROM. The memory content of eight sequentially accessed data banks is equivalent to accessing the entire memory content of one 27512 EPROM. This is an achievement in itself, and it allows *EOS* to manage and to load data from any sized EPROM simply and elegantly.

When RESET is pressed, the 74LS174 data control register and the 74LS74 high bank select register are cleared in order to select EPROM 0, force Bank 0 to be mapped into Apple][memory from 0xE000 to 0xFFFF, and turn the quikLoader ON. The 6502-microprocessor automatically loads the RESET vector at 0xFFFC:0xFFFD into the program counter and it continues to fetch instructions beginning from the address that is stored at that location. As an aside, the NMI vector is at 0xFFFA:0xFFFB and the IRQ/BRK vector is at 0xFFFE:0xFFFF. From EPROM 0, Bank 0 content is now in focus where *EOS* resides in the 0xE000 to 0xFFFF memory range, and this memory range includes the above three hardware vectors and all three vectors point to the start of *EOS* which begins at 0xE800. The *EOS* Catalog page resides at 0xE000 to 0xE0FF, the seven peripheral-card ROM memory pages reside from 0xE100 to 0xE7FF, and *EOS* utilizes the remaining 0x17FA bytes in data Bank 0. A 2764 EPROM, at a minimum, can therefore be used for EPROM 0 and still support *EOS*. Some sort of bank switching would be required in order to extend *EOS* processing into another EPROM bank, an option I did not wish to employ. Table V.8.2 shows the firmware entry points for one of the seven copies of peripheral-card ROM firmware that is mapped to the peripheral-card ROM memory of the quikLoader so that the quikLoader may reside in any of the seven peripheral-card slots. EOS can utilize this magnificent capability simply by incorporating that single, unused 74LS08 AND gate as shown in Figure V.7.1. I am sure a *knock-off* quikLoader hardware design would be extraordinarily silly if it did not incorporate that same simple modification including an LED and the SPDT switch at a minimum.

Bank	EPROM	EPROM Access	Memory Access	A1	A0	USR
0	2716	0x0000-0x07FF	0xF800-0xFFFF	0	0	0
0	2732	0x0000-0x0FFF	0xF000-0xFFFF	0	0	0
0	2764	0x0000-0x1FFF	0xE000-0xFFFF	0	0	0
0	27128	0x0000-0x1FFF	0xE000-0xFFFF	0	0	0
1		0x2000-0x3FFF	0xE000-0xFFFF	0	0	1
0	27256	0x0000-0x1FFF	0xE000-0xFFFF	0	0	0
1		0x2000-0x3FFF	0xE000-0xFFFF	0	0	1
2		0x4000-0x5FFF	0xE000-0xFFFF	0	1	0
3		0x6000-0x7FFF	0xE000-0xFFFF	0	1	1
0	27512	0x0000-0x1FFF	0xE000-0xFFFF	0	0	0
1		0x2000-0x3FFF	0xE000-0xFFFF	0	0	1
2		0x4000-0x5FFF	0xE000-0xFFFF	0	1	0
3		0x6000-0x7FFF	0xE000-0xFFFF	0	1	1
4		0x8000-0x9FFF	0xE000-0xFFFF	1	0	0
5		0xA000-0xBFFF	0xE000-0xFFFF	1	0	1
6		0xC000-0xDFFF	0xE000-0xFFFF	1	1	0
7		0xE000-0xFFFF	0xE000-0xFFFF	1	1	1

Table V.8.1. quikLoader Bank Switching

Offset	Name	Description
0x00	QLASEOS	Applesoft interface entry, parses command variables
0x5F	QLEXIT01	Return Unknown Command error, 0x01
0x62	QLEXIT02	Return Wrong Number of Parameters error, 0x02
0x65	QLEXIT03	Return Search Range Invalid error, 0x03
0x68	QLEXIT04	Return File Not Found error, 0x04
0x6B	QLEXIT00	Return no error, 0x00
0x9D	QLEXIT1	If ZipChip present flush cache and enable it, fall into QLEXIT2
0xC3	QLEXIT2	Turn quikLoader OFF, jump to (MEMJMP) at 0x0290
0xCB	QLUSER1	Return from DOS CMDUSER 1 command
0xCE	QLUSER2	Return from DOS CMDUSER 2 command
0xE0	QLBINEOS	Turn quikLoader ON, load QBMCODE, jump to BINEOS2 at 0xF229
0xF0	QLEOS	Turn quikLoader ON, jump to EOS at 0xE800
0xF8	QLBINTXT	ASCII text string *QLBINEOS* used to find the slot number for a quikLoader

Table V.8.2. quikLoader Firmware Entry Points

Bank	Offset	Memory	Size	Contents
0	0x0000	0xE000	0x0004	Synchronization bytes that preface Catalog
0	0x0004	0xE004	0x00FC	Catalog, terminated by 0x00
0	0x0100	0xE100	0x0100	Slot 1 *EOS* ASEOS/BINEOS interface
0	0x0200	0xE200	0x0100	Slot 2 *EOS* ASEOS/BINEOS interface
0	0x0300	0xE300	0x0100	Slot 3 *EOS* ASEOS/BINEOS interface
0	0x0400	0xE400	0x0100	Slot 4 *EOS* ASEOS/BINEOS interface
0	0x0500	0xE500	0x0100	Slot 5 *EOS* ASEOS/BINEOS interface
0	0x0600	0xE600	0x0100	Slot 6 *EOS* ASEOS/BINEOS interface
0	0x0700	0xE700	0x0100	Slot 7 *EOS* ASEOS/BINEOS interface
0	0x0800	0xE800	0x17FA	*EOS* software
0	0x1FFA	0xFFFA	0x0002	NMI vector, address of *EOS*
0	0x1FFC	0xFFFC	0x0002	RESET vector, address of *EOS*
0	0x1FFE	0xFFFE	0x0002	IRQ/BRK vector, address of *EOS*
1	0x2000	0xE000	0x2100	DOS4.5L, Build 05
2	0x4100	0xE100	0x2A00	DOS4.5H, Build 06
3	0x6B00	0xEB00	0x2800	LISA80.1 code segment
4	0x9300	0xF300	0x1000	LISA80.2 code segment
5	0xA300	0xE300	0x0640	LISA80.3 code segment
5	0xA940	0xE940	0x1914	*SETUP80*
6	0xC254	0xE254	0x01C0	*LOADLISA80*
6	0xC414	0xE414	0x1B04	RamDisk Install
6	0xDF18	0xFF18	0x1316	*FID*
7	0xF22E	0xF22E	0x064A	*Set Clock*
7	0xF878	0xF878	0x06D9	*ASLIST*
7	0xFF51	0xFF51	0x00AF	unused

Table V.8.3. quikLoader EPROM 0 Containing EOS and Programs

From 0xE800 to 0xFFF9 there is sufficient room for *EOS* to process the 26 commands that are shown in Figure V.8.1. There is even room for the EPROM Catalog function, the Applesoft interface or ASEOS, the assembly language interface or BINEOS, the ZipChip configuration software that supports a ZipChip if one is present, and the software to manage Primary files. Unlike the SCRG interface, *EOS* does not capture the state of the keyboard at the moment the RESET key is pressed. Rather, *EOS* displays an EOS Main Selection Menu, and any one of the displayed options may be selected. I simply chose those programs and those utilities I liked best and displayed them as menu options. Someone else may display a different set of favorite options. The way I have organized EPROM 0 is so simple that others may simply model their EPROM 0 after mine. The remaining seven banks in EPROM 0, a 27512, contain DOS 4.5.05L, DOS 4.5.06H, *Lisa80*, *SETUP80*, and *LOADLISA80*, RAM Disk Installation, *FID*, *Set Clock*, and *ASLIST*. Table V.8.3 shows the contents of my EPROM 0 that contains *EOS*. All other programs reside on the other quikLoader EPROMs. *EOS* uses the power and the flexibility of BINEOS to load and to run those other programs without regard to a specific EPROM number. An EPROM Catalog display is shown in Figures V.8.2. and V.8.3, and an example Catalog File Entry Values display is shown in Figure V.8.4 that displays the software components of a program that is based on its file Type. Simply press numbers 0-7 to display the Catalog contents for any EPROM.

```
        EOS Main Selection Menu

A DOS 4.5L Boot      N Copy ROM->RAM
B DOS 4.5H Boot      O goto RAM Reset
C Coldstart DOS      P goto ROM Reset
D Warmstart DOS      Q goto RAM Monitor
E EPROM Burner       R goto ROM Monitor
F Sourceror          S run HELLO on SDV
G Boot the Slot S    T CATALOG this SDV
H Hook the Slot S    U VTOC Manager
I Unhook a Slot S    V Volume Manager
J FID                W Volume Duplicate
K ADT                X Disk Window
L Lisa80             Y Real Time Clock
M RamDisk Config     Z ZipChip Config

0-7 EPROM Catalog    SDV S=7 D=01 V=000

RTN Toggle ZipChip   ZipChip State
^C Configure SDV        -> Off <-

Enter Selection:
```

Figure V.8.1. EOS Main Selection Menu

```
    quikLoader EOS - EPROM Catalog
        Slot 4              EPROM 0

  S 0x44  >DOS4.5.05L

  S 0x5C   DOS4.5.06H

  P 0x84   LOADLISA80

  S 0x48   LISA80.1

  S 0x50   LISA80.2

  S 0x44   LISA80.3

  B 0x04   SETUP80

  B 0x04   RamDisk Config

  RTN - File Info        (L)oad
  SPC - Next EPROM       (R)un
  0-7 - Select EPROM     (Q)uit
```

Figure V.8.2. EPROM 0 Catalog, Part 1

```
    quikLoader EOS - EPROM Catalog
        Slot 4              EPROM 0

  S 0x44   LISA80.3

  B 0x04   SETUP80

  B 0x04   RamDisk Config

  B 0x04   FID

  B 0x04   Set Clock

  B 0x04   Applesoft Formatter

  R 0x20   ROM Copy

  R 0x20  >Catalog Sync

  RTN - File Info        (L)oad
  SPC - Next EPROM       (R)un
  0-7 - Select EPROM     (Q)uit
```

Figure V.8.3. EPROM 0 Catalog, Part 2

```
    quikLoader EOS - EPROM Catalog
        Slot 4              EPROM 0


File Name - DOS4.5.06H
File Type - System
            Binary, LC Bank 2
            Binary, LC Bank 1
            Binary, main memory
File Size - 0x2A00

  EPROM Offset - 0x4100

Memory Address - 0xBE00



    Press Any Key to Continue
```

Figure V.8.4. EOS Catalog File Entry Values

Table V.8.4 shows the definition of the file Types that are utilized in *EOS*, the ASCII character that is used to display each file Type in the EPROM Catalog display, and the hexadecimal value for each file Type. Notice in Figure V.8.2 that the DOS.4.5.06H entry is file Type S having a value of 0x5C. This value is derived from the logical OR of System file, Binary file Bank 2 memory, Binary file Bank 1 memory, and Binary file lower Main memory because parts of DOS.4.5.06H reside in all these memory locations as shown in Figure V.8.4. Mathematically, the file Type for the DOS.4.5.06H entry is

$$\text{FILETYPE} = 0x40 \lor 0x10 \lor 0x08 \lor 0x04 = 0x5C$$

EOS provides Applesoft users with three commands when using the Applesoft or ASEOS interface for LOAD file, RUN file, and CATALOG. In order to access ASEOS by means of Applesoft, the quikLoader control register must be initially configured to EPROM 0, Bank 0, and disabled or turned OFF: the reason for the added 74LS08 AND gate. If the quikLoader resides in slot 4 for example, the program must POKE 49344,16 in order to initially configure the quikLoader hardware before making the CALL to ASEOS. This

CALL will bring *EOS* into focus when the peripheral-card ROM turns the quikLoader ON. In this example, CALL 50176 begins ASEOS processing. The CALL command must be followed with some required arguments, and there are some optional arguments that can be used as well. These arguments **must only be** integer variables, integer arrays, ASCII character strings, or ASCII character string arrays where indicated. Real variables and real arrays **must never** be used in an ASEOS CALL because real numbers are floating point numbers and they are **not** supported by the ASEOS routines.

Value	Catalog	Description
0x01	T	Text file, NULL terminated, an EXEC file for example
0x02	A	Applesoft file
0x04	B	Binary file or segment, lower Main memory
0x08	B	Binary file or segment, Bank 1 Language Card partition
0x10	B	Binary file or segment, Bank 2 Language Card partition
0x20	R	Reserved file
0x40	S	System file
0x80	P	Primary file

Table V.8.4. EOS File Types

1) LOAD file. This command loads a file into memory from a quikLoader EPROM using ASEOS:

```
QL    = quikLoader slot number      ; 1 - 7
OFF   = 16                          ; 0x10
DEV   = QL * 16 + 49280             ; QL * 0x10 + 0xC080
EOS   = QL * 256 + 49152            ; QL * 0x100 + 0xC000
C%    = 1                           ; LOAD file command
S%    = -1                          ; set Status to ERROR
E%    = EPROM search range          ; 0-7 or 0-7:0-7
F$    = Filename                    ; 1 to 24 upper ASCII
[A%]  = Alternate load address      ; optional

POKE DEV, OFF
CALL EOS, C%, S%, E%, F$ [, A%]
```

2) RUN file. This command loads a file into memory from a quikLoader EPROM and begins file execution using ASEOS:

```
QL    = quikLoader slot number      ; 1 - 7
OFF   = 16                          ; 0x10
DEV   = QL * 16 + 49280             ; QL * 0x10 + 0xC080
EOS   = QL * 256 + 49152            ; QL * 0x100 + 0xC000
C%    = 2                           ; RUN file command
S%    = -1                          ; set Status to error
E%    = EPROM search range          ; 0-7 or 0-7:0-7
F$    = Filename                    ; 1 to 24 upper ASCII
```

```
        [A%]       = Alternate load address                    ; optional

        POKE DEV, OFF
        CALL EOS, C%, S%, E%, F$ [, A%]
```

3) CATALOG files. This command reads the Catalog of the specified quikLoader EPROMs into a character string array using ASEOS:

```
        QL              = quikLoader slot number        ; 1 - 7
        OFF             = 16                            ; 0x10
        M%              = Maximum number of entries
        DEV             = QL * 16 + 49280               ; QL * 0x10 + 0xC080
        EOS             = QL * 256 + 49152              ; QL * 0x100 + 0xC000
        C%              = 3                             ; CATALOG command
        S%              = -1                            ; set Status to error
        E%              = EPROM search range            ; 0-7:0-7
        N%              = Last index used and returned  ; set to start index
        F$(N%)          = Filename array                ; 1 to 24 upper ASCII
        [P%(0,N%)]      = Parameter Array returned       ; optional

        M% = 128
        DIM  F$(M%), P%(4,M%)
        POKE DEV, OFF
        N% = 0
        CALL EOS, C%, S%, E%, N%, F$(N%) [, P%(0,N%)]
```

Returned Status values for all ASEOS commands:

```
        S% = 0          no error
        S% = 1          Unknown Command error
        S% = 2          Number of Parameters Invalid error
        S% = 3          Search Range Invalid error
        S% = 4          Requested File Not Found error
```

EPROM search range for all ASEOS commands:

```
        E% = 0-7 for a single, specific quikLoader EPROM
        E% = 0-7:0-7, or ( last EPROM number ) * 16 + ( start EPROM number )
```

Optional Parameter Array returned for the CATALOG command:

```
        P%(0,N%) = quikLoader EPROM number
        P%(1,N%) = file type
        P%(2,N%) = EPROM offset
        P%(3,N%) = file size in bytes
```

Offset	Length	Variable	Description
0	1	FILETYPE	File Type as defined in Table V.8.4
1	2	SRCVAL	EPROM source address (EPROM offset supplied by assembler)
3	2	LENVAL	File length or size in bytes
5	2	DSTVAL	Destination memory address (the Apple][memory address)
7	1-24	FILENAME	Filename, 1 to 24 ASCII bytes (in DCI format using apostrophes)

Table V.8.5. EOS Catalog File Entry Structure

EOS file Types were shown previously in Table V.8.4 with their value and their display designation in the EPROM Catalog function. *EOS* currently uses two Reserved Type files in the *EOS* EPROM Catalog. The Data Context Block or DCB for the ROM code that resides from 0xD000 to 0xFFFF and the DCB for the four Catalog synchronization bytes are both Reserved Type files. Primary files are Binary files that can utilize the BINEOS interface and Primary files may be activated directly by the quikLoader EPROM Catalog function in order to load or to run System files. The quikLoader EPROM Catalog function **cannot** directly load or run a System file. System files may be Text, Applesoft, or other assembly language files. System files may be attached to a Primary file, or they may be loaded or run by activating its associated Primary file either using the quikLoader EPROM Catalog function, ASEOS, or BINEOS. *EOS* is not designed to support Integer BASIC Type files because DOS 4.5 does not support Integer BASIC Type files. A DOS image and the software tool *Sourceror* are two examples of System Type files. The program that loads *Sourceror* into memory and begin its processing is an example of a Primary file. Primary and System files that are used in *EOS* are different in function and in concept than Primary and System files that are used in the SCRG interface. It is important that this distinction is fully understood in order to differentiate *EOS* functionality and SCRG functionality.

A quikLoader EPROM Catalog for the files that are contained in that EPROM is always prefaced with four synchronization bytes, 0xC4, 0xB8, 0x90, and 0xED. The actual catalog begins at offset 0x0004 and it may contain any number of entries, where each entry can vary in size because the entry size depends on the length in bytes for its filename. An EPROM Catalog filename is a character string that uses *lower* ASCII characters for all of its bytes except for the last byte which is an *upper* ASCII character. When a character string is comprised of lower ASCII characters except for the last character which is an upper ASCII character, the *Lisa* assembler designates this character string to be in the DCI format and the character string is defined within two apostrophes. An EPROM Catalog is terminated with a NULL or character 0x00. An example entry in a Catalog File structure is shown in Table V.8.5. All of the parameters in a Catalog file entry must be supplied by the EPROM developer except for the SRCVAL parameter. The SRCVAL parameter should only be supplied by the assembler as the assembler is creating the EPROM binary image from all of the program data that comprise the Catalog file entries.

EOS provides assembly language users with three commands when using the Binary or BINEOS interface for LOAD file, RUN file, and CATALOG. An eight-byte DCB is utilized for the input variables and for the returned status. The structure of the DCB is command specific. Any assembly language routine like a Primary file can use QLBINEOS in order to load and to run a System file. QLBINEOS is located at the 0xE0th byte in the peripheral-card ROM memory of the quikLoader as shown in Table V.8.2 as long as EPROM 0 and Bank 0 are latched in the control registers. For example, if the quikLoader resides in slot 4, QLBINEOS resides at memory address 0xC4E0. The code that is listed next in Figure V.8.5 shows how to utilize the QLBINEOS interface. This example code also contains the optional FINDQL routine that discovers in which peripheral slot the quikLoader resides for a generic interface.

271

```
0800                    1              ttl "QLBINEOS Utilization, QLBINEOS.L"
0800                    2    ;
0800                    3    ;
0800                    4    ; QLBINEOS.L
0800                    5    ;
002A                    6    SRCPTR    epz $2A
002E                    7    DSTPTR    epz $2E
0800                    8    ;
0000                    9    ZERO      equ $00
00FF                   10    NEGONE    equ $FF
0800                   11    ;
0000                   12    QLON      equ $00
0010                   13    QLOFF     equ $10
0800                   14    ;
C080                   15    QLSELC    equ $C080
0800                   16    ;
C0E0                   17    QLBINEOS  equ $C0E0
C0F8                   18    QLBINTXT  equ $C0F8
0800                   19    ;
C700                   20    PAGEC7    equ $C700
E700                   21    PAGEE7    equ $E700
0800                   22    ;
CFFF                   23    CLRROM    equ $CFFF
0800                   24    ;
0800                   25    ;
0800                   26              org $800
0800                   27              obj $800
0800                   28              usr
0800                   29    ;
0800 20 0C 08          30              jsr FINDQL          ; find quikLoader
0803 B0 07             31              bcs FINDERR
0805                   32    ;
0805 A0 6A             33              ldy #EOSDCBL        ; address of
0807 A9 08             34              lda /EOSDCBL        ;   LOAD DCB
0809                   35    ;
0809 20 5C 08          36              jsr QLBINJMP        ; LOAD the file
080C                   37    ;
080C                   38    ;         :::
080C                   39    ;
080C                   40    FINDERR:
080C                   41    ;         :::
080C                   42    ;
080C A0 00             43    FINDQL    ldy #PAGEC7         ; get 0xC700 slot
080E A9 C7             44              lda /PAGEC7         ;   address
0810                   45    ;
0810 84 2A             46              sty SRCPTR          ; store address at
0812 85 2B             47              sta SRCPTR+1        ;   source pointer
0814                   48    ;
0814 A9 E7             49              lda /PAGEE7         ; get EPROM Bank 0 address
0816                   50    ;
0816 84 2E             51              sty DSTPTR          ; store address at
0818 85 2F             52              sta DSTPTR+1        ;   destination pointer
081A                   53    ;
081A A9 07             54              lda #7              ; initialize
081C 8D 5F 08          55              sta QLSLOT          ;   for slot 7
081F                   56    ;
081F AD 5F 08          57    ^1        lda QLSLOT          ; get slot number
0822                   58    ;
0822 0A                59              asl                 ; multiply by 16
0823 0A                60              asl
```

272

```
0824 0A           61              asl
0825 0A           62              asl
0826              63  ;
0826 AA           64              tax                     ; use as index
0827              65  ;
0827 A9 00        66              lda #QLON               ; turn quikLoader ON
0829 9D 80 C0     67              sta QLSELC,X
082C              68  ;
082C 2C FF CF     69              bit CLRROM              ; detach shared slot memory
082F              70  ;
082F A0 F8        71              ldy #QLBINTXT           ; point to QLBIN text
0831              72  ;
0831 B9 6A 07     73  ^2          lda QLTEXT-QLBINTXT&NEGONE,Y ; get QLBIN text
0834              74  ;
0834 D1 2A        75              cmp (SRCPTR),Y          ; compare slot memory
0836 D0 16        76              bne >3
0838              77  ;
0838 D1 2E        78              cmp (DSTPTR),Y          ; compare EPROM memory
083A D0 12        79              bne >3
083C              80  ;
083C C8           81              iny
083D D0 F2        82              bne <2
083F              83  ;
083F A9 10        84              lda #QLOFF              ; turn quikLoader OFF
0841 9D 80 C0     85              sta QLSELC,X
0844              86  ;
0844 A5 2B        87              lda SRCPTR+1            ; get slot memory address
0846 8D 61 08     88              sta QLBINADR+1          ; save to vector
0849              89  ;
0849 2C FF CF     90              bit CLRROM              ; detach shared slot memory
084C              91  ;
084C 18           92              clc                     ; quikLoader found
084D              93  ;
084D 60           94              rts
084E              95  ;
084E C6 2B        96  ^3          dec SRCPTR+1            ; next slot memory
0850 C6 2F        97              dec DSTPTR+1            ; next quikLoader slot
0852              98  ;
0852 CE 5F 08     99              dec QLSLOT              ; next slot number
0855 D0 C8       100              bne <1
0857             101  ;
0857 2C FF CF    102              bit CLRROM              ; detach shared slot memory
085A            103  ;
085A 38         104              sec                     ; no quikLoader found
085B            105  ;
085B 60         106              rts
085C            107  ;
085C            108  ;
085C 6C 60 08   109  QLBINJMP jmp (QLBINADR)
085F           110  ;
085F           111  QLSLOT   dfs 1,ZERO                   ; quikLoader slot
0860          112  ;
0860 E0 C0     113  QLBINADR adr QLBINEOS                 ; QLBINEOS vector
0862          114  ;
0862 D1 CC C2  115  QLTEXT   asc "QLBINEOS"               ; QLBIN text
0865 C9 CE C5
0868 CF D3
086A         116  ;
086A         117  ;
086A         118  EOSDCBL:
```

273

```
086A              119  ;
086A 01           120  DCBLCMD  hex 01           ; LOAD command
086B 70           121  DCBLEP   hex 70           ; search all EPROMs
086C 00 00        122  DCBLOAD  hex 0000         ; no alternate LOAD address
086E FF           123  DCBLSTAT hex FF           ; return status
086F 0F           124  DCBLFLEN byt FILENDL-FILNAML ; filename length
0870 72 08        125  DCBLFADR adr FILNAML      ; filename address
0872              126  ;
0872 C1 F0 F0     127  FILNAML  asc "Apple File List"
0875 EC E5 A0
0878 C6 E9 EC
087B E5 A0 CC
087E E9 F3 F4
0881              128  FILENDL:
0881              129  ;

BSAVE QLBINEOS,A$0800,L$0081
0881              130           usr QLBINEOS
0881              131  ;
0881              132  ;
0881              133           end 000

*** End of Assembly
```

Figure V.8.5. Example Code for QLBINEOS Utilization

1) LOAD file. This DCB loads a file into memory from a quikLoader EPROM using BINEOS:

```
EOSDCBL      equ *                      ; LOAD file DCB
DCBCMDL      hex 01                     ; LOAD command
DCBEPNL      hex 70                     ; search all EPROMs
DCBFALTL     hex 0000                   ; no alternate address
DCBSTATL     hex FF                     ; return status
DCBFLENL     byt FILELENL               ; filename length
DCBFADRL     adr FILENAML               ; filename address

FILENAML     asc "Applesoft File List"
FILELENL     equ *-FILENAML
```

2) RUN file. This DCB loads a file into memory from a quikLoader EPROM and begins file execution using BINEOS:

```
EOSDCBR      equ *                      ; RUN file DCB
DCBCMDR      hex 02                     ; RUN command
DCBEPNR      hex 70                     ; search all EPROMs
DCBFALTR     hex 0000                   ; no alternate address
DCBSTATR     hex FF                     ; return status
DCBFLENR     byt FILELENR               ; filename length
DCBFADRR     adr FILENAMR               ; filename address

FILENAMR     asc "Volume Copy"
FILELENR     equ *-FILENAMR
```

3) CATALOG files. This DCB reads the Catalog of the specified quikLoader EPROMs into a buffer using BINEOS:

```
EOSDCBC      equ *                        ; CATALOG EPROMs DCB
DCBCMDC      hex 03                       ; CATALOG command
DCBEPNC      hex 70                       ; CATALOG all EPROMs
DCBCALT      hex 0000                     ; not used
DCBSTATC     hex FF                       ; return status
DCBCNUM      hex 00                       ; CATALOG entries start number
DCBCADR      adr CATBUFR                  ; CATALOG buffer address

CATBUFR      dfs 32*n,ZERO                ; n 32-byte entries
```

The call to BINEOS returns one of the following Status values:

```
0x00 = no error
0x01 = Unknown Command error
0x02 = Filename Length Invalid error
0x03 = Search Range Invalid error
0x04 = Buffer/Filename Address error
0x05 = Requested File Not Found error
```

Offset	Length	Variable	Description
0	1	FILEPNUM	EPROM number containing this file
1	1	FILETYPE	File Type
2	2	SRCVAL	EPROM source address (EPROM offset)
4	2	LENVAL	File length or size in bytes
6	2	DSTVAL	Destination memory address (Apple][memory)
8	24	FILENAME	Filename, space padded, upper ASCII

Table V.8.6. BINEOS Catalog File Entry

The quikLoader EPROM search range and file Types are the same in BINEOS as they are in ASEOS. The Catalog buffer contains the number of entries which is given by DCBCNUM. A maximum of 255 entries is provided. Even if the quikLoader contains eight 27512 EPROMs, the EPROMS would each have to exceed an average of thirty-two entries in order to exceed a total maximum of 255 Catalog entries. There is very little likelihood that DCBCNUM would ever exceed 255 entries. Each BINEOS Catalog entry is exactly thirty-two bytes in size regardless of the exact length in bytes for the filename. The filename characters are always upper ASCII characters and the filename is padded with the upper ASCII SPACE or character 0xA0 such that each filename is exactly twenty-four characters in length. A BINEOS Catalog file entry is structured as shown in Table V.8.6.

EOS makes extensive use of the 6502-microprocessor stack page from 0x0110 to 0x0194 for the QBMCODE that consists of the routines QLCONFIG, QLMOVE, QLJMP, QLJSR, QLRTN, and QLEXEC. When *EOS* is activated, *EOS* initializes the stack pointer to 0xFF in order to ensure that these temporary stack page routines are safe while *EOS* is active. And, it is extremely unlikely that the stack pointer will ever venture into the region where these stack routines are placed because Applesoft tightly controls this pointer. The same argument can be made for software that uses the BINEOS interface as long as the calling software is mindful of the stack pointer location and where the QBMCODE routines reside. *EOS* also makes extensive use of the text input page from 0x0280 to 0x02EF. It is extremely unlikely that a lengthy Applesoft or DOS command is ever issued during ASEOS or BINEOS processing. However, an Applesoft user should be aware that *EOS* does use the upper half of the INPUT page. *EOS* uses the stack and input pages so that the User buffer page from 0x0300 to 0x03CF is still left available for program loaders. The original loader for *Sourceror*, a Primary file, is one example of a short assembly language routine that uses 0x300 to 0x32C to load *Sourceror*, a System File, from a quikLoader EPROM to memory address 0x8900 using a LOAD DCB. The original code segment to set MAXFILES to one is unnecessary for DOS 4.5. The possibilities are virtually endless in how *EOS* can be utilized to easily obtain information and data from an EPROM or from all EPROMs that reside in a quikLoader.

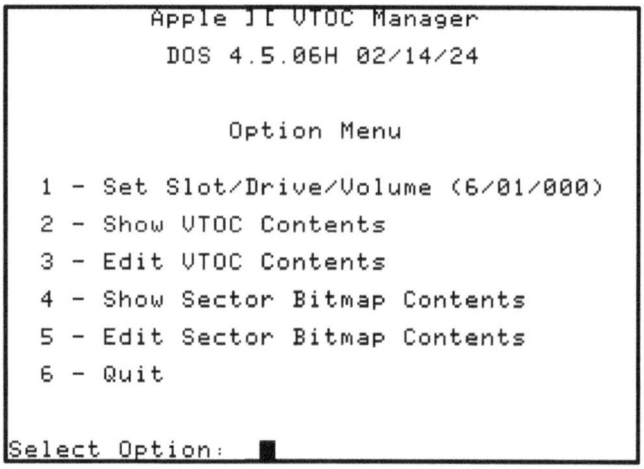

Figure V.9.1. VMGR Option Menu

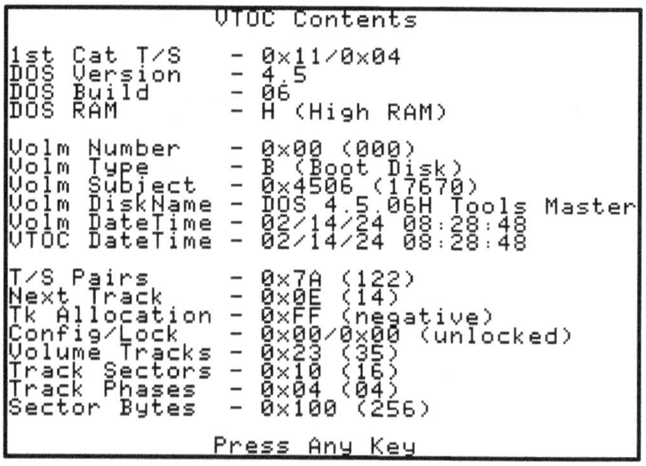

Figure V.9.2. Show VTOC for Option 2

9. VTOC Manager Utility

The Volume Table of Contents (VTOC) Manager, or *VMGR*, is a utility I developed while I was designing the enhancements to the DOS 4.1 VTOC and volume Catalog. *VMGR* provides the user with the ability to display and to change the contents of the VTOC of a volume for any slot, drive, and volume number. Figure V.9.1 displays the DOS release version and the Option Menu for *VMGR*. Initially, the program displays the slot, drive, and volume number values that is currently in focus. The user can change these values using Option 1. Option 2 reads the VTOC for the selected volume and displays the VTOC contents as shown in Figure V.9.2. Option 3 displays the same VTOC contents as in Option 2 except that the user can edit, or change that information. Great harm can easily be done to a volume, even making the volume unusable, if the VTOC information is changed inappropriately. It is critical that the user understands the effects of any change to the VTOC and to accept all consequences. Figure V.9.3 displays the VTOC contents and shows the arrow -> in front of the first catalog T/S location. Using the up and down arrow keys, the arrow can be positioned in front of any of the VTOC contents in order to change that content. Simply follow the directions after selecting a VTOC item to edit. The instruction Press ESC to Quit is printed at the bottom of the display while edits are being made. When ESC is pressed, the Save these changes (Y/N) screen is displayed as shown in Figure V.9.4. ESC may be pressed at any time in order to escape any function or when making any change so that that change does not become effective. When Option 4 is selected from the Option Menu, the contents of the sector bitmap for the selected volume is displayed as shown in Figure V.9.5. Selecting Option 5 allows one to change or to edit the contents of the sector bitmap for whatever reason as shown in Figure V.9.6. Again, for emphasis, great harm can easily be done to a volume, even making the volume unusable, if the VTOC information is changed inappropriately.

```
         Edit VTOC Contents
1st Cat T/S    ->0x11/0x04
DOS Version    - 4.5
DOS Build      - 06
DOS RAM        - H (High RAM)

Volm Number    - 0x00 (000)
Volm Type      - B (Boot Disk)
Volm Subject   - 0x4506 (17670)
Volm DiskName  - DOS 4.5.06H Tools Master
Volm DateTime  - 02/14/24 08:28:48
VTOC DateTime  - 02/14/24 08:28:48

T/S Pairs      - 0x7A (122)
Next Track     - 0x0E (14)
Tk Allocation  - 0xFF (negative)
Config/Lock    - 0x00/0x00 (unlocked)
Volume Tracks  - 0x23 (35)
Track Sectors  - 0x10 (16)
Track Phases   - 0x04 (04)
Sector Bytes   - 0x100 (256)
         Press ESC to Quit
```

Figure V.9.3. Edit VTOC for Option 3

```
         Edit VTOC Contents
1st Cat T/S    - 0x11/0x04
DOS Version    - 4.5
DOS Build      - 06
DOS RAM        - H (High RAM)

Volm Number    - 0x00 (000)
Volm Type      - B (Boot Disk)
Volm Subject   - 0x4506 (17670)
Volm DiskName  - DOS 4.5.06H Tools Master
Volm DateTime  - 02/14/24 08:28:48
VTOC DateTime  - 02/14/24 08:28:48

T/S Pairs      - 0x7A (122)
Next Track     - 0x0E (14)
Tk Allocation  - 0xFF (negative)
Config/Lock    - 0x00/0x00 (unlocked)
Volume Tracks  - 0x23 (35)
Track Sectors  - 0x10 (16)
Track Phases   - 0x04 (04)
Sector Bytes   - 0x100 (256)
Save these changes (Y/N): █
```

Figure V.9.4. Save VTOC for Option 3

```
         Sector Bitmap Contents

              35 Tracks

Trk|00001111 00001111 00001111 00001111
Num|C840C840 C840C840 C840C840 C840C840
Rng|FB73FB73 FB73FB73 FB73FB73 FB73FB73
---------------------------------------
00|00000000 00000000 00000000 00000000
04|00000000 00000000 00000000 00000000
08|00000000 00000000 00000000 00000000
0C|00000000 00000000 00000000 00000000
10|00000000 00000000 00000000 00000000
14|00000000 00000000 003F0000 00000000
18|00000000 00000000 00000000 00000000
1C|00000000 00000000 00000000 00000000
20|00000000 00000000 00000000
         Press Any Key
```

Figure V.9.5. Show VTOC Bitmap Option 4

```
      Edit Sector Bitmap Contents

              35 Tracks

Trk|00001111 00001111 00001111 00001111
Num|C840C840 C840C840 C840C840 C840C840
Rng|FB73FB73 FB73FB73 FB73FB73 FB73FB73
---------------------------------------
00|00000000 00000000 00000000 00000000
04|00000000 00000000 00000000 00000000
08|00000000 00000000 00000000 00000000
0C|00000000 00000000 00000000 00000000
10|00000000 00000000 00000000 00000000
14|00000000 00000000 003F0000 00000000
18|00000000 00000000 00000000 00000000
1C|00000000 00000000 00000000 00000000
20|00000000 00000000 00000000
Enter track number to edit:  0x█
```

Figure V.9.6. Edit VTOC Bitmap Option 5

Each track of a DOS 4.5 volume may contain either sixteen or thirty-two sectors depending on the hardware media. Also, the VTOC can contain the sector bitmap for a maximum of fifty tracks. Figure I.5.2 shows the complete sector bitmap that always begins at byte 0x38 in the VTOC. The sector bitmap allocates four bytes, or thirty-two bits, to every available track in that volume in order to determine if a sector in that track is available or not available. If a sector is available, its respective bit is set to one. If a sector is not available, its respective bit is set to zero. Table I.5.3 shows the sector order from left to right so that sectors 0x0F to 0x00 utilize the left two bytes followed by sectors 0x1F to 0x10 which utilize the right two bytes. DOS 4.5 indirectly interacts with the VTOC bitmap by means of the variable NEXTSECR exclusively OR'd with the value of 0x10. Therefore, if a volume only supports sixteen sectors per track, the right two bytes of every four bytes are set to zero. In Figures V.9.5 and V.9.6 track 0x16 contains six free sectors because its track bitmap is 0x003F0000. The hexadecimal value 0x003F contains six bits that are set to one for sectors 0x00 through 0x05.

10. Asynchronous Data Transfer Program

I have developed a serious amount of software programs for the Apple][computer using a MacBook Pro running the Virtual][emulation program by Gerard Putter. Virtual][can launch a utility called *A2V2* that is designed to transfer the image of a thirty-five track volume that is 143 KB to and from a physical Apple][computer that is concurrently running a program called Asynchronous Data Transfer, or *ADT* by Paul Guertin. *ADT* was further enhanced by Gerard Putter. My Apple //e uses a serial cable that is connected to a Super Serial peripheral interface card and to a Keyspan Serial to USB Adapter. The Keyspan uses a USB cable in order to connect the adapter to the MacBook Pro. Only a 143 KB volume image can be transferred. I typically utilize the RAM Disk 320 to receive disk images from the MacBook Pro. Because the RAM Disk 320 can support up to forty tracks for its volumes, I would like the 143 KB processing size increased to forty track images in *A2V2* and in *ADT*. I would even like to have Virtual][support up to forty-eight track diskettes. However, Mr. Putter has rejected both of my requests.

I did source *ADT* so that I could add an Update ADT command to its command repertoire as shown in Figure V.10.1. After a user has configured *ADT* to their requirements, Update ADT saves the *ADT* program with its new configuration values as its default when *ADT* is launched again in the future. This feature alone has saved me much time when I have had to transfer a volume image a number of times during the testing phase of software development. The testing phase can be a very lengthy, arduous, and iterative process, and it is quite helpful when changes to the configuration of a program like *ADT* can easily be saved and restored for the next iteration of tests. The ADT Configuration screen is shown in Figure V.10.2, and this screen utilizes lowercase characters that assist in helping the Apple screen text to be far easier for me to read in my opinion. If and when 163 KB and 196 KB volume images are supported, I will be ready. But let's not stop there! My RanaSystems EliteThree drive can support volumes that have forty tracks where each track contains thirty-two sectors, so 327 KB volume images are possible, too. In order to process 327 KB volume images, *ADT* may need to utilize the 80-column display. Furthermore, a CFFA volume can support up to forty-eight 32-sector tracks or forty-eight 16-block tracks that would require a 393 KB volume image. Now, that would be a seriously fun project that would utilize an 80-colum display in order to show the image transfer of volumes that have up to forty-eight tracks where each track can support either sixteen or thirty-two sectors or sixteen blocks. The *A2V2/ADT* data transfer protocol cannot be used to archive any diskette image other than a 143 KB sized volume. This somewhat limits the usefulness of the Rana and CFFA data storage containers in being able to archive their contents onto a MacBook Pro computer using the *A2V2/ADT* data transfer protocol. The ? command that is shown in Figure V.10.1 displays credits to Paul Guertin, Gerard Putter, and myself for adding the update command to *ADT*. These credits are displayed at the bottom of the screen in place of the *ADT* command repertoire as shown in Figure V.10.3.

```
SSC:S1,19200    ADT 2.1    Disk:S6,D1        ┌──────── ADT Configuration ────────┐
0000000000000000011111111111111111222          Disk Slot        6
0123456789ABCDEF0123456789ABCDEF012            Disk Drive       1
F                                  F           SSC Slot         1
E                                  E           SSC Speed        19200
D                                  D           Read Retries     1
C                                  C           Write Retries    0
B                                  B           Enable Sound     YES
A                                  A
9                                  9
8                                  8
7                                  7
6                                  6
5                                  5
4                                  4
3                                  3
2                                  2
1                                  1
0                                  0
                                                Use left/right Arrows to change value
Dir       Configure    Receive      Quit       Use up/down Arrows or SPACE to select
Send      Nibble Send  Update ADT   ?          RETURN to accept or CTRL-D for defaults
```

Figure V.10.1. ADT Window   Figure V.10.2. ADT Configuration

```
SSC:S1,19200    ADT 2.1    Disk:S6,D1        SSC:S1,19200    ADT 2.1    Disk:S6,D1
0000000000000000011111111111111111222        0000000000000000011111111111111111222
0123456789ABCDEF0123456789ABCDEF012          0123456789ABCDEF0123456789ABCDEF012
F                                  F          F                                  F
E                                  E          E                                  E
D                                  D          D                                  D
C                                  C          C                                  C
B                                  B          B                                  B
A                                  A          A                                  A
9                                  9          9                                  9
8                                  8          8                                  8
7                                  7          7                                  7
6                                  6          6                                  6
5                                  5          5                                  5
4                                  4          4                                  4
3                                  3          3                                  3
2                                  2          2                                  2
1                                  1          1                                  1
0                                  0          0                                  0
ADT 2.0 (SSC required) by Paul Guertin
'Nibble Send' added by Gerard Putter         File to receive:   @
'Update ADT' added by Philip Vrbancic
```

Figure V.10.3. ADT Software Credits   Figure V.10.4. ADT Receive Filename Entry

Both the Send and the Receive *ADT* commands require a filename as shown in Figure V.10.4. The filename is for a file that is found in the ~/Documents/Virtual][/A2V2 directory on the MacBook Pro computer. For example, if the hard drive is named MacOS 10.15.7 for the MacBook Pro computer and the Username is mozart, the diacritical mark tilde ~ that is used in the above pathname would be replaced such that the fully qualified pathname would be expressed as follows

    MacOS 10.15.7/Users/mozart/Documents/Virtual][/A2V2

However, there is a far easier way to specify the volume that is currently in focus within Virtual][rather than specifying a fully qualified pathname and filename for the 143 KB volume image. As shown in Figure V.10.4, entering the @ symbol tells *A2V2* to process and to send or to receive the contents of the volume that is currently in focus within Virtual][. This happens to be the exact procedure I have always utilized for *A2V2* and *ADT* communication.

11. Big Mac Assembler

I first started using the *Big Mac* assembler by Glen E. Bredon on my Apple][+ as soon as I took an interest in writing assembly language routines. Also, *Sourceror* is designed as a subsidiary tool to *Big Mac* because it creates *Big Mac* source code files from assembly language object code files. *Big Mac* and *Sourceror* are also capable of assembling and sourcing *SWEET16* instructions, respectively. The main menu for *Big Mac* is shown in Figure V.11.1. This menu is another example where I have incorporated lowercase characters to assist in making the Apple][screen text easier for me to read. When I started working at Sierra On-Line, all the programmers who wrote 6502 assembly only used the *Lisa* assembler and no one used the *Big Mac* assembler. However, whenever I source object code using *Sourceror* I am still dependent on *Big Mac* in order to perform some edits on the output source code that is generated by *Sourceror*. I use the ED/ASM Option E in *Big Mac* to make the necessary edits and then save the file as a TEXT file using Option W which happens to create a Text file that is compatible with *Lisa*. *Lisa* is able to EXEC a *Big Mac* TEXT file into its assembler quickly. And this is precisely the procedure I still use today. When Option Q is selected to quit *Big Mac*, *Big Mac* connects the DOS USER command to the *Big Mac* launch routine in order to restart *Big Mac* as shown in Figure V.11.2.

Big Mac made frequent use of DOS 3.3 internal variables and routines so it was not at all compatible with DOS 4.1 and, therefore, never compatible with DOS 4.5. I needed to find every instance where *Big Mac* utilized DOS 3.3 internals and then modify those dependencies to make use of the DOS 4.5 Data structure interfaces. *Big Mac* was certainly a challenge because it packaged a huge wallop of a program into the limited memory of the Language Card partition in Main memory. Creating source code for *Big Mac* that could be modified required a huge effort. It is one thing to have source code that assembles into object code which compares perfectly to the original object code. It is quite another thing to turn that source code into routines whose addresses may change as some code is modified, deleted, and added, and still assemble into a working, viable program. I did remove the ASSEM re-entry command because DOS 4.5 provides no visibility into its command tables, the command handler addresses, and the companion keyword tables for a reason. However, the new DOS 4.5 USER command is specifically designed to provide many functions. One of its functions can be used to restart *Big Mac* as shown in Figure V.11.2. DOS 4.5 does provide access to Data structures for drive number, file start address, and file length. I am satisfied that my sourced and modified version of *Big Mac* is fully DOS 4.5 compliant and, as a utility, *Big Mac* is still providing me with a terrific interface between *Sourceror* and *Lisa*.

In order to make *Big Mac* fully DOS 4.5 compliant, I had to relocate *Big Mac* to Auxiliary memory. Why? Because DOS 4.5 is designed to be resident in the Language Card partition in Main memory and *Big Mac* is designed to be resident in the Language Card partition in Main memory as well. Both cannot reside concurrently in the same Language Card partition. Auxiliary memory also contains its own Language Card partition. It seemed natural to relocate *Big Mac* to Auxiliary memory. It was definitely a challenge to understand how to master Auxiliary memory in terms of its operation and what it could provide and what it could not provide as far as resources. Certainly, to assist in Auxiliary memory utilization would be to decide which memory would handle input data, or keyboard and disk, and which memory would handle output data, or screen and disk. Once I established the operating rules for memory, it became very clear in how I would build the interface between Main memory and Auxiliary memory specifically for *Big Mac*. Fortunately, I was able to leverage on lessons learned from relocating *Lisa* into Auxiliary memory. Since DOS 4.5 occupies the Language Card partition in Main memory, it was quite logical to utilize Main memory for the input and the output of all disk data. It was totally unnecessary to duplicate two page-zeros particularly for the variables CH, CV, BASL, BASH, and the text window variables. So, all keyboard and screen display is handled within Auxiliary memory.

```
       ┌─────────────────────────────────┐  ┌─────────────────────────────────┐
       │           BIG MAC               │  │Type 'USER' to restart Big Mac   │
       │         By Glen Bredon          │  │                                 │
       │                                 │  │                                 │
       │C - Catalog                      │  │] *                              │
       │L - Load source                  │  │                                 │
       │S - Save source                  │  │                                 │
       │A - Append file                  │  │                                 │
       │R - Read TEXT file               │  │                                 │
       │W - Write TEXT file              │  │                                 │
       │D - Drive change                 │  │                                 │
       │E - Enter ED/ASM                 │  │                                 │
       │O - Save object code             │  │                                 │
       │Z - Zero tabs                    │  │                                 │
       │Q - Quit                         │  │                                 │
       │                                 │  │                                 │
       │          Source: A$0901,L$0000  │  │                                 │
       │Drive: 1                         │  │                                 │
       │                                 │  │                                 │
       │%                                │  │                                 │
       └─────────────────────────────────┘  └─────────────────────────────────┘
```

Figure V.11.1. Big Mac Main Menu Screen   Figure V.11.2. Big Mac Exit Screen

The original *Big Mac* contained its own version of the ROM Monitor. This Monitor mostly resembled the ROM Monitor that is found in the Apple][+. In order for *Big Mac* to utilize the current Apple //e ROM Monitor, the *Big Mac* installer simply copies the ROM Monitor into its same RAM memory space so that *Big Mac* can use the RAM Monitor for all of its functions. The interface between Main memory and Auxiliary memory is injected primarily at the COUT or 0xFDED routine. A small handler is needed for the GETFMCB, CALLFM, HOOKDOS, PRTERROR, GOTODOS, GOTOMON, GOTOCOLD, and GOTOWARM vectors. DOS errors have to be handled uniquely by the interface in order to always re-enter *Big Mac* appropriately. The state of the data Bank that is currently in focus in the Language Card partition must be captured in order to reconfigure Auxiliary memory for all of the subroutines that return to *Big Mac*. Because *Big Mac* utilizes data bank 1 in the Language Card partition for its symbol table and data bank 2 for its software routines, there is no way of knowing which data bank is in focus at any given stage during *Big Mac* processing.

The greater challenge was to align *Big Mac* and *Sourceror*, particularly in terms of assembling and sourcing all of the *SWEET16* instructions. *Big Mac* could process only some of the *SWEET16* instructions initially. And, as it turned out, *Big Mac* could not even process its own unique EVAL instruction because there is no entry in any of the *Big Mac* hash tables for that instruction. To this end, I chose to update *Sourceror* and *Big Mac* so that they are both able to process all of the *SWEET16* instructions that exist in my unique version of *SWEET16*. *Sourceror* is now able to *recognize* 65C02 instructions because my Apple //e ROM Monitor can now *display* 65C02 instructions. *Big Mac*, however, could not initially recognize nor could it process any of the new instructions in the 65C02 Instruction Set. It was fairly easy to update the ROM Monitor support logic for *Big Mac* so that it could at least parse and display those 65C02 instructions. It was not so easy to give *Big Mac* the ability to assemble the new 65C02 instructions. The original tables and the original logic in *Big Mac* that give *Big Mac* its ability to parse 6502 instructions and to handle all of their addressing mode rules is exceedingly dense. The original tables are found at 0xF339 to 0xF4DD. After I enhanced *Big Mac*, the tables are now found at 0xF339 to 0xF4FF. To make this enhancement even possible, a number of routines and ASCII tables must be moved elsewhere.

In order to add the STZ, TRB, and TSB hash table entries, for example, to the end of the table data starting at 0xF4EC, I have to move two ASCII tables. One table is at 0xF4E8 and the other table is at 0xF4EF. I only need twelve bytes for these three new instructions, and when combined, the ASCII tables are fifteen bytes in size. I did find an eighteen byte gap in the code at 0xE408 and this is where I moved those two

ASCII tables. The 10-byte table that is left at `0xF4DE` simply moves up to `0xF501`. To the best of my ability I have verified that *Big Mac* can assemble all of the additional 65C02 instructions and it can increment its program counter correctly for all of the addressing modes that these additional instructions can utilize. Furthermore, the *Big Mac* RAM Monitor support code can display all of the additional 65C02 instructions correctly with mnemonic, opcode, address, and displacement.

```
  :              :             :
E740 AD 34 02    640  GETHASH  lda H0234      ; get first character
E743             641  ;
E743 0A          642           asl            ; shift left
E744 0A          643           asl            ; shift left
E745 0A          644           asl            ; shift left
E746             645  ;
E746 85 EA       646           sta H00EA       ; save to hashA
E748             647  ;
E748 AD 35 02    648           lda H0235       ; get second character
E74B             649  ;
E74B 6A          650           ror             ; shift right
E74C 66 EB       651           ror H00EB       ; save bit to hashB
E74E             652  ;
E74E 6A          653           ror             ; shift right
E75F 66 EB       654           ror H00EB       ; save bit to hashB
E751             655  ;
E751 29 07       656           and #7          ; keep lower 3 bits
E753 05 EA       657           ora H00EA       ; add to hashA
E755 85 EA       658           sta H00EA       ; save to hashA
E757             659  ;
E757 AD 37 02    660           lda H0237       ; get fourth character
E75A 29 5F       661           and #$5F        ; mask; look for POPD
E75C             662  ;
E75C C9 44       663           cmp #$44        ; set carry if D
E75E F0 07       664           beq HE767       ; bypass if POPD
E760             665  ;
E760 AD 36 02    666           lda H0236       ; get third character
E763 49 BF       667           eor #$BF        ; looking for @
E765 C9 FF       668           cmp #NEGONE     ; set carry if 0x40
E767             669  ;
E767 AD 36 02    670  HE767    lda H0236       ; get third character
E76A 29 1F       671           and #$1F        ; keep lower 5 bits
E76C 2A          672           rol             ; shift in carry
E76D             673  ;
E76D 05 EB       674           ora H00EB       ; add to hashB
E76F 85 EB       675           sta H00EB       ; save to hashB
  :              :             :
```

Figure V.11.3. Big Mac Mnemonic Hashing Algorithm

Mr. Bredon utilizes a hashing algorithm in order to calculate a two-byte hash value for each assembly instruction that the *Big Mac* program encounters as *Big Mac* assembles each line of source code. The hash value is used to identify a table entry that provides additional data and/or format information that is used in order to process that particular assembly instruction. The GETHASH routine in *Big Mac* is found at `0xE740` and that routine is shown in its entirety in Figure V.11.3. The lower ASCII values of the four-character assembly instruction text, which may likely include a SPACE character 0xA0, is always placed starting at memory address 0x0234. The 2-byte hash value that is generated from these four characters is placed in page-zero at 0xEA:0xEB. The hash value must be unique for each assembly instruction, and this also includes the hash values for assembly directives, macro instructions, and *SWEET16* instructions. Mr. Bredon's hashing algorithm accomplishes that requirement.

Mnemonic	Table Address	Hash Value		Handler Address
		0xEA	0xEA	
]@	0xF339	0xE8	0x00	0xEFE0
EQU	0xF33D	0x2C	0x6A	0xEFE0
^^^	0xF341	0xF7	0xBC	0xF118
PMC	0xF345	0x83	0x46	0xF118
HEX	0xF349	0x41	0x70	0xEE80
DFB	0xF34D	0x21	0x84	0xEE68
DA	0xF351	0x20	0x40	0xEE42
DDB	0xF355	0x21	0x04	0xEE41
DS	0xF359	0x24	0xC0	0xF08C
LST	0xF35D	0x64	0xE8	0xEEB1
AST	0xF361	0x0C	0xE8	0xF04B
ORG	0xF365	0x7C	0x8E	0xF243
OBJ	0xF369	0xF2	0x42	0xF22A
SET	0xF36D	0x99	0x68	0xE892
SKP	0xF371	0x9A	0xE0	0xF048
PAG	0xF375	0x80	0x4E	0xF041
PAU	0xF379	0x80	0x6A	0xEB57
EXP	0xF37D	0x2E	0x20	0xEEB5
PUT	0xF381	0x85	0x68	0xF1DC
TR	0xF385	0xA4	0x80	0xEEA3
CHK	0xF389	0x1A	0x16	0xF20B
VAR	0xF38D	0xB0	0x64	0xEE35
SAV	0xF391	0x98	0x6C	0xF27B
KBD	0xF395	0x58	0x88	0xEF9E
END	0xF399	0x2B	0x88	0xF5B2

Table V.11.1. Hash Table 1 – Assembly Directives

Mnemonic	Table Address	Hash Value		Handler Address
		0xEA	0xEB	
ASC	0xF39D	0x0C	0xC6	0xEF60
DCI	0xF3A1	0x20	0xD2	0xEF5F
PLS	0xF3A5	0x33	0x26	0xEF53
INV	0xF3A9	0x4B	0x55	0xEF55

Table V.11.2. Hash Table 2 – Text Directives

The first table of hash values in *Big Mac* is found at 0xF339 and this table is shown in Table V.11.1. This table contains the hash values for assembly directives. In order to create the contents of this hash table, I had to reverse engineer each 2-byte hash value in order to derive its mnemonic. Table V.11.1 shows each 4-byte table entry beginning with the mnemonic for the directive, the memory address where the 4-byte entry begins, its 2-byte hash value, and the address of the software handler routine that processes this particular directive. The next hash table is found at 0xF39D and this table is shown in Table V.11.2. This second hash table is similar in structure to Table V.11.1, and this table contains the mnemonic for each text directive, the memory address where each 4-byte table entry begins, its 2-byte hash value, and the address of the software handler routine that processes this particular text directive. This table is terminated with a NULL or character 0x00 so that *Big Mac* can reconfigure its current indexing value and its pointers when the *Big Mac* scanner reaches the end of this table. The address bytes for each software handler that is listed in both of these tables are found decremented and reversed in byte order in memory so that they can be readily pushed onto the stack and in that byte order. The third hash table is shown in Table V.11.3 and this table contains the 4-byte table entries for all of the macro directives that can be used in *Big Mac*. This table is structured like Table V.11.2 and this table is terminated with a NULL or character 0x00 as well. Each 4-byte table entry begins with the mnemonic for the macro directive, the memory address where the 4-byte entry begins, its 2-byte hash value, and the address of the software handler routine that processes this particular directive. Again, the address bytes for each software handler is found in memory decremented and reversed in byte order so that these bytes can be readily pushed onto the stack and in that byte order.

Mnemonic	Table Address	Hash Value		Handler Address
		0xEA	0xEB	
\\\	0xF3AE	0xE7	0x38	0xF18F
DO	0xF3B2	0x23	0xC0	0xF101
ELS	0xF3B6	0x2B	0x26	0xF0F8
FIN	0xF3BA	0x32	0x5C	0xF18A
MAC	0xF3BE	0x68	0x46	0xF0B1
EOM	0xF3C2	0x2B	0xDA	0xF18F

Table V.11.3. Hash Table 3 – Macro Directives

Table V.11.4 includes all of the single byte 65C02 and *SWEET16* instructions along with the single byte 6502 instructions. This table is found at 0xF3C7 and each 3-byte table entry begins with the mnemonic of the instruction, its entry address, its 2-byte hash value, and the value of the opcode for that instruction. These instructions are the easiest to process and they require very little supporting code. It is to this table that I added the *SWEET16* RSNS instruction. All of the branch instructions for both the 65C02 Instruction Set and for the *SWEET16* instructions are contained in Table V.11.5 which is found at 0xF428. As in Table V.11.4 each 3-byte table entry begins with its mnemonic, its entry address, its 2-byte hash value, and the value of the opcode for that instruction. However, a displacement, or branch offset value also needs to be calculated for these instructions as well. *Big Mac* must refer to its symbol table and subtract the current program counter from the address of the symbol that the branch instruction references. This calculation provides a signed two's complement byte displacement value from -128 to +127 relative to the address of the following instruction. It is to this table that I added the *SWEET16* BSNS instruction. Tables V.11.4 and V.11.5 are both terminated with a NULL or character 0x00.

Mnemonic	Table Address	Hash Value 0xEA	Hash Value 0xEB	Opcode
CLC	0xF3C7	0x1B	0x06	0x18
DEX	0xF3CA	0x21	0x70	0xCA
DEY	0xF3CD	0x21	0x72	0x88
INX	0xF3D0	0x4B	0xB0	0xE8
INY	0xF3D3	0x4B	0xB2	0xC8
RTS	0xF3D6	0x95	0x26	0x60
SEC	0xF3D9	0x99	0x46	0x38
TAX	0xF3DC	0xA0	0x70	0xAA
TAY	0xF3DF	0xA0	0x72	0xA8
TXA	0xF3E2	0xA6	0x02	0x8A
TYA	0xF3E5	0xA6	0x42	0x98
PHA	0xF3E8	0x82	0x02	0x48
PHP	0xF3EB	0x82	0x20	0x08
PLA	0xF3EE	0x83	0x02	0x68
PLP	0xF3F1	0x83	0x20	0x28
TSX	0xF3F4	0xA4	0xF0	0xBA
TXS	0xF3F7	0xA6	0x26	0x9A
CLD	0xF3FA	0x1B	0x08	0xD8
SED	0xF3FD	0x99	0x48	0xF8
SEI	0xF400	0x99	0x52	0x78
RTI	0xF403	0x95	0x12	0x40
CLI	0xF406	0x1B	0x12	0x58
CLV	0xF409	0x1B	0x2C	0xB8
NOP	0xF40C	0x73	0xE0	0xEA
BRK	0xF40F	0x14	0x96	0x00
PHX	0xF412	0x82	0x30	0xDA
PHY	0xF415	0x82	0x32	0x5A
PLX	0xF418	0x83	0x30	0xFA
PLY	0xF41B	0x83	0x32	0x7A
RTN	0xF41E	0x95	0x1C	0x00
RS	0xF421	0x94	0xC0	0x0B
RSNS	0xF424	0x94	0xDC	0x0D

Table V.11.4. Hash Table 4 – Single Byte Instructions

Table V.11.6 contains the mnemonic, the table entry address, the 2-byte hash value, and the opcode/register value for the single byte *SWEET16* instructions that utilize a *SWEET16* register. Several of these opcode/register value entries may appear puzzling. The first entry, for example, is actually nibblized for the LD and the LD@ instructions. The second entry is nibblized for the ST and the ST@ instructions. It does not matter whether the actual opcode is in the upper nibble or in the lower nibble of the opcode/register value for these instructions. Whenever *Big Mac* processes an instruction from Table V.11.6, it knows how to formulate the upper nibble of the *SWEET16* opcode and to logically OR this nibble with a register number in order to complete the *SWEET16* instruction. Table V.11.6 is terminated with a NULL or character 0x00.

Mnemonic	Table Address	Hash Value 0xEA	0xEA	Opcode
BCC	0xF428	0x10	0xC6	0x90
BCS	0xF42B	0x10	0xE6	0xB0
BEQ	0xF42E	0x11	0x62	0xF0
BMI	0xF431	0x13	0x52	0x30
BNE	0xF434	0x13	0x8A	0xD0
BCC	0xF437	0x13	0x28	0x90
BCS	0xF43A	0x11	0xCA	0xB0
BPL	0xF43D	0x14	0x18	0x10
BVC	0xF440	0x15	0x86	0x50
BVS	0xF443	0x15	0xA6	0x70
BRA	0xF446	0x14	0x82	0x80
BR	0xF449	0x14	0x80	0x01
BNC	0xF44C	0x13	0x86	0x02
BC	0xF44F	0x10	0xC0	0x03
BP	0xF452	0x14	0x00	0x04
BM	0xF455	0x13	0x40	0x05
BZ	0xF458	0x16	0x80	0x06
BNZ	0xF45B	0x13	0xB4	0x07
BM1	0xF45E	0x13	0x62	0x08
BNM1	0xF461	0x13	0x9A	0x09
BS	0xF464	0x14	0xC0	0x0C
BSNS	0xF467	0x14	0xDC	0x0E

Table V.11.5. Hash Table 5 – Branch Instructions

Mnemonic	Table Address	Hash Value 0xEA	0xEB	Opcode/ Register
LD & LD@	0xF46B	0x61	0x00	0x24
ST & ST@	0xF46E	0x9D	0x00	0x35
LDD@	0xF471	0x61	0x08	0x06
STD@	0xF474	0x9D	0x08	0x07
POP@	0xF477	0x83	0xE0	0x08
STP@	0xF47A	0x9D	0x20	0x09
ADD	0xF47D	0x09	0x08	0xA0
SUB	0xF480	0x9D	0x44	0xB0
POPD	0xF483	0x83	0xE1	0x0C
CPR	0xF486	0x1C	0x24	0xD0
INR	0xF489	0x4B	0xA4	0xE0
DCR	0xF48C	0x20	0xE4	0xF0

Table V.11.6. Hash Table 6 – Single Byte SWEET16 Register Instructions

Mnemonic	Table Address	Hash Value 0xEA	Hash Value 0xEA	Valid Formats	Opcode Base Value
STA	0xF490	0x9D	0x02	0x3E	0x81
STX	0xF494	0x9D	0x30	0x01	0x82
STY	0xF498	0x9D	0x32	0x04	0x80
LDA	0xF49C	0x61	0x02	0xBE	0xA1
LDX	0xF4A0	0x61	0x30	0x83	0xA2
LDY	0xF4A4	0x61	0x32	0x8C	0xA0
ADC	0xF4A8	0x09	0x06	0xBE	0x61
AND	0xF4AC	0x0B	0x88	0xBE	0x21
ASL	0xF4B0	0x0C	0xD8	0x4C	0x02
CMP	0xF4B4	0x1B	0x60	0xBE	0xC1
CPX	0xF4B8	0x1C	0x30	0x80	0xE0
CPY	0xF4BC	0x1C	0x32	0x80	0xC0
DEC	0xF4C0	0x21	0x46	0x4C	0xC2
EOR	0xF4C4	0x2B	0xE4	0xBE	0x41
INC	0xF4C8	0x4B	0x86	0x4C	0xE2
JMP	0xF4CC	0x53	0x60	0x20	0x4C
JSR	0xF4D0	0x54	0xE4	0x00	0x20
SBC	0xF4D4	0x98	0x86	0xBE	0xE1
ORA	0xF4D8	0x7C	0x82	0xBE	0x01
LSR	0xF4DC	0x64	0xE4	0x4C	0x42
BIT	0xF4E0	0x12	0x68	0x8C	0x20
ROL	0xF4E4	0x93	0xD8	0x4C	0x22
ROR	0xF4E8	0x93	0xE4	0x4C	0x62
STZ	0xF4EC	0x9D	0x34	0x0C	0x64
TRB	0xF4F0	0xA4	0x84	0x00	0x10
TSB	0xF4F4	0xA4	0xC4	0x00	0x04
SOUT	0xF4F8	0x9B	0xEA	0x80	0x0A
SJMP	0xF4FC	0x9A	0x9A	0x00	0x0F

Table V.11.7. Hash Table 7 – Multiple Addressing Mode Instructions

Bit	7	6	5	4	3	2	1	0	–	–
Mode	IMM	ACC	(IND,X)	(IND),Y	ABS,X	ZP,X	ABS,Y	ZP,Y	ABS	ZP
Value	0x08	0x08	0x00	0x10	0x1C	0x14	0x18	0x14	0x0C	0x04

Table V.11.8. Format Byte Definition

The last table of hash values in *Big Mac* is shown in Table V.11.7 and it begins at 0xF490, and this table is terminated with a NULL or character 0x00. It is the most complex table to process because it contains the entries for those 6502 and 65C02 instructions that can be used in multiple addressing modes. This table also contains two *SWEET16* instructions because those instructions also require special processing. Each 4-byte table entry begins with the mnemonic, its entry address, its 2-byte hash value, its valid format byte, and its opcode base value byte. Depending upon how the instruction is utilized in context within the source code, this opcode base value byte is adjusted by one of the ten possible mode adjustment values. All ten mode adjustment values are located in memory beginning at 0xF501 (formally 0xF4DE) in the *Big Mac* source code. Those ten mode adjustment values are shown in Table V.11.8, and they are mapped to each of the ten possible addressing modes. It only takes a cursory look at the 65C02 Instruction Set to understand how Mr. Bredon was able to reconstruct the opcode values for all of the instructions in Table V.11.7. Mr. Bredon used the opcode base value byte and added that value to one of the ten mode adjustment value bytes based simply on how that instruction is utilized in context within the source code. The valid format byte for each table entry stipulates all of the legal addressing modes that can be utilized by that instruction. Each bit in the valid format byte is mapped to a particular addressing mode. When a bit is ON, that addressing mode is legal for that instruction. Table V.11.8 shows the mapping of which addressing mode is legal for each bit in the valid format byte.

The addressing modes shown in Table V.11.8 are Immediate (IMM), Accumulator (ACC), Indirect (IND) using the X-register, Indirect (IND) using the Y-register, Absolute (ABS) using the X-register, page-zero (ZP) using the X-register, Absolute (ABS) using the Y-register, and page-zero (ZP) using the Y-register. The remaining two modes, Absolute (ABS) and page-zero (ZP), are determined at the time of processing since a register is **not** associated with these two modes. Also, the standalone (IND) mode, new to the 65C02 Instruction Set except for the JMP indirect instruction, must be determined by how the instruction is used in context within the source code.

The source code that I have generated for the *Big Mac* program *is not perfect*. I have verified that two *SWEET16* branch displacements in the source code have the same value as to what exists in the original object code. I think Mr. Bredon somehow allowed two coding errors to pass his design reviews. More likely, Mr. Bredon hand-coded the two *SWEET16* routine displacements which are close in proximity, and for one reason or another these two displacements were simply not checked or not verified. The first displacement error occurs at 0xD2C0 for a BP instruction having a displacement of 0xD3. That displacement would put 0xD295 into the program counter register. There is a BZ instruction at 0xD294 and a ST instruction at 0xD296. I would choose the ST instruction as the more logical branch. The second displacement error occurs at 0xD2DE for a BNZ instruction having a displacement of 0x08. That displacement would put 0xD2E8 into the program counter register. There is a BZ instruction at 0xD2E7 and a SET instruction at 0xD2E9. I would choose the SET instruction as the more logical branch. I have not yet had an opportunity to do more than just document these two errors, so I have not yet changed these displacement values one way or the other. If I cannot ascertain a strategy in order to exercise these two sections of code, then I will not have any further information than I already have to make an educated decision as to what Mr. Bredon intended.

Another interesting anomaly in the *Big Mac* program occurs in the routine that begins at 0xDC60. For all intents and purposes that code looks unremarkable until 0xDC91. At that point there is a JSR instruction to 0xC9AA. How bizarre! I am aware of only one possible reason for this call. In the Apple //e CX ROM code there does exist a purposefully placed Pascal 1.0 output entry point at 0xC9AA called PXWRITE. The nearby routines in this region of code must either branch around or leave room for the PXWRITE entry point. PXWRITE loads the A-register from the variable CHAR located at 0x067B, and the routine jumps to 0xC356, an address in the Slot 3 peripheral-card ROM memory, presumably to write that data to a Pascal object. Why would Mr. Bredon make such a call in *Big Mac* when *Big Mac* was originally written for the Apple][+? This Pascal interface did not even exist for the Apple][+. If Mr. Bredon did update *Big Mac* for the Apple //e, why didn't he also update his *Big Mac* RAM Monitor to display the full 65C02 Instruction Set? So far this call to 0xC9AA is just an interesting anomaly in the *Big Mac* program. Perhaps Mr. Bredon modified the address for the JSR at 0xDC91 *on the fly*. I see no evidence of a label in that region of code to even suggest that such an address modification was even considered. The code could also simply be hogwash. I have yet to investigate this subject any further.

In order to display the 65C02 specific instructions in the Monitor, two format bytes need to be included in the FMT2 table. These two format bytes are for the (ZP) format and for the (ABS,X) jump format. For one reason or another every monitor or MiniAsm monitor that I have studied sets the (ZP) format to 0x4B and the (ABS,X) format to 0x5A. I have no problem with the value for the (ABS,X) format. However, I strongly believe that the value for the (ZP) format can only be 0x49 and never 0x4B. This (ZP) format value becomes even more critical in order to produce the correct opcodes that are generated by the ROM based mini-assembler. Even though *Big Mac* does not have the memory nor any reason to support the code for a mini-assembler, the FMT2 table is still necessary and its values are still critical in order to properly and correctly display the complete 65C02 Instruction Set.

12.   SCRG PROmGRAMER Card

The quikLoader, marketed by the Southern California Research Group, is of little value without a means to easily program EPROMs. So, SCRG marketed the PROmGRAMER which is designed by Bob Brice, and it can program or write EPROMs for the quikLoader, the Apple][family of character generator ROMs, and firmware ROMs. The PROmGRAMER is designed to be configurable using DIP switches in order to access 2708, 2716, 2732, 2764, 27128, 27256, and 27512 type EPROMs. Table V.12.1 shows the DIP switch settings that must be used in order to *correctly* configure the PROmGRAMER for each specific EPROM type. DIP switches 8, 9, and 10 control the level of programming voltage, and failure to orient these switches in their correct position may result in a catastrophic failure of the EPROM. The 2764A and the 27128A and higher EPROMs typically require a 12.5 volt programming voltage while the other EPROMs require a 21 or a 25 volt programming voltage. There are exceptions particularly the Toshiba 27256 which requires a 21 volt programming voltage. In order to utilize a 21 volt programming voltage, DIP switches 8 and 10 must be OFF and DIP switch 9 must be ON. DIP switch 9 must be OFF in order to utilize a 25 volt programming voltage.

EPROM Number	Switch Settings, ON is UP										Programming Voltage
	1	2	3	4	5	6	7	8	9	10	
2708		1		1		1					25.0
2716, 2716A		1		1		1					25.0
2732		1		1	1						25.0
2732A		1		1	1				1		21.0
2764				1			1		1		21.0
2764A				1			1	1		1	12.5
27128			1				1		1		21.0
27128A			1				1	1		1	12.5
27256			1				1	1		1	12.5
27512			1		1			1		1	12.5

Table V.12.1. PROmGRAMER DIP Switch Settings

The PROmGRAMER software by Bob Sander-Cederlof resides in memory beginning at 0x0803, and this program cannot extend beyond 0x0FFF because the desirable EPROM image start address is set at 0x1000. This is necessary particularly in order to program a 27256 or a 27512 EPROM. For a 27256 EPROM, its entire 0x8000 byte image must reside in memory for convenience, and if 0x1000 is its start address, then 0x8FFF will be its last address, and that is very close to the beginning of the third DOS 3.3 file buffer. When MAXFILES is set to 3 in DOS 3.3, HIMEM is set to 0x9600. To program a 27512 EPROM, a 0x10000 byte image must be divided into two or more parts and the EPROM must be programed in two or more sessions. It is for this reason that I highly recommend finding the midpoint for the contents of a 27512 EPROM so that it can be programmed in only two sessions where each session programs exactly 0x8000 bytes. Of course, these memory considerations are greatly alleviated when using DOS 4.5 since HIMEM is always set to 0xBE00. It is just interesting to remember that the original PROmGRAMER software had to consider memory availability when using DOS 3.3 for its disk operating system.

As shown in Figures V.16.10 and V.16.11 for the *Lisa* assembler, the 27512 EPROM image for *EOS* needs to be split at the 0x8000 byte halfway point. The *Lisa* source code directives are designed to direct the *Lisa* assembler to perform all of the work that is necessary in splitting the image at this desired location. Therefore, only two EPROM programming sessions are required in order to write the image of *EOS* into a 27512 EPROM. The software Mr. Sander-Cederlof provided for the PROmGRAMER allows the user to enter a command, such as F for Fast program, and the default parameters that are needed to program a 27256 or the first half of a 27512 EPROM image are automatically entered on the command line. There is **no** command available with default parameters that can program the second half of a 27512 EPROM, so those parameters have to be entered manually onto the command line. I found this to be rather unfortunate after I ruined one too many 27512 EPROM programming sessions where I mistakenly entered the wrong parameters. So, I sourced the PROmGRAMER object code software and I added all of the additional commands that I thought would be necessary in order to support the programming of a 27512 EPROM. Figure V.12.1 shows the new and enhanced configuration screen for PROmGRAMER and Figure V.12.2 shows all of the commands that are now available to the user. The commands that I added which support the programming of the 27512 EPROM are S, T, G, and A. I had to heavily modify the original source code in order to have enough code space that would support all of these new commands, and still have the entire program fit into memory at 0x0803:0x0FFF. The new PROmGRAMER program works incredibly well and it programs all of my EPROMs perfectly.

```
        S.C.R.G.  PROmGRAMER

Enter Slot number (1-7):   5


           EPROM Selection

    1 -- 2716        5 -- 27128
    2 -- 2732        6 -- 27128A
    3 -- 2732A       7 -- 27256
    4 -- 2764        8 -- 27512
Enter selection:   ※
```

```
Working with a 27512 in Slot 5

              Command Menu

     Start End  Offset
 R   1000 8FFF   0000     Read EPROM
 B   1000 8FFF   0000     Burn EPROM
 F   1000 8FFF   0000     Fast Burn & Compare
 C   1000 8FFF   0000     Compare RAM/EPROM
 S   1000 8FFF   8000     Read EPROM
 T   1000 8FFF   8000     Burn EPROM
 G   1000 8FFF   8000     Fast Burn & Compare
 A   1000 8FFF   8000     Compare RAM/EPROM
 D   1000 8FFF            Display RAM
 E   0000 FFFF            Erase Check EPROM
 H                        Help (Command Menu)
 Z                        Restart PROmGRAMER
 M                        Exit to Monitor
 Q                        Exit to DOS

Enter command:
```

Figure V.12.1. PROmGRAMER Configuration   Figure V.12.2. PROmGRAMER Command Menu

In addition to being able to configure the PROmGRAMER hardware to control the level of voltage that is used to program an EPROM, the hardware can be directed by two main programming algorithms to write each individual data byte to a unique EPROM address according to a timing schedule. Most EPROM manufacturers recommend a 50 millisecond programming pulse for every EPROM address. At this rate, it would require nearly 28 minutes to completely program a 27256 EPROM. The B and T commands in the Sander-Cederlof software are designed to program an EPROM using a 50 millisecond programming pulse. However, the F and G commands utilize another programming algorithm. This algorithm uses a much smaller programming pulse for every EPROM address, and it is coupled to a data verification routine. After the software issues the programming pulse, the software reads the EPROM and compares that value with the data from the EPROM image buffer that it is attempting to write to the EPROM. The software continues to loop back in order to issue another programming pulse until the EPROM value correctly matches the data from the EPROM image buffer. The fast programming pulse is set to 2 milliseconds. When the EPROM value matches the data from the EPROM image buffer, a final 4 millisecond programming pulse is issued to the EPROM. Programming time is drastically reduced and in nearly all programming sessions the EPROM is correctly programmed. A 27256 can be programmed in about 3.5 minutes using the fast programming algorithm. Most EPROM manufacturers do not guarantee that this algorithm and its method will successfully program an EPROM every session, though from the experience of most EPROM engineers, this algorithm is far more often utilized successfully. Personally, I have always used the F and G commands. If I am unable to successfully program an EPROM, I will resort to the B or T command. If the B or T command is unable to program an EPROM successfully, I will consider the EPROM to be damaged and unusable, and I will discard the EPROM. Both algorithms will skip any byte in the EPROM image buffer that has a value of 0xFF assuming, of course, that the EPROM was completely erased such that the value at each EPROM address is already set to 0xFF.

Erasing an EPROM requires exposing the EPROM to ultraviolet light for a period of time. The glass that covers the data storage circuits of an EPROM must pass the 253.7 nm or 2537 Å ultraviolet light. I found that the toothbrush sanitizer compartment of my Philips Sonicare was able to quickly erase either one or two EPROMs. The Personal Hygiene Appliance HX6150 or HX6160 uses a #6906 ultraviolet lamp in order to sanitize one or two toothbrushes by exposing the toothbrush bristles to ultraviolet radiation. It only requires two timed exposures by the Philips sanitizer to completely and safely erase any and all of my EPROMs. Ultraviolet lamps do contain mercury, so the lamp must be properly disposed of.

13.   CFFA Data Storage Card

The CompactFlash For Apple or CFFA card is an Apple II peripheral interface card that is able to read data from and write data to a CompactFlash memory card that is seated in its onboard CF card socket or to an external hard drive by means of a 40-pin IDE header socket. Later enhancements of the CFFA card replaced the 40-pin IDE header socket with a USB socket. This peripheral interface card is able to present the onboard flash memory as either a single hard drive or as a stack of floppy disks when using the supplied Disk][emulation firmware. Richard Dreher of R&D Automation created and distributed the CFFA card, and the first production run was released in 2002. I purchased my CFFA card in 2006, CFFA Version 2.0, revision B. It is my understanding that the CFFA card is most likely designed to be more compatible with ProDOS. Unfortunately, perhaps, I never participated in Apple's Disk Operating System changeover from DOS 3.3 to ProDOS. When ProDOS was first introduced my software interests had already been redirected to UNIX based high-end professional workstations that are manufactured by SGI running IRIX and SUN running SunOS. In view of my recent development of DOS 4.1 and now DOS 4.5, I began in earnest developing my own Disk][emulation firmware for my CFFA card, which sat unused for a number of years. I simply wanted to design a method that would digitally archive my hundreds, oh yes, many hundreds of 5.25-inch diskettes, and the CFFA card seemed to be the ideal reservoir. I understand, however, that Mr. Dreher has enhanced the CFFA card in many ways since my purchase in 2006. I have no idea if the hardware peripheral interface of the current version of the CFFA card resembles that of the past peripheral interface, and whether or not any firmware that is developed for CFFA Version 2.0 will even function on the current version of the hardware. As long as the current hardware design can still interface a CF memory card, I have no doubt that any previously designed CFFA firmware will also function without change on the current version of the CFFA hardware.

Address	Name	I/O	Description
0xC0n0	ATADATAH	R/W	Used with register #8 to R/W data. Write this byte first
0xC0n1	SETCSMSK	R/W	Disable 6502 pre-fetch when writing to CF
0xC0n2	CLRCSMSK	R/W	Enable 6502 pre-fetch when reading CF
0xC0n6	ATASTAT2	R	Secondary CF status register; does not clear IRQ
0xC0n6	ATADEVCT	W	Device control register to disable IRQ
0xC0n8	ATADATAL	R/W	Used with register #0 to R/W data. Read this byte first
0xC0n9	ATAERROR	R	Processing error source when register #15 is not zero
0xC0nA	ATASECCT	R/W	Number of blocks to read or write; always set to 1
0xC0nB	ATASECTR	R/W	Bits 07:00 of LBA
0xC0nC	ATACYLNL	R/W	Bits 15:08 of LBA
0xC0nD	ATACYLNH	R/W	Bits 23:16 of LBA
0xC0nE	ATAHEAD	R/W	Bits 27:24 of LBA; select LBA or CHS mode
0xC0nF	ATASTAT	R	Primary CF status register; does not clear IRQ
0xC0nF	ATACMD	W	Command register

Table V.13.1. CFFA Peripheral Interface Control Registers

The firmware that I designed and developed for my CFFA Version 2.0 peripheral interface card allows the complete access to each of the 512-byte data blocks on a CompactFlash memory card up to 8 GB in size. Each data block resides at a unique 24-bit Logical Block Address or LBA that is divided among three 8-bit bytes, and each byte is saved to three of the sixteen peripheral-card I/O memory locations or registers. There are also four upper address bits that are available in a fourth I/O register that can extend CFFA data block addressing to 28 bits. Table V.13.1 shows the peripheral-card I/O memory locations that are used in order to initiate a CF processing command for the CFFA hardware. In Table V.13.1 the value of n in 0xC0n0, for example, equals the slot number where the CFFA card resides plus eight. Even though 28 bits are available to specify an LBA, my CFFA firmware is limited to accessing an 8 GB CF memory card at most. Furthermore, my CFFA firmware is capable of reading and saving the Master BOOT Record or MBR. Only three processing commands are necessary in order to utilize the CFFA peripheral interface hardware and to access a CF memory card, and those processing commands are READ, WRITE, and ID. If the peripheral-card I/O locations have been changed to accept a 32-bit LBA, my CFFA firmware interface will still only address up to an 8 GB CF memory card.

Table V.13.2 shows the sizes of available CompactFlash cards in total data blocks based on their Cylinder, Head, and Sector or CHS geometry according to CompactFlash data sheets. Knowing the CHS geometry for a particular CF card allows one to convert CHS to LBA. However, it is not necessary to know or to even utilize this conversion to LBA in order to address the CFFA hardware in LBA mode. Also, the CFFA card that I own is designed and manufactured to address a CF card that is 8 GB in size or smaller. As stated above, the LBA value is 24-bits in size and divided among three bytes. The READ and the WRITE processing commands are the only commands that are necessary in order to read or to write any 512-byte data block within the CF card. The ID command can be used to read the IDENTIFY DEVICE block in the CF card. The ID block provides the serial number, the model number, and the capacity of the CF card in LBA addressable blocks as well as other useful information about the CF card.

Card Size	Cylinders	Heads	Sectors	Total Blocks
256 MB	0x03D4	0x10	0x20	0x07A800
512 MB	0x03E1	0x10	0x3F	0x0F45F0
1 GB	0x07C2	0x10	0x3F	0x1E8BE0
2 GB	0x0F82	0x10	0x3F	0x3D0FE0
4 GB	0x1F1C	0x10	0x3F	0x7A7E40
8 GB	0x3E08	0x10	0x3F	0xF43F80

Table V.13.2. CompactFlash Card CHS Geometry

Offset	Name	Description
0x00	CFBOOT	Entry point for the DOS PR# command in order to BOOT the selected DOS
0x10	ROMHOOK	Entry point to attach the CFFA to the DOS Disk Address table
0x18	ROMUHOOK	Entry point to detach the CFFA from the DOS Disk Address table
0x20	USRBOOT	BOOT selected CFFA DOS image
0x30	VOLBOOT	BOOT selected CFFA volume DOS image
0x3B	DISKRWTS	DOS 3.3 RWTS entry if DOS 3.3 is in memory
0x4B	CFRWTS	DOS 4.1 and DOS 4.5 RWTS entry if DOS 4.1 or if DOS 4.5 is in memory
0x5C	ROMBOOT	Simulate Disk][entry point for BOOT Stage 0 code that resides at 0x0801
0x64	CFRWTS3	Convert DVTS to LBA to seek, read, write, and format a CF volume
0xF3	MODOS3	Entry point to modify DOS 3.3 during BOOT Stage 2 for CFFA utilization
0xFE	VERSION	Version number of CF firmware (now 0x05)
0xFF	BUILD	Build number for CF firmware (now 0x06)

Table V.13.3. CFFA Firmware Entry Points

The firmware for the CFFA interface fits comfortably in the peripheral-card ROM memory and in the expansion ROM memory of the CFFA card. The peripheral-card ROM memory image utilizes the normal disk signature bytes and it includes a CFFA unique byte that is located at offset 0x00 for CFFA identification as shown in Table II.7.2. This ROM image also includes my standard DOS connection ON/OFF at offsets 0x10 and 0x18, respectively, a user BOOT entry at offset 0x20, and a volume BOOT entry at offset 0x30. Table V.13.3 shows all of the entry points in my CFFA firmware interface. The user can BOOT one of eight versions of DOS where twenty-four LBA blocks are reserved for each DOS image. The first six DOS images include DOS 3.3, DOS 4.1L, DOS 4.1H, DOS 4.3H, DOS 4.5.05L, and DOS 4.5.06H. Thus, there is room for two User Defined DOS images that may be installed at any time, and those images are called IMAGUSR1 and IMAGUSR2. Also, the CFFA firmware can BOOT any bootable volume on any drive that is within the memory of the CF card whether the BOOT tracks contain BOOT images for DOS 3.3, DOS 4.1, DOS 4.3, or DOS 4.5. ProDOS is **not** supported by this firmware.

The peripheral-card ROM memory image is saved to its own 256-byte file by the assembler. The expansion ROM memory image of the CFFA card firmware utilizes the full eight pages or 2048 bytes that are available to a peripheral interface card as long as that peripheral interface card contains the logic and the memory that can support that capability. The assembler saves the expansion ROM memory image separately from the peripheral-card ROM memory image. The expansion ROM memory image contains all of the routines that handle the BOOT of any of the DOS images as well as the BOOT of any of the User Defined DOS images on CF volumes. The entire BOOT process is highly monitored and it is based upon DOS version that is easily determined prior to the BOOT process. The monitor process implements certain modifications to either the DOS as in DOS 3.3, or modifications to the DOS BOOT Configuration Table as in DOS 4.1, DOS 4.3, or DOS 4.5. The purpose behind these *on the fly* modifications are, of course, to be able to utilize drive numbers that may be far greater than two. The expansion ROM memory image of the CFFA card must convert DVTS to LBA and range check the resulting LBA value. All of the CF routines that have specific protocols in addressing the CFFA peripheral interface control registers are also found in the expansion ROM memory image. These routines check the CF busy state, the CF ready state, and the CF status state. The routines can perform a CF software or hardware reset, utilize a specific CF delay routine, and implement a general status check by utilizing several of the lower level routines. There is a specific protocol that must be adhered to when loading the CF command register with a command value and when loading the LBA registers with a three-byte distributed LBA value. The most important routine is the DOCFCMD routine that directs all further processing based on the command that is extracted from the RWTS IOCB by the routines in the peripheral-card ROM memory image. All of the CFFA RWTS IOCB commands are shown in Table V.13.4 with a very cursory description of that command. All of the conversion table data that is used to convert DVTS to LBA and all of the Information Message data and the Error Message data is found at the end of the expansion ROM memory image. The Connect Message texts and the Disconnect Message texts both utilize offsets into the composite set of message data.

Command	Description
0x00	uses DVTS mode to seek that LBA
0x01	uses DVTS mode to read 256 bytes from that LBA
0x02	uses DVTS mode to write 256 bytes to that LBA
0x04	uses DVTS mode to format that volume
0x11	uses DVTS mode to read 512 bytes from that LBA
0x12	uses DVTS mode to write 512 bytes to that LBA
0x20	uses CF mode to reset the CFFA
0x21	uses LBA mode to read 512 bytes from that LBA
0x22	uses LBA mode to write 512 bytes to that LBA
0x30	uses CF mode to read the 512 byte ID from that CFFA

Table V.13.4. CFFA Firmware IOCB Commands

The RWTS IOCB commands 0x01 and 0x02 require highly complex processing in order to read either the first half or the second half of the 512-byte data block for the calculated LBA. The entire LBA must be read, so either the data in the second half is tossed or the data in the first half is tossed. The data in the first half is retained when sector number is 0x00:0x0F or the data in the second half is retained when sector number is 0x10:0x1F. When writing a sector of data to the CFFA, which is typically 256 bytes of data, those data bytes must replace the data in the first half of the 512-byte data block at the calculated LBA when the sector number is 0x00:0x0F. When the sector number is 0x10:0x1F, those 256 data bytes must replace the data in the second half of the calculated LBA. The entire LBA must first be read and the alternate half of that data block must be saved in its entirety. One of the important reasons why DOS 4.1, DOS 4.3, and DOS 4.5 provide the MSB page address for NBUF1 is so that the CFFA firmware can copy the alternate half of the calculated LBA for safe keeping. Therefore, the LBA is written from the IOCB specified data buffer and from the NBUF1 data buffer in the order that is dictated by the IOCB specified sector number. Care must also be given to disabling 6502 pre-fetch before ever writing to an LBA and ensuring that the 6502 pre-fetch is enabled after writing to an LBA. It is a very good policy to always enable 6502 pre-fetch before ever reading an LBA.

IOCB Parameter	Size in Bits	Address	Bit Range	Description
Sector	4	0x0578	03:00	maps into LBA0, the LSB
Track	6	0x05F8	09:04	maps into LBA0 and LBA1
Volume	8	0x0678	17:10	maps into LBA1 and LBA2
Drive	6	0x06F8	23:18	maps into LBA3, the MSB

Table V.13.5. RWTS IOCB Processing in LBA Mode

When LBA mode is utilized in order to process the RWTS IOCB commands 0x21 and 0x22, the entire LBA value must be assembled from the available parameters that are found within the RWTS IOCB. Table V.13.5 shows how the RWTS IOCB is utilized in order to directly specify which LBA is to be read or which LBA is to be written. Of course, the address of the data buffer that is specified in the RWTS IOCB must be able to accommodate 512 bytes of data. The LBA bytes are extracted from the RWTS IOCB and copied to the Public slot variable addresses that are shown in Table V.13.5. It is important that these RWTS IOCB parameters are cleared and initialized to zero except that Drive is initialized to one.

The peripheral-card ROM memory image and the expansion ROM memory image cannot be directly copied to the CFFA hardware using the ROM Monitor memory move routines. According to CFFA documentation, the EEPROM that is used in the CFFA hardware requires a minimum of a 200 μsec delay after writing each byte of data. The Volume Manager utility that I developed in order to manage the CFFA firmware utilizes a 225 μsec delay after writing each byte of data to both ROM memory locations. The 225 μsec delay is more than sufficient and comparison tests after writing each ROM memory location confirm that the ROM images are written successfully to each memory location.

I approached the design of my CFFA firmware as a means to communicate with a massive data storage container of many bootable devices. To that end, I devised an equation in order to utilize the parameters that I had available in DOS 4.5 that I could absolutely control, and these parameters are Sector, Track, Volume and Drive. My conversion algorithm collectively converts the Drive/Volume/Track/Sector parameters or DVTS to LBA and I provide another algorithm to perform the reverse conversion, or LBA to DVTS. There is only one unique solution for either conversion routine. Any DOS that is designed for the Apple][is limited by the variables that it can absolutely control. DOS 4.5 is no exception, of course, and the variables that are available to DOS 4.5 for the management of any collection of data volumes and bootable devices are sector number, track number, volume number, and drive number. The variables sector, track, and volume already have predefined limitations or ranges for their operational values. Drive number is typically thought of as being two disk devices for each peripheral interface card until Rana developed a peripheral interface card that supports up to four bootable devices. In order to utilize the extraordinary resources of a CF card, the concept of drive number must be re-imagined and thought of as a large bank of virtual disk resources that are strapped together such that each bootable device can accommodate a very large number of volumes up to 256. Being able to accommodate a large number of bootable devices or Drives is an opportunity to manage an exceedingly large collection of disk volumes with very little effort. The ranges that are allowed in my CFFA firmware for the IOCB variables Sector, Track, Volume, and Drive are shown in Table V.13.6.

The equations to convert DVTS to LBA where Drive > 0 are given by

```
   block = Sector & 0x0F
    page = Sector & 0x10
offset1 = 0x100

    LBA = ( ( Drive-1 ) * 0x30000 ) +
          ( Volume * 0x300 ) +
          ( Track * 0x10 ) + block + offset1
```

Parameter	Range	Description
Sector	0 - 31	supported by the DOS 4.5 VTOC
Track	0 - 47	supported by the DOS 4.5 VTOC
Volume	0 - 255	supported by the DOS 4.5 VTOC
Drive	1 - 81	supports up to an 8 GB CF card

Table V.13.6. DVTS Variable Range in CFFA Firmware

These equations conclude that each Volume contains 0x300 LBA blocks and each Drive contains 0x30000 LBA blocks. A Volume can consist of a maximum of forty-eight Tracks and each Track can consist of sixteen LBA blocks by definition. Since an LBA block contains 512 bytes of data, a block is partitioned by the page variable. When page is equal to zero, then disk sectors 0x00 to 0x0F reside on page 0, or the lower half of the LBA block. When page is not zero, then disk sectors 0x10 to 0x1F reside on page 1, or the upper half of the LBA block. I agree that forcing the size of a Volume to be 768 LBA blocks or 1536 disk sectors rather than a Volume that has 576 disk sectors with thirty-six tracks does potentially waste a lot of resource space on the CF card. DOS 4.5 has the potential to address a volume that has a maximum of fifty tracks, but I considered forty-eight tracks to be the better upper limit for mathematical reasons and for ease in converting DVTS to LBA. Because the VTOC can support thirty-two sectors per track and an LBA block contains 512 bytes, it makes sense to split an LBA block into a lower 256-byte disk sector and an upper 256-byte disk sector. The algorithm to convert a given DVTS to a unique LBA is exceedingly fast in the CFFA firmware because **all** of the multiplication is accomplished by using the addition of values that are obtained from three small conversion tables. The indexing into these three conversion tables use 4-bit nibbles that are derived from Volume and Drive.

Card Size	Blocks	Drives	Extra Volumes	Residue
256 MB	0x07A800	2	141	0x000
512 MB	0x0F45F0	5	22	0x2F0
1 GB	0x1E8BE0	10	46	0x0E0
2 GB	0x3D0FE0	20	90	0x0E0
4 GB	0x7A7E40	40	212	0x140
8 GB	0xF43F80	81	106	0x080

Table V.13.7. CompactFlash Drives and Volumes in CFFA Firmware

Block Start	Block End	Description
0x000000	0x000001	Not used
0x000002	0x000002	Saved peripheral-card slot firmware
0x000003	0x000006	Saved peripheral-card expansion ROM firmware
0x000007	0x000007	Saved Identify Device
0x000008	0x00000F	DOS descriptions, room for eight descriptions
0x000010	0x0000CF	DOS Images, room for eight 24-block images
0x0000D0	0x0000FF	Drive descriptions, room for 96 256-byte descriptions
0x000100	0x1E00FF	10 Drives each having 256 volumes
0x1E0100	0x1E8AFF	1 Drive having 46 volumes
0x1E8B00	0x1E8BDF	Not used

Table V.13.8. Block Utilization for a 1 GB CompactFlash Card

Using the values that are shown in Table V.13.2 for the Total Blocks in CF cards, the total number of drives and extra volumes can be easily determined, and they are shown in Table V.13.7. The conversion equation for DVTS to LBA stipulates that 0x30000 LBA blocks comprise one drive and that 0x300 LBA blocks comprise one volume. For example, a 1 GB CompactFlash card contains ten full drives and the last, or eleventh drive has room for only forty-six volumes. There is 0x0E0 unused LBA blocks remaining after accounting for offset1 which is set to 0x100 LBA blocks. Table V.13.8 shows an example of the block utilization for a 1 GB CF card. The only difference in CF card utilization for the other CF card sizes is the number of drives and extra volumes. Table V.13.8 shows that 0x30 blocks are allocated for drive descriptions so that there is enough room for 96 descriptions where each drive description is allocated 256 bytes. A drive description contains the drive name in the first twenty-four bytes, the date and time in the next six bytes when the drive description is first created, and the actual NULL-terminated drive description verbiage in the remaining 226 bytes.

The LBA and the page value for a particular drive description is calculated as follows

```
offset = 0xD0

   LBA = | ( ( Drive-1 ) / 2 ) | + offset

   page = ( Drive-1 ) - ( ( LBA - offset ) * 2 )
```

There is sufficient room reserved for eight DOS images that are up to 24 blocks in size, and these images begin at LBA block 0x000010 and the DOS images follow the DOS image descriptions that begin at LBA block 0x000008. The first six DOS images include DOS 3.3, DOS 4.1L, DOS 4.1H, DOS 4.3H, DOS 4.5.05L, and DOS 4.5.06H. Thus, there is also room for two User Defined DOS images that may be installed at any time, and those images are called IMAGUSR1 and IMAGUSR2. Each DOS image is assigned a volume number from one to eight and the image is fully contained within twenty-four LBA blocks that are reserved for that image. Each DOS image is saved to the CF card as it exists on disk after it is written to the BOOT tracks of a bootable DOS volume. The only difference between a BOOTing CFFA image and a BOOTing volume image is that a BOOTing CFFA image has a DRIVE value that is set to zero whereas a BOOTing volume image has a DRIVE value that is **not** set to zero.

Connecting the CFFA to DOS 4.5 is trivial because DOS 4.5 contains a reserved address location for each slot that contains a bootable peripheral interface card. As long as the peripheral interface card presents itself as a Disk][-like I/O device, DOS 4.5 will provide that device with an RWTS interface slot location. When the CFFA is BOOTed with one of its installed DOS images, DOS 4.5.06H for example, BOOT Stage 1 is monitored for the BOOTPGS parameter to become negative. Unlike DOS 3.3, BOOT Stage 1 in DOS 4.5 reads sectors 0x0F to 0x00 on track 0x00 in descending order into memory from Page 0xD0 to Page 0xDD and from Page 0xBE to Page 0xBF in ascending order. After sector 0x00 is read into memory at 0xBF00, all of the DOS 4.5 RWTS routines are now available to read into memory the remaining sectors or blocks of DOS 4.5. Normally, a Disk][-like I/O device only BOOTs from drive one of two possible drives regardless of the value of the volume number that is assigned to that diskette. However, the CFFA must also be able to BOOT **any** of its bootable volumes on **any** of its drives, so this puts a special burden on the CFFA firmware routines that monitor the BOOT Stage 1 process.

In addition to the BOOT variable BOOTPGS common to all varieties of DOS, and the DOS 4.5 Disk Address table, there is a variable called BCFGNDX that points to a structure on Page 0xBF. BCFGNDX points to the BOOTCFG table of variables that is used to initialize the RWTS IOCB by the RWPAGES routine at the beginning of BOOT Stage 2. It is at this crucial juncture when BOOT Stage 1 completes, but before BOOT Stage 2 begins, that the BOOTCFG table must be configured with the current CF Drive and the current Volume that is attempting to BOOT. The CHKDRVZ routine in the CFFA firmware is called during BOOT Stage 1 and during BOOT Stage 2 in order to ensure that the LBA block number for the given CFFA DOS is correctly calculated when the value for DRIVE is set to zero. When the value for DRIVE is **not** set to zero, the values for DNUM and VOLEXPT, the DRIVE and VOLUME values in BOOTCFG for the BOOTing CFFA volume, are utilized by BOOT Stage 2 and they are pushed onto the CFRWTS interface using the RWTS IOCB. This method ensures that the correct LBA is calculated from the given DVTS values. Unfortunately, the situation for BOOTing a DOS 3.3 volume is a complete nightmare for any firmware, and the CFFA firmware is no exception, but certainly it is not impossible to monitor and to manage the BOOTing of a DOS 3.3 volume correctly and with complete control.

BOOT Stage 1 for DOS 3.3 reads sectors 0x09 to 0x00 on track 0x00 in descending order into Apple][memory from Page 0xBF to Page 0xB6, also in descending order. After sector 0x00 is read into memory at Page 0xB6, all of the DOS 3.3 RWTS routines are now available to read into memory the remaining sectors or blocks of DOS 3.3. Before BOOT Stage 2 begins, DOS 3.3 initializes the RWTS IOCB with DNUM set to 0x01 and VOLEXPT set to zero, which allows any volume to BOOT in disk drive 1. These values must be patched, or overwritten in order for the CF firmware to calculate the correct LBA from the BOOTing DVTS values. Once the routine RWPAGES has read into memory the remaining pages of DOS 3.3 using the correct drive and volume values, the DOS 3.3 code must be patched yet again in order for it to function at all or properly within the CFFA environment. The prime issue with DOS 3.3 is how DOS 3.3 manages or mismanages volume number in my opinion. In the CFFA environment volume number cannot be ascertained from the Address Field header of a sector or a block because there are **no** Address Field headers to read when reading CF data blocks. Therefore, a DOS 3.3 routine such as CATHNDLR that handles the DOS CATALOG command must not presuppose any value for the BOOTing volume number. Similarly, the SETDFLTS routine must not initialize or change the current value for volume number so that other DOS 3.3 commands will work properly when the V keyword is not included with a DOS 3.3 command. Furthermore, in order for DOS 3.3 to read into memory any DOS 4.5 file, the maximum filename length must be adjusted down to twenty-four bytes in length. Before any CF volume is initialized with DOS 3.3, all patches like the ones just described probably should be removed. A simple tool can do this, of course, but in order for DOS 3.3 to communicate with the CFFA firmware and perform volume initialization, its CALLRWTS routine **must remain patched**. Thus, I believe the better solution is to leave DOS 3.3 patched and totally useable in the CF environment, initialize a CF volume as desired, and overwrite the DOS 3.3 image that resides on tracks 0x00, 0x01, and 0x02 with whatever *pure* DOS 3.3 image you require knowing full well that it may not BOOT or it may not function properly in the CF environment. There may be other equally viable solutions but this solution appears to be the most minimal. Table V.13.9 documents all of the patches that are applied by the CFFA firmware to a DOS 3.3 image before and after BOOT Stage 2 processing.

Address	Old	New	BOOT Stage 2	Description
0xB707	0x01	drive	before	update for DNUM
0xB7EB	0x00	volume	before	update of VOLEXPT
0xB748	0x84	#modos3	before	replace address of DOSSTRT with the #MODOS3
0xB749	0x9D	cfpage	before	routine and CFPAGE at 0xB748:0xB749
0xAA66	VOLVAL	volume	after	update VOLVAL with volume
0xB7EB	VOLEXPT	volume	after	update IOCB VOLEXPT with volume
0xA0DA	0x66	0x65	after	change address from VOLVAL to KYWRDIDX
0xA95B	0x02	cfmaxdrv	after	update KWRANGE for DRIVE
0xAD9E	0xF9	0xFE	after	change address from VOLNUMBR to unused address after File Manager Work Area
0xB203	0x1E	0x18	after	change NAMESIZE value for filename length
0xB707	drive	0x01	after	restore original value
0xB748	#modos3	0x84	after	restore the address of DOSSTRT (0x9D84) at
0xB749	cfpage	0x9D	after	0xB748:0xB749

Table V.13.9. DOS 3.3 Patches Used in CFFA Firmware

Referring to Table V.13.9, all of the variables that are listed in lowercase reside in CFFA firmware. All of the uppercase variables reside in DOS 3.3 source code. The first four substitutions are made just after BOOT Stage 1 completes and just before BOOT Stage 2 begins. The LSB address for the firmware entry point MODOS3 as shown in Table V.13.3 and the CFPAGE value for the MSB address of the CFFA peripheral-card slot firmware are used to replace the address at 0xB748:0xB749 for the DOSSTRT routine which is at 0x9D84. Once BOOT Stage 2 completes, these patches will force DOS 3.3 to re-enter the CFFA firmware in order to install the remaining patches and code replacements that are required so that DOS 3.3 is useable in the CF environment. After all of the patches have been installed, the CFFA firmware simply jumps to the intended DOSSTRT address at this time. I fondly recall meeting many software engineers, particularly those at Sierra On-Line, who I refer to as *DOS 3.3 Purists. Thou shalt not modify DOS 3.3!* Only when a few of the Sierra On-Line programmers were able to demonstrate to Ken Williams that they were able to make DOS 3.3 smarter, faster, and safer did Williams remove the DOS 3.3 Purity Shield. Now, from my current vantage point, I see that DOS 3.3 contains a lot of really horribly coded routines that are based on some very silly concepts, like how volume number is handled, and mishandled, and complimented, and substituted, and so on and so forth. So, I see nothing wrong with *adjusting* a few DOS 3.3 parameters in order for this DOS to function in the CF environment. Hopefully, DOS 4.5 demonstrates how simple and powerful it is when using volume number like the other DVTS parameters in the CF environment simply and without any further embellishment.

Index	Name	Phrase 1	Phrase 2	Phrase 3
0x00	IOTEXT1A	Unable to	disconnect CF and DOS	
0x03	IOTEXT1B	Unable to	connect CF and DOS	
0x06	IOTEXT2A	Able to	disconnect CF and DOS	3.3
0x09	IOTEXT2B	Able to	disconnect CF and DOS	4.1
0x0C	IOTEXT2C	Able to	disconnect CF and DOS	4.3
0x0F	IOTEXT2D	Able to	disconnect CF and DOS	4.5
0x12	IOTEXT3A	Able to	connect CF and DOS	3.3
0x15	IOTEXT3B	Able to	connect CF and DOS	4.1
0x18	IOTEXT3C	Able to	connect CF and DOS	4.3
0x1B	IOTEXT3D	Able to	connect CF and DOS	4.5
0x1E	ERRTEXT1	CF	reset	error
0x21	ERRTEXT2	CF	read	ID error
0x24	ERRTEXT3	Wrong	CF	card
0x27	ERRTEXT4	Wrong	BOOT image	value
0x2A	ERRTEXT5	Wrong	drive	value
0x2D	ERRTEXT6	LBA	range	error
0x30	ERRTEXT7	LBA	read	error

Table V.13.10. CFFA Firmware Messages

There are times when desperation leads to utilizing very creative and sneaky programming techniques. To be sure, I was desperate in finding enough memory space to include the DOS 4.5 interface into the CFFA firmware. I did not want to exclude the DOS 3.3 or the DOS 4.1 or the DOS 4.3 interfaces, and I did not want to remove any of the informational text messages when a DOS volume is attached to or when a DOS volume is detached from the CFFA. I had already faced a similar dilemma for the DOS 4.5 HELP command where I desperately needed a little more memory for some additional code. In that situation, I used every scheme in my programming arsenal and it was still not enough to give me the memory I required. What saved the day was recursive programming! Recursive programming depends upon solutions to smaller instances of the same problem. Recursive programming in C-language is very simple to implement and it is very much like winding up a spring. The spring continues to be *wound* until a solution end-point is reached, and then the spring is allowed to unwind transferring each *previous* solution to the *next* iteration. It was the final weapon to win the battle for more memory and code space in order to fully complete the DOS HELP handler. For the CFFA firmware, it was the utilization of phrases to formulate informational messages and error messages as shown in Table V.13.10. Each message contains three phrases so that the message data can be highly compacted. When a NULL byte or character 0x00 is encountered, that phrase is skipped, otherwise the byte is used as an offset to that phrase in memory. Not only was I able to include the DOS 4.5 interface and retain all informational message texts and all error message texts, but I succeeded in adding a new and more complex DOS image load manager and still have forty-six bytes remaining that can be used for new CFFA features I have yet to imagine. Using recursive programming and data phrases in these particular situations proved to be the right solution.

14. Volume Manager Utility

The Volume Manager or *VOLMGR* is a utility that I developed in order to manage the CFFA ROM memory firmware, manage the CFFA CompactFlash card utilization and identity, manage the CF Drives, manage all of the CF Volumes in a CF Drive, and manage the CF User DOS Images. In addition, the *BOOTDOS* utility can be used to BOOT any one of the six currently defined DOS images on the CF card as well as any one of the two User Defined DOS images on the CF card when and if a user makes them available. The *BOOTVOL* utility can be used to BOOT any one of the bootable CF volumes in any of the CF drives. Figures V.14.1 to V.14.4 show a few of the initial menu displays from *VOLMGR*. When *VOLMGR* first begins, it displays a warning screen as shown in Figure V.14.1. This warning display reminds the user that using powerful software like *VOLMGR* and its utilities can indeed cause damage to directories and file systems when this software is used carelessly. If a CFFA interface card is detected in one of the Apple][peripheral-card slots, the CFFA Volume Manager Main Menu is displayed as shown in Figure V.14.2. This menu shows that there are five main managers that comprise the *VOLMGR* utility. *VOLMGR* does detect a previously unmodified CFFA card by inspecting the first eight firmware bytes known as the signature bytes, and it continues its processing nevertheless for this single instance of the firmware configuration. This allows the user to save the current factory supplied CFFA firmware to a file on a diskette and to install new CFFA firmware onto the CFFA card as shown in Figure V.14.3.

The Manage Firmware menu provides for the installation of CFFA Slot and ROM firmware and the installation of all six default DOS images. After *VOLMGR* installs the CFFA firmware, the first eight firmware bytes, or signature bytes are changed to those that are listed for the CFFA card as shown in Table II.7.2. When *VOLMGR* is launched again anytime in the future, *VOLMGR* continues processing because the new CFFA signature bytes are read and they verify that the CFFA card contains the new CFFA firmware. Detecting any other firmware bytes will not allow *VOLMGR* to continue any further processing. *VOLMGR* copies the CFFA Slot Firmware that is written to the peripheral-card ROM memory of the CFFA card to LBA 0x0000002. It also copies the CFFA ROM Firmware that is written to the peripheral-card expansion ROM memory of the CFFA card to LBA 0x0000003-0x0000006. This allows *VOLMGR* to restore the critical firmware data that is located at 0xC804-0xC83C from LBA 0x0000003 and to restore all of the Slot Firmware from LBA 0x0000002. The CompactFlash device buffers all data that is written to a specific LBA block such that it is **not** necessary to throttle the speed at which data is written to the CFFA ATADATAL and ATADATAH registers. This is **not true** for data that is written to the CFFA peripheral-card ROM memory or to the peripheral-card expansion ROM memory. Data written to these memory areas must be actively throttled. However, data that is read from these memory areas do not require throttling such that these memory areas may be read like any other peripheral-card memory. The EEPROM memory that is utilized in the CFFA hardware meets the read data specifications and requirements for the Apple][address bus and data bus timing. To write a page of peripheral-card ROM memory for the CFFA peripheral interface card requires 63,233 µsec rather than 3841 µsec to write the same data without a delay throttle of 225 µsec. In other words, it is around 16.5 times slower to write any data to the CFFA peripheral-card and expansion ROM memory.

```
        CFFA Volume Manager

          DOS 4.5, Build 06

      Copyright (c) 2024 February 14
                  by
        Walland Philip Vrbancic Jr


      Use this CompactFlash For Apple
        installer and the accompanying
      software programs at your own risk.

     You are responsible for any damage or
    loss of productivity this installer or
    the accompanying software may cause.

         Press any key to continue if
         you agree to these terms, or
    press ESC to exit this program now.
```

Figure V.14.1. VOLMGR Product Warning

```
     CFFA Volume Manager Main Menu



    1 - Manage Firmware

    2 - Manage CompactFlash Card

    3 - Manage Drives

    4 - Manage Volumes

    5 - Manage Bootable DOS Images

    6 - Exit Volume Manager


Select Option:  ■
```

Figure V.14.2. VOLMGR Main Menu

```
           Manage Firmware


    1 - Save CFFA Firmware to Disk
    2 - Install CFFA Firmware from Disk
    3 - Install Default DOS from Disk
    4 - Restore CF Firmware Data
    5 - Restore CF Slot/ROM Firmware
    6 - Return to Main Menu



Select Option:
```

Figure V.14.3. Manage Firmware Menu

```
         Manage CompactFlash


    1 - Display CF Memory Utilization
    2 - Display Identify Device Contents
    3 - Save Identify Device to LBA 7
    4 - Save Selected LBA to Disk
    5 - Restore Selected LBA from Disk
    6 - Clear Selected LBA Range
    7 - Return to Main Menu


Select Option:  ■
```

Figure V.14.4. Manage CompactFlash Menu

The six default DOS images must be preprocessed into their BOOT image code format from their object code format before the images can be installed into the DOS Image region of the CFFA. For example, the **object image** format for a DOS 4.5 Binary file is shown in Table I.8.4, which shows the Binary file image as it maps to memory address. This object image format is in the order of object code data that the assembler generates when it assembles the source code for DOS 4.5. In order to write the object image that is contained in this Binary file to the BOOT tracks of a diskette in order to render that diskette bootable, the format of the object image must be transformed into the format of track and sector mapping to memory address that is shown in Table I.8.3. The result of this format transformation becomes the **BOOT image** for the DOS 4.5 object image in this example. The tool that is used to transform a DOS object image file into its BOOT image file is called INSTALL_DOS. The BOOT image file format gives any DOS its capability to BOOT by means of the CFFA firmware. The simplicity of this firmware to BOOT a DOS BOOT image makes it nearly magical in its power and in its flexibility.

The Manage CompactFlash menu as shown in Figure V.14.4 allows *VOLMGR* to provide visibility into how the resources of the CompactFlash card are utilized. This menu allows the 512-byte contents of the Identify Device block to be read into memory, it automatically saves a copy of the ID to LBA 0x0000007, and it displays the important aspects of the device data. This menu also provides complete LBA management as well. The contents of any LBA may be saved to a diskette, any LBA may be restored from a diskette, and a selected range of LBA blocks may be cleared where all 512 bytes of a block are set to zero. These routines are surprisingly fast in view of the amount of CF data that must be accessed. Figure V.14.5 shows an example display of a 1 GB CF card that is capable of hosting ten complete drives where each drive contains 256 volumes. In order not to waste the remaining resources on this card, an eleventh drive is available that contains forty-six volumes. Thus, 0x30000 * 10 + 0x300 * 46 = 0x01E8A00. The Identify Device contents for this same CF card is shown in Figure V.14.6. From this information, the LBA contents in this CF card is equal to 0x07C2 * 0x0010 * 0x003F = 0x01E8BE0.

```
     Display CF Memory Utilization

   CFFA slot - 5

   Card name - CF 1.0 GB Storage Media
   Date/Time - 02/14/24 08:28:48

 LBA sectors - 0x01E8BE0 (1 GB)

Total drives - 011 + 046 extra volumes

0000000-0000001 = Not used
0000002-0000002 = Saved Slot Firmware
0000003-0000006 = Saved ROM Firmware
0000007-0000007 = Saved Identify Device
0000008-000000F = DOS Descriptions (8)
0000010-00000CF = DOS Images (8)
00000D0-00000FF = Drive Descriptions
0000100-01E8AFF = Drives and Volumes
01E8B00-01E8BDF = Not used

             Press Any Key
```

Figure V.14.5. CF Memory Utilization

```
    Display Identify Device Contents


   Cylinders - 0007C2

       Heads - 000010

Sectors/Track - 00003F

 Maximum LBA - 1E8BE0

Serial Number - 020805J2806R5550

   Firmware - HDX 4.03

      Model - SanDisk SDCFB-1024



Status:  Okay, press any key
```

Figure V.14.6. Device Identity Contents

The Serial Number that is shown in Figure V.14.6 is used to verify that the same CF card matches the same critical firmware data that is located at 0xC804-0xC83C in the peripheral-card expansion ROM memory of the CFFA firmware. This Serial Number verification takes place whenever the CFFA firmware BOOTs a DOS image from the DOS Partition or whenever any volume is BOOTed from the Drive and Volume Partition. The firmware makes a call to READID that reads the Identify Device data to Page 0x08. A Serial Number mismatch between the seated CF card and the CFFA firmware is simply not tolerated, the Wrong CF card error message is issued, expansion ROM memory is deselected, and a jump is made to the ROM Monitor. When many CF cards need to be utilized in the same CFFA peripheral interface card, simply use *VOLMGR* to restore the CF firmware data using the Manage Firmware menu Option 4 in order to synchronize the CF card and the CFFA ROM firmware.

The Manage Drives menu is shown in Figure V.14.7. All of the drives that are contained in the CF card that is seated in the CFFA peripheral interface card are displayed in groups of no more than sixteen drives when Option 1 is selected. In Option 2 each drive is displayed showing its drive number, the number of volumes that are contained in that drive, and the Drive Name. All drives will contain 256 volumes except for the last drive. From Figure V.14.5, forty-eight LBA blocks from 0x00000D0-0x00000FF contain room for ninety-six drive descriptions. In other words, each LBA block in this region contains two drive descriptions, and each drive description can be displayed for viewing and each drive description can be easily changed. When Option 3 is selected in Figure V.14.7 and an accessible drive number is entered, a request to change the Drive Name is offered first, then followed by a request to update the Timestamp that is associated with this drive. The Original Drive Description is displayed in the upper part of the screen and the lower part of the screen provides enough room to enter a New Drive Description. If the RETURN key is entered before entering any new information for the Drive Name, the Timestamp, or the New Drive Description, no changes are made to the original data.

```
        Manage Drives


 1 - List All Drives
 2 - Display Drive Information
 3 - Change Drive Information
 4 - Return to Main Menu




Select Option:
```

Figure V.14.7. Manage Drives Menu

```
        Manage Volumes

 1 - Display Drive Volumes Catalog Size
 2 - Display Drive Volumes DOS
 3 - Display Volume LBA Range
 4 - Display Volume VTOC Information
 5 - Display Sector Bitmap Information
 6 - Initialize a CF Volume
 7 - Boot a CF Volume
 8 - Return to Main Menu

Select Option:
```

Figure V.14.8. Manage Volumes Menu

The Manage Volumes menu is shown in Figure V.14.8. When Option 1 is selected and an accessible drive number is entered, all volumes that are available on this selected drive are displayed showing the number of Catalog sectors that are contained in each volume. This is the most optimal way to quickly show whether a particular volume on a selected drive has already been initialized. If a volume has already been initialized, the number of its Catalog sectors will be some value other than zero and certainly not greater than fifteen. Option 2 is very similar to Option 1 in how the volume information is displayed for a selected and available drive. A DOS table is first displayed that lists the available DOS images from 1 to 8, with 0 for no DOS found, and 9 for an unknown DOS found. Instead of showing the number of Catalog sectors that are contained in each volume, a value from the DOS table is displayed for each volume. Option 3 displays the LBA ranges for the selected Volume that exists on the selected drive. This information may be quite useful in order to calculate a particular LBA that must be saved to or restored from a disk. Options 4 and 5 provide the same information as Options 2 and 4 in the *VMGR* utility that display VTOC information and Sector Bitmap information, respectively. *VOLMGR* does not provide the ability to edit the VTOC nor the Sector Bitmap information. Those capabilities are reserved solely for the *VMGR* utility. Option 6 may be selected in order to initialize a CF volume where several configuration options are available in order to select the number of tracks, the number of sectors, and the number of Catalog sectors. Option 7 may be selected in order to BOOT any bootable volume on any available drive.

```
       Manage Bootable DOS Images


  1 - List Installed DOS Images

  2 - Select DOS Image for Boot

  3 - Show DOS Image Description

  4 - Modify DOS Image Description

  5 - Return to Main Menu




Select Option:  ■
```

```
        List Installed DOS Images


  DOS Image 1 - DOS 3.3
  DOS Image 2 - DOS 4.1L
  DOS Image 3 - DOS 4.1H
  DOS Image 4 - DOS 4.3H
  DOS Image 5 - DOS 4.5L
  DOS Image 6 - DOS 4.5H
  DOS Image 7 - DOS User1 (Blank)
  DOS Image 8 - DOS User2 (Blank)







                Press Any Key
```

Figure V.14.9. Manage DOS Images Menu   Figure V.14.10. List DOS Images Display

The Manage Bootable DOS Images menu is shown in Figure V.14.9. When Option 1 is selected, all installed DOS images are displayed as shown in Figure V.14.10. If a User Defined DOS image has not yet been installed, its image number and category name is still listed but the image content is displayed as (Blank). Option 2 displays the same list of default and User Defined DOS images as shown in Figure V.14.10 in order to select the DOS image that will be automatically BOOTed by the CFFA card. Option 2 displays the current active DOS image number that is selected to BOOT and it provides an opportunity to enter a new DOS image number for the DOS that is selected to BOOT. Options 3 and 4 utilize the same list of default and User Defined DOS images in order to manage the eight DOS image descriptions. Option 3 displays the selected DOS image description if a description exists for that DOS image. From Figure V.14.5, eight LBA blocks at 0x0000008-0x000000F contain room for eight DOS image descriptions. In other words, each LBA block in this region contains one complete DOS image description, or enough room for 511 bytes of data. One byte is always reserved for the terminating NULL or character 0x00 in all text-entry buffers that are used in the *VOLMGR* utility. Each DOS image description can be displayed for viewing and each DOS image description can be easily changed. After selecting Option 4, the Original DOS image description is displayed in the upper two-thirds area of the screen and the lower one-third area of the screen provides enough room to begin entering a New DOS image description. Additional room will be made available in this area by automatically scrolling the previously entered text upwards only within this screen area. When the RETURN key or character 0x8D is entered after entering any and all new information for the selected DOS image, an opportunity is offered to save or not to save this new DOS image description. As in all text-entry menu options in the *VOLMGR* utility, Option 4 displays the number of characters that remain available in the data buffer that is reserved for completing that text-entry menu option. This remaining character count is extraordinarily useful in planning and in entering data into a text-entry menu option so that only the most critical and the most relevant information is included in order to use the available buffer space as efficiently as possible.

15. File Developer Utility

File Developer (*FID*) was an original Apple][assembly language utility that was written by Rich Williams who was an Apple Computer, Inc., employee from 1979 to 2009. The *FID* utility was found on the DOS 3.3 System Master diskette that I received with my new Apple][+. I suspect it was and it still is the most widely used DOS utility of all time. Instead of writing my own file management utility for DOS 4.1, and now for DOS 4.5, I decided to source *FID* and to add to that software what I needed, like volume number and phase number as additional input parameters. Anytime I start tearing into software that is written by someone else, I find it to be a real and sometimes a noteworthy educational experience. *FID* did not disappoint me in that regard. *FID* utilizes the RWTS and the File Manager interfaces as noted elsewhere in this book, which gave me a good insight in how the *Apple Experts*, such as Williams, made use of these interfaces. I received the most grief from *FID*'s hardcoded insistence that track 0x00 can never be utilized for data storage, and that it is a track that is used only for BOOTing DOS. There are only a few locations in the *FID* software where I had to insert the parameters TRKMASK or 0x3F and TRKZERO or 0x40 so that *FID* would accommodate track 0x00 as a data track, as it is properly accommodated in the DOS 4.X series of Disk Operating Systems.

```
*********************************************
*           Apple ][ File Developer         *
*       Version N with DOS 4.5, Build 06    *
*                                           *
*     Copyright 1979 Apple Computer Inc.    *
*********************************************


    Choose One of the Following Options

        <1>  Copy Files
        <2>  Catalog Volume
        <3>  Space on Volume
        <4>  Unlock Files
        <5>  Lock Files
        <6>  Delete Files
        <7>  Reset Slot, Drive, Volume
        <8>  Verify Files and Expunge TSL
        <9>  Undelete Files
        <Q>  Quit

Which Option would you like:   ※
```

```
                Copy Files

Source Slot:   6
       Drive:  1
      Volume:
       Phase:

Target Slot:   6
       Drive:  2
      Volume:
       Phase:

File (<name>/*):   FID

Insert Volume 000 and Volume 000.

Press <ctrl-C> to return to Main Menu.
Press any other key to begin.
※
```

Figure V.15.1. FID Main Menu   Figure V.15.2. FID Copy Files

I found that the most essential task was to implant the use of volume number into *FID* because I wanted *FID* to accommodate the CFFA hardware which greatly depends upon specifying a volume number. My CFFA firmware can access up to 81 drives in order to support an 8 GB CompactFlash card, where each drive can support 256 volumes. I originally derived this utilization of volume number from the Sider firmware that utilizes volume number in its calculation of the beginning sector number for the start of each DOS 3.3 volume image on its 10 MB hard drive. And, of course, I wanted *FID* to include my new DOS URM command in order to **undelete** files because that capability exists in DOS 4.5 by means of the File Manager. *FID* also makes use of the SUBCODE field for the DOS Catalog command in order to display the current list of files on a volume with or without listing the deleted files as well. *FID* must also use the free sector bitmap in the VTOC properly, as it is used properly in DOS 4.5, and not how it is used improperly in DOS 3.3. Finally, *FID* must include the phase number for the Source and Target volumes in order to share files between these two structurally different volumes when their phase numbers are different. Phase number is like any of the other physical parameters that are used in either the RWTS IOCB or in the File Manager Context Block.

The modified main menu for *FID* that supports the features in DOS 4.5 that have just been described is shown in Figure V.15.1. Option 9 has been added in order to undelete a selected file. This option uses the same interface as options 4, 5, 6, and 8 that operates on a single file. The Quit option has been given a new entry selection, or Q. The first part of Option 1 is shown in Figure V.15.2 in order to display the added volume number and phase number input variables. If RETURN is entered for those two variables, the default value of zero is entered for them. Unlike the DOS 3.3 version of *FID*, the current version of *FID* uses the asterisk for its *wild card* in order to replace any character before, after, or within a filename. When the asterisk is used by itself, then all filenames are included.

There are certain limitations that one needs to consider when using the *FID* utility because *FID* uses the File Manager in order to copy files from one volume to another. Whatever data sectors that are associated with a file that are specified in the TSL sector for that file are copied in total from the source volume to the destination volume. The very same track/sector numbers may not necessarily be selected on the destination volume that was used for data sectors on the source volume. The File Manager has no idea whether all or some of these data sectors are actually being used by that file. If the DOS command BSAVE TEST1,A$1000,L$6000 is issued on the DOS command line, for example, DOS 4.5 creates a file and allocates ninety-eight data sectors to that file. There is one sector that is allocated initially for the TSL sector and there will be ninety-seven Track/Sector entry pairs that will be specified in that TSL sector, one entry for each of the allocated data sectors on that volume. Then, if the DOS command BSAVE TEST1,A$1000,L$1000 is issued next, the DOS Catalog will show that ninety-eight sectors are still allocated for TEST1. *FID* blindly copies all ninety-seven data sectors even though only the first seventeen TSL entries specify the data sectors that now contain the valid data for TEST1. This same situation can occur with Applesoft files as well. If the original Applesoft file utilizes forty-one sectors and the file is edited to nearly half its size and saved to disk, the Applesoft file will continue to utilize the forty-one Track/Sector entry pairs in its TSL and not, say, just the first twenty TSL entries. There is simply no way for *FID* to know whether a file uses all or some of the data sectors that are specified in a TSL sector for a file unless additional and complex logic is included in *FID* that compares file size and TSL utilization. If disk space is truly a premium, then *FID* should not be used to copy files; the files should be copied manually or by another utility with the ability to expunge unused TSL entries.

Why does every Apple][DOS potentially waste valuable disk space when saving an edited and smaller file that already exists in the volume Catalog? There are probably many reasons, some of which are valid and some are merely cosmetic because they are easier to implement. I believe the most valid reason is for safety. In order to guarantee that a file only uses the disk space it truly requires when that file already exists in the volume Catalog would be to first delete the existing file, create a new file with the same name, and finally save the specified data to that new file. But would this procedure be entirely safe? What if something causes an error after the file is deleted but before the new file is created, or before the specified data of that file can be saved? Is having a DOS URM command enough insurance if such a situation like this should ever occur? Perhaps the specified data should be saved to a XXTEMPXX file first, then the original file can be safely deleted before the XXTEMPXX file is renamed? There may *not be* enough disk space in order to support two copies of the same file, or there may *not be* enough file entry space in the volume Catalog for an additional filename entry. This procedure would also rearrange the order of files in the volume Catalog which may *not be* appealing to some. I believe the best strategy is to save the specified data to the existing file using the existing TSL resources of that file, and if there are more TSL entries than needed, those entries should be marked as unused or cleared to zero, and those data sectors should be marked as unused in the VTOC bitmap of the volume. Of course, I would only use this strategy for the DOS SAVE, BSAVE, and LSAVE commands. It would be a moderately interesting exercise to implement this strategy, and certainly be the cause for the release of yet another version of *FID*. This may be a good time to implement this strategy as part of the Verify Option in *FID*.

At this time DOS 4.5 provides the use of the B keyword in order to implement the *File Delete/File Save* strategy for the DOS SAVE, BSAVE, LSAVE, SSAVE, and TSAVE commands if that strategy is desired. I have found this strategy to be quite useful and it has not caused me any concerns for the safety of my files though I do tend to back up my work regularly, regardless. If the *File Delete/File Save* strategy should fail, having a backup does ensure that all is not entirely lost. However, I believe I would be more inclined to suggest the creation of a simple utility that is devoted to the sole task of expunging unused TSL entries from the TSL sector of a file or files, and to return those data sectors to the VTOC bitmap of that volume. Applesoft, Binary, and *Lisa* files would be the easiest file Types to process and to expunge their unused data sectors since their file size in bytes for these particular file Types is found at the start of their first data sector. Random-Access Data files would be problematic to process because its data may contain many zeros. Sequential Text files would need to be processed byte by byte in order to locate its terminating NULL or character 0x00 before any extra TSL entries could be safely expunged and its unused data sectors returned to the VTOC bitmap. There is simply no way to actually identify whether a Text file is a Random-Access Data file or a Sequential Text file. I have previously stated that bytes 0x08:0x09 or 0x09:0x0A as shown in Figure I.7.2 could have been utilized for the value of the L keyword when the file is created initially instead of requiring the L keyword and its value in order to OPEN a Text file as a Random-Access Data file. Utilizing those bytes in the first TSL sector would have definitely distinguished a Random-Access Data file from a Sequential Text file without having to know anything about how the Text file is utilized programmatically.

```
     Verify Files and Expunge TSL

Source Slot:    6
       Drive:   1
      Volume:
       Phase:

File (<name>/*):    HELLO

Insert Volume 000.

Press <ctrl-C> to return to Main Menu.
Press any other key to begin.
```

Figure V.15.3. Verify Files and Expunge TSL

```
     Verify Files and Expunge TSL

Insert Volume 000.

Press <ctrl-C> to return to Main Menu.
Press any other key to begin.

   File:   HELLO

TS Track   - 0x12
TS Sector  - 0x0F
File Type  - 0x02
File Size  - 0x03
TSL Size   - 0x05
TSL Pairs  - 0x05

   Too many TSL entries, fix?     Y

Status:   Done

Press any key to continue*
```

Figure V.15.4. Expunge of TSL and Verify File

For the time being *FID* is perhaps the easiest utility to utilize in order to copy a set of files from one volume to another volume. Because *FID* can cross Volume and Phase barriers makes it exceedingly powerful in the DOS 4.5 environment. I decided to accept the challenge and to add the additional and very complex logic to *FID*, selectable of course, that would compare TSL utilization for its Track/Sector entry pairs and file size for Applesoft, Binary, and *Lisa* files. The appropriate option to include this complex logic would be Option 8 in order to implement the DOS VERIFY command once the Catalog and TSL entries have been corrected and adjusted. The decision to remove TSL entries from a TSL sector is based on whether the number of TSL entries matches the number of data sectors that are utilized by the file after examining the Catalog entry information. Of course, considerations must be made because the file size from the Catalog entry information also includes the TSL sector in its count. The file Type from the Catalog entry information is also used in order to select only those files that can actually be processed. Applesoft files that have the file Type of 0x20 are included with normal Applesoft files that have the file Type of 0x02. The final discrimination is to reject any file for processing that has a file size that is greater than 123 sectors. Files that utilize more than 122 data sectors require more than one TSL sector in order to accommodate those additional data sectors. An Applesoft file that is greater than 0x79FE bytes or a Binary or *Lisa* file that is greater than 0x79FC bytes would require more than one TSL sector. The algorithm to process an under-utilized TSL sector is complex enough without having to include the immense overhead that would be required in order to successfully process files that require multiple TSL sectors. Those large files should be processed manually using the simple *File Delete/File Save* strategy. The Verify Files and Expunge TSL option, or Option 8 in the main menu for *FID* is shown in Figure V.15.3 and it is ready to process the Applesoft HELLO file.

The file sizing information that is shown in Figure V.15.4 indicates that the Applesoft HELLO file is now greater than 0x1FD bytes and less than 0x2FE bytes in size. Therefore, this file only requires three data sectors and only three TSL entries in its TSL sector. Obviously, the Applesoft HELLO file was edited and reduced in size at some point in time after the original Applesoft HELLO file was saved which required five data sectors initially and five TSL entries in its TSL sector. The task to expunge the TSL involves extracting each TSL entry from the TSL sector that is not required by the Applesoft HELLO file starting with the fourth, or File Size + 1 entry. Those extracted track and sector values are submitted to a FREESECT routine that calls a RORBITMP routine in order to return that data sector to the VTOC bitmap of that volume. FREESECT and RORBITMP are two routines that are extracted from DOS 4.5 and modified for use in *FID*. The extracted TSL entry is cleared from the TSL sector and the next TSL entry is extracted and processed. This processing continues until the next TSL entry is already zero or the TSL sector index becomes greater than 0x7A. The TSL sector and the VTOC sector can both be written to the volume at this time. The final housekeeping task is to update the new file size in sectors in the Catalog sector that contains the entry for the Applesoft HELLO file. Once the new file size in sectors is updated, that Catalog sector can be written to the volume. After completing these processing steps for the Applesoft HELLO file, the remaining data sectors that are allocated to the Applesoft HELLO file can be read when *FID* issues the DOS VERIFY command to the File Manager. Of course, the processing steps appear to be complex and involved, and indeed they are, but this strategy is lightning fast and the updates only require three calls to the DOS RWTS interface in order to update the TSL sector, the VTOC sector, and the respective Catalog sector for the processed file.

16. Lazer's Interactive Symbolic Assembler

I have to say that I have spent a considerable amount of time and energy modifying, adjusting, and fine tuning Lazer's Interactive Symbolic Assembler or *Lisa* to my every whim and need. It truly has been a joy! First and foremost, my task was to modify *Lisa* to use the DOS 4.5 interfaces in order for *Lisa* to obtain the various pieces of information it requires for some of its special functions. Next, I wanted to eliminate the need for *Lisa* to save the first file of a multiple-file program as a .TEMP file before it completes its Pass 1 processing. That task required adding a new directive to *Lisa*. I wanted the Sort algorithm that is used to sort the Symbol table to be an integral part of *Lisa* as well as having a directive that would optionally not generate or generate one, two, or all of the Symbol table lists. I wanted to add an additional directive to define the text for the Symbol List title. I wanted LED, the Lisa EDitor, to be an integral part of *Lisa* and always be included whenever *Lisa* is activated. I wanted an easier way to enter a DOS PR# command and a ctrl-D in order to more easily enter and utilize any other DOS command. I wanted an additional command-line command besides A that would assemble source code and force the PRNTFLAG to be turned OFF as if the NLS directive is the first directive in the source code without actually having that directive there in the first place. I wanted *Lisa* to obtain the date and time directly from DOS 4.5 and not to negotiate with the clock hardware itself. I wanted to move *Lisa* into Auxiliary memory so that I could utilize the Language Card version of DOS 4.5. I wanted to fix some of the quirkiness *Lisa* sometimes displays. And, finally, I wanted to display a *Lisa* file in 80-column mode and I wanted to be able to fully edit *Lisa* source code in 80-column mode. While on this journey, I also found and fixed a few more coding errors that I discovered within *Lisa*. Ah, have I made *Lisa* absolutely perfect? Maybe. I certainly hope so! I certainly think I have done so!

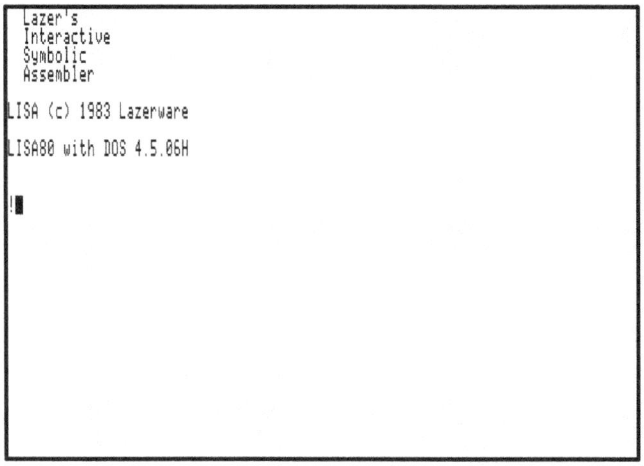

Figure V.16.1. Lisa80 Startup Display

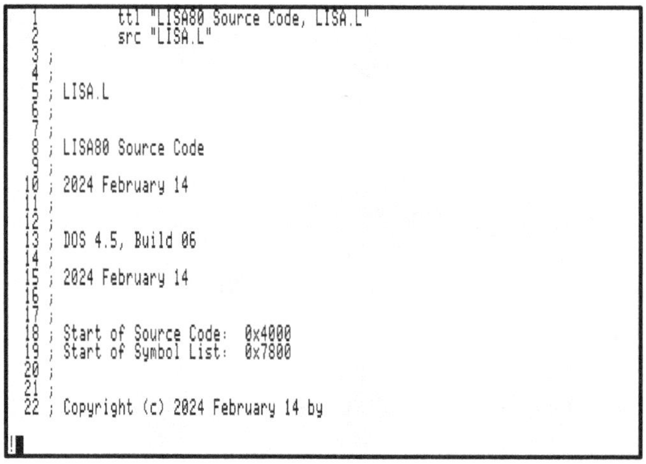

Figure V.16.2. Lisa80 Source Code List Display

Unlike the *Big Mac* assembler, the *Lisa* assembler resides in both Banks of the Language Card partition in Auxiliary memory, and LED, written by Bob Rosen of RSQ Software Products © 1983, now occupies the lower Main memory address space from 0xB967 to 0xBCC9. *Lisa* only requires one DOS file buffer but it no longer needs to change the number of DOS file buffers in DOS 4.5. The momentous task of sourcing *Lisa* took many, many hours, not just for the conversion of the assembly language object code into source code, but the laborious task of understanding the idiosyncrasies of how Randall Hyde designs and writes his software. The optimal desire is to understand the newly generated source code so that 1) it assembles and perfectly matches the original object code, and 2) it can be modified and all structures and tables and their lengths and sizes remain unaffected. Quite frequently an author may pass the address of a structure or of a data table in one or two registers, or as an index into a table of addresses or values, and initially the source code appears as if those structures or those tables of values are hardcoded. What needs to be done is to assign a variable name to that structure or that data table so if that structure or that data

310

table shifts up or down in memory, the registers will always contain the correct offset or the correct memory location for the variable name. It is necessary to find all such occurrences in order to reach that optimal state of perfectly sourced code. *Sourceror* can only do so much magic! Figure V.16.1 shows the *Lisa* startup display showing that *Lisa80* is running under DOS 4.5 in 80-column mode. Figure V.16.2 shows the first page of the *Lisa80* source code in 80-column mode.

In order to make *Lisa* fully DOS 4.5 compliant required me to relocate *Lisa* into Auxiliary memory. Why? Because DOS 4.5 is resident in the Language Card partition in Main memory and *Lisa* is resident in the Language Card partition in Main memory as well. Both cannot reside in the same Language Card partition concurrently. However, Auxiliary memory also contains its own Language Card partition. It seemed natural to relocate *Lisa* to the Language Card partition of Auxiliary memory. It was definitely a challenge to understand how to master Auxiliary memory in terms of its operation and what it could provide and what it could not provide in terms of resources. Certainly, to assist in its operation would be to decide which area of memory would handle input data or keyboard and disk data, and which area of memory would handle output data or display, printer, and disk data. Once I established the operating rules for memory it became very clear in how to build the interface between Main memory and Auxiliary memory specifically for *Lisa*. Since DOS 4.5 occupies the Language Card partition in Main memory, it was quite logical to utilize Main memory for the input and the output data for a volume. Thus, all keyboard, printer, and display data are handled within Auxiliary memory. It was totally unnecessary to maintain two page-zeros for the variables CH, CV, BASL, BASH, and all other text window variables.

Lisa contains its own version of the ROM Monitor. Previously, this monitor mostly resembled the ROM Monitor that is found in the Apple][+. In order to prepare *Lisa* to make use of the Apple //e 80-column display, the Apple //e ROM Monitor needs to be utilized, whatever version of the monitor it is. Unfortunately, Mr. Hyde embedded a few routines within his monitor that has no place in the Apple //e ROM Monitor. And, so, back to the drawing board in order to squeeze out even more code space within *Lisa* in order to provide a new location for those displaced routines. In order for *Lisa* to utilize any of the various iterations of the Apple //e ROM Monitor, *Lisa* simply copies the ROM Monitor for its RAM Monitor. The interface between Main memory and Auxiliary memory is injected primarily at the COUT or 0xFDED and the RDKEY2 or 0xFD18 routines in the RAM Monitor of *Lisa*. A small handler is needed for the HOOKDOS, DOSWARM, WRMSTRT, PRTERROR, and READCLK vectors. DOS errors have to be handled uniquely by the memory interface in order to re-enter *Lisa* appropriately. Finally, the state of the Language Card partition Bank that is currently in focus must be captured in order to reconfigure Auxiliary memory for all subroutines that are returning from Main memory. Because *Lisa* utilizes memory in both Banks of the Language Card partition, it is difficult to know which Bank is in focus at any given moment during *Lisa* processing. However, the greater challenge is to enhance the source code editing capabilities of *Lisa* while displaying *Lisa* source code in 80-column mode on the Apple //e.

The page-zero variable CH for the current line character index is used to address an ASCII character on the screen. The page-zero variable CV for the current screen line number is used to calculate the BASL/BASH pointer. As easy as it is to write to the screen, reading from the screen is just as easy. Mr. Hyde utilized these variables in his source code line editing routines. The Apple //e requires twice as much memory for the text buffer in order to display 80-column text. The additional buffer memory comes from Auxiliary memory such that every odd numbered screen character comes from Main memory and every even numbered screen character comes from Auxiliary memory. The variables OURCH or 0x057B and OURCV or 0x05FB are used instead for character index and line number, respectively. In order to provide the same line editing capabilities in 80-column display mode as in 40-column display mode it is necessary to read and write screen characters using a different and more complicated algorithm. The SETSCRN routine shown in Figure V.16.3 demonstrates one component of this complicated algorithm. The PAGE Soft Switch only functions in 80-column mode when 80-Column Store STR80ON, or 0xC001, is enabled as shown in that figure. The READSCRN routine that is shown in Figure V.16.4 utilizes SETSCRN in order to read the character of interest from the screen. The final routine SAVESCRN that is shown in Figure V.16.5 also utilizes SETSCRN in order to save the character of interest to the screen.

```
SETSCRN        sta STR80ON            ; enable PAGE Soft Switch
               sta PAGE1ON            ; assume Main memory
               lda OURCH              ; get character index
               sta CH                 ; save index to CH
               lsr                    ; shift LSB into carry flag
               tay                    ; copy |OURCH/2| to Y-reg
               bcs >1                 ; branch if odd (Main memory)
               sta PAGE2ON            ; enable Auxiliary memory
^1             rts                    ; return to caller
```

Figure V.16.3. Lisa80 SETSCRN Routine

```
READSRN1       sty OURCH              ; save character index
READSCRN       jsr SETSCRN            ; select screen PAGE
               lda (BASL),Y           ; read the screen character
               sta PAGE1ON            ; enable Main memory
               ldy CH                 ; get original index from CH
               rts                    ; return to caller
```

Figure V.16.4. Lisa80 READSCRN Routine

```
SAVESRN1       sty OURCH              ; save character index
SAVESCRN       pha                    ; save character on stack
               jsr SETSCRN            ; select screen PAGE
               pla                    ; retrieve character
               sta (BASL),Y           ; write the screen character
               sta PAGE1ON            ; enable Main memory
               ldy CH                 ; get index from CH
               rts                    ; return to caller
```

Figure V.16.5. Lisa80 SAVESCRN Routine

There are certainly other routines that are needed to handle all of the ctrl-key functions that *Lisa* provides, but the above display functions are the most basic and required routines. Because the 80-column ROM routines already support the left and the right arrow keys, I chose to replace the Cursor Left or

312

ctrl-J and the Cursor Right or ctrl-K options with the Go To Start of Line or ctrl-C and Go To End of Line or ctrl-D options. I liked these two cursor movement routines so much that I added them to my 40-column version of Auxiliary memory *Lisa*. The other configuration parameters in *Lisa* may be modified using the *SETUP80* utility. *SETUP80* may be invoked simply by typing the SE command on the *Lisa80* command line. The *SETUP80* utility is activated from the Lisa Image volume LISA80.Image that is in disk drive 1. Figure V.16.6 shows the main L.I.S.A. SETUP80 Utility screen and Figure V.16.7 shows the Screen Editing Definitions screen.

Having DOS in the Language Card partition in Main memory provides substantially more memory for object code, source code, and the symbol list. The judicious selection of memory locations and sizes for object code, source code, and the symbol list ensures a successful assembly no matter how large or how complex a program or a set of program modules are presented to *Lisa*. The values shown in Figure V.16.6 provide 56 memory pages for object code from 0x0800 to 0x3FFF, 56 memory pages for source code for a single program or for one module of a complex program from 0x4000 to 0x77FF, and nearly 64 memory pages for the symbol list from 0x7800 to 0xB7AF. Each symbol requires ten bytes, eight bytes for the symbol name and two bytes for the symbol value. This symbol list allocation provides enough memory for about 1600 symbols. *Lisa80* uses 0x1F36 bytes for its symbol list of 799 symbols. On the other hand, DOS 4.5 Build 06 uses 0x35E8 bytes for its symbol list of 1380 symbols. This information is found just before the symbol list is printed when the A command is used on the *Lisa* command line. These setup values are my recommended settings and they should be appropriate for nearly every program instance. But, of course, there are situations where a program or a program module may exceed 56 memory pages which is a file that is 57 sectors in size having one TSL.

```
   L.I.S.A. SETUP80 Utility


Current values are:

1) Start of Source Code    - 0x4000
2) Start of Symbol List    - 0x7800
3) Start of Page 2 Source  - 0x7800
4) Start of Page 2 Symbols - 0x9800
5) End of Symbol List      - 0xB7B0

6) Number of Lines/Page    - 68
7) Print Title on Page     - YES
8) Lower Case Mnemonics    - YES

9) Screen Editing Definitions

0) Quit

Enter option: █
```

```
   Screen Editing Definitions

A) Cursor up              ^O, 0x0F
B) Cursor down            ^L, 0x0C
C) Go to start of line    ^C, 0x03
D) Go to end of line      ^D, 0x04
E) Insert character       ^I, 0x09
F) Delete character       ^R, 0x12
G) Home and Clear         ^Q, 0x11
H) Clear to end of line   ^E, 0x05
I) Clear to end of screen ^F, 0x06
J) Insert a line          ^V, 0x16
K) Delete current line    ^N, 0x0E
L) Skip blanks character  ^S, 0x13
M) Show length of line    ^T, 0x14
N) Quit insert mode       ^A, 0x01

Enter Q to leave.

Enter option: █
```

Figure V.16.6. Lisa80 SETUP80 Utility   Figure V.16.7. Lisa80 Screen Editing Definitions

Command	Context	Description
USR	after OBJ $$	uses OBJ $$ address to save the start address for a future BSAVE
USR FN	at end of code	BSAVEs current code to filename FN; follow this with another USR
USR .FN	to BLOAD file	BLOADs the filename FN using the current value of the object code pointer

Table V.16.1. Lisa USR Command

I wish to give all credit to Robert Heitman who I met at Sierra On-Line for creating the USR directive software and the `ctrl-P` routine software that I have incorporated within *Lisa* and *Lisa80*. Heitman called the original software modules `LOADER.S` and `LINKER.S` for his USR and his `ctrl-P` routines, respectively. I may have adjusted them slightly for my own particular needs, but essentially their basic functionalities were all created by Heitman. The USR directive has a number of important uses depending upon how it is utilized in the source code and which arguments are utilized with the directive. Its syntax and usages are shown in Table V.16.1. The combination of

```
ORG $$/OBJ $$/USR/<some source code>/USR <filename>
```

is a very powerful set of directives.

The first use of the USR directive alone, at the top of a program after the `ORG` and `OBJ` directives, saves the current value of the object code pointer that is set by the `OBJ $$` directive, where `$$` is some hexadecimal address. After some source code has been assembled, the generated object code can be saved to a file using the USR FN directive, where FN is some filename. USR FN uses the object code pointer address value that is saved by the first USR, it calculates the length of the code segment knowing the memory location that is given by the current object code pointer, and it constructs a DOS BSAVE command. The USR `.FN` or *period* + FN directive is also useful in order to read a Binary file into memory at the memory location that is given by the current object code pointer. Once the Binary file is in memory, the object code pointer can be incremented using the DFS directive knowing the size of the included Binary file. I use the USR `.FN` directive in order to BLOAD into memory every Binary object file that is to be contained in an EPROM image that is used to program an EPROM so that the EPROM can reside in a quikLoader and be read by *EOS*, the EPROM Operating System.

Source code for programs such as *Big Mac* or *Lisa* or DOS 4.5 cannot possibly fit in the Apple][memory along with its generated object code, its complete symbol list, DOS, and the assembler. Large and complex software programs must be segmented into a number of manageable sized files and their assembled outputs can be saved to separate object code files that can be ultimately linked to form the complete executable program. At a minimum, *Lisa*, DOS, and some program source code must reside concurrently in memory and still have room for its generated object code and its complete symbol list. It is simply amazing what can be accomplished in such a ridiculously small amount of memory as that found in the Apple][computer when judicious values are chosen for memory configuration in *Lisa*.

The source code files that comprise DOS 3.3 are shown in Figure V.16.8. Several source code files are processed before their collective object code is saved to a Binary file. The convention used to name these object code files is to begin the filename with a SEG prefix and end the filename with a two digit number suffix generally beginning with `01`. The reason will become apparent shortly. It makes no difference how many SEG files are created, remembering, of course, that for each file that is created an additional disk sector is required for its TSL. In the case of DOS 3.3 there are ninety-five sectors remaining in the volume, so there are plenty of sectors left to make many significant changes and additions to this source code. When all SEG files are sequentially read into memory, the entire image for DOS 3.3 is created. I have the convention, if not the habit, to begin the load of an object code file at address `0x1000`. Loading the first SEG file is easy, as in BLOAD SEG01,A$1000. To what address is SEG02 loaded next? If the R keyword is used with the BLOAD command, the length of SEG01 is given, and one can simply calculate the load address for SEG02, which is BLOAD SEG02 at `0x1000` + length of SEG01 and so forth. There is an easier method built into *Lisa*: a `ctrl-P` user function that loads a range of sequentially numbered SEG files. Thank you again, Bob Heitman! *Lisa* provides software hooks into the two `0xDF` pages where a user can add any routine or routines of their choosing. The USR directive mentioned earlier is found at memory address 0xDF00 when Bank 2 is enabled using the BIT 0xC080 instruction. The ctrl-P user function is also found at memory address 0xDF00 when Bank 1 is enabled using the BIT 0xC088 instruction.

```
]CATALOG

S=6 D=02 V=000 F=0095 02/14/24 08:28:48

 L 005 DOS3.3.L          02/14/24  08:28:48
 L 037 INCL.L            02/14/24  08:28:48
 L 017 DISK.L            02/14/24  08:28:48
 L 008 BUFR.L            02/14/24  08:28:48
 L 054 CMD1.L            02/14/24  08:28:48
 L 045 CMD2.L            02/14/24  08:28:48
 L 040 CMD3.L            02/14/24  08:28:48
 L 040 CMD4.L            02/14/24  08:28:48
 L 037 MNGR1A.L          02/14/24  08:28:48
 L 032 MNGR1B.L          02/14/24  08:28:48
 L 033 MNGR2A.L          02/14/24  08:28:48
 L 040 MNGR2B.L          02/14/24  08:28:48
 L 036 RWTS1.L           02/14/24  08:28:48
 L 035 RWTS2.L           02/14/24  08:28:48

]
```

Figure V.16.8. DOS 3.3 Source Code Volume

```
]LSR,B Available = 0x23,0x05
B=4506H data T=EOS 512 Image Files
M=4506H P=04 L=0x3032 02/14/24 08:28:48
S=6 D=02 V=000 F=0013 02/14/24 08:28:48
 001 0x12,0x0F BURNER
 002 0x13,0x0F EOS1
 003 0x14,0x0F EOS2
 004 0x15,0x0F SEG01
 005 0x16,0x0F SEG02
 006 0x17,0x0F SEG03
 007 0x18,0x09 SEG04
 008 0x19,0x02 SEG05
 009 0x1C,0x0D SEG06
 010 0x1E,0x0C SEG07
 011 0x20,0x0E SEG08

]
```

Figure V.16.9. EOS Image Segment Files

```
!
 Segments = #4
First Seg = #1
  Address = $1000
BLOAD SEG01,A$1000
BLOAD SEG02,A$3000
BLOAD SEG03,A$5100
BLOAD SEG04,A$7B00

Load end = $9000
Save file = EOS1
BSAVE EOS1,B,A$1000,L$8000
!
```

Figure V.16.10. EOS1 Image Creation

```
!
 Segments = #4
First Seg = #5
  Address = $1000
BLOAD SEG05,A$1000
BLOAD SEG06,A$3300
BLOAD SEG07,A$5254
BLOAD SEG08,A$6F18

Load end = $9000
Save file = EOS2
BSAVE EOS2,B,A$1000,L$8000
!
```

Figure V.16.11. EOS2 Image Creation

The ctrl-P function allows the user to enter the number of segments to be loaded into memory, the segment start number, the object code start address, and optionally a filename in order to save the composite image which is comprised of all of the loaded SEG files. If a filename is not entered, the length of the image in bytes and its final memory address are displayed instead. Figure V.16.9 shows all of the SEG files that are created when the *EOS* source code is assembled. Those SEG files need to be linked into two 0x8000 byte files that are each used to program a 27512 EPROM. In order to perform this process most efficiently, SEG files 1 to 4 are linked into one file and SEG files 5 to 8 are linked into the second file. The ctrl-P user function is the perfect tool in order to perform this linking task.

Figure V.16.10 shows how SEG files 1 to 4 are linked into the first *EOS* image file, EOS1, and Figure V.16.11 shows how SEG files 5 to 8 are linked into the second *EOS* image file, EOS2. Notice that Lisa utilizes the B keyword to implement the *File Delete/File Save* strategy for the DOS BSAVE command. This strategy first deletes the file if it exists, returns the sector resources of the file back to the VTOC of the volume, and then saves the file using newly acquired VTOC resources. The two binary image files EOS1 and EOS2 are now ready to be programmed into an erased 27512 EPROM where EOS1 is programmed into the first half and EOS2 is programmed into the second half of the EPROM. In fact, the utility *BURNER* is conveniently located on the same volume with these two image files. This makes the process of preparing and programming an EPROM very simple, very reliable, and very accurate.

Lisa makes three passes through all data input source code files in order to create data output object code files. The first pass may be terminated using the ENZ directive, or ENd of page-Zero when all of the page-zero parameter definitions have been given. Pass 2 and Pass 3 must process all included source code files. In order to return to the first, or the initial source code file when an ICL, or InCLude filename directive is encountered, *Lisa* previously saved the initial source code file as an additional file named .TEMP. Therefore, processing can begin with a known first file for the next pass. Certainly, this method is the easiest to implement but it comes with an unfortunate price because it wastes some valuable disk space by duplicating the initial or first file. In the example above for the volume containing the DOS 3.3 source code, Figure V.16.8, there is enough disk space available for a sizeable .TEMP file having the same contents as the initial source code file, or DOS3.3.L. However, many times this may not be the case where there is sufficient disk space for a duplicate .TEMP file.

Lisa had a few unused opcodes available, so I added the SRC directive that requires a filename in parenthesis as shown in Figure V.16.2. The complete syntax is SRC "filename". I gave LED some additional memory at its end where I moved the .TEMP filename buffer, and that is where the SRC directive copies its filename. Naturally, if the SRC directive is not used and there is at least one use of the ICL directive, *Lisa* will still create a .TEMP file as usual. The filename that is specified in the SRC directive should be the filename of the file where the directive is found, but this is not necessarily required. Referring to Figure V.16.8, if the SRC directive in the DOS3.3.L file is SRC "INCL.L", the file DOS3.3.L would not be processed during Pass 2 and Pass 3, thus saving a little processing time, but at the expense of not including the DOS3.3.L file as part of the complete print listing, if an incomplete print listing is acceptable. Personally, I prefer to place the SRC directive on line 2, right after the TTL directive in the very first file when there are several source code files that comprise the program. Even if all of the source code resides in a single file, using the SRC directive does no harm.

I challenged myself to include the sort algorithm in *Lisa* and the code that is found in the external program called SYMBOLS. If SYMBOLS is activated immediately after *Lisa* processes some source code, SYMBOLS will print the complete symbol list alphabetized, and then print the list again with the symbols ordered by value or by their address. I liked what SYMBOLS offered but not well enough to fumble around locating a copy of the utility, even if I did have it in EPROM, especially after processing a huge project like DOS3.3. I never really considered adding another command-line command like SY to BRUN SYMBOLS similar in how I added the SE command-line command to BRUN SETUP80. Fortunately, SYMBOLS is a little program and it did not take much effort to source its code. Now I had some idea how much room it required to include SYMBOLS within *Lisa*. Of course, I could always make LED larger and rob memory from the symbol list, the source code, or the object code memory.

I know Randall Hyde used good sense when he developed his routines for each opcode in the Pass 2 implementation and separately in the Pass 3 implementation. Regardless of good sense, I studied those routines and I found a number of ways to compact a rather large amount of this code giving me more than enough code space so that I could include SYMBOLS within *Lisa*. Now that *Lisa* was headed down this path, I thought it would be exemplary to provide a means to give the symbol list a name on the page title line. I replaced the CSP directive (it mixes a JSR instruction with a .DA directive) with the STT directive whose syntax is STT "title". This directive copies the character string title to the buffer that is currently used by the TTL directive during Pass 3. If the symbol list is printed, its pages will contain the new TTL title. If the STT directive is not used, the symbol list pages are printed with the same title from the original TTL directive. Instead, if the TTL directive is used at the end of the source code in order to title the symbol list pages, the last printed page of the assembled code will contain the new symbol list title and not the original source code title. I did not care for that solution so that is the primary reason why I needed to add the separate STT directive.

To complete this challenge required one further modification, and that was to the END directive. This directive provided the perfect location to control which of three symbol lists to print after the assembled code listing. That is, no symbol lists, a new unsorted symbols list, an alphabetically sorted symbols list, and a numerically sorted symbols list. Regardless which if any symbol lists are desired, if at least one symbol list is selected, that symbol list is prefaced by and includes the memory address where the symbol list begins, the memory address where the symbol list ends, how many bytes are used for the symbol list, and the remaining bytes that are available in the symbol table partition. From Figure V.16.6, the absolute physical end of the symbol list internally to *Lisa* is set at 0xB7B0, or 0xB7C0 - 0x10. If there is substantial memory that is not utilized in the symbol table partition, the Start of Symbol List in Figure V.16.6 could be adjusted to allow for larger source code files. It is always better to have visibility in how effectively *Lisa* is configured particularly when problems due to source code file size begin to generate errors during assembly. Therefore, to complete this discussion, the END directive now allows a three-digit binary parameter to control which of the three symbol lists to print in the order stated above. The syntax for the directive is END nnn where **n** can be a 0 or a 1 for OFF and for ON, respectively.

I prefer to keep the default setting of the PRNTFLAG variable ON during Pass 3 in order to obtain a printed listing of the assembly, particularly when I am using Virtual][. Rarely do I use the LST and NLS directives anymore. However, when I am debugging software using real Apple][hardware along with the RAM Disk 320, leaving the PRNTFLAG variable ON greatly impacts assembly throughput, even with the ZipChip enabled and the Parallel Printer Buffer enabled. And, it is a nuisance having to insert and then delete the NLS directive in the source code during the debugging development phase. So, I added the Z command-line command to *Lisa* that functions exactly like the A command-line command in order to start the assembly process. However, the Z command-line command sets the PRNTFLAG variable to OFF instead of to ON as if the NLS directive is the first directive that is processed.

Many times it is necessary to enter a DOS command directly onto the *Lisa* command line. In order to do so requires having to enter a ctrl-D or character 0x84 that must precede the DOS command so that *Lisa* knows that it must send this command to DOS rather than to parse the command for itself. I found it cumbersome for me to enter a ctrl-D or character 0x84 before each and every DOS command when I needed some information from DOS. So, I added another *Lisa* command-line command, the single character / command, which is so much easier for me to enter before any DOS command on the *Lisa* command line. For example, to display the contents of the VTOC sector for the volume that is currently in focus, the following command can be entered on the *Lisa* command line

!/TS A17

The *Lisa80 SETUP80* utility that is shown in Figure V.16.6 no longer provides the options to select the clock slot number and its 0xCs05 and 0xCs07 values, where **s** is the clock slot number. *Lisa* used to obtain the date and time information similarly in how DOS 4.5 obtains that information, and *Lisa* also required a value for the current year because the Thunderclock card lacks a year register. Instead of having a duplicate date and time algorithm and a duplicate YEARVAL variable in order to manage in *Lisa*, I simply removed the date and time algorithm and the YEARVAL variable from *Lisa* and utilized the DOS 4.5 RDCLKVSN vector at 0x3E1. I placed the CLKBUFF buffer conveniently at 0x3C8. Now, whenever *Lisa* requires the current date and time, it requests that information from DOS 4.5. The *SETUP* utility and the *SETUP80* utility no longer configures the clock slot, its 0xCs05 and 0xCs07 values since *Lisa* no longer utilizes that information.

It is always an unspoken goal whenever sourcing software that is written by someone else to never introduce new and unwanted problems. On the other hand, there is always a very good opportunity in finding and repairing mistakes made by someone else due to the intensity in concentration that is needed in order to understand every single line of code in context with the surrounding lines of code. I suspect there might be some mistakes still resident in *Lisa* that I have yet to uncover, but for the moment *Lisa* is rock solid stable and it is providing me with output object code files that are totally true to their input source code files. Whether the input source code files are necessarily perfect is quite another story.

Relocating *Lisa* to Auxiliary memory was an exhilarating experience. Much of the action of an assembler is to display the assembled code to the screen and, quite often, to the printer. The assembler code can function virtually in any memory space; the screen and printer display code cannot. Main memory and Auxiliary memory in the Apple //e can be partitioned in a variety of ways. I chose to keep the fundamental *Lisa* code in the Language Card partition in Auxiliary memory. Doing so drove the relocation design in using only two Soft Switches in order to control memory management: AUXZPOFF or 0xC008 and AUXZPON or 0xC009. The default Apple //e memory configuration is with AUXZPOFF such that Main memory is enabled with its own page-zero, stack, and Language Card partition. Using the AUXZPON Soft Switch, Auxiliary memory page-zero, the stack, and its Language Card partition are enabled, thus leaving the bulk of lower memory in Main memory still enabled, or memory from 0x0800 to 0xBFFF. In other words, whether AUXZPOFF or AUXZPON are enabled, the object code, the source code, and the symbol list are all visible to both *Lisa* and to DOS 4.5 because these data areas occupy memory from 0x0800 to 0xBDFF. This area of memory is not toggled using these two particular Soft Switches. *Lisa* and DOS 4.5 never utilize Auxiliary memory from 0x0800 to 0xBDFF for any reason whatsoever and that area of memory is never enabled.

The *Lisa* loader *LOADLISA80* cannot load two of the three object code files that comprise *Lisa* directly into Auxiliary memory from disk. Either the Language Card partition in Main memory or the Language Card partition in Auxiliary memory is in focus and not both at the same time, and one memory Partition cannot be read-enabled while the other memory Partition is write-enabled. So, the *LOADLISA80* loader calls on DOS to load each of the first two *Lisa* object code files into lower Main memory sequentially, starting at 0x1000. Then the loader copies the contents of each of the files from lower Main memory into the target memory of the Language Card partition in Auxiliary memory after setting AUXZPON. The third *Lisa* object code file contains the Main/Auxiliary control and interface routines as well as LED, and that file is loaded directly to 0xB7C0. Hence, the End of Symbol List, or SYMEND is set to 0xB7B0, or sixteen bytes before 0xB7C0 for safety. The DOS MON C,I,O command is issued, AUXZPON is enabled again, Bank 2 of the Language Card partition in Auxiliary memory is enabled, and a jump is made to the *Lisa* COLDSTRT entry point at 0xE000.

The functional relocation of *Lisa* to Auxiliary memory is only made possible by the Main/Auxiliary control and interface routines that I have developed. It is this code, from 0xB7C0 to 0xB96D that makes this relocation functional. Some of the routines have familiar names because they are the necessary counterpart routines that toggle between AUXZPOFF and AUXZPON. These routines include XHOOKDOS, XCONSOLE, CONSOLE, XOUTPORT, XDOSCOLD, XDOSWARM, XWRMSTRT, XCSWL, XKSWL, GETVALS, PUTVALS, READCLK, PUTZP, GETZP, ROMON, and AUXRTN. Both DOS 4.5 and *Lisa* share the Text Page from 0x400 to 0x7FF in both Main and Auxiliary memory, but they do not share the same page-zero or stack memory. It is necessary to record when a DOS command is issued by *Lisa* and when that command is completed by DOS. It is also necessary to handle additional CSWL interface traffic when the printer is enabled. KSWL interface traffic is not as complex, but it still must be managed. Because *Lisa* operates in both Banks of the Language Card partition in Auxiliary memory, the current Bank that is in focus must be read using 0xC011, saved, and restored using 0xC080 or 0xC088 in order for external routines to re-enter *Lisa* properly. Again, successfully relocating *Lisa* to Auxiliary memory such that *Lisa* is fully operational in all aspects is an exhilarating experience.

Command	Usage	Description
BR	BR	Break, enter RAM Monitor with beep from speaker
LO	LO filename	Load *Lisa* file into memory
LE	LE	Print length of source code currently in memory in HEX
SA	SA filename	Save source code currently in memory to a *Lisa* file
SE	SE	BRUN SETUP utility
AP	AP filename	Append source code currently in memory from another *Lisa* file
EX	EX	Exit Lisa into DOS
U	U	BRUN INSTALL utility
I	I line number	Insert more source code at optional <line number>
D	D start,end	Delete range of source code using line number start,end
L	L start,end	List range of source code at optional line number start,end
A	A	Assemble the source code currently in memory, PRNTFLAG=ON
Z	Z	Assemble the source code currently in memory, PRNTFLAG=OFF
N	N	Clear all source code from memory and begin new code
M	M start,end	Modify range of source code using line number start,end
W	W start,end	Write a range of source code to a TEXT file at optional line start,end
F	F string	Find all occurrences of character string in source code
FC	FC n	CATALOG volume or optional disk drive <n>
FT	FT token	Find all occurrences of a *Lisa* token or directive in source code
FM	FM start,end>new	Move lines of source code to a new line location
FR	FR start,end>new	Replicate lines of source code to a new line location
FP	FP n	Show source code Page number; select source code Page
FX	FX ##	Check for damaged source code; optional # enables print flag
R	R n, filename	Read TEXT file into memory as source code; optional at line number
P	P #	Issue a PR# command to DOS to change CSW address
^P	^P	ctrl-P command to sequentially load SEG files into memory
^M	^M	allows a blank command line by executing a RTS instruction
/	/DOS command	Call HOOKDOS, issue ctrl-D, send command to DOS

Table V.16.2. Lisa80 Command-Line Commands

The *Lisa80* installer *INSTALL80* can be used to copy the *Lisa80* object code files, the *LOADLISA80* utility, and the *SETUP80* utility to another volume. Like the *SETUP80* utility, *Lisa80* contains a built-in command-line command to invoke this action. When the command U is entered on the *Lisa80* command line, the *INSTALL80* utility is activated from the Lisa Image volume LISA80.Image in disk drive 1. The target volume that receives the *Lisa80* object code files, the *LOADLISA80* utility, and the *SETUP80* utility must be in disk drive 2. Table V.16.2 lists all of the available *Lisa80* command-line commands as well as all of the available LED commands. The last command-line command that I added to *Lisa80* was the EX command that allows *Lisa80* to exit directly and cleanly into DOS. This command was extremely difficult to implement: *LOADLISA80* installs at the beginning of LISA80.3 at 0xB7C3 a copy of the real DOSCOLD vector, the first eight bytes of the INITVALS Data structure, and all forty-eight bytes of the Page 0x03 Interface Routines and Vectors from 0x03D0 to 0x03FF.

How does a software design engineer accomplish a task of this magnitude, of moving a software program having the complexity and the size of *Lisa* from being resident in Main memory to now being resident in Auxiliary memory? I believe the first paragraph in Section I.3 helps to answer this question.

In order to design reliable and powerful software
for a particular machine or platform,
one must understand the complete architecture of that machine.

Start any task with a complete list of requirements. From those requirements decide how hardware can be or should be utilized. It is not necessary to know **how** to accomplish this hardware utilization for the moment, but you should be able to decide how the hardware might be or could be or should be **configured**. As you develop the scope of your software design, that capacity should drive or identify the list of software *knowns* and *unknowns* for each software and/or hardware segment of the design. A list of *unknowns* can be very frustrating to the software engineer when that list contains unknown hardware functionality. Segmenting a single *unknown* into smaller components and pairing those components with sufficient unit testing usually yields the necessary knowledge that can move the task forward. The task becomes an incredible mosaic of many hundreds if not thousands of bits of knowledge that are woven together in order to allow only a precise stream of consciousness, or intellectual flow to occur as I like to imagine a software design that is taking form. At this stage in the software design and development process, the scope and the capacity of the software design should be well under control. The primary key to be gained here is derived solely from *sufficient unit testing*.

The unit testing for each design segment is incredibly important. After a functional segment has been thoroughly tested and verified to provide the intended results as per its design requirements, the development of another functional segment can be initiated. When all of the functional segments of the software design have been developed in this manner, the completed task will only require a simple system verification test. I have been developing simple, difficult, and highly complex software tasks using this methodology for so long that it has become ingrained in how I approach each and every software design whether that design is for a simple, for a difficult, or for a highly complex program. This methodology assures me that the final product will conform to **all** established requirements.

Lisa80 is indeed a remarkable assembler and a remarkable Apple //e program. Surely, *Lisa80* is an example of a software program that contains many possibilities that can be designed into Apple //e software. Having a complete and thorough understanding of the Apple //e hardware design can only *assist* in driving the design of any software program in order to utilize that hardware to its fullest potential.

Being able to literally *see* more of the source code for any software project allows for far easier and far faster software development, and *Lisa80* certainly does show more of its source code in every screen display. Being able to edit *Lisa* source code in 80-column mode can never be overstated in its significance and in its overall utility. *Lisa80* is absolutely beautiful in every dimension and in every detail!

17. Program Global Editor Utility

When I received my new Apple][+ in the early 1980's, I spent my first few months writing Applesoft programs. I was fortunate to obtain a copy of the Program Global Editor or *PGE* written by C. A. Greathouse and Garry Reinhardt. *PGE* certainly helped to make programming Applesoft much easier especially when one has excellent tools at hand. I have to say that there is one particular difficulty when writing Applesoft programs, and that is dealing with program line numbers. So many functions depend upon program line numbers, thus making the line numbers a highly critical element of any Applesoft program. There are not many ways to partition an Applesoft program into functions and subroutines except by using program line numbers that may use large line increments from function to function, and smaller line increments within a function. Or, many REM *** statements can be used to partition an Applesoft program, but those statements consume program line numbers as well as memory, which also impacts program execution. Here is where *PGE*'s forte provides me with the most assistance: its capability to quickly renumber program line numbers within a program or within a section of a program.

PGE functionality requires the ability to modify the WARMADR and RESETADR vectors, and to obtain the values found at ADRVAL and LOADLEN within DOS. *PGE* simply modified those vectors and it read the ADRVAL and LOADLEN parameters directly from within DOS 3.3 knowing the memory location for these vectors and these parameters. DOS 4.5 has these vectors and parameters, of course, and a set procedure to read and to modify them. As shown in Table I.8.1, the address of INITVAL is 0xBFFA. The address contained by INITVAL points to the table of address vectors called INITVALS as shown in Table I.8.5. This is where the vectors WARMADR at offset 0x00 and RESETADR at offset 0x06 can be found. The address of the MNGVALS vector is located at 0xBFF4 as shown in Table I.8.1. Section IV.3.4 shows how to access or to change the value of any variable within the CMDVALS Data structure using MNGVALS. According to Table I.12.1, the offset for ADRVAL is 0x2E and the offset for LOADLEN is 0x36. The representative code in Figures I.12.1 and I.12.2 that access and change any 8-bit or 16-bit variable in the CMDVALS Data structure can be used as a model in order to access and change the value for the variables ADRVAL and LOADLEN. Programs like *PGE* do not utilize memory in the Language Card partition for any purpose, thus a user may also safely employ those same procedures when using DOS 4.5. After I adjusted the *PGE* software to locate the vectors and parameters it needs from within DOS 4.5 using the same procedures just outlined, *PGE* executes its commands flawlessly.

One of the worst designed Applesoft functions is the LIST function because of the 40-column width of the display, program lines are truncated, multiple SPACE characters of 0xA0 are used between tokens and data, and there are only twenty-four text lines that comprise the entire display. The LIST function in *PGE* parses the Applesoft tokens and displays them as well as the remaining ASCII program data without using **any** spaces whatsoever. Perhaps the screen is a bit more difficult to read, a bit more cluttered, but considering the *day and the age* when *PGE* was utilized for program editing, having a little screen clutter was a small sacrifice, perhaps even respected. Printer paper and ink were expensive at that time and it was not practical to print programs a multitude number of times during their development. In those early days most software engineers initially wrote out their software instructions using paper and pencil, and typed in their programs after reviewing their program for structural logic and for the most obvious programming errors. I found that the activity of typing in a program from my written notes served as another major review process as well. So, *PGE* is very useful in displaying far more code within the available screen area for my review. The 80-column card allows the Applesoft `LIST` function to display far more program code as shown in Figure V.17.1. The *PGE* `LIST` function is shown in Figure V.17.2 for the beginning lines of the same `HELLO` file. I believe that Figure V.17.1 is far more readable when displaying program code. Although, if the two displays were compared in 40-column mode, the *PGE* `LIST` function would be for more practical in displaying more program code.

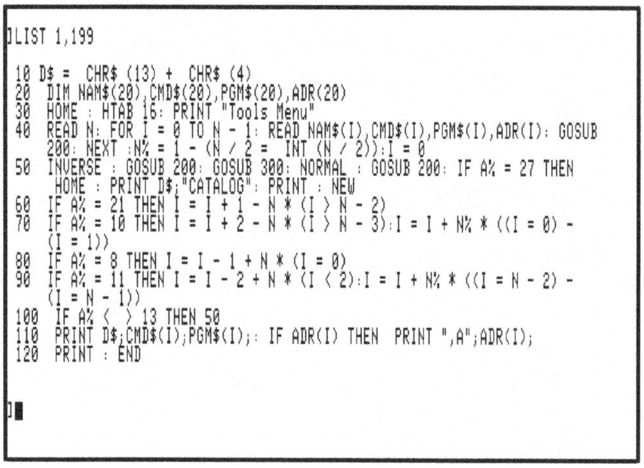

```
]LIST 1,199

 10 D$ =  CHR$ (13) +  CHR$ (4)
 20  DIM NAM$(20),CMD$(20),PGM$(20),ADR(20)
 30  HOME : HTAB 16: PRINT "Tools Menu"
 40  READ N: FOR I = 0 TO N - 1: READ NAM$(I),CMD$(I),PGM$(I),ADR(I): GOSUB
     200: NEXT :N% = 1 - (N / 2 =  INT (N / 2)):I = 0
 50  INVERSE : GOSUB 200: GOSUB 300: NORMAL : GOSUB 200: IF A% = 27 THEN
      HOME : PRINT D$;"CATALOG": PRINT : NEW
 60  IF A% = 21 THEN I = I + 1 - N * (I > N - 2)
 70  IF A% = 10 THEN I = I + 2 - N * (I > N - 3):I = I + N% * ((I = 0) -
     (I = 1))
 80  IF A% = 8 THEN I = I - 1 + N * (I = 0)
 90  IF A% = 11 THEN I = I - 2 + N * (I < 2):I = I + N% * ((I = N - 2) -
     (I = N - 1))
 100  IF A% <  > 13 THEN 50
 110  PRINT D$;CMD$(I);PGM$(I);: IF ADR(I) THEN  PRINT ",A";ADR(I);
 120  PRINT : END

]
```

Figure V.17.1. Applesoft LIST Function 1

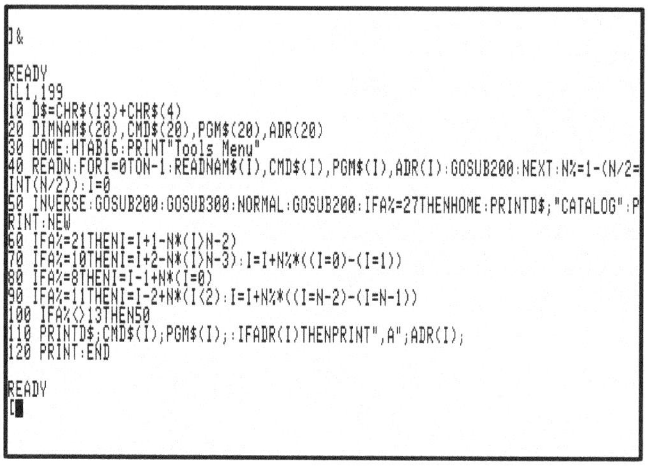

```
]&

READY
[L1,199
10 D$=CHR$(13)+CHR$(4)
20 DIMNAM$(20),CMD$(20),PGM$(20),ADR(20)
30 HOME:HTAB16:PRINT"Tools Menu"
40 READN:FORI=0TON-1:READNAM$(I),CMD$(I),PGM$(I),ADR(I):GOSUB200:NEXT:N%=1-(N/2=
INT(N/2)):I=0
50 INVERSE:GOSUB200:GOSUB300:NORMAL:GOSUB200:IFA%=27THENHOME:PRINTD$;"CATALOG":P
RINT:NEW
60 IFA%=21THENI=I+1-N*(I>N-2)
70 IFA%=10THENI=I+2-N*(I>N-3):I=I+N%*((I=0)-(I=1))
80 IFA%=8THENI=I-1+N*(I=0)
90 IFA%=11THENI=I-2+N*(I<2):I=I+N%*((I=N-2)-(I=N-1))
100 IFA%<>13THEN50
110 PRINTD$;CMD$(I);PGM$(I);:IFADR(I)THENPRINT",A";ADR(I);
120 PRINT:END

READY
[
```

Figure V.17.2. PGE LIST Function

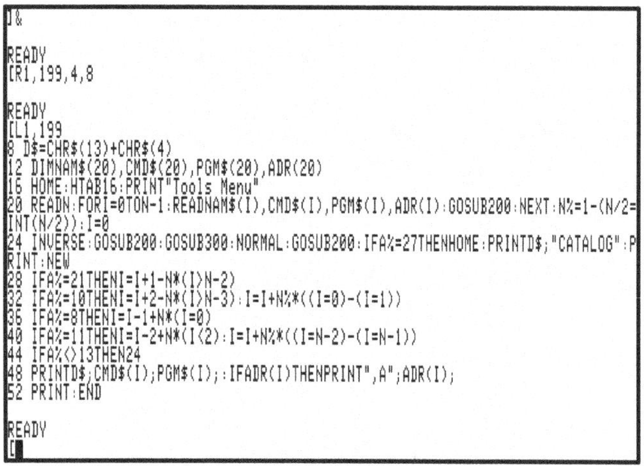

```
]&

READY
[R1,199,4,8

READY
[L1,199
8 D$=CHR$(13)+CHR$(4)
12 DIMNAM$(20),CMD$(20),PGM$(20),ADR(20)
16 HOME:HTAB16:PRINT"Tools Menu"
20 READN:FORI=0TON-1:READNAM$(I),CMD$(I),PGM$(I),ADR(I):GOSUB200:NEXT:N%=1-(N/2=
INT(N/2)):I=0
24 INVERSE:GOSUB200:GOSUB300:NORMAL:GOSUB200:IFA%=27THENHOME:PRINTD$;"CATALOG":P
RINT:NEW
28 IFA%=21THENI=I+1-N*(I>N-2)
32 IFA%=10THENI=I+2-N*(I>N-3):I=I+N%*((I=0)-(I=1))
36 IFA%=8THENI=I-1+N*(I=0)
40 IFA%=11THENI=I-2+N*(I<2):I=I+N%*((I=N-2)-(I=N-1))
44 IFA%<>13THEN24
48 PRINTD$;CMD$(I);PGM$(I);:IFADR(I)THENPRINT",A";ADR(I);
52 PRINT:END

READY
[
```

Figure V.17.3. PGE RENUMBER Function

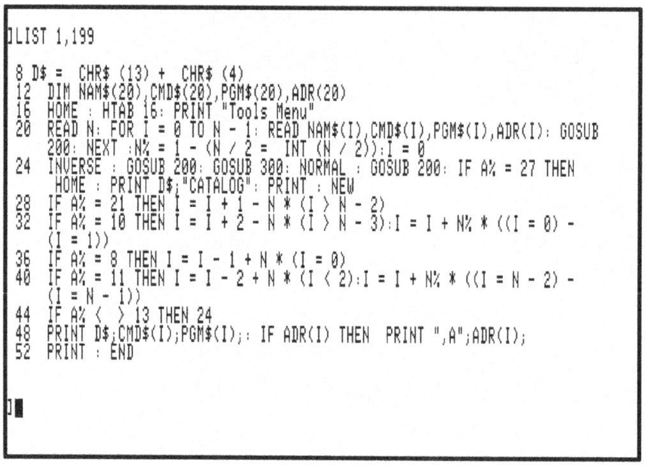

```
]LIST 1,199

 8 D$ =  CHR$ (13) +  CHR$ (4)
 12  DIM NAM$(20),CMD$(20),PGM$(20),ADR(20)
 16  HOME : HTAB 16: PRINT "Tools Menu"
 20  READ N: FOR I = 0 TO N - 1: READ NAM$(I),CMD$(I),PGM$(I),ADR(I): GOSUB
     200: NEXT :N% = 1 - (N / 2 =  INT (N / 2)):I = 0
 24  INVERSE : GOSUB 200: GOSUB 300: NORMAL : GOSUB 200: IF A% = 27 THEN
      HOME : PRINT D$;"CATALOG": PRINT : NEW
 28  IF A% = 21 THEN I = I + 1 - N * (I > N - 2)
 32  IF A% = 10 THEN I = I + 2 - N * (I > N - 3):I = I + N% * ((I = 0) -
     (I = 1))
 36  IF A% = 8 THEN I = I - 1 + N * (I = 0)
 40  IF A% = 11 THEN I = I - 2 + N * (I < 2):I = I + N% * ((I = N - 2) -
     (I = N - 1))
 44  IF A% <  > 13 THEN 24
 48  PRINT D$;CMD$(I);PGM$(I);: IF ADR(I) THEN  PRINT ",A";ADR(I);
 52  PRINT : END

]
```

Figure V.17.4. Applesoft LIST Function 2

PGE excels in renumbering small portions, large portions, and even entire portions of programs. Upon initialization, *PGE* remaps the ampersand vector to its `READY [` prompt. The renumber command `R` requires four parameters for the old start number, the old end number, the increment, and the new start number. *PGE* scours the entire Applesoft program and changes every occurrence of a program line number within the given specified range to the new program line number that is based on the new start number and some program line number increment, say 5 or 10 or 100. To say that the results were marvelous would be an understatement. As one's Applesoft programming capabilities mature, better choices for line numbers are usually made, and it becomes far easier to create sections of Applesoft code that resemble a function or a subroutine. In these instances, being able to renumber a small section of code is quite powerful. Figure V.17.3 demonstrates how simple it is to renumber the beginning lines of the HELLO program that is shown in Figure V.17.1. This program now begins with line number 8 and the line increment is set to 4 for all lines up to line 199. The line numbers following line 199 in Figure V.17.1 are not affected except when those earlier line numbers are *referenced* within the later line numbers. An astute observer will notice that *PGE* only accepts uppercase ASCII commands. I have no doubt that it would be easy to modify *PGE* to accept lowercase ASCII commands as well. That same renumbered program is shown in Figure V.17.4 using the Applesoft LIST function. It appears identical to Figure V.17.1 except for its line numbers.

The downside in using *PGE* occurs when *PGE* is used to renumber an Applesoft program that has one or more attached Binary programs. When the renumber function finds the triple-zero termination marker for an Applesoft program, it sets the end of program at ASPEND or 0xAF:0xB0 to that memory location. In other words, *PGE* processing loses the original *end of program* address and changes it to the address where the triple-zero termination marker is found regardless whether the Applesoft program has any attached Binary programs or not. This situation is not insurmountable because the assembly language routines may be easily re-attached using Binary File Installation as described in Section V.2. Though it is a little inconvenient having to re-install Binary programs after *PGE* processing, it is certainly nothing compared to the staggering convenience of the line renumbering capability of *PGE*.

PGE activation required a small program loader to load the *PGE* program into memory and to initialize FRETOP or 0x6F:0x70, HIMEM or 0x74:0x75, and the ampersand vector at 0x3F5. The *PGE* program used the upper part of the INPUT buffer from 0x2D0 to 0x2FF for variables. Two 256-byte buffers are used at the end of the *PGE* program as well as a number of variables at the end of a third 256-byte buffer from 0xnnE0 to 0xnnFF, where **nn** is the page number for that third buffer. I had already completed the sourcing of the *PGE* code so that *PGE* can function at another memory location. I decided to combine the *PGE* loader, the page-two variables, and the variables at the end of the third buffer into a page that precedes the main *PGE* code. Now, the *PGE* system has been drastically simplified and only one file is launched. *PGE* still depends upon reading and writing directly to the TEXT pages using CH and BASL. There are some *PGE* problematic functions that still do not work properly if the 80-column card in enabled. The renumber function is **not** one of those problematic functions.

DOS 4.5 is required by this new formulation of *PGE*. Seriously, there is not enough room in lower Main memory to support DOS 4.5L, *PGE*, and a large Applesoft program. An interested user can always reassemble my single file version of *PGE* to function in the Language Card partition. As of now, I have placed *PGE* at 0x8E00 and HIMEM is set at 0x8DF0. This configuration should be able to accommodate a massive Applesoft program. The two 256-byte *PGE* buffers are now located at pages 0xAB and 0xAC. Also, *GPLE* can be placed at 0xAD00 so that *GPLE* does not overwrite the DOS 4.5 interface at 0xBE00 that controls and manages DOS 4.5 that resides in the Language Card partition.

18. Global Program Line Editor Utility

Another invaluable and powerful Applesoft program editing tool that I was fortunate enough to obtain early in my Apple][programming career was Global Program Line Editor (*GPLE*). Neil Konzen published *GPLE* in 1982, and I obtained version V3.4. *GPLE* uses the entire Bank 1 of the Language Card partition beginning at 0xD000, so it is obviously not compatible with DOS 4.5 in its original format. *GPLE* did not utilize any vectors or parameters within DOS 3.3 so I did not have to adjust any of my sourced code for *GPLE* whatsoever in order for it to execute at another memory location. What I like about *GPLE* is that it works very much like a global word processor specifically for Applesoft programs. It has the ability to globally search and replace any variable, word, or character with any other variable, word, or character within an Applesoft program. And *GPLE* does its work extremely fast.

The original *GPLE* loader first verifies that the Apple][computer contains at least 48 KB of memory and that there is an available Language Card partition. Then, the loader write-enables Bank 1 of the Language Card partition and issues a DOS BLOAD command in order to load *GPLE* to memory address 0xD000. Finally, the *GPLE* loader copies a set of routines that are comprised of the ctrl-Y entry location, the ampersand entry location, and the CSWL and KSWL interface pointers to memory at 0xB6B3 to 0xB6F9, a small, unused area within DOS 3.3. These routines also control the Bank switching of the Language Card partition as well as providing the entry location for a modifiable JSR instruction that is used in *GPLE* processing.

```
            Global GPLE
Copyright (C) 1982 Neil Konzen


]LOAD HELLO
]EDIT "VOLUME"
 1040  DATA  VOLUME COPY, BRUN, VOLUME C
OPY, 0
 1120  DATA  VOLUME MANAGER, BRUN, VOLMG
R, 0
 1130  DATA  BOOT CFFA VOLUME, BRUN, BOO
TVOL, 0

] *
```

Figure V.18.1. GPLE EDIT Function

I decided to combine the *GPLE* loader, the ctrl-Y and the CSWL and KSWL interface routines, and the *GPLE* program into one, drastically simplified program. Thus, only one file is required to be launched. I specifically redesigned *GPLE* to function in lower Main memory since DOS 4.5 resides in the Language Card partition. *GPLE* still depends upon reading and writing directly to the TEXT pages using CH and BASL. Therefore, some *GPLE* capabilities still do not function properly if the 80-column card is enabled. I disabled the ampersand entry location since its primary function is to initialize *GPLE*. Instead, I reserve the ampersand function entirely for *PGE*. *GPLE* provides a host of ctrl shortcuts that are intended to issue certain DOS commands, calculate the size of an Applesoft program in memory, or calculate the number of free sectors in a volume. Because I only use *GPLE* to find and to replace text in Applesoft programs, I have ignored those other, special capabilities of *GPLE*. Those capabilities are primarily intended to be used within the DOS 3.3 architecture and I have not had the interest nor the desire to modify or to update these particular routines in *GPLE*. Figure V.18.1 shows *GPLE* after it has initialized. The `ctrl-E` function, or EDIT, provides access to all of the editing capabilities that are available in *GPLE*. It is this *GPLE* function that I use exclusively.

I made a gallant attempt to modify *GPLE* so that it would perform its functions with the 80-column card enabled. I even utilized some of the routines that I had developed for *Lisa* so that *Lisa* would function with the 80-column card enabled. Even after several bouts of frustration I finally had to shelve that effort from sheer mental exhaustion. I did, however, manage to update the *GPLE* CSWL and KSWL interface routines and capture the state of the Bank that is currently in focus in the Language Card partition. These two vectors must restore not only the state of the Language Card partition, but they must also restore which Bank is enabled at the very moment when either vector is entered since DOS 4.5 utilizes both Banks of memory in the Language Card partition for all of its processing capabilities.

Once the modified *GPLE* has been launched, my generic HELLO program on my DOS.4.5.Tools volume cannot capture any `ctrl` codes in order to select which programs to launch, like *PGE* for example. All keystrokes are filtered through *GPLE*, and any `ctrl` character such as the arrow keys are trapped. The HELLO program requires that arrow key information in order to properly select any of the available programs to launch. When the user requires the services of both *GPLE* and *PGE*, the global editor *PGE* should be launched **first**. Once *PGE* is operational, HELLO can be used to launch *GPLE* so that both utilities are available and glorious Applesoft programming and editing can begin again!

19.   Axlon RAM Disk Data Storage

I first became aware of the Axlon RAM Disk 320 when I was self-employed and working under contract for Sierra On-Line around 1985. Living in Oakhurst, California, was totally awesome, and being able to work at home was even better. Except when thunderstorms developed in the Oakhurst area and electrical power was temporarily interrupted, it was heavenly to live and work in Oakhurst. Due to the propensity of thunderstorms in the California Sierra mountains, I was alert to any hardware solutions that I might find in the various Apple and computer subscriptions I maintained. Perhaps I might find an affordable solution offered in one of the many advertisements throughout those magazine subscriptions. UPS battery backups, or Uninterrupted Power Supplies were not easy to obtain and they were not very affordable at that time. But when I was in the middle of a massive software development session and I lost power to the house that caused me to lose hours of work, the cost of a UPS seemed trivial. That was the time when I decided to purchase an Axlon RAM Disk. Actually, I purchased two because a friend wanted a RAM Disk, too, after I described to him all of its features. The RAM Disk emulates two 40-track disk drives using DRAM memory, and it has its own built-in power supply and backup lead-acid battery. As long as the power outage did not last more than four hours, all of my files would be safe within the RAM Disk memory. My software development pace vastly accelerated as well because files were assembled from RAM and not from diskette. And when the RAM Disk was mated with the ZipChip, large projects could be assembled and linked in seconds rather than in many, many minutes.

Axlon provided excellent software utilities with the RAM Disk. Their RAM Disk initialization software could transfer the contents of an entire diskette to one of the RAM drives in the time it took the Disk][, whose diskette is spinning at 300 revolutions per minute, to make thirty-five revolutions, one revolution per track, in seven seconds, or 35 * 60 / 300 seconds. That is impressive! From their software and from the hardware design of their peripheral interface card I truly learned the importance of reading the CLRROM address or 0xCFFF in order to detach peripheral-card expansion ROM memory. Whenever the 6502-microprocessor fetches an instruction in peripheral-card ROM memory, or 0xCs00 to 0xCsFF, where s is the slot number of the peripheral interface card, the peripheral interface card typically enables its peripheral-card expansion ROM memory, or 0xC800 to 0xCFFF, if the hardware is designed to do so and if it contains the memory for that use. The RAM Disk peripheral interface card was designed to enable its peripheral-card expansion ROM memory *only* when the card was accessed in the address range of 0xCs00 to 0xCs7F. Interesting. Software that resides in the upper half of its peripheral-card ROM memory can read the CLRROM address in order to detach the expansion ROM memory without re-enabling that same memory. That was indeed a very, very clever design. In fact, I made good use of that hardware design in all of my versions of RAM Disk firmware. Another interesting design of the RAM Disk peripheral interface card was its use of a static RAM IC, a 6116, for its firmware memory. The static RAM IC needs to be programmed only once when power to the computer is first turned ON, and regardless how many times the Apple][is powered OFF and back ON again, the static RAM IC retains its memory because its operating power comes from the RAM Disk and not from the Apple][.

The first page of the static RAM IC is mapped to the peripheral-card ROM memory or 0xCs00 to 0xCsFF and its 0xC8 page is mapped to the selected page of RAM Disk DRAM. The remaining seven pages of static RAM IC memory are mapped to the peripheral-card expansion ROM memory from 0xC900 to 0xCFFF. I made good use of the idea of utilizing a static RAM IC instead of an EPROM when I was testing my new firmware for the Sider Host adapter card. It was amazing how much easier it was to test different software algorithms for the Sider without having to program yet another, and another EPROM. However, I have recently replaced the RAM Disk static RAM IC with a 28C16A EEPROM. I connected Pin 18, its IC enable, to an SPDT switch in order to write-protect the EEPROM. This EEPROM needs to be programmed only once, and it retains its data until it is re-programmed at a later time. It has the conveniences of both a static RAM IC and an EPROM. This EEPROM cannot be programmed quickly like a static RAM IC, so care must be taken in developing any EEPROM programming software to include the appropriate time delay between program bytes.

I no longer remember when and where I became an owner of a 128 KB RAM peripheral interface card, or RAM Card. It may have been left inside a used Apple //e that I purchased at a garage sale. And, I have no idea who manufactured this RAM Card either. This RAM Card is designed to operate much like a Language Card in any peripheral slot in an Apple][+ or in an Apple //e, and it can be easily configured as one of eight Language Card partitions. Since Address Bit A02 is ignored when configuring the Language Card partition using its dedicated Soft Switches, this RAM Card utilizes Address Bit A02 in order to select a Language Card partition block. Table V.19.1 shows the memory management Soft Switches that are used by this RAM Card. Simply reading address 0xC084 selects RAM Card block 0 or reading address 0xC08D selects RAM Card block 5.

The original hardware circuit of the RAM Card is shown in Figure V.19.1. The circuit utilizes an Intel 3242 address multiplexer and refresh counter in order to periodically refresh the sixteen dynamic RAM ICs that are on board. This address multiplexer is designed to refresh 16 Kb dynamic RAM ICs, not 64 Kb dynamic RAM ICs like those that are found on this RAM card. Therefore, the RAM Card circuit derives Row Address 7 from the selected RAM Card block number. Data that is read from or written to the RAM Card is latched in the 0xD000 to 0xFFFF memory address range. The RAM Card must pull the *INH* line low in order to disable the Apple][ROMs appropriately and to enable the memory of the respective Language Card partition block according to the last read configuration Soft Switch as shown in Table V.19.1. In order to utilize the RAM Card for anything useful, software must be specifically designed to access the RAM Card as eight individual Language Cards, or an interface driver must reside in Apple][memory in order to provide RAM Card memory access. Neither of these ideas appealed to me, and I wanted to use all of the 128 KB of memory in a more generic fashion.

Address	Access	Name	Description
0xC080	R	RAM2WP	Select Bank 2; write-protect RAM
0xC081	R || RR	ROM2WE	Deselect Bank 2; enable ROM || write-enable RAM
0xC082	R	ROM2WP	Deselect Bank 2; enable ROM; write-protect RAM
0xC083	R || RR	RAM2WE	Select Bank 2 || write-enable RAM
0xC084	R	RCBLK0	Select RAM Card block 0
0xC085	R	RCBLK1	Select RAM Card block 1
0xC086	R	RCBLK2	Select RAM Card block 2
0xC087	R	RCBLK3	Select RAM Card block 3
0xC088	R	RAM1WP	Select Bank 1; write-protect RAM
0xC089	R || RR	ROM1WE	Deselect Bank 1; enable ROM || write-enable RAM
0xC08A	R	ROM1WP	Deselect Bank 1; enable ROM; write-protect RAM
0xC08B	R || RR	RAM1WE	Select Bank 1 || write-enable RAM
0xC08C	R	RCBLK4	Select RAM Card block 4
0xC08D	R	RCBLK5	Select RAM Card block 5
0xC08E	R	RCBLK6	Select RAM Card block 6
0xC08F	R	RCBLK7	Select RAM Card block 7

Table V.19.1. RAM Card Memory Configuration Soft Switches

The hardware of the RAM Disk, on the other hand, responds only to the first two of sixteen peripheral-card I/O memory locations that are dedicated to the RAM Disk in order to select the sector and the track variables, so Address Bit A02 is always **low**. The RAM Card is designed to latch Address Bits A00, A01, and A03 when Address Bit A02 is always **high**. Thus, the active peripheral-card I/O memory locations for the RAM Disk and for the RAM Card are mutually exclusive in selecting RAM Disk sector and track variables versus RAM Card block number. For example, when the RAM Disk interface card resides in slot 7, sector number is saved to 0xC0F0 and track number is saved to 0xC0F1. When the RAM Card resides in slot 7, block number is selected by reading 0xC0F4 to 0xC0F7 or 0xC0FC to 0xC0FF. Once I understood the hardware circuit of the RAM Card vis-á-vis its utilization by means of software, I thought perhaps the circuit could be easily re-engineered. I also had some unused space within the RAM Disk peripheral-card ROM memory and I had plenty of unused space for additional software within the RAM Disk peripheral-card expansion ROM memory. From within the RAM Disk peripheral-card ROM memory, I knew I could turn off the RAM Disk peripheral-card expansion ROM memory and use that address space to possibly access eight continuous pages of the RAM Card. Therefore, instead of accessing RAM Card data in the 0xD000 to 0xFFFF memory address range, I could access RAM Card data in the peripheral-card expansion ROM memory from 0xC800 to 0xCFFF as one of sixty-four 8-page data blocks.

It was around 1992 when I figured out a procedure to physically modify the RAM Card in order to allow the firmware of the RAM Disk to control it, and to access it as if it was a RAM disk drive that has thirty-two tracks. However, this modification required me to connect the RAM Card to the RAM Disk using a single control wire. I found that Slot 3 was the perfect slot for the RAM Card because the RAM Card no longer needs to respond to its own *DEVICE SELECT* signal, but instead, it responds to the simulated control *DEVICE SELECT* signal that is generated by the RAM Disk firmware. When the RAM Disk connects to DOS 4.5, it calls the MNGDISK routine on behalf of the RAM Disk **and** on behalf of the RAM Card in order to add the addresses of its Disk handlers to the Disk Address table DISKADRS, one address for the RAM Disk that resides in slot 7 and one address for the RAM Card that resides in slot 3. To be sure, the RAM Disk firmware is handling all of the RWTS IOCB traffic for the RAM Disk as well as the RWTS IOCB traffic for the RAM Card. Regardless which slot the RAM Card occupies, the RAM Disk firmware saves the track and the sector from the RWTS IOCB to the 0xC0n4 peripheral-card I/O memory location on behalf of the RAM Card, where **n** is equal to the slot number of the RAM Disk plus eight. Formatting either the RAM Disk drives for forty tracks or the RAM Card for thirty-two tracks is fundamentally trival in DOS 4.5 because the DOS INIT command can set the ENDTRK variable to those specific values using the A keyword.

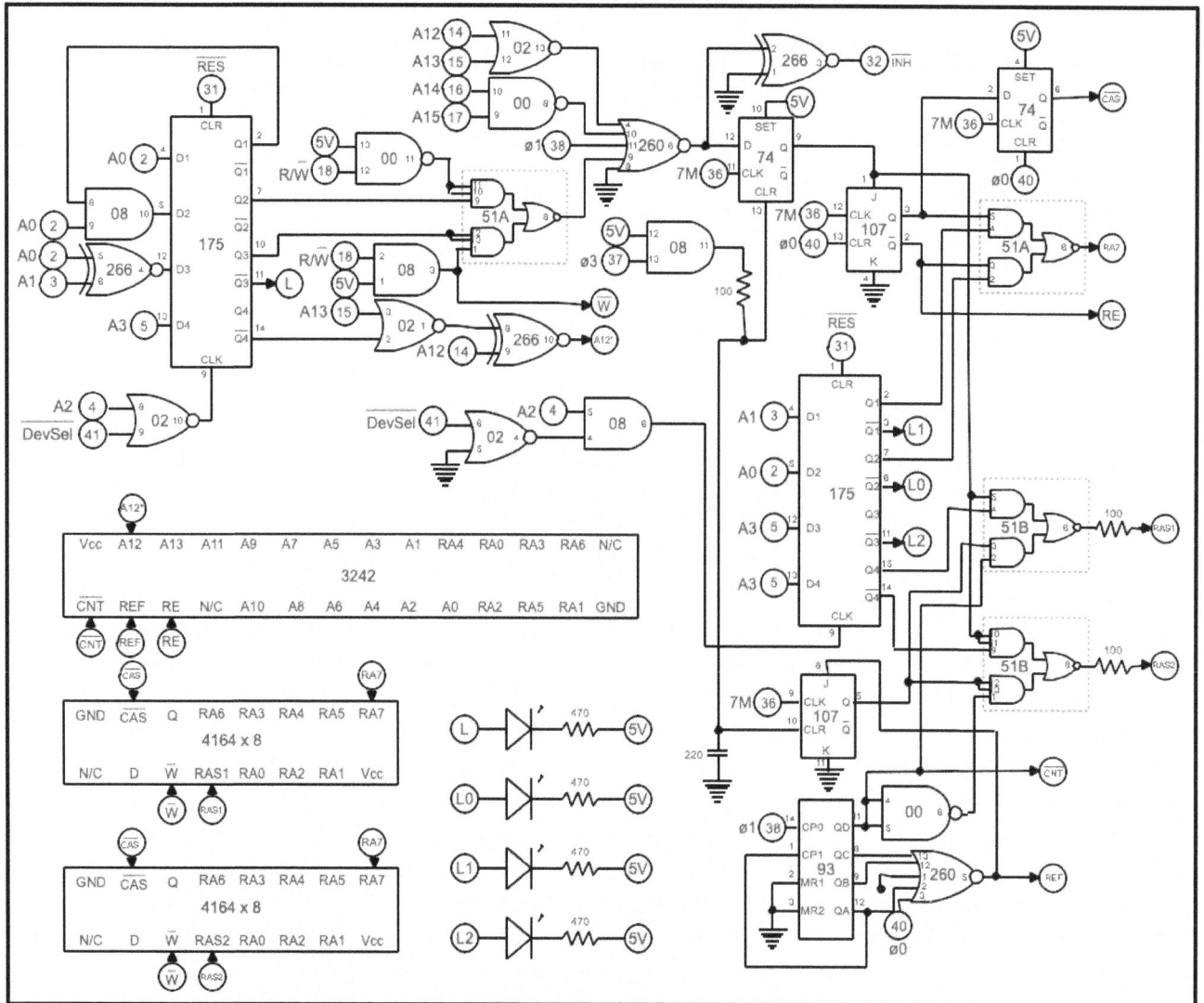

Figure V.19.1. Original RAM Card Hardware Circuit Diagram

Figure V.19.2 shows the modified RAM Card hardware circuit diagram. The 74LS175 quad D flip-flops latch the data bus bits except for data Bit D6. Data Bits D0 to D5 contain the desired sector/track number and data Bit D7 is used to enable the RAM Card. The desired 6-bit sector/track Data Block and the sector Page value are calculated as follows

$$B = (\text{ track number} * 2) + (\text{ sector number} / 8)$$
$$P = \text{ sector number} \& 7$$

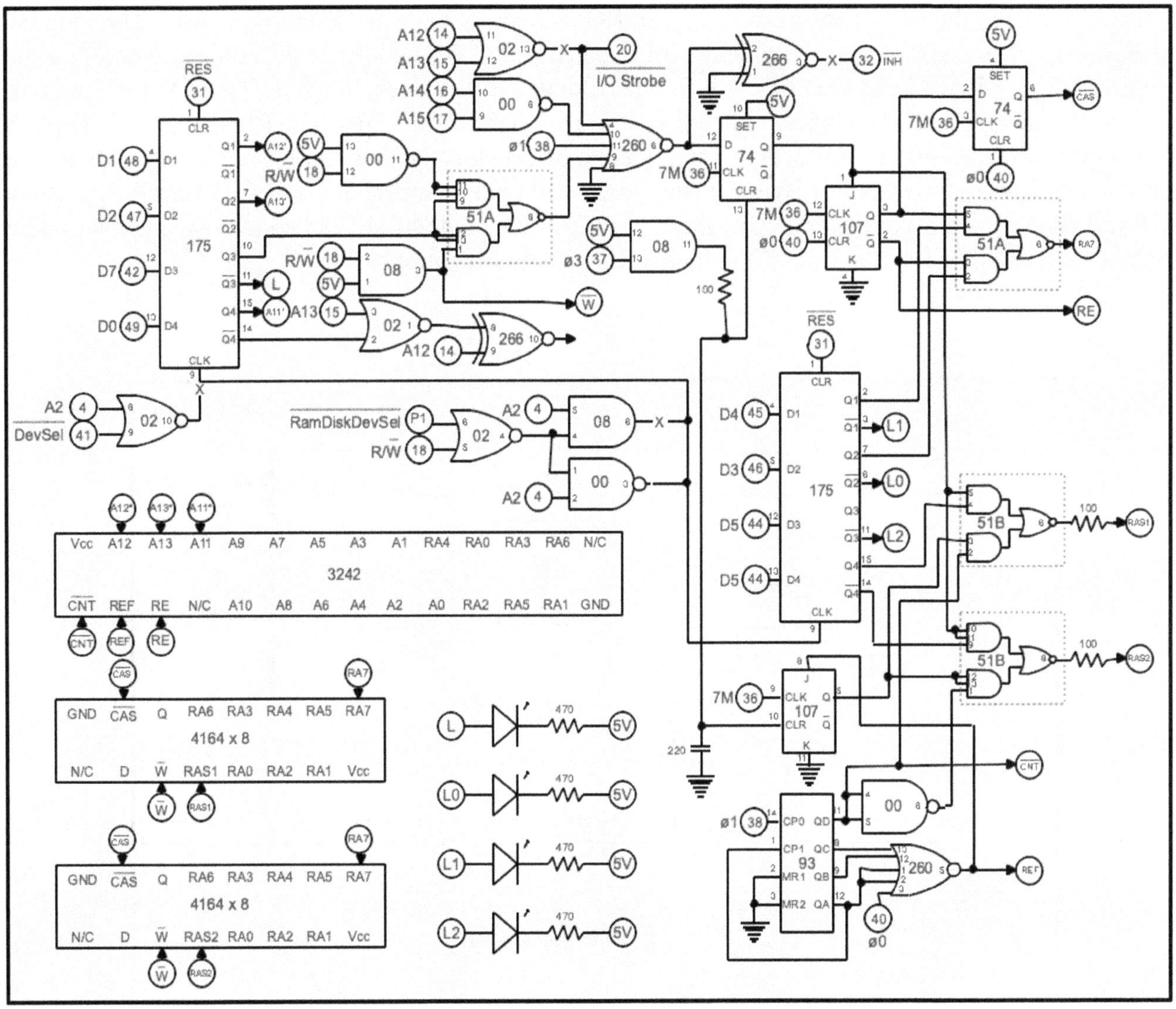

Figure V.19.2. Modified RAM Card Hardware Circuit Diagram

The selected data Block B within the total memory of the RAM Card is determined by doubling the track number and adding in the sector number divided by eight. The selected page P value within that data Block B that is mapped to the RAM Card peripheral-card expansion ROM memory is determined from the first three bits of the sector number. That data Block is either the first eight sectors or the last eight sectors of the specified track. These calculations show that the 128 KB RAM Card provides sixty-four

Data Blocks and each Data Block provides eight pages of data. Now, the modified RAM Card circuit is not required to bring *INH* low because it is **no longer** necessary to disable the Apple][ROMs. Figure V.19.3 shows the actual modifications that must be made to Figure V.19.1 in order to obtain Figure V.19.2. Fortunately, a 74LS00 gate is available in order to clock the 74LS175 control registers.

In Figure V.19.3, the Control Byte is latched into the two control registers on the RAM Card only when Address Bit A02 is high as in STA 0xC084,X where the X-register contains the slot number of the RAM Disk times sixteen. The RAM Disk hardware does not respond to any value that is written to its peripheral-card I/O memory location when Address Bit A02 is high, but it does generate a suitable *DEVICE SELECT* signal that can be used by the RAM Card. Before the RAM Card is enabled, the CLRROM address is read in order to disable the peripheral-card expansion ROM memory from 0xC800 to 0xCFFF. The moment the RAM Card is enabled, the peripheral-card expansion ROM memory is instantly mapped to eight selected pages of RAM Card memory. Bit 0 of the Control Byte that is shown in Figure V.19.3 contains bit 3 of the desired sector number. Therefore, the peripheral-card expansion ROM memory displays sectors 0x00 to 0x07 when Control Byte bit 0 is zero and sectors 0x08 to 0x0F when Control Byte bit 0 is one. Bits 1 to 5 of the Control Byte contain the desired track number. Bit 6 of the Control Byte is not used and bit 7 is used to enable or disable the RAM Card. The RAM Card can no longer function as a set of eight Language Cards after having had these hardware modifications.

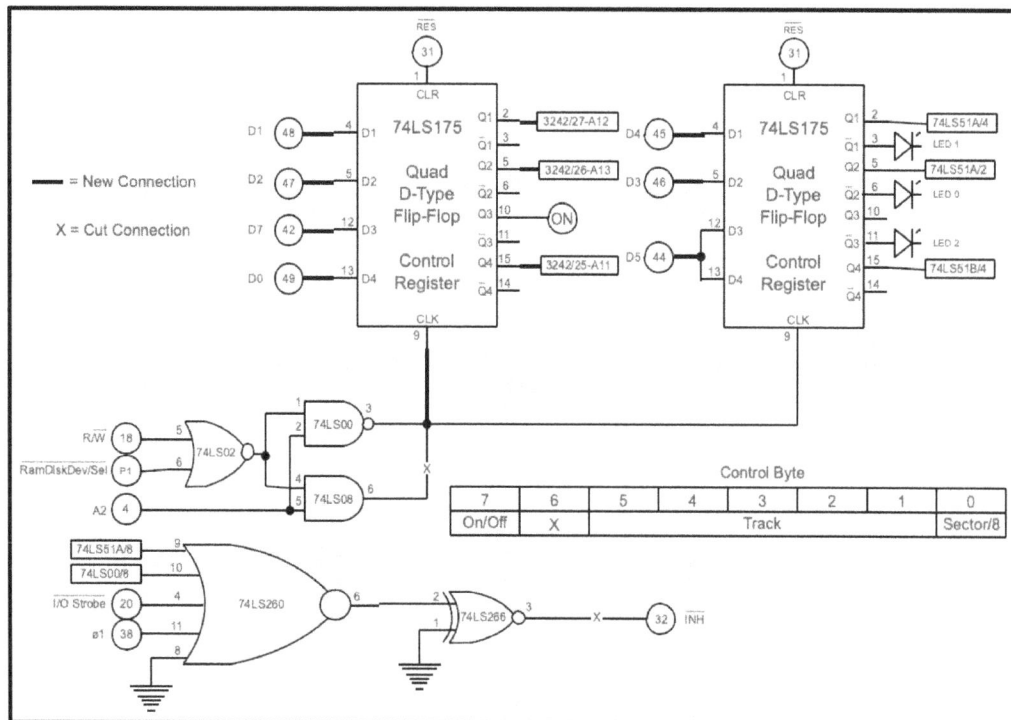

Figure V.19.3. RAM Card Hardware Modifications

Table V.19.2 shows the DOS RWTS entry points for the RAM Disk and for the RAM Card in the firmware that is mapped to the peripheral-card ROM memory that resides in the EEPROM of the RAM Disk. The RAM Card hardware does not contain an EPROM or an EEPROM and, therefore, does not contain any firmware. The RAM Card depends entirely on the RAM Disk for its complete operation and for its connectivity to DOS RWTS. According to manufacturing documentation, the 28C16A is a fast, low power, 5V-only CMOS Parallel EEPROM organized as 2K x 8-bits. It requires a simple interface for in-system programming. Integrated circuit address and data latches, Vcc power up/down write-protection, and self-timed write cycle with auto-clear eliminates the need for additional timing and protection hardware. This EEPROM is designed to endure a minimum of 10,000 program/erase cycles and this EEPROM has a data retention of ten years. Fast read access time is 200 nanoseconds and fast write cycle time is 10 milliseconds maximum. The algorithm I developed to program this integrated circuit writes a byte of data to the EEPROM, reads the EEPROM, and then compares the byte that was read to the byte that was written until they are the same. The continuous read-loop for this EEPROM is 300 μsec, and the loop is enabled for a maximum of 48 retries. This algorithm provides a generous 14.4 milliseconds for the write cycle time for each byte written, though data is typically written in far less time. If, for some reason, a data byte cannot be written within 14.4 milliseconds, programming is terminated and an error routine is called. Once each byte of the EEPROM is programmed, a verification routine is called in order to confirm the accuracy of the entire EEPROM data image. The complete programming process does take several minutes to fully program an EEPROM of this size, but the EEPROM only needs to be programmed once rather than having to program a static RAM IC each and every time the RAM Disk is first powered ON.

Offset	Name	Description
0x00	RDBOOT	Entry point for DOS PR# command to BOOT DOS that is in drive 1
0x10	ROMHOOK	Entry point to attach the RAM Disk/RAM Card to the DOS Disk Address table
0x18	ROMUHOOK	Entry point to detach the RAM Disk/RAM Card from the DOS Disk Address table
0x20	RDENTRY3	Entry for DOS 3.3 RAM Disk RWTS processing, IOCB in Y-/A-registers
0x40	RDENTRY	Entry for DOS 4.1-4.5 RAM Disk RWTS processing, IOCB in Y-/A-registers
0x50	RCENTRY	Entry for RAM Card RWTS processing, IOCB in Y-/A-registers
0x5C	ROMBOOT	Simulate Disk][entry point for BOOT Stage 0 code that resides at 0x0801
0x70	MODOS3	Patch DOS 3.3 after BOOT Stage 2
0x80	BOOTEXIT	Issue CLRROM, jump to 0x0801
0x87	RCEXIT	Turn RAM Card OFF, fall into RDEXIT
0x90	RDEXIT	Save RWTS error code, issue CLRROM, return to caller
0x9E	HOOKEXIT	Exit for ROMHOOK and ROMUHOOK
0xA5	EXIT3	Exit for MODOS3
0xAC	RCRDWRT	Enable RAM Card, read/write RAM Card, exit to RCEXIT
0xD4	RCFORMT	Issue CLRROM, enable RAM Card, clear sectors, exit to RCEXIT
0xFE	VERSION	Version number of RAM Disk firmware (0x05)
0xFF	BUILD	Build number for RAM Disk firmware (0x06)

Table V.19.2. RAM Disk 320 Firmware Entry Points

20. RanaSystems EliteThree Data Storage

I met a very knowledgeable engineer at Hughes Aircraft Company a year or so after I was hired into the Digital Simulation and Integration Laboratory in 1986. Kathryn provided private consulting services to small companies and she designed proprietary databases for her customers. In order to document and record her services, she used a database system of her own design that is hosted on an Apple][computer

331

connected to a single Disk][drive and a RanaSystems EliteThree drive as her massive database data storage container. She preferred the large storage capacity of the Rana and she thought the access time was a bit faster than the Disk][. When she sold her consulting business, she offered to sell me the Rana drive for $100 on November 14, 1988. I recently found her dated invoice in a folder along with the Rana manual. Obviously, the Rana is used, but certainly still useable, and I jumped at her offer. My early investigations into the Rana and its installation software revealed to me how tightly coupled it is to DOS 3.3. I didn't much care for all of the modifications the installation software had to make to DOS 3.3 in order to provide the various configurations the hardware was capable of supporting. These modifications were provided by Rana Enhancement Utilities and they were designed to modify DOS and *FID* on a Master DOS diskette. The Rana can read and write either side of a diskette and it can create tracks half the size of Disk][tracks so it can create eighty tracks on each side of a diskette. The RanaSystems EliteThree Controller card is capable of hosting up to four disk drives of any manufacture. I basically left it at that, and put the Rana away for another time to explore its capabilities.

That time has arrived to have another look at the RanaSystems EliteThree vis-à-vis DOS 4.5. Any configuration that utilizes the hardware capabilities of the Rana needs to consider the current VTOC structure and how the VTOC can possibly be expanded in order to provide the resources for more than fifty tracks in a volume. The Rana can seek up to eighty tracks on a double-sided, double-density diskette. The Rana can also access both sides of a diskette without having to manually flip the diskette over in order to access its backside, thereby providing direct access to one hundred sixty tracks.

I fondly recall the time in 1968 when I sat in the Audio Music Library in Schoenberg Hall at UCLA listening to magnetic tape recordings for my class on Johann Sebastian Bach. The library used an array of four Viking 80 magnetic tape recorders to playback audio assignments for students who are enrolled in various music classes. I happened to own a Viking 880 which used vacuum tubes for its audio recording and playback circuits. The only difference the Viking 880 had to the Viking 80 is that the 880 came installed in a suitcase with two 2x6 inch speakers and a small, solid state stereo audio amplifier. This recorder has the ability to adjust the physical position of the erase, record, and playback heads in order to playback magnetic tapes that are recorded in half-track mode as well as magnetic tapes that are recorded in quarter-track mode. The signal-to-noise ratio for a half-track recording is obviously far superior to a quarter-track recording because twice as much magnetic material is used for the recorded signal. Even though the Viking used a quarter-track playback head to read a half-track audio recording, the increased signal-to-noise ratio was still quite apparent. Why I mention half-track versus quarter-track magnetic audio recording playback is that the concepts are quite similar when they are applied to magnetic disk recording using a Disk][recorder versus a RanaSystems EliteThree recorder. The recording head gap length, or track size in the Rana is half the recording head gap length in the Disk][, so recordings that are made by the Rana would have a lower signal-to-noise ratio than recordings that are made by the Disk][because half as much magnetic material is used for the recorded signal in the Rana. Pure havoc would occur if the Disk][tried to read recordings from an eighty track Rana diskette.

Information is recorded in a magnetic material when that material is brought close to an electromagnet that contains a small gap where changing magnetic flux can easily flow across that gap. The width of that physical gap, its spacing, is critical and it is an important design component of the recording and of the playback circuitry. The required magnetic flux to impose changes in the magnetic material is determined by the current that is flowing in, the voltage across, and the impedance of the magnetic coil that is contained in the read/write disk head. The generated magnetic flux is imposed across the width of the gap of the electromagnet that is formed by that internal magnetic coil. I simply point this out so that there is no confusion between the gap width that induces a magnetic flux and the gap length or track size of a read/write disk head because the gap width and the gap length specifications are easily confused and thought to be synonymous when referring to the read/write disk head gap.

It would be possible to differentiate between diskettes that are recorded using the standard prologue bytes in the Address Field header and in the DATA Field header and those diskettes that use other prologue header bytes. This simply makes this diskette readable by one RWTS and not by another RWTS. The Rana could certainly use such a protocol but I believe there is simply not enough code space in its peripheral-card expansion ROM memory in order to support more than one or two configurations regarding the number of tracks in the volume, the number of sectors per track, and the expansion of any of its VTOC bitmap data. Whatever configuration that uses the full capabilities of the Rana will most likely not be compatible with the full capabilities of the Disk][. The DOS 4.5 VTOC is the only common structure that exists between the Rana and the Disk][. I believe that whatever is defined in the DOS 4.5 VTOC is what should be utilized in order to decide how best to support the Rana, though whatever configuration that is defined will most likely leave the Rana somewhat under-supported.

Considering the lessons learned from half-track and quarter-track magnetic audio recording, and in view of the rather limited availability of double-sided, double-density magnetic media, I chose to implement full-track recording for the Rana, thus providing forty tracks on each side of the diskette knowing full well that the physical length of the recording head gap in the Rana is half the length of the recording head gap in the Disk][. I also chose to implement recording all track sectors 0x00 to 0x0F on the notched side of the diskette and recording all track sectors 0x10 to 0x1F on the un-notched side of the diskette. The VTOC can fully accommodate this configuration. The Rana EPROM can also accommodate this configuration within its available code space and implement all of the RWTS commands for DOS 4.5. This configuration provides forty tracks, each track having thirty-two sectors, in order to comprise a volume that has a total of 1280 addressable sectors. If the VTOC and the Catalog together use twelve of those sectors, a data disk would potentially provide 1268 sectors for data storage, a rather massive amount of disk space that is accessible on a single diskette. This is precisely the configuration I chose to implement. Table V.20.1 shows the firmware entry points for the firmware that is mapped to the peripheral-card ROM memory in the RanaSystems EliteThree Controller card.

Offset	Name	Description
0x00	RANABOOT	Entry point for PR# DOS command in order to BOOT the diskette that is in drive 1
0x10	ROMHOOK	Entry point to attach the Rana to the DOS 4.5 Disk Address table
0x18	ROMUHOOK	Entry point to detach the Rana from the DOS 4.5 Disk Address table
0x20	RANARWTS	Issue CLRROM; enter RWTS processing
0x5C	BOOTFW	Simulate Disk][entry point to read BOOT Stage 0 code that resides at 0x0801
0x83	FNDADDR	Read Address Field header for volume, track, and sector; checksum ignored
0xA6	FNDDATA	Read 342 disk nibbles, post-nibblize to memory, and jump to 0x0801
0xFE	VERSION	Version number of Rana firmware (0x05)
0xFF	BUILD	Build number for Rana firmware (0x06)

Table V.20.1. Rana Disk Firmware Entry Points

The signal-to-noise ratio for the Rana drive is still very much a concern of mine because the Rana RWTS FORMAT algorithm rejects many of the double-sided/double-density diskettes that I recently purchased.

The FORMAT algorithm marks these diskettes as not safely recordable, but they are perfectly recordable using the Disk][. Diskettes that have been previously recorded by a Disk][will still contain residual and problematic magnetic information even after the Rana overwrites such a diskette using its FORMAT algorithm due to its smaller head gap length. Even after formatting, the bleed-through residual information still remains between tracks. It was after the successful formatting of a few virgin diskettes that allowed me to finally test the Rana firmware that I had designed. Designing this firmware gave me the opportunity to learn more about how the volume format was originally conceived to use a free sector bitmap that supports up to fifty tracks, where each track can support thirty-two sectors. These bitmap findings are thoroughly discussed in Sections I.5 and I.6. Needless to say, a CFFA volume that utilizes forty-eight tracks, where each track can support thirty-two sectors is just a minor extension to what I designed and implemented for a Rana volume. Truth be said, the education I received from exploring the Rana and its capabilities proved to be absolutely invaluable in the design of DOS 4.5 and the CFFA software. Perhaps a future enhancement to DOS 4.5 would be an extension to the VTOC bitmap area?

VTOC bytes 0xF8 through 0xFF are normally used for the sector bitmaps for tracks 48 and 49, but these bytes are currently unused even by the CFFA firmware. I believe these eight bytes could easily serve as some sort of VTOC continuation bridge to another available or designated sector in order to extend the free sector bitmap of a Rana volume in particular. Perhaps the Rana firmware could carry the burden of expanding the free sector bitmap rather than DOS 4.5, since it is the Rana that is able to read and write far more tracks than most other disk hardware. I believe it is quite possible to modify the RanaSystems EliteThree Controller card in order to access a far larger EPROM that could possibly bank switch the peripheral-card expansion ROM memory area. Having substantially more expansion ROM memory could easily support the additional software that may be necessary in order to extend the free sector bitmap of the Rana VTOC. The calculation of Free Space on a volume would have to ignore these last eight bytes and perhaps utilize those eight bytes in order to address and process those expanded VTOC bitmap bytes that are continued and bridged onto another sector.

DOS 4.5 uses a new and unique algorithm to move the read/write disk head from one track to an adjacent track. Section I.10 describes the DOS 4.5 RWTS interface and the spacing of adjacent tracks in terms of half-phases. I have replaced the Rana firmware with my own firmware that uses and supports this new DOS 4.5 technology. This new firmware includes all of the algorithms from DOS 4.5 for stepping the read/write disk head in half-phase increments. Whether the Rana interface firmware attaches to the DOS 4.5 DISKADRS table makes little difference because the same algorithms are used in both my own Rana firmware and in the RWTS that is found in DOS 4.5. Even the FORMAT routines are essentially identical in both the Rana firmware and in DOS 4.5. However, if the Rana firmware does attach to the DOS 4.5 DISKADRS table, the Rana firmware will be able to utilize its ability to access four disk drives as it is designed to handle. Because the Rana can access forty four-half-phase spaced tracks, it would be reasonable to expect the Rana to easily access forty-eight three-half-phase spaced tracks as well. Not only is this expectation reasonable, it is absolutely possible. Such a configuration would provide a total of 1536 sectors for data, nearly three times that of a single Disk][diskette.

I recently became quite fascinated with yet another format design for a Rana volume after I finished designing and building my EPROM Reader card. I also thought it was interesting why I hadn't explored this particular Rana format design earlier. Why not utilize the physical capabilities of the read/write disk head and format a volume with eighty tracks, yet retain a phase value of four for each track? That is, if the RWTS IOCB specifies the format of drive four having thirty-two sectors per track, the tracks that contain sectors 0x00 to 0x0F will be written every four half-phases and the tracks that contain sectors 0x10 to 0x1F will be written two half-phases next. Using this strategy would place a physical track every two half-phases such that a pair of these tracks would comprise all thirty-two sectors for that track number.

The calculation to move the read/write disk head is trivial and would simply add two half-phases to the computation when and if the requested sector number is greater than 0x0F. Only the Rana drive would connect to drive four on the Rana Controller card and only the read/write disk head for the notched side of the diskette in the Rana would be utilized. Therefore, the volume would need to be flipped if the unnotched side of the volume is ever formatted for use. Having a volume formatted with eighty tracks, where each pair of disk tracks contains thirty-two sectors for each track number is easily handled by the DOS 4.5 VTOC and this design provides for 1280 sectors. When both sides are utilized, a single diskette that is formatted with this design can provide a total of 2560 sectors for data storage.

Figure V.20.1 indeed shows a volume has been formatted with forty tracks, each having thirty-two sectors, and each track spaced four half-phases. The Catalog consists of seven sectors so this Catalog can accommodate up to forty-nine entries. The HELLO file's TSL is written to sector 0x1F on track 0x13. Figure V.20.2 is captured from *Disk Window* and it shows the utilization of nearly the entire VTOC. The VTOC and Catalog sectors are allocated by entry byte 0x7D and the HELLO file's TSL and data sectors are allocated by entry byte 0x86. This particular Rana volume is designated as a DOS 4.5 BOOT volume, so its total sector capacity is calculated as 1224 + 42 (DOS 4.5) + 8 (VTOC and Catalog) + 6 (HELLO file) = 1280 sectors. If a suitable VTOC continuation bridge can be constructed, I would definitely favor formatting a Rana volume with eighty tracks on both sides of a double-sided/double-density diskette and utilize both read/write disk heads for a volume with 2560 sectors. Otherwise, I would favor formatting a Rana volume with eighty tracks on a single side of a double-sided/double-density diskette and utilize a single read/write disk head for a volume with 1280 sectors.

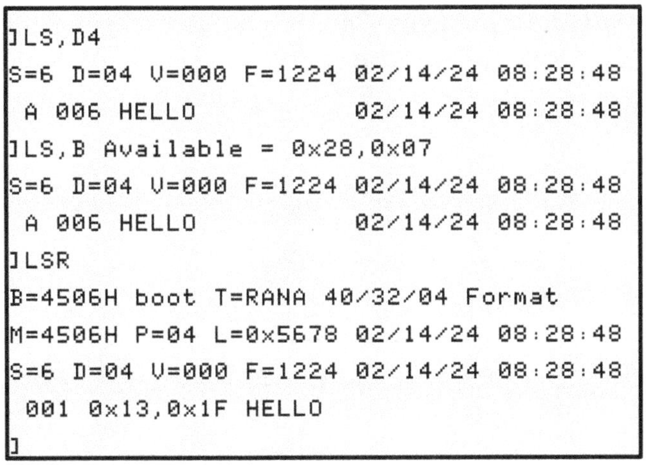

Figure V.20.1. Initialized Rana Volume

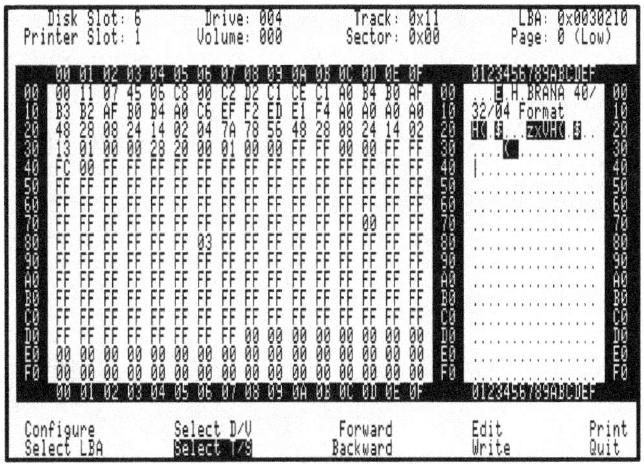

Figure V.20.2. Rana Volume VTOC

21. First Class Peripherals Data Storage

Around 1985 my mother asked me to put together a computer system that would store all of her genealogy records and data. She was becoming overwhelmed with family ancestry documentation, and she knew and understood how invaluable a computer would be that could store and link all of her data and information. I knew of a software product called *Family Roots* by Stephen C. Vorenberg and marketed by Quinsept, Inc., that would give my mother the power and the flexibility that she needed in order to contain and organize all of her ancestry information. Her *Family Roots* database initially filled four data

335

diskettes besides the three *Family Roots* program diskettes when she asked me if there was a better alternative than swapping these various diskettes using her two disk drives in order to generate a family report. In its documentation, *Family Roots* suggested using the Sider from First Class Peripherals, a fixed disk drive subsystem that features a 10 MB hard disk drive that has its data storage partitioned mostly as DOS 3.3 volumes. And, to tell the truth, I had been very interested in the Sider when I first heard about this drive, but I just didn't have the reason or the bankroll to afford such a luxury. Mom had both. When I inherited her Apple //e computer system, she had filled more than sixteen DOS 3.3 volumes on her Sider with genealogy data. The Sider proved to be the perfect data storage system for all of my mother's genealogy data.

The Sider consists of a Host Adapter peripheral interface card that is connected to an external housing by means of an IDE cable. The housing contains a Xebec 1410A controller board and a Winchester 10 MB hard drive. The Host adapter card contains a 2716 EPROM and it uses only two of its sixteen peripheral-card I/O memory locations in order to communicate with the Xebec controller. Essentially, the firmware transfers the first six bytes of an eight-byte Data Context Block, or DCB to the Host adapter card. The firmware uses the last two bytes of the DCB, the buffer address, to transfer 256-bytes of data to or from the Xebec controller. The DCB contains the command, a 24-bit Logical Block Address or LBA, a block count, a step option, and a buffer address. The LBA buffer address specifies one 256-byte page of memory. A DOS 3.3 volume is configured to contain 560 256-byte pages, or Sider blocks of data. Even though a Sider may be configured not to use CP/M or ProDOS or Pascal formatted volumes, some Sider blocks are still set aside for those partitions according to the Sider documentation. The Sider is partitioned only once in order to configure the sizes of the DOS 3.3, CP/M, ProDOS, or Pascal partitions. In the case of my mother's Sider, we partitioned her Sider for the maximum number of DOS 3.3 volumes and the minimum number of CP/M, ProDOS, and Pascal volumes. After this partitioning process, her 10 MB Sider contains 69 DOS 3.3 volumes that begins with Volume 0. *Family Roots* utilizes volume number exclusively in order to locate all *Family Roots* system programs and all *Family Roots* genealogy data. Of course, I was fascinated to learn how the Sider modified DOS 3.3 in order to *tame* volume number such that a program like *Family Roots* could utilize this *invaluable* parameter.

| LBA Range | | Description |
Start	End	
0	0	Sider BOOT block
1	1	Sider parameter block
2	36	DOS 3.3 BOOT image (35 blocks)
37	84	RAM card image (DOS) (48 blocks)
85	135	CP/M BOOT image point #1 (51 blocks)
136	255	Reserved for future use (120 blocks)
256	258	CP/M BOOT image point #2 (3 blocks)
259	463	Free area for any application (205 blocks)
464	1023	DOS 3.3 volume 0xFD (Back Up volume)
1024	????	User data area
????	????	12 alternate tracks

Table V.21.1. Sider Original Logical Block Structure

Table V.21.1 shows the original logical block structure of the Sider that is based on LBA number. The Xebec controller determines how this LBA number, or Sider block number is mapped to the hard drive. It is important to note that a volume is a contiguous group of blocks and that each volume follows the previous volume, or group of blocks. Table V.21.2 shows the modifications that I made to the Sider Logical Block structure in order to support DOS 4.1, DOS 4.3, and DOS 4.5. The new Sider peripheral-card ROM firmware that I designed BOOTs the DOS 4.5H image starting at block 184. Alternately, the DOS 4.5L image can be BOOTed by calling 0xCs20, where s is the slot number of the Sider Host Adapter card, typically slot 7. The DOS 4.5H image can also be BOOTed by calling 0xCs28. When a Sider DOS image BOOTs, the Sider firmware inserts its RWTS handler address, or 0xCs80, into the Disk Address table. Table V.21.3 shows all of the Sider firmware entry points for the firmware that is mapped to the Sider peripheral-card ROM memory. There is a mathematical relationship between LBA and volume, track, and sector that are found in the RWTS IOCB. The first volume is Volume 0 and it is defined to begin at LBA address 464, or 0x01D0. A Sider volume is configured with thirty-five tracks and each track contains sixteen blocks, one block for each sector, or 560 blocks for each volume.

$$LBA = (\text{volume} * 0x230) + (\text{track} * 0x10) + \text{sector} + 0x01D0$$

| LBA Range | | Description |
Start	End	
0	0	Sider BOOT block
1	1	Sider parameter block
2	36	DOS 3.3 BOOT image (35 blocks)
37	84	RAM card image (DOS) (48 blocks)
85	135	CP/M BOOT image point #1 (51 blocks)
136	183	DOS 4.5L Build 05 BOOT image (48 blocks)
184	231	DOS 4.5H Build 06 BOOT image (48 blocks)
232	255	reserved for future use (24 blocks)
256	258	CP/M BOOT image point #2 (3 blocks)
259	263	Free blocks (5 blocks)
264	311	DOS 4.1L BOOT image (48 blocks)
312	359	DOS 4.1H BOOT image (48 blocks)
360	407	DOS 4.3H BOOT image (48 blocks)
408	455	DOS SPR1 BOOT image (48 blocks)
456	463	Free blocks (8 blocks)
464	1023	Volume 0 (560 blocks)
1024	39103	Volumes 1 to 68 (38080 blocks)
39136	39136	Park heads block

Table V.21.2. Sider Modified Logical Block Structure

In order to calculate the LBA efficiently and with great speed, lookup tables are employed that can essentially perform all of the multiplication by using simple addition. There is sufficient room in the 2716 EPROM for the four lookup tables that are required to perform this calculation. The RWTS IOCB volume, track, and sector values are range-checked before the track and volume values are used as indices into a pair of tables, one pair of tables each for track and volume, and the extracted values are added to the sector value. The offset 0x01D0 is already incorporated within the data of the volume tables. I added the address of the DOS 4.5L image at index 69, the address of the DOS 4.5H image at index 70, the address of the DOS 4.1L image at index 71, the address of the DOS 4.1H image at index 72, the address of the DOS 4.3H image at index 73, and the address of the DOS Spare image at index 74 to the volume tables. Any of these DOS images or a selected Sider volume having a bootable DOS image can be BOOTed using the BOOTVOL entry point from Table V.21.3 at 0xCs40, and a regular DOS BOOT sequence is initiated. If the Sider BOOT image is a DOS 3.3 image, the SDRWTS3 address is used to replace the RWTS address that is found at 0xB7B8:0xB7B9 in DOS 3.3. Otherwise, if the Sider BOOT image is a DOS 4.1, DOS 4.3, or a DOS 4.5 image, the SDRWTS4 address is added into their respective DOS Disk Address table using the slot number in which the Sider resides.

Offset	Name	Description
0x00	BOOTHR	Entry point for PR# DOS command to BOOT DOS 4.5H
0x10	ROMHOOK	Entry point to attach the Sider to the DOS Disk Address table
0x18	ROMUHOOK	Entry point to detach the Sider from the DOS Disk Address table
0x20	SDOS4.5L	Entry point to BOOT DOS 4.5L
0x28	SDOS4.5H	Entry point to BOOT DOS 4.5H
0x40	BOOTVOL	Entry point to BOOT any bootable volume on the Sider
0x50	PARK	Entry point to call ROMUHOOK and park the disk heads
0x5C	ROMBOOT	Simulate Disk][entry point for BOOT Stage 0 code that resides at 0x0801
0x70	SDRWTS3	RWTS handler for DOS 3.3
0x80	SDRWTS4	RWTS handler for DOS 4.1, DOS 4.3, or DOS 4.5
0xA0	DRIVER	Read/write a Sider LBA using an eight-byte DCB in Y-/A-registers
0xC0	GETSTAT	Get Sider status in C-flag
0xD0	READSTAT	Read Sider status into a four-byte user buffer
0xF0	MODOS3	Patch DOS 3.3 after BOOT Stage 2
0xFE	VERSION	Version number of Sider firmware (0x05)
0xFF	BUILD	Build number for Sider firmware (0x06)

Table V.21.3. Sider Firmware Entry Points

Family Roots utilizes Diversi-DOS in order to accelerate the loading of its humungous Applesoft programs, and it also utilizes DDMOVER by Diversi-DOS to relocate most of DOS 3.3 into the Language Card partition. Still, *Family Roots* requires four file buffers, and even after DDMOVER has moved DOS 3.3, these file buffers must remain in lower Main memory. *Family Roots* chains from program to program keeping all of its global values in memory. This technique certainly makes *Family Roots* appear to seamlessly transfer control from one program to the next program particularly when the disk acceleration routines are utilized in Diversi-DOS. I have to say that I derived some of my inspiration from Diversi-DOS to incorporate native disk acceleration routines in DOS 4.1, and to move an early version of DOS 4.1, perhaps Build 32 or Build 33, into the Language Card partition. DOS 4.5H is based upon that early Language Card version of DOS 4.1H. Diversi-DOS moves bits and pieces of DOS 3.3 into the Language Card and it must modify the addresses of all JMP and JSR instructions. Diversi-DOS creates a software interface between the routines it leaves in lower Main memory and the routines it moves into the Language

Card partition in order to perform all necessary Bank switching protocol for the Language Card partition. Designing DDMOVER must have been a momentous effort to be sure, and having most of DOS 3.3 in the Language Card partition certainly gives *Family Roots* the *breathing room* it needs in view of the size of its Applesoft programs and the size of its variable and ASCII data arrays. And yet, the memory in the Language Card partition is not fully utilized by Diversi-DOS.

I certainly understand how Diversi-DOS, designed by Bill Basham at Diversified Soft Research, is able to accelerate the I/O routines in the File Manager, and I understand how SPEEDOS from Applied Engineering accelerated its RamWorks products as well. I also looked at David DOS by David Weston and TurboDOS that is used with the original *Lisa* software. I am sure there are others who have forsaken the DOS INIT command routines and utilize that code space for their particular ingenious acceleration algorithm. Even Don Worth and Pieter Lechner went so far as to suggest modifying the DOS sector interleave table in order to speed up the reading of large Applesoft programs and assembly language routines. None of these algorithms seemed to be the very best solution for managing disk I/O in DOS 3.3. At Sierra On-Line, a software engineer colleague of mine, a gentleman from the United Kingdom, did provide an additional BLOAD keyword that provided a Page parameter. This keyword parameter provided an additional and new *read pages* subcode for the File Manager. His BLOAD implementation was certainly fast and, if I recall correctly, it is used on the first version of King's Quest.

I decided that my goal to accelerate DOS I/O was not to rewrite the File Manager, but to add some additional logic to the File Manager. This logic would read pages of a file only when it was appropriate to do so. For example, the first two bytes of an Applesoft file must be read in order to calculate the address of its program end before the remaining sectors of the file are read into memory. After reading the initial sector, the remaining 0xFE bytes in its file buffer are copied to the target address, one byte at a time. However, the remaining sectors of the file, except for the last sector most likely, can be read directly into memory one page at a time. If there is a last sector that contains some bytes, that sector can be read into its file buffer and the remaining few bytes copied to the target address, again one byte at a time. Binary files are handled in the same way except that the first four bytes are copied into the DOS parameter area from its file buffer, which includes the target memory address and the size of the file in bytes. The remaining 0xFC bytes in its file buffer are copied to memory one byte at a time. The remaining sectors of the file can be read directly into memory one page at a time.

I am quite sure that if DSR, Inc., had access to the source code for Apple DOS 3.3, it could have generated a native version of DOS 3.3 that would be resident in the Language Card partition and not require software like DDMOVER. A fundamental requirement for my vision of a DOS is that it must BOOT directly into the Language Card partition and be wholly resident in the Language Card partition for the most part. It is one thing to cobble together a system from bits and pieces of a previous system, but it is quite another thing when a complete Disk Operating System is fully designed from the ground up to reside specifically in the Language Card partition. Initially, I designed DOS 4.1H to occupy the Main memory Language Card partition natively. It has all of the functionality that is found in DOS 4.1L and more. All file buffers, up to five, are fully contained in the Language Card partition. There is even enough code space to provide a DOS HELP command that displays the basic syntax for all DOS commands. It is from this initial version of DOS that became DOS 4.5H. Therefore, regardless of the number of file buffers in use, HIMEM is always set to 0xBE00, the highest possible address in order to provide an Applesoft environment that can support monster programs like those found in *Family Roots*.

DOS 4.5 contains the same CHAIN algorithm that is found in DOS 4.1 with a few minor enhancements. Furthermore, preliminary tests show that DOS 4.5 and the DOS CHAIN command function beautifully with *Family Roots*. There are empty volumes on the Sider that can be used to conduct further tests with

339

Family Roots and its association with DOS 4.5. Also, the *Family Roots* programs and data volumes can be moved to a drive on the CFFA and tested in that environment. Either hardware location would certainly verify the migration of *Family Roots* to DOS 4.5. I believe my mother would have certainly been very impressed, and she would have provided me with hours of hands-on verification testing.

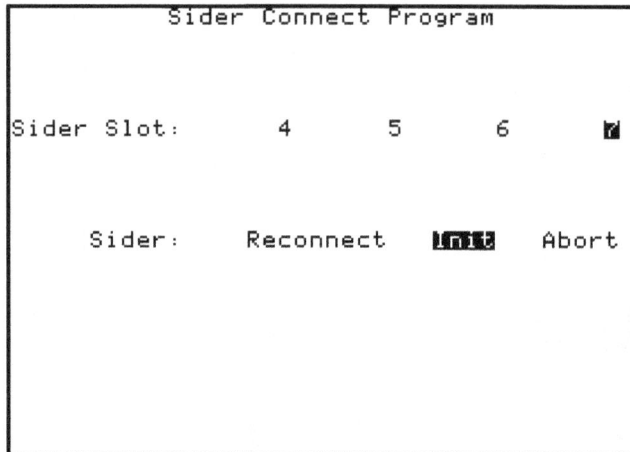

```
      Sider Connect Program                    Useful Entry Points

                                                         Type From Type From
                                                         Applesoft   Monitor
Sider Slot:     4      5      6      ▶     DOS 4.5H Boot:    CALL -14592   C700G
                                          DOS Connect:      CALL -14576   C710G
                                          DOS Disconnect:   CALL -14568   C718G
                                          DOS 4.5L Boot:    CALL -14560   C720G
                                          DOS 4.5H Boot:    CALL -14552   C728G
    Sider:    Reconnect    Init    Abort  DOS Volume Boot:  CALL -14528   C740G

                                          Park Heads:       CALL -14512   C750G

                                          DOS 3.3 RWTS:     CALL -14480   C770G
                                          DOS 4.5 RWTS:     CALL -14464   C780G

                                          Sider DCB Driver: CALL -14432   C7A0G
                                          Request Status:   CALL -14400   C7C0G
                                          Receive Status:   CALL -14384   C7D0G

                                            Press Any Key to Continue
```

Figure V.21.1. Sider Connect Program   Figure V.21.2. Sider Entry Points

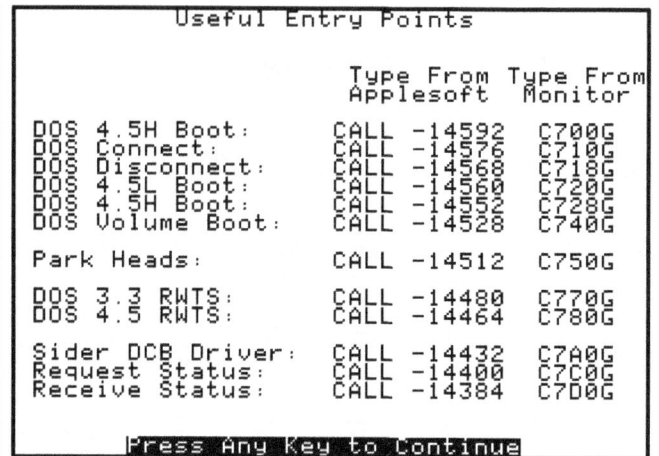

I replaced the Xebec 2716 EPROM with a 6116 static RAM IC and connected its R/W pin to finger 18 of the Host Adapter card. This allows me to easily conduct experiments with my own firmware for the Sider in order to test its ability to BOOT different DOS images. Early versions of this firmware utilized some memory in the static RAM in order to save variables such as slot number, slot number times sixteen, and the version of DOS that is currently in memory. Using the static RAM for certain variables was the easiest path in order to implement communication with the Xebec controller. I simply ported over the RAM Disk Connect Program since the RAM Disk interface card also uses a 6116 static RAM. Figures V.21.1 and V.21.2 show the Sider Connect Program that I use in order to load this static RAM with the Sider firmware. Now that I have established a strong confidence level in the operation of this firmware, I have re-engineered the firmware to utilize the public and the private memory bytes on the TEXT screen that are reserved for peripheral interface cards. This allows me to either utilize a 2716 EPROM or a 28C16A EEPROM for the Sider firmware.

It is interesting to note that the hardware logic on the Sider Host Adapter card maps the first seven pages of its EPROM data to the peripheral-card expansion ROM address range 0xC800 to 0xCEFF. The last page of its EPROM data is mapped to its peripheral-card ROM address range 0xCs00 to 0xCsFF, where s is the slot number of the Sider Host Adapter card. With the Sider peripheral-card expansion ROM enabled, the 0xCF00 to 0xCFFF data is the same as the 0xCs00 to 0xCsFF data. The hardware engineers at RanaSystems designed their Controller card for the EliteThree disk drive using the very same EPROM to memory mapping. There really isn't a better EPROM to memory mapping scheme when a 2716 EPROM is selected. I believe a 2732 EPROM would be a far better choice, however! The first eight pages of the 2732 would be mapped to the peripheral-card ROM memory, one page for each slot after skipping the first page. The bytes in the first page would be programmed to 0xFF and left unused. Absolute addressing instructions could be used for the software routines that are utilized by each slot like the software I designed for *EOS* where the software is identical in each slot except for their absolute addressing instructions that enable or disable the quikLoader. The last eight pages of the 2732 would be mapped to the entire peripheral-card expansion ROM memory. This memory would contain the generic routines that are used by each slot no matter in which slot the Sider Host Adapter card resides. More importantly, the hardware logic design of the Host Adapter card would be greatly simplified. I wonder if the availability of 2716 verses 2732 EPROMs drove the design of the Sider Host Adapter and the RanaSystems Controller card. Perhaps cost was chosen over simplicity. An additional page of peripheral-card expansion ROM memory would have been rather nice to have. Perhaps this would be an interesting hardware upgrade project for these two peripheral interface cards?

22. Sourceror Program

I first *sourced Sourceror* so that I could modify its source code in order to create a more pleasing display for its available commands by using a mixture of uppercase and lowercase ASCII while I was processing source code into object code. *Sourceror*, like *Big Mac*, was written by Glen Bredon. *Sourceror* is an assembly language utility that originally executed at 0x8900 after MAXFILES is set to 1. This placed *Sourceror* just below the first file buffer in DOS 3.3 and in DOS 4.1L. I found only one coding error in *Sourceror*, a missing CLC instruction where the software processes 65C02 opcodes. Occasionally, not always, the program counter was incremented one byte too many because a *Sourceror* routine assumed that the C-flag would always be clear upon the return from a call to GETNUM at 0xFFA7. Obviously, the C-flag was **not** always clear after making this call. After I developed DOS 4.1H, I was able to relocate *Sourceror* to 0xAC00 thus allowing the sourcing of far larger assembly language routines. DOS 4.1H can now provide more lower Main memory for the input object code and more memory for the output source code. A few more changes to the source code of *Sourceror* allows *Sourceror* to function beautifully in concert with the Language Card version of DOS 4.5.

Sourceror already contains the text for a number of symbols in order for *Sourceror* to generate a symbol listing at the end of its generated source code file as per the convention that *Big Mac* follows for its input source code file. I added a number of additional symbols to the *Sourceror* source code that includes CLRROM, RAM2WP, ROM2WE, ROM2WP, RAM2WE, RAM1WP, ROM1WE, ROM1WP, RAM1WE, STROBE, LATCH, DATAIN, and DATAOUT.

```
Press RETURN to accept default Source
Code address 0x4000, or enter 0x

If the present location of the code
to be disassembled is at its original
location, press RETURN.  If not,
enter PRESENT location 0x900

In disassembling, use the ORIGINAL
location 0xAC00
```

Figure V.22.1. Sourceror Initialization

```
SOURCEROR - 65C02 - DOS 4.5.06
           by Glen Bredon
A HEX byte nn after commands T or H
limits the output to nn bytes.

Commands (alone or after HEX address):
L - Disassemble (current mode)
N - Normal (next mode)
S - Sweet 16 (next mode)
T - Text (TT defeats DCI)
W - Address (W-: Address-1, WW: DDB)
H - HEX data (1 byte default)

R - Read (does not create source)
/ - Retrieve last default address
I - Instructions
Q - Quit

$*
```

Figure V.22.2. Sourceror Startup/Help Display

Figure V.22.1 shows the initialization display after launching *Sourceror*. A loader program such as *Loadsrcrr* is no longer necessary because the HELLO file simply loads *Sourceror* at 0xAC00 and jumps to that address. Figure V.22.2 shows the startup, or Help display that *Sourceror* displays with its command-line prompt $. Figure V.22.3 shows the RAM Monitor listing of *Sourceror* in response to the first L command. Figure V.22.4 continues the sourcing of *Sourceror* using the H command followed by multiple T commands. Of course, these figures and these commands are shown for demonstration only. I have a tremendous debt of gratitude to Glen Bredon, his software utilities, and his brilliant insight into Apple][hardware and software architecture. Thank you Mr. Bredon for a peek into your exciting and insightful assembly language world!

```
$AC00L
                         ORG  $AC00
AC00-   78              SEI
AC01-   20 58 FF        JSR   $FF58
AC04-   BA              TSX
AC05-   BD 00 01        LDA   $0100,X
AC08-   58              CLI
AC09-   C9 AC           CMP   #$AC
AC0B-   F0 03           BEQ   $AC10
AC0D-   4C D3 03        JMP   $03D3
AC10-   4C 07 B0        JMP   $B007
AC13-   8D 8D 3C        STA   $3C8D
AC16-   09 0E           ORA   #$0E
AC18-   16 05           ASL   $05,X
AC1A-   12 13           ORA   ($13)
AC1C-   05 3D           ORA   $3D
AC1E-   03              ???
AC1F-   0E 14 12        ASL   $1214
AC22-   2E 20 03        ROL   $0320
AC25-   08              PHP
AC26-   2E 3E 20        ROL   $203E
AC29-   7C 46 4C        JMP   ($4C46,X)
$*
```

Figure V.22.3. Sourceror Source Listing 1

```
AC29-   7C 46 4C        JMP   ($4C46,X)
$AC13H2
AC13-                   HEX   8D8D
$T
AC15-           ASC   '<'
$T
AC16-           INV   'INVERSE=CNTR. CH.> '
$T
AC29-           FLS   '<FLASH=LOWER CASE>'
$T
AC3B-
$AC3BH
AC3B-                   HEX   8D
$T
AC3C-           ASC   "^ IS BELOW BYTES WITH HIGH
   BIT SET."
$*
```

Figure V.22.4. Sourceror Source Listing 2

23. JFD Parallel Printer Buffer Device

When I saw the advertisement for the JFD Parallel Printer Buffer in one of my 1985 Apple magazines, I just had to have this printer buffer. As I recall there were two, or perhaps more configurations for the printer buffer. One could choose a configuration that has a single set of parallel input/output ports, two sets of parallel input/output ports, or perhaps a combination of these two configurations. Always budget minded I chose the printer buffer with one set of parallel input/output ports. If I had more than one computer or more than one printer I may have chosen differently.

I spent so much time waiting for my computer and for my printer to print hundreds of pages of code that I was more than ready to put this printer buffer to work. This printer buffer would allow me to work on the computer while the printer buffer is supplying data to the printer, especially data from large graphic files. The printer buffer provides 256 KB of dynamic RAM to store data. Once an ASCII listing or a page of graphics is printed, the printer buffer is equipped with a Copy pushbutton in order to select the number of additional copies, up to 255, to print if they are desired.

The printer buffer connects to the Grappler+ Printer Interface card that is inside the computer and to my Epson MX100 printer by means of parallel interface flat-ribbon cables. A large wall transformer powers the printer buffer supplying it with nine volts DC. Besides the Copy pushbutton there is a Reset pushbutton. The Reset pushbutton causes the printer buffer software to initialize. This initialization forces the input data of the next print job to be stored at the beginning of printer buffer memory. This feature is useful particularly when multiple copies of only that print listing is needed. Otherwise, when the Copy pushbutton is pressed after printing multiple items, the printer buffer prints everything again that resides in its memory.

The manual that comes with the printer buffer did not discuss what happens when input data overflows memory. I had already seen some bizarre behavior when some paragraphs were not printed after many listings were sent to the printer buffer, or when I forgot to press the Reset pushbutton prior to printing the next printer listing. Momentarily pressing the Copy pushbutton puts the printer buffer into Pause Mode such that the printer buffer can still accept input data; it just does not send any further data to the printer. Momentarily pressing the Copy pushbutton a second time takes the printer buffer out of Pause Mode and data is again output to the printer. I took advantage of Pause Mode and sent a known, and very large amount of data to the printer buffer. Then I took the printer buffer out of Pause Mode and sent another known, and very large amount of data to the printer buffer. When printer buffer memory was filled, it appeared to me that the printer buffer started to accept 256 bytes of data after it printed approximately 256 bytes of data, but for only a short period of time. Then the printer buffer started to drop data, perhaps 256 bytes at a time, but I wasn't absolutely sure. I could force this bizarre behavior every time I forced the printer buffer memory to overflow. It appeared to me that the firmware contained some sort of software bug. I saw a challenge waiting for me.

I opened the printer buffer and found a voltage regulator, an 8035-microprocessor, a 2716 EPROM, eight 1257-15 NMOS dynamic RAM ICs, and an assortment of eight-bit latches and logic ICs. There is a PCB location for an additional input parallel connector and for an additional output parallel connector. The Ready LED is inconveniently located on the rear apron of the cabinet. I moved this LED to the front apron since there is only one input parallel connector and plenty of cabinet space next to it. Ideally, I would have liked to have moved that input parallel connector to the rear apron alongside the output parallel connector. I worked at Hughes Aircraft at that time, so I had access to virtually any data book available, and I was able to obtain data sheets on the microprocessor and on the RAM ICs.

Being able to source and compile the MCS-8048 Instruction Set was certainly going to be a challenge, but I had already had some experience doing something similar for an external keyboard that used a 6802-microprocessor on its interface board. My technique is to set up a series of equates within *Lisa*, one equate for each MCS-8048 instruction. I have to keep in mind which instructions require additional parameters, however. Actual coding within *Lisa* only requires the BYT directive followed by an MCS-8048 instruction equate, and then followed by any required parameter when it is needed. On each line I put a comment documenting what the BYT directive and the instruction equate are actually doing. The next step is to reverse engineer the software that is contained in the EPROM that is located on the PCB.

Obtaining the data content in the 2716 EPROM on the PCB is easy using the PROmGRAMER. Sourcing that data is also easy because I wrote an Applesoft program that translated the MCS-8048 instructions into a Text file that uses the BYT directive that *Lisa* can easily EXEC into its memory. Analyzing that sourced code takes the most time and the most effort because I have to fully understand the architecture of the 8035-microprocessor, the operation of the 1257-15 dynamic RAM for data access and refresh requirements, and the hardware function of all of the eight-bit latches and supporting logic ICs that comprise the printer buffer. The Grappler+ and the Epson printer also have handshake and data acknowledgement requirements as well. Slowly, I plowed my way through this code and I found all of the necessary logic that performs RAM refresh, access to RAM data, read Input data and write Output data, as well as all of the logic that performs data initialization, printing diagnostic status information, reading the Reset and Copy pushbuttons, and controlling the Ready LED to be ON or OFF.

I could not locate an error in the logic of this software that could possibly cause the bizarre behavior that I observed. I did locate the general logic where the printer buffer would wait for a free 256 byte page of memory whenever the write pointer address approached the read pointer address. I thought a page of memory was dropped or skipped somewhere in this area of logic, when the data pointers were near the end of memory or they were close to each other somewhere just past the end of memory. But I could not find any unreasonable logic. I'm sure it is some silly addition error, perhaps involving the C-flag, or perhaps when the pointers transition from the 0x3FFxx page to the 0x000xx page in order to access data as those pointers overflow and wrap around to the beginning of the 256 KB buffer.

I decided to scrape the original code and write my own version of this firmware. Of course, I had to borrow some of the original logic in order to access and refresh RAM, but I thought I could do a better job at controlling the data pointers and handling the memory overflow situation. I set up hardware on a breadboard to emulate a 2716 EPROM so that I could compile and test my new software strategies without having to program an actual EPROM. This hardware setup made it extremely easy to develop MCS-8048 software for the 8035-microprocessor. Sometime in May, 1989, I was successful in developing new firmware for this printer buffer that did **not** fail any of my previous overflow tests. This new firmware also behaved exactly like the original firmware for the Pause Mode and for the Copy function. The Reset function also behaved exactly like that function in the original firmware. I programmed a 2716 EPROM, installed it, and used the printer buffer with this firmware thereafter.

I performed timing tests and documented the results for the original firmware and for my new printer buffer firmware. I had calculated the time it **should** take the firmware to test all 256 KB of RAM using the minimum instructions of a write followed by a read and a compare. The initialization routine for the original firmware did not take nearly the amount of time to complete that I thought was required. My initialization routine took precisely the amount of time to complete in the time that I had calculated. I also timed how long each firmware version took to fill memory with the Pause Mode enabled and the Pause Mode disabled. With Pause Mode enabled, the original firmware took about 2.5 times longer to fill memory, or 2.91 KB/sec versus 7.28 KB/sec for my firmware. With the Pause Mode disabled the results were 2.91 KB/sec versus 6.90 KB/sec for my firmware. I sent a letter to JFD explaining what I had observed when memory overflow occurs, my timing test calculations and my observed results, and a printed copy of my new printer buffer firmware. I did not receive even an acknowledgement to my letter from JFD. I was terribly hurt and thoroughly disappointed. Whatever.

I recently took some time to look over and review the printer buffer firmware that I had designed back in 1989. I have had a lot of time over the last forty years to increase my knowledge and my programming skills vis-à-vis various hardware architectures. I noticed that I used the built-in 8035-microprocessor Interval Timer in the same fashion as the Interval Timer is used in the original printer buffer firmware for timing events and for handling pushbutton debounce. My first thought was, "What a waste of a perfectly good Interval Timer!" To use an Interval Timer in order to handle pushbutton debounce was idiocy. What became especially clear to me is how to use the Interval Timer in order to schedule dynamic RAM refresh without having to guess or to wonder if the RAM refresh routine is called often enough. In my version of the firmware, like that in the original JFD firmware, the MAIN loop calls the REFRESH routine, the CHECKT0 routine, and, if the printer is ready to accept another data character, the SENDMEM routine in that order in an infinite loop. The CHECKT0 routine checks if the Copy pushbutton is being pressed, and if so, that routine would flash the LED ON and OFF at a 0.5 Hz rate in order to set the number of copies if they are desired. CHECKT0 alone can consume huge amounts of time within the MAIN loop and, hence, time away from the REFRESH routine which left me pondering why memory never became corrupted. Or, did it? I wonder. The REFRESH routine is totally ignored during any CHECKT0 processing no matter how much time is consumed. I wondered if this logic design contributed to the actual cause of the bizarre behavior

344

that I had observed so many years ago? Did this printer buffer RAM have built-in refresh capabilities? I really didn't think so.

Byte Offset	Size	Name	Description
0x00	8 bytes	SELRB0	Primary registers, Bank 0
0x08	16 bytes	PSW	12-bit program counter and 4-bit status in an 8 level stack for subroutine return addresses
0x18	8 bytes	SELRB1	Secondary registers, Bank 1
0x20	32 bytes	USERRAM	User RAM for indexed word locations

Table V.23.1. 8035-Microprocessor Memory Map

Bit	Name	Description
0	S0	Bit 0 of Stack Pointer
1	S1	Bit 1 of Stack Pointer
2	S2	Bit 2 of Stack Pointer
3	–	not used, set to 1
4	BS	Register Bank Select
5	F0	User Flag 0
6	AC	Auxiliary Carry Flag
7	CY	C-flag

Table V.23.2. User Flag or F1

Port:Bit	Name	Description
1:0	n/a	not used, set to 1
1:1	PDATENBL	Processor data enable, 1=disable
1:2	OLATENBL	Outport latch enable, 1=disable
1:3	n/a	not used, set to 1
1:4	ODATRDY	Outport data ready, 1=ready
1:5	n/a	not used, set to 1
1:6	n/a	not used, set to 1
1:7	PMEMENBL	PPB memory enable, 1=disable
2:0	ADR08ON	Address bit ADR08, 1=ON
2:1	LED1TGL	Test LED 1, 1=ON
2:2	LED2TGL	Test LED 2, 1=ON
2:3	RDLEDON	Ready LED, 1=ON
2:4	IDATENBL	Inport data strobe, 1=disable
2:5	n/a	not used, set to 1
2:6	n/a	not used, set to 1
2:7	OCTLENBL	Octal latch enable, 1=disable

Table V.23.3. Port Utilization

I have heavily documented the printer buffer source code as I developed the routines that utilize the Interval Timer as the basic timer for timing **all** functions. The 8035-microprocessor utilizes sixty-four bytes of internal memory for its complete operation. The configuration of its memory map is shown in Table V.23.1. There are two banks of eight 8-bit registers, an eight level stack for subroutine return addresses and status, and thirty-two bytes of indexed User RAM. When designing software for this microprocessor, one must be mindful that the stack only provides eight levels of subroutine return addresses. And, it is this indexed User RAM that is only slightly cumbersome to access. My printer buffer firmware does use four bytes of this indexed user RAM. The definition of User Flag 1, or F1, is shown in Table V.23.2. F1 is **not** part of the Program Status Word, or PSW. Table V.23.3 shows the utilization of Port 1 and Port 2 and how each of their eight bits are used in both of these variables. The utilization of SELRB0 is shown in Table V.23.4 and the utilization of SELRB1 is shown in Table V.23.5. The R/W Block Number Bits in Primary Register R3 is shown in Table V.23.6. The System Flag Bits in Secondary Register R3 are shown in Table V.23.7.

Register	Description
R0	Input/output working register
R1	EXTIRQ A-register save
R2	Temporary data byte
R3	R/W block number for address bits 0x08 and 0x11; see Table V.23.6
R4	Address bits 0x00-0x07, read data RAS
R5	Address bits 0x09-0x10, read data CAS
R6	Address bits 0x00-0x07, write data RAS
R7	Address bits 0x09-0x10, write data CAS

Table V.23.4. SELRB0 Utilization

Register	Description
R0	Input/output working register
R1	REFRESH A-register save
R2	Temporary data byte
R3	System flag bits; see Table V.23.7
R4	Copy number
R5	Refresh counter, LSB
R6	Timer counter, LSB
R7	Timer Counter, MSB

Table V.23.5. SELRB1 Utilization

If I followed the 1257-15 dynamic RAM data sheet requirements in order to perform a RAS-only refresh every 4.0 milliseconds or less, I could easily use the Interval Timer to schedule a dynamic RAM refresh at that interval rate. The Interval Timer could also serve as the basis for all of the other timing requirements such as pushbutton debounce and LED flash rate. Central to the 8035-microprocessor is the RESET interrupt, the EXTIRQ interrupt, and the TIMRIRQ interrupt. The Reset pushbutton is connected to the RESET Interrupt pin, the Input connector from the Apple][computer is connected to the External Interrupt pin, and the Interval Timer is connected to the Timer Interrupt pin of the 8035-microprocessor. Each of these interrupt events is handled by a unique interrupt handler routine whose vector address resides at a hard-wired offset in page-zero of EPROM memory at offsets 0x00, 0x03, and 0x07. And, as mentioned earlier, there are thirty-two bytes of indexed User RAM in internal microprocessor memory that is only slightly cumbersome to access, but nevertheless available in order to store program variables, vectors, pointers, and data.

Bit	Description
0	Read block number, LSB
1	Read block number, MSB
2	zero
3	zero
4	Write block number, LSB
5	Write block number, MSB
6	zero
7	zero

Table V.23.6. Primary R3 R/W Block Number Bits

Bit	Description
0	Refresh counter, ADR08
1	zero
2	zero
3	Overflow state flag, 0=OFF
4	Message state flag, 0=OFF
5	Copy state flag, 0=OFF
6	Pause state flag, 0=OFF
7	EXTIRQ state flag, 0=OFF

Table V.23.7. Secondary R3 System Flag Bits

The 8035-microprocessor is clocked using a 6.0 MHz external crystal. This crystal frequency is divided by fifteen, which is internal to the microprocessor, so that the cycle time, or Tcy for instruction decoding is 2.5 microseconds. Most instructions decode within one Tcy cycle and the remaining instructions require only two Tcy cycles. The Interval Timer pre-scaler divides Tcy by thirty-two so that each Interval Timer period is 80 microseconds in duration. Thus, loading the timer counter with a value of 0xFF causes a TIMRIRQ interrupt in only 80 microseconds when the timer counter overflows to zero after one count. Loading the timer counter with a value of 0xCF causes a TIMRIRQ interrupt in 3.920 milliseconds. However, the microprocessor instructions that are necessary to rearm the Interval Timer require eight Tcy cycles, so reloading the timer counter with the value of 0xCF actually generates a TIMRIRQ interrupt every

3.940 milliseconds. This interval time is certainly within the specifications to refresh the 1257-15 dynamic RAM ICs.

Another function of the Interval Timer handler routine is to increment a 2-byte counter. Whatever value that is pre-loaded into this counter is incremented every 3.94 milliseconds. Naturally, a number that represents the negative of a value would be ideal to use in this application. In other words, when the most significant byte of this counter becomes `zero`, the desired time is reached. For example, if a 63-millisecond debounce time is desired, then -16 must be pre-loaded into the 2-byte counter, or `0xFFF0`. Furthermore, an approximate 1.0 second wait time can be easily achieved by loading `0xFF00` into a 2-byte counter such that `3.940 milliseconds * 256 = 1.0086 seconds`.

Using the Interval Timer as the primary method to refresh the dynamic RAM of the printer buffer changed the code only in the `MAIN` routine. Now, in an infinite loop, `MAIN` simply calls the `CHECKT0` routine and the `SENDMEM` routine when the printer is ready to accept another data character. The `CHECKT0` can take all the time it requires in order to count the number of LED flashes that represent the desired number of copies. I added another bit-flag to the System Flag byte called the Overflow state flag. If the write memory pointer should ever reach `0x00000` and new incoming data now overflows memory, the Overflow state flag is turned `ON`. When the Overflow state flag is `ON`, the printer buffer software will now bypass the copy counting logic in the `CHECKT0` routine and, as a protection, not even allow whatever data there is currently in memory to be sent to the printer as another copy. Of course, pressing the Reset pushbutton will reset all of the state flag bits including the Overflow state flag bit, and Reset re-enables the ability of the printer buffer to send as many copies of whatever data there will be in memory to the printer again. If additional printer copies is selected using the Copy pushbutton immediately after pressing the Reset pushbutton, nothing is printed as expected. I programmed a 2716 EPROM with this version of the firmware, installed it, and this is the firmware that I have been using in the JFD parallel printer buffer. I have seen no further bizarre behavior even when the printer buffer has reached and passed the end of the 256 KB memory buffer.

Whenever you have access to an interval timer, utilize it preciously and carefully in order to exact the great benefits from its phenomenal usefulness in nearly all computer utilities. An interval timer is always worth far more than its weight in measuring timing events accurately.

24. TrackScan Program

I found that the process of developing an algorithm to control the movement of the read/write disk head in a Disk][drive using half-phase increments to be extremely exciting, if not down-right challenging. There are so many physical parameters to consider while designing such an algorithm. In order to verify whether an algorithm is even working or even approaching the desired results, good tools are absolutely essential. Visual inspection that the Cam Table is being controlled appropriately is also invaluable information. As shown in Figures I.10.2 and I.10.3, I used a very fine liquid-ink pen to mark where the Cam Rider stops along the Cam Channel as I positioned the read/write disk head over tracks `0x00`, `0x01`, `0x02`, and `0x03` before I started to test various half-phase track stepping algorithms. I already knew that tracks on a Master DOS diskette are separated by four half-phases, so those ink marks indicated where the first four tracks are located that have a separation of four half-phases along the Cam Channel. I also noticed that track `0x00` was not precisely at the Cam Stop, but very, very close to the Cam Stop. That indicated to me that Electromagnet `0` must be held in the `ON` state to ensure that Phase `0` coincides precisely with track 0x00. No matter how many half-phases the Cam Table is turned in order to return the read/write disk head once again to track 0x00, Electromagnet 0 is always the last electromagnet to be de-energized and track 0x00 always coincides with Phase 0.

During the development of DOS 4.1, I spent a considerable amount of time and energy mapping the processing steps of the RWTS routines. I needed to include additional processing logic at the entry point of RWTS in order to obtain the correct Disk Address table entry for the peripheral interface card that is based on the specified slot number that is used to index into the Disk Address table. If a non-Disk][peripheral interface card handler is ever entered into the Disk Address table, additional provisions would be needed in order to ensure that its peripheral-card expansion ROM memory is fully detached after its RWTS processing. After determining an even better set of processing steps for the RWTS routines in DOS 4.5, I reviewed the RWTS disk formatting routine again with far more knowledge. I was already well acquainted with the read and the write Address Field header routines as well as the read and the write DATA Field header routines. I also knew the lead-in and the lead-out requirements for these header fields so that the peripheral interface card firmware could always synchronize with the data that it is about to read. It is critical that the write Address Field header routines and the write DATA Field header routines incorporate these requirements in their processing.

A minimum of **five** 40-microsecond auto-synchronization bytes are necessary for the Disk][Interface Card hardware to read in order to synchronize with the data of the Address Field header or with the DATA Field header that follow auto-synchronization bytes. At least one 32-microsecond synchronization byte must follow the final three epilogue bytes of an Address Field header or of a DATA Field header in order to correctly read the final epilogue byte even though only the first two epilogue bytes are verified. Synchronization bytes are always set to 0xFF and they require thirty-two microseconds to write and auto-synchronization bytes are set to 0x3FF and they require forty microseconds to write. Timing is absolutely critical in the RWTS write routines in order to write all (6 + 8 + 1) = 15 32-microsecond Address Field header data bytes and all (6 + 343 + 1) = 350 32-microsecond DATA Field Data bytes. Disk][Interface Card firmware has the capability and the capacity to read 32-microsecond disk bytes and 40-microsecond auto-synchronization bytes using its current PROMs. There are severe restrictions that are imposed on the interface card hardware that determine which bytes, from 0x80 to 0xFF, that can be used as valid disk bytes. Only sixty-six unique bytes can be used in order to implement the *6 and 2* encoding algorithm that is used by DOS 3.3 and, therefore, by DOS 4.5. Thus, the write Address Field header routine and the write DATA Field header routine can only write 32-microsecond disk bytes from the *6 and 2* Write Translate table and 40-microsecond auto-synchronization bytes equal to 0x3FF.

The copy protection algorithm that is used on many of the software products that are produced by Sierra On-Line such as *ScreenWriter* can only be implemented by using specialized diskette duplicating hardware. Even though Sierra On-Line owned the Form Master duplicating hardware, Sierra On-Line had to create the Form Master software that utilizes the duplicating capabilities of this machine. The Form Master must duplicate all of the features of the Apple][disk format and any other specific byte patterns that only this hardware can create. Sierra On-Line hired Mark Duchaineau to write the control software for the Form Master, but his copy-protection scheme required the end user to utilize a well maintained disk drive that is adjusted to operate only at the factory specified disk rotational speed. Any deviation from that factory specified rotational speed causes major problems for the copy protection scheme that Duchaineau designed. The rendering algorithm that Duchaineau developed as it is implemented within *ScreenWriter*, stops reading disk data for a specific period of time and then reads the next available disk byte. That raw disk byte must be a specific value for the rendering algorithm to accept and, therefore, pass the diskette as a valid product that is produced by the Form Master. If the Sierra On-Line diskette is copied, even by *Locksmith*, the special region that the rendering algorithm skips reading cannot be precisely duplicated because the Form Master writes a series of invalid disk bytes that the Disk][Interface Card PROMs cannot physically reproduce. That is, the Form Master manufactures specific disk bytes that it can write, but these disk bytes cannot be written by the Disk][because this data does not reside in the *6 and 2* Write Translate table. Once I became acquainted with Duchaineau's rendering algorithm, I could easily spot its presence simply by viewing the sectors of any copy protected Sierra On-Line diskette using *Disk Window*. And, I could use *Disk Window* to *adjust* or to *modify* the rendering algorithm routine on the diskette so that it would *pass* any value that the Disk][should read for that special raw disk byte when the rendering algorithm starts reading disk data again.

A year or so later while I was self-employed and assigned to a Sierra On-Line project, I was challenged by the remaining software programmers who had not yet been laid off from Sierra On-Line. That challenge was to break the copy protection of a new product that Sierra On-Line had recently received for its evaluation. Armed with my personal arsenal of disk tools and utilities, all of which I had created, I rendered the new product free of copy protection within ninety-five seconds. To be sure, the copy protection scheme that was used by this new product revealed itself early in my investigation and I was able to defeat its implementation by using NOP and CLC instructions that I strategically placed. Of course, *Disk Window* made the task of rendering this new product free of copy protection in short order. There are hundreds of stories about other people who were very much like Mark Duchaineau, how his achievements became interwoven in the fascinating history of the personal computer, and how those achievements fueled the computer revolution. I happened to be working for Sierra On-Line as an employee when Steven Levy came to Sierra On-Line in order to interview several individuals for his forthcoming book *hackers*. Ken Williams was but one of many hundreds of individuals Mr. Levy found interesting and compelling to include in *hackers*. I have to admit that it is a fascinating book to read.

When I started to analyze the volume formatting routines in RWTS, I began to develop software tools that could read and store the raw disk bytes into memory for an entire track. I knew that a sector requires $15 + 350 = 365$ 32-microsecond bytes for the Address Field header, the DATA Field header, and the prologue and epilogue bytes for those fields, and a bare minimum of ten auto-synchronization bytes in total. However, the routine WRITADR writes SYNCNT auto-synchronization bytes before an Address Field header and the routine WRITSCTR writes **six** auto-synchronization bytes before a DATA Field header. A track that is comprised of sixteen sectors would require $365 * 16 = 5840$ 32-microsecond bytes and $6 * 16 = 96$ 40-microsecond auto-synchronization bytes. The Disk][Interface Card firmware would require a minimum of $5840 * 32 + 96 * 40 = 190,720$ microseconds to read all of those disk bytes. A diskette that is spinning at 300 revolutions per minute would make five revolutions in one second, or it would take 200,000 microseconds to make one revolution. For each track, this would leave $200,000 - 190,720 = 9280$ microseconds available for all of the auto-synchronization bytes before the Address Field header of each sector assuming the Disk][is well maintained and has perfect rotational velocity of the diskette.

The DISKFMT routine initializes SYNCNT to thirty-two, the number of auto-synchronization bytes that are written before an Address Field header. Before the TRACKFMT routine begins writing the Address Field header for sector 0x00 on track 0x00, it writes 128 auto-synchronization bytes. Before each Address Field header for the sectors that follow sector 0x00, the TRACKFMT routine writes SYNCNT auto-synchronization bytes. The TRACKFMT routine then analyzes the track it just wrote in order to determine if it can read the Address Field header for sector 0x00. Obviously, an initial $128 + 32 * 15 = 608$ auto-synchronization bytes are about $608 - 9280 / 40 = 376$ auto-synchronization bytes too many, but this exercise provides a good start to determine the **optimal** value for SYNCNT. TRACKFMT then reduces SYNCNT and tries to format track 0x00 again. As soon as TRACKFMT can discover the Address Field header for sector 0x00, TRACKFMT reduces SYNCNT a final time and uses that stored value for the number of auto-synchronization bytes it writes before the Address Field header of all sectors on all tracks other than sector

0x00 because TRACKFMT always begins the format of a track with 128 auto-synchronization bytes. Typically, the epilogue bytes that are written after the DATA Field Data for the last sector, or sector 0x0F, are written somewhere within those initial 128 auto-synchronization bytes. In order to verify that TRACKFMT, as I just described, performs its function correctly and as intended, I wrote a utility that reads and stores the raw disk bytes into memory for an entire track, and the utility analyzes that data so that the track properties can be uniquely displayed. That utility is *TrackScan*, and its Main Menu is shown in Figure V.24.1. I developed *TrackScan* using the *VMGR* program as its structural model. However, instead of specifying VOLUME as in *VMGR*, *TrackScan* uses PHASE in order to format a diskette using that parameter before *TrackScan* displays the properties of any selected track or track range. *TrackScan* can format a diskette with 35, 36, 40, or 48 tracks which is user selected and shown in Figure V.24.2.

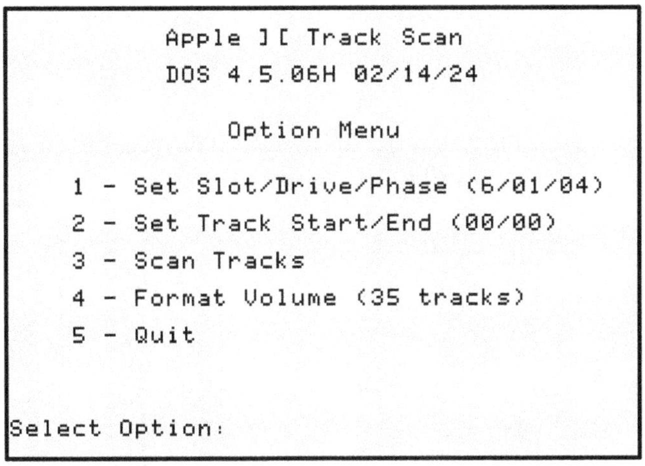

```
      Apple ][ Track Scan              Apple ][ Track Scan
      DOS 4.5.06H 02/14/24             DOS 4.5.06H 02/14/24

         Option Menu                      Option Menu

 1 - Set Slot/Drive/Phase (6/01/04)   1 - Set Slot/Drive/Phase (6/02/04)
 2 - Set Track Start/End (00/00)      2 - Set Track Start/End (00/00)
 3 - Scan Tracks                      3 - Scan Tracks
 4 - Format Volume (35 tracks)        4 - Format Volume (35 tracks)
 5 - Quit                             5 - Quit




Select Option:                       Enter LAST Track (35/36/40/48):  35
```

Figure V.24.1. TrackScan Main Menu 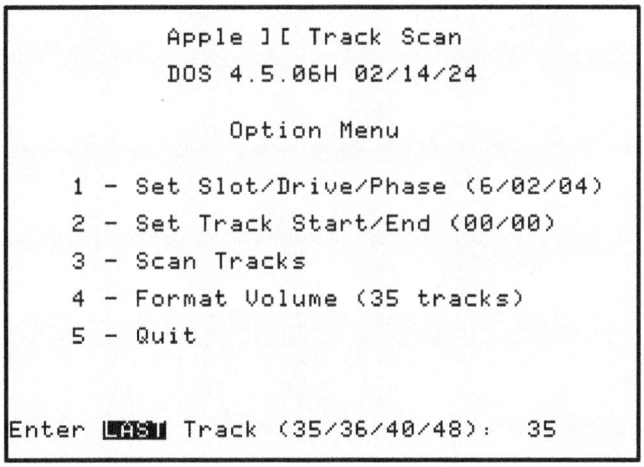   Figure V.24.2. TrackScan Format Volume

TrackScan can scan and process any track on any volume, and *TrackScan* does not have to format a volume before it scans that volume. After *TrackScan* has scanned a selected track, it analyzes the raw track data after it locates the Address Field header for sector 0x00 and verifies that it can locate the next instance of the Address Field header for sector 0x00. *TrackScan* uses a total of eight processing steps in order to analyze the raw track data for each sector. It decodes the Address Field header data and it displays that information first along with the number of synchronization bytes that come prior to the Address Field header and the number of data bytes that comprise the Address Field header. Recall that a synchronization byte is 0xFF in value and that it requires thirty-two microseconds to write that byte. It is not possible to distinguish synchronization bytes from auto-synchronization bytes except indirectly. *TrackScan* processing continues by locating the DATA Field header that follows the Address Field header, and *TrackScan* analyzes its Data structure and data contents. The number of synchronization bytes that are found prior to the DATA Field header, the number of data bytes that comprise the DATA Field Data, and the error status are displayed next for that sector. The error status shows the number of successful processing steps *TrackScan* completed during its analysis of that sector and a final error value for the processing step that it could not complete or zero for no errors. *TrackScan* continues its processing for each of the sectors that are contained in the raw track data.

351

```
        Apple ][ Track Scan                        Apple ][ Track Scan
        DOS 4.5.06H 02/14/24                        DOS 4.5.06H 02/14/24

           Option Menu                                 Option Menu

 1 - Set Slot/Drive/Phase (6/02/04)        1 - Set Slot/Drive/Phase (6/02/04)
 2 - Set Track Start/End (00/00)           2 - Set Track Start/End (00/34)
 3 - Scan Tracks                           3 - Scan Tracks
 4 - Format Volume (35 tracks)             4 - Format Volume (35 tracks)
 5 - Quit                                  5 - Quit
                        SYNCNT=0x0D
                        RETRYCNT=0x1F
Return code from Format:  0x00.           Select Option:  3█
```

Figure V.24.3. TrackScan Format Results   Figure V.24.4. TrackScan Scan Tracks

```
           Apple ][ Track Scan                         Apple ][ Track Scan

Vol  Trk  Sec  Gap  Hdr  Gap  Data  Err   Vol  Trk  Sec  Gap  Hdr  Gap  Data  Err
---  ---  ---  ---  ---  ---  ----  ---   ---  ---  ---  ---  ---  ---  ----  ---
000  00   00   062   4   10   343   8-0   000  17   00   051   4   10   343   8-0
000  00   01   018   4   10   343   8-0   000  17   01   018   4   10   343   8-0
000  00   02   018   4   10   343   8-0   000  17   02   018   4   10   343   8-0
000  00   03   018   4   10   343   8-0   000  17   03   018   4   10   343   8-0
000  00   04   018   4   10   343   8-0   000  17   04   018   4   10   343   8-0
000  00   05   018   4   10   343   8-0   000  17   05   018   4   10   343   8-0
000  00   06   018   4   11   343   8-0   000  17   06   018   4   10   343   8-0
000  00   07   018   4   10   343   8-0   000  17   07   018   4   10   343   8-0
000  00   08   018   4   10   343   8-0   000  17   08   018   4   10   343   8-0
000  00   09   018   4   10   343   8-0   000  17   09   018   4   10   343   8-0
000  00   10   018   4   10   343   8-0   000  17   10   018   4   10   343   8-0
000  00   11   018   4   11   343   8-0   000  17   11   018   4   10   343   8-0
000  00   12   018   4   10   343   8-0   000  17   12   018   4   10   343   8-0
000  00   13   018   4   10   343   8-0   000  17   13   018   4   10   343   8-0
000  00   14   018   4   10   343   8-0   000  17   14   018   4   10   343   8-0
000  00   15   018   4   10   343   8-0   000  17   15   018   4   10   343   8-0
Avg Header Gap = 18, Remainder = 00/15   Avg Header Gap = 18, Remainder = 00/15
```

Figure V.24.5. TrackScan for Track 0x00   Figure V.24.6. TrackScan for Track 0x11

TrackScan displays the final value it determines for SYNCNT when *TrackScan* is used to format a volume as shown in Figure V.24.3. SYNCNT is used for the number of auto-synchronization bytes that are written prior to the Address Field header for a sector after track 0x00 has been successfully formatted. HDRSYNC, or six auto-synchronization bytes are always written prior to the DATA Field header for every sector. Figure V.24.4 shows that *TrackScan* is prepared to scan tracks 0x00 to 0x22. The results of the scan for track 0x00 is shown in Figure V.24.5 and the results of the scan for track 0x11 is shown in Figure V.24.6. These scans were obtained from scanning a volume that was formatted by *TrackScan* with thirty-five tracks and a PHASE of four as previously shown in Figure V.24.2. *TrackScan* reported obtaining a value of 0x0D for SYNCNT in Figure V.24.3. This information and the data that is shown in Figures V.24.5 and V.24.6 can be used to determine if the actual number of auto-synchronization bytes that are recorded can be verified indirectly. Once the disk data latch has been loaded with a synchronization byte, data one's are clocked out by the firmware and recorded onto the disk.

When WRITADR finishes writing an Address Field header, it exits via WRITEXIT and a synchronization byte is left stored in the data latch before it returns the latch configuration to read-mode. By the time

352

WRITSCTR begins its processing and enables the data latch for write-mode again, already 92 microseconds has elapsed. After WRITSCTR has written six auto-synchronization bytes, the total time from the end of the Address Field header to the start of the DATA Field header is 92 + 6 * 40 = 332 microseconds. The DOS 4.5 TRACKFMT routines calculate that 332 / 32 = 10.38 bytes should be observed. Figures V.24.5 and V.24.6 show that the average of the second Gap column of numbers is observed to be (30 * 10 + 2 * 11) / 32 = 10.06 bytes. Assuming only minor fluctuations in drive speed, the calculated and the observed results through raw data track analysis are very much in agreement for the size of the synchronization gap that exists between the Address Field and the DATA Field headers.

Previously, it was determined that 9280 microseconds should be available for all auto-synchronization bytes that are found prior to an Address Field header assuming perfect rotational velocity of the Disk][hardware. The total number of 32-microsecond synchronization bytes that are observed before all Address Field headers for track 0x00 is 62 + 15 * 18 = 332 bytes from Figure V.24.5. The total number of 32-microsecond synchronization bytes that are observed before all Address Field headers for track 0x11 is 51 + 15 * 18 = 321 bytes from Figure V.24.6. Strategically reducing SYNCNT from 0x0F to 0x0D for all tracks ensures that sector 0x00 is always found, even on the very last track of the volume. The summation of all observed synchronization bytes that are found through raw data track analysis before an Address Field header for track 0x00 would be 332 * 32 = 10,624 microseconds. This is only 1344 microseconds more than the calculated value of 9280 microseconds. The summation of all observed synchronization bytes that are found through raw data track analysis before an Address Field header for track 0x11 would be 321 * 32 = 10,272 µsec. This is only 992 microseconds more than the calculated value of 9280 microseconds.

Another way to demonstrate how closely the raw data track analysis results compare with reality is to sum all of the data results that are shown separately in Figures V.24.5 and V.24.6.

From raw data track analysis for track 0x00, the sum of the values for all sectors would be

$$(332 + 14 * 10 + 2 * 11) * 32 + (16 * 15 + 16 * 350) * 32 = 202,688 \text{ microseconds}$$

This is only 2688 microseconds more than the time it takes to rotate the diskette once.

From raw data track analysis for track 0x11, the sum of values for all sectors would be

$$(321 + 16 * 10) * 32 + (16 * 15 + 16 * 350) * 32 = 202,272 \text{ microseconds}$$

This is only 2272 microseconds more than the time it takes to rotate the diskette once.

It is obvious that *TrackScan* is a very important tool that can be used to verify the efficacy of the DOS 4.5 TRACKFMT routines. Being able to initialize a volume with precision and being able to scan and analyze each track on that volume for accuracy provides the necessary insight that confirms the validity of the TRACKFMT routines that comprise this algorithm in DOS 4.5. Now that a suitable volume formatting algorithm can be certified using *TrackScan*, a new algorithm to control the movement of the read/write disk head in a Disk][drive that is any multiple of a single half-phase can be rationally developed. *TrackScan* was instrumental in developing such an algorithm for it absolutely demonstrates its ability to read, analyze, and display every sector on every track after a volume has been initialized utilizing useful values for track PHASE separation.

25. ClientServer Program

As my previous publications on Disk Operating Systems for the Apple][computer have shown, I have certainly demonstrated that I have developed and created a serious amount of software for this computer. I typically develop Apple][computer software using a MacBook Pro computer that is hosting the Virtual][emulation program by Gerard Putter. Virtual][can launch a utility that is called *A2V2* and this utility can transfer a 143 KB disk volume image to and from a real Apple][computer. The Apple][computer must be concurrently running a program called Asynchronous Data Transfer, or *ADT* by Paul Guertin which is enhanced by Gerard Putter. My Apple //e computer hosts a Super Serial peripheral interface card that uses a serial cable to connect to a Keyspan serial to USB adapter. The Keyspan adapter uses a USB cable to connect the adapter to my MacBook Pro computer which is running MacOS 10.12.6. These three components are shown in Figure V.25.1.

About a year after Apple introduced the Disk][floppy disk drive, probably around 1979, the Disk][Cam Table and supporting hardware were slightly modified in order to access thirty-six tracks rather than thirty-five tracks. For one reason or another this information never found its way into the Apple user community. Regardless, *ADT* only supports volumes that have been formatted with thirty-five tracks, so it only allows a 143 KB disk volume image to be transferred to and from an Apple][computer and a MacBook Pro computer, or any other similar personal computer device. Certainly, there are advantages in using a program like *A2V2* on the MacBook Pro.

1. *A2V2* does not depend on the Virtual][emulation of the Apple][computer
2. *A2V2* has full access to the MacBook Pro file system
3. *A2V2* allows the user to archive ~.dsk images of diskettes in the MacBook Pro file system

On the other hand there are a few disadvantages in using *A2V2*.

1. *A2V2* only supports 35-track disk or Disk][-like volume images
2. *A2V2* requires a USB to serial communication adapter like the Keyspan adapter
3. There is no Keyspan driver available for an operating system beyond MacOS 10.12.6

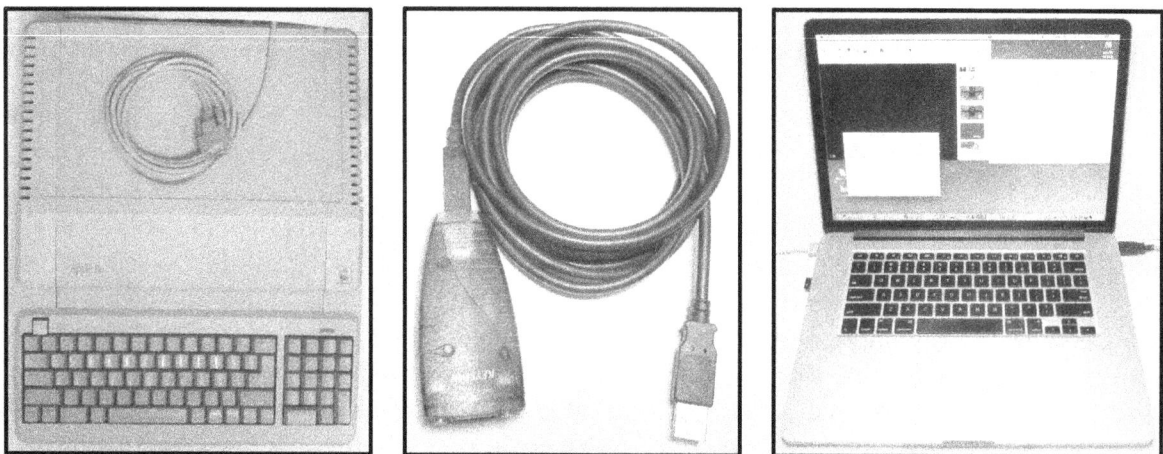

Figure V.25.1. Apple //e Computer, Keyspan Adapter, MacBook Pro Computer

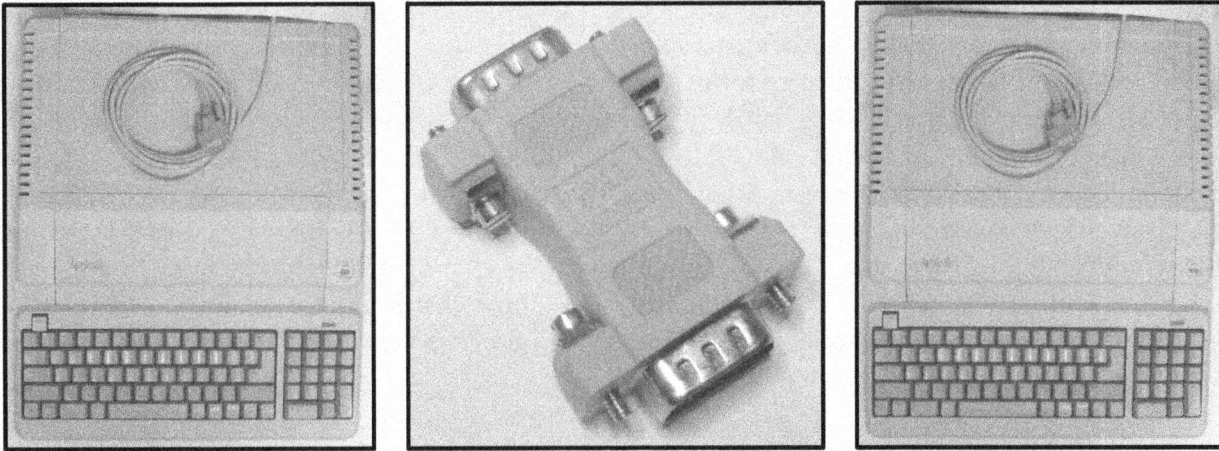

Figure V.25.2. Apple //e Computer, Null Modem Adapter, Apple //e Computer

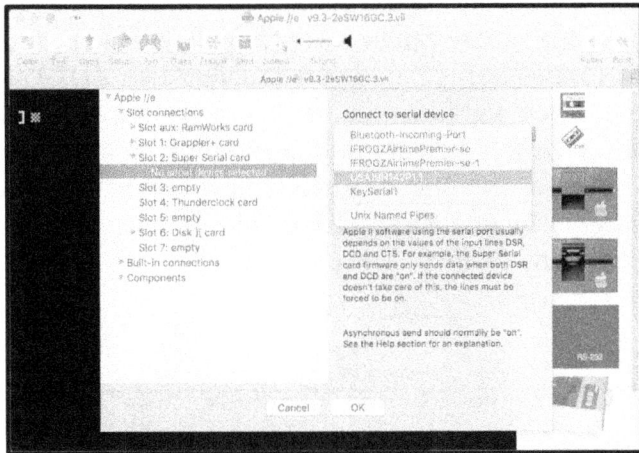

Figure V.25.3. Selecting the USA19H142P1.1

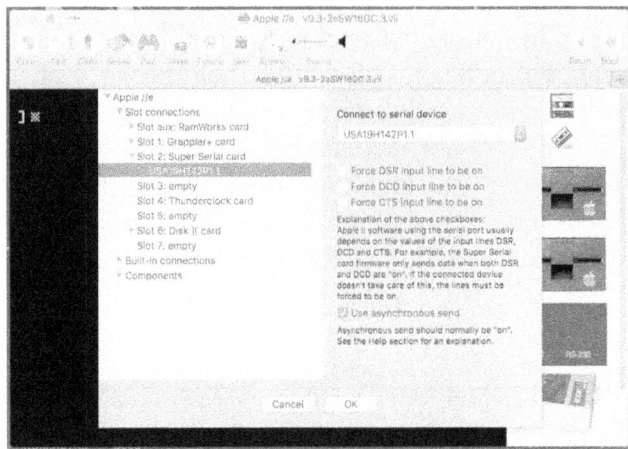

Figure V.25.4. Keyspan Connection Complete

In order for two Apple][computers to communicate with each other, a Super Serial peripheral interface card or an equivalent RS232 communication serial card must reside in each Apple][computer. Their external serial cables must be connected using a Null Modem adapter like a DB9 male to male adapter as shown in Figure V.25.2 along with both Apple computers. The DB9 adapter may be obtained for around $1.58 from www.sfcable.com, for example. Figure V.25.3 shows how to connect the Keyspan driver USA19H142P1.1 to the Super Serial card that is emulated in Virtual][. Figure V.25.4 shows that the connection of the Keyspan serial to USB adapter to the Virtual][program is complete.

I have developed specific firmware for the CFFA Slot Card as discussed in Section V.13, firmware for the Axlon RAM Disk 320 Interface Slot Card as discussed in Section V.19, and firmware for the RanaSystems EliteThree Disk Drive Interface Slot Card as discussed in Section V.20. My CFFA firmware can access up to eighty-one drives, where each drive can access 256 volumes, and each volume may be formatted with up to forty-eight tracks, where each track may contain either sixteen or thirty-two sectors. My Rana firmware can access forty four-half-phase spaced tracks, where each track contains thirty-two sectors, sixteen sectors on the notched side and sixteen sectors on the unnotched side of the diskette. Many

355

Disk][compatible drives became available in the early 1980's that could access up to forty four-half-phase spaced tracks, where each track contains sixteen sectors. Even the Axlon 320 can access its memory which is equivalent to a volume that is formatted with forty tracks, where each track contains sixteen sectors. Mr. Putter even provides the capability for his Virtual][software to read and to write a ~.woz version 2 diskette that may be initialized with forty-eight three-half-phase spaced tracks, where each track contains sixteen sectors. In other words, my CFFA volumes, regardless of their number of tracks, may be archived on a MacBook Pro as a ~.woz version 2 file as long as the CFFA volume is formatted with tracks that only contain sixteen sectors. The *A2V2/ADT* data transfer protocol cannot be used to archive any diskette image other than a 143 KB sized volume. This somewhat limits the usefulness of the CFFA, Axlon, and Rana data storage containers in being able to archive their contents onto a MacBook Pro computer using the *A2V2/ADT* data transfer protocol.

My analysis of the *ADT* software that transfers data to and from an Apple][computer was primarily focused in order to incorporate changes in that software. For example, lowercase characters could be utilized in all menus in order to assist in helping to make the Apple screen text easier for me to read in my opinion. My analysis also enabled me to incorporate an Update feature to the software that would allow me to save the *ADT* program back onto its disk volume when its slot/drive configuration is modified. This feature alone has saved me much time when I have had to transfer a volume image a number of times during the testing phase of software development. The testing phase can be a very lengthy, arduous, and iterative process, and it is quite helpful when changes to the configuration of a program like *ADT* can easily be saved and restored for the next iteration of tests. The documentation I found for the Super Serial Slot Card did not include the information that I required so that I could design serial communication software that uses this card. The *ADT* program provided me with one example in how to transmit and how to receive serial data that uses the various configurations that are available on the Super Serial Slot Card. These configurations include baud rate, data format, and parity.

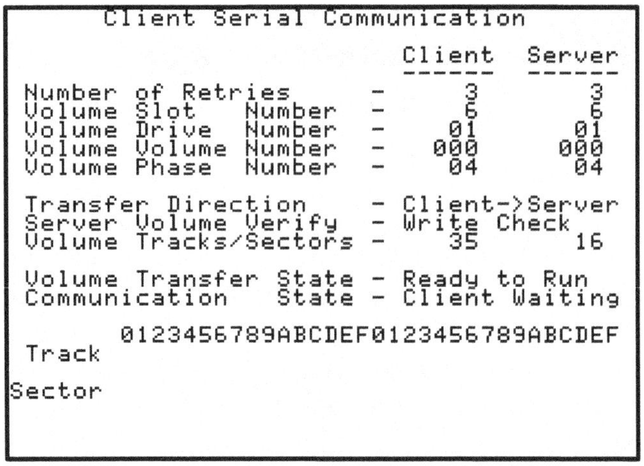

Figure V.25.5. Client Waiting Synchronization 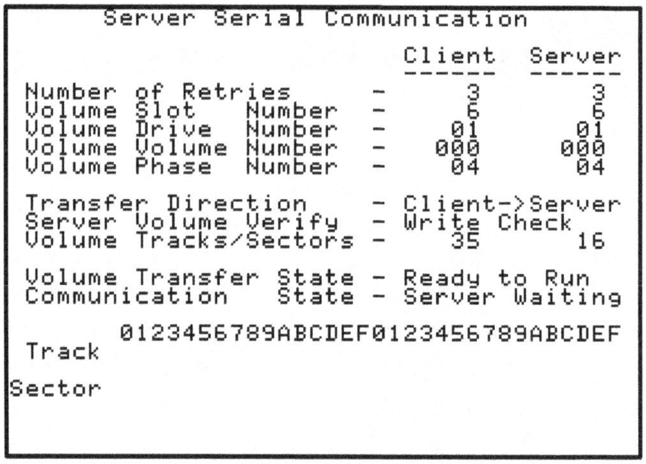   Figure V.25.6. Server Waiting Synchronization

The Client program handles the complete operation of configuring and of transferring a volume image from one Apple][computer to another Apple][computer. A volume image may be transferred from the Client to the Server computer or from the Server to the Client computer. The Server program displays the same ongoing operation menu details for the volume image transfer as that shown by the Client program for its menu details. The Server program, on the other hand, is not utilized in order to configure the data transfer setup. The Server is utilized to show its real time processing of the data that is being transferred. However, both programs at startup automatically locate the slot number of their respective Super Serial Slot Card, perform its firmware initialization for baud rate in order to set the maximum data transfer rate, and to initiate its auto-synchronization to the serial communication program that is processing on the other Apple][computer. Figures V.25.5 and V.25.6 show the text screens of the Client and the Server programs before auto-synchronization has occurred. Figures V.25.7 and V.25.8 show the text screens of both programs after auto-synchronization is achieved.

```
   Client Serial Communication              Server Serial Communication

                     Client   Server                         Client   Server
                     ------   ------                         ------   ------
Number  of Retries      -       3       3    Number  of Retries      -       3       3
Volume Slot    Number   -       6       6    Volume Slot    Number   -       6       6
Volume Drive   Number   -      01      01    Volume Drive   Number   -      01      01
Volume Volume  Number   -     000     000    Volume Volume  Number   -     000     000
Volume Phase   Number   -      04      04    Volume Phase   Number   -      04      04

Transfer Direction      - Client->Server     Transfer Direction      - Client->Server
Server Volume Verify    - Write Check         Server Volume Verify    - Write Check
Volume Tracks/Sectors   -      35      16    Volume Tracks/Sectors   -      35      16

Volume Transfer State  ->Ready to Run        Volume Transfer State   - Ready to Run
Communication  State   - Synchronized        Communication  State    - Synchronized

       0123456789ABCDEF0123456789ABCDEF              0123456789ABCDEF0123456789ABCDEF
Track                                        Track

Sector                                       Sector
```

Figure V.25.7. Auto-Synchronized to Server   Figure V.25.8. Auto-Synchronized to Client

Super Serial Slot Card documentation is absolutely necessary in order to understand the software *environment* that is required by its firmware. That is, its page-zero utilization, its addressing and control logic, how the ROM/RAM memory space is utilized in the computer, the operation of its Asynchronous Communications Interface Adapter or ACIA, and its Input/Output routine entry points all contribute to the software *environment* of the Super Serial Slot Card. Analyzing and understanding how others have utilized the various configurations and registers that are supported by the Super Serial Slot Card certainly help to coordinate and assimilate the written documentation to practical realizations for the design of serial communication software on the Apple][computer. My goal was to design serial communication software that would utilize a Super Serial Slot Card in one Apple][computer and another Super Serial Slot Card in a second Apple][computer. The ultimate design goal is to transfer the contents of a diskette volume from one Apple][computer to a second Apple][computer. Whether the Apple][computer was, in fact, a Virtual][emulation of an Apple][computer should not matter. If a Virtual][emulation of an Apple][computer is utilized, it is important to remember to always configure the virtual machine to the normal clock speed of an Apple][computer, which is 1.0 MHz. The emulated Super Serial Slot Card will not operate correctly if the virtual machine is configured to any of the other available higher processing clock speeds.

As shown in Figure V.25.2, two Apple][computers are connected by means of two serial cables, each connected to their Super Serial Card or SSC, and the two serial cables are in turn connected to each other by means of a Null Modem adapter. The Null Modem adapter connects the RX data line of one serial cable to the TX data line of the other serial cable. The serial communication software package that I developed is comprised of two separate software programs, a Client Serial communication program and a Server Serial communication program. The Client Serial communication program processes data on the first Apple][computer and the Server Serial communication program processes data on the second Apple][computer. It is critical that the Client and the Server programs synchronize with each other so that the transfer of data can transpire as efficiently as possible. In earlier versions of *A2V2* and *ADT*, program synchronization was always problematic, and I could never find a reliable strategy to achieve immediate and repeatable program synchronization when these programs began their processing. That is, I could not ascertain whether it was preferable to begin *A2V2* first, and then begin *ADT*, or if it was better to begin *ADT* first, and then begin *A2V2*. I tabulated conflicting results every time I changed the start order or the amount of time one program had already been processing before the other program, and I could never resolve my collected data to prefer one start order over another. Fortunately, the current version of *A2V2* that runs on MacOS 10.12.6 is Version 2.4, and in this version of *A2V2*, *A2V2* appears to have solved its problematic and timely synchronization with *ADT*. Of course, my design of Client and Server serial communication software must auto-synchronize immediately irrespective of start order or the amount of time one program is processing before the other program.

Command	Sent By	Description
A	Client	Command to Server to initiate auto-synchronization
B	Server	Response to Client that the auto-synchronization command was received
C	Client	Command to Server followed by CFDCB Data or configuration data
D	Server	Response to Client that CFDCB Data was correctly received
E	Server	Response to Client that CFDCB Data was not correctly received
F	Client	Command to finish data transfer in order to calculate data transfer time duration No response needed from Server
H	Reader or Writer	Command to halt further data transfer and exit program
L	Reader	Command to Writer followed by TSDCB Data or Track/Sector data
M	Writer	Response to Reader that TSDCB Data was correctly received
N	Writer	Response to Reader that TSDCB Data was not correctly received
O	Reader	Command to Writer followed by RWDCB Data to tell Writer that Reader is Pausing to read disk
P	Writer	Response to tell Reader that RWDCB Data was correctly received
Q	Writer	Response to tell Reader that RWDCB Data was not correctly received
R	Client	Command to tell Server to read/write/format verify its data disk
S	Server	Response to tell Client that Server is ready for data transfer
T	Reader	Command to Writer followed by TXDCB Data or sector data
U	Writer	Response to Reader that TXDCB Data was correctly received
V	Writer	Response to Reader that TXDCB Data was not correctly received

Table V.25.1. Client/Server Commands and Responses

The Client program communicates to the Server program using specific commands and, in some instances, with specific Data Control Blocks, or DCBs. The complete list of Client/Server commands is shown in Table V.25.1. During auto-synchronization, the Client continuously transmits an A command every 250 milliseconds and waits for a B response from the Server. The Server must ignore any extra A commands it may receive after it responds with a B command response. It must be understood that prior to auto-synchronization, the Client and Server programs are processing their software asynchronously to each other and that each program is independent of the other. Once the Client and Server programs have auto-synchronized, their commands, DCBs, and sectors of data are transferred totally synchronously.

Entry	Index	Size	Value Range	Description
VOLXFER	0x00	0x01	R = 0, W = 1	Volume transfer direction
INITFLAG	0x01	0x01	NO = 0, YES = 1	Volume initialization flag
VOLTRKS	0x02	0x01	18 to 48	Volume number of tracks
VOLSECS	0x03	0x01	16 or 32	Volume number of sectors
CLNTRTRY	0x04	0x01	1 to 9	Client number of retries
CLNTSLOT	0x05	0x01	1 to 7	Client drive slot number
CLNTDRV	0x06	0x01	1 to 81	Client drive number
CLNTVOL	0x07	0x01	0 to 255	Client volume number
CLNTPHAS	0x08	0x01	1 to 16	Client phase number
SRVRRTRY	0x09	0x01	1 to 9	Server number of retries
SRVRSLOT	0x0A	0x01	1 to 7	Server drive slot number
SRVRDRV	0x0B	0x01	1 to 81	Server drive number
SRVRVOL	0x0C	0x01	0 to 255	Server volume number
SRVRPHAS	0x0D	0x01	1 to 16	Server phase number
CLSRSTAT	0x0E	0x01	WAIT = 0, SYNC = 1	Client/Server Status
CLSRRUN	0x0F	0x01	WAIT = 0, RUN = 1, QUIT = 2	Client/Server RUN state
CFDCBXOR	0x10	0x01	0 to 255	Checksum XOR
CFDCBSUM	0x11	0x01	0 to 255	Checksum ADC

Table V.25.2. CFDCBTBL Configuration Data Control Block Table Contents

As noted earlier, a volume image may be transferred from the Client to the Server computer or from the Server to the Client computer. Once the user has configured the serial communication system using the Client program, both Client and Server programs transfer their control to either a Reader function or to a Writer function. In other words, if the Client configures the system as a Client→Server volume image transfer, the Client will function as the Reader and the Server will function as the Writer. Alternatively, if the Client configures the system as a Server→Client volume image transfer, the Client will function as the Writer and the Server will function as the Reader. The Reader and Writer functions simply refer to which function reads data from a disk volume and which function writes data to a disk volume, respectively. Once the Reader/Writer functions have been established, all further commands will be initiated by the Reader and all command responses will be initiated by the Writer. After a volume image is transferred, the Reader/Writer functions are complete and the Client/Server roles can resume so that data throughput calculations can be completed and displayed by the Client. The Server re-initializes its display and it retains the previous data transfer menu selections in order to present itself such that the Server may receive its next command from the Client. For example, the next command the Server may likely receive from the Client would be the Quit command.

Initialization data that is displayed on both the Client and the Server text screens is transmitted by the Client to the Server using the C command followed by the transmission of the contents of the CFDCB Configuration Data Control Block. This data block contains all of the information necessary to configure both the Reader and the Writer functions that perform the task of transmitting a data volume image from one Apple][computer to another Apple][computer. The size in bytes of the CFDCB Data block is given by CFDCBLEN, which is equal to eighteen bytes. Every time the user makes any change on the Client menu, the CFDCB Data block is transmitted to the Server program. Once the Server program receives the CFDCB Data block it calculates its own values for CFDCBXOR and CFDCBSUM. CFDCBXOR and CFDCBSUM are the two checksum variables that are found at the end of the CFDCB Data block. If the calculated values for these checksum variables that is performed by the Server are equal to their respective values in the CFDCB Data block, the Server returns the D command response, otherwise the Server returns the E command response indicating a checksum mismatch error. If the Client receives an E command response, the Client will attempt to re-transmit the C command followed by the transmission of the CFDCB Data block. The Client will attempt this re-transmission up to CLNTRTRY times, or the number of retries that are assigned to the Client. The CFDCB Data block contents are shown in Table V.25.2 with a brief description for each entry. Both the Client and the Server programs will terminate with an error number when the number of retries is exceeded.

```
+--------------------------------------------+   +--------------------------------------------+
|     Client Serial Communication            |   |     Server Serial Communication            |
|                                            |   |                                            |
|                       Client   Server      |   |                       Client   Server      |
|                       ------   ------      |   |                       ------   ------      |
| Number  of Retries   -    3        3       |   | Number  of Retries   -    3        3       |
| Volume Slot   Number -    6        6       |   | Volume Slot   Number -    6        6       |
| Volume Drive  Number -    01       01      |   | Volume Drive  Number -    01       01      |
| Volume Volume Number -    000      000     |   | Volume Volume Number -    000      000     |
| Volume Phase  Number -    04       04      |   | Volume Phase  Number -    04       04      |
|                                            |   |                                            |
| Transfer Direction   - Client->Server      |   | Transfer Direction   - Client->Server      |
| Server Volume Verify - Write Check         |   | Server Volume Verify - Write Check         |
| Volume Tracks/Sectors -   35       16      |   | Volume Tracks/Sectors -   35       16      |
|                                            |   |                                            |
| Volume Transfer State - Data Transfer      |   | Volume Transfer State - Data Transfer      |
| Communication    State - Synchronized      |   | Communication    State - Synchronized      |
|                                            |   |                                            |
|       0123456789ABCDEF0123456789ABCDEF     |   |       0123456789ABCDEF0123456789ABCDEF     |
| Track                                      |   | Track                                      |
|                                            |   |                                            |
|Sector                                      |   |Sector                                      |
|                                            |   |                                            |
|  Volume must be in slot #6, drive #01      |   |  Volume must be in slot #6, drive #01      |
|         Press any key to continue          |   |                                            |
+--------------------------------------------+   +--------------------------------------------+
```

Figure V.25.9. Client Volume Verify Message Figure V.25.10. Server Volume Verify Message

When the CFDCB variable CLSRRUN is set to RUN, or CLSRRUN = 1, the Client program and the Server program will both extract variables from their CFDCB Data block in order to initialize either their Reader function or their Writer function based on the value of VOLXFER. Both programs will display a message at the bottom of their text screen as shown in Figures V.25.9 and V.25.10. As soon as the RETURN key is pressed on the Client computer, the Client program will issue the R command to the Server program to read-verify or to write-verify or to initialize-verify its target disk volume while the Client program performs the appropriate task for its target disk volume. For example, if VOLXFER = 0, then the Client becomes the Reader and it will read-verify its volume; the Server becomes the Writer and it will write-verify its volume if INITFLAG = 0 or initialize-verify its volume if INITFLAG = 1. On the other hand, if VOLXFER = 1, then the Client becomes the Writer and it will write-verify its volume if INITFLAG = 0 or initialize-verify its volume if INITFLAG = 1; the Server becomes the Reader and it will read-verify its volume. VOLTRKS, VOLSECS, CLNTVOL or SRVRVOL, and CLNTPHAS or SRVRPHAS are used as input initialization parameters to RWTS in order to create a DATA Type volume in the DOS 4.5 environment if a volume is selected to be initialized for its verification. All disk access, whether a volume is read from or written to, is handled exclusively by the DOS 4.5 external RWTS interface using an RWTS IOCB that is internal to the Client software and internal to the Server software. Once the Server program completes its target disk volume verification, the Server will issue the S command response to the Client program. If either program receives a return error value in their respective RWTS IOCB, the appropriate error message will be displayed at the bottom of the text screen and the program will wait for appropriate, corrective action to be made. If no errors are reported during the disk volume verification check process by RWTS, the Client and Server software will transition into their role as a Reader or as a Writer function at this time.

The Client/Server serial communication programs are designed to process and to transmit batches of data that are comprised of ten tracks of data when those tracks contain sixteen sectors. If those tracks contain thirty-two sectors, then a data batch will be comprised of five tracks of data. I conducted a plethora of timing tests to determine the optimal number of tracks that would comprise a data batch. Initially, the Reader must read a data batch into memory before any data can be transmitted to the Writer. During the data read/write process, as the Reader is reading the next data batch, the Writer is writing the previous data batch. After the Reader has transmitted the final data batch to the Writer, the Writer is left to finish the volume transfer by writing the final data batch. To my surprise it did not matter how many tracks of data that comprise a data batch irrespective of disk drive type. My tests included real Disk][drives, simulated Disk][drives like those found in Virtual][, RAM drives, and CFFA drives. I simply set the number of tracks that comprise a data batch to ten because DOS 4.5 provides that much memory from 0x1E00 to 0xBE00. Therefore, the Reader begins the actual serial communication and transmission of disk volume data by reading the first ten tracks of its target volume into memory.

Data is transmitted from Reader to Writer one sector at a time. The same process is repeated over and over for each sector of data until the entire data batch is transmitted. The last data batch may or may not contain ten tracks of data. For example, a disk volume that contains thirty-five tracks will be transmitted using three full data batches and a partial final data batch that contains five tracks. Since both the Client and the Server know the value of VOLTRKS, their respective Reader or Writer function know when the final track has been transmitted. The order of sector data transmission is always from sector 0x00 to sector VOLSECS-1 for each track, and from track 0x00 to track VOLTRKS-1.

As the Reader program reads each track of data from disk into computer memory, it records its activity by writing an ASCII R under its appropriate track number for the first 0x20 tracks. For track numbers beyond 0x20, it writes an ASCII R on the next line under its modulo 0x20 track number. This scheme does support a value for VOLTRKS up to sixty-four, but VOLTRKS is capped at forty-eight. As the Reader prepares and processes each sector for transmission, it records its activity by writing an ASCII R under its appropriate sector number up to a maximum of sixteen or thirty-two sectors. During the time the Reader is transmitting each sector of a given track, it records its track activity by writing an ASCII * in place of the previous ASCII R until the entire track has been transmitted. When all sectors have been transmitted, an ASCII + is used to replace the ASCII * in order to indicate that the entire track was transmitted successfully. Otherwise, a hexadecimal value from 0x01 to 0x0F is written in place of the ASCII * to indicated how many sectors were successfully transmitted for that track.

The preparation and processing of a sector before the sector data can be transmitted to the Writer program occurs in two steps. Certainly, there exists two major counters: TSTRACK and TSSECTOR. Both counters are initialized to zero by the Reader program. After the data for a sector is transmitted, the value of TSSECTOR is incremented until it reaches the value of VOLSECS. When that happens, TSSECTOR is reset to zero and TSTRACK is incremented until it reaches the value of VOLTRKS. When TSTRACK reaches VOLTRKS, the Reader program commands the Writer program to write the final data batch to its disk volume. In addition to these two counters, there is a third counter TRACKCNT that is initialized to BUFRTRKS, the number of tracks that comprise a data batch. The Reader program prepares the transmission of sector data by using the L command followed by the transmission of the contents of the TSDCB Data block. The size in bytes of the TSDCB Data block is given by TSDCBLEN, which is equal to four bytes. Once the Writer program receives the TSDCB Data block, it calculates its own values for TSDCBXOR and TSDCBSUM which are the two checksum variables that are found at the end of the TSDCB Data block. If the calculated values for these variables by the Writer equal the respective values in the TSDCB, the Writer returns the M command response, otherwise the Writer returns the N command response indicating a checksum mismatch error. If the Reader receives an N command response, the Reader will attempt to re-transmit the L command followed by the transmission of the contents of the TSDCB Data block. The Reader will attempt this re-transmission up to the number of retries that are assigned to the Reader which is the number of retries of whichever program is hosting the Reader, either CLNTRTRY or SRVRRTRY. The TSDCB Data block contents are shown in Table V.25.3 with a brief description for each entry. The Reader program will terminate with an error number when the number of retries is exceeded.

Entry	Index	Size	Value Range	Description
TSTRACK	0x00	0x01	0 to 47	Transfer track
TSSECTOR	0x01	0x01	0 to 31	Transfer sector
TSDCBXOR	0x02	0x01	0 to 255	Transfer checksum XOR
TSDCBSUM	0x03	0x01	0 to 255	Transfer checksum ADC

Table V.25.3. TSDCBTBL Track/Sector Data Control Block Table Contents

Once the Reader has communicated the information of which sector onto which track the sector data belongs, the Reader begins the second step which is the data transmission of sector data to the Writer program. The Reader program begins the transmission of sector data by sending the T command, then the transmission of sector data that is compressed in real time, and followed by the TXDCB Data block. The size in bytes of the TXDCB Data block is given by TXDCBLEN, which is equal to four bytes. Once the Writer program receives the TXDCB Data block, it calculates its own values for TXDCBBYT, TXDCBXOR, and TSDCBSUM which are the sector data contents in bytes and the checksum variables that are found in the TXDCB Data block. Because the contents of the sector data is compressed in real time to an unknown total number of bytes, the value in TXDCBBYT is not a known value until after data compression is complete. If the calculated values for these variables by the Writer equal the respective values in the TXDCB Data block, the Writer returns the U command response, otherwise the Writer returns the V command response indicating a data size error or a checksum mismatch error. If the Reader receives a V command response, the Reader will attempt to re-transmit the T command, then the transmission of the compressed sector data, and finally the TXDCB Data block. The Reader will attempt this re-transmission up to the number of retries that are assigned to the Reader which is the number of retries of whichever program is hosting the Reader, either CLNTRTRY or SRVRRTRY. The TXDCB Data Control Block contents are shown in Table V.25.4 with a brief description for each entry. The Reader program will terminate with an error number when the number of retries is exceeded.

362

Entry	Index	Size	Value Range	Description
TXDCBBYT	0x00	0x02	0 < n < 512 + 2	Transfer bytes
TXDCBXOR	0x02	0x01	0 to 255	Transfer checksum XOR
TXDCBSUM	0x03	0x01	0 to 255	Transfer checksum ADC

Table V.25.4. TXDCBTBL Transfer Data Control Block Table Contents

I developed the compression algorithm that is used to process a sector of data in real time exclusively for serial data transmission. There is **no** pre-processing required to determine the value for TXDCBBYT. TXDCBBYT, as well as TXDCBXOR and TXDCBSUM are continuously being determined while the sector data is processed, compressed, and transmitted in real time. Obviously, the Writer is processing and decompressing the sector data in parallel, and also in real time. Hopefully, the compression algorithm does not, in fact, cause more than 256 bytes of data to be transmitted, but there can exist certain data sets where this may occur, unfortunately. It is always a matter of weighing the benefits and the advantages of such an algorithm over the possible disadvantages that the algorithm might cause more data to be transmitted when the sector data contains many groups of identical byte-pairs.

The Client and Server programs initialize their Super Serial Slot Card to transmit serial data at the highest possible baud rate, which is 19,200 baud. That is, the Super Serial Slot Card is capable of transmitting one bit of information in a little over 52 microseconds. To transmit a full byte of information, a Super Serial Slot Card requires nearly 417 microseconds. A 6502-microprocessor operating at 1.0 MHz can certainly perform a great deal of work within 417 microseconds, the time the Super Serial Slot Card is transmitting the previous data byte. So, it is completely reasonable to be able to design a data compression algorithm as well as a data decompression algorithm that iterates through a sector of data: it looks for sequential data bytes that have the same value. As long as sector data bytes change in value from byte to byte, the sector data will be transmitted without modification. However, when two or more sequential bytes have the same value, that group of bytes will be transmitted uniquely as a sequence of three bytes: two bytes with the same value as sequential *duplicate* bytes and a third byte that is equal to the index of the next *different* byte. For example, if the next four bytes of sector data at index 0x10 are equal to 0x0A as in the ASL instruction four times, the transmitted data will be 0x0A, 0x0A, 0x14. When the Writer encounters sequential duplicate bytes, it understands that it is being directed to start filling its sector data buffer with the duplicate byte value until it reaches the index that is given by the byte immediately following the duplicate bytes. If these same four duplicate bytes come at the end of the sector data stream, the transmitted data will be 0x0A, 0x0A, 0x00. Obviously, the index value of 0x00 would be the index of the next sector data buffer, which really does not exist, but it is a value that also concludes the transmission of the duplicate compressed data for that sector. The next four bytes that are received by the Writer would be those bytes of the TXDCB.

One may reach the erroneous conclusion that the real time sector data compression algorithm will transmit only three data bytes when all of the data in a sector has the same value. Many times a disk volume will contain a few sectors that have not been utilized, and the data in those sectors will be set to 0x00 from the original initialization process of that disk volume. Unfortunately, it is not possible for the Writer to set all bytes in a sector to the same value within 417 microseconds so that the Writer will still be able to receive the four TXDCB bytes that follow. What happens, regrettably, is a hardware disconnect between Reader and Writer, synchronization is lost, and no further data can be correctly transmitted and/or received. I found this situation to be rather interesting and I studied it quite closely. The test programs that I developed which monitor all data transmission and data receive transactions essentially filled specific buffers with data that I could analyze when the compression algorithm loses synchronization and starts to go awry. I did not know what I was looking for initially, but as I started to accumulate more and more data transactions, the better I could refine my test programs and capture the specific data that helped me formulate a diagnosis. As with all remedies, I did not want the solution to be worse than the problem at hand, and I certainly wanted no impact, or at least minimal impact on the Writer decompression algorithm. In fact, the solution should not even affect the Writer, therefore leaving the entire management of the compression algorithm fully on the shoulders of the Reader.

```
:            :         :
15F5         459   ; Calculate the memory page for the sector and track values
15F5         460   ; contained in the Y-register and A-register, respectively.
15F5         461   ;
15F5         462   GETPAGE:
15F5 CD 34 19 463   ^1        cmp BUFRTRKS
15F8 90 05   464             bcc >2
15FA         465   ;
15FA ED 34 19 466             sbc BUFRTRKS
15FD 10 F6   467             bpl <1            ; always taken
15FF         468   ;
15FF 2C 35 19 469   ^2        bit BUFRFLAG
1602 10 01   470             bpl >3
1604         471   ;
1604 0A      472             asl
1605         473   ;
1605 AA      474   ^3        tax
1606         475   ;
1606 98      476             tya
1607 7D 57 19 477             adc TRACKTBL,X
160A         478   ;
160A 60      479             rts
:            :         :
1934         22   BUFRTRKS dfs 1,ZERO
1935         23   BUFRFLAG dfs 1,ZERO
:            :         :
1957 1E 2E 3E 44   TRACKTBL hex 1E2E3E4E5E
195A 4E 5E
195C 6E 7E 83 45             hex 6E7E8E9EAE
195F 9E AE
:            :         :
```

Figure V.25.11. Calculation of GETPAGE

My analysis of all of the test program data that I collected demonstrated that the Reader and the Writer programs will **not** lose synchronization as long as the Writer is not required to fill its sector data buffer with more than 0x40 consecutive data bytes having the same value. This was certainly very good news indeed, and it was a very simple modification to implement within the compression algorithm for the Reader program. When all 256 bytes of a data sector are identical in value, any value, that sector can be transmitted using just twelve bytes. Those twelve bytes can be generated, transmitted, and expanded to completely fill the memory buffer of a specific data sector in real time within the time that is required for the transmission of duplicate bytes and an index. Assuming an initialized sector is zero-filled, the twelve bytes that would be transmitted to the Writer program would be: 0x00, 0x00, 0x40, 0x00, 0x00, 0x80,

`0x00, 0x00, 0xC0, 0x00, 0x00, 0x00`. The time to transmit these twelve bytes would be approximately 5.0 milliseconds rather than 106.7 milliseconds in order to transmit the entire sector of 256 bytes that have the same value. Accumulatively, this would amount to a very substantial time savings if many such sectors comprised the bulk of a disk volume. What is most incredible about my sector data compression algorithm is that it is applied continuously, in real time, to all consecutive bytes of sector data that have the same value without requiring **any** sector data pre-processing.

I know that *A2V2* and *ADT* both assume that when the sector data of one sector is fully transmitted, the sector number whose data will be transmitted next will be one less than the previous sector number. In other words, sector number is decremented in descending order in these two programs. Sector number is first initialized to `0x0F`, decremented until it becomes negative, and re-initialized to `0x0F` while track number is incremented. When track number becomes equal to `0x23`, *A2V2* and *ADT* are both finished transmitting and receiving sector data. My solution in communicating both sector and track number using the TSDCB ensures that both the Reader and the Writer programs are addressing the same relative page of data in memory. The variables TSSECTOR and TSTRACK are used to calculate the memory page number from where the sector data is read or to where the sector data is written using a very simple look-up table which can actually be generated programmatically. The routine that calculates GETPAGE is shown in Figure V.25.11. If the disk volumes both have tracks that contain sixteen sectors, BUFRTRKS contains the value of `0x0A` and BUFRFLAG contains the value of `0x00`. On the other hand, if these tracks contain thirty-two sectors, BUFRTRKS contains the value of `0x05` and BUFRFLAG contains the value of `0xFF`. The target page number is returned in the A-register and saved to a page-zero pointer.

When the Reader program begins its processing, the very first call it makes is to GETRACKS in order to fill its memory with the contents of the first ten tracks, or five tracks if the volume has tracks containing thirty-two sectors, of its target disk volume. Later in its processing when the TRACKCNT variable becomes zero, the Reader program calls the SNDRWDCB routine to inform the Writer program that it is time to write its accumulated memory contents, or final data batch to its target disk volume. The RWDCB provides the Writer with all of the information it requires in order to write a data batch to its target disk volume. The Reader program prefaces the transmission of the RWDCB by using the O command followed by the transmission of the contents of the RWDCB Data block. The size in bytes of the RWDCB Data block is given by RWDCBLEN, which is equal to four bytes. Once the Writer program receives the RWDCB Data block, it calculates its own values for RWDCBXOR and RWDCBSUM which are the two checksum variables that are found at the end of the RWDCB Data block. If the calculated values for these variables by the Writer equal the respective values in the RWDCB, the Writer returns the P command response, otherwise the Writer returns the Q command response indicating a checksum mismatch error. If the Reader receives a Q command response, the Reader will attempt to re-transmit the O command followed by the transmission of the contents of the RWDCB Data block. The Reader will attempt this re-transmission up to the number of retries that are assigned for the Reader which is the number of retries of whichever program is hosting the Reader, either CLNTRTRY or SRVRRTRY. The RWDCB Data block contents are shown in Table V.25.5 with a brief description for each entry. The Reader program will terminate with an error number when the number of retries is exceeded.

Once the Writer program receives the O command from the Reader program, the Writer calls the RCVRWDCB routine so that it can receive the RWDCB Data block in order to have the parameters that are necessary before the PUTRACKS routine is called. Working in parallel with the Writer, the Reader program calls GETRACKS in order to fill its memory with the next data batch unless its TSTRACK has reached the value found in LASTTRK which was originally initialized to the value found in VOLTRKS that is found in the CFDCB Data Control Block. After the Reader completes its work in preparation to transmit the next data batch, the Reader waits for the P command response from the Writer before it can continue any further processing. Essentially, this gives the Writer all the time it requires in order to write the data batch that is saved in its memory to its target disk volume. After the Writer completes writing data to its disk volume, it sends the P command response to the Reader. If the Reader takes longer to fill its memory with the next data batch that it reads from its disk volume, the P command response will already be available to the Reader when it reads its Super Serial input data register.

Entry	Index	Size	Value Range	Description
RWTRACK	0x00	0x01	0 to 47	Start track
NTRACKS	0x01	0x01	0 to BUFRTRKS	Number of tracks to R/W
RWDCBXOR	0x02	0x01	0 to 255	Transfer checksum XOR
RWDCBSUM	0x03	0x01	0 to 255	Transfer checksum ADC

Table V.25.5. RWDCBTBL Read/Write Data Control Block Table Contents

One may rightfully reach the conclusion that many bytes of control data are transmitted to the Writer program and many bytes of response data are transmitted to the Reader program. I happen to strongly agree with that assessment. I could have followed more closely the design method that is used by the *A2V2/ADT* software programs, but I was more intrigued with the micro-management control that is used in my data transmission design. The transmission of the various ASCII commands and their associated DCB Data blocks is rather minimal overhead, in my opinion, and they provide extraordinary control over the transmission of the contents of a disk volume from one Apple computer to another Apple computer. One needs to realize that the Client and Server programs, like all other programs, are designed with a certain underlying strategy such that they can be developed quickly, effortlessly, and flawlessly. I have always designed software with parallel *unit testing* in mind. When all of the individual pieces of a software program have been *unit tested*, or tested individually outside of the scope of a program, there is a very strong likelihood that when those individual pieces of software are combined, the completed program will more than likely perform as designed. Other software engineers may utilize another strategy when they design their software. I would always consider another approach to software design if I thought its strategies would provide me with a similar end product and its implementation would require less effort.

The Client and Server software programs contain many potential locations where failure of one kind or another can terminate the transmission of sector data. Of course, the user may terminate data transmission at any time by pressing the ESCAPE key on either computer. And, the user may pause data transmission at any time by pressing any other key on either computer. Why one would want to pause data transmission is questionable, but nevertheless its function is available. Pausing data transmission will simply increase the total time that data transmission is active, and that will factor into the calculation of data transmission rate. I could have factored out all of the time that data transmission is paused, but it seemed like too much work for a rarely used, if at all, feature. Because of the high volatility of potential transmission errors beyond what can easily be accommodated, I designed a very large set of error codes that would precisely indicate where a transmission error occurs in either software program. Because there is so much time that is available between the transmission of one data byte and the next data byte, pre-loading a register with an error code that would point to a transmission error at that precise location in the software would not affect the overall transmission rate whatsoever. And this is precisely the technique I employed in order to assist me in performing Client/Server program unit and verification testing and Client/Server program functional testing with real time error reporting. A very comprehensive list of routines that are found in the Client and Server programs that can generate an error code is shown in Tables V.25.6 and V.25.7. The Client/Server functional design allocates a group of error codes to specific routine functions rather than assigning error codes sequentially. Either method would be acceptable, but I considered this approach to have far more organization as well as far more ease in adding additional errors to a routine function if it should become necessary.

The SSC00 routines for transmit or TX and for receive or RX do not wait indefinitely for an empty ACIA transmit or receive register, respectively. These two routines will wait until the X-register has counted no more than 256 iterations of a sixteen microsecond loop that tests for DCD or Data Carrier Detect and DSR or Data Set Ready to be both TRUE. If this loop counter should expire, the routine will simply return with the carry flag **set**, otherwise the carry flag is returned **clear** after writing data to the transmit register or reading data from the receive register. The transmit register and the receive register are actually the same ACIA register, and the function of this register is determined simply by how it is utilized. The SSC80 routines for transmit and for receive will wait indefinitely for an empty ACIA transmit or receive register, respectively. There is no way to interrupt the eleven microsecond loop that tests for DCD and DSR to be both TRUE. Inspection of Tables V.25.6 and V.25.7 show that if the Client program or the Server program appears to be hanged, more than likely it is due to a call to the RXSSC80 routine. Throughout all of my testing I have yet to document a failure in reading the ACIA Data register. It would be terribly inconvenient if it is necessary to differentiate the press of the ESCAPE key if it should be captured in a call to the RXSSC80 routine rather than captured from the GETKEY routine which is far more desirable. Again, the RXSSC80 routine cannot be interrupted.

Several of the Client and Server routines require a call to the GETKEY function in order to obtain input direction from the user. It is during these routines where the user may immediately terminate the Client or Server program. Less immediate are the routines that utilize the GETKEY function that simply require any press of a key. If the ESCAPE key should be pressed, then responsible action will be taken when it is most appropriate to do so. For example, if the ESCAPE key is pressed while sector data is being transmitted, it would not be appropriate to interrupt that function until the data transfer has completed. Delaying the response to the ESCAPE keypress until after the transmission of sector data has completed would leave the Super Serial card registers in a far better state. Furthermore, if the key press is not the ESCAPE key and sector data is being transmitted, that key press would be interpreted as a command to pause further transmission of sector data once the current transmission of data has completed. That is the implementation that is used for the Reader routine. Before the Reader sends the TSDCB Data block, the keyboard is checked for any keypress. This would be the most appropriate time to pause sector data transmission. On the other hand, the Writer checks the keyboard for any keypress after receiving the TSDCB but before responding with the M response after it has successfully verified the TSDCB checksum bytes. That would be the most appropriate time to pause sector data transmission because the Reader can wait forever for the M response without losing synchronization with the other computer.

Tables V.25.8 and V.25.9 transform the information that is found in Tables V.25.6 and V.25.7 as well as provide additional information about each error code, the routine that issues that error code, and the calling routines. Of course, the user would be required to have a copy of the Client and the Server software source code listing in order to fully appreciate the precise reason why any particular error code is generated. Considering all of the data that is transmitted to and from the Reader and the Writer functions, approximately 268 bytes of data are transmitted for every sector of data assuming that the data transmission is for all of the data bytes in a sector, and that every sector is filled with data that contains no sequential duplicate bytes. For a volume that contains thirty-five tracks, this amounts to transmitting approximately 150,080 bytes of data without incurring an error. This is quite a significant benchmark to achieve, and to be able to repeat this performance every single time is simply outstanding.

I am often amazed how easy this benchmark can be achieved with the Apple][computer, with its accessory vintage hardware, and with such an ancient, though exceedingly reliable communication protocol such as RS232. But, indeed, the Client and Server programs perform this function flawlessly. Voltage spikes, noise, lost data bits, skewed timing, and a host of many other problems can cause failure during the transmission of sector data. When such intermittent failures occur, there is sufficient logic in the Client and in the Server programs to handle a modest level of failure. However, when there are serious communication problems, no level of error handling will ever be adequate.

The Client program obtains the current time of day and date by indirectly jumping to the RDCLKVSN vector at 0x03E1 with the carry flag **clear**, which is the protocol in DOS 4.5 to obtain the date and time data. DOS 4.5 fills the supplied 6-byte CLKBUFR, whose address is in the Y- and A-registers, with three bytes of time data and three bytes of date data. This data is suppled in Binary-Coded Decimal or BCD format. In order to calculate elapsed transmission time, a call is made to RDCLKVSN before transitioning to the Reader/Writer functions and after returning from the Reader/Writer functions only in the Client program. The 6502-microprocessor can perform BCD arithmetic after it has processed the SED or Set Decimal instruction. Once the BCD arithmetic is complete, the 6502-microprocessor must be returned to hexadecimal mode by processing the CLD or Clear Decimal instruction. The two BCD time buffers must be subtracted in order to obtain elapsed time in seconds. The math is trivial knowing that there are 3600 seconds in one delta hour and 60 seconds in one delta minute. The total amount of data in bytes that is transferred from one Apple][computer to another Apple][computer is calculated by the successive addition of 0x4096 when VOLSECS is sixteen or 0x8192 when VOLSECS is thirty-two in a processing loop that is iterated VOLTRKS times. As shown in Figures V.25.12 and V.25.13, the Client program displays how many bytes are transferred and the number of elapsed seconds that transpired for that data transfer to take place both as decimal values, and utilizing hexadecimal display routines that are found in the ROM Monitor. These calculations demonstrate the power in using the BCD Data format for integer values when the 6502-microprocessor is set to decimal mode. This is the first opportunity I have had to utilize BCD arithmetic for date and time values when I chose to represent date and time with the BCD format in the design of DOS 4.5. I believe the simplicity of these calculations demonstrate that I did indeed make the best design choice in choosing the BCD format to represent date and time in DOS 4.5.

```
 Client Serial Communication

                              Client   Server
                              ------   ------
Number of Retries        -       3        3
Volume Slot    Number    -       6        6
Volume Drive   Number    -      01       01
Volume Volume  Number    -     000      000
Volume Phase   Number    -      04       04

Transfer Direction       - Client->Server
Server Volume Verify     - Write Check
Volume Tracks/Sectors    -      35       16

Volume Transfer State    - Data Transfer
Communication   State    - Synchronized

         0123456789ABCDEF0123456789ABCDEF
Track    ++++++++++++++++++++++++++++++++
         +++
Sector

  Moved 143360 bytes in 000165 seconds
         Press any key to continue
```

Figure V.25.12. Client Transfer Complete

```
 Server Serial Communication

                              Client   Server
                              ------   ------
Number of Retries        -       3        3
Volume Slot    Number    -       6        6
Volume Drive   Number    -      01       01
Volume Volume  Number    -     000      000
Volume Phase   Number    -      04       04

Transfer Direction       - Client->Server
Server Volume Verify     - Write Check
Volume Tracks/Sectors    -      35       16

Volume Transfer State    - Data Transfer
Communication   State    - Synchronized

         0123456789ABCDEF0123456789ABCDEF
Track    WWWWWWWWWWWWWWWWWWWWWWWWWWWWWWWW
         WWW
Sector
```

Figure V.25.13. Server Transfer Complete

Routine	SSC00		SSC80		GETKEY	Error Number	Description
	TX	RX	TX	RX			
MAIN	F					01-02	
FINDSSC						10	C-flag set if SSC not found
INITSSC						[14-17]	resets, enables SSC registers; sets baud rate
AUTOSYNC	A^	(B)			18	[19-1F]	AUTOSYNC terminated by ESC keypress
EDITMENU					21	20	CLSRRUN = 2 or ESC; causes H to be sent
SHOWMENU						[28-2F]	no error handling; returns C-flag clear
CHK4DISK	R			(H, S)	36,37	30,34	extract CFDCB, CALLRWTS/RWTSREAD
DOREADER				(S)	47	40,41	SNDTSDCB, SNDTXDCB, SNDRWDCB, GETRACKS
DOWRITER	S			(H, O, S, T)		50,54-55	RCVRWDCB, PUTRACKS, RCVTXDCB, RCVTSDCB
SNDCFDCB*	C, CFDCB			(D, E)		60-65	send C, CFDCB; get D, E; return CLC, ESC
SNDTSDCB*	L, TSDCB			(M, N)		70-73	send L, TSDCB; get M, N; return CLC, ESC
RCVTSDCB	M, N	TSDCB				78-79	get TSDCB; send M, N; return CLC, ESC
SNDRWDCB*	O, RWDCB			(P, Q)		80-82	send O, RWDCB; get P, Q; return CLC, ESC
RCVRWDCB	P, Q	RWDCB				88-89	get RWDCB; send P, Q; return CLC, ESC
SNDTXDCB*	T, TXDCB			(U, V)		90-92	send T, TXDCB; get U, V; return CLC, ESC
RCVTXDCB	U, V	TXDCB				98-99	get TXDCB; send U, V; return CLC, ESC
PUTDATA	data					A0-A4	TX loop timeout
GETDATA		data				B0-B2	RX loop timeout
GETRACKS						C0-C1	calls CALLRWTS with RWTSREAD
PUTRACKS						D0	calls CALLRWTS with RWTSWRIT
EXITPGM			H				jumps to DOSCOLD

* = uses NRETRIES   ^ = no timeout   (*,*) = looking for   [*-*] = available, not used

Table V.25.6. Error Handling Error Codes for Client Routines

Routine	SSC00		SSC80		GETKEY	Error Number	Description
	TX	RX	TX	RX			
FINDSSC						10	C-flag set if SSC not found
AUTOSYNC	B			(H, A)		18-19	look for H, A
SHOWMENU						[28-2F]	no error handling; returns C-flag clear
CHK4DISK	R			(H, S)	37	30,34	extract CFDCB, CALLRWTS/RWTSREAD
DOREADER				(S)	47	40-41	SNDTSDCB, SNDTXDCB, SNDRWDCB, GETRACKS
DOWRITER	S			(H, O, S, T)		50,54-55	RCVRWDCB, PUTRACKS, RCVTXDCB, RCVTSDCB
RCVCFDCB	D, E	CFDCB		(H, C)		68-69	get CFDCB; send D, E; return CLC, ESC
SNDTSDCB*	L, TSDCB			(M, N)		70-73	send L, TSDCB; get M, N; return CLC, ESC
RCVTSDCB	M, N	TSDCB				78-79	get TSDCB; send M, N; return CLC, ESC
SNDRWDCB*	O, RWDCB			(P, Q)		80-82	send O, RWDCB; get P, Q; return CLC, ESC
RCVRWDCB	P, Q	RWDCB				88-89	get RWDCB; send P, Q; return CLC, ESC
SNDTXDCB*	T, DXDCB			(U, V)		90-92	send T, TXDCB; get U, V; return CLC, ESC
RCVTXDCB	U, V	TXDCB				98-99	get TXDCB; send U, V; return CLC, ESC
PUTDATA	data					A0-A4	TX loop timeout
GETDATA		data				B0-B2	RX loop timeout
GETRACKS						C0-C1	calls CALLRWTS with RWTSREAD
PUTRACKS						D0	calls CALLRWTS with RWTSWRIT
EXITPGM			H				jumps to DOSCOLD

* = uses NRETRIES   ^ = no timeout   (*,*) = looking for   [*-*] = available, not used

Table V.25.7. Error Handling Error Codes for Server Routines

Error	Error Name	Set in Routine	Called by Routine	Description
01	MAIN1.E	START	CLIENT	received carry set from call to PRESNCLR
02	MAIN2.E	START	CLIENT	received carry set from call to TXSSC00
10	FSSC.E	FINDSSC	INITPGM	unable to find a Super Serial Card in a slot
18	ASYNC.E	AUTOSYNC	CLIENT	received carry set from call to GETKEY
20	EMENU1.E	EDITMENU	START	when value of CLSRRUN becomes 2 (QUIT)
21	EMENU2.E	EDITMENU	START	received carry set from call to EDIT subprogram
30	CHK4D1.E	CHK4DISK	START	received carry set from call to TXSSC00
34	CHK4D2.E	CHK4DISK	START	received H from call to RXSSC80
36	CHK4D3.E	CHK4DISK	START	received carry set from call to PRESNCLR
37	CHK4D4.E	CHK4DISK	START	received carry set from call to PRESNCLR
40	READ1.E	DOREADER	START	did not receive S from call to RXSSC80
41	READ2.E	DOREADER	START	did not receive S from call to RXSSC80
47	READ3.E	DOREADER	START	received carry set from call to GETKEY
50	WRIT1.E	DOWRITER	START	received carry set from call to TXSSC00
54	WRIT2.E	DOWRITER	START	received H from call to RXSSC80
55	WRIT3.E	DOWRITER	START	received H from call to RXSSC80
60	SNDCF1.E	SNDCFDCB	START	received carry set from call to TXSSC00
61	SNDCF1.E+1	SNDCFDCB	EDITMENU	received carry set from call to TXSSC00
62	SNDCF2.E	SNDCFDCB	START	received carry set from call to TXSSC00
63	SNDCF2.E+1	SNDCFDCB	EDITMENU	received carry set from call to TXSSC00
64	SNDCF3.E	SNDCFDCB	START	RETRYCNT is zero or did not receive D or E
65	SNDCF3.E+1	SNDCFDCB	EDITMENU	RETRYCNT is zero or did not receive D or E
70	SNDTS1.E	SNDTSDCB	DOREADER	received carry set from call to TXSSC00
71	SNDTS2.E	SNDTSDCB	DOREADER	received carry set from call to TXSSC00
72	SNDTS3.E	SNDTSDCB	DOREADER	received H from call to RXSSC80
73	SNDTS4.E	SNDTSDCB	DOREADER	RETRYCNT is zero or did not receive M or N
78	RCVTS1.E	RCVTSDCB	DOWRITER	received carry set from call to RXSSC00
79	RCVTS2.E	RCVTSDCB	DOWRITER	received carry set from call to TXSSC00
80	SNDRW1.E	SNDRWDCB	DOREADER	received carry set from call to TXSSC00
81	SNDRW2.E	SNDRWDCB	DOREADER	received carry set from call to TXSSC00
82	SNDRW3.E	SNDRWDCB	DOREADER	RETRYCNT is zero or did not receive P or Q
88	RCVRW1.E	RCVRWDCB	DOWRITER	received carry set from call to RXSSC00
89	RCVRW2.E	RCVRWDCB	DOWRITER	received carry set from call to TXSSC00
90	SNDTX1.E	SNDTXDCB	DOREADER	received carry set from call to TXSSC00
91	SNDTX2.E	SNDTXDCB	DOREADER	received carry set from call to TXSSC00
92	SNDTX3.E	SNDTXDCB	DOREADER	RETRYCNT is zero or did not receive U or V
98	RCVTX1.E	RCVTXDCB	DOWRITER	received carry set from call to RXSSC00
99	RCVTX2.E	RCVTXDCB	DOWRITER	received carry set from call to TXSSC00
A0	PDATA1.E	PUTDATA	SNDTXDCB	received carry set from call to TXDATA4
A1	PDATA2.E	TXDATA4	PUTDATA	received carry set from call to TXSSC00
A2	PDATA2.E+1	PUTDATA	SNDTXDCB	received carry set from call to TXDATA2
A3	PDATA3.E	TXDATA2	PUTDATA	received carry set from call to TXSSC00
A4	PDATA3.E+1	PUTDATA	SNDTXDCB	received carry set from call to TXDATA2
B0	GDATA1.E	GETDATA	RCVTXDCB	received carry set from call to RXDATA2
B1	GDATA2.E	GETDATA	RCVTXDCB	received carry set from call to RXDATA2
B2	GDATA3.E	GETDATA	RCVTXDCB	received carry set from call to RXDATA2
C0	GTRACK.E	GETRACKS	DOREADER	received carry set from call to PRTRWERR
C1	GTRACK.E+1	GETRACKS	DOREADER	received carry set from call to PRTRWERR
D0	PTRACK.E	PUTRACKS	DOWRITER	received carry set from call to PRTRWERR

Table V.25.8. Client Source Routines for Error Codes

Error	Error Name	Set in Routine	Called by Routine	Description
10	FSSC.E	FINDSSC	INITPGM	unable to find a Super Serial Card in a slot
18	ASYNC1.E	AUTOSYNC	SERVER	received H from call to RXSSC80
19	ASYNC2.E	AUTOSYNC	SERVER	received carry set from call to TXSSC00
30	CHK4C1.E	CHK4DISK	START	received carry set from call to TXSSC00
34	CHK4C2.E	CHK4DISK	START	received H from call to RXSSC80
37	CHK4C3.E	CHK4DISK	START	received carry set from call to PRESNCLR
40	READ1.E	DOREADER	START	did not receive S from call to RXSSC80
41	READ2.E	DOREADER	START	did not receive S from call to RXSSC80
47	READ3.E	DOREADER	START	received carry set from call to GETKEY
50	WRIT1.E	DOWRITER	START	received carry set from call to TXSSC00
54	WRIT2.E	DOWRITER	START	received H from call to RXSSC80
55	WRIT3.E	DOWRITER	START	received H from call to RXSSC80
68	RCVCF1.E	RCVCFDCB	START	received carry set from call to RXSSC00
69	RCVCF2.E	RCVCFDCB	START	received carry set from call to TXSSC00
70	SNDTS1.E	SNDTSDCB	DOREADER	received carry set from call to TXSSC00
71	SNDTS2.E	SNDTSDCB	DOREADER	received carry set from call to TXSSC00
72	SNDTS3.E	SNDTSDCB	DOREADER	received H from call to RXSSC80
73	SNDTS4.E	SNDTSDCB	DOREADER	RETRYCNT is zero or did not receive M or N
78	RCVTS1.E	RCVTSDCB	DOWRITER	received carry set from call to RXSSC00
79	RCVTS2.E	RCVTSDCB	DOWRITER	received carry set from call to TXSSC00
80	SNDRW1.E	SNDRWDCB	DOREADER	received carry set from call to TXSSC00
81	SNDRW2.E	SNDRWDCB	DOREADER	received carry set from call to TXSSC00
82	SNDRW3.E	SNDRWDCB	DOREADER	RETRYCNT is zero or did not receive P or Q
88	RCVRW1.E	RCVRWDCB	DOWRITER	received carry set from call to RXSSC00
89	RCVRW2.E	RCVRWDCB	DOWRITER	received carry set from call to TXSSC00
90	SNDTX1.E	SNDTXDCB	DOREADER	received carry set from call to TXSSC00
91	SNDTX2.E	SNDTXDCB	DOREADER	received carry set from call to TXSSC00
92	SNDTX3.E	SNDTXDCB	DOREADER	RETRYCNT is zero or did not receive U or V
98	RCVTX1.E	RCVTXDCB	DOWRITER	received carry set from call to RXSSC00
99	RCVTX2.E	RCVTXDCB	DOWRITER	received carry set from call to TXSSC00
A0	PDATA1.E	PUTDATA	SNDTXDCB	received carry set from call to TXDATA4
A1	PDATA2.E	TXDATA4	PUTDATA	received carry set from call to TXSSC00
A2	PDATA2.E+1	PUTDATA	SNDTXDCB	received carry set from call to TXDATA2
A3	PDATA3.E	TXDATA2	PUTDATA	received carry set from call to TXSSC00
A4	PDATA3.E+1	PUTDATA	SNDTXDCB	received carry set from call to TXDATA2
B0	GDATA1.E	GETDATA	RCVTXDCB	received carry set from call to RXDATA2
B1	GDATA2.E	GETDATA	RCVTXDCB	received carry set from call to RXDATA2
B2	GDATA3.E	GETDATA	RCVTXDCB	received carry set from call to RXDATA2
C0	GTRACK.E	GETRACKS	DOREADER	received carry set from call to PRTRWERR
C1	GTRACK.E+1	GETRACKS	DOREADER	received carry set from call to PRTRWERR
D0	PTRACK.E	PUTRACKS	DOWRITER	received carry set from call to PRTRWERR

Table V.25.9. Server Source Routines for Error Codes

26.   CHAR Editor and LENGTH Programs

I was thrilled when I obtained my copy of Sierra On-Line's *ScreenWriter* product years before I finally invested in a Videx UltraTerm video display card. *ScreenWriter*, copyrighted by David Kidwell in 1982, was able to display up to seventy various graphic characters on a HIRES mixed graphics screen whose character font was designed to be only as wide as the graphic character needed to be. Upper case characters were compressed in width, but they were still seven pixels high. The lower case characters were also compressed in width, and they extended below the line. Combined together, the entire font used the full eight pixels in height similar to what is required in a normal mixed-case Text line. *ScreenWriter* did not provide a blank single-pixel line between text lines in order to help assist in making its font more readable on my Amdek color monitor. It was not until several years later did I discover that the embedded RUNOFF commands that are used by *ScreenWriter* are modeled after an IBM mainframe word processor that I used extensively in order to document my Preliminary Design Reviews or PDR and my Critical Design Reviews or CDR for software that I developed while I was employed at Hughes Aircraft Company. And, it didn't take me long to find the code in *ScreenWriter* that was used to draw its graphic characters onto the HIRES screen of my Apple][+. When I was first employed by Sierra, I assisted in converting *ScreenWriter* to utilize the Apple //e 80-Column text card. My Videx UltraTerm video display card would never support the new *ScreenWriter* for the Apple //e.

ScreenWriter utilizes a data table that contains the width in pixels for each of its graphic characters and graphic symbols. This table is used extensively to determine if the next word and the single pixel space between words can be displayed on the current line without overflowing the right side of the HIRES screen. *ScreenWriter* did a fantastic job in moving words from one line to another line as characters are added to the current line while in Insert Mode or as characters are deleted from the current line while in Change Mode. The pixel width table is also consulted anytime a group of words are centered on a line. Centering calculations are easy to execute simply by subtracting the sum of all font, symbol, and space between characters in pixels from 40 columns * 7 pixels/column = 280, and logically shifting half that difference to the right. Thus, words could be drawn starting at a calculated number of pixels from the left side of the HIRES screen. This pixel number can be converted to a byte index or window number that ranged from 0x00 to 0x27 and a bit index or cell number that ranged from 0x00 to 0x06. Using these two indices enables any character string to be drawn anywhere on the current line or on any other line with the understanding that each byte index contains seven HIRES pixels.

I adapted the **concept** of the *ScreenWriter* HIRES graphic font characters for *BFI* and I developed the *CHAR Editor* and the *LENGTH* programs to support that effort. And, I modeled *CHAR Editor* from my previous program that I called *EDITROM*. I described *EDITROM* in Section II.6 and this program uses LORES graphics in order to assist in the creation of the HIRES screen font for *BFI*. I only had to create the graphic font characters from ASCII 0x20 to 0x7F and not the graphic symbols that are used in *ScreenWriter* since I had no use for those symbols. Unlike the *ScreenWriter* graphic characters, the *BFI* upper case graphic characters are only six pixels high so they are not as tall and compressed. Combined with the lower case graphic characters, the entire *BFI* font is only seven pixels high. These ninety-six graphic characters require ninety-six bytes of data for each of the seven character data tables, one table for each scan line, and there is an additional table that contains forty-eight entries that is called the character width table. The goal in designing a HIRES screen font is to use the smallest width that is practical for each of the font characters and still allow each character to be understood. The brain does an admirable job in filling in what the eyes do not necessarily see, and typically a person will recognize a word when, at the minimum, only the first two and/or the last two characters of the word are clearly recognized. Certain symbols like $ and & can only be created when their widths are five pixels, but their usage is not that frequent. Similarly, letters like M and W can only be understood when their widths are also five pixels. Even though the graphic representation of a character using LORES graphics appears to be boxy in *CHAR Editor*, when that graphic character is displayed on the HIRES screen, its edges do not appear as sharp because the brain tends to smooth out all of those sharp transitional edges.

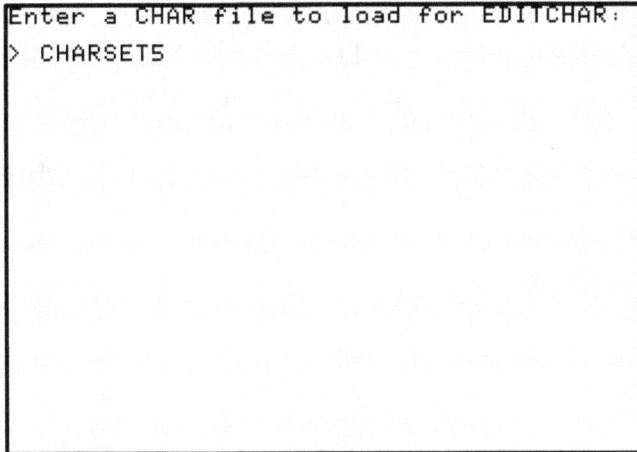

Figure V.26.1. Load CHAR File for EDITCHAR

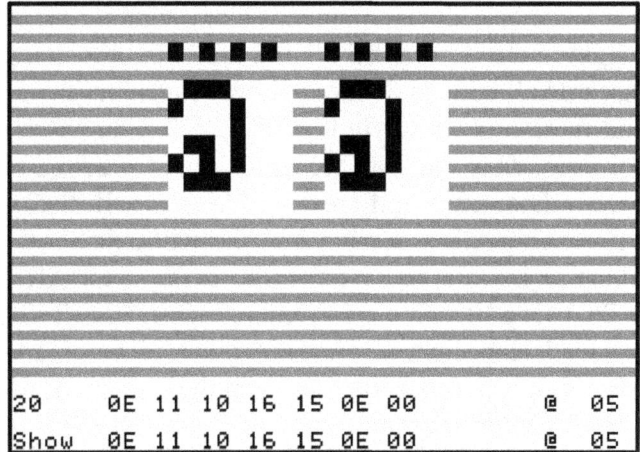

Figure V.26.2. CHAR Data Show Mode

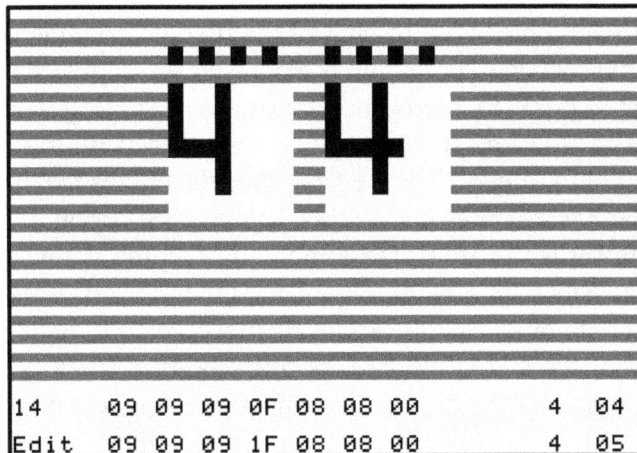

Figure V.26.3. CHAR Data Edit Mode

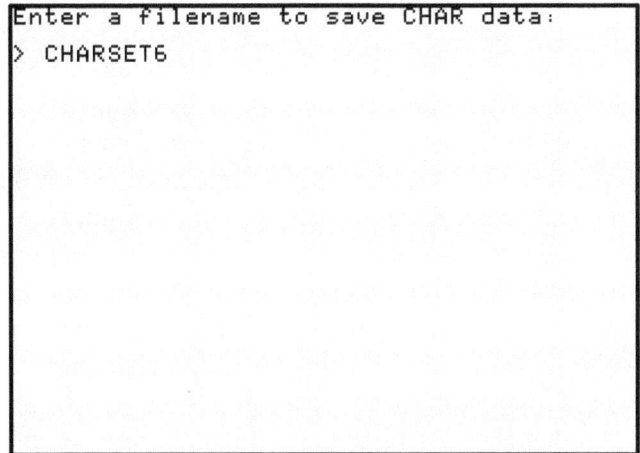

Figure V.26.4. Save CHAR Data for EDITCHAR

To begin a graphic character font editing session with *CHAR Editor*, a suitable filename for CHAR Data may be entered as shown in Figure V.26.1. Simply press RETURN if there is no new CHAR Data file to read. The complete CHAR Data file is 7 * 96 + 48 = 720 bytes in size and it is read into memory at memory address 0x0E80. There is no particular rationale for this load address; it is where the program *CHAR Editor* ends in memory. Figure V.26.2 shows the LORES display of the character @ entry in the CHAR Data file and four lines of Text at the bottom of the display. Line twenty-two in this display shows the HEX offset of the character @ in the CHAR Data, the seven bytes of character DATA, one byte from each of the seven tables, how the character is currently displayed by the Apple][for normal text, and its width in pixels. There are two modes of operation that are used in *CHAR Editor*: Show Mode and Edit Mode. Show Mode simply duplicates the LORES character that is displayed on the left side and displays that character on the right side of the screen, and the character DATA that is displayed on line twenty-two is duplicated on line twenty-four. As in *EDITROM*, there are only four commands that are used in Show Mode: B goes back one character, E enters Edit Mode, RETURN displays the next character, and ESCAPE exits the program. Each character is initially displayed in Show Mode.

There are only three commands along with the arrow key movements that are used in Edit Mode: SPACE toggles a character pixel ON and OFF, RETURN saves all edits to memory and enters Show Mode, ESCAPE discards all edits and enters Show Mode, and the arrow keys move the pixel cursor up and down or left and right. As shown in Figure V.26.3, Edit Mode updates the character DATA on line twenty-four that corresponds to the LORES character as it is edited on the **right** side of the screen. Pressing RETURN will accept those edits and pressing ESCAPE will discard those edits. Once all edits have been made to the CHAR character, pressing ESCAPE will exit Show Mode and the *CHAR Editor* program will ask for a filename in order to save the 720 bytes of CHAR Data that is currently in memory as shown in Figure V.26.4. If a filename is not entered when *CHAR Editor* begins or when *CHAR Editor* exits, no file is read or saved, respectively. The DOS 4.5 DIFF command can be used to compare both the input and the output CHAR files in order to ensure that the output CHAR file contains only those edits that were made by the CHAR *Editor* program.

For those who are interested in understanding the correspondence with CHAR Data and the display of that data by the Apple][HIRES hardware, a few data samples will easily illustrate their relationship by saving those data samples to the HIRES graphics screen. On the Apple Command Line enter HGR and then enter CALL-151. Assuming MIXEDON or 0xC053 is enabled, enter 2000:1 and 2400:40 on the Monitor Command Line. Now you will see that the least significant bit or LSB or bit 0 of the first data sample is displayed to the far left of the screen whereas bit 6 of the second data sample is displayed seven pixels to the right of the far left of the screen. Therefore, the Apple][HIRES hardware processes data starting with the LSB to the MSB and displays that data from left to right, respectively. The same hardware logic displays the CHAR Data in the same fashion. Looking at Figure V.26.3, the first three data bytes for the edited character 4 that is displayed on the right side of the screen is 0x09. In this data, the LSB or bit 0 is ON. The next two bits in the data while moving left towards the MSB, are zero, thus keeping the next two pixels OFF while moving to the right of the screen. Since bit 3 is ON in the data, the top pixel of the right column of the character 4 is also ON. The fourth data byte, or 0x1F turns all five pixels ON, which becomes the new width for the edited character. All of the CHAR characters from 0x20 to 0x7F are designed to begin its character pixels on the far left column of the display and utilize the smallest pixel width that is practical, thus leaving the character understandable. I would not consider the edited version of the character 4 as shown in Figure V.26.3 to be practical. Figure V.26.5 shows all of the graphic characters in the CHAR font file that is used in *BFI*.

The String Draw or SD program that is mentioned in Section V.2 that discusses Binary File Installation is used to draw any character string variable on a HIRES screen at any location on that screen. The interface to SD is defined by its CALL statement: CALL SD,S$[,H%,L%,W%,C%,I%]. In other words, at a minimum SD only requires a string variable S$ in its CALL statement and the other parameters in the CALL statement are optional. As previously discussed, the SD routine begins at 0x6000 in memory. The H% parameter sets the MSB of the HIRES page to 0x20 or 0x40, otherwise the parameter is ignored if it is set to 0x00. The L% parameter tells SD on which screen line to draw S$, and its valid values range from 0 to 23. The W% parameter defines the window to begin drawing in, and its valid values range from 0 to 39. This parameter corresponds to the character byte number on a normal Text screen line. The C% parameter defines the cell within the current window in which to begin drawing, and its valid values range from 0 to

6. This parameter corresponds to the bit number that is within a character byte. Both the W% and the C% parameter values are returned to the caller only if one or both of these parameters are included in the CALL statement once SD processing has completed and S$ has been drawn. The I% parameter enables the drawing of S$ in INVERSE anytime I% is not zero. Once SD processing has completed and S$ has been drawn, I% is automatically reset to zero.

Figure V.26.5. Complete BFI CHAR Font

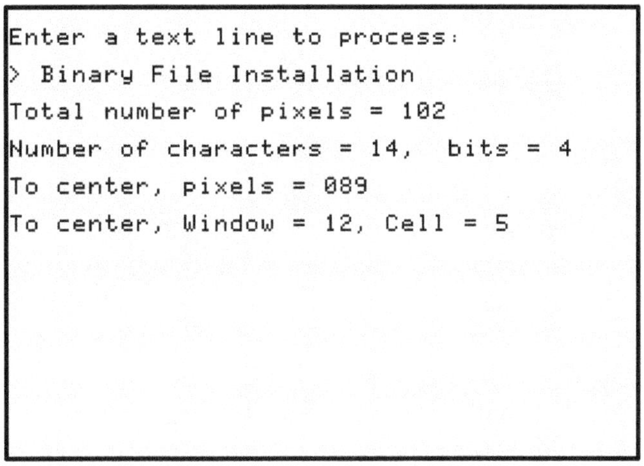

Figure V.26.6. Using LENGTH for String Draw

None of the characters in the CHAR font that is shown in Figure V.26.5 include a pre- or a post-character pixel that provides some pixel space after the previous character or before the next character is drawn, respectively. Pixel space between all characters is automatically inserted by SD. Even the SPACE or character 0x20 that is used between words is given an additional pixel insertion. After a cursory inspection of the figures that are shown in Section V.2 for *BFI*, nearly all of the character strings appear centered on the HIRES screen. It would be a significant challenge to manually process even one of these character strings in order to calculate how many pixels to the right the character string must be moved in order for that character string to appear centered on the HIRES screen. Not only must the size of each character be considered, but also consideration must be given for that single pixel space that is automatically inserted between each character and, of course, discounting the single pixel space after drawing the last character in the character string. What better time than now to develop a program that can provide this critical centering information in the form that is useable by SD.

BFI is introduced by Figure V.2.1 where the character string Binary File Installation appears centered on the HIRES screen. The parameters that are used to display this particular character string include L% = 8, W% = 12, and C% = 5 according to my Applesoft source code. When this same character string is entered into the *LENGTH* program as shown in Figure V.26.6, the entire character string is found to be 102 pixels in length if it is drawn on the HIRES screen by SD. Knowing that there are 280 pixels on each HIRES scan line, the character string would need to be moved to the right 89 pixels for the character string to appear centered on the HIRES screen. For SD to accomplish this, the parameters W% and C% in the CALL statement need to be set to 12 and 5, respectively. I processed all of the character strings that appear centered in *BFI* using the program *LENGTH*. It is fairly obvious that I saved more time in creating and utilizing the program *LENGTH* than the total time it would have taken to determine the values for the parameters W% and C% manually for all of the character strings that appear centered in *BFI*, let alone

375

guarantee the accuracy of these values when they are determined manually. What an utter illogical use of time that would have been. Furthermore, I now own a valuable and useful program, a tool that I can utilize at any time if I should develop another Applesoft program that uses SD to draw character strings that appear centered on a HIRES screen. This alone should be sufficient inducement to anyone who considers spending their time pursuing a repetitive task manually rather than using their time to write a valuable and useful program, a tool to perform that repetitive task.

27. ICON Maker Program

During my discussion of the Applesoft hybrid program *BFI* in Section V.2, I introduced the subject of *ICON Maker*, the HIRES editing tool that I developed for Sierra On-Line. I use *ICON Maker* to generate the *shape table* data for the screen icons that I use in *BFI*. I wrote the original *ICON Maker* tool in Applesoft and utilized ROM routines to draw lines on the HIRES graphics screen. I knew that the same ROM routines would be utilized by Sierra On-Line's customers in displaying the icons I had designed for its products. Actually, I never completed the Applesoft *ICON Maker* tool and there were several features that were still incomplete. These incomplete features, however, were not important nor were they critical in delivering the icons and the icon display routines for the various Sierra products. My present day *ICON Maker* tool is complete and it is written entirely in assembly language, and this assembly language version incorporates the same very high speed HIRES line drawing routines that are used in Draw ICON. Draw ICON, or DI is also introduced in Section V.2 for *BFI*. *ICON Maker* and Draw ICON do **not** utilize any of the flawed HIRES drawing routines that are found in the Apple ROM.

The icon window defines an area on the HIRES graphics screen where the *shape table* objects are drawn. The location of the first pixel that is in the upper left-hand corner of the icon window defines the start location for the entire icon. The icon is drawn relative to this start location which occurs at some index bit that is within some index byte from the left side of the screen on some index scan line from the top of the screen. In other words, the icon start location is some number of pixels to the left from the left side of the HIRES screen and some number of pixels or scan lines down from the top of the HIRES screen. When the icon window is defined, its location is specified by its X- and Y-coordinates in pixels. These coordinates are used additively to the *shape table* data when drawing each component of an icon.

In order to speed up and accelerate the drawing of lines and shapes in *ICON Maker* and in Draw ICON and in any other utility or game that utilizes HIRES graphics and animation, lookup tables are necessary in order to obtain maximum calculation speed. Given an X-location on a scan line that is some number of pixels from the left side of the screen, that location must be converted into a bit index that is within some byte index. There are forty bytes of memory that comprise each visible scan line and these bytes contain the data for the 280 pixels that can be displayed, amounting to seven pixels for each byte of data. Obviously, converting pixel number to bit index and byte index requires the division by seven with some remainder. This is a terrible division to implement without using lookup tables. The first set of lookup tables are called XBASEL and XBASEH, and these tables accomplish this division easily at the expense of 0x118 bytes of data. XBASE simply determines the byte index from the base screen location that is found in GBAS, a page-zero pointer at 0x26:0x27. Pixel number is also used to index into a MASKNDX table in order to determine which index bit will be turned OFF or turned ON within the index byte, so this table provides the value for the remainder in the division by seven operation. The MASKNDX table is 0x100 bytes in size. In order to support color on the HIRES graphics screen, *ICON Maker* uses a COLORNDX table that is also 0x100 bytes in size and this table is also indexed by pixel number. COLORNDX determines which color byte is selected from the 8-byte COLORBYT table. Specific bytes are copied from the COLORTBL table to form the COLORBYT table that supports a selected color for the icon component that is currently being drawn. The COLORTBL is 0x20 bytes in size. At this point, 0x340 bytes of table data are required just to support the X-location in pixels in order to accelerate the calculations for drawing lines and shapes in *ICON Maker*.

The Y-location in pixels or scan lines is used to initialize the base screen location or address for the page-zero pointer GBAS. Steven Wozniak constructed the Apple][HIRES graphics screen in three sections where each section consists of eight Text lines and each Text line consists of eight scan lines. Therefore, there are a total of 192 scan lines that are available for the entire HIRES graphics screen. Within each of the three screen sections, the address of one Text line to the next Text line or group of eight scan lines to the next group of eight scan lines is incremented by 0x80, and each screen section is incremented by 0x28. Within one Text line, its eight scan lines are each incremented by 0x400. Wozniak's design of the hardware that displays the data to the HIRES graphics screen that resides in memory requires the least number of hardware components when the data in memory is addressed for display using these specifications. In view of the above specifications, it is quite understandable that using a lookup table in order to initialize GBAS by using scan line as the index into the YBASE table will definitely accelerate the calculations for drawing lines and shapes in *ICON Maker*. YBASE consists of two tables called YBASEL and YBASEH that define the full 16-bit base screen address for the start of each scan line. Obviously, these two tables are each 192 bytes in size.

The total number of bytes that are found in the lookup tables that are used to accelerate the calculations for drawing lines and shapes in *ICON Maker* and in Draw ICON is 0x4C0 bytes. Is using nearly five pages of memory just for lookup tables really worth it? You bet it is! When lookup tables are utilized, an icon can be drawn nearly instantaneously. If the ROM HPLOT routine at 0xF457 and the ROM HLIN routine at 0xF53A are used instead, the icon and all of its components would be drawn comparatively at a snail's pace. There is **no** faster way to accelerate the calculations for drawing dots and lines on the HIRES graphics screen than using these lookup tables for initializing the base screen address, the index byte, the index bit within that index byte, and the desired color mask. Another advantage for not using the ROM HPLOT and the ROM HLIN routines is that the ROM HLIN routine is fundamentally flawed as I discuss in Section II.1. My analysis of the assembly language instructions for the ROM HLIN routine shows that the algorithm does not correctly calculate the delta difference of the horizontal and of the vertical start to end points before the routine draws a line. This calculation error severely affects the appearance of all diagonally drawn lines in my opinion. The HLIN routine that is used in *ICON Maker* and in Draw ICON does not contain this flaw. All diagonal lines are drawn precisely and diagonal lines are segmented equally in all instances and the results will always be the same without regard to the direction in which the lines are drawn. The ROM HLIN routine cannot make these same guarantees.

Graphic tools such as *ICON Maker* are not particularly suited for building colorful icons. Typically, *ICON Maker* initializes the color of a new icon to White1 that has all bits ON except for the MSB, or color-group bit. It is only necessary to set color once, at the beginning of a *shape table*, and that color will be used to draw all of the components of the icon. If color is used in any one shape and white in all other shapes, then every shape will be required to initialize its color space using its first entry command. Of course, it is possible to use color in some of the components that are contained in an icon and white in the remaining components, or multiple colors within the same icon. The subject of Apple][HIRES color is complicated, yet very interesting. Color pairs are best used on the same scan line within a group of bytes, and the color pair may remain the same or change on the previous or next scan line. Color pairs are Green and Purple because the MSB is OFF in both of these colors, and Orange and Blue because the MSB is ON in both of these colors. Black1 and White1 are compatible with Green and Purple and Black2 and White2 are compatible with Orange and Blue. Any of the four colors may be used from byte pair to byte pair as long as the color bits begin on a byte boundary. If the icon is shifted, even by one bit left or right, its colors will shift, perhaps making the icon very difficult to interpret. If the icon is shifted up or down one or more scan lines, the colors will remain consistent. Creating a colorful icon in *ICON Maker* does not guarantee that that icon will even look like the same icon or have the same color palette when it is drawn *in situ* by its target program. However, for those willing to develop strategies that can properly place a colorful icon as it is designed on the correct byte boundary, then *ICON Maker* will provide the necessary color commands that can be utilized in order to create an icon that will meet the needs of the target program.

Command Name	Value	Command Size	Description
COLORCMD	0xF0	2 bytes	set COLOR index command
HORZCMD	0xF1	4 + n bytes	draw HORZ shape command
VERTCMD	0xF2	4 + n bytes	draw VERT shape command
DIAGCMD	0xF3	4 + n bytes	draw DIAG shape command
CURVECMD	0xF4	4 + n bytes	draw CURVE shape command
BOXCMD	0xF5	5 bytes	draw BOX shape command
PARLLCMD	0xF6	7 bytes	draw PARALLEL shape command
DOTCMD	0xF7	3 + 2n bytes	draw DOT shape command
CHAINCMD	0xF8	1 byte	exit ICONPROC with C-flag set command
GRPAGCMD	0xF9	2 bytes	set HIRES graphics page command
GROFFCMD	0xFA	4 bytes	set ICON window coordinates command
GRSIZCMD	0xFB	3 bytes	set ICON window size command
GRWIDCMD	0xFC	2 bytes	set ICON window frame thickness command
FRCLRCMD	0xFD	1 byte	clear ICON window frame command
FRSETCMD	0xFE	1 byte	draw ICON window frame command
EXITCMD	0xFF	1 byte	exit ICONPROC with C-flag clear command

Table V.27.1. Drawing Commands Available in ICONPROC

The routine ICONPROC in *ICON Maker* utilizes a total of sixteen commands. Five commands are used for initialization, two commands are used to draw or clear an ICON window frame, seven commands are used to actually draw lines and shapes, and two commands are used to chain to another *shape table* or exit the current *shape table*. These commands begin with the value of 0xF0 and they end with the value of 0xFF. The data in a *shape table* is specifically designed to never equate to a command value, particularly the data for the CURVE and the PARALLEL commands as will be explained. The ICONPROC commands are shown in Table V.27.1 with their command name, their value, and a brief description of their function. Table V.27.2 lists all of the simple colors that are available in ICONPROC. These colors, as well as the complex colors that are shown in Table V.27.3, are referenced by their Index number which is the number that is used in conjunction with the COLORCMD, 0xF0. As previously explained above, the Index number for a color is used to copy specific bytes from the COLORTBL table to form the COLORBYT table. The complex colors are included in the *ICON Maker* and in the Draw ICON source code, but the color values are not included in the assembly code. Additional changes to the source code for ICONPROC would be necessary in order to include all of the complex colors, though these changes would be trivial. The COLORBYT table is set to eight bytes in size and it will only support the complex colors that are six bytes or less in length because only six bytes can be indexed when using the COLORNDX table in its present form. The COLORNDX table would need to be expanded in order to index all ten color bytes that are associated with the last four complex colors that are listed in Table V.27.3.

Color Name	Index	Color Value	Description
Black1	0x00	0x00000000	turn all graphic data bits OFF, MSB OFF
Green	0x01	0x2A552A55	set odd bit in even byte, even bit in odd byte, MSB OFF
Purple	0x02	0x552A552A	set even bit in even byte, odd bit in odd byte, MSB OFF
White1	0x03	0x7F7F7F7F	turn all graphic data bits ON, MSB OFF
Black2	0x04	0x80808080	turn all graphic data bits OFF, MSB ON
Orange	0x05	0xAAD5AAD5	set odd bit in even byte, even bit in odd byte, MSB ON
Blue	0x06	0xD5AAD5AA	set even bit in even byte, odd bit in odd byte, MSB ON
White2	0x07	0xFFFFFFFF	turn all graphic data bits ON, MSB ON

Table V.27.2. Simple Colors Available in ICONPROC

Color Name	Index	Color Value
Green/Black1	0x08	0x22440811
Purple/Black1	0x09	0x11224408
Orange/Black2	0x0A	0xA2C48891
Blue/Black2	0x0B	0x91A2C488
Green/White1	0x0C	0x3A5D2E57 6B75
Purple/White1	0x0D	0x5D2E576B 753A
Orange/White2	0x0E	0xBADDAED7 EBF5
Blue/White2	0x0F	0xDDAED7EB F5BA
White1/Green/Black1	0x10	0x3A746851 23470E1D
White1/Purple/Black1	0x11	0x74685123 470E1D3A
White2/Orange/Black2	0x12	0xBAF4E8D1 A3C78E9D
White2/Blue/Black2	0x13	0xF4E8D1A3 C78E9DBA
White1/Green/Black1/Green	0x14	0x3A510B5D 68452E74 2217
White1/Purple/Black1/Purple	0x15	0x510B5D68 452E7422 173A
White2/Orange/Black2/Orange	0x16	0xBAD18BDD E8C5AEF4 A297
White2/Blue/Black2/Blue	0x17	0xD18BDDE8 C5AEF4A2 97BA

Table V.27.3. Complex Colors Not Available in ICONPROC

When I originally designed *ICON Maker*, I had already created a number of icons using graph paper. I knew the range of sizes that I needed for the ICON window. The ICON window must be large enough to accommodate the largest icon that I needed to create, but not so large as to limit the number of icons I wanted to display at the bottom of a HIRES screen. And, the ICON window could not be so small as to prevent the display of an icon that could not represent the visual concept that I needed to convey. For example, an icon showing a standard dot-matrix printer of the day had to contain enough features of a

379

typical printer to make it recognizable, but not so large and complex as to limit the number of other icons that needed to be displayed as well. During the process of creating a number of icons on graph paper, I kept in mind what I needed to distill from these icons. These icons are simply a collection of fundamental components, each a basic and easy-to-define shape. The purpose of using a collection of basic shapes to create the components of an icon is to generate an icon *shape table* whose data set is reasonably small in size yet powerful enough to draw each component of an icon quickly and easily.

Command	Usage	Example
0xF0	F0nn	F003
0xF1	F1xxyyXxYyXxYy ...	F10B1808210310
0xF2	F2xxyyYyXxYyXx ...	F20C1909220411
0xF3	F3xxyyXxYyXxYy ...	F30B18200E1128
0xF4	F4xxyyXYXYXY ...	F40C1929229299
0xF5	F5xxyyXxYy	F50B182824
0xF6	F6xxyyXxYyXYnn	F60C191B189203
0xF7	F7xxyyXXYYxxyyXXYY ...	F70B181D100D1B1B13
0xF8	F8	F8
0xF9	F9nn	F940
0xFA	FAxxXXyy	FA640032
0xFB	FBxXyY	FB2828
0xFC	FCnn	FC02
0xFD	FD	FD
0xFE	FE	FE
0xFF	FF	FF

Table V.27.4. Using ICONPROC Drawing Commands

Table V.27.4 defines the usage of each Drawing command including an example that contains actual data. This example data is for demonstration purposes only. The HORZCMD command, or the 0xF1 command first establishes a fully qualified starting coordinate relative to the upper left-hand corner of the icon window. The upper left-hand corner of the icon window is defined as the pixel location where the X-coordinate equals zero and the Y-coordinate equals zero. In the example data given for this command, the fully qualified starting coordinate is X = 11 and Y = 24. The remaining bytes of data following the fully qualified starting coordinate toggle between horizontal coordinate and vertical coordinate, starting with the horizontal coordinate in this command. The HORZCMD as well as the VERTCMD only draw straight lines that are either horizontal or vertical. From the example data of seven bytes in Table V.27.4, the first byte of data changes the X-coordinate so that X = 8 while leaving the Y-coordinate unchanged for Y = 24. A straight is drawn from 11,24 to 8,24. The next data byte changes the Y-coordinate so that Y = 33 while leaving the X-coordinate unchanged for X = 8. A straight line is drawn from 8,24 to 8,33; then from 8,33 to 3,33; and finally from 3,33 to 3,16. With this command, seven bytes of data will draw four straight lines, eight bytes of data will draw five lines, *et cetera*.

The VERTCMD command, or the 0xF2 command functions exactly like the HORZCMD except the first byte of data that comes after the fully qualified starting coordinate changes the Y-coordinate first. From the example data of seven bytes in Table V.27.4, four lines are drawn: a line is drawn from 12,25 to 12,9; then from 12,9 to 34,9; then from 34,9 to 34,4; and finally from 34,4 to 17,4.

The DIAGCMD command, or the 0xF3 command draws diagonal lines from fully qualified coordinate data. This is a far more expensive command in terms of data utilization because fully qualified coordinate data must specify both the X- and the Y-coordinates for every point to which a line is drawn. Therefore, seven bytes of data will draw only two lines, nine bytes of data will draw three lines, *et cetera*. From the example data of seven bytes in Table V.27.4, two diagonal lines are drawn: a line is drawn from 11,24 to 32,14; and finally a line is drawn from 32,14 to 17,40.

```
:               :           :
4F59 48        152  DELTA    pha
4F5A           153  ;
4F5A 29 0F     154           and #CMDMASK
4F5C C9 08     155           cmp #$08
4F5E 90 02     156           bcc >1
4F60           157  ;
4F60 49 F7     158           eor #DLTACOMP
4F62           159  ;
4F62 A8        160  ^1        tay
4F63           161  ;
4F63 68        162           pla
4F64           163  ;
4F64 4A        164           lsr
4F65 4A        165           lsr
4F66 4A        166           lsr
4F67 4A        167           lsr
4F68           168  ;
4F68 C9 08     169           cmp #$08
4F6A 90 03     170           bcc >2
4F6C           171  ;
4F6C 49 F7     172           eor #DLTACOMP
4F6E           173  ;
4F6E 18        174           clc
4F6F           175  ;
4F6F 60        176  ^2        rts
:               :           :
```

Figure V.27.1. DELTA Calculation in ICONPROC

The CURVECMD command, or the 0xF4 command draws diagonal lines from a fully qualified start coordinate to any direction that has a ±7 pixel displacement. Each byte of data that follows the fully qualified start coordinate contains a ±7 pixel displacement for the X-coordinate in the upper nibble and a ±7 pixel displacement for the Y-coordinate in the lower nibble. The extraction of the coordinate displacements is performed by the DELTA routine. The A-register must contain the *shape table* data value for the input to this routine, and the DELTA routine exits with the displacement of the X-coordinate in the A-register and the displacement of the Y-coordinate in the Y-register and the C-flag is always **clear**. The DELTA routine is shown in Figure V.27.1. Any negative displacement of a coordinate produces a two's compliment value that will provide the desired displacement when that value is added to the current coordinate value with the C-flag clear. In other words, a negative displacement of -1 is affected when the upper or lower nibble contains 0x8, a negative displacement of -2 is affected when the upper or lower nibble contains 0x9, *et cetera*. Therefore, the upper negative limit for any delta displacement data must be 0xEE which would affect a -7 displacement to both coordinates. This upper negative limit will ensure that the values for the Drawing commands in ICONPROC are protected. From the example data of seven bytes in Table V.27.4, four diagonal lines are drawn: a line is drawn from 12,25 to 14,23; then from 14,23 to 16,25; then from 16,25 to 14,27; and finally from 14,27 to 12,25. This results in a perfectly drawn diamond shape.

The BOXCMD command, or the 0xF5 command draws a square or rectangular box given the fully qualified coordinate values for its upper left-hand corner and for its lower right-hand corner. With only five bytes of data, a box having four sides is perfectly drawn anywhere within the ICON window. From the example data of five bytes in Table V.27.4, a rectangular box is drawn: a line is drawn from 11,24 to 40,24; then from 40,24 to 40,36; then from 40,36 to 11,36; and finally from 11,36 to 11,24. This is certainly one of the more powerful Drawing commands in ICONPROC.

The PARRLCMD command, or the 0xF6 command draws multiple, equally positioned, and equally offset parallel lines within the ICON window. To be sure, this command is the more complex of all the Drawing commands, but it provides so many unique features that make it a highly desirable command to use often. The PARRLCMD command requires seven bytes of data to draw at least two parallel lines, but it is capable of drawing up to 255 parallel lines in total however impractical that may be. *ICON Maker* does not limit the parallel line count for this command. What *ICON Maker* does is limit the number of parallel lines to those that can be **drawn within** the ICON window given the specifications of the first line, the offsets to the second and remaining lines, and the line count for additional parallel lines. From the example data of seven bytes in Table V.27.4, the initial diagonal line is drawn from two fully qualified coordinates from 12,25 to 27,24. The next byte of data provides the delta value for the second and remaining lines that will be drawn parallel to the initial diagonal line. The number of additional diagonal lines that are drawn is provided by the last byte of data which is the line count. The delta value, as in the CURVECMD command, can provide up to a ±7 pixel displacement to the initial fully qualified coordinate. In this example data, the delta value is 0x92 giving a -2 displacement to the X-coordinate and a +2 displacement to the Y-coordinate that is applied to the **first** initial coordinate. Thus, the second diagonal line is drawn from 10,27 to 25,26. The same delta values are applied to this coordinate again in order to draw a total of three additional parallel lines. The last two parallel lines are drawn from 8,29 to 23,28 and from 6,31 to 21,30. It is absolutely exquisite how the parallel lines appear on the display after they have been drawn so quickly and so easily!

The DOTCMD command, or the 0xF7 command draws one or more single dot pixels within the ICON window given the fully qualified coordinate that provides the X- and the Y-coordinate values for each pixel or dot that is drawn. Multiple pixels may be specified with a single DOTCMD command. With this command, three bytes of data will draw one pixel, five bytes will draw two pixels, *et cetera*. From the example data of nine bytes in Table V.27.4, four pixels are drawn at 11,24; at 29,16; at 13,27; and at 27,19. A colorful icon would be the most difficult of all icons to create if a single pixel of a particular color is necessary at a required ICON window location since two adjacent pixels are required in order to express a single dot of color. The difficulty would be compounded if multiple colored pixels were necessary at required locations since a color will only appear when its pixel pair is ON in even bits of even bytes or in even bits of odd bytes or in odd bits of even bytes or in odd bits of odd bytes throughout a scan line. The DOTCMD command is the most costly in terms of its shape size to its data size for all of the Drawing commands in ICONPROC. However, this command, with only two bytes of data for the fully qualified coordinate for a single pixel, is still the better option than wastefully using any of the other commands to implement turning ON a single pixel.

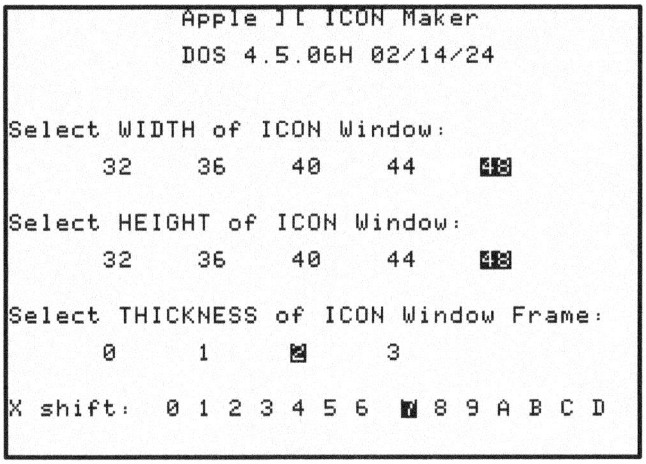

Figure V.27.2. Initialization of ICON Maker

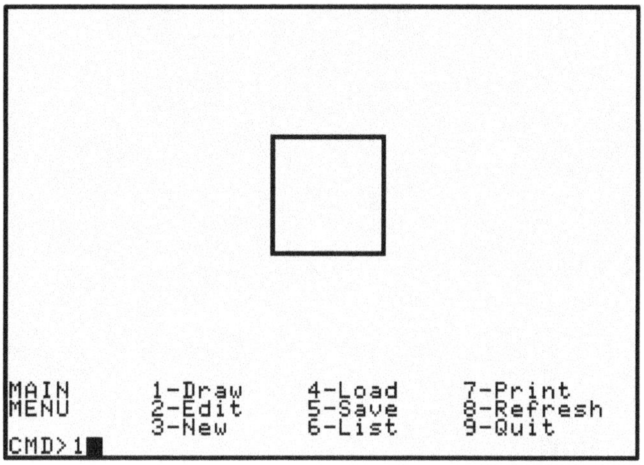

Figure V.27.3. ICON Maker Main Menu

BFI uses two sizes for its ICON windows: `0x28` x `0x28` and `0x30` x `0x30`. *BFI* only uses ICON window frames that are two pixels in thickness. These parameters are the first values that *ICON Maker* requests, so when *ICON Maker* first initializes as shown in Figure V.27.2, the WIDTH and the HEIGHT of the ICON window, the THICKNESS of the ICON window frame, and a bit shift to the X-coordinate for the entire ICON window can easily be selected. I believe that values smaller and/or larger than those offered would be excessive or not within the purview of *ICON Maker*. The Main Menu for *ICON Maker* is shown in Figure V.27.3 with an ICON window frame that is drawn based on the selected values for WIDTH, HEIGHT, THICKNESS, and XSHIFT. The ICON window is placed on the HIRES screen at predetermined coordinates in order to place the window at a workable height in the display and at a byte boundary that may be shifted no more than thirteen pixels to the right. This shift in the X-coordinate places the ICON window anywhere within two data bytes so that a colorful icon may be created for a specific color group. When XSHIFT is zero, the X- and Y-coordinates are set so that the ICON window is placed at the seventeenth character and at the start of the eighth text line in the display.

$$X = 16 * 7 + XSHIFT$$
$$Y = 8 * 7$$

The ICON window and the ICON window frame are drawn by ICONPROC after *ICON Maker* has initialized an ICON Shape structure using the Drawing commands `0xF0`, `0xF9`, `0xFA`, `0xFB`, and `0xFC` and the values that are selected from Figure V.27.2. Regardless of the size that is selected for the ICON window, the coordinates for the window are X = 112 + XSHIFT and Y = 56. The ICON window frame is always drawn exterior to the ICON window such that all *shape table* values will be added to the upper left-hand coordinate that is equal to 112+XSHIFT,56 as shown in Figure V.27.3. All calculations involving the X-coordinate will automatically set the most significant byte to zero. Assuming that a **48x48** ICON window is selected and XSHIFT = 0, the ICON window frame will be drawn from 111,55 to 160,55 to 160,104 to 111,104 and to 111,55 and from 110,54 to 161,54 to 161,105 to 110,105 and to 110,54 because the THICKNESS of the ICON window frame is equal to two from Figure V.27.2. *ICON Maker* initializes a number of variables such as ERRORNDX, ASONERR, PROMPT, ASRUN, and the configuration of the HIRES screen. The ICONBUFR is initialized with the color command and the color value for WHITE1. When building an icon in ICONBUFR, if the color command is chosen first with a different color, that color replaces WHITE1 at the beginning of the data buffer for the new icon.

383

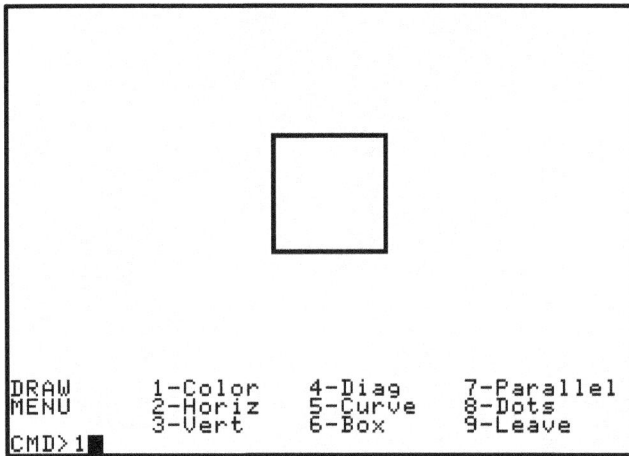

Figure V.27.4. ICON Maker Draw Menu

```
DRAW      1-Color   4-Diag    7-Parallel
MENU      2-Horiz   5-Curve   8-Dots
          3-Vert    6-Box     9-Leave
CMD>1█
```

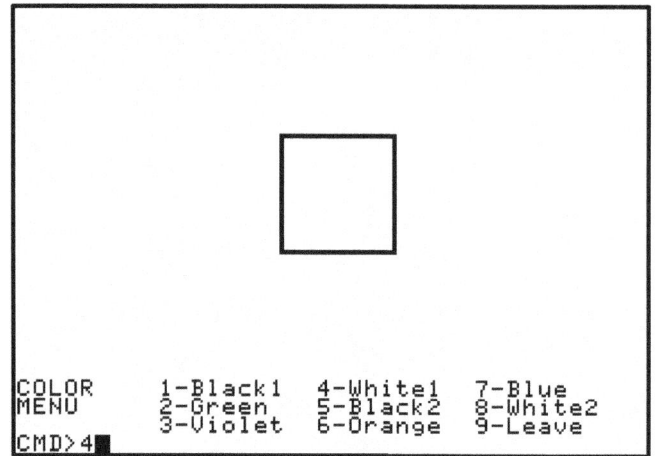

Figure V.27.5. Draw Menu for Color

```
COLOR     1-Black1  4-White1  7-Blue
MENU      2-Green   5-Black2  8-White2
          3-Violet  6-Orange  9-Leave
CMD>4█
```

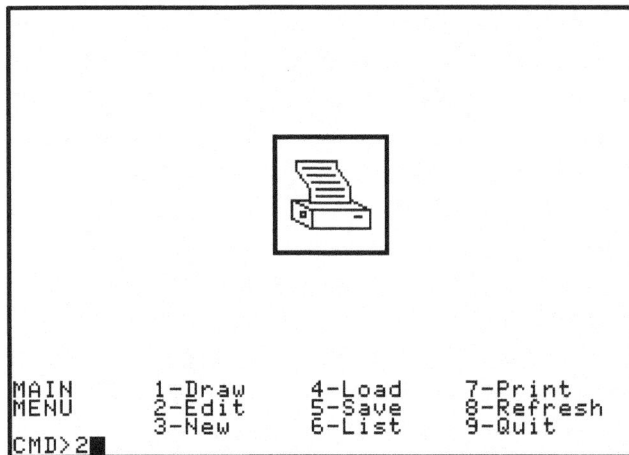

Figure V.27.6. Main Menu for Edit

```
MAIN      1-Draw    4-Load    7-Print
MENU      2-Edit    5-Save    8-Refresh
          3-New     6-List    9-Quit
CMD>2█
```

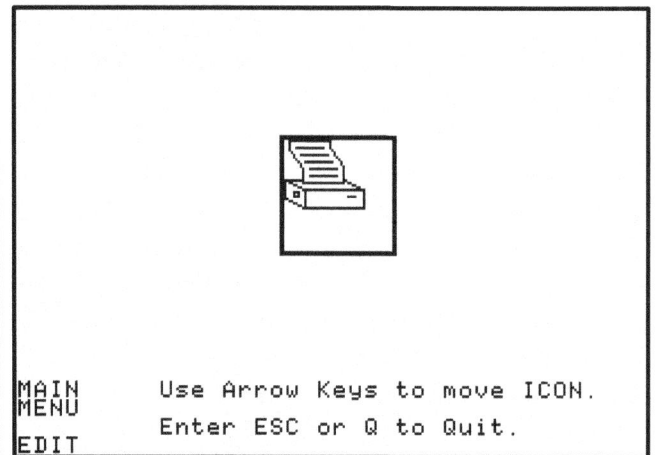

Figure V.27.7. Moving an Icon in Edit

```
MAIN      Use Arrow Keys to move ICON.
MENU
          Enter ESC or Q to Quit.
EDIT
```

The first option that is available in the Main Menu that is shown in Figure V.27.3 is the Draw option, and the Draw option displays the Draw Menu as shown in Figure V.27.4. Color is the first option that is available in the Draw Menu, and the Color option displays the Color Menu as shown in Figure V.27.5. This menu allows the user to select any of the simple colors that are available in ICONPROC as shown previously in Table V.27.2. Once a complete icon has been created or any time during its creation, the Edit option in the Main Menu enables an entire icon to be shifted left, right, up, or down within the ICON window. The complete icon can never be shifted out of the ICON window. Perhaps an icon is first designed within a large ICON window; the complete icon can be shifted towards the upper left-hand corner using Edit, then Saved, and finally Loaded into a smaller ICON window for display. An example in using Edit to shift a complete icon within an ICON window is shown in Figures V.27.6 and V.27.7. This icon can presumably be placed within a smaller ICON window. Selecting the New option in the Main Menu simply clears ICONBUFR except for the initial color command and the color WHITE1. Selecting the Load option in the Main Menu provides the ability to enter a filename as shown in Figure V.27.8. Any DOS disk error is reported immediately as shown in Figure V.27.9. When a DOS disk error does occur, the appropriate error message is displayed without causing an interruption to the *ICON Maker* program.

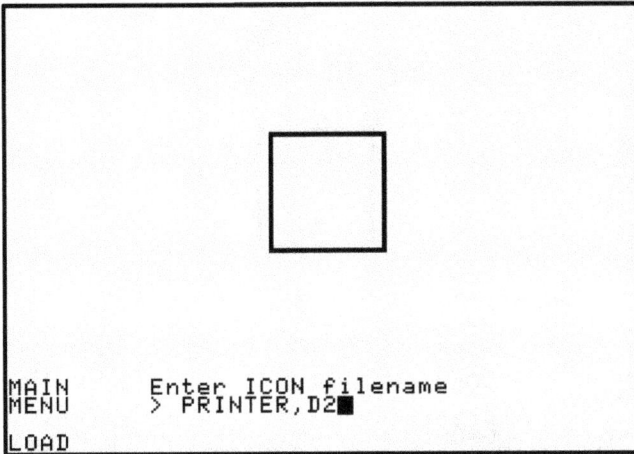

Figure V.27.8. Main Menu for Load

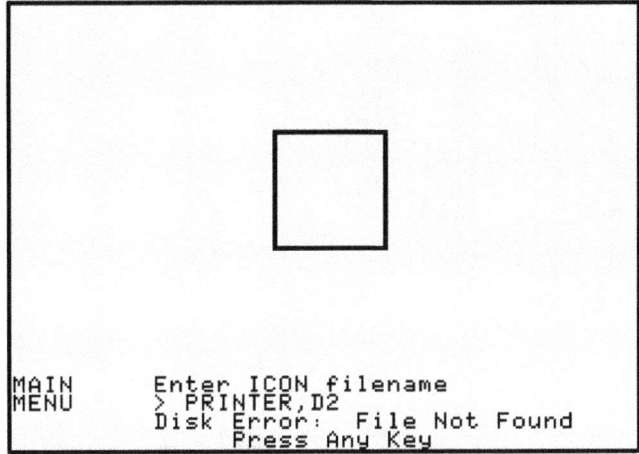

Figure V.27.9. Disk Errors in ICON Maker

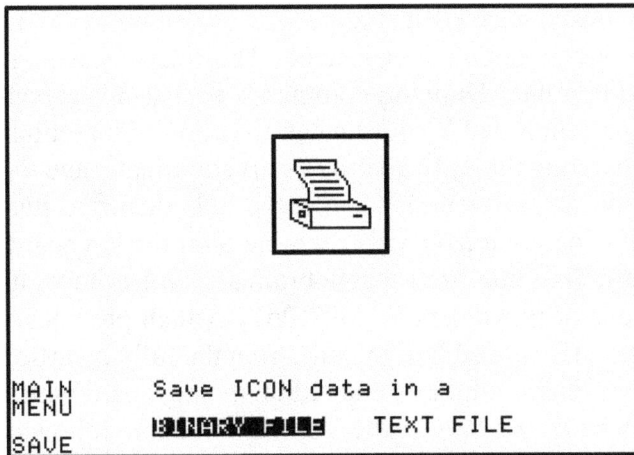

Figure V.27.10. Main Menu for Save

Figure V.27.11. Entering Filename in Save

Selecting the Save option in the Main Menu provides the ability to save the data that is currently in memory in ICONBUFR into either a Binary file or into a Text file as shown in Figure V.27.10. Following the data selection type, the actual filename that is used to save the icon data is requested next as shown in Figure V.27.11. Example Text data for an icon that is in memory and whose binary data is currently in ICONBUFR is shown in Figure V.27.12. This is the same Text data that would be written into a Text file after selecting the Save option and displayed after selecting the List option or sent to the printer after selecting the Print option, where all three option selections are from the Main Menu. *ICON Maker* formats the binary data that is in memory such that each Text line begins with a Drawing command which is followed by the data that is utilized to draw the shape that is specified by that command. All Drawing commands and their data are expressed in hexadecimal. The last option in the Main Menu is the Refresh option. Refresh clears the contents of the ICON window and the ICON window frame. Refresh then redraws the ICON window frame and sends the contents of ICONBUFR to ICONPROC in order for that data to be drawn as a complete icon. Refresh ensures that the data that currently resides in ICONBUFR is correct and it verifies that all of the Drawing commands and their data elements draw the shapes that are specified in ICONBUFR without error.

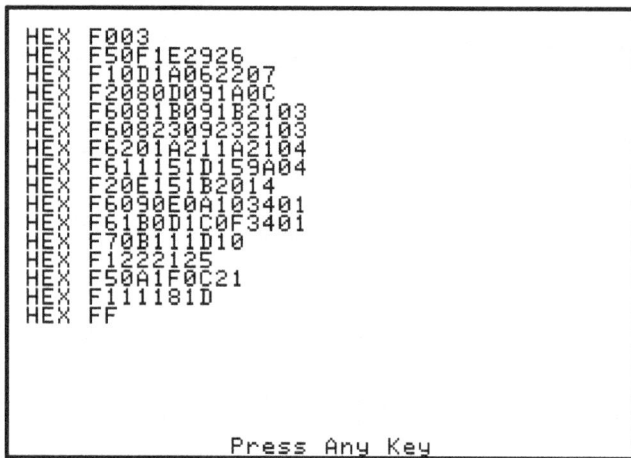

```
HEX F003
HEX F50F1E2926
HEX F10D1A062207
HEX F2080D091A0C
HEX F6081B091B2103
HEX F6082309232103
HEX F6201A211A2104
HEX F611151D159A04
HEX F20E151B2014
HEX F6090E0A103401
HEX F61B0D1C0F3401
HEX F70B111D10
HEX F1222125
HEX F50A1F0C21
HEX F111181D
HEX FF
                    Press Any Key
```

Figure V.27.12. ICON Maker Text Data for Icon

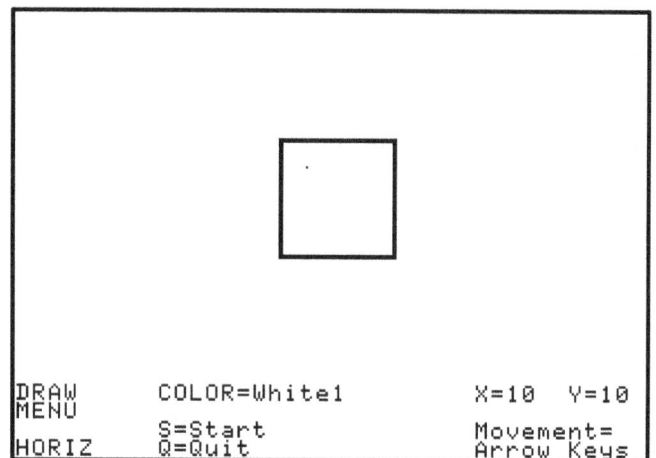

```
DRAW        COLOR=White1        X=10   Y=10
MENU
            S=Start             Movement=
HORIZ       Q=Quit              Arrow Keys
```

Figure V.27.13. Draw Menu for Horizontal

Returning to the Draw Menu where Color was previously selected in Figure V.27.4, Figure V.27.13 shows the Draw Menu screen for Horiz when the Horiz option is selected. This menu screen is representative of the menu screens that are shown for the other Drawing commands in that this screen displays the current color that is in effect as well as the current X and Y coordinates, the allowed directions for cursor movement which are the Arrow Keys when entering the fully qualified start coordinate, and the allowed keyboard inputs, or S and Q. The purpose of this screen menu is to enter the fully qualified start coordinate for the shape that will be drawn by this Drawing command after pressing S on the keyboard. Once the fully qualified start coordinate is specified, the first line from that coordinate can be drawn as shown in Figure V.27.14. In this figure the allowed cursor movement is HORZ Only, which previously was Arrow Keys from Figure V.27.13. As the cursor point is moved horizontally from the fully qualified start location, a line that continues to change in length is drawn until D is entered on the keyboard which fixes the final length of the first line. The next line can be drawn only in the Vertical direction, followed by the third line in the Horizontal direction, and followed by the fourth line in the Vertical direction as shown in Figure V.27.15 that ends at X = 5 and Y = 25.

After selecting the Vert option in Figure V.27.4 and entering the fully qualified start coordinate as in the example for the Horiz option that is shown in Figure V.27.13, the first Vertical line can be drawn as shown in Figure V.27.16 where the allowed cursor movement is VERT Only. As the cursor point is moved vertically from the fully qualified start location, a line that continues to change in length is drawn until D is entered on the keyboard which fixes the final length of the first line. The next line can be drawn only in the Horizontal direction, followed by the third line in the Vertical direction, and followed by the fourth line in the Horizontal direction as shown in Figure V.27.17 that ends at X = 25 and Y = 10.

The Diag option in Figure V.27.4 allows the drawing of a diagonal line in any direction from the fully qualified start coordinate after that coordinate has been specified. This diagonal line may be drawn having any length, and when D is pressed on the keyboard, its final fully qualified end coordinate is recorded into ICONBUFR as shown in Figure V.27.18. Any number of diagonal lines may be drawn from end to end where each time D is pressed on the keyboard, the current fully qualified coordinate is recorded into ICONBUFR as shown in Figure V.27.19. As noted earlier, the DIAGCMD is a far more expensive command in terms of data utilization because every line ends at a fully qualified coordinate.

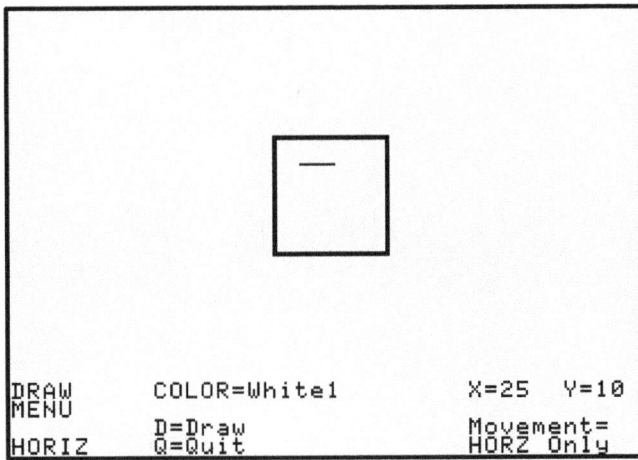

Figure V.27.14. Drawing Lines in Horizontal

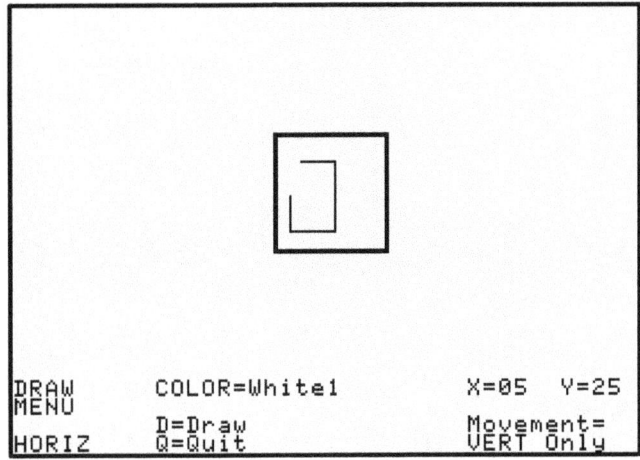

Figure V.27.15. Drawing More Lines in Horizontal

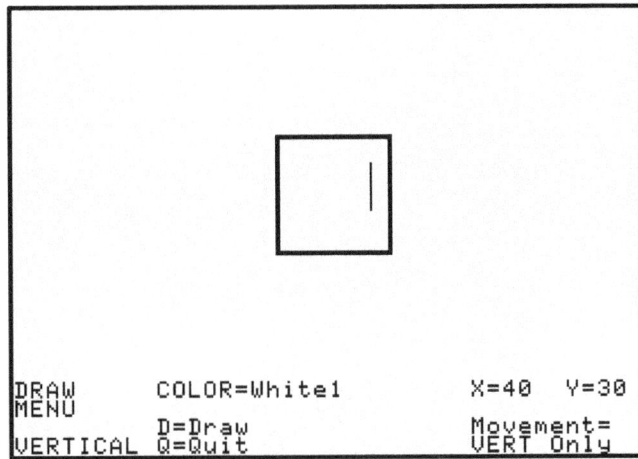

Figure V.27.16. Draw Menu for Vertical

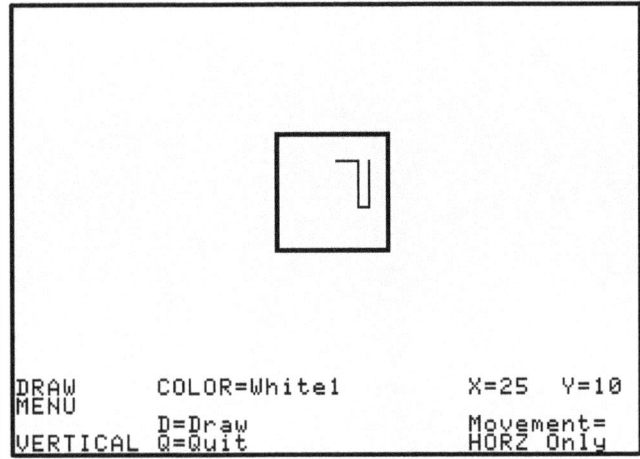

Figure V.27.17. Drawing Lines in Vertical

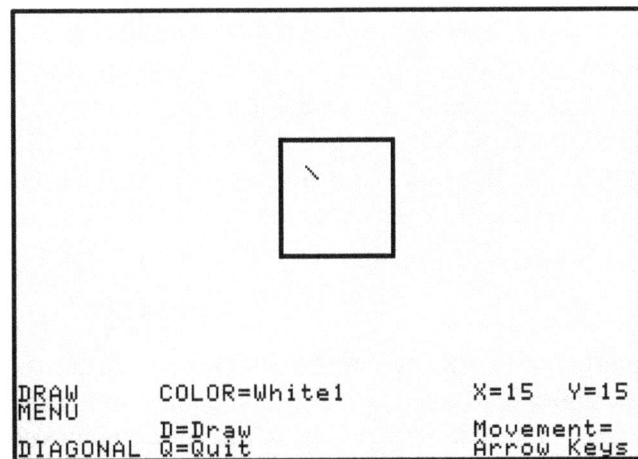

Figure V.27.18. Draw Menu for Diagonal

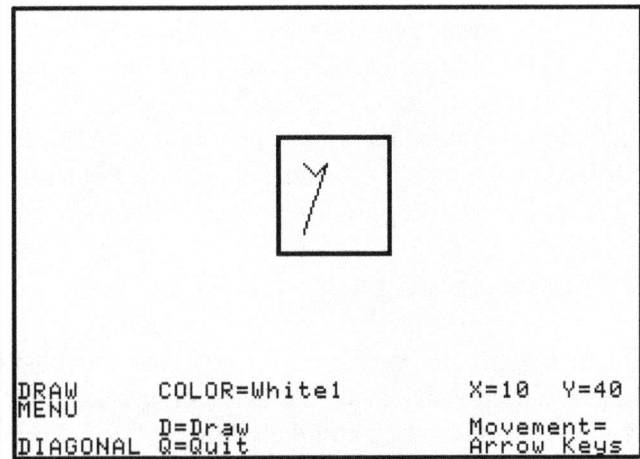

Figure V.27.19. Drawing Lines in Diagonal

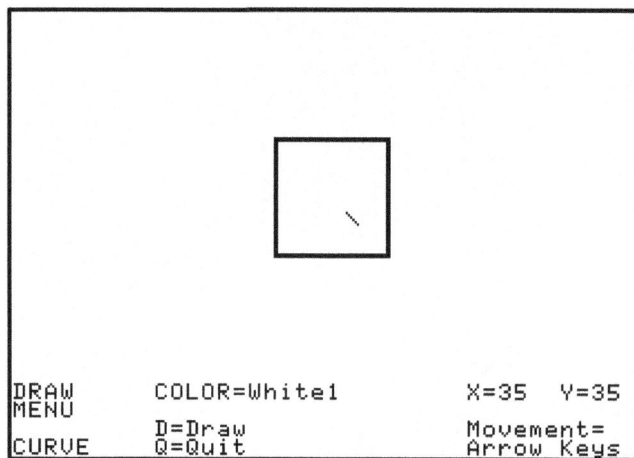

Figure V.27.20. Draw Menu for Curve

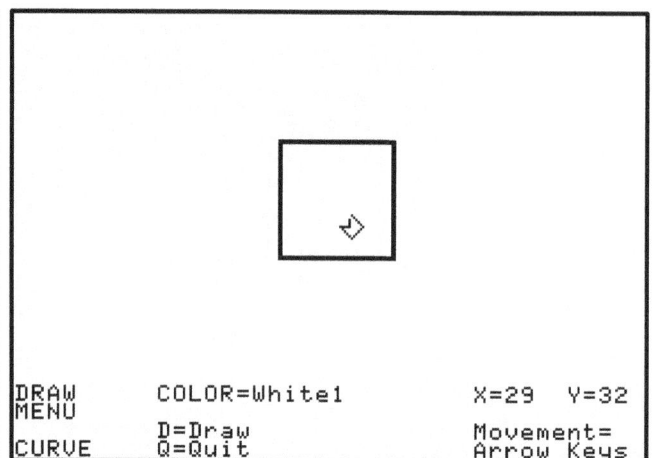

Figure V.27.21. Drawing Lines in Curve

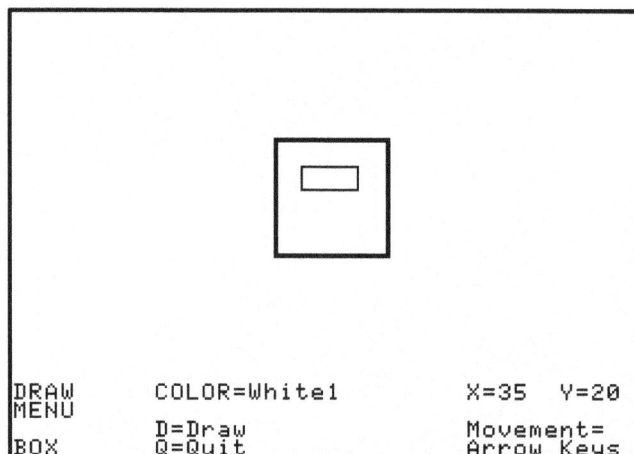

Figure V.27.22. Draw Menu for Box

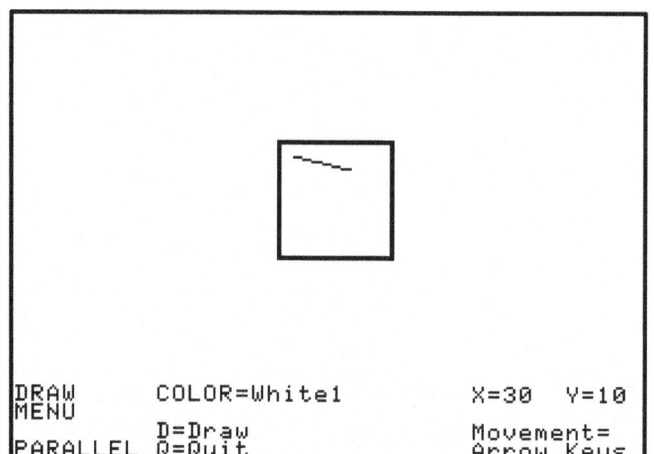

Figure V.27.23. Draw Menu for Parallel

The Curve option in Figure V.27.4 allows the drawing of a diagonal line in any direction from the fully qualified start coordinate after that coordinate has been specified. This diagonal line is limited to be drawn that has no more than a ±7 pixel displacement from the fully qualified start coordinate as shown in Figure V.27.20. This displacement is recorded into ICONBUFR as a single byte containing both the X and the Y displacements with the X displacement in the upper nibble and the Y displacement in the lower nibble. Any number of diagonal lines may be drawn from end to end that have no more than a ±7 pixel displacement. Each time D is pressed on the keyboard, a single byte displacement value is recorded into ICONBUFR as shown in Figure V.27.21.

The Box option in Figure V.27.4 is one of the most entertaining Drawing commands to draw. After the fully qualified start coordinate has been specified for the upper left-hand corner of a box, the lower right-hand corner of the box can then be specified. A new box is continuously drawn as the cursor is moved either vertically or horizontally until D is pressed on the keyboard. Of course, if Q or ESCAPE is pressed, the Box option is immediately terminated and the Draw Menu of Figure V.27.4 is displayed. As soon as

388

D is pressed on the keyboard, the current fully qualified coordinate of the lower right-hand corner of the box is recorded into ICONBUFR as shown in Figure V.27.22.

The Parallel option in Figure V.27.4 is used to create one of the more complex icon elements of all the Drawing commands. This option begins by first creating a diagonal line similarly in how a diagonal line is initially created for the Diag option as shown in Figure V.27.18. This diagonal line may be drawn in any direction and it may have any length from the fully qualified start coordinate, and when D is pressed on the keyboard, its fully qualified end coordinate is recorded into ICONBUFR as shown in Figure V.27.23. The diagonal lines that will be drawn parallel to this initial diagonal line will be drawn having no more than a ±7 pixel displacement from the start and the end coordinates that were established by the initial diagonal line. When D is pressed on the keyboard, that displacement byte from the start coordinate is recorded into ICONBUFR and the Arrow Keys are used to increment or decrement the number of additional parallel lines that are drawn in addition to the initial diagonal line as shown in Figure V.27.24. When D is pressed on the keyboard one final time for Done, the line count for the additional parallel lines that are drawn is recorded into ICONBUFR. Of all of the Drawing commands, and for only seven bytes of data that this command requires, the PARRLCMD command provides so many unique features that makes this command a highly desirable command to use often.

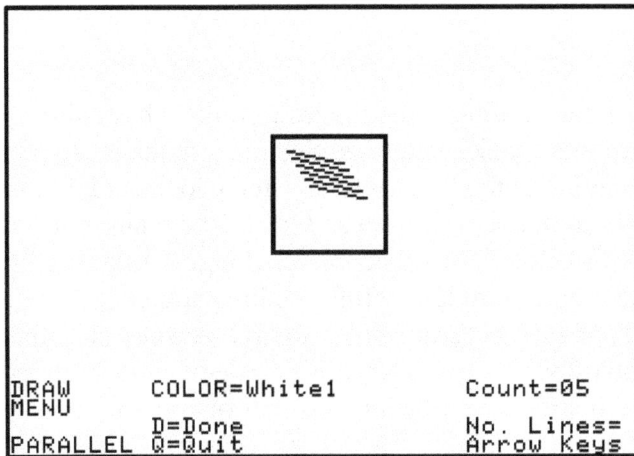

Figure V.27.24. Drawing Lines in Parallel

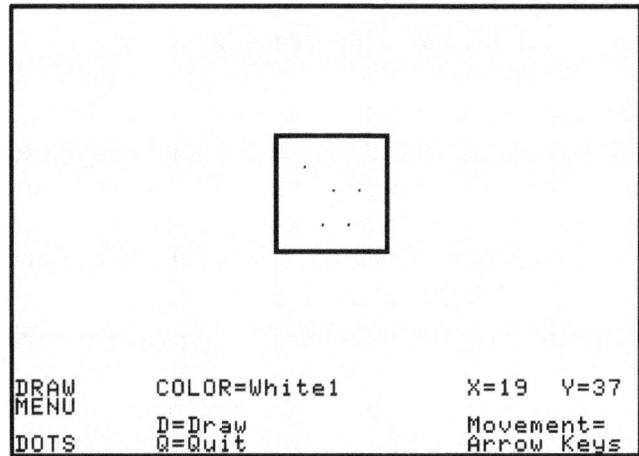

Figure V.27.25. Drawing Single Points in Dots

The Dots option is the last drawing option that is shown in Figure V.27.4, and this option is used to create one or more shapes that are a single dot pixel. When D is pressed on the keyboard, the fully qualified coordinate is recorded into ICONBUFR which is for the X- and the Y-coordinate values of the pixel that is drawn as shown in Figure V.27.25. The Arrow Keys are used to select the coordinate values for each desired dot pixel.

Draw ICON is designed to draw a specific set of icon elements on a HIRES screen. *BFI* utilizes five sets of icons for HIRES display in all of its menu screens. In two of these sets of icons is the icon for a file cabinet that has different drawers that are open and closed. In order to reduce the amount of data that is used for each *shape table*, the common portion of the file cabinet is drawn followed by a unique portion that is found in two other icons. However, to prevent Draw ICON from moving on to the next icon to draw in the Draw ICON loop before the unique portion of the file cabinet can be drawn as part of the current file cabinet icon, the CHAINCMD Draw command is utilized. The CHAINCMD Draw command terminates the *shape table* of an icon while leaving the C-flag **set** instead of leaving the C-flag **clear** as the EXITCMD Draw command does. This allows the Draw ICON loop to operate on the state of the C-flag and to select another *shape table* in order to complete the drawing of the icon that was started by the previous *shape table*. The CHAINCMD Draw command cannot be added by *ICON Maker* as the terminator of a *shape table*; this command can only be added manually. For example, when a Text file that contains a *shape table* is read into a *Lisa* file using EXEC, the source code for that *shape table* can be modified at that time and the EXITCMD Draw command can be changed to the CHAINCMD Draw command. *BFI* only uses the CHAINCMD Draw command once in order to draw one particular file cabinet icon in several different ways. It is quite extraordinary how nicely the CHAINCMD Draw command operates and how much *shape table* data can actually be saved as its by-product.

ICON Maker is a unique HIRES drawing and editing tool that I created and programmed using assembly language, a tool which I have used to design and to generate the *shape table* data for all *BFI* screen icons. *ICON Maker* does not depend on any of the ROM HIRES routines that are used by the Applesoft drawing command repertoire such as the HPLOT and HLIN Applesoft commands. On the other hand, *ICON Maker* uses only the very high speed HIRES line drawing routines that I designed and developed.

28. EPROM Reader Card

I have wanted to design and build my own *quikLoader* card according to the suggestions that I have already outlined ever since I first wrote Section V.7 that describes the quikLoader and Section V.8 that describes the EPROM Operating System, *EOS*. However, after having built my own Real Time Clock card, I have been hesitant in building another peripheral slot card for a number of reasons. One of the major reasons why I am hesitant is due to the difficulty in working with a double sided copper clad board, masking the copper for integrated circuit or IC sockets and connection tracings, carefully etching the copper with dangerous chemicals, and having to precisely drill all of the necessary holes for IC sockets and other components. It is now possible to obtain a perforated board whose holes contain a circle of copper around each hole and each hole connects to both sides of the board. Even better, one can obtain an Apple][prototyping board from ReActive Micro that is made by Glitch Works. This board has a standard 0.062" thickness and it provides an area that is 67 holes by 24 holes where the holes are spaced 0.10 inch apart. This board contains an Apple][slot finger with two rows of twenty-five holes above the finger that connect to the gold plated fifty pin slot finger. Certainly, this board alone eliminates the need to cut and to prepare a circuit board that will fit within the available space in the Apple][computer, and this board considerably reduces the labor that is needed before any IC sockets or components can be soldered in place and wire wrapped. With the board from Glitch Works, only the fun stuff is left to do, like developing a circuit diagram and wiring together all of its components.

The circuit logic in the Apple][computer that supports peripheral slot cards is so incredibly well-designed that one can utilize a rather large number of serially connected logic gates up to the point where the final resultant signal can be used to drive data onto the data bus if that signal is clocked by either $\phi0$ or $\phi1$ in the last logic gate. The quikLoader utilizes up to six serially connected logic gates before EPROM data is finally driven onto the data bus. Even the EPROM Reader must utilize five serially connected logic gates before the EPROM Reader can drive specific EPROM data onto the data bus, and only one logic gate is needed in order to enable a selected EPROM.

Address	Operation	Description
0xC0n0	write	select EPROM data bank 0
0xC0n1	write	select EPROM data bank 1
0xC0n2	write	select EPROM data bank 2
0xC0n3	write	select EPROM data bank 3
0xC0n4	write	select EPROM data bank 4
0xC0n5	write	select EPROM data bank 5
0xC0n6	write	select EPROM data bank 6
0xC0n7	write	select EPROM data bank 7

Table V.28.1. Peripheral-Card I/O Memory Locations for EPROM Reader

Bit	Name	Source	Description
0	E0	D0	EPROM number, bit 0
1	E1	D1	EPROM number, bit 1
2	E2	D2	EPROM number, bit 2
3	E3	D3	EPROM number, bit 3
4	B0	A0	EPROM data bank, bit 0
5	B1	A1	EPROM data bank, bit 1
6	B2	A2	EPROM data bank, bit 2
7	C1	D7	EPROM Reader enable, 0 = ON

Table V.28.2. Control Register for EPROM Reader

B2	B1	B0	Bank	EPROM	EPROM Access	Memory Access
0	0	0	0	2716	0x0000-0x07FF	0xF800-0xFFFF
0	0	0	0	2732	0x0000-0x0FFF	0xF000-0xFFFF
0	0	0	0	2764	0x0000-0x1FFF	0xE000-0xFFFF
0	0	0	0	27128	0x0000-0x1FFF	0xE000-0xFFFF
0	0	1	1		0x2000-0x3FFF	0xE000-0xFFFF
0	0	0	0	27256	0x0000-0x1FFF	0xE000-0xFFFF
0	0	1	1		0x2000-0x3FFF	0xE000-0xFFFF
0	1	0	2		0x4000-0x5FFF	0xE000-0xFFFF
0	1	1	3		0x6000-0x7FFF	0xE000-0xFFFF
0	0	0	0	27512	0x0000-0x1FFF	0xE000-0xFFFF
0	0	1	1		0x2000-0x3FFF	0xE000-0xFFFF
0	1	0	2		0x4000-0x5FFF	0xE000-0xFFFF
0	1	1	3		0x6000-0x7FFF	0xE000-0xFFFF
1	0	0	4		0x8000-0x9FFF	0xE000-0xFFFF
1	0	1	5		0xA000-0xBFFF	0xE000-0xFFFF
1	1	0	6		0xC000-0xDFFF	0xE000-0xFFFF
1	1	1	7		0xE000-0xFFFF	0xE000-0xFFFF

Table V.28.3. EPROM Data Bank Selection for EPROM Reader

I believe every peripheral interface card that I have worked with utilizes some sort of control register. A peripheral interface card could even utilize several control registers. When I designed my Real Time Clock card, I wanted to be able to capture what was previously loaded into the register that configures the clock. Every register, EPROM, or even a data generator such as the clock IC in this example, requires some sort of octal 3-state line driver like a 74LS244 or a 74LS245 IC in order to display its data contents. The Real Time Clock card uses two 74LS244 ICs in order to drive control data values and clock data values onto the data bus when those values are requested. Unlike the quikLoader, I want to display the data values in the control register that resides in the EPROM Reader. Like the quikLoader, I want to use an octal driver to drive the data of the selected EPROM onto the data bus. Unlike the quikLoader, I want to capture eight control bits which requires an octal D flip-flop IC that has a common clock and a master reset, and a 74LS273 IC fits that job description nicely. I can place eight twenty-eight pin EPROM sockets and three twenty pin IC sockets comfortably on the Glitch Works card and still have room for up to four fourteen or sixteen pin IC sockets. These physical requirements form the beginning specifications that I considered when I designed the circuit for the EPROM Reader card.

My development of *EOS* allowed me to design software routines that viewed an EPROM as a series of addressable banks of data. When a program requires data from multiple data banks, the *EOS* software simply initializes its pointer to an offset within the first data bank and selects the next following data banks as necessary by using the protocol that is designed into its hardware. At most, the EPROM Reader must be able to address up to eight data banks where each data bank is 0x2000 or 8192 bytes in size in order to read without interruption all of the contents in a 27512 EPROM that contains 64 KB of data. As in the quikLoader, an EPROM is easily selected by saving its EPROM number from 0x00 to 0x07 into the control register. This register utilizes the peripheral-card I/O memory locations that are dedicated to a peripheral slot card, and these memory locations reside from 0xC0n0 through 0xC0nF where n is equal to the slot number where the peripheral card resides plus eight. Only eight of the available sixteen peripheral-card I/O memory locations are necessary in order to select one of eight data banks within each EPROM that resides on the EPROM Reader card. In other words, the EPROM Reader only latches the state of the first three address bits in order to select a data bank. Table V.28.1 lists the peripheral-card I/O memory locations and the EPROM Reader data bank that these memory locations select. Table V.28.2 lists the contents of the EPROM Reader control register. I have duplicated Table V.8.1 and modified it for the EPROM Reader card as Table V.28.3. Table V.28.3 shows the Apple][memory locations where EPROM data is found and the number of data banks each EPROM size is capable of addressing. A major structural EPROM difference exists between the 16/32/64 EPROMs and the 128/256/512 EPROMs. The 16/32/64 EPROMs are manufactured in 24-pin dual in-line packages or DIPs whereas the 128/256/512 EPROMs are manufactured in 28-pin DIPs. The EPROM Reader hardware circuit must take this EPROM structural difference into consideration in being able to electrically support both EPROM sizes without having to cut traces and solder bubbles as in the quikLoader hardware circuit design.

I have no reason to design the EPROM Reader circuit to be fully compatible with the design of the quikLoader circuit in selecting which control register bit enables or disables the EPROM Reader card. The quikLoader uses control register bit 4 for its ON/OFF hardware function. Personally, I would rather utilize control register bit 7 or the MSB for the ON/OFF function in the EPROM Reader, so that design choice is shown in Table V.28.2. It just makes more sense to me to use the MSB for the ON/OFF function, and I believe it is far more logical. Any system software can certainly control all hardware functionality of the quikLoader or of the EPROM Reader by simply utilizing an assembly directive. This directive would optionally assemble the specific system software for one hardware design or the other hardware design and assemble the remaining identical system software for both. Thus, whenever an EPROM card must be turned ON and if *EOS* is being assembled for the quikLoader, its hardware design would be utilized and control register bit 4 would be set to zero. If *EOS* is being assembled for the EPROM Reader, its hardware design would be utilized and control register bit 7 would be set to zero. *EOS* that is assembled for the quikLoader would only be utilized by the EPROM that resides in socket 0 of the quikLoader.

When I first began working on *EOS*, I had no intention in supporting more than one EPROM card in an Apple][computer and I made that decision quite clear when I wrote Section V.8. Now that I am at that stage of gathering specifications and requirements for the EPROM Reader card, I need to decide whether *EOS* can truly support multiple EPROM cards in an Apple][computer and if so, what additional circuitry does that capability require? What is the function or all of the functions of the USR bit in the quikLoader and how necessary is it to incorporate the USR bit in the EPROM Reader? What additional circuitry does the USR bit capability require? It is my understanding that the functions of the USR bit are to select the odd data bank and to utilize a quikLoader in an Apple][and in an Apple][+. Two unmarked locations on the underside of the Apple][motherboard must be jumpered in order to make the USER1 connection. After this connection is made and after the quikLoader is jumpered or soldered appropriately, the quikLoader can be utilized in an Apple][computer according to quikLoader documentation. Furthermore, if the Apple][computer uses a 16 KB RAM card in Slot 0, it must also be electrically modified as well. It appears to me that a number of hardware modifications must be made in order to utilize a quikLoader in these Apple computers. I do not fully understand the effect of turning the USR bit ON and OFF in order to select the odd data bank in a quikLoader vis-à-vis when that quikLoader is utilized in an Apple][computer. Regardless, the USR bit is simply **not** utilized in the EPROM Reader card, yet the EPROM Reader is fully functional in an **unmodified** Apple][or Apple][+ as will be explained shortly.

From my analysis of the quikLoader hardware and my design of *EOS* and purposefully tailoring the Apple][data bank window to include **only** the memory range at 0xE000:0xFFFF, the EPROM Reader circuit can be greatly simplified. There is absolutely no need to extend the data bank window any lower than 0xE000 and restrict access to ROM or RAM memory below 0xE000. A 27512 EPROM can be accessed entirely by means of eight 8 KB data bank windows. These eight data bank windows can easily be selected by storing the desired EPROM number into the control register at any one of the first eight addresses of the peripheral-card I/O memory locations that are dedicated to that slot as shown in Table V.28.1. Even if the next eight peripheral-card I/O memory locations are utilized instead, the same data bank will be selected. Thus, the fourth address bit is not captured and it is not utilized by the EPROM Reader hardware. The primary circuit design task is the attempt to provide all of the EPROM Reader control logic within any four ICs that can fit into either a fourteen or a sixteen pin package. The quikLoader circuit is able to control all of its functionality using five ICs though it is unable to control an additional 74LS244 octal driver, thus it is unable to display the contents of its control register.

I have now decided to include additional software logic into *EOS* in order to support multiple EPROM cards if they should reside in the same Apple][computer. The version of *EOS* that supports multiple EPROM cards in the same Apple][computer is now called *EOS+*. Therefore, my circuit design for the EPROM Reader card must also utilize the DMA IN and DMA OUT protocol as in the quikLoader in order to prioritize multiple EPROM cards in an Apple][computer by slot number where the Apple][sets the higher priority to the lower slot number. Therefore, EPROM cards must follow the rules for using DMA IN and DMA OUT. Simply put, there can be no interruption of the DMA OUT of one card to the DMA IN of the card in the next higher slot. No connection must be made to the DMA IN of the highest priority EPROM card or to the DMA OUT of the lowest priority EPROM card, but both DMA IN and DMA OUT must be connected for all cards in between the EPROM cards. My circuit design for the EPROM Reader card that supports all *EOS+* functionality, utilizes DMA IN and DMA OUT protocol, and controls all of the capabilities of the EPROM Reader hardware using only four fourteen or sixteen pin IC packages, is presented in Figure V.28.1.

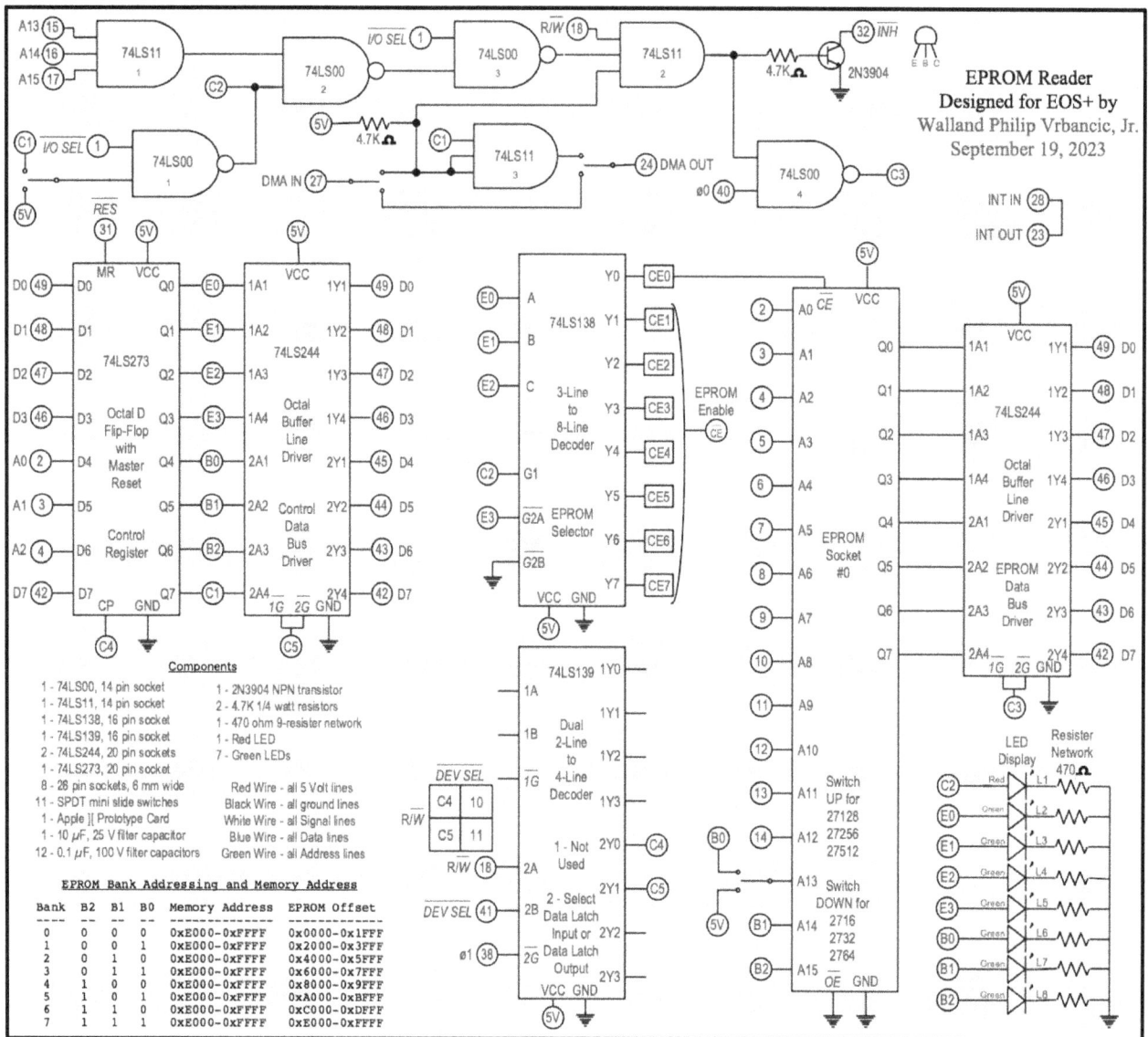

Figure V.28.1. Schematic Diagram for the EPROM Reader Card

It is a bit odd having to design a hardware circuit where the ON/OFF enable bit is opposite to normal logic. That is, when the control register enable bit, or bit 7 is 0, the EPROM Reader hardware is turned ON as if *RESET* had just been pressed. When the control register enable bit is 1, the EPROM Reader hardware is turned OFF. The first 74LS00 dual input gate inverts either the C1 control signal or the *I/O SELECT* control signal in order to generate the C2 control signal. The C2 control signal is used to enable the 74LS138 decoder IC that enables the selected EPROM which uses all four bits from the control register called E0, E1, E2, and E3. It is important to enable the selected EPROM as soon as possible particularly for an EPROM that has an access time well over 300 ns. When the EPROM Reader is enabled by pressing *RESET*, any address on the Apple][address bus that is within the data bank window address 0xE000:0xFFFF will enable the first 74LS11 gate. These two gates together will enable the second 74LS00 gate. The third 74LS00 gate behaves as an OR gate in that if either the second 74LS00 gate is enabled OR the *I/O SELECT* control signal is enabled, each enabled to a logic level of 0, the output of the third 74LS00 gate will be at a logic level of 1. How beautiful is that?

The *I/O SELECT* control signal in the Apple][is always enabled whenever the ROM firmware of a peripheral-card is accessed as when 0xCs00:0xCsFF, where **s** is the slot number of the peripheral slot card, is put onto the address bus. Thus, the EPROM Reader responds to its dedicated *I/O SELECT* control signal whenever its peripheral-card ROM memory is accessed regardless whether the EPROM Reader is ON or OFF. In either case, the output of the third 74LS00 gate will be at logic level 1 though it really is not possible for both the data bank window (0xE0:0xFF) and the *I/O SELECT* control signal (0xC1:0xC7) to be enabled at the very same time. The output of the third 74LS00 gate, the Apple's R/W or read/*write* control signal, and the Apple's DMA IN line are the inputs to the second 74LS11 gate and it outputs the control signal that drives the fourth 74LS00 gate and the 2N3904 transistor. The fourth 74LS00 gate uses this control signal along with ϕ0 in order to generate the control signal C3, the control signal that enables the EPROM octal line driver, or 74LS244. The 2N3904 transistor is configured having an open collector output which safely drives the Apple's *INH* control line low in order to deselect the motherboard ROM(s) from responding to any address that is within the data bank window of the EPROM Reader. I was quite successful in using this same transistor configuration in my Real Time Clock card in order to generate both the IRQ and the NMI interrupts. One half of the 74LS139 uses R/W, *Dev Sel*, and ϕ1 in order to generate the control signals C4 and C5. The other half of the 74LS139 is not utilized. The control signal C4 is used to latch new configuration data into the control register of the EPROM Reader. The control signal C5 is used to enable its octal line driver, or 74LS244, in order to display the contents of the EPROM Reader control register. Finally, the DMA IN line along with the control signal C1 are presented to the third 74LS11 gate and the output of this gate becomes the DMA OUT signal in the EPROM Reader card.

I was able to obtain miniature SPDT slide switches that have a 0.1 inch pinout which is perfect for mounting them on the Glitch Works card. These SPDT switches are rugged enough for their limited usage and they certainly are a far better choice than having to cut traces and solder bubbles as in the quikLoader. One switch is used for every EPROM socket in order to select whether a 16/32/64 EPROM or a 128/256/512 EPROM is seated in that socket. One switch is used to disable the EPROM Reader hardware. However, even if the EPROM Reader is disabled, the EPROM Reader will still respond to its *I/O SELECT* control signal and its control register can still be written and the contents of the control register can still be displayed. One switch is used to enable the DMA IN input control line and one switch is used to enable the DMA OUT output control line. When both DMA lines are disabled, both DMA lines are connected to each other. A red LED is connected to the control signal C2, green LEDs are connected to EPROM selection bits E0, E1, E2, and E3, and green LEDs are connected to data bank selection bits B0, B1, and B2. The electrical current through all LEDs is limited by a resistor network. Low and high frequency transients are filtered by a 10.0 µF and 0.1 µF capacitor, respectively, before any power is distributed to the card, and 0.1 µF capacitors are used to filter transients for each EPROM and each IC socket. Various colored wire wrapping wire is used to connect all of the components on the back side of the Glitch Works card.

The advanced EPROM Operating System *EOS+* is very similar to its predecessor *EOS*, and *EOS+* contains all of the functionality that is found in the original EPROM Operating System as well as the new mapping function for the Apple][slots and their respective contents. The new mapping function provides *EOS+* with the ability to access multiple EPROM cards that may reside in the same Apple][computer in a hierarchical structure. Table V.28.4 lists all of the firmware entry locations that are available whenever the firmware code or the peripheral-card ROM memory of an EPROM Reader is in focus and is accessed. In other words, whenever an address within 0xCs00:0xCsFF, where **s** is the slot number of the EPROM Reader, is put onto the Apple's address bus **only** when EPROM 0 and when Bank 0 are both selected, the firmware locations that are shown in Table V.28.4 can be utilized in order to process *EOS+* routines such as EPASEOS, EPBINEOS, and EPEOS. Table V.28.5 lists all of the software routines and the program content that is found in the EPROM that resides in the EPROM 0 socket of the EPROM Reader card or in the quikLoader card that contains the *EOS+* assembly language program.

Offset	Name	Description
0x00	EPASEOS	Applesoft entrance to parse a CALL statement for ASEOS command and variables
0x50	ASEXIT	ASEOS exit and to RUN Applesoft files
0x80	BINEXIT	BINEOS exit and to RUN binary files; address of EPBINEOS put in Y-reg and A-reg
0xA8	RTNEXIT	*EOS+* exit assuming a return to *EOS+* by means of EPUSER1/2 or EPMAPEOS
0xB8	EPOFF	Special location for the software routine that can turn this EPROM card OFF
0xC0	EPUSER1	Return from *EOS+* CMDUSER 1 command
0xC8	EPUSER2	Return from *EOS+* CMDUSER 2 command
0xD0	EPMAPEOS	Entrance into *EOS+* by means of SLOTMAP, from the *EOS+* mapping function
0xE0	EPBINEOS	Program entrance to process a BINEOS DCB command structure
0xF0	EPEOS	Manual entrance into *EOS+*
0xF8	EPBINTXT	ASCII text string *EPBINEOS* used to find the slot number for an EPROM card

Table V.28.4. Firmware Locations in EOS+

Bank	Offset	Memory	Size	Contents
0	0x0000	0xE000	0x0004	Synchronization bytes that preface Catalog
0	0x0004	0xE004	0x00FC	Catalog, terminated by 0x00
0	0x0100	0xE100	0x0100	Slot 1 *EOS+* ASEOS/BINEOS interface
0	0x0200	0xE200	0x0100	Slot 2 *EOS+* ASEOS/BINEOS interface
0	0x0300	0xE300	0x0100	Slot 3 *EOS+* ASEOS/BINEOS interface
0	0x0400	0xE400	0x0100	Slot 4 *EOS+* ASEOS/BINEOS interface
0	0x0500	0xE500	0x0100	Slot 5 *EOS+* ASEOS/BINEOS interface
0	0x0600	0xE600	0x0100	Slot 6 *EOS+* ASEOS/BINEOS interface
0	0x0700	0xE700	0x0100	Slot 7 *EOS+* ASEOS/BINEOS interface
0	0x0800	0xE800	0x17FA	*EOS+* assembly language program
0	0x1FFA	0xFFFA	0x0002	NMI vector, address of *EOS+*
0	0x1FFC	0xFFFC	0x0002	RESET vector, address of *EOS+*
0	0x1FFE	0xFFFE	0x0002	IRQ/BRK vector, address of *EOS+*
1	0x2000	0xE000	0x2100	DOS4.5L, Build 05 file image
2	0x4100	0xE100	0x2A00	DOS4.5H, Build 06 file image
3	0x6B00	0xEB00	0x2800	LISA80.1 code segment, Auxiliary memory
4	0x9300	0xF300	0x1000	LISA80.2 code segment, Auxiliary memory
5	0xA300	0xE300	0x0640	LISA80.3 code segment, Main memory
5	0xA940	0xE940	0x1914	*SETUP80*
6	0xC254	0xE254	0x01C0	*LOADLISA80*
6	0xC414	0xE414	0x1B04	RamDisk Install
6	0xDF18	0xFF18	0x1316	*FID*
7	0xF22E	0xF22E	0x064A	*Set Clock*
7	0xF878	0xF878	0x06D9	*ASLIST*
7	0xFF51	0xFF51	0x00AF	unused

Table V.28.5. Contents of EPROM 0 Showing EOS+ and Programs

```
:             :           :
0000          56 QLCARD   equ 0
0001          57 EPCARD   equ 1
:             :           :
0008         130 EPUSR    equ %00001000
:             :           :
0294         169 EPNMBR   equ $294
0295         170 EPBANK   equ $295
:             :           :
0001         187 HWCARD   equ EPCARD
:             :           :
0110         209 ; Configure the X-reg and A-reg based on EPNMBR and EPBANK.
0110         210 ;
0110         211 EPCONFIG:
0110         212         .if HWCARD
0110 AE 95 02 213         ldx EPBANK
0113 AD 94 02 214         lda EPNMBR
0116 60      215         rts
0117         216         dfs 6,NEGONE
011D         217         .el
011D         218         lda EPBANK
011D         219         lsr
011D         220         tax
011D         221         lda EPNMBR
011D         222         bcc >1
011D         223         ora #EPUSR
011D         224 ^1      rts
011D         225         .fi
:             :           :
```

Figure V.28.2. Utilizing EPNMBR and EPBANK in EPCONFIG

The two major hardware design differences between the quikLoader and the EPROM Reader is the utilization of the USR bit in the quikLoader in order to select the odd or even data bank and how each card is enabled and disabled. The EPROM Reader does **not** utilize the USR bit. Figure V.28.2 shows the EPCONFIG routine that is used by the EPMOVE and EPEXEC routines in order to configure the control register in either EPROM card. The quikLoader control register may or may not use the EPUSR value of 0x08 depending upon whether the selected data bank or EPBANK is even or odd. The assembly directive HWCARD determines whether EPCONFIG is being assembled for the quikLoader or for the EPROM Reader, that is, when HWCARD = QLCARD or when HWCARD = EPCARD, respectively. For the EPROM Reader, the X-register is loaded with EPBANK and the A-register is loaded with EPNMBR. For the quikLoader, the A-register is loaded with EPBANK, shifted right to detect oddness, and then copied to the X-register. Next, the A-register is loaded with EPNMBR and OR'd with EPUSR only when EPBANK is odd. In the remaining common code that follows, the control register can now be configured by using the initial peripheral-card I/O memory location 0xC0n0 with the desired EPROM number in the A-register and the desired data bank number in the X-register so that the first byte of the desired EPROM data may be read and copied to the specified memory location in the Apple][computer.

The quikLoader uses bit 4 to enable or to disable its hardware control logic and the EPROM Reader uses bit 7 to enable or to disable its hardware control logic. While the *EOS+* mapping function is processing, the firmware entry location EPOFF that is shown in Table V.28.4 is fundamental to this function in that this special firmware location can disable either the quikLoader or the EPROM Reader depending upon

397

the value of the assembly directive HWCARD. Using **s** for the slot number of an EPROM card, EPOFF is located at 0xCsB8 in all seven peripheral-card ROM memory locations in *EOS+* when Bank 0 is enabled. Since both the quikLoader and the EPROM Reader are required to utilize an EPROM in the EPROM 0 socket, that EPROM must contain a **version** of *EOS+* that is unique for that specific hardware. Thus, *EOS+* differs only in the value that is assigned to HWCARD and in the value that is utilized in order to disable its hardware control logic. Thus, 0x10 is used to disable the quikLoader and 0x80 is used to disable the EPROM Reader. It is extraordinary that there are only twenty-six differences in the entire contents of these two EPROMS whose EPROM card can reside in any available peripheral-card slot.

EOS+ first initializes the stack pointer, XMODE, the configuration of CX ROM memory, the ZipChip if it is found, and the annunciators before the EPROM card determines its slot number. If more than one EPROM card resides in a computer, only the highest priority EPROM card will control the data bus at this time assuming, of course, that all EPROM cards utilize their DMA IN connections, provide DMA OUT connections, and follow all of the rules for using DMA IN and DMA OUT. *EOS+* can now call the BUILDMAP routine that is designed to locate all EPROM cards and record its findings in a variable called SLOTMAP. For example, if SLOTMAP contains the value of 0xA4 which is %10100100 in binary, there are EPROM cards in slots 2, 5, and 7. There is no slot 0, so BUILDMAP initializes bit 0 in the SLOTMAP variable to zero as a placeholder. In this example, the EPROM card that resides in slot 2 has the highest priority and **is** the EPROM card that determines the value that is stored into SLOTMAP. While any EPROM card is in control, the variables within 0x0290:0x02EF in the INPUT buffer are used exclusively by *EOS+*. The clock uses the INPUT buffer at 0x02F0:0x02FD. Any reasonably sized CALL statement to ASEOS in an Applesoft program can easily be accommodated within this smaller INPUT buffer such that Applesoft is still able to parse the CALL statement before and after ASEOS processing. Naturally, if a person wishes to disregard any of these clarifications, warnings, explanations, and suggestions, that person will undoubtedly experience unfortunate behaviors of even the most robust software routines even on well-designed hardware. It is my sincere intention to provide a computing experience that provides expected results successfully while using acceptable program values for each and every iteration. All of the variables that reside in the INPUT buffer are available to all other EPROM cards that may also reside in the same computer as long as each EPROM card utilizes *EOS+*. When the next EPROM card begins its processing, it will use the value that it finds in SLOTMAP in order to select the next lower priority EPROM card or, if there is not a lower priority EPROM card, then the first, or highest priority EPROM card will be selected next.

EOS+ uses the display of a Main Menu that lists all of the routines and the functions that it can either launch, load, or provide in one simple location. All of the programs that *EOS+* can launch or load from the Main Menu is accomplished by using an internal DCB for that program which is processed internally by BINEOS. If a program is simply loaded into memory, BINEOS automatically returns to the *EOS+* Main Menu for further direction. There is absolutely no difference in how *EOS+* loads and runs programs internally than how an external user uses EPBINEOS at 0xCsE0 in order to load and run programs using an external DCB. It would be ludicrous for *EOS+* to process a DCB otherwise from an external source. It would be quite possible to design and to implement multiple menus where each menu pane could provide the ability to launch or to load twenty-six additional programs. I simply selected those programs that I most often use for the Main Menu display and then use the *EOS+* EPROM Catalog function in order to launch any of the other programs that I use occasionally. Figures V.28.3 and V.28.4 show the *EOS+* Main Menu Selection for an EPROM Reader that resides in slot 4 and a quikLoader that resides in slot 5. Both menus are identical because their EPROM 0 are nearly identical. The EPROM Reader can address sixteen EPROMs in its Catalog and the quikLoader can address eight EPROMs in its Catalog. Figure V.28.5 shows an example Catalog display of the contents of EPROM 0 from the EPROM Reader. The file entry values for the file that is named DOS4.5.06H are read from the Catalog structure that is found at the beginning of that same EPROM and those values are shown in Figure V.28.6. A two-digit hexadecimal entry beginning with 0 is required to select an EPROM number in order to display its full Catalog.

```
EOS+ Main Menu Selection for Slot 4
A DOS 4.5.05L         N Copy ROM->RAM
B DOS 4.5.06H         O Run HELLO on SDV
C Coldstart DOS       P CATALOG this SDV
D Warmstart DOS       Q BigMac
E Boot the Slot S     R Scan Disk
F Hook the Slot S     S Applesoft List
G Unhook a Slot S     T Binary Install
H Sourceror           U VTOC Manager
I EPROM Burner        V Volume Manager
J FID                 W Volume Duplicate
K ADT2                X Disk Window
L Lisa80              Y Real Time Clock
M RamDisk Config      Z ZipChip Config

  S=7 D=01 V=000      00-0F EPROM Catalog

^C Configure SDV      RTN Toggle ZipChip
^S Skip EPROM Card        -> Off <-

Enter Selection:
```

Figure V.28.3. EPROM Reader Main Menu

```
EOS+ Main Menu Selection for Slot 5
A DOS 4.5.05L         N Copy ROM->RAM
B DOS 4.5.06H         O Run HELLO on SDV
C Coldstart DOS       P CATALOG this SDV
D Warmstart DOS       Q BigMac
E Boot the Slot S     R Scan Disk
F Hook the Slot S     S Applesoft List
G Unhook a Slot S     T Binary Install
H Sourceror           U VTOC Manager
I EPROM Burner        V Volume Manager
J FID                 W Volume Duplicate
K ADT2                X Disk Window
L Lisa80              Y Real Time Clock
M RamDisk Config      Z ZipChip Config

  S=7 D=01 V=000      00-07 EPROM Catalog

^C Configure SDV      RTN Toggle ZipChip
^S Skip EPROM Card        -> Off <-

Enter Selection:  ■
```

Figure V.28.4. quikLoader Main Menu

```
      EPROM Card - EPROM Catalog
        Slot 4          EPROM 0

  S 0x44   DOS4.5.05L

  S 0x5C  >DOS4.5.06H

  P 0x84   LOADLISA80

  S 0x48   LISA80.1

  S 0x50   LISA80.2

  S 0x44   LISA80.3

  B 0x04   SETUP80

  B 0x04   RamDisk Config


  RTN - File Info        (L)oad
  SPC - Next EPROM       (R)un
  0-F - Select EPROM     (Q)uit
```

Figure V.28.5. EPROM Reader Catalog

```
      EPROM Card - EPROM Catalog
        Slot 4          EPROM 0


File Name - DOS4.5.06H

File Type - System
            Binary, LC Bank 2
            Binary, LC Bank 1
            Binary, main memory

File Size - 0x2A00

From EPROM Offset - 0x4100

To Memory Address - 0xBE00


      Press any key to Continue
```

Figure V.28.6. EPROM Reader Entry Values

Main Menu selections E, F, G, O, and P depend on the current values that are assigned to Slot, Drive, and Volume, or SDV. Those assigned values can easily be changed by pressing CTRL-C and entering the requested values. It is easy to select the next, lower priority EPROM card by pressing CTRL-S. The Catalog function may be selected for any of the EPROMs that reside on that EPROM card by first pressing 0 and then pressing its EPROM number. Pressing any of the alpha keys from A to Z will launch that program or execute that function. Obviously, the *EOS+* Main Menu is very straightforward, easy to understand, and easy to use. This menu is designed to launch or to execute any of the desired programs or functions as quickly and as easily as possible. Furthermore, the utilization of ASEOS and BINEOS has not changed in *EOS+*. The documentation that is presented in Section V.8 is still current and has not changed for *EOS+*. All of the *EOS+* exit routines leave the EPROM card selected for EPROM 0 and data

Bank 0. Therefore, an Applesoft program should always find an EPROM card configured for EPROM 0 and for data Bank 0. However, all of the recommendations that are given for using ASEOS in an Applesoft program should still be followed as outlined in Section V.8.

I have taken a very deep dive into the data that is found in the EPROM that was furnished with my quikLoader hardware when I purchased that quikLoader sometime in 1983. There are a few Givens or Knowns for a quikLoader EPROM 0. That is, when an Apple][is powered ON or when the RESET key is pressed, EPROM 0 and Bank 0 are both enabled. The RESET vector address that is put onto the address bus is found at 0xFFFC:0xFFFD. The design of EPROM 0 for the quikLoader puts the address of its Katalog at bytes 0xFFF8:0xFFF9 if an EPROM Katalog exists in that data bank. All data banks in EPROM 0 contain vectors or JMP instructions that begin at 0xFFF8. The EPROM that was supplied with my quikLoader is a 27256 EPROM that has four 8 KB data banks, and this EPROM can hold up to 32 KB of data. Its RESET address is 0xFF00 in Bank 0 and its Katalog address is 0xFF00 in Bank 3 at 0xFFF8:0xFFF9. EPROM 0 contains a number of data files and an Overhead file that comprise the two parts of QLOS, the quikLoader Operating System. QLOS provides a list of ten selectable RESET vectors for various routines that execute when a particular key is pressed before the RESET key is pressed. In order to produce QLOS compatible EPROMs, each QLOS EPROM must contain both the data files and the Overhead file that comprise QLOS. Typically, the QLOS Overhead begins at 0xFF00 in **each** data Bank of the EPROM and the Katalog begins at 0xFF00 and is included in the very last bank of the EPROM. There is no recourse that is provided in QLOS if 255 bytes are insufficient to contain the entire contents of files within that EPROM given that the Katalog must terminate with the value of 0x86. **Mr. Sather could not have designed a more complex and more convoluted operating system for the quikLoader**.

QLOS is limited to only coping its EPROM resources into memory and QLOS does not provide any ability to view its EPROM resources by any external means nor can one even obtain the resource content information of an EPROM by any external means. Bank switching is prolific such that it becomes difficult, tedious, and nearly unfathomable to follow program flow and the operation of QLOS, if such an operation is even quantifiable. QLOS is engineered to utilize a configuration register such that the upper three bits are intended for the exited EPROM number and the lower five bits are intended for the entered EPROM number. This strategy is employed entirely by quikLoader primary routines that ping pong EPROM data bank control from EPROM to EPROM and from data bank to data bank. In Mr. Sather's words, "The operational philosophy of The quikLoader and QLOS is to transfer programs to RAM for execution. However, programs can be run while they reside in the quikLoader. There are some limitations on this capability, though." The quikLoader documentation that I received with my quikLoader contained little if any information on how QLOS conducts its operations vis-à-vis the presence of multiple quikLoaders that may reside in the same Apple][computer. The page-zero variable QLMAP at 0x2D is constructed by the successive OR of values from the Slot Map table that is found at 0xFF95 in Bank 0. Even Bank 2 contains a copy of this very same table at 0xFC00. In QLOS, QLMAP uses the MSB to denote whether there is an EPROM card in slot 1 and QLMAP uses bit 1 to denote whether there is an EPROM card in slot 7. I do not fully comprehend the logic of this strategy.

Looking at the EPROM Reader using the same oversight lens, the RESET vector address that is put onto the address bus when an Apple][is powered ON or when the RESET key is pressed, its vector address is found at 0xFFFC:0xFFFD which is at EPROM offset 0x1FFC:0x1FFD. The EPROM Catalog for all *EOS+* EPROMS begins on the fourth byte after the thirty-two bit word 0xC4B890ED which begins each and every *EOS* and *EOS+* EPROM. The EPROM Catalog may extend as far into the EPROM memory as necessary except for EPROM 0 because the Slot 1 interface for ASEOS and BINEOS must begin at EPROM offset 0x0100 as shown in Table V.28.5. All *EOS+* resource Catalogs are terminated with 0x00. Except in EPROM 0 which must contain the *EOS+* assembly language routine from EPROM offset

0x0800 to 0x1FFF, the **remainder** of EPROM 0 and the **remainder** of all other EPROMs after their Catalog, can be used sequentially, without interruption, for contiguous data using multiple data banks. EPROMs 1 through 7 are not required to contain any *EOS+* data or Overhead in order to transfer any EPROM file to memory. The only locations in *EOS+* where bank switching occurs are in the EPMOVE and EPEXEC routines that call EPCONFIG in order to initialize the EPROM number and the data bank number where the start of EPROM data is first located. Where necessary, the next successive data bank is enabled to obtain the remaining EPROM data that is requested. An eight-byte DCB is utilized in order to load or to launch any EPROM resource whether that resource is requested internally by *EOS+* or externally by a user by means of the binary interface called BINEOS. Even an external Applesoft user has full access to all EPROM resources by means of an Applesoft interface called ASEOS. Both interfaces have the capability to read and to extract the content of Catalogs that reside on each and every EPROM of an EPROM card whether that card is a quikLoader or an EPROM Reader. Multiple EPROM cards are supported by *EOS+* and *EOS+* uses a SLOTMAP variable that is found at 0x292 and whose bits are defined uniquely for *EOS+*. Each EPROM card may transfer its control to another EPROM card by utilizing two entry locations that are found in the peripheral-card ROM memory and the bit settings that are found in SLOTMAP which determines the slot number of the next EPROM card. *EOS+* simply exits one EPROM card via RTNEXIT at 0xCuA8 and enters another EPROM card via EPMAPEOS at 0xCvD0. The u and v slot numbers are usually not the same. If only one EPROM card resides in an Apple][computer, *EOS+* can certainly exit itself and re-enter itself using RTNEXIT and EPMAPEOS that are located in the same peripheral-card ROM memory. The *EOS+* that resides on the next EPROM card will handle its EPROM resources uniquely. As long as an Applesoft program knows the slot number of each EPROM card, that program will be able to obtain the Catalog contents of all EPROMs on all EPROM cards as well as load or launch any resource that is contained in any EPROM that resides on any EPROM card.

I found it to be the most exhausting and the most extensive exercise when I attempted to make sense out of the data that I found in the EPROM that was supplied with my quikLoader. All I wanted was to obtain an overview of the general layout of this EPROM and where Mr. Sather placed the various data for DOS 3.3, *FID*, *COPYA*, QLOS HELP, the ROM Monitor, quikLoader initialization, and the EPROM Katalog structure. I also wanted to understand how Mr. Sather utilized the USR bit, other than for specifying data bank selection, in order for the quikLoader to operate successfully in the Apple][or in the Apple][+ computers. That is, I wanted to understand why the USR bit is sometimes set ON and other times set OFF, yet it is expected to always control the 74LS138 IC at motherboard location H12 which generates the slot *I/O SELECT* control signals in the Apple][. In other words, when the USR bit is ON, the 74LS138 at location H12 will **not** be enabled, thus the slot *I/O SELECT* control signals will **not** be provided, and each slot will **not** be able to utilize its peripheral-card ROM memory. Obviously, this functionality in QLOS can only be accomplished when this function resides in an odd data bank which is the only time when the USR bit **is** turned ON. It seems that the EPROM Reader solves all of these peripheral-card and ROM memory issues because it only responds to a data bank window within 0xE000:0xFFFF. There is no need to disable the 0xC100:0xCFFF memory range because the EPROM Reader does not need to respond to this particular memory range. Tables V.28.6 to V.28.9 list the general contents of EPROM 0 by bank number for the EPROM that was provided with the quikLoader that I purchased. These tables contain a great wealth of information and I believe that information is far easier to assimilate if that information is displayed according to bank number as I have done. It is very apparent that this EPROM contains a large number of Overhead routines that prevent QLOS from loading a very large number of contiguous data bytes. The loading of DOS 3.3 is one such example where a part of DOS 3.3 is found at the beginning of Bank 1 and the remaining part of DOS 3.3 is found well into the first half of Bank 2. Certainly, the file image of DOS 3.3 is not presented in contiguous pages and transferring a non-contiguous image of any program would require additional Overhead routines. Such routines are not required and do not exist in *EOS+*.

EPROM Offset	Memory Address	Name	Description
0x0000 - 0x124D	0x0803 - 0x1A50	FID	Primary routine, Katalog, binary data in Bank 0
0x124E - 0x1378	0x02A0 - 0x03CA	QLOS	src/len/dst in Bank 3 control, 0x7F00
0x1379 - 0x1AC9	0x0803	COPYA	Primary routine, Katalog, Applesoft data in Bank 0
0x1ACA - 0x1E7E	0x0803	QLOS	Applesoft code used for QLOS HELP processing
0x1E7F	0xFE7F	0x3A	HEX 3A
0x1E80 - 0x1EFF	0xFE80 - 0xFEFF	0xFF	Unused, set to 0xFF
0x1F00 - 0x1FF7	0xFF00 - 0xFEF7	Control	Bank 0 control page
0x1FF8 - 0x1FF9	0xFFF8 - 0xFFF9	0x0000	Katalog vector, no catalog vector address found here
0x1FFA - 0x1FFB	0xFFFA - 0xFFFB	0x0000	NMI vector, no vector address found here
0x1FFC - 0x1FFD	0xFFFC - 0xFFFD	0xFF00	RESET vector, address found here is 0xFF00
0x1FFE - 0x1FFF	0xFFFE - 0xFFFF	0xFFFF	IRQ vector, no vector address found here

Table V.28.6. Contents of Original quikLoader EPROM 0, Bank 0

EPROM Offset	Memory Address	Name	Description
0x2000 - 0x3DFF	0x9D00 - 0xBAFF	DOS 3.3	DOS 3.3 pages in Bank 1 Control
0x3E00 - 0x3EFF	0xBD00 - 0xBDFF	DOS 3.3	DOS 3.3 page in Bank 1 Control
0x3F00 - 0x3FF7	0xFF00 - 0xFFF7		Bank 1 control page
0x3FF8 - 0x3FF9	0xFFF8 - 0xFFF9	0x0000	Katalog vector, no vector address found here
0x3FFA - 0x3FFB	0xFFFA - 0xFFFB	0x03FB	NMI vector, address is 0x03FB
0x3FFC - 0x3FFE	0xFFFC - 0xFFFE	JMP 0xBC45	JMP instruction, address is 0xBC45
0x3FFF	0xFFFF	0x00	HEX 00

Table V.28.7. Contents of Original quikLoader EPROM 0, Bank 1

EPROM Offset	Memory Address	Name	Description
0x4000 - 0x57FF	0xE000 - 0xF7FF	ROM Monitor	ROM Monitor code
0x5800 - 0x59FF	0xBE00 - 0xBFFF	DOS 3.3	DOS 3.3 pages in Bank 1 Control
0x5A00 - 0x5BFF	0xFA00 - 0xFBFF	quikLoader	Check power up byte,][or //e, copy ROM Monitor
0x5C00 - 0x5CC5	0xFC00 - 0xFCC5	quikLoader	QL bitmap bits
0x5CC6 - 0x5D03	0xFCC6 - 0xFD03	quikLoader	Initialization code
0x5D04 - 0x5D2F	0xFD04 - 0xFD2F	quikLoader	QL EPROM to memory copy routine
0x5D30 - 0x5D52	0xFD30 - 0xFD52	quikLoader	EPROM to EPROM transfer control routine
0x5D53 - 0x5EFF	0xFD53 - 0xFEFF	0x00	unused, set to 0x00
0x5F00 - 0x5FF7	0xFF00 - 0xFFF7	Control	Bank 2 control page
0x5FF8 - 0x5FF9	0xFFF8 - 0xFFF9	0x0000	Katalog vector, no catalog vector address found here
0x5FFA - 0x5FFB	0xFFFA - 0xFFFB	0x03FB	NMI vector, address is 0x03FB
0x5FFC - 0x5FFD	0xFFFC - 0xFFFD	0xFB89	RESET vector, address found here is 0xFB89
0x5FFE - 0x5FFF	0xFFFE - 0xFFFF	0x00	HEX 00

Table V.28.8. Contents of Original quikLoader EPROM 0, Bank 2

EPROM Offset	Memory Address	Name	Description
0x6000 - 0x6013	0xE000 - 0xE013	QLOS	Routine to copy QLOS code to 0x01D0
0x6014 - 0x61E3	0x01D0 - 0x039F	QLOS	QLOS code
0x61E4 - 0x6598	0x0803	QLOS HELP	Applesoft code used for QLOS HELP processing
0x6599 - 0x7EFF	0xE599 - 0xFEFF	0xFF	unused, set to 0xFF
0x7F00 - 0x7FF7	0xFF00 - 0xFFF7	Control	Bank 3 control page
0x7FF8 - 0x7FF9	0xFFF8 - 0xFFF9	0xFF00	Katalog vector, address is 0xFF00
0x7FFA - 0x7FFB	0xFFFA - 0xFFFB	0x03FB	NMI vector, address is 0x03FB
0x7FFC	0xFFFC	0x09	HEX 09
0x7FFD - 0x7FFF	0xFFFD - 0xFFFF	JMP 0xB385	JMP instruction, address is 0xB385

Table V.28.9. Contents of Original quikLoader EPROM 0, Bank 3

Index	Subroutines	Description of Function
0x00	MOVEBLK	Move data block from quikLoader to memory
0x02	MOVEINT	Move Integer Basic from quikLoader and copy Monitor to LC memory
0x04	MOVEDOS	Move DOS from quikLoader to memory and initialize
0x06	DOJSR	Execute a subroutine in memory
0x08	GOMRBRD	Enter a memory address and begin execution
0x0A	MBRDRST	Perform a computer RESET
0x0C	LOADFP	Do MOVEDOS; move Applesoft program from quikLoader to memory; enter Applesoft Basic
0x0E	RUNFP	Do LOADFP; RUN the Applesoft program
0x10	LOADINT	Do MOVEINT; do MOVEDOS; move Integer program from quikLoader to memory; enter Integer Basic
0x12	RUNINT	Do LOADINT; RUN the Integer program

Table V.28.10. QLOS Subroutines Used by Primary Routines

Indeed, the quikLoader Operating System QLOS is definitely a wild beast and it certainly is a programming nightmare compared to the rather simplistic structure of *EOS+*. Mr. Sather utilized the quikLoader USR bit in conjunction with the Apple USER1 control line in an Apple][or in an Apple][+ as he used the CXROMOFF/CXROMON and the C3ROMOFF/C3ROMON Soft Switches in the Apple //e. The purpose of the USR/USER1 control line or the Apple //e Soft Switches is to inhibit all *I/O SELECT* and *I/O STROBE* control signals in all peripheral slot cards in order to deactivate any and all peripheral slot card memory in the 0xC100:0xCFFF addressing range. Once this addressing range is deactivated, the quikLoader is free to utilize this addressing range for its own purposes which is particularly important to quikLoader Primary routines. Primary routines are free to utilize ten subroutines that are available in QLOS simply by initializing the Y-register with the subroutine number from 0x00 to 0x12 and *dropping in* or bank switching into the control page of Bank 0 or Bank 1 at a specific address location. These ten subroutines are shown in Table V.28.10 and they are all part of the QLOS Overhead. Since DOS 3.3 supports both Applesoft and Integer Basic Type files and programs, QLOS also must support Applesoft and Integer Basic Type files and programs. I have already pointed out that the EPROM Reader only responds to a data bank window within 0xE000:0xFFFF and that it is totally unnecessary for the EPROM Reader to deactivate the peripheral slot card memory in the 0xC100:0xCFFF addressing range. However, the EPROM Reader does manipulate the Soft Switches CXROMOFF/CXROMON and C3ROMOFF/C3ROMON in the Apple //e in order to determine its peripheral slot card number and to determine the bit settings that are saved in SLOTMAP. These EPROM Reader routines are designed to work as they are intended in an Apple][or an Apple][+.

Primary routines that are found in a quikLoader that employ any QLOS Overhead routine **must** be utilized when a software application cannot be implemented using straightforward Applesoft or assembly language files according to QLOS documentation. Primary routines in QLOS **must** be utilized when

1. The program is made up of more than one contiguous EPROM data bank
2. The program exceeds the capacity of a single EPROM
3. The program must be activated by *n-reset*
4. The program must use the first 0x100 bytes of a 27128 or a 27256 EPROM
5. The program must be the power-up program when EPROM 0 is moved to EPROM socket 6

It is rather unfortunate that the above requirements suggest a need to utilize a Primary routine in QLOS in view of *EOS+* and its simplicity of use. I strongly suspect that these requirements stem from the original quikLoader design that utilizes a single address bit. That single address bit in conjunction with the USR bit can only address up to a 27256 EPROM. When 27512 EPROMs became readily available, the quikLoader was redesigned and a second address bit was added in order to increase EPROM addressing and to accommodate the 27512 EPROM. Thus, requirement #2 is no longer viable. The Primary routine that loads all of the *Lisa* modules from EPROM into various areas of memory, for example, makes three calls to BINEOS, and the Primary routine constructs a fourth call within the *Lisa* program that calls BINEOS in order to load the *Lisa* setup program from EPROM into memory when and if that program is ever needed. Now, requirement #1 becomes unimportant and is easily managed in *EOS+*. *EOS+* does not utilize *n-reset* programs nor does *EOS+* capture the last pressed key before RESET is initiated. Rather, *EOS+* displays a Main Menu in order to select from a very large number of programs or functions. I find it difficult to justify the cost in memory and programming logic in order to support *n-reset* or other various keyboard RESET commands. Do these *n-reset* commands, indeed, accelerate and augment one's creative outputs or game playing? I do not believe it does. *EOS+* utilizes a Main Menu structure that can easily be tailored to another person's individual needs, so requirement #3 does not exist by default in *EOS+*. The hardware design of the quikLoader that defines its humongous data bank window parameters prevents all but Primary routines access to the first 0x100 bytes of an EPROM which I believe is an unfortunate design choice. When the data bank window only responds to the 0xE000:0xFFFF memory range, other strategies may be utilized that **does** include the first 0x100 bytes of an EPROM. For example, my design strategy for *EOS+* is to use those first 0x100 bytes, more or less, for the Catalog of that EPROM, so requirement #4 does not exist in *EOS+*. The *EOS+* Catalog **must** begin with the thirty-two bit control word 0xC4B890ED in order for *EOS+* to quickly and to efficiently determine if a particular EPROM socket is occupied by a readable *EOS* or *EOS+* EPROM. If this unusual control word is found in the first four bytes of EPROM memory, the Catalog of that EPROM can quickly be read in order to display the file Types and the EPROM parameters that are shown in Figures V.28.5 and V.28.6.

Once an external Primary routine is copied from EPROM into memory by *EOS+*, that routine can utilize the resources of BINEOS **any number of times** in order to LOAD or to RUN a System file such as *Big Mac*, *Sourceror*, or even DOS4.5.06H. I simply cannot imagine one reason why an *EOS+* Primary routine would require the need for any of those quikLoader Overhead subroutines that are shown in Table V.28.10. If the quikLoader and the EPROM Reader both utilize *EOS+* rather than QLOS, there appears to be no need to consider the state of the USR bit except for data bank selection in the quikLoader. The quikLoader USR bit in conjunction with the Apple USER1 control line in an Apple][or in an Apple][+ is totally unnecessary in *EOS+*. Both the quikLoader and the EPROM Reader cards operate flawlessly in an Apple][and in an Apple][+ when both cards utilize *EOS+* and its Catalog and file structure. Neither card is required to drive the USER1 control line in the Apple][or in the Apple][+. In fact, the EPROM Reader does not even include the USR bit in driving USER1 ON or OFF for any of its functions. The quikLoader, of course, requires the USR bit in order to select the odd data bank when data is found in that bank of an EPROM. Otherwise, the USR bit is not utilized in controlling the visibility of the 0xC100:0xCFFF addressing range in the Apple][or in the Apple][+. *EOS+* is capable of reading the entire contents of an EPROM by means of its vastly smaller data bank window at 0xE000:0xFFFF. Being able to obtain all EPROM information through a smaller data bank window provides many other advantages as well. It is very interesting to note that one major advantage in using a smaller data bank window is how it simplifies the software routines that copy EPROM information into Apple][memory. A corollary advantage in utilizing a smaller data bank window is how it simplifies the hardware circuit design of the EPROM Reader card. Fewer components are required in the EPROM Reader circuit in order to address an entire EPROM and to provide its data to the requested programs and functions. Smaller software routines and fewer hardware components for the same end result always confirms that simplicity in design as a target goal is worth the extra developmental time and effort, and simplicity in design appears to be a far better accomplishment yet a far more difficult achievement.

I have found it uncanny, perhaps even alarming, that data retention in the memory of an Apple][computer can last for many moments after the computer has been powered OFF. This memory data retention provides many false positives that can suggest that DOS has been loaded into memory when in fact it has not. There are four ROM routines or structures in the Apple //e, for example, that are part of the ability of the Apple //e to manage and to detect the power up nature of that machine. These routines or structures are NEWMON at 0xFA81, PWRUP at 0xFAA6, PWRCON at 0xFAFD, and SETPWRC at 0xFB6F. Even before DOS has had an opportunity to initialize its concept of a power up state at PWRSTATE at 0x3F4, at least one ROM routine has managed to initialize the value that is found at 0x3F4. It is very unpredictable what happens when an Apple //e is powered ON with the quikLoader disabled, when a disk drive is not available to BOOT DOS, and when the quikLoader is then enabled and RESET is pressed, everything crashes and falls into the ROM Monitor if one is lucky. The machine believes DOS is loaded and ready to manage files! Even when the computer is quickly turned OFF and then ON, even over and over many times, the quikLoader or the EPROM Reader never seems to be able to stop dumping itself into the ROM Monitor. But if the value at 0x3F4 is altered ever so slightly, everything appears to be fixed. For these reasons, *EOS+* does not utilize the AUTORSET nor the PWRSTATE values at 0x3F2:0x3F3 and 0x3F4, respectively, in order to detect a hardware power ON situation. The AUTORSET and the PWRSTATE values tend to generate false positives all too often, even when power is turned OFF for several moments and then turned ON again. These false positives are simply due to memory data retention.

Every peripheral slot card has available to it eight memory locations that are indexed by slot number. These eight memory locations are for private variables that are designed to be available only to that peripheral slot card. These memory locations reside in TEXT Page 1 and these locations are not displayed by the screen hardware. In addition, all peripheral slot cards may utilize the eight public memory locations that begin each indexed array of seven private memory locations, one location for each slot in each indexed array. For example, the public memory location 0x478 is available for immediate or for temporary processing by all peripheral slot cards, but the memory location 0x479 is a private memory location for Slot 1, 0x47A for Slot 2, and so forth. *EOS+* uses four of its eight private indexed memory locations at 0x478, 0x578, 0x678, and 0x778, all indexed by the slot number of the slot where the quikLoader or the EPROM Reader card resides. The other four private memory locations are indexed from 0x4F8, 0x5F8, 0x6F8, and 0x7F8. *EOS+* uses the first set of four private indexed memory locations to store one sequential byte of the thirty-two bit Catalog control word 0xC4B890ED. Using four bytes rather than one byte to detect power up verification helps to minimize false positives that are due to memory data retention.

I still stand by my previous statement that, "Essentially, the quikLoader is a very simple, though elegantly designed peripheral interface card that can hold up to eight 2716 to 27512 EPROMs." I just happen to believe that the circuit diagram of my EPROM Reader card is just a bit **more** elegant and my *EOS+* software is a bit **better** designed EPROM controller, though I am still standing on the shoulders of one of the most prolific Apple][peripheral card developer, software designer, and author, Mr. James Fielding Sather! If it was not for Mr. Sather's initial investigations and all of the risks that he managed and endured while designing and marketing his remarkable quikLoader hardware and his software controller QLOS, I could have never been able to design and develop my own EPROM Reader card and my own EPROM controller *EOS+*. For that and for many, many additional reasons, I extend my thanks and my appreciation to Jim Sather. He is quite a remarkable genius and entrepreneur!

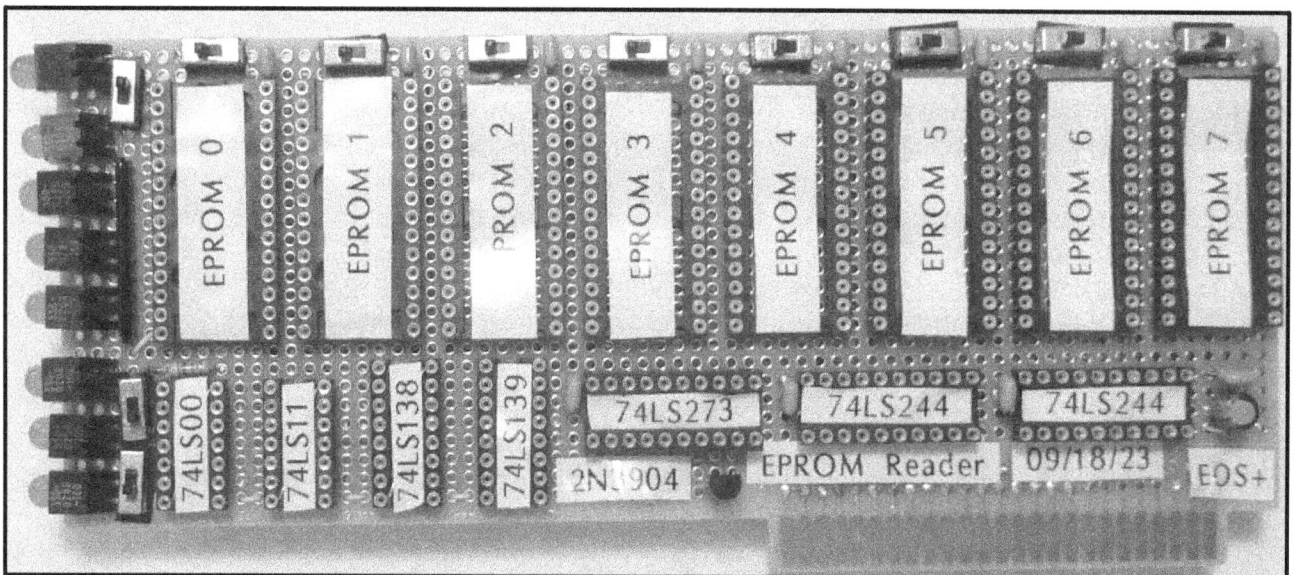

Figure V.28.7. EPROM Reader Card Top View

Figures V.28.7 and V.28.8 show photographs of the top and bottom views, respectively, of the completed and functional EPROM Reader circuit board that uses the Glitch Works Apple][prototyping board from ReActive Micro. As is readily apparent, this board is completely produced and wire wrapped by hand. Perhaps the components are not perfectly aligned and aesthetically looking as would be expected in a manufactured board, yet this board is fully functional. I have to say that continual and incremental testing prevented any wire wrapping errors to propagate any further than one or two pins at most. I also used an LED lighted magnifying lens and found it to be absolutely necessary in order to verify that I was wrapping the intended pin at all times. I have to say that I still have a very steady hand and that I am still capable of making very precise movements.

I explained near the beginning of this Section when I presented Figure V.28.1 that control signal C2 is used to enable the 74LS138 IC. The 74LS138 IC uses all four EPROM selection bits from the control register which are called E0, E1, E2, and E3 in order to enable the desired EPROM. I utilize all four selection bits purposefully in order to allow for the attachment of an Extension EPROM board to the

EPROM Reader card so that eight additional EPROMs may easily be addressed. Thus, the *EOS+* Main Menu allows for the selection of sixteen EPROMs for an EPROM Reader Catalog function whereas eight EPROMs can be selected for the quikLoader Catalog function as shown previously in Figures V.28.3 and V.28.4. A 28-pin connector must plug into any EPROM socket and a 16-pin connector must plug into the 74LS138 socket in the EPROM Reader card. The switch for the selected EPROM socket must be enabled in order to provide all sixteen address bits to the Extension EPROM board. An inverter gate or a transistor is required in order to invert the E3 signal for the second and new 74LS138 IC that is resident on the Extension EPROM board. The Extension EPROM board should include ten EPROM sockets, one socket for the 28-pin connector, one socket for the EPROM that was removed from the EPROM Reader card, and eight sockets for new EPROMs. Also, the Extension EPROM board should include three 16-pin sockets, one socket for the 16-pin connector, one socket for the 74LS138 IC that was removed from the EPROM Reader card, and one socket for the second and new 74LS138 IC for the Extension EPROM board, and a location for a 2N3904 transistor and its associated resistors. The second and new 74LS138 IC will enable each of the eight additional EPROMs that reside on the Extension EPROM board when the E3 signal in the control register is high.

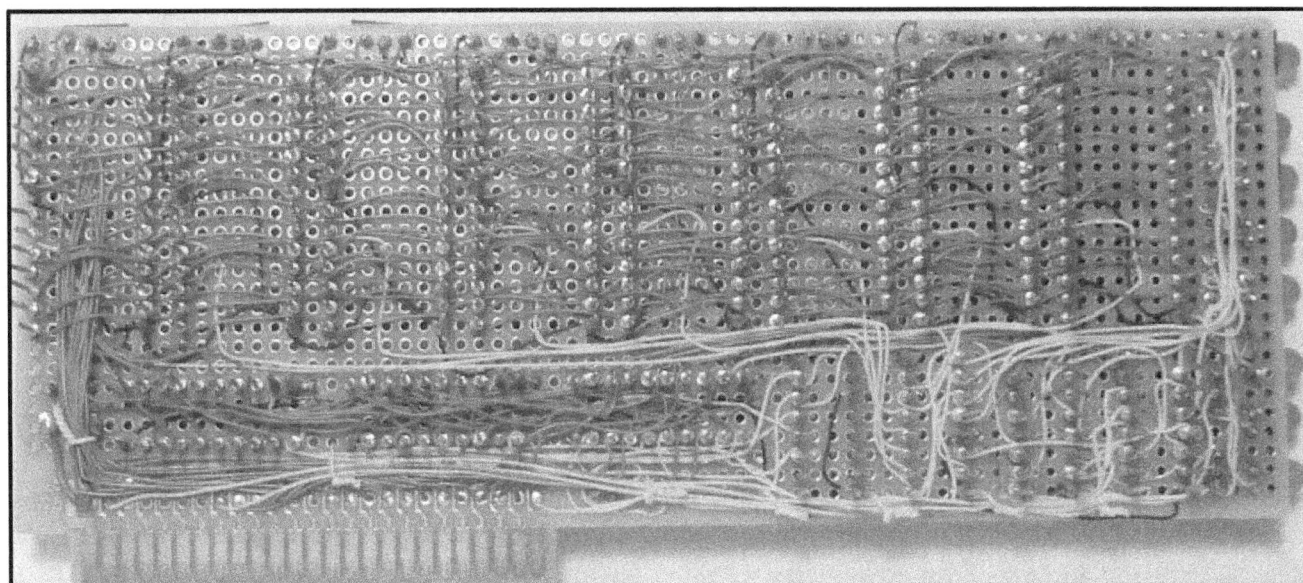

Figure V.28.8. EPROM Reader Card Bottom View

Figure V.28.9 shows the schematic diagram of my design for an EPROM Reader Extension Card. This solution would be more favorable than having two individual EPROM Reader cards in the same Apple][computer because only one slot would be required for an EPROM Reader card and its EPROM Reader Extension card. Together, the EPROM Reader card and its Extension card could easily address sixteen EPROMs rather than utilizing two slots in order to accommodate two separate EPROM Reader cards. In addition, it may be more difficult to adhere to all of the DMA IN and DMA OUT restrictions in order to support two separate EPROM Reader cards. Certainly, the Glitch Works prototyping board can be utilized for the Extension EPROM board and this board could be plugged into any unused and available slot since none of the slot finger connectors would be utilized in order to obtain any computer signals. All necessary signals would emanate from the EPROM Reader card. I believe this would be a fantastic rainy day project.

EPROM Reader Extension
Designed for EOS+ by
Walland Philip Vrbancic, Jr.
December 18, 2023

LED Display   Resister Network 470Ω

C2 Red   L1
E0 Green L2
E1 Green L3
E2 Green L4
E3 Green L5
B0 Green L6
B1 Green L7
B2 Green L8

DMA IN 27
DMA OUT 24
INT IN 28
INT OUT 23

5V
4.7K C2
2N3904
4.7K
E B C
5V

74LS138
3-Line to 8-Line Decoder
EPROM Selector

E0 A   Y0 CE8
E1 B   Y1 CE9
E2 C   Y2 CEA
        Y3 CEB
        Y4 CEC
G1   Y5 CED
G2A   Y6 CEE
G2B   Y7 CEF
VCC GND

EPROM Enable CE

5V 5V

EPROM Socket #8
A0 A0 CE VCC
A1 A1
A2 A2   Q0
A3 A3   Q1
A4 A4   Q2
A5 A5   Q3
A6 A6   Q4
A7 A7   Q5
A8 A8   Q6
A9 A9   Q7
A10 A10
A11 A11 Switch UP for 27128 27256 27512
A12 A12
A13 Switch DOWN for 2716 2732 2764
A14 A14
A15 OE GND

EPROM Socket from EPROM Reader
A0 A0 CE VCC
A1 A1   Q0
A2 A2   Q1
A3 A3   Q2
A4 A4   Q3
A5 A5   Q4
A6 A6   Q5
A7 A7   Q6
A8 A8   Q7
A9 A9
A10 A10
A11 A11
A12 A12
B0 A13
B1 A14
B2 A15 OE GND

74LS138 Socket from EPROM Reader
E0 A   Y0
E1 B   Y1
E2 C   Y2
        Y3
C2 G1   Y4
E3 G2A Y5
        Y6
G2B   Y7
VCC GND
Switch UP for ON
5V

B0
A12
5V
B1 A14
B2 A15

Components

1 - 74LS138, 16 pin socket
2 - 16 pin sockets
10 - 28 pin sockets, 6 mm wide
10 - SPDT mini slide switches
1 - Apple][Prototype Card
10 - 0.1 µF, 100 V filter capacitors

1 - 2N3904 NPN transistor
2 - 4.7K 1/4 watt resistors

1 - 470 ohm 9-resister network
1 - Red LED
7 - Green LEDs

Red Wire - all 5 Volt lines
Black Wire - all ground lines
White Wire - all Signal lines
Blue Wire - all Data lines
Green Wire - all Address lines

EPROM Bank Addressing and Memory Address

Bank	B2	B1	B0	Memory Address	EPROM Offset
0	0	0	0	0xE000-0xFFFF	0x0000-0x1FFF
1	0	0	1	0xE000-0xFFFF	0x2000-0x3FFF
2	0	1	0	0xE000-0xFFFF	0x4000-0x5FFF
3	0	1	1	0xE000-0xFFFF	0x6000-0x7FFF
4	1	0	0	0xE000-0xFFFF	0x8000-0x9FFF
5	1	0	1	0xE000-0xFFFF	0xA000-0xBFFF
6	1	1	0	0xE000-0xFFFF	0xC000-0xDFFF
7	1	1	1	0xE000-0xFFFF	0xE000-0xFFFF

Figure V.28.9. Schematic Diagram for the EPROM Reader Extension Card

Verification tests are not at all difficult to design that will confirm the functionality of the EPROM Reader hardware. The most basic tests would verify the operation of the configuration register of the EPROM Reader hardware and verify the readability of the peripheral-card ROM memory and the EPROM data of an EPROM that is seated in one of the EPROM sockets. Testing the configuration register would employ routines to increment and decrement the register and verify the write ability and the read ability of the register with an array of values. Referring to the schematic diagram for the EPROM Reader as shown in Figure V.28.1, reading the peripheral-card ROM memory may be problematic for some EPROMs that have a significant access time. The *I/O SELECT* control signal alone must be sufficient to enable the EPROM when the EPROM Reader is disabled or turned OFF, and that signal may not provide the required access time in order to enable some slow EPROMs. Various tests should be designed to verify the read ability of the peripheral-card ROM memory that can be configured for all Banks of an array of EPROMs that are seated in the EPROM sockets of the EPROM Reader. The ROM memory should be compared to its EPROM data for that particular data bank, and the EPROM Reader and its target EPROM should be enabled for a minimum of thirty-two retries. The most exhausting tests should be designed to read an EPROM data bank and compare that data to the data that was originally used to create the EPROM in the first place. This test should be repeated a number of times for each data bank of that target EPROM, perhaps beginning with a minimum of thirty-two retries. If there is a comparison discrepancy, the incremented error number should be reported along with the EPROM address, the EPROM data that was incorrectly read, and the correct data from the EPROM data file at the time of the data discrepancy. The EPROM Reader is designed to tolerate EPROMs that have an access time of 300 ns or less without incurring a read error from either peripheral-card ROM data or from EPROM bank data.

I have utilized all of the above requirements in order to design and to create a most comprehensive series of EPROM Reader verification tests. These tests are designed not only to verify the functionality of the EPROM Reader card, but to also verify the physical wiring of the EPROM Reader card. Wire wrapping a card of this size and of this type where there are eight parallel data lines, sixteen parallel address lines, and several control lines to eight EPROM sockets is not an easy task to perform without incurring some trivial wiring error. Each EPROM socket must be thoroughly tested such that all data banks must be available and correctly read from the seated EPROM. There must be at least one additional verification test that must utilize the configuration register in order to verify the operation of all LEDs to glow appropriately. I found this exercise in creating these EPROM Reader verification tests to actually be a goodly amount of fun. It amazes me even more that I have designed and built such a magnificent piece of hardware when all of these comprehensive tests correctly pass without error over and over. I could not conceive of any software verification test that fails to pass my new EPROM Reader card.

29. Last Concluding Thoughts

There have been many published books and articles that tell the story about the history, the evolution, and the people, some of whom are definitely characters, who have been involved in the Computer Revolution. I must say that I was part of that revolution, though perhaps more realistically on the periphery of that revolution. Ken Williams did attract a host of other entrepreneurs to Oakhurst, California, where Sierra On-Line was located. Like these other entrepreneurs, he was involved in developing certain software programs and products that were targeted for the soon-to-be-released Apple //c. The Apple //c was a very restricted project, and, indeed, access was strictly *on a need to know* basis. It was fascinating to be living in Oakhurst at that period of time and to witness those events personally, and to know that Wozniak and Jobs were among those who occasionally visited Williams. I know that there are many others like me who look back upon those years with a high degree of nostalgia. It was a glorious time to be writing software for the Apple][family of computers!

Even today I must admit that the Apple][computer holds a unique charm for me, and that charm continuously draws me into its technical and software environment. People like Gerard Putter and Richard Dreher certainly must also experience this Apple][charm as well. They have created invaluable tools, one software and the other hardware, that keep Apple][enthusiasts like me motivated and excited about creating more useful software and utilizing more hardware products for this computer today. I believe that in creating DOS 4.5 is my way of acknowledging and demonstrating the level of my understanding and my proficiency for the Apple][computer primarily in terms of its hardware. It was fortunate that I studied Electrical Engineering at University rather than Computer Science. I certainly absorbed enough Computer Science during my professional career where I designed and built very, very high speed tactical radar and sensor data collection and processing engines and data storage software structures.

DOS 4.5 is also the culmination of all of my ideas that are derived from my original DOS 4.1 Wish List and from the *parameter needs* of a large number of commercial software programs. Understanding those commercial software programs was vital in focusing my attention in order to design and to provide an interface between DOS 4.5 internals and DOS 4.5 externals. I suppose that studying Control Systems and viewing DOS similarly as a system having inputs, outputs, and feedback loops all contributed in how I wanted to design DOS 4.5 as the proverbial *black box* not to have its internals recklessly poked and prodded. At least for the most part I believe that I have succeeded in designing an Apple][Disk Operating System and Volume and File Management System that fulfills all of my software needs for the Apple][computer and for the Apple //e computer. I certainly believe that DOS 4.5 is capable of fulfilling the needs of others, particularly the owners of the CFFA card and the users of commercial programs like *Family Roots* who do not utilize ProDOS. This has been an incredible journey for me and I have enjoyed solving every problem and every issue while I was developing, designing, and programming DOS 4.5.

I still believe that there is a huge potential for using the 6502-microprocesser IRQ and NMI interrupts in some sort of hardware/software product. What that product is, is yet another mystery to me. But I still keep thinking about potential uses of interrupts in view of how much joy I had in implementing interrupts on my clock card. And that is part of the charm that the Apple][generates because of its open architecture. It allows people to build their own peripheral interface cards and to seat them into a real computer slot! I was so fortunate to have the opportunity to experiment and to design and to try out my ideas that significantly increased my knowledge and my understanding of digital electronics and software design. There is no better classroom than the laboratory of an engineer, and my laboratory happened to be my garage. Others may have a basement or a spare room for their laboratory. The point is, book knowledge is essential for understanding theory, but the real learning happens when you can apply that theory and build something that is your own design, be it something intellectual or something tangible, for both are meaningful and both stimulate creativity. At least that is the case for me especially when I recall that the original Apple and Apple I computers were first designed and built in a garage.

I have yet to explore integrating my love for the Apple][hardware and software and my love for model railroading, specifically S-gauge that is used by the American Flyer model trains. I have boxes and boxes of these trains and many accessories of that scale that are stored in my garage even today. Perhaps it is time I introduce Mr. American Flyer to Mr. Apple. The relationship could be rather exciting if not downright explosive. Oh, not in the sense of Addams Family explosive, but in the sense of opening up a whole new world of awesome challenges, struggles, creativity, and a whole lot of downright fun.

The generation of young engineers of today have the opportunity to explore computer-assisted or computer-associated projects particularly with the affordable Raspberry Pi computer. The Raspberry Pi is the size of a credit card that has four USB ports, an Ethernet port, HDMI video and audio, raw video and stereo sound outputs, and it only requires an input voltage of five volts at 2.4 amps for full operation and control. The Pi computer uses a micro Secure Digital or SD memory card that hosts its UNIX-like operating system and its C language compiler and linker. It provides twenty-six General Purpose Input/Output or GPIO pin connections or ports to the outside world. The GPIOs are software configurable to be an input or an output port that accept or provide a 3.3-volt digital signal, respectively. That is totally genius.

I designed my Sunrise/Sunset computer assisted controller around the Raspberry Pi in order to control all of my outside decorative lightening. My control software considers my location on planet Earth in terms of longitude, latitude, and azimuth in order to calculate precisely when sunrise and sunset occurs each day of the year. The software refers to an input CFG configuration file that has selectable offsets in order to adjust program timing so that my decorative lights turn ON thirty minutes after sunset and they turn OFF forty-five minutes before sunrise. One GPIO pin is used as a 3.3-volt output port in order to illuminate the LED of a TRIAC controller. When the TRIAC is turned ON, 120 volts of Alternating Current or AC is gated to a medium-duty 120 volt AC electromagnetic relay. This relay can control a load of up to fifteen amps at 240 volts AC. The AC transformer that provides the twelve volts AC to my decorative lights draws no more than eight amps at 120 volts AC through this relay. As the days become longer and the nights shorter my decorative lights turn ON and they turn OFF according to sunset and sunrise, respectively. And, as the days become shorter and the nights longer my decorative lights are turned ON and they are turned OFF appropriately.

There is absolutely no need to make any further adjustments to this decorative light controller throughout the year. The Raspberry Pi assisted controller is totally maintenance free because it receives its time-of-day from the Internet by means of a USB wireless adapter that communicates with my wireless Internet Router. There must be an interesting project or two that could tie Mr. Apple to Mr. Raspberry Pi. I already use a Keyspan serial to USB adapter with my Apple //e and my Apple MacBook Pro. And, I already have the programming tools on the Raspberry Pi to write even more C language programs. The best part is that the Raspberry Pi only costs around $45.00. The Raspberry Pi has massive programming power and agility for just pennies in investment cost. The only thing remaining is the application of a little knowledge, a little enthusiasm, and a little creativity.

Would I trade those early years in learning how to program on an Apple][for present day years to learn how to program on the Raspberry Pi or other similar UNIX computer? I am very fond of all of my past memories, and software and hardware versions in those years did not change quite so often. It is surprising how many years DOS 3.3 actually survived. Today, it seems like my iPad or my iPhone receives a new iOS update every other month or so. Software development occurs at a frenzied pace now, and considerations for size of application and available memory are totally unimportant it seems. Of course, I could not last even ten minutes in the aerospace industry of today because I do not have the understanding or the experience of the tools that today's young engineers have access to, nor do I have their current intellectual growth processes as a foundation. My intellectual foundation was the slide rule where the knowledge of concepts was tested rather than having to reach a particular numerical result. So I am satisfied with my memories and the fascinating experiences that I had, and the interesting characters that I happened to meet along the way. It is comforting to know that through my travels in time I may have touched someone else's curiosity.

Curiosity in and of itself is the driving force for all intellectual achievements. Without curiosity nothing would have been created in my opinion. There would simply be no interest in building the world of today without curiosity. Furthermore, curiosity paired with mankind's fundamental and stubborn laziness would never have prompt the design and the development of the Industrial Revolution. The Industrial Revolution was sparked by that great mathematician, physicist, astronomer, theologian, and author Isaac Newton. It was Isaac Newton's *Philosophiae Naturalis Principia Mathematica* that directly paved the way to our modern world. Laziness, a fundamental human character, is what drives mankind to create a world of comfort, pleasure, and safety. Laziness is the star ingredient in the First Postulate that formulates the Theory of Volitional Science.

It was pure laziness that prompt me to create the theoretical design equations for a multiple input operational amplifier summer while I was an Electrical Engineering student. My paper detailing the process in how I arrived at these theoretical design equations was published by IEEE and my paper is the reason why my Electrical Engineering professors submitted me for the Alton B. Zerby Outstanding Student Award. Furthermore, it was my curiosity that continuously drove all of my Electrical Engineering pursuits. Here is my story in how my laziness, paired with my curiosity, drove me to write my paper on the design of multiple-input operational amplifier summers.

Back in 1981 I registered for Professor Gene H. Hostetter's course in Operational Amplifiers or op amps, which was about seven years before his untimely death in 1988. Dr. Hostetter, still a young man, presented the course materials in syllabus format because this syllabus would eventually become the basis of an

Electrical Engineering textbook. He believed that for learning to be successful it was necessary and important for the student to apply all of the new theories and the new concepts that he presented in lecture format to solving real-life design problems. Dr. Hostetter created a huge array of design problems that were generic to the design of multiple input op amp summers. He also wanted his students to filter out those problems that best helped them to learn the course material, and those selected design problems would be included in his forthcoming textbook. I recall when Dr. Hostetter assigned fifty design problems on a beautiful Friday afternoon and he expected their solutions by the following Monday afternoon. The assignment was given in two parts: solve all fifty problems using the basic techniques that he had discussed in class that week and then solve all fifty problems again and remove all Direct Current or DC voltage imbalances at the input connections to the op amp. A total of one hundred homework problems due Monday would surely prevent any other weekend plans, and I did have plans to party that weekend.

I solved the first two design problems Friday evening. They each took about thirty minutes to complete before and after considering all DC voltage imbalances. I could not believe that this weekend was going to be spent doing nothing but this homework, and only this homework: no food, no sleep, and no party. Being basically lazy by nature drove my initial curiosity to apply Kirchhoff's Voltage Law for a closed loop circuit and Ohm's Law for parallel resistance vis-à-vis what Dr. Hostetter presented in class for general op amp theory. It seemed as though that the more I manipulated those op amp equations with these two fundamental laws, the more I started to see interesting and new relationships begin to develop between the input variables on the positive side of the op amp and the input variables on the negative side of the op amp. Of course, feedback from the output of the op amp had to be considered as well. By the end of the evening I had developed a set of equations that I called the *front door equations* and a set of equations that I called the *back door equations*. Incredible as it seems, these two independent sets of equations actually reduced to a shared commonality. I now had a tremendously powerful set of theoretical design equations that I could use in order to solve any multiple input op amp summer design problem. By Saturday afternoon I had solved all one hundred of Dr. Hostetter's homework problems mostly by visual inspection! That is, I performed little if any calculations in order to solve these problems. To be sure, I spent the rest of the weekend at a well-deserved party totally enjoying myself.

Early Monday morning I met with Dr. Hostetter in his office and presented to him the process I used to develop my op amp design equations. Please understand, Dr. Hostetter had been teaching this subject for nearly twenty years. He was amazed, flabbergasted, excited, and could not wait for class that afternoon. I declined his invitation to present my design equations to my classmates because Dr. Hostetter used a brilliant lecture technique that made any topic that he presented easy to follow and easy to understand. I did not have this capability at that time, and this subject was too important to me not to allow Dr. Hostetter to articulate this subject to my fellow classmates. In summary, all of my classmates scored 100% on their midterm exam. A year or two later my professor Clement J. Savant, Jr., asked if he could publish my design equations in his forthcoming textbook *Electronic Circuit Design An Engineering Approach*. I gave him a resounding **YES!**

Whatever your particular talents might be or whatever your personal aspirations are, your innate curiosity of perhaps building a star ship, or programming a computer, or growing a garden of flowers, will always be realized when you utilize the power of your fundamental human laziness. It is this wonderful human character from which we can all benefit and for which we can all utilize. Use your curiosity to unlock your full potential and let your desire for more leisure, more down-time, and more pleasure reward you with a better understanding of Mother Nature. She is the ultimate judge on what is good, what works, and what will always survive!

VI. Autobiographical Information

Grandfather Vrbančić was born in Trg, Croatia, once a province of Yugoslavia, and he was named Vid. Vid decided to immigrate to the United States around 1907, and he joined his older brother in Rankin, Pennsylvania. There, he and Marko worked in the coal mines. This work did not appeal to him, so he moved to Cleveland, Ohio, to work in the steel mill industry. Vid did not have a profession and he had no desire to learn a trade, so he became one of the many immigrant laborers living in the Cleveland area. There were many other Croatian and Slovenian immigrant laborers living in the same suburbs, and they tended to retain their European style of living and speak their native languages. Vid had lived in America for nearly ten years when he met Veronika Sneperger. Veronika had not been in America as long as Vid, but she became far more fluent in English than he. She was also fluent in six other languages. Vid and Veronika were married on June 25, 1917, in Saint Paul's Church and they moved into a lovely, but small apartment on the east side.

Veronika's mother Tvka (Eva) Stefančić had already died in 1910 and the steel mill industry was no longer manufacturing wartime supplies by the 1920's. Vid was finally laid off in 1921 and he could not find any other work in the Cleveland area. He did not want to move his wife, daughter Josephine, and son Andrew to Rankin where his younger brother Franjo was now living and working as a policeman. Veronika's father Jure, a widower for over ten years now, wrote many letters to Vid and to Veronika and he pleaded with them to return to Croatia. He even promised to give them his home in Maklen and all of his farm land if they would agree to care for him in his old age. Vid finally relented and he and his family set sail back to Croatia. Unfortunately, Jure had blatantly lied to both Vid and to Veronika as he never intended to give them his home or any of his farm land. He also did not want Vid working his farm land using the methods Vid had learned while he was growing up in Trg. Regardless of their near hopelessness, Mathew was born in February, 1922, in Maklen.

By 1923 the steel mill industry in Cleveland had converted back to manufacturing household and industrial supplies, and they sent pleas to European countries for mill workers. The industry even offered to pay the man's passage and assist him in finding an apartment. Even though Josephine and Andrew were American citizens, Vid, Veronika, and Mathew were not. When Vid inquired about bringing his family to America, he was told he would need to become an American citizen, have $2000 in a savings account, provide an adequate home for his family to live, and have the required fare for their passage from Maklen to Cleveland. So, if Vid took the job offer, he would have to leave his family behind. After much soul searching and in view of being duped and lied to by Jure, Vid did accept the job offer to return to Cleveland. But, to make financial matters even worse, Vid left Croatia six months before the birth of his fourth child in February, 1924. Grandmother named him Valentin because Father was born on Saint Valentine's Day.

413

Jure's property would have rightfully gone to his son George (Jure in Croatian) before it would go to Veronika if Jure should die. But George had left for America in 1899 and was never heard from again. Jure never trusted banks or a hiding place at home for his money, so he carried all of his cash with him and he made this fact known to all. In 1925, while he was taking a shortcut through the woods, Jure's cousin shot him through the heart and decapitated him. To this day there is tree with a four foot cross carved into its bark marking the crime spot. It is believed that teenage boys in the neighborhood keep that cross scrapped clean of bark and retell the killing of Jure. No one was officially charged with the crime, but Jure's cousin admitted to the crime on his deathbed. Even though Veronika inherited her father's home in Maklen and all of his farm lands, life was still very hard for Grandmother raising and feeding her four growing children without her husband there.

Josephine and Andrew both attended a one-room school in Brod Moravice; Mathew and Valentin were still too young to attend school. They explored the surrounding villages and farms, but were afraid to venture into the woods where their grandfather had been murdered. They

did explore several of the caves in the area only when an older boy accompanied them. Grandmother's farm had many fruit trees they could climb and they would feast on the fruit. Vid wrote to his family often and told them he was progressing well with all of the requirements that were needed to bring everyone to Cleveland. He sent Veronika sufficient funds for her to obtain passport photos, visas, clothes, and luggage that was necessary for the long journey to America. Many government officials had to stamp their passport papers. These included officials in Brod Moravice, officials in the municipality of Delnice, officials in the district of Rijeka, officials in the city of Zagreb (the capital of Croatia), and finally officials in the city of Belgrade (the capital of Yugoslavia). In each case there were fees to be paid to the official for each paper and visa they stamped, and for every outstretched hand, otherwise the papers and visas would be confiscated. In 1930 Veronika and her four children left Maklen, Croatia, forever and boarded the USS Paris in Le Havre, France, for their voyage to the United States of America.

Father says he remembers when the Statue of Liberty first became visible because all of the passengers crowded to that side of the ship to get a good look at the Lady who promised so much to the newly arriving immigrants. When he gazed upon the statue, he was puzzled why everyone seemed so excited at the sight, but he was only six years old. The ship docked at Ellis Island and everyone had to file through the various designated checkpoints. Father remembers having his hair and body examined, and he was given a mental aptitude test which he thought was some sort of game. Once everyone was examined and tested, Veronika gathered up her children and their luggage and boarded a train to Cleveland. When they arrived in Cleveland, Father met his father Vid for the first time. I can only imagine what that stern-faced man had to say, if anything, to his youngest son? Everyone was ushered up to a second floor apartment that had three bedrooms. No one seems to remember when Father's name was changed from Valentin to Walland. Since Father did not speak English, it is believed that a teacher at East Madison Grade School misunderstood the name Valentin when Father pronounced it for her, and she changed it to Walland. Father has been called Wally ever since.

I was named after Father so I was given the Junior designation. Over the years the name Walland coupled with the last name Vrbančić has given many of my teachers and counselors tremendous pause in how to address me and how to pronounce my name. The diacritic marks over the two "c's" of my last name provided even more confusion except to another Eastern European raised speaking any of the Serbo-Croatian dialects. I have always been called Philip in

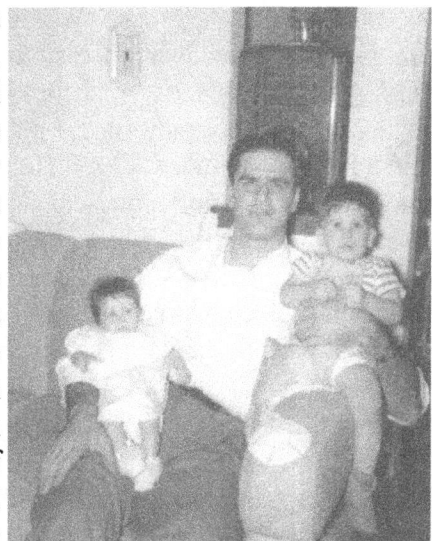

order to differentiate me from Father. That part of my journey through time has always been very interesting to me. The fact that I was born with a moderately severe speech impediment, a stutter, has not been so interesting, and only those who also have a stutter know precisely what I mean.

We lived in California and I still have very vivid memories when I was very young, lying on a throw rug in our living room listening to Mother practice her violin. She produced the most wonderful music to my ears and it was then that I became very much attracted to that instrument. Mr. Joe Burger came to my fourth grade classroom looking for potential music students. When he played *The Flight of the Bumblebee* by Nikolai Rimsky-Korsakov, I was forever charmed. I immediately requested a permission slip for my parents to sign so that I could study the violin under Mr. Burger. Mother rented a student-sized violin to see how well I would progress before considering buying a decent instrument. She must have been very happy with my progress that year because she convinced Father to invest in a "very nice" instrument. Mother took me to meet Mr. Lewis Main in central Long Beach to select my violin. Mr. Main took me alone into his studio at the back of his home where I saw hundreds of instruments, some still wet with varnish and hanging from wires stretched high across the room. He wanted to talk to me privately in order to evaluate what sort of personality I had. He said he could match the violin to the student, much like in the Harry Potter book where Mr. Ollivander matched the wand to the student wizard. I had to wait some months before Mother received a call from Mr. Main. Mother was so excited and she told me that Mr. Main had found my violin!

Mr. Main told us that many appraisers traveled about England to attend estate sales, and the appraiser who worked with Mr. Main only purchased instruments at those particular sort of sales. My violin, a *Gemünder Art* violin, model A266, was handcrafted in 1930 by Oscar A. Gemünder of August Gemünder & Sons, New York, New York. It was purchased new, originally for a young English girl who was beginning her studies on the violin. So, this instrument has traveled across the Atlantic Ocean twice before I became its second owner. Not only did Mr. Main match the instrument to me perfectly, he also matched an 1801 French violin to my younger sister a year later. Many years passed when I discovered that the American violinist Camilla Wicks was a close friend to the Main family, and when she and Mr. Main's son were teenagers, they would spar endlessly to see who was the better violinist! When my parents purchased my violin, Mr. Main's son was already a professional violinist and he performed primarily in Las Vegas, Nevada. Camilla Wicks performed as an international soloist. As for my study of the instrument after Mr. Burger, my private violin teachers included Carol Higley in Lakewood, California, during elementary and junior high school, Professor Frank Bellino at Denison University, Granville, Ohio, during high school, Professor Stanley Plummer at the University of California, Los Angeles, California, while I was a student at University, and Mr. Allan Carter in Long Beach, California, when I wanted to study and perform chamber music in my mid-forties. Plummer and Carter were both students of Vera Barstow in Pasadena, California, though perhaps nearly a generation apart.

I always excelled in mathematics and science classes during high school, so I decided to study Zoology at UCLA as an undergraduate in the mid-sixties after I was graduated from high school. At that time Mother, a registered nurse, was managing the department of surgery at a local hospital and her vision was to send me to medical school after graduation from University. Father, on the other hand, thought my talents were more inclined towards engineering. He was a graduate of the University of Southern California, school of Industrial Engineering, and he was a licensed Professional Engineer. My secret dream or illusion was to become a concert violinist, or at least a professional orchestral musician. Honestly, I was too immature when I attended UCLA, let alone live on campus at Sproul Hall. I was not passionate enough about any of my studies and, unfortunately, I did not have sufficient time nor talent to adequately prepare my lessons for Professor Plummer. It was a dynamic, historical time to attend University during the mid-sixties. The political arena was in an uproar with President Reagan in office. The war in Vietnam was still being waged. Communists like Angela Davis, a student of Herbert Marcuse, was teaching and giving lectures in the adjacent lecture hall where I was attending my required Political Science (clearly, an oxymoron) class. She and others were permitted to corrupt the minds of children with their lectures on political fantasy, socialism, and the destruction of God-given values and rights. In hindsight, I should have stepped back, attended a community college for a year or two, so I could mature a bit more emotionally.

One particularly horrifying experience I had while I was a student at UCLA was when I walked into my second quarter German class and saw my instructor's name written on the blackboard: Frau Milovanović. She pronounced my name perfectly and clearly, rolling the "r" in my last name majestically, when she took attendance, and she ordered me to stay after class. I knew she was Serbian, or, at least her husband was Serbian, but that did not matter to me. When the other students left the classroom and were out of earshot, she told me I was a "dirty, filthy Croatian" and she wanted to know if I was going to give her any "trouble", and she used other colorful language as well. Literally, shaking in my boots, I told her I was born an American and I did not have any resentment towards any ethnic group of people. I worked my tail off in that class and I managed to squeak by with a "C" grade. She found fault in most everything I wrote. After the final exam I thanked her for all of the "special" attention she gave me! At least I did not have a "melt down" entirely, but finished my studies, and was graduated with a Bachelor's of Science degree in Zoology.

Father suggested that I enroll in a two-year program through the USC Medical Center for training as an Orthopedic Physician's Assistant or OPA. I thoroughly enjoyed every aspect of that program, I completed all of the requirements, and I earned my certificate to work as an OPA. I was quickly hired by a local hospital where I worked for over nine years. By the mid-seventies I had already worked as an OPA for about four years when I experienced some sort of intellectual "awakening" and I decided Father was right after all, and I should have studied engineering, particularly Electrical Engineering. My epiphany to return to another tour of undergraduate studies was perhaps precipitated by the lectures I was attending at that time. The lectures were given by the renowned Astrophysicist Andrew J. Galambos, PhD. Professor Galambos was now an entrepreneur giving lectures on Volitional Science. I had already enrolled in his V-201 course which continued for over a year, one three-hour lecture once a week with a few weekend sessions as well. Previous to the V-201 course, I had enrolled in Professor Galambos's V-50 course which was now being presented by J. S. Snelson. It would not be possible for me to summarize here the knowledge that I gained from the V-50 and from the V-201 courses, and from several other lectures that I attended in order to celebrate unique and historical events.

Before I enrolled in the OPA program at the USC Medical Center, I did work as a phlebotomist in a doctor's office for nearly two years. Both doctors treated obese patients using diet and an array of medications they prescribed and provided on-site. In the early 1970's it was common practice to prescribe either Dextroamphetamine Sulfate or Levoamphetamine Sulfate, the enantiomer of amphetamine, or any of the combinations of these very powerful and very addicting drugs with other ingredients to help promote weight loss. More importantly, I had a lot of spare time during working hours, and my manager allowed me to read. In fact, she encouraged me to read the works of Ayn Rand. I even attended a few meetings where I was introduced to laissez-faire capitalism. Years later I suppose that when I heard Snelson's presentation of V-50, I was entirely comfortable with the subject of capitalism, and I was amazed at how far the concepts of Galambos had surpassed those of Rand. After attending the V-201 course, it was very difficult for me to manage the "blab forth syndrome", and I was guilty of trying to explain some of the concepts from V-201 to my colleagues for many, many years. Once again, it is something that is difficult and complicated to explain in short order.

It was completely normal for me to take apart, dismantle, and study the innards of every toy, train, erector set, chemistry set, or electrical set that Santa brought to me when I was young, and reconstruct that toy to working order, without inflicting any significant internal damage. Countless times Father would see a radio or a tape recorder completely disassembled on the floor of my room and ask me, laughingly, "How long until that works again?" This sense of curiosity even when I was very young should have given me a clue as to what I should have initially studied at University. I have felt some degree of regret that it took me nearly ten years after high school to realize my mistake. Electrical Engineering became my absolute passion. I worked full time on second shift at the hospital and during the morning hours I attended at least three lecture classes and I always included one laboratory class each semester for the next five years. IEEE published my original paper that detailed my theoretical design equations for multiple input operational amplifier summers, and my professors submitted me for the Alton B. Zerby Outstanding Student Award. I won first place in the Region Six IEEE Student Paper contest and placed third nationally that same year during WESCON in 1982. My operational amplifier design equations were also published in a textbook written by one of my professors on that subject. All of these accomplishments coupled with a 4.0 GPA gave me many choices for my next employer. Father worked for Rockwell International, though it was originally known as North American Aviation. I did interview at TRW and I received a very lucrative job offer, but I decided to join the team at Rockwell, in the Space Shuttle Simulation Laboratory. I was hired about five months before the launch of STS-1, thus changing my hospital scrubs for a coat and tie, and a whole lot more money!

About three months after Rockwell hired me, the Simulation Laboratory manager hired a Computer Science Engineer to join the ranks of Initialization Engineers. He and I had the daunting task of learning how to initialize the computers and the electronics that comprised the total simulation of a Space Shuttle trajectory from Main Engine Cutoff or MECO to landing at a few selected sites within the United States. The computers that were initialized with flight and target parameters included a PDP-11 and two Xerox mainframes. The mainframes were initially programmed using front-panel rocker switches: the Sigma 5 had 16 KB of magnetic core memory and the Sigma 9 had 64 KB of magnetic core memory. We used Hollerith cards to insert faults into the General Purpose Computers or GPCs just like those that were aboard the shuttle. We used a color Eidophor projector to project visual images of our landing site runways into a shuttle cockpit simulator in which the astronauts trained. Finally, we used Nova computers by DEC and DEC word processing software in order to generate all of the required customer documentation and, I might add, to play the Adventure game.

My system initialization colleague was an early Apple][owner when Integer Basic was first available in ROM. The following year Rockwell offered a home computer purchase program and the offer provided

us with the choice between an IBM PC or the Apple][+ which now came with the Autostart ROM. My colleague strongly encouraged me to request the Apple computer, and he assisted me in selecting the monitor, the disk drive, and the printer accessories. The total cost was a lot of money for me, but the Rockwell offer also loaned me the money and paid the cost in full. I repaid the interest-free loan through weekly payroll deductions making this computer purchase relatively painless. Thus, my dream of having my own personal computer was fulfilled. My ever-constant V-50 and V-201 "blab forth syndrome" did interest another colleague of mine who actually enrolled in the V-50T course, where "T" stand for Tape. Later, he enrolled in the V-201 course and many other "V" courses after completing V-50T. In fact, he became the personal assistant to Professor Galambos during the last and final trip Galambos made to Budapest, Hungary, his native country. Mrs. Galambos stayed behind to manage the curriculum of their Free Enterprise Institute or FEI. Professor Galambos recognized that he was beginning to display the symptoms of Alzheimer's disease and he entrusted my colleague with handling more and more of the private living affairs for both he and his wife. Andrew J. Galambos and Suzanne J. Galambos established their Natural Estates Trust that was to manage all of their Intellectual Property. From my vantage point it appeared to me that my colleague participated in and contributed to what I considered to be dishonorable activities not in the favorable interests of this Natural Estates Trust. My colleague's activities primarily involved the convoluted publishing of *Sic Itur Ad Astra* by Andrew J. Galambos after his death on April 10, 1997.

I became fascinated with all aspects of the Apple][+ computer, and I wanted to incorporate it into my studies for my Master's degree. My assigned advisor was analyzing tomographic reconstructions of the human spinal column, and he thought perhaps I could assist him. He wanted to be able to make measurements between any two points within the computer image of a spinal column, even after rotating or enlarging the image. I was tasked to develop the Fortran programs that could be launched on a Microsoft Z80 Softcard in an Apple][+ that would provide him with these capabilities. I found an ingenious way to reduce the size of the three-dimensional rotational matrix in order to accelerate data image processing and the remapping of the resulting HIRES image to the computer display. My professor was very pleased with my progress. However, I was becoming increasingly interested in high-speed graphics animation, and the only way I thought I could learn that technology was to work for Ken Williams at Sierra On-Line. I terminated my work on my Master's degree, I gave notice to Rockwell, I packed my bags, and I moved to Oakhurst, California.

At Sierra On-Line I was tasked to assist a colleague in migrating *ScreenWriter* to the new Apple //e which was recently available for purchase. On another project I wrote all of the I/O routines and ICON drawing routines for HomeWord Speller. When I started working as a self-employed contractor, I was given the *Goofy's Word Factory* project which was a children's computer game to teach English grammar. Williams had a license to display certain Disney characters on a bit-mapped computer display per approval by Disney for visual likeness, color, and movement. I would have finished *Goofy's Word Factory* if John Williams, Ken Williams's brother, the assigned designer of the game, could have developed the third game feature and its strategy in a timely fashion. He apparently could not do so before I secured a position at Hughes Aircraft Company back in Los Angeles. I did utilize Williams's high-speed graphics animation algorithms in *Goofy's Word Factory*, which I had to somewhat redesign in order to include collision detection on a dithered background. No other computer game could detect collisions on a dithered background at that time. Williams was impressed, and it was really hard to impress Williams. I stayed all of 18 months at Sierra On-Line.

The major observation that I made after I was hired by Hughes Aircraft was how different its culture was to the culture that I had experienced at Rockwell. At Rockwell I found it to be exceedingly difficult to have anyone who had written a software tool or program to explain to me how that tool or that program worked, and the algorithms the software utilized or exploited. When I was tasked to migrate a software tool from Fortran to C language at Rockwell, I found some incorrect logic that eventually affected the final output data. Given certain input parameters, this tool could calculate a three-dimensional corridor in space and either interpolate points within or extrapolate points outside of that corridor. I presented my findings to its original Fortran programmer showing him how I could insert the same incorrect logic into the C code in order to generate the same wrong output data. He told me to keep the incorrect logic and not to disclose my findings to management. I absolutely refused. This was totally unthinkable to me, and this would never have happened at Hughes. In fact, CIP awards were presented to engineers who found such errors in software and who reported those errors to management. The Hughes culture encouraged the aggressive sharing of knowledge, and it gave rewards to those who made significant software improvements. The Rockwell culture cultivated self-preservation tactics where knowledge was thought to be job security and not to be shared, but to be kept undisclosed to others. Hughes certainly provided me with a great opportunity in the Digital Simulation Laboratory where I learned about real time executive software that was hosted on Gould SEL mainframe computers like the 2750, the 6750, the 8780, and the 9780. I also learned about MIL-STD-1553 communication software protocol and real time software interface drivers to a host of various external data processors. Our purpose was to create a digital time frame in order to simulate in real time the environment for a tactical Radar Digital Processor or RDP that was being flown above the surface of the earth.

Due to the general slowdown in the engineering industry, I returned to Rockwell in 1990. I believed that my knowledge in real time executive software that is hosted on SEL mainframe computers would be my passport to a nice software engineering career closer to where I wanted to live. How I regret that major blunder in judgment because my employment at Rockwell was terminated just a few years later. I had co-authored a *White Paper* outlining the risks that are associated with using off-the-shelf RISC processors in certain applications, and the response from my colleagues was very unfavorable. This and my disclosure of software errors that I uncovered during a Fortran-to-C language software conversion eventually led to my dismissal. Fortunately, my former Hughes management was able to reinstate my position, and I was tasked to gain further expertise in very, very high speed real time data collection software engines for tactical radar systems and other tactical sensor devices.

Hughes tactical radar systems are programmed to operate in many different modes depending upon various situations and the immediate needs that are faced by that particular military aircraft. During the development of a tactical radar mode, its processing is heavily instrumented which generates a large volume of output data as the mode progresses through its various processing stages. It is critical to capture all of this generated data, primary and incidental in nature, in order to ensure and to verify that the mode is behaving as expected and is generating its data according to pre-established boundaries, much like comparing the data to some gold standard of expectations. My task was to capture all of the In-phase and Quadrature or I/Q components of radar data in real time, process certain other data components, package that data according to generated source code and timestamp, and save the resulting files using some recording device. It is important to understand that there are many independent generating sources of data in a tactical radar system whose timestamps are totally asynchronous. At a later time the collected data that is packaged in those files by my software engine would be analyzed using various data analysis tools in order to determine if, in fact, the processing modes operated as expected. Physically collecting this I/Q data during real time tactical maneuvers was quite a challenge, and recorders that are designed to operate in this environment were costly. Preparing for a data collection session involved securing a particular military aircraft, a flight crew, a ground crew, and people to securely transport the recorded data back to my tempested lab. This certainly added to my responsibilities, and my mantra was to neither add, subtract, nor modify any data word or data bit while that data was in my immediate possession and while my software algorithms extracted and processed that data into prescribed data formats. Those data formats would allow the data analysis tools to function more efficiently for the tactical radar mode builders.

I was thoroughly vetted and held maximum-security clearances that allowed me to process data from many different and independent classified programs not only in Los Angeles, but also in other locations, and even in other states. The general data collection software engines that I began designing in the unclassified world served as my software library for every classified program to which I was assigned. Perhaps I was simply in the right place at the right time that steered my career to become the sole resident expert in Transcription Software Engines. That is, to process, to encrypt, and to store in real time at least a terabyte of data every second. Or, perhaps I was in the right place at the right time that allowed me to develop a task far beyond its envisioned potential. There is a direct ancestral linkage between my unclassified software library of tools, routines, and transcription engines and every single classified program with which I was associated that required my tools, my routines, my engines, and my expertise. I was practicing *code reuse* light-years before it became a topic that some managers greedily thought could reduce software development costs. "How insightful!" I jokingly thought of management, silently, and very highly disrespectfully in my private thoughts. "How insightful, indeed."

I was given the initial opportunity to host my current Transcription Software engine on a newly acquired SGI Origin 300 having four bricks, or sixteen CPUs. *Code reuse* made this task fairly straightforward, thus demonstrating the Origin's practicality for this feasibility study. After a fact-finding tour to the SGI facilities at Mountain View, California, I was assigned the momentous task of designing a Transcription Software engine for an SGI Origin 3000 that has eight bricks or thirty-two CPUs and is running IRIX, and using Big Endian memory management. This turned out to be one of my greatest individual achievements. Even at this time, little did my management understand how effortlessly I could build my Transcription Software engines primarily using *code reuse*. I was extremely fortunate to have had one very intelligent manager who casually asked me to consider the possibility of building a digital playback system. Such a system did not yet exist. Some highly respected engineers with Ph.D. degrees had tried building an analog playback system a few years earlier with absolutely no success. Instead of analyzing the collected instrumented data, one could observe how the RDP hardware behaved when the recorded high-speed I/Q data and the slow-speed environment data were injected back into its system using a playback system. A few months later I presented my first digital playback recorder and pre-processing system, my last and greatest achievement at Raytheon which is the former Hughes Aircraft. I was assigned the unique privilege to design and build a second digital playback recorder and pre-processing system for another classified program. That program, like the previous program which used my first digital playback recorder and pre-processing system, saved countless hours of analysis time and mission costs before I scheduled my overdue retirement.

A few years after I retired, I was presented with an astonishing diagnosis by my partner that seemed to explain some, if not all of the idiosyncrasies that I have displayed my entire life as far back as elementary school: I may have been living with Asperger's. Indeed, how does one know what is truly normal; that which falls under the umbrella of a Gaussian curve? We are all volitional beings and our behavior is internal to each of us. Our brain is composed of carbon-based synapses whose trillions of inter-connections and cross-connections compose the very person and personality we have become or have allowed ourselves to become. It is simply miraculous that any of our species can reach total fulfillment of their

dreams. I would like to believe that I have come closer than most in reaching many of my major dreams and unique aspirations.

Now, I have the time and the continuing curiosity to delve into the Disk Operating System, the Volume and File Disk Management System for the Apple][computer. Also, I now have the opportunity to create my own version of a Volume and File Disk Management System that contains the power and the flexibility I always believed that an Apple][Disk Operating System ought to and could have.

I called my previous versions of Apple][DOS, DOS 4.1 and DOS 4.3. DOS 4.1 was complete with its 46th build in 2019. DOS 4.3 was complete with its eighth build in 2020. DOS 4.5 was complete with its fifth build in 2022. And, the second edition of DOS 4.5 was complete with its sixth build in 2024. What a ride I have been on! Why? To see what I could do for this wonderful machine and its magnificent architecture!

I completed DOS 4.1 in March, 2019, after I agreed to have the Build 45 Manual published by *Call-A.P.P.L.E.* I requested no fees, no incentives, and no royalties. But I continued to innovate DOS 4.1 and Build 46 contains the final modifications that I wanted to include into this DOS. I felt that I could not take DOS 4.1 any further due to the memory constraints of DOS 4.1L, and I did not want to increase its size nor add additional sectors to its volume image. However, I could continue to develop Apple][DOS if I concentrated only on the version that resides in the memory of the Language Card partition. I naïvely thought perhaps I could utilize Auxiliary Memory and move DOS there. To that end, I copied my source code for DOS 4.1H into a new directory and gave it a new name, and that was the birth of DOS 4.3. In the same fashion and nearly in the same way, from DOS 4.3 came the birth of DOS 4.5. I continued to develop DOS 4.5 for the remainder of 2020 and through 2021 and I developed a DOS 4.5L that resides in lower Main memory. As in the development of DOS 4.1 and in DOS 4.3, I reached a point with the fifth build where I did not wish to continue any further development of DOS 4.5L. The very last and final modifications are now complete and installed into the sixth build of DOS 4.5 that only resides in the memory of the Language Card partition. It is now time to complete the DOS 4.5 documentation for the Second Edition of the DOS 4.5 Volume and File Disk Management System. Yes! It is The End of a magnificent journey into the incredible Apple][and Apple //e computers that began a true revolution.

After all that I have seen and all that I have done during my life and in my travels through time, I am always comforted when I recall the following beautiful thought

The diversity in the human family should be the cause of love and harmony,
as it is in music where many different notes blend together
in the making of a perfect chord.

~~~ Abdu'l-Bahá ~~~

Index

I have always viewed software development
as a set of very complex strategies that involve
highly developed problem solving techniques.

To develop such programming skills requires
passion, perseverance, and practice.

One cannot be expected to perform a
Fiorillo Caprice overnight without expending
a little passion, a little perseverance, and a little practice.

Learning how to utilize and manage the memory
of the Language Card partition in the Apple][machine is,
in itself, very complicated, problematic, and certainly not intuitive.

When that memory is managed correctly,
the utilization of the Language Card partition provides
great opportunities to expand one's programming skills.

But those skills are still considerably simple
compared to the skills that are required to
utilize and manage Auxiliary memory.

Only with passion, perseverance, and practice
will the Apple][hardware reveal itself
and yield its total computational power to
that competent software and hardware engineer.